February 21–23, 2011
San Antonio, TX, USA

**Association for
Computing Machinery**

Advancing Computing as a Science & Profession

CODASPY'11

Proceedings of the First ACM Conference on

Data and Application Security & Privacy

Sponsored by:

ACM SIGSAC

Supported by:

**The Institute for Cyber Security, Center for Education & Research in
Information Assurance & Security and
Purdue University Cyber Centerx**

**Association for
Computing Machinery**

Advancing Computing as a Science & Profession

The Association for Computing Machinery
2 Penn Plaza, Suite 701
New York, New York 10121-0701

Notice to Past Authors of ACM-Published Articles

ACM intends to create a complete electronic archive of all articles and/or other material previously published by ACM. If you have written a work that has been previously published by ACM in any journal or conference proceedings prior to 1978, or any SIG Newsletter at any time, and you do NOT want this work to appear in the ACM Digital Library, please inform permissions@acm.org, stating the title of the work, the author(s), and where and when published.

ISBN: 978-1-4503-0466-5 (Digital)

ISBN: 978-1-4503-1376-6 (Print)

Additional copies may be ordered prepaid from:

ACM Order Department
PO Box 30777
New York, NY 10087-0777, USA

Phone: 1-800-342-6626 (USA and Canada)
+1-212-626-0500 (Global)
Fax: +1-212-944-1318
E-mail: acmhelp@acm.org
Hours of Operation: 8:30 am – 4:30 pm ET

Printed in the USA

Foreword

It is our great pleasure to welcome you to the inaugural edition of the *ACM Conference on Data and Application Security and Privacy (CODASPY 2011)*. This conference series has been founded to foster novel and exciting research topics in this arena and to develop directions for further research and development. The initial concept came up in a conversation between the two co-founders when both happened to be at the same meeting. This was followed by discussions with a number of fellow cyber security researchers. Their enthusiastic encouragement persuaded us to move ahead with the always daunting task of creating a high-quality conference.

Data and the applications that manipulate data are crucial assets in today's information age. With the increasing drive towards availability of data and services anytime anywhere, security and privacy risks have increased. Vast amounts of privacy-sensitive data are being collected today by organizations for a variety of reasons. Unauthorized disclosure, modification, usage or denial of access to these data and corresponding services may result in high human and financial costs. New applications such as social networking and social computing provide value by aggregating input from numerous individual users and the mobile devices they carry with them and computing new information of benefit to society and individuals. To achieve efficiency and effectiveness in traditional domains such as healthcare there is a drive to make these records electronic and highly available. The need for organizations and government agencies to share information effectively is underscored by rapid innovations in the business world that require close collaboration across traditional boundaries and the dramatic failure of old-style approaches to information protection in government agencies in keeping information too secret to connect the dots. Security and privacy in these and other arenas can be meaningfully achieved only in context of the application domain. Data and applications security and privacy has rapidly expanded as a research field with many important challenges to be addressed.

In response to the call for papers of CODASPY 2011 a total of 69 papers were submitted from Asia, Australia, Europe and North America. The program committee selected 21 papers that cover a variety of topics, including security and privacy of social networks, novel privacy techniques and applications, secure data outsourcing, secure provenance, insider threats and data leakage. The program is complemented by three applications and industry papers focusing on insights and experience from real-world applications. We are also very fortunate to have as part of the program three outstanding keynote speeches by Moti Yung, N. Asokan, and John Dickson. In addition, as a special feature, the program includes an inaugural keynote by the General Chair and Co-Founder of CODASPY. Finally, the program includes a panel, chaired by X. Sean Wang, on a "Research Agenda for Data and Application Security."

The organization of a conference like CODASPY requires the collaboration of many individuals. First of all, we would like to thank the authors for submitting to the conference, the keynote speakers for graciously accepting our invitation, and the panel chair and the panelists for contributing to the program. We express our gratitude to the program committee members and external reviewers for their efforts in reviewing the papers, engaging in active online discussion during the selection process and providing valuable feedback to authors. Our special thanks go to our local arrangement chair Jeffrey Reich and to our Web master Ram Krishnan. Special thanks also go to Gail-Joon Ahn for publicizing the conference. Finally, we would like to thank our sponsor, ACM SIGSAC, for their support of this conference.

We hope that you will find this program interesting and that the conference will provide you with a valuable opportunity to interact with other researchers and practitioners from institutions around the world. Enjoy!!

Ravi Sandhu
CODASPY'11 General Chair & Co-founder
University of Texas at San Antonio, USA

Elisa Bertino
CODASPY'11 Program Chair & Co-founder
Purdue University, USA

Table of Contents

Foreword iii
Ravi Sandhu *(University of Texas at San Antonio)*, Elisa Bertino *(Purdue University)*

CODASPY 2011 Conference Organization viii

CODASPY 2011 Sponsor & Supporters x

Keynote Talks

- **The Challenge of Data and Application Security and Privacy (DASPY):
  Are We Up to It?** 1
  Ravi Sandhu *(University of Texas at San Antonio)*

- **Key Dependent Message Security: Recent Results and Applications** 3
  Tal Malkin *(Columbia University)*, Isamu Teranishi *(NEC Corporation & Columbia University)*,
  Moti Yung *(Google Inc. & Columbia University)*

- **Old, New, Borrowed, Blue — A Perspective on the Evolution of Mobile Platform
  Security Architectures** 13
  Kari Kostiainen *(Nokia Research Center)*, Elena Reshetova *(Nokia)*,
  Jan-Erik Ekberg, N. Asokan *(Nokia Research Center)*

- **Software Security: Is OK Good Enough?** 25
  John B. Dickson *(Denim Group, Ltd.)*

Session 1: Security and Privacy Techniques for Social Networks
Session Chair: Murat Kantarcioglu *(University of Texas at Dallas)*

- **Towards Active Detection of Identity Clone Attacks on Online Social Networks** 27
  Lei Jin, Hassan Takabi, James B. D. Joshi *(University of Pittsburgh)*

- **Virtual Private Social Networks** 39
  Mauro Conti, Arbnor Hasani *(Vrije Universiteit Amsterdam)*, Bruno Crispo *(University of Trento)*

- **A Probability-Based Approach to Modeling the Risk of Unauthorized Propagation
  of Information in On-Line Social Networks** 51
  Barbara Carminati, Elena Ferrari, Sandro Morasca, Davide Taibi *(University of Insubria)*

Session 2: Insider Threats and Data Leakage
Session Chair: Ram Krishnan *(University of Texas at San Antonio)*

- **Detection of Anomalous Insiders in Collaborative Environments Via Relational
  Analysis of Access Logs** 63
  You Chen, Bradley Malin *(Vanderbilt University)*

- **LeakProber: A Framework for Profiling Sensitive Data Leakage Paths** 75
  Junfeng Yu *(Huazhong University of Science and Technology & The Pennsylvania State University, University Park)*,
  Shengzhi Zhang, Peng Liu *(The Pennsylvania State University, University Park)*,
  Zhitang Li *(Huazhong University of Science and Technology)*

- **Distributed Data Usage Control for Web Applications:
  A Social Network Implementation** 85
  Prachi Kumari, Alexander Pretschner *(Karlsruhe Institute of Technology)*, Jonas Peschla, Jens-Michael Kuhn *(TU
  Kaiserslautern)*

Session 3: Performance Evaluation and Enhancement
Session Chair: James Joshi *(University of Pittsburgh)*

- **MyABDAC: Compiling XACML Policies for Attribute-Based Database Access Control** 97
  Sonia Jahid, Carl A. Gunter, Imranul Hoque, Hamed Okhravi *(University of Illinois, Urbana-Champaign)*

- **Implementation and Performance Evaluation of Privacy-Preserving Fair Reconciliation Protocols on Ordered Sets** 109
  Daniel A. Mayer, Susanne Wetzel *(Stevens Institute of Technology)*,
  Dominik Teubert, Ulrike Meyer *(RWTH Aachen University)*

- **An Empirical Assessment of Approaches to Distributed Enforcement in Role-Based Access Control (RBAC)** 121
  Marko Komlenovic, Mahesh Tripunitara, Toufik Zitouni *(University of Waterloo)*

Session 4: Secure Provenance
Session Chair: Ravi Sandhu *(University of Texas at San Antonio)*

- **A Language for Provenance Access Control** 133
  Tyrone Cadenhead, Vaibhav Khadilkar, Murat Kantarcioglu, Bhavani Thuraisingham *(University of Texas at Dallas)*

- **Non-Interactive Editable Signatures for Assured Data Provenance** 145
  Haifeng Qian *(East China Normal University)*, Shouhuai Xu *(University of Texas at San Antonio)*

Session 5: Privacy Threats and Protection Techniques
Session Chair: Barbara Carminati *(University of Insubria)*

- **Identifying a Critical Threat to Privacy Through Automatic Image Classification**...............157
  David Lorenzi, Jaideep Vaidya *(Rutgers University)*

- **k-out-of-n Oblivious Transfer Based on Homomorphic Encryption and Solvability of Linear Equations** 169
  Mummoorthy Murugesan *(Teradata Corporation)*, Wei Jiang *(Missouri University of Science and Technology)*,
  Ahmet Erhan Nergiz, Serkan Uzunbaz *(Purdue University)*

- **Mixture of Gaussian Models and Bayes Error Under Differential Privacy** 179
  Bowei Xi *(Purdue University)*, Murat Kantarcioğlu *(University of Texas at Dallas)*, Ali Inan *(Isik University)*

Session 6: Novel Models and Systems for Access Control
Session Chair: Dan Thomsen *(Sandia National Laboratories)*

- **Relationship-Based Access Control: Protection Model and Policy Language** 191
  Philip W. L. Fong *(University of Calgary)*

- **Enforcing Physically Restricted Access Control for Remote Data** 203
  Michael S. Kirkpatrick, Sam Kerr *(Purdue University)*

- **Towards Defining Semantic Foundations for Purpose-Based Privacy Policies**.................213
  Mohammad Jafari, Philip W. L. Fong, Reihaneh Safavi-Naini, Ken Barker *(University of Calgary)*,
  Nicholas Paul Sheppard *(Queensland University of Technology)*

Session 7: Invited Industry and Application Papers
Session Chair: Elisa Bertino *(Purdue University)*

- **Practical Policy Patterns** 225
  Dan Thomsen *(Independent Consultant)*

- **The Optimization of Situational Awareness for Insider Threat Detection** 231
  Kenneth Brancik *(Northrop Grumman Corporation)*, Gabriel Ghinita *(Purdue University)*

Session 8: Secure Data Outsourcing
Session Chair: Gabriel Ghinita *(Purdue University)*

- **Fair and Dynamic Proofs of Retrievability** 237
  Qingji Zheng, Shouhuai Xu *(University of Texas at San Antonio)*

- **RASP: Efficient Multidimensional Range Query on Attack-Resilient Encrypted Databases** 249
  Keke Chen, Ramakanth Kavuluru, Shumin Guo *(Wright State University)*

Session 9: Novel Applications of Privacy Techniques

Session Chair: Keke Chen *(Wright State University)*

- **Privacy-Preserving Activity Scheduling on Mobile Devices** 261

  Igor Bilogrevic, Murtuza Jadliwala, Jean-Pierre Hubaux *(Ecole Polytechnic Fedérale Lusanne)*,
  Imad Aad, Valtteri Niemi *(Nokia Research Center)*

- **Privacy-Enhanced Reputation-Feedback Methods to Reduce Feedback Extortion
  in Online Auctions** 273

  Michael T. Goodrich *(University of California, Irvine)*, Florian Kerschbaum *(SAP Research, Germany)*

- **Research Agenda for Data and Application Security** 283

  X. Sean Wang *(National Science Foundation & University of Vermont)*

Author Index 284

CODASPY 2011 Conference Organization

General Chair: Ravi Sandhu *(University of Texas at San Antonio, USA)*

Program Chair: Elisa Bertino *(Purdue University, USA)*

Proceedings Chair: Gail-Joon Ahn *(Arizona State University, USA)*

Local Arrangements Chair: Jeffrey Reich *(University of Texas at San Antonio, USA)*

Web Master: Ram Krishnan *(University of Texas at San Antonio, USA)*

Publicity Chair: Gail-Joon Ahn *(Arizona State University, USA)*

Program Committee: Gail-Joon Ahn *(Arizona State University, USA)*
Lujo Bauer *(Carnegie Mellon University, USA)*
Barbara Carminati *(University of Insubria, Italy)*
Isabel Cruz *(University of Illinois at Chicago, USA)*
Elena Ferrari *(University of Insubria, Italy)*
Gabriel Ghinita *(Purdue University, USA)*
Carl Gunter *(University of Illinois at Urbana-Champaign, USA)*
Murat Kantarciouglu *(University of Texas at Dallas, USA)*
Günter Karjoth *(IBM Research, Switzerland)*
Anupam Joshi *(University of Maryland at Baltimore County, USA)*
Peng Liu *(The Pennsylvania State University, USA)*
Wenbo Mao *(EMC, China)*
Sharad Mehrotra *(University of California at Irvine, USA)*
Gunther Pernul *(University of Regensburg, Germany)*
Ning Shang *(Microsoft, USA)*
Elaine Shi *(PARC, USA)*
Philippe Pucheral *(University of Versailles, France)*
Dan Thomsen *(Sandia National Labs, USA)*
Bhavani Thuraisingham *(University of Texas at Dallas, USA)*
Vijay Varadharajan *(Macquarie University, Australia)*
Xinwen Zhang *(Samsung, USA)*
William Winsborough *(University of Texas at San Antonio, USA)*
Duminda Wijesekera *(George Mason University, USA)*
Shouhuai Xu *(University of Texas at San Antonio, USA)*

Additional reviewers:

Masoom Alam
Tristan Allard
Shamim Ashik
Ali Bagherzandi
Luc Bouganim
Christian Broser
Tyrone Cadenhead
Mustafa Canim
Ee-Chien Chang
Omar Chowdhury
Mamadou Diallo
Stefan Dürbeck
Christoph Fritsch
Ludwig Fuchs
Rigel Gjomemo
Aries Gkoulalas-Divanis
Oliver Gmelch
Omar Hasan
Raymond Heatherly
Bijit Hore
Ali Inan
Saiful Islam
Sonia Jahid

Yoon-Chan Jhi
Basel Katt
Vaibhav Khadilkar
Michael Kirkpatrick
Fengjun Li
Jingqiang Lin
Michael Netter
Benjamin Nguyen
Robert Nix
Kerim Oktay
Murillo Pontual
Andreas Reisser
Moritz Riesner
Jun Shao
Limin Wang
Xiong Xi
Li Xu
Ziye Yang
Zhenxin Zhan
Wanying Zhao
Yunlei Zhao
Qingji Zheng
Lan Zhou

CODASPY 2011 Sponsor & Supporters

Sponsor:

Supporters:

The Challenge of Data and Application Security and Privacy (DASPY): Are We Up to It?

Ravi Sandhu
Institute for Cyber Security
Univ of Texas at San Antonio
San Antonio, TX, USA
ravi.sandhu@utsa.edu

ABSTRACT

This talk gives a personal perspective on the topic area of this new conference on data and application security and privacy, the difficult nature of the challenge we are confronting and possible research thrusts that may help us progress to an effective scientific discipline in this arena.

Categories and Subject Descriptors

D.4.6 [**Operating Systems**]: Security and Protection—Access controls; K.6.5 [**Management of Computing and Information Systems**]: Security and Protection—Unauthorized access

General Terms

Security, Privacy

Keywords

Data and Application Security and Privacy

1. INTRODUCTION

It is a privilege and honor to start this new conference on data and application security and privacy (DASPY), in collaboration with my colleague and co-founder Elisa Bertino as well as the numerous volunteers who have worked hard to put it together. Before launching into a formal proposal to establish this conference, both of us chatted informally with various colleagues. Their unqualified enthusiasm for a high-quality research forum on this topic motivated us to push ahead. The response from the research community in terms of submissions and the caliber of the resulting program has been truly gratifying, confirming our intuition that this new conference serves a real need.

The term data security has been used for over three decades [2, 3, 8]. The connotation of privacy as an element of data security has often been emphasized [3]. Many of the fundamental problems and solution approaches were identified early on, such as the confinement or covert channel problem [10], statistical inference [6] and the promise of homomorphic encryption [12]. The general understanding of the term data security and privacy is probably not significantly changed since these early days, although of course in the details and nuances there have been considerable advances.

The term application security on the other hand has been and continues to be more amorphous. There isn't much usage of this term in the literature until relatively recently. In the past decade it has become a popular term but in a very narrow sense. For example, it has been equated to a subset of the more general term software security specifically applying to "protection of software after it has been built" [11]. In industrial practice this equates to scanning applications for vulnerabilities before deployment or filtering activity with application firewalls that detect or prevent application-layer attacks. This is particulary so in context of web application security [7, 13].

The intent of this conference is to use the term application security in a much broader sense. The connotation of the narrow sense of application security given above is that the application developer understands the security controls that the application should be enforcing but enforces them incorrectly by focussing entirely on functional aspects. Attackers are able to circumvent this enforcement by exploiting techniques such as SQL injection and cross-site scripting [14]. The much bigger challenge in application security is to understand what security policies need to be incorporated into the application logic. Of course, we still need to understand how these application-layer policies can be correctly coded so that we have high assurance that they cannot be bypassed. In other words the problem of software security is the how part of the problem of application security. This makes software security (i.e., how) a subset of the bigger problem of application security (i.e., what and how).

Is the what question really that big a deal? I definitely think so. Web applications deployed in the past decade have been e-commerce or e-business applications where the security policy of each individual transaction is fairly straightforward. Hence, industrial practice and consequent security breaches in this arena have been dominated by the how aspect. As we look to the future we anticipate the emergence of new applications wherein the what question is not going to be that straightforward. We are already seeing this in social networking, secure information sharing, secure collaboration, secure data provenance, electronic health records, location-based services, secure smart grid, and similar emerging applications. In these applications the security and privacy requirements are not at all obvious. It is a major research challenge to discover, articulate and formulate these requirements.

To summarize, the scope of data security and privacy has been fairly stable over the past three decades although many challenging research still remain. Usage of the term application security has become prevalent only in the last decade. Thus far it has been primarily used in the narrow sense of software failure to enforce fairly straightforward e-commerce and e-business policies due to unforeseen errors in how the security controls were coded. As we look ahead the challenge of securing emerging new applications is going to be driven as much or more by the what question rather than the how question.

2. THE DASPY SYSTEM CHALLENGE

Now that we have clarified the terms used in the DASPY topic we can turn to consideration of the DASPY system challenge. The essence of this challenge was actually articulated long ago as follows.

> "Generally, security is a system problem. That is, it is rare to find that a single security mechanism or procedure is used in isolation. Instead, several different elements working together usually compose a security system to protect something." [5]

Simply stated, the DASPY system challenge is how to develop a systems perspective on DASPY.

3. POSSIBLE RESEARCH THRUSTS

At a very high level I characterize the major research thrusts that are needed to make progress on DASPY as follows.

- We should continue to make progress on point solutions for various problems in data security and privacy.

- We should continue to make progress on the how aspect of application security in the narrow sense of software security.

- We should embark on research to understand the what elements of application security. There are some excellent examples of such research [1, 4, 9]. Nonetheless it needs further and explicit encouragement.

- We should embark on research to address the DASPY system challenge. Today this is largely ignored.

All four of these thrusts are deserving of support. The DASPY system challenge in particular needs special and urgent consideration. Advances in understanding the what aspects of application security are likely to be a prerequisite for progress on the DASPY system challenge.

4. CONCLUSION

The excitement generated by this inaugural conference is evidence of the growing interest in the DASPY topic, even as we develop it conceptually. I am confident this conference will contribute to advancing research in this arena.

Acknowledgment

Ravi Sandhu is partially supported by a grant from the State of Texas Emerging Technology Fund.

5. REFERENCES

[1] A. Barth, A. Datta, J. Mitchell, and H. Nissenbaum. Privacy and contextual integrity: Framework and applications. In *IEEE Symposium on Security and Privacy*, pages 15–198. IEEE, 2006.

[2] D. Denning. *Cryptography and data security*. 1982.

[3] D. Denning and P. Denning. Data security. *ACM Computing Surveys (CSUR)*, 11(3):227–249, 1979.

[4] P. Fong, M. Anwar, and Z. Zhao. A privacy preservation model for facebook-style social network systems. *Computer Security–ESORICS 2009*, pages 303–320, 2010.

[5] R. Gaines and N. Shapiro. Some security principles and their application to computer security. *ACM SIGOPS Operating Systems Review*, 12(3):19–28, 1978.

[6] M. Haq. Insuring individual's privacy from statistical data base users. In *Proceedings of the ACM National Computer Conference*, pages 941–946. ACM, 1975.

[7] Y. Huang, S. Huang, T. Lin, and C. Tsai. Web application security assessment by fault injection and behavior monitoring. In *Proceedings of the 12th international conference on World Wide Web*, pages 148–159. ACM, 2003.

[8] H. Katzan. *Computer data security*. Van Nostrand Reinhold, 1973.

[9] R. Krishnan, R. Sandhu, J. Niu, and W. H. Winsborough. Foundations for group-centric secure information sharing models. In *SACMAT '09: Proceedings of the 14th ACM symposium on Access control models and technologies*, pages 115–124, New York, NY, USA, 2009. ACM.

[10] B. Lampson. A note on the confinement problem. *Communications of the ACM*, 16(10):613–615, 1973.

[11] G. McGraw. Software security. *IEEE Security & Privacy*, 2(2):80–83, 2005.

[12] R. Rivest, L. Adleman, and M. Dertouzos. On data banks and privacy homomorphisms. *Foundations of Secure Computation*, pages 169–178, 1978.

[13] D. Scott and R. Sharp. Abstracting application-level web security. In *Proceedings of the 11th international conference on World Wide Web*, pages 396–407. ACM, 2002.

[14] D. Scott and R. Sharp. Developing secure web applications. *IEEE Internet Computing*, 6(6):38 – 45, 2002.

Key Dependent Message Security: Recent Results and Applications

Tal Malkin
Columbia University
tal@cs.columbia.edu

Isamu Teranishi
NEC Corporation
Columbia University
teranisi@ah.jp.nec.com

Moti Yung
Google Inc.
Columbia University
moti@cs.columbia.edu

ABSTRACT

An encryption scheme is *Key Dependent Message (KDM) secure* if it is secure even against an attacker who has access to encryptions of messages which depend on the secret key. Recent studies have revealed that this strong security notion is important both theoretically and practically. In this paper we review the definition, and survey recent results and applications of KDM security.

Categories and Subject Descriptors

C.2.0 [**COMPUTER-COMMUNICATION NETWORKS**]: General—*Security and protection*; K.4.4 [**COMPUTERS AND SOCIETY**]: Electronic Commerce—*Security*; D.4.6 [**Software**]: OPERATING SYSTEMS—*Security and Protection*

General Terms

Security, Cryptography, Encryption

Keywords

Key Dependent Message Security, KDM, Circular Encryption, Survey

1. INTRODUCTION

The design of public key systems that are secure against attackers which are given a class of functons, and are allowed to request ciphertexts that are each a chosen function (from the given class) of the system's secret keys is a very active area of research. The initial schemes designed in this area were called "circular" [17] and allowed encryption of a secret key or a linear function of a secret key. Later on, more general functions were considered and the security of these schemes was called *Key Dependent Message (KDM) security* [11]. In particular, we say that a public-key encryption (PKE) scheme is *KDM[$\mathcal{F}$] secure* (where $\mathcal{F}$ is a class of functions), if it is secure even against an adversary who is given

public keys $\mathrm{pk}_1, \ldots, \mathrm{pk}_n$ and has access to encryptions of key dependent messages $f(\mathrm{sk}_1, \ldots, \mathrm{sk}_n)$ for adaptively selected functions $f \in \mathcal{F}$.

Originally motivated by the fact that in some systems, keys encrypt other keys (by design or by misuse of protocols), recent research has revealed sdditional important motivation for studying KDM security. On the theoretical side, KDM security can be used to "reconcile" the two fundamental views of security, indistinguishability-based security and Dolev-Yao security [1, 11, 3, 7]. This notion also has surprising connections with other fundamental notions: cryptographic agility [2], obfuscation [18], and encryption with weakly random keys [18]. On the practical side, KDM security is crucial for designing some recent cryptographic protocols. For instance, this notion is used in an anonymous credential system [17], where a KDM secure encryption is used to discourage delegation of credentials. Another example is fully homomorphic encryption, where KDM security is used to achieve the full unbounded construction of [20]. KDM security is also used in the applied case of arguing the security of disk encryption utilities [12] where the disc encryption key may end up being stored in the page files and thus is encrypted along with the disc content.

2. HISTORY OF KDM SECURITY

In this section we briefly overview the history of the KDM security definitions and results. We provide more details (in particular, regarding the technical aspects of these works) in later sections.

2.1 Prehistory of KDM Security

Cryptographers traditionally thought of this kind of "self-encryption" as a dangerous abuse of an encryption scheme. For instance, the seminal work of Goldwasser and Micali [22] already observed that semantic security may not hold if an adversary gets to see an encryption of the secret key.

Another example of a group who considered self-encryption as abuse are the members of the IEEE P1619 standard group [31, 32]. When this group was developing a standard for sector level encryption, they discussed an attack on the tweakable cipher of [29] using self-encryption, and argued whether this self-encryption is a real problem or just a theoretical possibility. They then found that the implementation of disk encryption in Windows Vista^{TM} stored this kind of self-encryption on the disk in some situations. Consequently, they switched to a different scheme based on [37]. Note that, after that event, self-encryptions of tweakable cipher was extensively studied in [26].

2.2 Proposing the KDM Security Notion

Positive aspects of self-encryption were first studied by Camenisch and Lysyanskaya [17] and independently by Black, Rogaway, and Shrimpton [11]. In [17] it was realized that self-encryption could be used to discourage delegation of credentials in the setting of anonymous credential systems. They then formalized the security of self-encryption, called this security notion *circular security*, and proposed circular secure encryption based on the random oracle model.

On the other hand, the authors of [11] studied self-encryption in a different context. Their motivation came from the progress in studies of the Dolev-Yao model [19], which is a formal (symbolic) model of security of encryptions. In this area, Abadi and Rogaway [1] showed that formally equivalent formulae in the Dolev-Yao model give rise to computationally indistinguishable ciphertexts, if there is no "encryption cycle" (some general types of self-encryption) in the formulae. The authors of [11] studied self-encryption in order to overcome this restriction and formalized the security of self-encryption as *KDM security*, which is a more general notion than the circular security. They also proposed KDM secure encryption w.r.t. all functions based on the random oracle model. Later, Adão, Bana, Herzog, and Scedrov [3] proved formally that the above restriction could be removed if an encryption is KDM secure.

2.3 The Seminal Work of Boneh, Halevi, Hamburg, Ostrovsky and Recent Studies

The most important problem, at the time, was constructing a KDM secure public key encryption without relying on the random oracle idealization. Hofheinz and Unruh [28] partially solved this problem. Later, Boneh, Halevi, Hamburg, and Ostrovsky finally succeeded and proposed the first feasible KDM secure scheme in the standard model in their seminal paper [12]. They achieve KDM secure scheme w.r.t. affine functions, which is quite inefficient.

After this breakthrough, two main lines of research have emerged. The first is the theoretical direction: we want to know the largest function ensembles $\mathcal{F}$ such that there exists a feasible KDM secure scheme w.r.t. $\mathcal{F}$. The second direction considers the more practical side: we want to construct an efficient KDM secure scheme w.r.t. a reasonably large $\mathcal{F}$.

In the first direction, Brakerski, Goldwasser, and Kalai [15] succeeded in proposing an encryption scheme which is KDM secure beyond affine functions. Then later, Barak, Haitner, Hofheinz, and Ishai [8] succeeded in constructing KDM secure scheme w.r.t. all bounded size circuits. On the other hand, an impossibility result of Haitner and Holenstein [25] (which is improved by [8]) showed that there is no black-box construction of KDM secure scheme w.r.t. all (unbounded size) circuits.

In the second direction, constructions that do not encrypt messages bit by bit were considered, but rather do it block-wise. Applebaum, Cash, Peikert, and Sahai [5] proposed an efficient KDM secure scheme w.r.t. affine functions based on lattices. Recently, Malkin, Teranishi, and Yung [30] proposed a KDM secure scheme w.r.t. quite larger function set than the affine function set (i.e. a rational function over Straight Line Programs). The scheme is block-wise and the resulting ciphertext is a function of the function degree and not that of the computational program size.

2.4 Other Works

Next we mention a number of KDM related investigations. Backes, Dürmuth, and Unruh [6] showed that the well-known OAEP encryption is KDM secure. Halevi and Krawczyk [26] generalized the notion of KDM to pseudorandom functions and studied its KDM security. Camenisch, Chandran and Shoup [16] proposed the first KDM and CCA2 secure PKE in the standard model. Green and Hohenberger [23] gave an example of PKE which satisfies the indistinguishability but does not satisfy 2-circular security.

The connection between the adaptive Dolev-Yao model and generalized versions of KDM security were studied by Backes, Pfitzmann, Scedrov [7]. Finally, surprising connections between KDM security and the notions of agility and obfuscation are shown by Acar, Belenkiy, and Bellare, and Cash [2] and Canetti, Kalai, Varia, and Wichs [18], respectively.

3. KDM SECURITY

Next, we define the notion of KDM security, give example of function classes, and discuss a security proof methodology. The reader is assumed to be familiar with basic traditional definitions of public-key encryption schemes and of cryptographic attacks on such systems (i.e., chosen plaintext (CPA) and chosen ciphertext (CCA) attacks).

3.1 Definition

For a public key encryption scheme $\mathcal{PKE} = (\mathsf{Kg}, \mathsf{Enc}, \mathsf{Dec})$ a security parameter κ, and a natural number n, let

$$(\overrightarrow{\mathsf{pk}}, \overrightarrow{\mathsf{sk}}) \leftarrow \overrightarrow{\mathsf{Kg}}_n(1^\kappa)$$

denote the algorithm which executes Kg n times and outputs the n-tuples of public keys and secret keys. Let pk_i and sk_i denote the i-th element of $\overrightarrow{\mathsf{pk}}$ and $\overrightarrow{\mathsf{sk}}$, respectively.

For the secret key space SkSp and message space MeSp of $\mathcal{PKE}$, let

$$\mathcal{F}^{(n)} \subset \{f \: : \: \mathsf{SkSp}^n \rightarrow \mathsf{MeSp}\}, \qquad \mathcal{F} = \cup_{n=1}^\infty \mathcal{F}^{(n)}.$$

For $\mathrm{ATK} \in \{\mathrm{CPA}, \mathrm{CCA}\}$, a natural number n, a bit b, and an adversary A, consider the following game:

$$(\overrightarrow{\mathsf{pk}}, \overrightarrow{\mathsf{sk}}) \leftarrow \mathsf{Kg}_n(1^\kappa), \quad b' \leftarrow \mathsf{A}^{\mathcal{O}_{\mathsf{Enc}}^{(b)}, \mathcal{D}_{\mathrm{ATK}}}(\overrightarrow{\mathsf{pk}}), \quad \text{Output } b'.$$

Above, A is allowed to make polynomial number of queries to oracles:

- If $(i, f) \in [n] \times \mathcal{F}^{(n)}$ is sent to $\mathcal{O}_{\mathsf{Enc}}^{(b)}$, $\mathcal{O}_{\mathsf{Enc}}^{(b)}(i, f)$ answers the following C. Below, 0 be some fixed element of MeSp.

$$C \leftarrow \begin{cases} \mathsf{Enc}(\mathsf{pk}_i, f(\overrightarrow{\mathsf{sk}})) & \text{if } b = 1 \\ \mathsf{Enc}(\mathsf{pk}_i, 0) & \text{Otherwise.} \end{cases}$$

- If $(i, C) \in [n] \times \{0, 1\}^*$ is sent to $\mathcal{D}_{\mathrm{ATK}}$, $\mathcal{D}_{\mathrm{CPA}}$ always sends back $\perp$. On the other hand, $\mathcal{D}_{\mathrm{CCA}}$ sends back $\mathsf{Dec}(\mathsf{sk}_i, C)$, as long as C was not an output of $\mathcal{O}_{\mathsf{Enc}}^{(b)}(i, f)$ for some f.

We say that $\mathcal{PKE}$ is $KDM^{(n)}[\mathcal{F}]$-ATK *secure* (or $KDM^{(n)}$-ATK *secure with respect to* $\mathcal{F}$) if the following advantage is negligible for any polynomial time adversary A.

$$\mathsf{Adv.KDM_A}[\mathcal{F}, n] = \big| \Pr[b' = 1 \mid b = 1] - \Pr[b' = 1 \mid b = 0] \big|.$$

We say that $\mathcal{PKE}$ is $KDM[\mathcal{F}]$-ATK *secure* if it is $\text{KDM}^{(n)}[\mathcal{F}]$-ATK secure for any n. In this survey, we simply call *KDM security* KDM-CPA security.

The following proposition is simple to verify:

PROPOSITION 1 (**KDM-ATK $\Rightarrow$ IND-ATK**). $KDM[\mathcal{F}]$-*ATK security imply indistinguishability against ATK if $\mathcal{F}$ contains all constant functions* $\{f_M : \overrightarrow{\text{sk}} \mapsto M\}_M$ *on* MeSp.

3.2 Stronger Definitions

KDM Security for Adaptive Public Key Generations: A stronger definition of KDM security can be considered, where an adversary can get new public keys adaptively by making a query to the challenger.

Some known schemes (e.g. [14]), however, may not satisfy this stronger security notion. This is because they require the maximum n to be fixed before key generation and KDM security is be proved only when n is less than the predetermined maximum.

KDM Security with Corruptions: Backes, Pfitzmann, and Scedrov [7] and Backes, Dürmuth, and Unruh [6] studied stronger variants of KDM security where an adversary can obtain some secret keys adaptively by "corrupting users". This kind of "KDM security with corruption" is required to study Dolev-Yao model, as we will see in Section 5.1.

Defining this notion is not easy because an adversary may get unexpected secret keys other than queried one. E.g. if she knows $\text{Enc}(\text{pk}_1, \text{sk}_2)$, she can get sk_2 also by making reveal query for the secret key sk_1 corresponding to pk_1.

The authors of [7] therefore imposed the following restriction on reveal queries: An adversary can make reveal queries for sk_i only when she has not made encryption query under key pk_i.

However, the authors of [6] then found that the security definition of [7] cannot be used to prove some useful examples of protocols. They therefore gave another definition of "KDM security with corruption" where the restriction on reveal queries is weaker than that of [7], and then they showed that the well-known OAEP encryption scheme [10] satisfies their security notion.

3.3 Examples of KDM function ensembles

Constants. The trivial example of KDM function ensemble $\mathcal{F}$ is the set of all constant functions

$$\{f_M : \overrightarrow{\text{sk}} \mapsto M\}_M$$

on MeSp. KDM security w.r.t. this ensemble is clearly equivalent to indistinguishability (namely semantic security).

Clique and Circular. A simple non trivial example is the set of all selector functions

$$\mathcal{CLQ} = \{P_j : \overrightarrow{\text{sk}} \mapsto \text{sk}_j\}_j.$$

KDM security w.r.t. this ensemble is called *clique security* [12]. This security notion against CPA attacks is clearly equivalent to the following statement:

$\{\text{Enc}(\text{sk}_j, \text{sk}_i)\}_{i,j}$ is indistinguishable from $\{\text{Enc}(\text{sk}_j, 0)\}_{i,j}$.

Circular security has two meanings: the original definition in [17] is equivalent to clique security, but it sometimes refers to a weaker security notion (Strictly Circular Security):

$\{\text{Enc}(\text{sk}_i, \text{sk}_{i+1 \bmod n})\}_i$ is indistinguishable from $\{\text{Enc}(\text{sk}_i, 0)\}_i$.

Projections. *Projection security* [4] refers to KDM security w.r.t.

$$\mathcal{PRJ} = \mathcal{F}_0 \cup \mathcal{F}_1,$$

where

$$\mathcal{F}_0 = \{f_{i,j} : \overrightarrow{\text{sk}} \mapsto (\text{the } j\text{-th bit of sk}_i)\}_{i,j}$$
$$\mathcal{F}_1 = \{f_{i,j} : \overrightarrow{\text{sk}} \mapsto 1\text{-(the } j\text{-th bit of sk}_i)\}_{i,j}.$$

Linear and Affine. If the message space is a linear space over $\mathbb{Z}_p$, we can define

$$\text{Lin}(\mathcal{F}) = \{\sum_j a_j f_j \mid a_j \in \mathbb{Z}_p, f_j \in \mathcal{F}\},$$

$$\text{Aff}(\mathcal{F}) = \{c + \sum_j a_j f_j \mid c, a_j \in \mathbb{Z}_p, f_j \in \mathcal{F}\}.$$

for a function ensemble $\mathcal{F}$.

(Bounded Degree) Quotient Straight-Line Program. A function $f(X_1, \ldots, X_n)$ is called *SLP computable* over $\mathbb{Z}_K$ if it can be computed from constants of $\mathbb{Z}_K$ and variables X_k by applying $+$, $-$, and $\cdot$ a polynomial number of times. Clearly, SLP computable function is a polynomial over $\mathbb{Z}_K$ but it may have superpolynomial number of terms[30].

A function f is called *QSLP computable* (stands for Quotient SLP) if we also consider division it satisfies the same definition as above, except division is allowed as well, and we consider a ratio (division) of two SLP computable functions [13]. We require that a QSLP is well-defined in the sense that all denominator of divisions have inverses.

The following ensembles [30] can be defined:

$$\mathcal{SLP}_{\text{poly}}[K] = \{f \mid \deg f \leq \text{poly}(\kappa), f \text{ is SLP computable}\}$$
$$\mathcal{QSLP}_{\text{poly}}[K] = \left\{f \, \middle| \, \begin{array}{l} \deg f \leq \text{poly}(\kappa), \\ f \text{ is well-defined QSLP computable} \end{array}\right\}$$

Recall that κ above is the security parameter.

(Bounded) Boolean Circuits [8]. The largest ensemble for which it is feasible to achieve KDM security, is that of bounded Boolean circuits.

$$\mathcal{C}_{\text{poly}} = \left\{f \, \middle| \, \begin{array}{l} \exists C : \text{circuit with size}(C) \leq \text{poly}(\kappa), \\ f \text{ is computable by } C. \end{array}\right\}$$

3.4 Important Factors

The following factors are important when one constructs a KDM secure scheme:

- The function ensemble $\mathcal{F}$.

- Security: CPA or CCA.

- Idealized random oracle model or not.

- Efficiency.

- Flexibility of parameters.

About efficiency, public key encryption schemes are considered efficient (in some general sense) if they encrypt messages as entire blocks (and not "bit by bit"). Hence, being block-wise encryption or bit-wise encryption scheme is an important factor, for approaching practicality. Many known schemes [12, 16, 8, 15, 14] are bit-wise encryption, although some known schemes are more efficient block-wise ones [5, 30].

"Flexibility of parameters" means whether one can select parameters such as the number of users flexibly. This factor is also an important parameter for assessing efficiency and practicality. In [30] three types of flexibility levels were identified (based on when a parameter is chosen):, "KeyGen bounded," "Enc bounded," and "Unbounded."

"KeyGen bounded" means that one has to fix the maximums of these parameters before the key generation, KDM security holds only when the parameters are less than these maxima, and efficiency of the scheme depends on these maxima.

"Enc bounded" means that we do not have to fix such maxima, and KDM security hold for all values of parameters, but efficiency of the scheme (the size of the ciphertext) depends on the values of parameters (given at encryption time).

"Unbounded" is the same as "Enc bounded" except that efficiency of the scheme is independent of the values of parameters.

3.5 How to Prove KDM Security

Malkin, Teranishi, and Yung [30] gave a general framework for proving KDM security, called *triple mode proof framework*, by abstracting the proof techniques of known schemes [12, 5, 14]. Specifically, a triple mode proof framework is the notion which enables us to overcome the following inherent dilemma.

Dilemma for Proving KDM Security. A simulator in the proof should produce the view of an adversary without knowing the secret keys, because the secrecy of the secret keys should be used in the proof as the intractable problem. However the simulator has to know the secret keys because it has to compute (an encryption of) the value $f(\mathrm{sk}_1, \ldots, \mathrm{sk}_n)$.

Solution. The triple mode proof framework is the mechanism that overcomes the above dilemma by using *two* simulators for the security proof, where the first one knows the secret key but the second one does not.

These two simulators are used to show the indistinguishability of *standard ciphertext*, *faked ciphertext*, *hiding ciphertext*. (See Fig.1.) The standard ciphertext is the same as the ciphertext of the scheme. On the other hand, the *faked ciphertext* can be computed by using query (i, f) of an adversary but without using the secret keys. The *hiding ciphertext* can be computed by using neither a query nor the secret keys.

Since a hiding ciphertext does not depend on the query of an adversary, the indistinguishability of a standard ciphertext and a hiding one clearly implies the KDM security.

4. KNOWN SCHEMES

4.1 Comparisons

Fig.2, taken from [30], shows a comparison among the known schemes in the regular (non idealized) model. Here κ

is the security parameter. Note that all schemes except for [16] are KDM-CPA secure, and [16] is KDM-CCA2 secure. Only two schemes [5, 30] are efficient block-wise schemes. Only one scheme [8] provides KDM security against the most general class of all bounded size circuits.

In Fig.2, the "Flexibility of Parameters" category is the one explained in Section 3.4. $\mathcal{F}$ of [5] is the set of functions $f(\vec{\mathrm{sk}})$ which outputs some blocks of sk. In the row of [8] (resp. [30]) the "size" ℓ represents the number of gates in a circuit (resp. the number of $\{+, -, \cdot, /\}$ in a QSLP) which computes a function $f(\vec{\mathrm{sk}})$. The value N of [30] is an RSA modulus and s is a constant.

4.2 Scheme in the Random Oracle Model

Schemes in the random oracle (idealized and unrealizable) model are relatively easy due to availability of truly random strings.

Black, Rogaway, and Shrimpton [11] showed that the following simple encryption scheme of Bellare and Rogaway [9] is the KDM-CPA secure with respect to the set of all functions.

$$\mathsf{Enc}(\mathrm{pk}, M) = (\phi_{\mathrm{pk}}(R), \mathcal{H}(R) \oplus M).$$

Above, ϕ_{pk} is a trapdoor one-way permutation, R is a random, and $\mathcal{H}$ is a random oracle. A secret key sk of this scheme is the trapdoor of ϕ_{pk}.

The proof of KDM security is straight forward. The output $\mathcal{H}(R)$ of the random oracle is a truly random string, and therefore hides M perfectly, even if M depends on the secret key. This means that a ciphertext is indistinguishable from random and the KDM security of the scheme therefore holds.

Camenisch and Lysyanskaya [17] also gave another example of KDM secure scheme in the random oracle model which details we omit.

4.3 The [12] scheme w.r.t. Affine Functions

In their seminal work [12] Boneh, Halevi, Hamburg, and Ostrovsky proposed the first KDM secure scheme in the standard model. Let $\mathbb{G}$ be a group of prime order p and g be a fixed generator of $\mathbb{G}$. Their scheme is as follows.

- **Key Generation.** Let $\ell = \lfloor 3 \log_2 p \rfloor$. $g_1, \ldots, g_\ell \overset{\$}{\leftarrow} \mathbb{G}$, $s \leftarrow (s_1, \ldots, s_\ell) \overset{\$}{\leftarrow} \{0, 1\}^\ell$, $h \leftarrow g_1^{s_1} \cdots g_\ell^{s_\ell}$. Output the following pk and sk:

$$\mathrm{pk} := ((g_j)_{j \in [\ell]}, h), \qquad \mathrm{sk} := (g^{s_j})_{j \in [\ell]}.$$

- **Encryption of** $M \in \mathbb{G}$. Choose $r \overset{\$}{\leftarrow} \mathbb{Z}_p$ and output the ciphertext

$$((g_j^r)_{j \in [\ell]}, Mh^r)$$

- **Decryption of** $(c_1, \ldots, c_\ell, d) \in \mathbb{G}^{\ell+1}$. Compute $(s_1, \ldots, s_\ell$ from $\mathrm{sk} = (g^{s_1}, \ldots, g^{s_\ell})$. (One can do it in polynomial time because $s_i \in \{0, 1\}$.) Output

$$M \leftarrow d \cdot c_1^{s_1} \cdots c_\ell^{s_\ell}.$$

THEOREM 1 ([12]). *The above scheme is KDM secure with respect to* $\mathsf{Aff}(\mathcal{PRJ})$ *for any n under the DDH assumption.*

Dependency of Ciphertexts	sk	(i,f)	
Ciphertext	Yes.	Yes.	} Sim. knows sk.
Faked Ciphertext	No.	Yes.	} Sim. does not know sk.
Hiding Ciphertext	No.	No.	

Figure 1: Triple Mode Simulatable Encryption[30]

	Block-wise?	Functions	$|$Ciphertext$|$ per $|$Message$|$	Flexibility of Parameters			Assumption
				# of Users n	max deg d	Size ℓ	
[12] [16]		Aff(PRJ)	$O(\kappa^2)$		-	-	DDH LDDH
[15]		Polynomial of Bits with deg= $O(1)$	$O(\kappa^{d+1})$	Unbounded	KeyGen	-	DDH LWE
[14]	No.	Aff(PRJ)	$O(n\kappa^2 + \kappa^{d+1})$	KeyGen		-	QR DCR
[8]		Bounded Size Circuit	$O(n\mathsf{poly}(\kappa) + \kappa\ell)$	Enc	-	Enc	DDH LWE
[5]	Yes.	Aff($\mathcal{F}$)	$O(1)$		-	-	LWE
[30]		$\mathcal{QSLP}_{\mathsf{poly}}[N]$	$O(d)$	Unbounded	Enc	Unbounded	DCR

Figure 2: Comparison of Known Results [30]

Idea Behind the Proof. A starting point of the proof is showing that the ElGamal encryption is KDM secure w.r.t. function $f(s) = (g^a)^s$. Here $a \in \mathbb{Z}_p$ is some constant. We can divert the idea for proving it into the proof of the KDM security of the scheme [12], because the scheme [12] coincides with ElGamal if we let $\ell = 1$, take s_i not from $\{0,1\}^\ell$ but $\mathbb{Z}_p$, and finally set the secret key not to $(g^{s_j})_{j\in[\ell]}$ but to $s = \log_g h$, where (g,h) is a public key.

KDM security of ElGamal w.r.t. $f(s) = (g^a)^s$ is shown as follows. A ciphertext $C = (g^r, Mh^r)$ for a key dependent message $M = (g^a)^s$ can be re-written as follows, by setting $t = r + a$:

$$C = (g^r, (g^a)^s(g^s)^r) = (g^r, g^{s(a+r)}) = (g^{-a}g^t, g^{st}) = (g^{-a}g^t, h^t).$$

The above discussion shows that a ciphertext C is (statistically) indistinguishable from a "faked ciphertext" $(g^{-a}g^t, h^t)$, which is computable from a public key (g,h), the random value t, and a, without using the secret key s!

The DDH assumption implies that (g^t, h^t) is indistinguishable from random pair of group elements. In other words, a faked ciphertext $(g^{-a}g^t, h^t)$ is indistinguishable from a "hiding ciphertext" (random,random).

The above discussion shows that a ciphertext C is indistinguishable from a the hiding ciphertext, which is independent from the function $f(s) = (g^a)^s$ queried by an adversary. This means that the KDM security holds.

We can prove KDM security of [12] based on the above idea, although it is much harder involving linear algebra arguments.

4.4 A Lattice based Scheme

Applebaum et.al. [5] constructed a KDM secure scheme using the Learning With Errors (LWE) assumption [35], which is a lattice based assumption. Their public key and an encryption of a message M is as follows:

$$\mathsf{pk} = (A, B), \qquad C = (Ar, Br + Mp + e) \bmod p^2,$$

where p is a prime, A and B are some matrix over $\mathbb{Z}_{p^2}$, r is a random value, and e is some randomly selected "error".

Their scheme is similar to ElGamal encryption in some sense: In fact, if we remove e and p, a ciphertext becomes

$$C = (Ar, Br + M),$$

which is an "additive version" of ElGamal. The KDM security of ElGamal was given above in Section 4.3, and the security proof of the current scheme indeed resembles that proof.

4.5 Scheme w.r.t. Bounded Boolean Circuits

Barak, Haitner, Hofheinz, and Ishai [8] constructed a KDM secure scheme w.r.t. the set of bounded Boolean circuits.

The starting point of their scheme is fully homomorphic encryption [20]. A *fully homomorphic encryption* is an encryption scheme such that $\mathsf{Enc}(\mathsf{pk}, f(M))$ can be computed from $\mathsf{Enc}(\mathsf{pk}, M)$ for any polynomial size circuit f.

If a fully homomorphic encryption also satisfies the property $\mathsf{Enc}(\mathsf{pk}, \mathsf{sk}) \simeq \mathsf{Enc}(\mathsf{pk}, \mathsf{random})$, it is immediately KDM secure for all functions because the fully homomorphic property, the above property, and the semantic security of Enc imply $\mathsf{Enc}(\mathsf{pk}, f(\mathsf{sk})) \simeq \mathsf{Enc}(\mathsf{pk}, f(\mathsf{random})) \simeq \mathsf{Enc}(\mathsf{pk}, 0)$.

However, there is no known scheme that satisfies all of the above properties. The authors of [8] therefore replace the fully homomorphic encryption of the above scheme with Yao's garbled circuits. Informally, a *garbled circuit* $\mathsf{GC}(h, K)$ is a polynomial time computable function which takes a bounded Boolean circuit h and a "key" $K = (K_{i,j})_{i\in\{0,1\}, j\in[m]}$. For a bit string $x = x_1||\cdots||x_m$, let K_x be $(K_{x_j,j})_{i\in\{0,1\}, j\in[m]}$. Then the garbled circuit satisfies the following properties:

- If one knows K_x, one can compute the value $h(x)$ from $\mathsf{GC}(h, K)$.

- Even if one knows K_x, $\mathsf{GC}(h, K)$ and $\mathsf{GC}(h', K)$ are indistinguishable for every h and h' satisfying $h(x) = h'(x)$.

- If one does not know K, $\mathsf{GC}(h, K)$ and $\mathsf{GC}(h', K)$ are indistinguishable for every h and h'.

A public key pk and an encryption $C = \mathsf{Enc}(\mathrm{pk}, M)$ of a message M in [8] are as follows. Bellow, $\mathsf{TEnc}^{(i,j)}$ is an encryption satisfying some special property which we will explain later, $\mathrm{pk}_{i,j}$ is a public key for $\mathsf{TEnc}^{(i,j)}$, and h_M is a circuit which always outputs M.

$$\mathrm{pk} = (\mathrm{pk}_{i,j})_{i,j}$$

$$\mathsf{Enc}(\mathrm{pk}, M) = ((\mathsf{TEnc}^{(i,j)}(\mathrm{pk}_{i,j}, K_{i,j}))_{i,j}, \mathsf{GC}(h_M, K)).$$

To decrypt the above ciphertext, K is recovered from the first part of the ciphertext using the secret keys, and then $h_M(0)$ is computed from $\mathsf{GC}(h_M, K)$ and K. Since h_M always outputs M, the recovered message $h_M(0)$ is equal to M.

$\mathsf{Enc}^{(i,j)}$ is an encryption function of a *target encryption scheme* [8]. Informally, a target encryption scheme (TKg, $(\mathsf{TEnc}^{(i,j)})_{i,j}$, TDec) is a tuple of polynomial time algorithms satisfying the following properties, where $(\mathrm{pk}, \mathrm{sk})$ is a key pair generated by $\mathsf{TKg}(1^\kappa)$, sk_i is the i-th bit of sk, and $\overline{\mathrm{sk}}_i$ is $1 - \mathrm{sk}_i$.

- $\mathsf{TDec}(\mathrm{sk}, \mathsf{TEnc}^{(i,\mathrm{sk}_i)}(\mathrm{pk}, M)) = M$ holds for any M and i.

- $\mathsf{TEnc}^{(i,\overline{\mathrm{sk}}_i)}(\mathrm{pk}, M)$ and $\mathsf{TEnc}^{(i,\overline{\mathrm{sk}}_i)}(\mathrm{pk}, M')$ have statistically indistinguishable distributions for any M, M' and i.

- $(\mathrm{pk}, \mathsf{TEnc}^{(i,j)}(\mathrm{pk}, M))$ and $(\mathrm{pk}, \mathsf{TEnc}^{(i,j)}(\mathrm{pk}, M'))$ have computationally indistinguishable distributions for any M, M' and i.

The authors of [8] showed that target encryptions can be constructed based on DDH and LWE assumptions. Hence KDM secure scheme w.r.t. bounded size circuits can be constructed based on a DDH or LWE assumption (and the existence of garbled circuits). We note that, obviously, the resulting ciphertext in the scheme is a very large function of the circuit size.

4.6 CCA and KDM secure scheme

Camenisch, Chandran, and Shoup [16] gave a general method to construct KDM-CCA secure scheme based on Naor-Yung dual encryption technique [33]. Specifically, they construct their scheme based on a KDM[$\mathcal{F}$]-CPA secure encryption $\Pi_{\mathsf{KDM}} = (\mathsf{Kg}_{\mathsf{KDM}}, \mathsf{Enc}_{\mathsf{KDM}}, \mathsf{Dec}_{\mathsf{KDM}})$, IND-CCA2 secure encryption $\Pi_{\mathsf{CCA}} = (\mathsf{Kg}_{\mathsf{CCA}}, \mathsf{Enc}_{\mathsf{CCA}}, \mathsf{Dec}_{\mathsf{CCA}})$, and a NIZK (Non-Interactive Zero-knowledge Proof). The details of their scheme are as follows.

- **Key Generation.** Generate key pairs $(\mathrm{pk}_1, \mathrm{sk}_1)$ and $(\mathrm{pk}_2, \mathrm{sk}_2)$ of Π_{KDM} and Π_{CCA}. Generate a CRS σ for NIZK. Output $\mathsf{PK} = (\mathrm{pk}_1, \mathrm{pk}_2, \sigma)$ and $\mathsf{SK} = \mathrm{sk}_1$.

- **Encryption of** M**.** Compute and output the following C.

$$C = (\mathsf{Enc}_{\mathsf{KDM}}(\mathrm{pk}, M), \mathsf{Enc}_{\mathsf{CCA}}(\mathrm{pk}, M), \mathsf{pf}).$$

Here pf is a NIZK which proves that the first two components of C encrypt the same messages.

- **Decryption of** C**.** Parse C as (C_1, C_2, pf). If pf is invalid, output $\bot$. Otherwise, recover message from C_1 using SK.

The KDM[$\mathcal{F}$] security and the CCA security of C follows from those of $\mathsf{Enc}_{\mathsf{KDM}}(\mathrm{pk}, M)$ and $\mathsf{Enc}_{\mathsf{CCA}}(\mathrm{pk}, M)$. The scheme of [16] is therefore KDM[$\mathcal{F}$]-CCA secure.

Camenisch et.al. [16] also gave the concrete scheme, more secure than the generic one, where Π_{KDM} is (a LDDH based variant of) [12], Π_{CCA} is [38, 27], and NIZK is Groth-Sahai proof system [24].

4.7 KDM$^{(1)}$ Secure Scheme w.r.t. $\mathsf{Lin}((\phi_j)_{j \in [m]})$

Brakerski, Goldwasser, and Kalai [15] proposed a KDM$^{(1)}$ secure scheme w.r.t. $\mathsf{Lin}((\phi_j)_{j \in [m]})$, where $\phi_1, \ldots, \phi_m$ are polynomial time computable functions $\mathsf{SkSp} \rightarrow \mathsf{MeSp}$ *fixed in advances*. (Here KDM$^{(1)}$ security means that KDM security for a single key. See Section 3.1 for the definition of this.)

Their scheme is constructed by modifying the scheme of [12]: Their key generation selects secret key $\mathrm{sk} \leftarrow s \leftarrow (s_1, \ldots, s_k) \xleftarrow{\$} \{0,1\}^k$ randomly and sets

$$s_{k+i} \leftarrow \phi_i(s_1, \ldots, s_k), \text{ for } i \in [m], \quad \bar{s} \leftarrow (s_1, \ldots, s_\ell),$$

where k is some parameter and $\ell = k + m$. The other parts of the scheme are the same as those of [12] except that one uses $\bar{s}$ instead of s when generating pk and decrypting a ciphertext.

Specifically, their scheme is as follows (bellow, k and m are parameters).

- **Key Generation.** Let $\ell \leftarrow k + m$. $g_1, \ldots, g_\ell \xleftarrow{\$} \mathbb{G}$, $s \leftarrow (s_1, \ldots, s_k) \xleftarrow{\$} \{0,1\}^k$, $s_{k+i} \leftarrow \phi_i(s_1, \ldots, s_k)$ for $i \in [m]$, $h \leftarrow g_1^{s_1} \cdots g_\ell^{s_\ell}$. Output the following pk and sk:

$$\mathrm{pk} := ((g_j)_{j \in [\ell]}, h), \qquad \mathrm{sk} := (g^{s_j})_{j \in [\ell]}.$$

- **Encryption of** $M \in \mathbb{G}$**.** Choose $r \xleftarrow{\$} \mathbb{Z}_p$ and output the ciphertext

$$((g_j^r)_{j \in [\ell]}, Mh^r)$$

- **Decryption of** $(c_1, \ldots, c_\ell, d) \in \mathbb{G}^{\ell+1}$**.** Compute $(s_1, \ldots, s_\ell$ from $\mathrm{sk} = (g^{s_1}, \ldots, g^{s_\ell})$. (One can do it in polynomial time because $s_i \in \{0,1\}$.) Output

$$M \leftarrow d \cdot c_1^{s_1} \cdots c_\ell^{s_\ell}.$$

For suitable choice of k, their scheme become KDM secure under the DDH assumption.

They also showed that their scheme became KDM secure w.r.t. the set of polynomials of bits of secret keys with degree $\leq d$, by setting $\phi_i = s_1^{\varepsilon_1} \cdots s_k^{\varepsilon_k}$ for $i = \varepsilon_1 || \cdots || \varepsilon_k$ and $\varepsilon_1 + \cdots + \varepsilon_k \leq d$.

They also gave a sufficient condition characterizing when their technique is applicable to a scheme, and use it to apply their technique to the scheme of [5], resulting in a scheme based on the LWE assumption.

4.8 KDM Secure Schemes w.r.t. Affine Functions based on QR and DCR Assumptions.

Brakerski and Goldwasser [14] proposed a general framework of assumptions (implying the QR and the DCR assumptions as special cases) and proposed a KDM secure scheme w.r.t. the set $\mathsf{Aff}(\mathcal{PRJ})$ of affine functions based on assumptions contained in this framework.

Their scheme itself is similar to that of [12], that is

$$\mathrm{sk} = (s_1, \ldots, s_\ell), \quad \mathrm{pk} = ((g_j)_{j \in [\ell]}, h), \quad \text{where } h = g_1^{s_1} \cdots g_\ell^{s_\ell}$$

$$\mathsf{Enc}_{\mathsf{pk}}(M) = ((g_j{}^r)_{j \in [\ell]}, T^M h^r) \bmod N,$$

where $M \in \{0,1\}$ is a message, and T is -1 or $1+N$ if the assumption is QR or DCR, respectively. They also showed that their scheme is leakage resilient and auxiliary input resilient.

The security proof of their scheme, in turn, is based on a new proof technique. If we use the term of triple mode proof framework of [30], their proof technique can be described as follows: they prove the computational indistinguishability of the ciphertext of the message $M = b + \sum_j a_j s_j$ and a "faked ciphertext" $((T^{a_j} g_j{}^r)_{j \in [\ell]}, T^b h^r)$ based on the secrecy of the random value r.

4.9 Scheme w.r.t. Bounded Degree SLP and QSLP

The scheme of Malkin, Teranishi, and Yung [30], called *d-Cascaded Paillier ElGamal*, is computed recursively as follows: Let N be an RSA modulus and $s \geq 2$ be a natural number. First, a "Paillier ElGamal" encryption $(e_0, c_0) = (u_0{}^{-1}, T^M v_0) \bmod N^s$ of a message M is computed, where $T = 1 + N$ and $(u_0, v_0) \leftarrow (g^{r_0}, h^{r_0})$. Next, the left component e_i of the ciphertext is encrypted by "Paillier ElGamal" encryption and $(e_{i+1}, c_{i+1}) = (u_{i+1}{}^{-1}, e_i v_{i+1})$ is obtained for $i = 1, \ldots, d-1$, where $(u_{i+1}, v_{i+1}) \leftarrow (g^{r_{i+1}}, h^{r_{i+1}})$. We finally let c_{d+1} be e_d.

The d-cascaded Paillier ElGamal encryption of message M is the tuple

$$C = (c_{d+1}, c_d, c_{d-1}, \ldots, c_0)$$
$$= (u_d{}^{-1}, u_{d-1}{}^{-1} v_d, u_{d-2}{}^{-1} v_{d-1}, \ldots, T^M v_0) \bmod N^s.$$

The details of the scheme are as follows: Bellow, we assume that N which is a product of two safe primes and $g \in \{u^{2N} \bmod N^s \mid u \in \mathbb{Z}_N\}$ are public. We will let T denote $1 + N$.

- $\mathsf{Kg}(prm)$: Select $\mathsf{sk} \leftarrow x \xleftarrow{\$} [2^\xi \cdot \lfloor N/4 \rfloor]$ randomly, compute $\mathsf{pk} \leftarrow h \leftarrow g^x \bmod N^s$, and output $(\mathsf{pk}, \mathsf{sk})$.

- $\mathsf{Enc}_{prm}(\mathsf{pk}, M)$ for $M \in \mathbb{Z}_{N^{s-1}}$: Select $r_0, \ldots, r_d \xleftarrow{\$} [\lfloor N/4 \rfloor]$ randomly, compute the following $c_0, \ldots, c_{d+1}$ and output $C \leftarrow (c_{d+1}, \ldots, c_0)$.

$$c_j \leftarrow \begin{cases} T^M h^{r_0} & \bmod N^s & \text{if } j = 0 \\ g^{-r_{j-1}} h^{r_j} & \bmod N^s & \text{if } j \in \{1, \ldots, d\} \\ g^{-r_d} & \bmod N^s & \text{if } j = d+1. \end{cases}$$

- $\mathsf{Dec}_{prm}(\mathsf{sk}, C)$: Parse C as $(c_{d+1}, \ldots, c_0)$ and compute and output the following M:

$$M \leftarrow L(c_0 c_1{}^x \cdots c_{d+1}{}^{x^{d+1}} \bmod N^s).$$

where L is the function such that for all $M \in \mathbb{Z}_{N^{s-1}}$, $L(T^M) = M \bmod N^{s-1}$.

Their scheme is KDM secure w.r.t. SLP (i.e., straight line program) computable polynomial f with degree $\leq d$ modulo N^s. The idea behind the proof is as follows: Let $f(x)$ be a polynomial with degree d (which is a special case of a SLP computable function). Based on the technique of [14], they showed that $(g^{-r}, T^{f(x)} h^r)$ is indistinguishable from $(T^{f'(x)} g^{-r}, T^b h^r)$, where $f(s) = f'(s)s + b$. Now the right term is independent of the secret key, and the left term does

depend on the secret key, but only as a degree $d-1$ polynomial $f'(x)$. Hence, recursive encryption of [30] enables us to reduce the degree to 1.

The authors of [30] also gave a KDM secure scheme w.r.t. QSLP which is a quotient of SLP's computable polynomial f with degree $\leq d$ modulo N. Intuitively, the scheme has two ciphertexts where the first and the second ciphertexts correspond to the numerator and the denominator of the Quotient SLP, respectively (which are encryptions of non-zero representing SLP's).

5. APPLICATIONS

5.1 Dolev-Yao Model

The *Dolev-Yao model*[19] is the security model of an "ideal world" which is defined by a formal symbolic logic. Intuitively, this model treats an ideal encryption $\{M\}_K$ of a bit string M, wher one can decrypt it only if he "knows" the key K.

In this model words of bit strings, keys and encryptions, such as $K_1 || \{M || \{K_1\}_{K_2}\}_{K_1}$, are considered. Each word called *expression* can be simplified by decryption. E.g. the above expression can be simplified by obtaining K_1 from it and decrypting $\{M || \{K_1\}_{K_2}\}_{K_1}$ by K_1. The process of the simplification is called *entailment*. Two expressions are called *equivalent* if their entailed forms have essentially the same pattern.

The Dolev-Yao model is related to KDM security because "self-encryption," e.g., $\{K\}_K$ can be symbolically described in this model.

The result of Abadi and Rogaway [1] (improved by [11, 3, 7]) shows the following facts:

THEOREM 2. *(Soundness Theorem, informal) Let* $\Pi = (\mathsf{Kg}, \mathsf{Enc}, \mathsf{Dec})$ *be a public key encryption scheme which is KDM secure w.r.t. any functions. Then, if two expressions X and Y are equivalent, $[|X|]_\Pi$ and $[|Y|]_\Pi$ are indistinguishable. Here $[|X|]_\Pi$ is a bit-string which is obtained by replacing $\{\cdot\}$. in X with $\mathsf{Enc}(\cdot, \cdot)$.*

Backes, Pfitzmann, and Scedrov [7] generalized the above soundness theorem to the case of active attacks. Specifically, they formalized a notion "KDM security with corruption" called this notion DKEM security, and showed that the soundness theorem of (BRSIM)/UC [34] holds under DKEM security.

5.2 Fully Homomorphic Encryption

Recall that a *fully homomorphic encryption* is an encryption scheme such that $\mathsf{Enc}(\mathsf{pk}, f(M))$ can be computed from $\mathsf{Enc}(\mathsf{pk}, M)$ for any polynomial size circuit f.

In a seminal work [20], Gentry succeeded in proposing a *leveled* fully homomorphic encryption scheme. His scheme uses as a component a leveled scheme, leveled in the sense that the encryption algorithm Enc depends on a parameter d and a homomorphic operation can be applied to a ciphertext only when the size of f is smaller than d (and the ciphertext is computed using d). Specifically, $\mathsf{Enc}^{(0)}(f(M))$ can be computed from f with size $\leq d$ and $\mathsf{Enc}^{(d)}(M)$. That is,

$$(f, \mathsf{Enc}^{(d)}(\mathsf{pk}, M)) \mapsto \mathsf{Enc}^{(0)}(\mathsf{pk}, f(M)).$$

The scheme is constructed as follows. First, an encryption scheme $(\mathsf{Kg}', \mathsf{Enc}', \mathsf{Dec}')$ is constructed such that $\mathsf{Enc}'(\mathsf{pk}_{i+1},$

$f(M))$ can be computed from f whose size is bounded by small constant, $\mathsf{Enc}'(\mathrm{pk}_i, M)$ and $\mathsf{Enc}'(\mathrm{pk}_{i+1}, \mathrm{sk}_i)$. That is,

$$(f, \mathsf{Enc}'(\mathrm{pk}_i, M), \mathsf{Enc}'(\mathrm{pk}_{i+1}, \mathrm{sk}_i)) \mapsto \mathsf{Enc}'(\mathrm{pk}_{i+1}, f(M)). \tag{1}$$

Here i is an integer and $(\mathrm{pk}_i, \mathrm{sk}_i)$ and $(\mathrm{pk}_{i+1}, \mathrm{sk}_{i+1})$ are key pairs generated by $\mathsf{Kg}'(1^\kappa)$.

Second, the public key pk of the scheme is allowed to be $(\mathrm{pk}_i, \mathsf{Enc}'(\mathrm{pk}_i, \mathrm{sk}_{i-1}))_{i \in [d]}$, where $(\mathrm{pk}_i, \mathrm{sk}_i)$ is a key pair generated by $\mathsf{Kg}'(1^\kappa)$. Gentry then let

$$\mathsf{Enc}^{(d)}(\mathrm{pk}, M) := \mathsf{Enc}'(\mathrm{pk}_d, M).$$

The leveled fully homomorphic property of his scheme can be achieved by applying equation (1) above d times.

Gentry then points out that KDM security can be used to achieve the full non-leveled construction of a fully homomorphic encryption: Indeed, the above scheme achieves non-leveled fully homomorphic property if it holds that $(\mathrm{pk}_i, \mathrm{sk}_i) = (\mathrm{pk}_{i+1}, \mathrm{sk}_{i+1})$. The KDM security ensures the secrecy of sk_i in a ciphertext $\mathsf{Enc}'(\mathrm{pk}_{i+1}, \mathrm{sk}_i)$ even if $(\mathrm{pk}_i, \mathrm{sk}_i) = (\mathrm{pk}_{i+1}, \mathrm{sk}_{i+1})$.

5.3 Anonymous Credential System

An *Anonymous Credential System* is a system in which a user can obtain a credential from organizations and can prove the possession of these credentials anonymously.

Specifically, each user has k keys pairs $(\mathrm{pk}_i, \mathrm{sk}_i)$ (or "credentials") representing notions like a driver licence or a passport, and can prove the possession of credentials by executing zero-knowledge proofs.

To discourage delegation of credentials, we make the user publish "circular" encryption

$$\mathsf{Enc}(\mathrm{pk}_1, \mathrm{sk}_2), \mathsf{Enc}(\mathrm{pk}_2, \mathrm{sk}_3), \ldots, \mathsf{Enc}(\mathrm{pk}_n, \mathrm{sk}_1).$$

Then the user is in an "all-or-nothing" situation where he has to reveal all secret keys if he wants to delegate only one of them! For the above publication the encryption scheme Enc should be KDM secure.

5.4 Relationship with Agility

We call a function ensemble $\mathcal{E}$ *k-agile* w.r.t. weak PRF (Pseudo Random Function) if any adaptively selected k-element $F_1, \ldots, F_k$ of $\mathcal{E}$ is weak PRF even if the components use the same key K. Here a polynomial time computable deterministic function F is called *weak PRF* if $(F(x_1), F(x_2), \cdots)$ is indistinguishable from random when $x_1, x_2, \ldots$ are selected randomly.

Acar, Belenkiy, Bellare, and Cash [2] showed by using KDM security that the set of all weak PRF is not k-agile for any $k \geq 2$ (or this set is empty).

This fact was proved by contradiction as follows. From the assumption, there exists weak PRF f. For a public key (or secret key) encryption scheme $\Pi = (\mathsf{Kg}, \mathsf{Enc}, \mathsf{Dec})$, key $\bar{K} = (L, K_1, K_2)$, and an input x, let

$$F_{\bar{K}}^{(1)}(x) := \mathsf{Enc}(K_1, K_2; f_L(x))$$
$$F_{\bar{K}}^{(2)}(x) := \mathsf{Enc}(K_2, K_1; f_L(x)).$$

Then they showed that, if $\{F^{(1)}, F^{(2)}\}$ are 2-agile, assuming IND-R ("Indistinguishable from random") security for Π implies the following property (2-circularity):

$$(\mathsf{Enc}(K_1, K_2), \mathsf{Enc}(K_2, K_1)) \simeq (\mathrm{Rand}_1, \mathrm{Rand}_2)$$

They finally showed that there existed an encryption scheme which was IND-R but is not 2-circular. Hence the set of all weak PRF is not k-agile for any $k \geq 2$ (or this set is empty).

5.5 Relationship with Point Obfuscation

An algorithm O is called (multi-bit) *point obfuscator* if it satisfies the following two properties:

- One can compute M easily from $O(K, M)$ and "key" K.

- One cannot compute M from $O(K, M)$ if she does not know K.

Canetti, Kalai, Varia, and Wichs [18] showed that O was point obfuscator iff the following symmetric key encryption scheme was CPA secure for weak key K:

$$\mathsf{Enc}(K, M) = O(K, M)$$

They also showed that the above theorem hold even if M was related to K, when we replace "CPA" with "KDM".

6. OTHER WORKS

6.1 Impossibility Results

Haitner and Holenstein [25] showed an impossibility results about KDM security. To this end they defined two notions whose intuitive meanings are as following.

- A *cryptographic game* is a polynomial time algorithm which takes a security parameter as an input, interacts with a polynomial time adversary, and outputs 1 or 0. An example of a cryptographic game is the game of DDH.

- A *strongly black-box reduction* from KDM security w.r.t. $\mathcal{F}$ to a cryptographic game is a polynomial time reduction which uses an adversary for KDM security *and* queries of the adversary as black-boxes.

The first impossibility result of Haitner and Holenstein [25] is:

THEOREM 3. *(informal) There exists no strongly black-box reduction from KDM security of a public key encryption w.r.t. all functions to any cryptographic game.*

Note that the above result is strengthened by [8].

The second impossibility result of [25] is formalized using the following notion [36]:

- A *fully black-box reduction* from KDM security w.r.t. $\mathcal{F}$ to a one way permutation that consists of the following two algorithms:

  - A polynomial time algorithm which takes a description of a one way permutation f and outputs a description of a public key encryption Π^f.

  - A polynomial time reduction from KDM security of Π^f w.r.t. $\mathcal{F}$ to one way permutation f such that the reduction uses f and an adversary for KDM security as black-boxes.

THEOREM 4. *(informal) There exists no fully black-box reduction from KDM security w.r.t. all functions to a one way permutation.*

6.2 CPA Does Not Imply KDM

Known CPA secure scheme may remain secure even if one encrypts secret keys. A natural question [12] is whether CPA security implies KDM security. Green and Hohenberger [23] gave a counter example to this. Specifically, they gave an example of a CPA secure public key encryption such that one can recover secret keys when given 2-circular encryption $(\mathsf{Enc}(\mathsf{pk}_1, \mathsf{sk}_2), \mathsf{Enc}(\mathsf{pk}_2, \mathsf{sk}_1))$. Note that Acar, Belenkiy, Bellare, and Cash [2] also gave another counter example independently. The authors of [23] also gave a counter example for the case of CCA secure scheme.

6.3 KDM Security of Other Primitives

KDM security of primitives other than public key encryption were studied, considering symmetric key encryptions and PRFs, where KDM security is called *KDI security* [26] (stand for Key Dependent Input).

KDI Security for PRFs. KDI Security for PRFs is defined [26] as following: Let $\{F_K : X \to Y\}$ be a family of PRFs, $\mathcal{K}$ be a key space of F, and $\mathcal{F}$ be a ensemble of functions from $\mathcal{K}$ to X. For a bit b, a security parameter κ, consider the following game:

$$K \leftarrow (\text{rand.}), \quad b' \leftarrow \mathsf{A}^{\mathcal{O}_K^{(b)}, \mathcal{O}_K'^{(b)}}(1^\kappa), \quad \text{Output } b'.$$

Here $\mathcal{O}_K^{(b)}$ and $\mathcal{O}_K'^{(b)}$ are the following oracles:

- $\mathcal{O}_K^{(0)}(\cdot)$ is $F_K(\cdot)$ and $\mathcal{O}_K^{(1)}(\cdot)$ is a random oracle from X to Y.

- On inputting a function $f \in \mathcal{F}$, $\mathcal{O}_K'^{(b)}$ returns $\mathcal{O}_K^{(b)}(f(K))$.

We say that PRF F_K is *KDI secure w.r.t.* $\mathcal{F}$ if the following advantage is negligible for any polynomial time adversary A:

$$\mathsf{Adv.KDM}_\mathsf{A}[\mathcal{F}] = \left| \Pr[b' = 1 \mid b = 1] - \Pr[b' = 1 \mid b = 0] \right|.$$

The aspects of KDI security of PRFs is quite different from that of KDM security of public key encryptions, because of the determinism of PRFs. For instance, it is impossible to construct KDI secure PRFs w.r.t. all function because of the following reason[26]:

Let g_i and g_i' be functions such that $g_i(K) = g_i'(K)$ holds iff the i-th bit of K is 0. Then an adversary A can know the i-th bit of the secret key K by making query g_i and g_i' to the oracle $\mathcal{O}'^{(b)}$ (if $b = 0$). Hence, A can gets the secret key K and can distinguish whether $b = 0$ or not by using K.

KDM Security for Symmetric Key Encryptions. KDM security [11, 5] for symmetric key encryptions is defined in the same way as the definition of KDM security for public key encryptions. We therefore omit the details.

KDM security for symmetric key encryptions was first studied by Black, Rogaway, and Shrimpton [11]. They showed that the following scheme $(\mathsf{Kg}, \mathsf{Enc}, \mathsf{Dec})$ is KDM-CPA secure w.r.t. all functions in the random oracle model. Bellow $\mathcal{H}$ is a random oracle and κ is a security parameter.

- $\mathsf{Kg}(1^\kappa)$: Choose $K \xleftarrow{\$} \{0,1\}^\kappa$ and output K.

- $\mathsf{Enc}(K, M)$: Choose $R \xleftarrow{\$} \{0,1\}^\kappa$ and output
$$C \leftarrow (R, \mathcal{H}(K\|R) \oplus M)$$

- $\mathsf{Dec}(K, C)$: Parse C as (R, C'). Compute and output
$$M \leftarrow \mathcal{H}(K\|R) \oplus C'.$$

Later, Halevi and Krawczyk [26] succeeded in constructing KDM secure scheme w.r.t. a single function in the standard model based on PRF, (although their definition of security is different from ours.)

Then Applebaum, Cash, Peikert, and Sahai [5] proposed a KDM secure scheme w.r.t. affine sum of blocks of the secret key. Their scheme is constructed based on similar idea to their public key encryption scheme and the security of their scheme is proved under the LPN assumption (stand for Leaning Parity with Noise) [35].

7. REFERENCES

[1] M. Abadi and P. Rogaway. Reconciling two views of cryptography (the computational soundness of formal encryption). *J. Cryptology*, 20(3):395, 2007.

[2] T. Acar, M. Belenkiy, M. Bellare, and D. Cash. Cryptographic agility and its relation to circular encryption. In Gilbert [21], pages 403–422.

[3] P. Adão, G. Bana, J. Herzog, and A. Scedrov. Soundness of formal encryption in the presence of key-cycles. In S. D. C. di Vimercati, P. F. Syverson, and D. Gollmann, editors, *ESORICS*, volume 3679 of *Lecture Notes in Computer Science*, pages 374–396. Springer, 2005.

[4] B. Applebaum. Key-dependent message security: Generic amplification and completeness theorems. Cryptology ePrint Archive, Report 2010/513, 2010. http://eprint.iacr.org/.

[5] B. Applebaum, D. Cash, C. Peikert, and A. Sahai. Fast cryptographic primitives and circular-secure encryption based on hard learning problems. In S. Halevi, editor, *CRYPTO*, volume 5677 of *Lecture Notes in Computer Science*, pages 595–618. Springer, 2009.

[6] M. Backes, M. Dürmuth, and D. Unruh. Oaep is secure under key-dependent messages. In J. Pieprzyk, editor, *ASIACRYPT*, volume 5350 of *Lecture Notes in Computer Science*, pages 506–523. Springer, 2008.

[7] M. Backes, B. Pfitzmann, and A. Scedrov. Key-dependent message security under active attacks - BRSIM/UC-soundness of Dolev-Yao-style encryption with key cycles. *Journal of Computer Security*, 16(5):497–530, 2008.

[8] B. Barak, I. Haitner, D. Hofheinz, and Y. Ishai. Bounded key-dependent message security. In Gilbert [21], pages 423–444.

[9] M. Bellare and P. Rogaway. Random oracles are practical: A paradigm for designing efficient protocols. In *ACM Conference on Computer and Communications Security*, pages 62–73, 1993.

[10] M. Bellare and P. Rogaway. Optimal asymmetric encryption. In *EUROCRYPT*, pages 92–111, 1994.

[11] J. Black, P. Rogaway, and T. Shrimpton. Encryption-scheme security in the presence of key-dependent messages. In K. Nyberg and H. M. Heys, editors, *Selected Areas in Cryptography*, volume 2595 of *Lecture Notes in Computer Science*, pages 62–75. Springer, 2002.

[12] D. Boneh, S. Halevi, M. Hamburg, and R. Ostrovsky. Circular-secure encryption from decision Diffie-Hellman. In D. Wagner, editor, *CRYPTO*, volume 5157 of *Lecture Notes in Computer Science*, pages 108–125. Springer, 2008.

[13] D. Boneh and R. Venkatesan. Breaking RSA may not be equivalent to factoring. In *EUROCRYPT*, pages 59–71, 1998.

[14] Z. Brakerski and S. Goldwasser. Circular and leakage resilient public-key encryption under subgroup indistinguishability - (or: Quadratic residuosity strikes back). In T. Rabin, editor, *CRYPTO*, volume 6223 of *Lecture Notes in Computer Science*, pages 1–20. Springer, 2010.

[15] Z. Brakerski, S. Goldwasser, and Y. Kalai. Circular-secure encryption beyond affine functions. Cryptology ePrint Archive, Report 2009/485, 2009. http://eprint.iacr.org/ to appear in TCC 2010.

[16] J. Camenisch, N. Chandran, and V. Shoup. A public key encryption scheme secure against key dependent chosen plaintext and adaptive chosen ciphertext attacks. In A. Joux, editor, *EUROCRYPT*, volume 5479 of *Lecture Notes in Computer Science*, pages 351–368. Springer, 2009.

[17] J. Camenisch and A. Lysyanskaya. An efficient system for non-transferable anonymous credentials with optional anonymity revocation. In B. Pfitzmann, editor, *EUROCRYPT*, volume 2045 of *Lecture Notes in Computer Science*, pages 93–118. Springer, 2001.

[18] R. Canetti, Y. T. Kalai, M. Varia, and D. Wichs. On symmetric encryption and point obfuscation. In D. Micciancio, editor, *TCC*, volume 5978 of *Lecture Notes in Computer Science*, pages 52–71. Springer, 2010.

[19] D. Dolev and A. C.-C. Yao. On the security of public key protocols. *IEEE Transactions on Information Theory*, 29(2):198–207, 1983.

[20] C. Gentry. Fully homomorphic encryption using ideal lattices. In M. Mitzenmacher, editor, *STOC*, pages 169–178. ACM, 2009.

[21] H. Gilbert, editor. *Advances in Cryptology - EUROCRYPT 2010, 29th Annual International Conference on the Theory and Applications of Cryptographic Techniques, French Riviera, May 30 - June 3, 2010. Proceedings*, volume 6110 of *Lecture Notes in Computer Science*. Springer, 2010.

[22] S. Goldwasser and S. Micali. Probabilistic encryption. *J. Comput. Syst. Sci.*, 28(2):270–299, 1984.

[23] M. Green and S. Hohenberger. CPA and CCA-secure encryption systems that are not 2-circular secure. Cryptology ePrint Archive, Report 2010/144, 2010. http://eprint.iacr.org/.

[24] J. Groth and A. Sahai. Efficient non-interactive proof systems for bilinear groups. In Smart [39], pages 415–432.

[25] I. Haitner and T. Holenstein. On the (im)possibility of key dependent encryption. In O. Reingold, editor, *TCC*, volume 5444 of *Lecture Notes in Computer Science*, pages 202–219. Springer, 2009.

[26] S. Halevi and H. Krawczyk. Security under key-dependent inputs. In P. Ning, S. D. C. di Vimercati, and P. F. Syverson, editors, *ACM Conference on Computer and Communications Security*, pages 466–475. ACM, 2007.

[27] D. Hofheinz and E. Kiltz. Secure hybrid encryption from weakened key encapsulation. In A. Menezes, editor, *CRYPTO*, volume 4622 of *Lecture Notes in Computer Science*, pages 553–571. Springer, 2007.

[28] D. Hofheinz and D. Unruh. Towards key-dependent message security in the standard model. In Smart [39], pages 108–126.

[29] M. Liskov, R. L. Rivest, and D. Wagner. Tweakable block ciphers. In M. Yung, editor, *CRYPTO*, volume 2442 of *Lecture Notes in Computer Science*, pages 31–46. Springer, 2002.

[30] T. Malkin, I. Teranishi, and M. Yung. Efficient block-wise PKE with KDM security under a flexible slp queries. Cryptology ePrint Archive, 2011. http://eprint.iacr.org/ (to appear).

[31] IEEE P1619. Standard for cryptographic protection of data on block-oriented storage devices, 2007.

[32] IEEE P1619 email archive, 2007. http://grouper.ieee.org/groups/1619/email.

[33] M. Naor and M. Yung. Public-key cryptosystems provably secure against chosen ciphertext attacks. In *STOC*, pages 427–437. ACM, 1990.

[34] B. Pfitzmann and M. Waidner. Composition and integrity preservation of secure reactive systems. In *ACM Conference on Computer and Communications Security*, pages 245–254, 2000.

[35] O. Regev. On lattices, learning with errors, random linear codes, and cryptography. *J. ACM*, 56(6), 2009.

[36] O. Reingold, L. Trevisan, and S. P. Vadhan. Notions of reducibility between cryptographic primitives. In M. Naor, editor, *TCC*, volume 2951 of *Lecture Notes in Computer Science*, pages 1–20. Springer, 2004.

[37] P. Rogaway. Efficient instantiations of tweakable blockciphers and refinements to modes ocb and pmac. In P. J. Lee, editor, *ASIACRYPT*, volume 3329 of *Lecture Notes in Computer Science*, pages 16–31. Springer, 2004.

[38] H. Shacham. A Cramer-Shoup encryption scheme from the linear assumption and from progressively weaker linear variants. Cryptology ePrint Archive, Report 2007/074, 2007. http://eprint.iacr.org/.

[39] N. P. Smart, editor. *Advances in Cryptology - EUROCRYPT 2008, 27th Annual International Conference on the Theory and Applications of Cryptographic Techniques, Istanbul, Turkey, April 13-17, 2008. Proceedings*, volume 4965 of *Lecture Notes in Computer Science*. Springer, 2008.

Old, New, Borrowed, Blue – A Perspective on the Evolution of Mobile Platform Security Architectures

Kari Kostiainen
Nokia Research Center
kari.ti.kostiainen@nokia.com

Elena Reshetova
Nokia
elena.reshetova@nokia.com

Jan-Erik Ekberg
Nokia Research Center
jan-erik.ekberg@nokia.com

N. Asokan
Nokia Research Center
n.asokan@nokia.com

ABSTRACT

The recent dramatic increase in the popularity of "smartphones" has led to increased interest in smartphone security research. From the perspective of a security researcher the noteworthy attributes of a modern smartphone are the ability to install new applications, possibility to access Internet and presence of private or sensitive information such as messages or location. These attributes are also present in a large class of more traditional "feature phones." Mobile platform security architectures in these types of devices have seen a much larger scale of deployment compared to platform security architectures designed for PC platforms. In this paper we start by describing the business, regulatory and end-user requirements which paved the way for this widespread deployment of mobile platform security architectures. We briefly describe typical hardware-based security mechanisms that provide the foundation for mobile platform security. We then describe and compare the currently most prominent open mobile platform security architectures and conclude that many features introduced recently are borrowed, or adapted with a twist, from older platform security architectures. Finally, we identify a number of open problems in designing effective mobile platform security.

Categories and Subject Descriptors

D.4 [**Operating Systems**]: Security and Protection

General Terms

Security, Design

1. INTRODUCTION

In the past few years, there has been a dramatic increase in the popularity of the category of mobile phones commonly known as "smartphones." Consequently there is increased interest in the security and privacy research community in

"smartphone security". What exactly constitutes a "smartphone" is a matter of debate [16]. But from the perspective of a security researcher, some attributes of smartphones stand out. One is the ability to extend the functionality of phone by incorporating new software components. At the moment, this takes the form of installing new applications. Another is the ability to access (and be accessed from) the Internet. A third is the presence of private or sensitive information like personal messages, location etc.

These security-relevant attributes lead us to two important observations. First, these attributes are also present in a large class of mobile phones commonly known as "feature phones". For example, Java Platform Micro Edition (Java ME), which makes it possible for application developers to develop and deploy Java midlets to mobile devices, is reportedly present on over three billion phones [23]. Therefore, we argue that instead of focusing on "smartphone security", security researchers should study mobile platform security more generally.

Second, these attributes are instantly recognizable as characteristics of any personal computer (PC) platform. PC platforms started out as open systems with no platform security schemes in place. Even today, security mechanisms in PC platforms are based primarily on perimeter control, like firewalls, and reactive mechanisms like anti-virus tools. Although various platform security architectures (such as Security-Enhanced Linux [17]) have been designed and implemented, none has seen widespread deployment.

In contrast all significant mobile phone platforms have widely deployed platform security schemes. The primary reason for this is how the business, regulatory, and end-user requirements on mobile phones have shaped the evolution of mobile platform security over the last decade or so.

In this paper, we begin by taking a brief look at the motivation and background for mobile platform security and the requirements they implied. Then we describe the types of hardware-security mechanisms that provide the foundation for mobile platform security. After that we describe and compare the currently most prominent open mobile platform security architectures. Finally, we identify a number of open problems in designing effective mobile platform security.

2. BACKGROUND AND MOTIVATION

In contrast to PC platforms, mobile phones began as closed systems with limited functionality. Right from the beginning different stakeholders had certain clear security requirements for mobile devices. For example, in many parts of the world, several *mobile network operators* provide subsidized mobile phones to their customers in return to commitment to a specified contract period. They require mobile phones to incorporate mechanisms to enforce *subsidy locks*, to prevent a customer who received a subsidized mobile phone from changing operators before the subsidy contract was ended. *Regulators*, like the Federal Communication Commission in the United States, are interested in aspects affecting the public good. For example, during manufacture a mobile phone undergoes a configuration process where the parameters for radio frequency (RF) operations (like transmission power) are calibrated and stored. Regulators want to ensure *secure storage* of such RF parameters for end-user safety. Additionally, if a malicious user could manipulate these parameters he could gain unfair advantage (bigger communication bandwidth than was intended for him) or disrupt communications for other users. Regulators are also interested in theft-deterrent mechanisms such as the means to track stolen devices.

Some of these requirements made their way into standards specifications. The European Telecommunications Standards Institute (ETSI), the body that originally specified the Global System for Mobile Communications (GSM) standard had representatives from mobile device manufacturers, mobile network operators as well as regulators. In the early 1990s, a version of the ETSI recommendation on "security aspects" recommended protection of the IMEI (International Mobile Equipment Identifier, a unique code for a specific device) and the IMSI (International Mobile Subscriber Identifier, a unique code for each subscription) by specifying that "Both IMSI and IMEI require physical protection. Physical protection means that manufacturers shall take necessary and sufficient measures to ensure the programming and mechanical security of the IMEI" [10]. Immutability of IMEI and IMSI is essential for enforcing subsidy lock. Immutability of IMEI also serves as a theft-deterrent mechanism.

Ten years later, by the time the first "smartphone" (the Nokia 9210) appeared, the importance of these basic requirements grew. A subsequent version of the same ETSI specification re-iterated the requirement that "The IMEI shall not be changed after the ME (mobile equipment) final production process. It shall resist tampering, i.e. manipulation and change, by any means (e.g. physical, electrical and software)" [11]. It also implied that compliance to this requirement would be needed for type approval by stating that "This requirement is valid for new GSM . . . MEs type approved after 1st June 2002."

In addition to operator and regulator requirements, it was also evident that *end-users* had come to expect a certain level of predictability and reliability from mobile phones. Unlike in PC platforms, where malfunctioning system software or malicious applications are usually merely a nuisance to the user, in mobile domain such software can cause considerable harm to him, e.g. in the form of monetary losses due to an increased phone bill. To retain that level of end-user trust while opening up mobile phone platforms for application installation and Internet connectivity, the platforms needed to support appropriate platform security schemes.

Mobile platform vendors responded to these operator, regulator and end-user needs by developing "hardware-security mechanisms" and by integrating "platform security architectures" to the mobile operating systems and application plat-

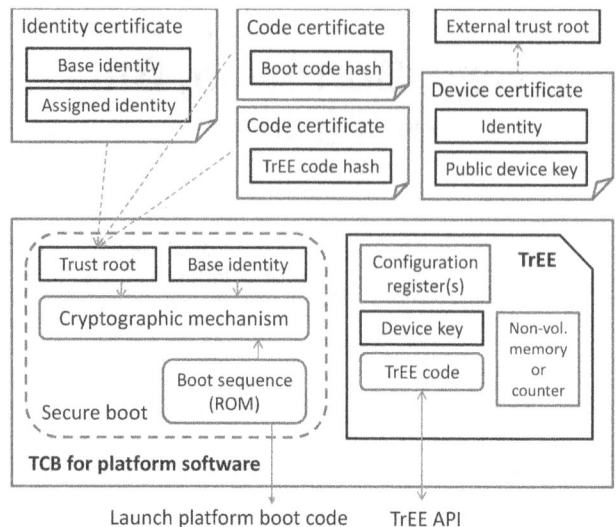

Figure 1: Common hardware-security mechanisms used in mobile devices.

forms. In the next sections of this paper, we describe typical hardware-security mechanisms used in mobile phones and compare widely deployed open platform security architectures.

3. HARDWARE-SECURITY MECHANISMS

The augmentation of device hardware to support operating system security is by no means a new invention. As early as in 1971, Lampson examined the concept of protection domains [15] and e.g. the Cambridge CAP computer [37] developed in the 1970s provided hardware support for such a feature. The first standardization efforts for hardware-assisted security took place in late 1990s when the Trusted Computing Platform Alliance (TCPA) [25], a predecessor of current Trusted Computing Group (TCG) [34], defined a hardware-based security element for PCs. Roughly at the same time, the first large scale deployments of hardware-assisted security started when mobile device manufacturers added hardware-based integrity protection of booted system software. The mechanism was originally designed as a safety feature rather than a security one, but in the context of mobile devices its primary purpose was to prevent software replacement in the field.

In this section we describe common hardware-security mechanisms used in mobile devices today (see Figure 1), and explain the rationales of mobile device manufacturers for introducing such security mechanisms. Then we briefly list some existing and standardized hardware-security architectures in the mobile domain that implement some or all of the explored mechanisms.

3.1 Base identity and trust root

For typical mobile devices, two pieces of immutable information are needed in hardware. First, virtually all devices need at least one *base identity* that uniquely identifies the device hardware. The base identity can be the IMEI of the device or any other (statistically) unique identifier. Immutability of the device identifier can be achieved e.g. by storing the value in a read-only memory (ROM) during the manufacturing of the application-specific integrated circuit (ASIC).

Second, mobile devices need to authenticate external information (see e.g. assigned identities and secure boot in Sections 3.2 and 3.3). A pre-condition for external information authentication is that another piece of immutable information, a *trust root*, is stored on the device hardware during manufacturing. A typical trust root is a hash of the device manufacturer public key [32, 33], and thus the trust root is usually shared within a family of manufactured devices, unlike the device-specific immutable identity which is typically unique.

3.2 Assigned identities

Mobile devices usually need more than one identity, e.g. for MAC addresses of all supported radio interfaces. The ability to assign additional device identities after the ASIC manufacturing, rather than to fixing them into ROM at the time of manufacturing, gives more flexibility to the device manufacturers. The combination of a trust root and at least one base identity gives the device manufacturer or integrator the possibility to assign arbitrarily many other identities to a chosen device.

One way to achieve this is to issue an *identity certificate* for the device. This certificate is signed with respect to the device trust root and it binds the an *assigned identity* to the base identity. Additionally, the device hardware must be enhanced with a *cryptographic mechanism* that can verify the identity certificate (or a certification chain). The operational integrity of the cryptographic mechanism implementation must be trustworthy, and thus such algorithms, say RSA implementation, are often part of the ROM on the ASIC, where they can be deployed during the boot sequence at a stage where no untrusted code has yet been run.

3.3 Secure boot

Due to regulatory, operator and end-user requirements some mobile device manufacturers assert the integrity of system software during device boot-up and stop the boot process if system software has been modified. This process is called *secure boot*. To implement secure boot, a typical approach is to make the beginning of the *boot sequence* immutable, e.g. by the virtue that it resides in ROM, and that the processor unconditionally starts executing from that memory area. The device manufacturer can issue a set of *code certificates* that contain *boot code hashes* and are signed with respect to the device trust root. Again, the hardware must be enhanced with a cryptographic mechanism that validates the first executed system component (e.g. boot loader) before it further validates and executes the next one (e.g. OS kernel). If any of the validation steps fail, the boot process aborts.

This "measure-before-execute" principle can be iterated as many times as necessary to include not just the initially launched OS kernel (or hypervisor) binary, but also any other code or configuration data whose integrity needs to be validated. Secure boot based on code signing does not necessarily imply that only a single code set-up can be booted on a given device. The launched image may be one of several certified alternatives, depending on user selection (see Section 5) or other external or internal context.

3.4 Trusted Execution Environment

All the hardware-security mechanisms listed so far have been integrity-related, and implementation of these mechanisms does not require storage of or operation on secrets. There are, however, security services and use cases (see Section 3.7) that require secure storage and isolated execution.

A way to construct an isolated execution environment is to validate the Trusted Computing Base (TCB) using secure boot, since TCB by definition is isolated from the rest of the system. This approach may suffice, especially in cases where the TCB is small, like a hypervisor. For complete operating systems (kernels) this is not a viable approach, since these are so large that implementation bugs that enable software-attacks against TCB are inevitable.

When dealing with confidential information, the attack model also changes. When attacking integrity features, isolation must be broken at every boot, whereas a breach against confidentiality needs to succeed only once and the secret falls into the hands of the attacker. Thus, where confidentiality is concerned, at least simple hardware attacks like memory-bus monitoring or side-channel attacks must be considered as plausible attack vectors in addition to software-based attacks.

To overcome the security problems of TCB that consists of entire OS kernel, mobile device manufacturers have enhanced their ASICs with support for *Trusted Execution Environment* (TrEE). A typical TrEE includes secure storage for a (statistically) unique *device key* and an execution environment in which small pieces of code (*TrEE code*) can be executed isolated from the rest of the system. The isolated execution environment is typically based on on-chip memory to alleviate memory-bus attacks. Combined with the secure boot features, trust roots and identities described above, this set effectively can become a minimal *TCB for platform software* to be leveraged by the booted operating system or platform software on the device.

Like with any TCB, since the TrEE will contain and provide access to secrets, there must be some assurance that code that is run inside it will not, as part of its operation, reveal the secrets to outside, either accidentally or by malice. This assurance can be achieved either by code-signing (code certificates that contain TrEE code hashes) or by constructing the TrEE such that any code run in it gets only indirect access to the confidential data (e.g. a secret key can be applied to a cryptographic algorithm, but it is never directly accessible to TrEE code). The same applies to run-time protected data that may be stored in TrEE memory. TrEE typically provides an API for loading executed code.

3.5 Configuration registers

Additionally, TrEEs often support *configuration registers*. These registers can be used to store measurements from the (possibly validated) booted software or an aggregate of the non-validated code the TCB executes over time. Also hardware configuration options, configuration file contents or user inputs can be stored on these registers. The integrity of configuration registers must be guaranteed, but it is not persistent across boot cycles. The information contained in such registers can be used in two ways. First, code run inside the TrEE can adjust their logic based on the current system state, or e.g. user input received at boot when no untrusted software still was running. Secondly, the state of the system can be attested to a remote party (see Section 3.7).

3.6 Authenticated boot

A boot process in which (1) the measure-before-execute principle is followed during boot without certificate validation nor possible boot termination, and (2) all intermediary measurement results are added to configuration registers (without the possibility of data rollback), is often called *authenticated boot*. The aggregate information from the registers will uniquely identify the system state up to the instance where the first piece of untrusted code is launched. Put another way, if no untrusted code was launched, this fact can later be attested to external parties without the need for certificate checking or halting during boot.

3.7 Sealing and attestation

A persistent device key initialized during ASIC manufacturing and only accessible within the TrEE, can be used for various security mechanisms. First, with this key, or any derivation from it, the TrEE can locally encrypt data, and then give the result to an unprotected domain, such as external memory, for persistent storage. This mechanism is often called *sealing*.

If the device key is usable for public key cryptography, then an external certification authority (CA, typically run by the device manufacturer) may issue a *device certificate* that binds the public part of the device key to any of the device identities (base or assigned). The certification process can take place e.g. during device manufacturing, when the CA can still trust the integrity of the public part of the device key.

The *public device key* together with the device certificate can be used to set up an authenticated and confidential communication channel from an external party into the TrEE, e.g. for provisioning or data migration purposes. Also, the TrEE can by means of a signed statement to a third party remotely attest any state information inside it, e.g. the measurements stored to configuration registers from an authenticated boot sequence.

3.8 Statefulness

Many services in which the user can be considered an adversary, such as digital rights management, device lock PIN retry control or micropayment protocols, need reliable rollback protection of system state. During one device boot cycle, rollback protection is implementable using the configuration registers described in Section 3.5. To implement *off-line* rollback protection, stored data needs to be bound to reliable time information within the TrEE. Straightforward ways to implement this is to include either a monotonic *counter* or *non-volatile memory* in the TrEE.[1]

3.9 Hardware-security architectures

Most of the hardware-security mechanisms described above have seen widespread deployment in proprietary mobile *hardware-security architectures*, such as ARM TrustZone [3, 4] or M-Shield [32]. TrustZone architecture augments the processing core to provide a new set of processing (register) contexts, as well as memory management unit (MMU) and direct memory access (DMA) security integration. ASICs with TrustZone architecture support secure boot, and can also be populated with isolated RAM and ROM residing within the ASIC package to provide memories resistant to simple hardware attacks. For confidential information, trust roots and identifiers some amount of chip-specific "write once, read many times" persistent memory (typically implemented with E-fuses) is also available. Thus TrustZone provides secure boot, integrity protected trust roots and device identifiers, confidential device keys and isolated execution for TrEE code, but typically lacks secure non-volatile memory and counters, and thus rollback protection must be set up with external means.

On the PC side, the most widely deployed hardware-security architecture is the Trusted Platform Module (TPM) [35] defined by Trusted Computing Group (TCG). TPM by definition is a self-contained, stand-alone secure element. TPM does not provide secure boot, but combined with an associated processor feature, the Dynamic Root of Trust for Measurement (DRTM), it can be used to set up a limited TrEE [19] within the logic confines of an Intel VTx or AMD processors. In this context TPM has trust roots, device secrets, device certificate capability, counters, i.e. all features listed above.

TCG has also defined a standard called Mobile Trusted Module (MTM) [9] for mobile devices. Unlike TPM, MTM is an interface specification that can be implemented using various means, e.g. using TrustZone. MTM specification supports most TPM features, with a few mobile-domain specific additions.

4. OPEN MOBILE PLATFORMS

In this section we briefly describe the prominent open mobile operating systems and application platforms: Symbian, Java ME, Android and MeeGo. We focus on mobile platforms for which reference implementations and security architectures are publicly available, and exclude other popular mobile platforms, such as iPhone, Windows Phone 7 and Blackberry, that are open to third-party application development but the internals of which are not public.

4.1 Symbian

Symbian is an evolution from EPOC operating system used in Psion devices in 1990s. In Symbian most of the operating system services, such as file system and networking, are implemented as user-space system servers. Communication between system servers and user applications takes place via built-in interprocess communication (IPC) framework [28]. Symbian platform security architecture was added in 2005 and at the time Symbian was the first smartphone OS to incorporate a platform security architecture. Symbian is currently the most used smartphone OS [12] and primarily used in Nokia devices. Application development in Symbian is done in C++ and using Qt framework. Symbian operating system supports three types of executables: UI applications, background servers and libraries.

Symbian developers define two configuration files for each application: a project definition file (MMP file) defines project settings, such as the identifier of the application and source code files and libraries used, and a packaging file (PKG file) controls how an installation package in constructed.

In the Symbian platform security architecture, access to

---

[1]Many existing mobile devices support neither non-volatile secure memory nor secure counters (see e.g. [30] for rationale). In some cases the need for *local* rollback protection can be mitigated; e.g. when on-line server communication is an unconditional requirement of the use case at hand, the rollback-protection can be server-assisted, i.e. the server provides authenticated time information.

protected APIs is controlled using a finite set of permissions which are called "capabilities". Applications that access protected APIs must be signed by a central trusted authority (SymbianSigned). During the signing process the trusted authority checks that the application conforms to publication criteria and assigns a globally unique application identifier (Secure Identifier, SID) from a *protected range* of application identifiers. The authority maintains a mapping between the issued identifiers and identities of the software issuers. For most applications the developer identity verification is based on simple online registration (nominal fee of 1 euro). For applications that require restricted capabilities, the application developer must purchase a publisher identity certificate (200 USD per year). Nokia Ovi Store is the primary distribution channel for Symbian applications.

Symbian applications that do not require access to protected APIs can be self-signed and distributed via other channels. In such a case, the developer picks the application identifier from an *unprotected range*.

4.2 Java ME

Java Micro Edition (Java ME) is an application platform supported by various devices from embedded devices to mobile phones and set-top boxes. Java ME platform consists of device "configurations" that define the used Java virtual machine and the core APIs, and "profiles" that define additional APIs for building complete applications. Mobile phones typically support Connected, Limited Device Configuration (CLDC) and Mobile Information Device Profile (MIDP). Java ME is the most widely supported third-party application development platform for feature phones with over 3 billion devices deployed [23]. However, many latest high-end smartphone platforms, including Android, iPhone and MeeGo, do not support Java ME.

The current MIDP standard [21] supports only standalone UI applications, or *midlets*.[2] Midlets are packaged into JAR files before deployment. Applications specific attributes, such as name, version, vendor and requested permissions, are shipped in a Java Desriptor (JAD) file or manifest file.

In Java ME platform security architecture access to protected APIs is controlled with permissions. Application signing binds the application to a *protection domain* according to a local security policy. The policy defines the permissions that applications of each protection domain can have. Typically mobile phones have four predefined protection domains: device manufacturer domain, network operator domain, and domains for identified and unidentified third-party applications.

4.3 Android

Android is a Linux-based smartphone OS developed by Google. Android was released in 2008 and currently it is the second most used smartphone operating system [12]. Application development in Android is primarily done in Java, although applications can include native components as well. Each Android application runs in a separate Dalvik virtual machine in its own process context. Android provides an IPC framework for communication between Java applications.

---

[2]Next MIDP version [22] adds support for background midlets, shared libraries and inter-midlet communication. We exclude analysis of these features from our discussion, because this version is not yet widely supported.

In Android platform security architecture access to protected APIs is controlled with permissions. Android applications are distributed as Android packages. A manifest file inside the package defines the permissions requested by the application and permissions required to use the services (IPC APIs) offered by the application. Android applications must be signed before installation to the device. Most third-party Android applications can be self-signed (applications accessing system APIs must be signed by Google). Android Market is the primary distribution channel for Android applications. Publishing an application requires a registration fee of 25 USD.

4.4 MeeGo

MeeGo is an upcoming Linux-based mobile platform developed jointly by Intel and Nokia. MeeGo is an evolution from Nokia's Maemo platform and Intel's Moblin OS. Compared to Android, MeeGo is much closer to a standard Linux distribution. Application development is primary done in native C/C++ and using Qt framework. MeeGo supports IPC between applications via standard Unix sockets and with Desktop Bus (D-Bus) framework [6].

MeeGo provides a new platform security architecture called Mobile Simplified Security Framework (MSSF) [14, 13]. MSSF is an evolution from Maemo 6 platform security solution, which was initially developed by Nokia. In this paper we will concentrate on the latest design of MSSF framework [20]. In MSSF access to sensitive APIs and files on the device can be controlled using both traditional Linux access control rules and permissions that are called "resource tokens".

MeeGo applications may be installed from various software sources. The notion of a "software source" is abstract and can represent a different range of entities starting from central software repository, such as Nokia Ovi Store, to single developers. Individual software sources are part of a tree-like structure, and a *trust level* is associated with each software source in hierarchical manner.

MeeGo applications are distributed as RPM packages. Each package must be signed by the software source. MeeGo devices have a local list of known software sources and their public keys. A local security policy on a MeeGo device defines *trust levels* for known software sources and permissions that each software source is allowed to grant. The local security policy can either be defined by a manufacturer, operator or even a device user, when a device booted in "developer mode" (see Section 5).

5. OPERATING SYSTEM BOOTSTRAPPING

In this section we start a comparative security analysis of the open mobile platforms described in the previous section. We begin our analysis be comparing different operating system validation and bootstrapping approaches that are used in these platforms.

Symbian. Most Symbian devices support secure boot, with hardware-security architectures like ARM TrustZone, as described in Section 3. Thus, with Symbian devices developers cannot boot their own custom kernels.

Android. In Android, the bootstrap issue is up to the device manufacturer. There is little information available about the different bootstrapping schemes chosen by different Android device manufacturers, but at least in principle developers can update devices with custom kernels [36].

MeeGo. Also in MeeGo different device manufacturers

may implement different OS bootstrapping strategies. Nokia MeeGo devices can support a dual boot approach in which the device can be booted to *normal mode* with official OS kernel image provided by the device manufacturer or to *developer mode* with custom kernel provided by any developer [26]. Integrity of each component of the boot sequence, starting from the bootloader, is verified using boot certificates (see Section 3.3 for more details). However, unlike in usual secure boot, if the integrity verification of operating system image fails, the boot process is not halted, but the user is notified and asked permission to continue the boot. If the user decides to continue, this information is stored in a configuration register inside TrEE.

Later, when the OS requests access to certain device secrets, such as digital rights management keys, this access is prevented (inside TrEE) if the device was booted to developer mode. Both modes allow user space applications to utilize cryptographic services provided by the TrEE. The keys for these services are derived from the device key, and the derivation process includes information about the device mode. This guarantees that the content, encrypted in the normal mode, can not be decrypted in the developer mode.

6. PLATFORM SECURITY ARCHITECTURE COMPARISON

Next, we compare the platform security architectures of mobile platforms described in Section 4. The key differences and similarities are summarized in Table 1.

6.1 Application identification

Symbian. During application installation and at runtime each executable (application or background server) has two identifiers: Secure Identifier (SID) uniquely identifies the executable and Vendor Identifier (VID) identifies the software vendor. These identifiers are typically assigned by the central trusted authority; for self-signed applications the developer may pick any SID from the unprotected range. Libraries inherit SID and VID from the executable that loads them.

Java ME. During installation, a midlet is identified based on installation package signature key and midlet attributes, such as package name. Midlets are standalone applications that do not communicate with each other, and thus runtime code identification is not applicable to Java ME.

Android. During installation Android applications are identified based on signing key and package name. The installation process assigns a locally unique Linux user identifier (UID) to each installed application and at runtime Android applications can be identified either based on UID or package name (one should note that package names are not globally unique, developers may freely use any package name). Only applications that are signed with the same key can be assigned the same UID.

MSSF. During installation applications are identified by software source (signing key) and package name. At runtime applications can be identified by a globally unique application identifier that consists of three parts: software source, package name and package-specific application identifier.

6.2 Application update

Symbian. Centrally signed Symbian application can only by updated by an installation package that has been assigned the same SID by the central trusted authority. Self-signed applications can be updated by any installation package that has the same SID from the unprotected range.

Java ME. Update of signed midlets is allowed only if the new midlet package is signed by the same key as the previous version was. This approach is often called *same-origin policy*. For signed midlet update the application persistent storage is retained. In unsigned application update the user is asked whether the new application should have access to the persistent storage of the old application.

Android. In Android, application update is always based on same-origin policy, i.e. an application can be updated only from an installation package that is signed with the same developer key as the currently installed application. Updated application gets access to the same data storages as its previous version.

MSSF. Application can be updated if the installation package is signed by the same software source from which it was originally installed or by another software source that has higher trust level. Also in MSSF, the updated application automatically gets access to data of previous application version.

6.3 Permission granularity

Symbian. Symbian platform security architecture defines a fixed number (21) of permissions (capabilities). The capabilities are divided into four categories: User Capabilities can be granted by the user during application installation. System Capabilities require application signing by the central trusted authority. Restricted Capabilities require application signing with stronger application developer identity checking (publisher identity certificate). Manufacturer Capabilities are reserved for device manufacturer.

Java ME. Java ME provides more fine-grained permission set. System API developers can define their own permissions. The permissions are mapped into coarse-grained "function groups". The purpose of the function groups is to present permission requests to the user in human understandable format. The MIDP specification recommends 15 function groups for mobile devices.

Android. The default permission set defined by Google includes 112 permissions. The permission names are intended to be user understandable, but in practice this is not the case with all permissions (e.g. a permission named "BROADCAST_STICKY"). Android developers may define their own permissions, and thus the number of permissions is unlimited. Permissions are categorized into four protection levels: Normal, Dangerous, Signature and SystemOrSignature.

MSSF. In MSSF architecture access control can be defined using traditional Linux access control mechanisms and using permissions (resource tokens). Resource tokens names should be understandable for users. MSSF provides a standard set of global resource tokens. Additionally, applications can define their own local resource tokens. The number of permissions in MSSF is unlimited.

6.4 Permission assignment

Symbian. A developer declares the requested permissions in MMP file. For most applications the permission assignment is done by the central trusted authority during application signing. During application installation the Symbian installer validates application signature if System,

	Symbian	Java ME	Android	MSSF
application identification at runtime	application and vendor identifier assigned by central authority	not applicable	local UID and package name	sotware source, package name and package-specific application identifier
application update	application identifier assigned by central authority	same-origin policy and user approval	same-origin policy	trust level of software source
permission granularity	coarse-grained	fine-grained and coarse-grained groups	unlimited permissions	unlimited permissions
permission assignment	signature by central authority and user at installation	signature by protection domain owner and user at runtime	user at installation	signature by software source
runtime application integrity	dedicated directory (manufacturer permissions)	Java sandboxing	Linux access control and Java sandboxing	Linux access control and permissions and IMA [27]
offline application integrity	not supported	not supported	not supported	hardware-assisted EVM [31]
access control policy declaration	permissions and application and vendor identifier	permissions	permissions	permissions and Linux access control and application identifier
access control policy scope	system APIs and application IPC	system APIs	system APIs and application IPC	system APIs and application IPC and file access
runtime application data protection	dedicated directory (manufacturer permissions)	Java sandboxing	dedicated directory	fine-grained permission-based policies
offline application data protection	hardware-assisted with restricted API	not supported	not supported	hardware-assisted with file system integration

Table 1: Summary of key features in mobile platform security architectures.

Restricted or Manufacturer Capabilities are requested. For requested User Capabilities a user prompt is generated during application installation.

The permission set that an application gets during installation remains the same throughout the application lifetime. When an executable loads a library, the operating system checks the capabilities of the library. The library must have all capabilities of the executable, otherwise loading fails. (Because of this Symbian system libraries typically have almost all capabilities.)

Java ME. The developer declares the permissions that his application needs in JAD or manifest file. When an application is installed, the signature is checked against the protection domains on the device. If the protection domain does not support the requested permissions the installation is denied. At application runtime API calls that require user-grantable permission trigger a prompt to the user. The prompts are presented in terms of function groups. If the user grants the requested permission, the decision applies to all permissions of the same function group. The user can grant permissions to a midlets permanently, for midlet execution lifetime or for one-time access. The permissions of a midlet remain constant during midlet lifetime.

Android. Android developers declare the requested permissions in a manifest file. Normal permissions do not require explicit user granting. Each application that requests such permissions will get them. Dangerous permissions must be granted by the user during application installation. Signature permission can be given to an application, only if it is signed by the same key as the application that declared the permission. SystemOrSignature permissions are additionally granted to OS manufacturer applications. The permissions set that an Android application gets during application installation remains constant during application lifetime.

MSSF. Developer declares requested permissions (resource tokens) in the application manifest file. The manifest file can additionally declare a requested Linux UID, GID and POSIX permissions. When an application is installed, the installer checks the requested permissions against the permissions of the software source from a local policy file. The application is granted the intersection of these two permission sets. A special resource token type, unique application identifier, is generated by the installer for all applications.

At runtime applications can request the kernel to drop some of their permissions. When an application loads a shared library, its set of permissions stays the same, but the library loading may fail if a library comes from a software source that cannot grant all the permissions that the application currently possesses. The permission set of an installed applications can also increase during the lifetime of the application. This happens when a plugin library is installed as an extension to an already installed application.

If the plugin requires permissions currently not possessed by the application, these permissions can be added to the permission set of the application, if software sources of both the application and the plugin are allowed to grant the missing permissions.

6.5 Application integrity

We use term "application integrity" to refer to the protection of installed applications against unauthorized modifications both when the system is running (runtime application integrity) and when the device is powered down (offline application integrity).

Symbian. Executable files are kept in and exclusively loaded from a dedicated directory (/sys/bin) in the device internal memory. Only processes with manufacturer capabilities are allowed to access this directory which provides runtime application integrity.

Symbian supports also application installation to removable memory elements. In such a case, the installer calculates a hash of the executable binary and stores the hash to device internal memory and the executable itself to removable element. When an executable is loaded from the removable memory element, a hash of the executable is calculated again and compared to the one stored on internal memory.

Symbian platform security model does not support offline application integrity protection. Instead, the platform security architecture relies on the assumption that the device internal memory cannot be accessed, and thus the already installed applications cannot be modified, by the attacker when the device is powered down.

Java ME. Midlets are executed in a sandbox of Java virtual machine and do not have direct access to the device file system which prevents them from modifying each other. Java ME platform security architecture does not address offline application integrity.

Android. Applications are stored in directories that are assigned unique Linux UIDs during installation. Standard Linux access control mechanisms prevent applications from modifying each other. Additionally, Android devices do not have root account available and third party applications cannot run with root UID, which preserves integrity of these directories. Java sandboxing prevents applications from modifying their own stored attributes such as permissions.

MSSF. Running processes as root is not explicitly prevented in MeeGo devices, and thus relying on UID-based access control is not enough. Instead a combination of Integrity Measurement Architecture (IMA) [27] and Extended Validation Module (EVM) [31] is used. During application installation a reference hash for executable binaries (and also other executable file, such as scripts) is calculated. The reference hashes are stored in an extended Linux file system attribute called security.ima for each file. IMA/EVM verifies these hashes when applications are executed. The security.ima attribute is automatically recalculated, when an application binary is modified during system run-time. MSSF uses the Smack kernel module in order to enforce the access control permissions of the filesystem in addition to standard Linux filesystem permissions.

The offline integrity of security.ima attribute and other file attributes is preserved using hardware-based TrEE. EVM module calculates a keyed message authentication code using a key that is protected by TrEE. This prevents unnoticed modification of security.ima when the device is powered down.

6.6 Access control policy

We use term "access control policy" to refer to both the declaration and scope of rules that control access to the system APIs and IPC services provided by installed applications.

Symbian. Symbian servers can provide services to other Symbian executables through Symbian IPC framework. Developer of a Symbian server defines access control policy for the server APIs by assigning required permissions and application identifiers (SID and VID) for each API function call. The access control policy declaration is done by writing C++ code. The Symbian IPC framework automatically enforces permission-based access control rules for IPC function calls (SID or VID based access control enforcement must be implemented in code).

Java ME. In Java ME platform system APIs provide access to protected resources. Midlets themselves cannot communicate with each other in current MIDP version. System API developers define access control policies by assigning required permission to appropriate API function calls in Java code. The API developer may either reuse existing permissions or define their own.

Android. Android applications can provide services to each other through Android IPC framework. Developers declare access control policies by defining the set of permissions that are needed to use entire service (defined in manifest file) or to use an individual function from an IPC service interface (implemented in code). Also Android IPC framework automatically enforcement permission based access control rules.

MSSF. Applications can communicate with each other through D-Bus and local socket interfaces. Application developers may declare access control policies for such IPC in terms of permissions (resource tokens) or traditional Linux access control mechanisms (e.g. UID or GID). The access control policy declaration is done in the application manifest file. Developers can use common system wide permissions or declare their own application specific permissions. Unlike in other platforms MSSF access control policies can also be defined for file access (e.g. an application developer may define the resource tokens needed to access any of the files created by the application). Internally, the access control enforcement is done by Smack kernel module [29].

6.7 Application data protection

We use term "application data protection" to refer to the protection of application persistent storage (e.g., files on device file system) against unauthorized modification and eavesdropping both when the device is running (runtime protection) and powered down (offline protection).

Symbian. In Symbian platform security model a dedicated directory is created in the file system for each application. This directory can only be accessed by the owner application or a process with manufacturer capabilities. Application developers may define whether the contents of application private directory should be included to backups that are made from the device data. The default policy is to exclude private directory contents from backups.

Nokia Symbian devices provide a restricted API for sealing (authenticated encryption) data with TrEE-resident device key (or derivation of it). This feature provides support for offline data protection for certain Symbian applications.

Java ME. In Java ME architecture applications do not have direct access to device file system, instead database system is provided for persistent storage. Databases are either private to the application itself or shared with all other applications on the same device. Java ME platform security model does not address offline application data protection.

Android. Each application has a dedicated directory protected with Linux UID and GID. By default, the files in this directory can be written and read only by the application itself. During file creation, the application may explicitly define that the created file should be readable or writable by other applications as well. Android platform provides an automatic backup feature that creates backups of application data to an online server. These backups are protected by Google account authentication.

MSSF. MSSF architecture provides fine-grained data caging model. Application developers can define in manifest file required permissions for each type of file access (read, write etc.) for each application file. By default applications files can be accessed only by the application itself.

MSSF allows applications to encrypt data using a TrEE-resident device key. The key derivation can be based on application identifier or specified resource token which allows an application to encrypt data only for itself or to a set of applications. This encryption feature is integrated to the device file system which allows legacy applications to utilize offline data protection without changes.

7. DISCUSSION

Modern mobile platform security architectures have generously borrowed from old ideas but with new twists to adapt these ideas to the needs of mobile devices. For example, all of the software security architectures discussed in Section 4 incorporate access control schemes built around the notion of permissions that are granted to the subjects and checked at the time of access control. This is similar to the VAX/VMS notion of "privileges" introduced back in the late 1970s [24]. However, while privileges in VAX/VMS are typically granted to a user of the system, in modern platform security architectures, they are granted to software modules. Similarly, the notion of secure bootstrapping was discussed in the 1990s [2], but saw widespread adaption when smartphones started to be deployed. As described in Section 5 MSSF borrows from the notion of "authenticated boot" introduced by the Trusted Computing Group, with a new twist: allowing any OS software image to be booted, but if the booted image is not authorized by a trusted party (e.g., device manufacturer), the user is alerted to the fact; furthermore access to sensitive resources (such as cellular network access) or data (such as encrypted device-specific keys) are rendered inaccessible by the OS.

Other examples of old techniques adapted, sometimes with new twists, include the use of code signing for code identification and as the basis for permission assignment. Offline data caging (discussed in Section 6.7) makes use of hardware-assisted secure storage similar to the notion of sealing in Trusted Computing Group specifications, but with the addition that sealed data can be bound to application identities or permissions.

Despite the widespread deployment of mobile platform security architectures, a number of open problems remain.

7.1 Permission granularity

Symbian platform security took the approach of using a fixed number of pre-defined permissions. Resource and service providers who need access control attempt to find the most relevant pre-defined permission to protect their resource or service but may not always succeed. This may lead to developer confusion.

Java ME, Android and MSSF on the other hand allow fine-grained permissions and make it possible to define new permissions. But this does not completely address the problem either. Having numerous permissions can be a cause of potential confusion among users and developers [5]. For this reason some of these architectures allow permissions to be grouped together for presentation to the user.

Designing a flexible and sufficiently rich platform security architecture without sacrificing usability remains a challenge. Solutions like Security Enhanced Linux are not widely adapted because of their perceived complexity. This choice may need to be revisited.

7.2 Permission assignment

Perhaps the most serious problem with mobile platform security architectures is the issue of permission assignment. Android (and also partially Java ME and Symbian) take the approach of relying on the user to decide whether an application can be grated dangerous permissions. Two basic approaches are used: the user can be prompted to grant permissions during application installation (Android and Symbian) or during application runtime (Java ME). Both of these approaches have drawbacks. Runtime permission prompts are often considered annoying by the users while permission assignment during application installation suffers from the lack of relevant context (e.g., the user might know only at runtime whether Internet access should be granted to an application). In both cases users are ill-equipped to make permission assignment decisions and may become habituated to click-through access control prompts.

7.3 Software appropriateness

The problems of user-based permission assignment can be avoided by having a central authority that does permission assignment by means of code signing as in the case of iTunes AppStore or SymbianSigned. While centralized permission assignment is preferable from a usability perspective, it is problematic in cases where subjective judgement is involved. This is particularly so in cases where centralized judgement regarding the appropriateness of applications (e.g., classifying applications as offensive or otherwise inappropriate) is made [8]. One alternative is to rely on the wisdom of crowds (e.g., the WhatApp service at http://whatapp.org) or the wisdom of smaller and more personalized "cliques" [8, 7].

7.4 Access control policy enforcement

Two basic approaches for platform internal access control policy enforcement exist. First, a *reference monitor* (e.g. the platform security architecture on a mobile device) can enforce access control policies over *subjects* (e.g. caller application and callee application in IPC communication) [1]. Second, the full responsibility of access control enforcement can be left to the callee application, assuming that the underlying platform provides the needed information about the caller to the callee.

Most of the platform security architectures described in

this paper use a hybrid approach. The platform security architecture typically enforces access control policies defined in application manifest files automatically, but the application developers can implement additional access control checks, e.g. based on IPC call input data, on top. In Symbian and MSSF callee application can query attributes of caller, such as application identity and possessed permissions.

Pure reference monitor approach preserves application privacy, i.e. the callee does not learn more about the caller than what is needed to make the access control decision, while providing full information about the caller to the callee enables useful security services, such as attestation of untrusted application attributes to an external party by a trusted callee application. Finding the optimal balance between these two approaches remains an open challenge.

7.5 Colluding applications

All of the mobile platform security architectures discussed above grant and enforce accesss control to individual pieces of software. Two such pieces could collude over overt or covert inter-process communication channels so that they gain access to resources or services that neither was able to acting along [18]. Defending against this problem appears to be very hard. In particular, in cases where the user is responsible for granting permissions, visualizing the different potential collusion scenarios and their implications to the user is a security usability challenge.

8. CONCLUSIONS

"Smartphone security" is becoming a popular research topic. The fundamental security issues with smartphones are also present in a larger class of personal mobile communication devices, as well as in personal computers. However, unlike PC platforms, all dominant mobile platforms incorporate widely deployed mobile platform security architectures. The history of mobile platform security goes back long beyond the current popularity of smartphones. The widespread deployment of mobile platform security architectures is due to specified and perceived business, regulatory and end-user requirements for mobile communication devices.

We surveyed four mobile platform security architectures. In all of these architectures the fundamental concepts are borrowed from older commercial or research systems, but some of them have been adapted with new twists to suit the needs of mobile platforms. We also discussed a number of issues that are insufficiently addressed by the current generation of mobile platform security architectures. They constitute fertile ground for further research on the topic.

9. REFERENCES

[1] James Anderson. Computer security technology planning study. Technical Report ESD-TR-73-51, Electronic Systems Division, 1972.

[2] William A. Arbaugh, David J. Farber, and Jonathan M. Smith. A secure and reliable bootstrap architecture. In *IEEE Symposium on Security and Privacy*, pages 65–71. IEEE Computer Society, 1997.

[3] ARM. Trustzone-enabled processor. `http://www.arm.com/products/processors/technologies/trustzone.php`.

[4] ARM. *Building a Secure System using TrustZone^{TM} Technology*, 2009. Available from `http://infocenter.arm.com/help/topic/com.arm.doc.prd29-genc-009492c/PRD29-GENC-009492C_trustzone_security_whitepaper.pdf`.

[5] David Barrera, Hilmi Günes Kayacik, Paul C. van Oorschot, and Anil Somayaji. A methodology for empirical analysis of permission-based security models and its application to android. In Ehab Al-Shaer, Angelos D. Keromytis, and Vitaly Shmatikov, editors, *ACM Conference on Computer and Communications Security*, pages 73–84. ACM, 2010.

[6] Desktop bus project page. website. `http://www.freedesktop.org/wiki/Software/dbus`, 2010.

[7] Pern Hui Chia, Andreas Heiner, and N. Asokan. Use of ratings from personalized community for trustworthy application installation. In *Proceedings of the the 15th Nordic Conference in Secure IT Systems*, 2010.

[8] Pern Hui Chia, Andreas Heiner, and N. Asokan. The wisdom of cliques: Use of personalized social rating for trustworthy application installation. Technical Report NRC-TR-2010-001, Nokia Research Center, July 2010. Available at `http://research.nokia.com/files/tr/NRCTR2010001.pdf`.

[9] Jan-Erik Ekberg and Markku Kylänpää. Mobile trusted module. Technical Report NRC-TR-2007-015, Nokia Research Center, November 2007. Available at: `http://research.nokia.com/files/NRCTR2007015.pdf`.

[10] ETSI. *ETSI GSM 02.09 Security Aspects*. European Telecommunication Standards Institute, April 1993. Version 3.1.0; Available from `http://www.3gpp.org/ftp/Specs/html-info/0209.htm`.

[11] ETSI. *ETSI GSM 02.09 Security Aspects*. European Telecommunication Standards Institute, June 2001. Version 8.0.1 Release 99; Available from `http://www.3gpp.org/ftp/Specs/html-info/0209.htm`.

[12] Gartner. Press release; worldwide mobile phone sales in trhid quarter 2010. `http://www.gartner.com/it/page.jsp?id=1466313`, 2010.

[13] Gitorious. Mssf project source code. `http://meego.gitorious.org/meego-platform-security`, 2010.

[14] Dmitry Kasatkin. Mobile simplified security framework. In *Proceedings of the 12th Linux Symposium*, 2010.

[15] Butler Lampson. Protection. In *Proceedings of the 5th Princeton Conference on Information Sciences and System*, pages 18–24, 1971.

[16] Steve Litchfield. Defining the smartphone. On-line article at AllAboutSymbian.com, July 2010. Available at `http://www.allaboutsymbian.com/features/item/Defining_the_Smartphone.php`.

[17] Peter Loscocco and Stephen Smalley. Integrating flexible support for security policies into the linux operating system. In Clem Cole, editor, *USENIX Annual Technical Conference, FREENIX Track*, pages 29–42. USENIX, 2001.

[18] Claudio Marforio, Srdjan Capkun and Auŕelien Francillon. Personal communication, November 2010. Paper in submission.

[19] Jonathan M. McCune, Bryan Parno, Adrian Perrig,

Michael K. Reiter, and Arvind Seshadri. Minimal TCB Code Execution (Extended Abstract). In *Proc. IEEE Symposium on Security and Privacy*, May 2007.

[20] MeeGo. Mobile simplified security framework overview. http://conference2010.meego.com/session/mobile-simplified-security-framework-overview, 2010.

[21] Sun Microsystems. Mobile information device profile for java 2 micro edition, version 2.1. http://www.oracle.com/technetwork/java/index-jsp-138820.html, 2006.

[22] Motorola. Mobile information device profile for java micro edition, version 3.0. http://opensource.motorola.com/sf/projects/jsr271, 2009.

[23] Oracle. Java technology. http://www.java.com/en/about/, 2010.

[24] Hewlett Packard. Openvms guide to system security. Available from http://www.hp.com/go/openvms/doc/, June 2010.

[25] Siani Pearson, editor. *Trusted Computing Platforms: TCPA technology in context*. Prentice Hall, 2003.

[26] Elena Reshetova. Mobile simplified security framework overview. http://userweb.kernel.org/~jmorris/lss2010_slides/reshetova_LinuxCon_overview_v_final.pdf, 2010.

[27] Reiner Sailer, Xiaolan Zhang, Trent Jaeger, and Leendert van Doorn. Design and implementation of a tcg-based integrity measurement architecture. In *SSYM'04: Proceedings of the 13th conference on USENIX Security Symposium*, pages 16–16, Berkeley, CA, USA, 2004. USENIX Association.

[28] Jane Sales. *Symbian OS Internals*. Wiley, 2005.

[29] Casey Schaufler. Smack in embedded computing. In *Proceedings of the 10th Linux Symposium*, 2008.

[30] Dries Schellekens, Pim Tuyls, and Bart Preneel. Embedded trusted computing with authenticated non-volatile memory. In *Proc. of the 1st International conference on Trusted Computing and Trust in Information Technologies (TRUST 2008)*, 2008.

[31] SourceForge. An overview of the linux integrity subsystem. http://heanet.dl.sourceforge.net/project/linux-ima/linux-ima/Integrity_overview.pdf, 2010.

[32] Jay Srage and Jerome Azema. M-Shield mobile security technology, 2005. TI White paper. http://focus.ti.com/pdfs/wtbu/ti_mshield_whitepaper.pdf.

[33] Harini Sundaresan. OMAP platform security features, July 2003. TI White paper. http://focus.ti.com/pdfs/vf/wireless/platformsecuritywp.pdf.

[34] Trusted Computing Group. https://www.trustedcomputinggroup.org/home.

[35] TCG. Trusted Platform Module (TPM) Specifications. Available at: https://www.trustedcomputinggroup.org/specs/TPM/.

[36] Android-DLS wiki. Howto: Unpack, edit, and re-pack boot images. http://android-dls.com/wiki/index.php?title=HOWTO:_Unpack%2C_Edit%2C_and_Re-Pack_Boot_Images, 2010.

[37] Maurice Wilkes. *The Cambridge CAP computer and its operating system*. North-Holland Publishing Co., Amsterdam, The Netherlands, The Netherlands, 1979.

Keynote Talk

Software Security: Is OK Good Enough?

John B. Dickson, CISSP
Denim Group, Ltd.
San Antonio, Texas USA
john@denimgroup.com

Abstract

Widely publicized breaches regularly occur involving insecure software. This is due to the fact that the vast majority of software in use today was not designed to withstand attacks encountered when deployed on hostile networks such as the Internet. What limited vulnerability statistics that exist confirm that most modern software includes coding flaws and design errors that put sensitive customer data at risk. Unfortunately, security officers and software project owners still struggle to justify investment to build secure software. Initial efforts to build justification models have not been embraced beyond the most security conscious organizations. Concepts like the "Rugged Software" are gaining traction, but have yet to make a deep impact. How does an organization – short of a breach – justify expending critical resources to build more secure software? Is it realistic to believe that an industry-driven solution such as the Payment Card Industry's Data Security Standard (PCI-DSS) can drive secure software investment before headlines prompt government to demand top-down regulation to "fix" the security of software?

This presentation will attempt to characterize the current landscape of software security from the perspective of a practitioner who regularly works with Fortune 500 chief security officers to build business cases for software security initiatives. Given the current status of software security efforts, and the struggles for business justification, industry would be well-served to look further afield to other competing models to identify future justification efforts. There is still much that can be learned from models outside the security and information technology fields. For example, the history of food safety provides lessons that the software security industry can draw from when developing justification models. We can also learn from building code adoption by earthquake-prone communities and draw comparisons to communities that have less rigorous building codes. Finally, we can learn much from certain financial regulations that have or have not improved confidence in our financial system.

Categories & Subject Descriptors: Economics, Human Factors, Management, Measurement, Security, Standardization.

General Terms: Management, Measurement, Documentation, Design, Economics, Reliability, Security, Human Factors, Standardization, Theory, Legal Aspects, Verification.

Bio

John Dickson, CISSP, has over 15 years in the information security field including hands-on experience with intrusion detection systems, telephony security, and application security in the commercial and government sectors. In his current position as a Principal at Denim Group, he helps Chief Security Officers of Fortune 500 clients and Federal organizations launch successful software initiatives. John is a member of the US Space Command Commander's Group, the Founders Council, Institute for Cyber Security Studies, University of Texas at San Antonio, and is President Elect of the Texas Lyceum, a statewide leadership group in the State of Texas.

Towards Active Detection of Identity Clone Attacks on Online Social Networks

Lei Jin
School of Information Sciences
University of Pittsburgh
Pittsburgh, PA, USA

lej17@pitt.edu

Hassan Takabi
School of Information Sciences
University of Pittsburgh
Pittsburgh, PA, USA

hatakabi@sis.pitt.edu

James B.D. Joshi
School of Information Sciences
University of Pittsburgh
Pittsburgh, PA, USA

jjoshi@sis.pitt.edu

ABSTRACT

Online social networks (OSNs) are becoming increasingly popular and Identity Clone Attacks (ICAs) that aim at creating fake identities for malicious purposes on OSNs are becoming a significantly growing concern. Such attacks severely affect the trust relationships a victim has built with other users if no active protection is applied. In this paper, we first analyze and characterize the behaviors of ICAs. Then we propose a detection framework that is focused on discovering suspicious identities and then validating them. Towards detecting suspicious identities, we propose two approaches based on *attribute similarity* and *similarity of friend networks*. The first approach addresses a simpler scenario where mutual friends in friend networks are considered; and the second one captures the scenario where similar friend identities are involved. We also present experimental results to demonstrate flexibility and effectiveness of the proposed approaches. Finally, we discuss some feasible solutions to validate suspicious identities.

Categories and Subject Descriptors

H.2.7 [**Information Systems**]: Database Administration-*Security, integrity, and protection*; K.6.5 [**Management of Computing and Information Systems**]: Security and Protection-*Authentication*

General Terms

Security, Algorithm, Experimentation, Measurement

Keywords

Identity Clone Attack, Detection, Security, Online Social Networks, Profile Similarity

1. INTRODUCTION

The popularity of online social networks (OSNs) is growing significantly. At the same time, they are also being increasingly targeted by adversaries interested in extracting privacy sensitive information about users. The security and privacy threats on OSNs are mainly raised by the increasing amount of publicly available personal information posted by users in their profiles.

Recently, a new attack called Identity Cloning Attack (ICA), which focuses on forging user profiles on OSNs, has been introduced [1]. The key goal of an adversary in ICA is to obtain personal information about a victim's friends after successfully forging the victim, and to establish increased levels of trust with the victim's social circle for future deceptions. In this attack, the adversary first tries to find ways to obtain a victim's personal information, such as name, location, occupation and friends list from his public profile on OSNs or his personal homepage(s). Then, the adversary forges the victim's identity and creates a similar or even identical profile on OSN sites. Afterwards, he sends friend requests to the victim's contacts. Once the friend requests are accepted, he builds the victim's friend network and gains access to profiles of the victim's friends. In addition, he can launch ICAs on the victim's friends based on these personal data. The adversary can also implement an automated, cross-site profile cloning attack [1] in which the adversary can clone the identity of a victim in one site where the victim is registered, and forge it on another OSN site where the victim is not registered yet. After having successfully created the forged identity on the site where the victim has no account, the adversary can automatically attempt to rebuild the social networks of the victim by contacting his friends who have accounts on both sites. The experimental results show that both of these ICA schemes are effective and adversaries do not raise much suspicion in users who have been compromised [1].

The ICA on OSN sites is not only a privacy attack for the victims but also may cause potential financial loss and severely affect the trust they have built on OSNs [1]. Most users may be apt to trust their friends' activities on OSN sites more than their activities on other websites. This is because OSNs are built on the core concept of making friends and sharing information with each other. However, due to users' lack of awareness, they are more likely to trust both OSN sites and their friends there. Such trust makes it easier for adversaries to obtain a victim's personal information and then clone the identity. Thus, it is urgent to build mechanisms to detect ICAs and try to reduce the loss on OSN sites.

In regard to defending against ICAs, most solutions focus on educating users to control the distribution of their sensitive personal information and digital identities [6, 7]. *FightIDTheft* [6] and *Facebook Identity Theft* [7] focus on providing detailed suggestions to help users to define their privacy policies. Typically, well-designed OSN sites allow users to customize their privacy policies. For example, *Facebook* has a "Privacy Settings" page that allows users to specify which pieces of profile data each user is allowed to view. It also allows users to set fine-grained access policies by specifying whether a piece of profile data is visible or not to some friends. However, configuring fine-grained privacy settings on OSNs are often complicated and time-consuming task that many users feel confused about and usually skip. Unfortunately, most of users are apt to stand in side of popularity and usability rather than security and privacy.

There are several third-party applications of OSN sites proposed and employed for protecting users against ICAs. For instance, in *Facebook*, *Identity Badge* identifies a user via a passport check [4], and *mysafeFriend* validates a user's identity by asking user's friends to verify him and doing a credit card check [5]. Although these applications may help users to validate who they are and protect their identities, they are passive protections and only used to identify users themselves but cannot defend against ICAs targeting them. The faked identities still exist on OSN sites and adversaries continue to deceive more victims using them without any restrictions. Therefore, an active security mechanism to detect faked identities on OSNs is required and urgent.

However, detection of faked identities is a challenging work. The key challenges are as follows:
- It is quite common that several people have similar names in real world; and hence their identities on OSNs may be similar. We cannot arbitrarily infer all the similar identities that have similar names as faked identities.
- The characteristics of a faked identity have not been analyzed and summarized.

In this paper, we address these challenges and propose an active detection framework to detect existing faked identities on OSNs. We first investigate and characterize a faked identity. We observe that a cleverly crafted faked identity may not only forge attributes of the victim but may also add friends into its networks that are also in the victim's networks. We propose two approaches to calculate profile similarity between two identities based on *attribute similarity* and *friend network similarity*. Based on profile similarity, we propose a framework to detect faked identities on OSNs that includes three steps. The first step is to search and filter identities in profile set where the input is a profile. The second step is to discover a list of suspicious identities related to the input profile using profile similarity schemes, and the last one is to verify the identities in suspicious identity list and remove the faked ones. In our detection process, we use a flexible set of parameters, which can be adjusted to distinguish a victim from its clones and may achieve accurate detections on different OSNs where the faked identities may have different behaviors.

The contribution of this paper is three fold. First, to the best of our knowledge, our work is the first attempt to characterize the faked identities, and detect them on OSN sites using an active approach based on profile similarity. Second, we propose two profile similarity schemes to discover suspicious identities. Third, we present experiments to demonstrate that our detection schemes are flexible and effective.

The rest of the paper is organized as follows. In Section 2, we characterize attribute and friend networks of a faked identity. In Section 3, we introduce the detection framework with two profile similarity schemes: *Basic Profile Similarity* and *Multiple-Faked Identities Profile Similarity*. Then, we build the dataset, discuss the relationships between parameters and detection results and evaluate our proposed models in Section 4. In Section 5, we discuss the related work and discuss limitations in Section 6. Finally, Section 7 concludes the paper and discusses future work.

2. CHARACTERISTICS OF FAKED IDENTITIES
In this section, we discuss the limitation of friend adding process in existing OSNs and introduce characteristics of a faked identity based on its attribute and friend network characteristics.

2.1 Friend Adding Process on OSNs
In typical existing OSN sites, when user B receives a friend request from user A, or user B gets user A's link as a result of a friend search function or friend recommender feature of OSN, there is no immediate approach for B to verify the authenticity of A. Furthermore, user B can see only the public features of user A. An adversary can create a faked identity by copying the victim's public attributes and adding the individuals in the victim's friend networks into its networks. In addition, an adversary can also first become a friend of the victim to gain access more features that are visible to his friends, which may be used to forge the victim more successfully. Due to the similarity of the public features between the victim and the faked identity, it is difficult for users to distinguish them when they receive friend requests.

2.2 Definition of a User Profile
A social network is a social structure modeled as a graph, where nodes represent users or other entities (e.g. group) embedded in a social context, and edges represent specific types of relationships between entities. Such relationship may be based on real-world friendship, common values, shared visions and ideas, kinship, shared likes and dislike, etc. [3].

In this paper, we only model users' attributes and their friend networks since the main target of ICAs is to forge the victims' attributes and rebuild the victims' friend networks to establish trust from their friends [1]. We assume that each identity may have three different lists associated with it; a *friend list* that indicates other users in his friend network, a *recommended friend list* that OSN sites generate to recommend potential new friends to users based on activities or common interests, and an *excluded friend list* that indicates people who users avoid from having in their friend network such as parents, boss, etc. We define an identity profile (or simply a profile) in an OSN site as follows:

DEFINITION 1. : *Let x be a user in an OSN system, we define public profile of x, represented as P_x, as a tuple (A_x, G_x), where*
  a) $A_x = \{(a, v) \mid a$ *is an attribute name and v is its value}represents x's public attribute-value set;*
  b) $G_x = (FL_x, RFL_x, EFL_x)$ *represents x's public friend networks, where FL_x, RFL_x, and EFL_x are x's friend list, recommended friend list and excluded friend list respectively.*

We assume that friendship relationships in the *friend list* are bidirectional while relationships in the *recommended friend list* and *extended friend list* may not be bidirectional.

2.3 Attribute as Target
In most OSN sites, *Name* of a user, *e.g.* a full name "*Martin Luther King*", is usually public to everyone and is treated as a key piece of identification information. Consequently, as the first step of ICA, an adversary usually creates a faked identity that has a name that is same or similar to that of the victim, such as "*Martin L. King*" and "*Martin King*". Besides *Name*, we note that a faked identity may have several attributes whose values are similar to those of the victim, if not the same. In this paper, "similar" means "equivalent" when values of these attribute are numeric, such as

Birthday and *Age* while it means "equivalent", "synonymous" or "abbreviation" when the values are strings. Some of attributes of a victim may be easily obtained from his homepage or his public profile on OSNs. Sometimes, an adversary may not obtain such information easily when a user does not have a homepage or is careful enough to publicly disclose as little personal information as possible. However, even if a victim's public information is little, it cannot prevent an adversary from implementing ICAs. He can arbitrarily set the values of fake identity's attributes when he does not know the victim's corresponding attribute value, and then hide them as private attributes. As users not connected to the faked identity only see the public attributes, they may not be able to distinguish the faked identity from the genuine identity.

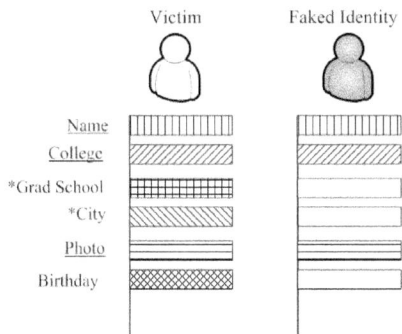

Figure 1. Attribute characteristics of a faked identity

An experienced adversary may also be able to easily guess the victims' privacy settings by checking the blank values in the victim's public profiles. By doing this, the adversary can forge not only the values of the attributes they do not know, but also hide some information that is regarded as private in general but is set as public by the victims. This activity may make the faked identities more genuine. In Figure 1, the left part represents the victim's profile and the right part is the faked identity created by an adversary. In the victim's profile, the *Grad School* and *City* are set to be private (indicated by an *) and other attributes are public. The adversary, if he is not a friend of the victim, can obtain the values of the victim's *Name*, *College*, *Photo* and *Birthday*, but he may not know the values of *Grad School* and *City*. However, he can create a faked identity which has the same *Name*, *College* and *Photo* as the victim. For *Grad School* and *City*, he may simply configure the privacy settings similar to that of the victim, sets random values for these attributes and hides them. For *Birthday* which is usually sensitive and is set to be private by most of users, the adversary can set it as private, while the victim in Figure 1 has it set as public. Such an activity may make the victim's friends believe the faked one more than the real one because it complies with the general trends regarding privacy settings.

Based on the above analysis, we summarize the key targets while creating attributes of a faked identity as follows:
- *Attribute value* **as target**: An adversary creates a faked identity that has several similar attributes to those of the victim.
- *Privacy setting* **as target**: An adversary creates a faked identity that has several similar attributes to those of the victim but also follows his privacy settings.

2.4 Friend Networks as Target
The main goal of ICA is to add victim's friends and build the trust relationship with them [1]. Therefore, after an adversary creates a faked identity based on attributes similar to that of the victim, his

next step is typically to forge friend networks of the victim. Earlier we introduced the friend networks in definition 1. We elaborate on these lists below.

Friend List (FL)
At first, an adversary may try to obtain the *friend list* of a victim's profile. Then, he may send friend requests to all of these friends in order to forge the victim more accurately. Experimental results reported in [1] suggest that a typical user tends to accept a friend request from a fake identity although its real counterpart is already in his *friend list*. Thus, the adversary may add many friends of the victim successfully in his networks. After he gets enough friend requests accepted, he can forge the victim successfully.

Recommended Friend List (RFL)
A cautious user may check his friend list before he makes a decision to accept a suspicious friend request. However, an experienced adversary can still forge the victim successfully even when he cannot add enough existing friends of the victim. Many OSN sites generate a list of recommended friends for every identity based on some of his attributes, such as Educations and Interests. These recommended friends are probably friends of the victim or the ones who are familiar with him, but they are not in the *friend list* of the victim. The victim may add these people as friends in future. However, the recommended friends generated for a faked identity may be same as those of the victim, since the adversary has successfully forged related attributes of the victim. Then, an adversary can send friend requests to these recommended friends before the victim does. After the friend requests are accepted, it may make the faked identity more genuine than the victim and makes it difficult for the victim to add these friends. Therefore, besides the existing friends of the victim, the recommended friends of the victim should be considered in characterizing the friend networks of a faked identity.

Excluded Friend List (EFL)
In order to avoid social embarrassments within OSNs, some users may be less likely to add some individuals that they are very familiar with into their friend list. For instance, teenagers may want to make sure they do not add their parents, elder relatives and tutors to their *friend list*. These people may or may not be listed in his *recommended friend list*. In this paper, we add these people into a special group, called *excluded friend list*. It is also possible that an adversary, such as a neighbor or a colleague of the victim, may be familiar with the victim and his relatives who may be in his *excluded friend list*. The adversary can forge the victim's identity on OSN sites and send friend requests to these users who are in the victim's *excluded friend list*. If such a friend request is accepted, this faked identity may appear to be more authentic and hence it may be easier for the adversary to add the victim's other friends who do not know the victim's potential *excluded friend list*.

Based on the above analysis, we characterize the friend networks of a faked identity as follows:
- *Friend List* **as target**: An adversary creates a faked identity that has several common friends with the victim. F1 in Figure 2 belongs to this type. In F1, all of friends of the faked identity are also the friends of the victim.
- *Recommended Friend List* **as target**: An adversary creates a faked identity and adds some friends who are in the victim's *recommended friend list*. An example is shown in F3 in Figure 2.

- *Excluded Friend List* as target: An adversary creates a faked identity and some friends of this faked identity are the users in the victim's *excluded friend list*. An example is shown in F6 of Figure 2.
- *Combined Friend List* as target: An adversary creates a faked identity that has some friends, who are in *friend list* of the victim, some friends who are in *recommended friend list* of the victim, some friends who are in *excluded friend list* of the victim, and some friends who are not connected to the victim. Examples of these attacks are shown in F2, F4, F5, F7, F8, F9 and F10 of Figure 2. For instance, F10 shows the most complicated *friend list* of a faked identity that has four mutual friends with the victim, and has one *recommended friend* and one *excluded friend* of the victim. It also has one friend who does not connect with the victim. Specially, in F9, the faked identity does not connect with the victim directly but there is one *recommended friend* and two *excluded friends* of the victim in its *friend list*.

Note that these characteristics introduced above are basic and used for one of our profile similarity schemes: *Basic Profile Similarity*. For *Multiple-FID Profile Similarity*, we introduce several additional characteristics in Section 3.2.4.

3. PROFILE SIMILARITY SCHEMES AND DETECTION PROCESS
Based on the characteristics of a faked identity, we introduce our profile similarity schemes and detection process in this section.

3.1 Profile Similarity
We first introduce definitions of *attribute similarity* and *friend network similarity* in two identity profiles. Several different similarity measures exist in the literature which may be useful to define these two similarity measure such as *overlap similarity*, *Jaccard similarity, dice coefficient* and *cosine similarity*. We adopt the *cosine similarity* [8, 9, 14] in this work because of the following reasons:

- The vectors in our framework are binary vectors and *cosine similarity* is especially suitable for binary data [8]. For computing *attribute similarity*, the vector we expect is the value of *similar* or *not similar* for the same attribute between two profiles. For computing *friend network similarity*, the vector is the value of *mutual friend* (Y) or *not mutual friend* (N) between two sets for *Basic Profile Similarity*, while it is the value of *similar friend* (Y) or *not similar friend* (N) for *Multiple-Faked Identities Profile Similarity*.
- The equations using *Cosine Similarity* have special representations in these definitions. In *attribute similarity*, the equation represents the portion of similar attributes in the average size of two sets, while the other equations in *similarity of friend networks* represents the portion of mutual and similar friends in the average size of two sets.

Based on *attribute similarity* and *friend network similarity*, we introduce two profile similarity measures: *Basic Profile Similarity* (BPS) and *Multiple-Faked Identities Profile Similarity* (MFIPS). We consider both of similarities of attributes and friend networks in these schemes for two reasons. First, after an adversary creates a faked identity by forging attributes similar to that of the victim, some victim's friends may add the faked one as their friend without noticing any suspicion, while some of them may notice such attacks and add the genuine one. Thus, some of the victim's friends are in the *FL* of the faked identity, whereas some of his

friends are in *FL* of the authentic identity of the victim. When only considering *friend network similarity*, we may overlook the faked identities that have few mutual friends with the identity of the victim but have victim's many friends that do not add the victim as friend in their profiles. Second, some users that have similar names may be cautious enough to not disclose enough attributes to the public. When only considering similarity of attributes, we may make mistakes and identify some of these genuine and similar identities as faked ones.

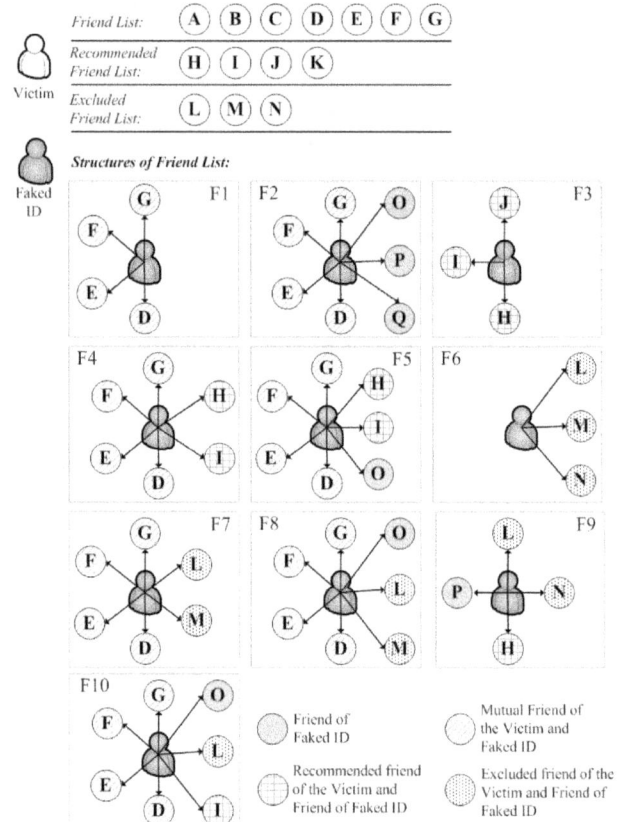

Figure 2. Friend networks of a faked identity

3.1.1 Attribute Similarity Measure
The *attribute similarity* calculates the similarity between two profiles' attributes and its value is based on similar values of the attributes in two profiles. The attribute similarity based on *cosine similarity* is formalized as follows:

DEFINITION 2. *Let P_c be the public profile of a candidate identity c and P_v be the public profile of a victim v. Let SA_{cv} denote the number of the attributes for which P_c and P_v have similar values. We define the attribute similarity of two profiles, S_{att}, as:*

$$S_{att}(P_c, P_v) = \frac{SA_{cv}}{\sqrt{|A_c| \times |A_v|}} \qquad (1)$$

where $|A_c|$ and $|A_v|$ represents the number of attributes in P_v and P_v, respectively.

For instance, for the victim in Figure 1, *Name, College, Phone* and *Birthday* are public attributes ($|A_v|$=4). For the faked identity, *Name, College* and *phone* are public and $|A_f| = 3$. The values of

30

Name, *College* and *Phone* are same for the victim and the faked identity. Thus, $SA_{fv}=3$ and $S_{att}=\frac{3}{\sqrt{3\times4}} \approx 0.866$.

3.1.2 Friend Network Similarity Measure

As another key component of our detection models, *friend network similarity* calculates the similarity of two identities' friend networks. As discussed earlier, we should count not only the victim's and the faked identity's *friend list* but also their *recommended friend list* and *excluded friend list*. For the *friend list*, it can be obtained directly from user's profile, when it is set to be public. Users can set their friend network as private and such activity may defend against ICAs. However, most of users do not prefer this activity as it also makes their profiles less popular. The *recommended friend list* is usually generated by an OSN system. This list may be dynamic. In our detection framework, we only consider the *recommended friend list* at the time the detection process runs. For the *excluded friend list*, we assume that a user creates them. For example, a user is able to input a list of e-mail addresses as the identifications of individuals in his *excluded friend list*. Also, a user can input user IDs or profile links on OSN sites to identify his *excluded friend list*.

In order to calculate the of *friend network similarity* between a candidate identity and a victim identity, we first define similarities with respect to *FL*, *RFL* and *EFL* of the victim:

DEFINITION 3. *Let P_c be the public profile of a candidate identity c and P_v be the public profile of a victim v. We define the similarity between the FLs in two identities as S_{ff}, similarity between FL of P_c and RFL of P_v as S_{frf}, and similarity between FL of P_v and EFL of P_v as S_{fef}:*

$$S_{ff}(P_c,P_v) = \frac{|MFF_{cv}|}{\sqrt{|F_c|\times|F_v|}} \qquad (2),$$

$$S_{frf}(P_c,P_v) = \frac{|MFRF_{cv}|}{\sqrt{|F_c|\times|RF_v|}} \qquad (3),$$

$$S_{fef}(P_c,P_v) = \frac{|MFEF_{cv}|}{\sqrt{|F_c|\times|EF_v|}} \qquad (4),$$

where

- *MFF_{cv} denotes the set of mutual friends common in the FLs of P_c and P_v*
- *$MFRF_{cv}$ denotes the set of mutual friends common in FL of P_c and RFL of P_v*
- *$MFEF_{cv}$ denote the set of mutual friends common between FL of P_c and EFL of P_v*
- *$|X|$ represents the number of elements in the set X.*

We define the overall *friend network similarity* for Basic Profile Similarity approach as follows:

DEFINITION 4. *Given a public profile P_c of a candidate identity c and a public profile P_v of a victim identity v, we define the friend networks similarity of these two identities for BPS as S_{bfn}:*

$$S_{bfn}(P_c,P_v) = (\alpha S_{ff} + \beta S_{frf} + \gamma S_{fef}), \ \alpha+\beta+\gamma=1 \qquad (5),$$

where α, β and γ are parameters that are used to balance the weights of similarities related to FL, RFL and EFL for the overall similarity of the friend networks in two identities.

We assume that the similarity of *FL*s between two identities is the most important component and the similarity between *FL* of the candidate and *RFL* of the victim is the second most important element. Thus, we set $\alpha > \beta > \gamma$. These three parameters can be estimated by distributions of dataset before the detection process runs. For example, we can estimate their values based on average values of S_{ff}, S_{frf} and S_{fef}. In Section 4, we determine these values by estimating the minimum values of S_{ff}, S_{frf} and S_{fef}.

Note that definition 4 is only used for *Basic Profile Similarity*. We will update this equation for *Multiple-Faked Identities Profile Similarity* in definition 12.

3.1.3 Basic Profile Similarity (BPS)

In the BPS scheme, we assume that the adversary does not create faked identities that forge friends of the victim. In this case, all of the friends in friend networks of both victim and faked identity are assumed to be authentic identities. Therefore, BPS is based on the number of similar attributes and the number of mutual friends in the two identities. We formalize the BPS in two identities as follows:

DEFINITION 5. *Given a public profile P_c of a candidate identity c and a public profile P_v of a victim v, we define the Basic Profile Similarity of these two identities as S_{BPS}:*

$$S_{BPS}(P_c,P_v) = \frac{\sqrt{(\kappa S_{att})^2 + (\chi S_{bfn})^2}}{\sqrt{\kappa^2 + \chi^2}} \qquad (6),$$

where κ and χ are the parameters to balance the effect of attribute similarity and friend network similarity on the BPS..

The values of κ and χ can be determined based on the pre-calculated results of *attribute similarity* and *friend network similarity*. Usually, we adjust κ and χ to make similarities of attributes and similarity of friend networks contribute equally to the overall similarity. However, their values can be adjusted based on requirements of the detection. In particular, when $\kappa = 0$ and $\chi = 1$, BPS is switched to the case that only similarity of the friend networks contributes to its result. We specially use this case in our experiments in Section 4 to compare the differences of our two schemes of *profile similarity*.

3.1.4 Multiple-Faked Identities Profile Similarity (MFIPS)

In previous sections, we characterized the friend networks of a faked identity based on assumption that an adversary does not create faked identities that forge friends of the victim. However, an intelligent adversary can create multiple faked identities related to a single victim. In addition to forging a victim, the adversary may also fake the identities of the victim's friends. It is possible that some of the victim's cautious friends notice friend requests from a potentially faked identity and reject such requests. In such scenarios, this attack of faking friends of the victim can be especially effective. In particular, after multiple faked identities related to a victim are created and added as friends of the faked identity targeting the victim, an adversary can forge friend networks of the victim more successfully. Figure 3 illustrates two examples of such ICAs.

As shown in F11 of Figure 3, in order to get *FL* of the victim, an adversary first creates a faked identity *E'* that forges identity *E*. Then he sends friend request from *E'* to the victim. After the friend request is accepted and then *FL* of the victim is exposed, the adversary creates a faked identity to forge the victim. In *FL* of the faked identity, we see identity *K*, who is a *recommended friend* of the victim, and identity *L*, who is an *excluded friend* of the victim. In addition to these friends related to the victim, the adversary also creates two faked identities - *C'* and *D'* - to forge victim's friends. Lastly, although the faked identity targeting the victim has only one mutual friend with the victim, it has four indirect friends: *C'*, *D'*, *K* and *L*. In F12 of Figure 3, it is a more successful example of a faked identity whose *FL* is almost the same as that of the victim. In this graph, the faked identity has connected and forged all of the friends of the victim (friends *D*, *E*, *F'* and *G* are connected, friend *B* and *C* are forged by *B'* and *C'*), except friend *A*. Such attack makes it more difficult for the victim's friends to notice the attacks.

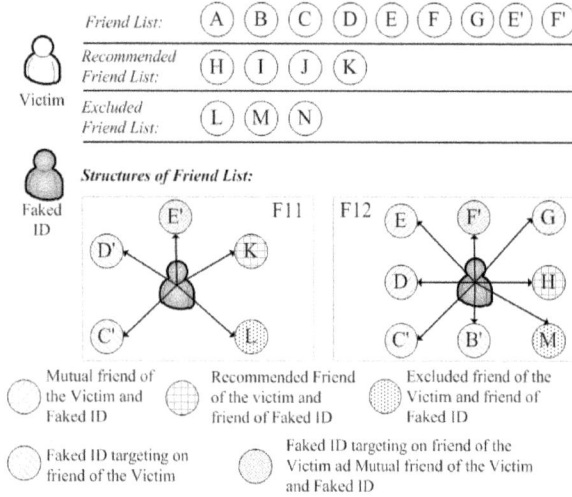

Figure 3. e.g. 1: Multiple faked identities in friend networks

It is worth noting that some features on OSNs may help defend against such an ICA. For instance, in *Facebook*, showing mutual friends between two identities when a user is looking at another user's public profile may help to defend against such ICA that is creating multiple faked identities of the victim's friends. However, these features do not work for the victims who have a large number of friends (e.g. the number of friends larger than 100). This is because it is difficult for a user to remember all the friends he added. Furthermore, an adversary can first create a faked identity of the victim, send friend requests to all of the victim's friends and may successfully add some of the victim's friends who are less cautious. Then, he can create some faked identities that are interesting for the victim, and try to make them as the victim's friends. After that, he can create some faked identities of the victim's friends, make all of them as the friends of the identity that forges the victim and then try to add these faked identities into the victim's friend list. He can repeat these three steps to succeed in adding and forging a large number of the victim's friends. At this point, the number of the mutual friends between the friend list of the faked identity targeting the victim and the victim may be large and complex enough that makes it difficult for the victim's friends to distinguish which one is real. In addition, recent statistic from *Facebook* supports the possibility of our proposed arguments since the average user in *Facebook* has more than 130 friends [2]. Therefore, attacks by creating multiple identities forging the victim as well as his friends cannot be neglected and should be actively detected.

In order to detect multiple faked identities targeting one victim, we update BPS and design a similarity scheme called MFIPS to

detect such complicated attacks. In MFIPS, we apply the same definition of attribute similarity but update the equations to calculate the similarity of friend networks. Here, we focus on similar friends between *FL* of the candidate identity and friend networks (*FL*, *RFL* and *EFL*) of the victim.

In the following, we categorize types of attacks related to multiple faked identities targeting one victim while introducing new definitions to capture them.

TYPE A: The adversary first creates identities that forge the identities in the victim's *FL*, *RFL* and *EFL*. Then, these faked identities are added as friends of a faked identity targeting the victim. For instance, in F11 of Figure 3, the faked identity has friends of C' and D'. They are the faked identities of C and D, who are the friends of the victim. However, potential friends of the victim may not discover such attack and add the faked identity of the victim as friend since friend networks of faked identity are similar to those of the victim. As more friends of the victim make wrong decisions and add faked identity as friend, the friend networks of the faked identity become more complex: both authentic friends and faked friends of the victim exists. It may confuse the future friends of the victim and make it more difficult for them to distinguish which one is genuine.

In order to detect such attack, we introduce the following definitions in which similar friends between *FL* of the candidate identity and the friend networks of the victim are captured.

DEFINITION 6. *Let P_x and P_y be the public profiles of two identities. We define P_x and P_y as similar if and only if $S_{BPS}(P_x, P_y) > \mu$, where μ is a threshold of profile similarity.*

DEFINITION 7. *Let P_c be the public profile of a candidate identity c and P_v be the public profile of a victim v. We update the similarity between the FLs in two identities as $S_{s\text{-}ff}$, similarity between FL of P_c and RFL of P_v as $S_{s\text{-}frf}$, and similarity between FL of P_v and EFL of P_v as $S_{s\text{-}fef}$:*

$$S_{s\text{-}ff}(P_c, P_v) = \frac{|SFF_{cv}|}{\sqrt{|F_c| \times |F_v|}} \qquad (7),$$

$$S_{s\text{-}frf}(P_c, P_v) = \frac{|SFRF_{cv}|}{\sqrt{|F_c| \times |RF_v|}} \qquad (8),$$

$$S_{s\text{-}fef}(P_c, P_v) = \frac{|SFEF_{cv}|}{\sqrt{|F_c| \times |EF_v|}} \qquad (9)$$

where,

- *SFF_{cv} denotes the set of similar friends between FLs of P_c and P_v.*
- *$SFRF_{cv}$ denotes the set of similar friends between FL of P_c and RFL of P_v.*
- *$SFEF_{cv}$ denotes the set of similar friends between FL of P_c and EFL of P_v.*

TYPE B: We also consider the influences of similar identities which are in the friend networks of the victim and are also mutual friends of both the faked identity and the victim. In this case, an adversary, who creates a faked identity targeting a victim, can create multiple faked identities corresponding to those in the victim's friend list, add them as friends of the faked identity and try to add them into the friend networks of the victim. After enough mutual faked identities are added into the victim's friend networks, the faked identity forging the victim will appear authentic to the victim's friends.

First, we capture the case that at least one of the identities in the pairs of similar identities exists in *FL* of the victim. There are two attack schemes in this scenario:

- **Case 1:** Both of the similar identities exist in *FL* of the victim. One of them is a friend of the faked identity. For example, in F11 of Figure 3, E' is a faked identity of E and both of them are the friend of the victim. In addition, E' is also a friend of the faked identity.
- **Case 2:** One of the identities in the pairs of similar identities is in *FL* of the victim and is a friend of the faked identity. The other one in this pair exists in *RFL* of the victim. For instance, in F14 of Figure 4, K' is a faked identity of K that is a *recommended friend* of the victim. It is also a mutual friend of the victim and the faked identity.

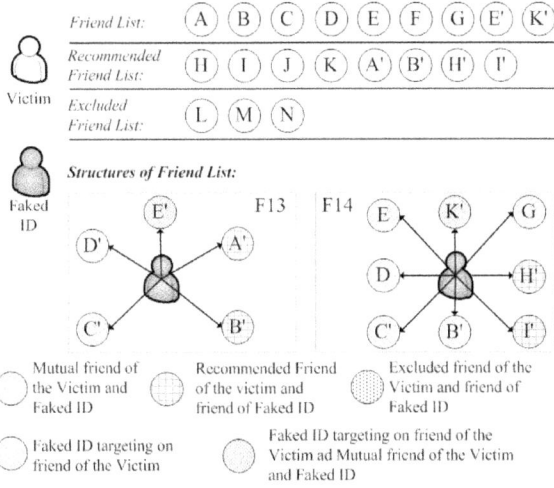

Figure 4. e.g. 2: Multiple faked identities in friend networks

However, we do not count the pairs of similar identities between the victim's *EFL* and *FL*, since identities in *EFL* are the ones that the victim never adds as friends. Thus, the common or similar identities in them do not contribute to the overall similarity.

DEFINITION 8. *Let P_c be the public profile of a candidate identity c and P_v be the public profile of a victim v. We define the similarity S_{s-cf} to capture the scenarios in Case 1 and 2:*

$$S_{s-cf}(P_c, P_v) = \frac{|SCF1_{cv}| + |SCF2_{cv}|}{\sqrt{|F_c| \times |F_v|}} \quad (10),$$

where

- $SCF1_{cv}$ *denote the set of similar but no same identities between CF and FL of the victim.*
- $SCF2_{cv}$ *denotes the set of similar but no same identities between CF and RFL of the victim.*
- $CF = F_c \cap F_v$

Second, we capture the case where at least one of the identities in a pair of similar identities exists in the *RFL* of the victim. There are also two attack schemes in this scenario:

- **Case 3:** Both of the similar identities exist in *RFL* of the victim. One of them is a friend of the faked identity. For instance, in F13 of Figure 5, A' and B' are in *RFL* of the victim and they

forge A and B respectively. Also, they are the friends of the faked identity.

- **Case 4:** One of the identities in the pair of similar identities is in *RFL* of the victim and is a friend of the faked identity. The other one in this pair exists in *FL* of the victim. In F13 of Figure 4, A' and B' exist in *RFL* of the victim and they forge A and B respectively. Also, they are friends of the faked identity.

As in the previous cases, we do not count the pairs of similar identities between the victim's *EFL* and *RFL*. The next definition captures these cases.

DEFINITION 9. *Let P_c be the public profile of a candidate identity c and P_v be the public profile of a victim v. We define the similarity S_{s-cfrf} to capture the scenarios in Case 3 and 4:*

$$S_{s-cfrf}(P_c, P_v) = \frac{|SCFRF3_{cv}| + |SCFRF4_{cv}|}{\sqrt{|F_c| \times |RF_v|}} \quad (11)$$

where,

- $SCFRF3_{cv}$ *denotes the set of similar (but not same) identities between CFRF and RFL of the victim.*
- $SCFRF4_{cv}$ *denotes the set of similar (but no same) identities between CFRF and FL of the victim.*
- $CFRF = F_c \cap RF_v$

Based on definitions 7, 8 and 9, we update the definition of *friend network similarity* and then the profile similarity for MFIPS as follows:

DEFINITION 10. *Given a public profile P_c of a candidate identity c and a public profile P_v of a victim v, we define the friend network similarity of these two identities for MFIPS as $S_{mfn}(P_c, P_v)$:*

$$S_{mfn}(P_c, P_v) = \alpha(S_{s-ff} + S_{s-cf}) + \beta(S_{s-frf} + S_{s-cfrf}) + \gamma S_{s-fef} \quad (12).$$

DEFINITION 11. *Given a public profile P_c of a candidate identity c and a public profile P_v of a victim v, we define the Multiple-Faked Identities Profile Similarity of these two identities as S_{MFIPS}:*

$$S_{MFIPS}(P_c, P_v) = \frac{\sqrt{(\kappa S_{att})^2 + (\chi S_{mfn})^2}}{\sqrt{\kappa^2 + \chi^2}} \quad (13).$$

Compared to definition 5 which is used for BPS, this definition employs refined notion of *friend network similarity* to capture the influences of multiple faked identities that forge the victim and his friends. We argue that MFIPS is more accurate and is able to discover more suspicious identities, although it increases the complexity of detection process.

3.2 The Detection Process
In order to detect faked identities on OSN sites, we design a detection process. Our detection process is mainly based on the profile similarity measures we introduced above.

3.2.1 Overview of Detection Process
As shown in Figure 5, our detection process has the following phases:

- *Discovery*: Given an *input identity (IID)* and a *Profile Set*, we search and collect all the identity profiles that have *Name* similar to that of IID into a *Candidate List (CL)*.
- *Compute Profile Similarity*: After obtaining *CL*, we calculate profile similarity between each candidate identity in *CL* and

IID based on our profile similarity schemes. When the similarity of a candidate identity for *IID* is larger than a pre-defined threshold, it is added into *Suspicious Identity List* (*SIL*). *IID* is also added into *SIL* since we do not know whether *IID* itself is authentic or not.

- *Validation*: We validate every identity in *SIL* in this step. When an identity is verified to be a faked one, it is put into the *Faked Identity List* (FIL). On the other hand, when an identity is verified to be genuine, its trust value (will be explained in Section 3.5) is increased to avoid future multiple validations. Finally, the faked identities in *FIL* are temporarily closed or eliminated and the existing friends of these identities will receive notifications that their friends are determined to be faked.

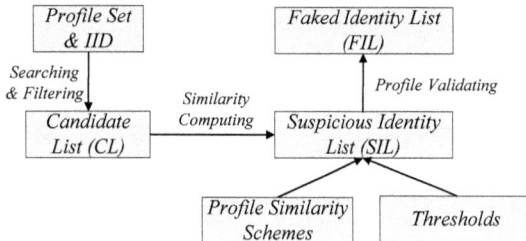

Figure 5. The detection process

Note that we do not do the similarity computation and validation in parallel since validation phase may take significant amount of time depending on the adopted approaches, some of which may involve user responding time.

3.2.2 Thresholds in Detection Process

In our detection process, we have introduced several threshold parameters in order to help to determine the suspicious identities while computing *profile similarity*.

We use threshold parameters ε and δ during *attribute similarity* computation. The ε is used as the threshold for SA_{cv} to indicate that whether we consider this measure in overall similarity. When SA_{cv} is less than ε, we believe that *attribute similarity* will not have significant influence on the value of overall *profile similarity* computed for a given candidate identity and the victim. Then, we set the *attribute similarity* between this candidate identity and the victim as δ, which is the threshold of *attribute similarity*. For example, $\varepsilon = 2$ means that we do not care about the *attribute similarity* for a candidate identity that has only two similar attributes to that of the victim. For δ, it is the minimum value of *attribute similarity*. Sometimes, due to the large number of public attributes in two identities, S_{att} may be less than δ but we set it as δ. This is because we also claim *attribute similarity* contributes less to *profile similarity* in this case.

The third threshold λ we use is to select values of *friend network similarity*. Sometimes, the number of mutual friends in two identities' friend networks may be small compared to the relatively large number of friends in each of them. In this case, similarity of friend networks does not make significant contribution to the results of *profile similarity*. Thus, we set the similarity of friend networks as λ when it is less than λ.

The last threshold we adopt in the detection process is μ for both BPS and MFIPS. We use μ to directly determine whether a candidate identity is suspicious or not. When the *profile similarity* value calculated via BPS or MFIPS is less than μ, we consider this

candidate identity as not suspicious identity to the victim; otherwise, we consider it as suspicious and add it into *SIL*.

The values of these thresholds should be estimated before running the detection process. We show how to determine them based on the distribution of the data set in Section 4. Note that there are other thresholds that used in various definitions but we do not discuss those it in this paper.

3.3 The Validation Process

We discuss several possible approaches for validation of the identities once they have been identified as suspicious.

An intuitive approach to identify users is to ask users to input a unique real world ID. For example, *Identity Badge* requires users to input a passport in order to verify them [4]. However, this kind of approach may be difficult to apply for all of the users in the world. Furthermore, since user's unique ID in the real world may be difficult to change, it is hard for the victim to recover from ICA when the adversary knows the victim's unique ID and uses it to pass the identity validation on OSN sites. Another approach currently applied for identifying users is proposed by *mysafeFriend* [5], which is a third-party application in Facebook. It sets five levels of trust for one identity. At the lower levels (level 1 to level 3), it asks an identity to choose his friends to verify himself. The more friends verify this identity, the more points it gets and eventually it gets promoted to a higher level. At the high levels (level 4 and 5), this application checks the identity's credit card to verify it. However, we argue that this is not secure enough to ask user's friends directly verify whether a user's identity is genuine no not. It may be better to ask user's friends to design questions for a user and validate the answers from him. The validation of an identity should be based on the percentage of questions that a user answers right. In addition, we claim that asking users to input their private information, such as credit card, may not be effective as users are likely to avoid them.

Social authentication, which is similar to the identification method of *mysafeFriend*, is proposed by *Schechter et.al* [10]. In this approach, when the user has answered most of the questions from his friends correctly, he is verified to be valid. We believe that social authentication is the ideal approach for identifying users on OSNs because this method does not request any personal information for validation. However, the current approaches of social authentication are not secure enough and have not been well tested. There are several problems of these identifying approaches that need to be solved before they can be used in practical environments:

- A mechanism is required for an identity to choose his appropriate friends, not suspicious identities, to design or select questions to identify him.
- A research on how to design or select questions to identify identities effectively on OSN systems.
- This identifying approach based on the questions should not expose more private information of identities. Otherwise, the adversaries may get more private information of identities when faked identities created by them are chosen by the validation service.

Another potential approach we consider is to monitor and analyze activities of the faked identities, such as their login times and times of checking friends' posts. However, we cannot guarantee that it works until a practical research is applied and we can monitor suspicious identities for substantially long period of time.

Finally, the validation process may verify the duplicated identities of a user as the faked identities when the user refuses to respond to the validation processes for his multiple identities. In addition, there is a possible case that some real identities may fail during the validation process for various reasons, such as not responding to validation questions within a certain time period. As a result, an appeal mechanism should be applied for the identities that have been erroneously flagged as a faked identity.

3.4 Detection Resistant for Future Attack

It is possible that the faked identities may claim they are authentic and request validation many times. In addition, as the candidate identity of the validation process, the victim may be added into *SIL* and need to be verified. Therefore, the genuine identities may be asked to validate too many times, which is inconvenient. In order to prevent too many validations for identities, we define the number of times a user passes the validation as his trust value. After *SIL* is generated, we refine the similarity of every identity in this list as per definition below:

DEFINITION 12. *Given a public profile P_c of a candidate identity and its result of profile similarity ω_c (calculated by BPS or MFIPS) to a public profile P_v of a victim, we refine it as ω_c^r by counting the times of validation the candidate identity has passed:*

$$\omega_c^r = \omega_c * a^{K_c}, a \in (0,1), K_c \geq 0, K_c \in N \qquad (14)$$

where a is a pre-defined parameter to reduce the value of the similarity between P_c and P_v, and K_c is the times of successful validations (trust value) of P_c.

The value of a needs to be determined empirically to suit the requirements of the detection phase. Based on this value, when a user has been validated enough number of times, its profile similarity value with respect to a victim will be reduced to be less than a threshold μ, and will be removed from *SIL*. We claim that his trust value will be reset to zero once a user alters any value of his attributes. This setting is used to avoid an attack where an adversary creates a genuine identity and wins enough trust value at first and then he changes some values of his attributes to forge the victim and clone the victim's friend networks as well.

4. SIMULAITONS AND EXPERIMENTS

In this section, we present our experimental results to validate out detection models. We used offline dataset of *Facebook* [16] and added *recommended friends* and *excluded friends* of users in them for our detection process. We do not validate our detection framework in a real system because it is difficult to find verified identities and their suspicious identities on OSN sites. Also, we cannot create faked identities into the real system as such activity interferes with OSN sites [1]. In the offline dataset, we assumed a special set of identities as faked identities, in order to verify our detection framework.

4.1 Data Initialization

In the original *Facebook* data, the total number of users is 63,731 (User ID is from 1 to 63,731), the total friend links are 1,634,115, with the average user's friend links of 25.6 [16]. Specially, there are 60,102 users that have the whole friend networks, with the remaining 3,629 users who may not show their full friend links in this dataset because they appear in the friend list of users but do not exist in the profile ID index.

In order to implement our detection schemes, we have updated this data by creating user's attributes, recommended friends and excluded friends for every user:

- **Attribute Generation**: in our updated data, we have ensured that every user has 2 to 10 non-hidden attributes.
- **Recommended Friend Generation**: the number of the recommended friends for a user is a random number between 10 and 42 and these friends are random users whose IDs are from 1 to 63,731, excluding the users that are already in his friend list.
- **Excluded Friend Generation**: they are also random users from 1 to 63,731 with the exclusion of the existing users in this user's *friend list* and *recommended friend list*. The total number of the excluded friend for a user is a random number between 5 and 40.

We also need to choose the victims and assume faked identities in this data set.

Victim Selection
We have randomly selected 179 users (1%) from 17,880 users (excluding the 3,629 users who may not show their full friend links), who have more than 25 friends, as the victims. These victims have 11,723 friend links in total and have average friend links of 65.5 with the minimum and maximum friend links of 26 and 266 respectively. The reason we selected such victims is that adversaries usually like to forge victims who are popular on OSN sites [1].

Faked Identity Assumption
We assumed that the 3,629 users, who do not show their full friend links in original data, are the faked identities that randomly forge the 179 candidates (average faked identities for a victim is 20.3). The reason we set these users as faked identities is that they may not show their full friend links and then it may not affect a lot when friends of victims are added into their friend lists, in order to make them forge the victims.

We also assume that similar attributes between a victim and a faked identity is a random number between 2 and the minimum number of public attributes of the victim and the faked identity. We also randomly created 25 to 50 friend links and added into *friend list* of each faked identity. These links are chosen from corresponding victim's *friend list*, *recommended friend list* and *excluded friend list*. Besides 88,494 friend links that already exist in the faked identities (we infer this number based on the fact that A must be in B's friend list if B is in A's friend list), we have created 136,527 faked links with an average faked identity's friend links of 62.0 (minimum and maximum friend links of 26 and 759 respectively). Table 1 shows the statistic of our data.

Table 1. Statistics of the dataset

Total Users	Original Friend Links	Original Average Friend Links
63731	1634115	25.6
Victims	**Victims' Friend Links**	**Victims' Average Friend Links**
179	11723	65.5
Faked Identities	**Friend Links of Faked Identities**	**Average Friend Links of Faked Identities**
3629	225021	62.0
Victims' Public Attributes	**Public Attributes of Faked Identity**	**Similar Attributes**
2 to 10	2 to 10	2 to min (V's attributes, F's attributes)

4.2 Initialization of Parameters

Before running experiments, we should determine the appropriate parameters in the detection framework. In this section, we set and estimate these parameters by computing their average values and minimum values.

Setting parameters for *attribute similarity*

In our experiments, we first set the minimum value of ε as 2. Based on the attribute distribution in data initialization – an identity has 2 to 10 public attributes, we infer the minimum value of S_{att} is 0.2 (refer to equation 1). We also set the minimum value of δ is equal to 0.2.

Estimating parameters for *friend network similarity*

We first infer α, β and γ in the equations 5 and 12. The values of these parameters can be estimated by the minimum sizes of friend networks of faked identities. According to data initialization, the average size of a faked identity's FL is 62, while the average sizes of its RFL and EFL are 26 and 22.5 in our simulation. Thus, we get $\alpha:\beta:\gamma=\sqrt{62}:\sqrt{26}:\sqrt{22.5} \approx 1.7:1.1:1$ (refer to equation 5 or 12), in order to ensure that FL, RFL and EFL equally contribute to the *friend network similarity* in two identities. In our experiments, however, we assume that the contribution of FL to *friend network similarity* is the largest while contribution of RFL is the second largest. Then, we set $\alpha:\beta:\gamma=5:3:2$ and get $\alpha=0.5$, $\beta=0.3$ and $\gamma=0.2$.

Next, we estimate the minimum value of *friend network similarity* in two identities is approximately $0.2 \times 26/\sqrt{40 \times 759} \approx 0.03$, where 26 is the minimum value of mutual friends in two identities, 40 is the largest size of EFL for a victim and 759 is the largest size of FL for a faked identity (refer to equation 5). Thus, λ should be no less than 0.03.

Estimating parameters for *profile similarity*

Based on the previous settings of *attribute similarity* and estimations of *friend network similarity*, we calculate *attribute similarity* and friend *network similarity* for all pairs of faked identity and victim based on equations 2 and 5. We then get the average values of *attribute similarity* and friend *network similarity* for an identity as 0.56 and 0.31 respectively. Since 0.56: 0.31≈1.8:1 (based on equation 6), we set $\kappa=1$ and $\chi=1.8$ in order to balance the contribution of the similarities of attributes and friend networks to the overall *profile similarity* in two identities. Finally, we get the minimum value of μ as 0.1 by using minimum values of *attribute similarity* (0.2) and friend *network similarity* (0.03) in equation 6.

4.3 Experimental Results and Analysis

In order to demonstrate the effects of the key parameters in detection results, we first design four experiments for the BPS scheme to illustrate the sensitivity of μ, ε, δ and λ under the given values of κ and χ.

Relationship between μ and detection results

In Figure 6, with $\varepsilon = 2$, $\delta = 0.2$ and $\lambda = 0.03$, the detection result drops quickly from 100% to 11.13% with μ increasing from 0.1 to 0.5. It shows that our detection results are very sensitive to μ.

Relationship between ε and detection results

Figure 7 demonstrates the sensitivity of ε for $\delta = 0.2$, $\lambda = 0.03$ and $\mu = 0.2$. The experimental result illustrates that the detection result drops slowly when ε is larger than 6. Thus, we infer that the sensitive values of ε are the integers between 2 to 5 (20% to 50% in total number of attributes).

Relationship between δ and detection results

The experiment that shows the trend of detection results with the values of δ under the condition of $\varepsilon=2$, $\lambda=0.03$ and $\mu=0.4$ is illustrated in Figure 8. This figure shows that detection result increases gradually with the increasing of δ from 0.2 to 0.8.

Relationship between λ and detection results

Figure 9 illustrates the influence of λ in detection. With $\varepsilon = 2$, $\delta = 0.3$ and $\mu = 0.3$, the detection result increases slowly for λ from 0.12 to 0.27. However, in the range of λ between 0.27 and 0.3, the result increases sharply. This is because current minimum value of *friend network similarity* is 0.3. This makes the minimum value of the overall *profile similarity* to be larger than 0.3, which is the current threshold of overall *profile similarity*.

Contributions of friend network similarity to detection results

Next, we design an experiment to demonstrate influence of only the *friend network similarity* on the detection result. This experiment can be regarded as a supplementary to compare detection results between BPS and MFIPS.

To do this, we first filter the candidates by setting $\varepsilon = 2$. When the number of similar attributes between a candidate identity and the victim is not less than 2, we set it as the suspicious identity and calculate its similarity to the victim. Then, we remove the influence of *attribute similarity* in the detection results by setting $\kappa=0$ and $\chi=1$. The result of this experiment is illustrated in Figure 10. The detection result decreases slowly with μ increasing from 0.1 to 0.2. At μ beyond 0.2 the detection result drops quickly to a value around 10%. The comparison of this experiment with the first experiment presented above is also demonstrated in the same figure. After comparing their differences, we find that *friend network similarity* influences the overall *profile similarity* significantly when the detection results are from 90% to 10%. Thus, we may only consider *friend network similarity* for *profile similarity* in MFIPS when comparing its detection results to that of BPS.

Comparisons of detection results of MFIPS and BPS

In this experiment, we only consider *friend network similarity* for *profile similarity* in both of BPS and MFIPS .We adopt $\varepsilon = 2$, $\delta = 0.3$, $\lambda=0.03$ and apply the same values of α, β, γ for both MFIPS and BPS. Our experimental results are illustrated in Table 2. The MFIPS approach detect more faked identities than BPS, e.g. it detects 114 more faked identities than BPS when $\mu=0.5$. However, MFIPS does not change the percentages of the detection results significantly, compared to the detection results of BPS. The main reason is that we randomly chose 179 candidates as the victims from 17,880 users and there are fewer similar and faked identities in friend networks of these victims. Considering the key difference between BPS and MFPIS that we count similar identities rather than mutual identities in MFIPS when computing *profile similarity*, these experimental results are expected. This is because the number of similar and faked identities are not enough large that it cannot update the percentages significantly, compared to the larger denominator (3,629).

5. RELATED WORK

The clone attack (or node replication attack) in sensor networks is similar to ICA on OSNs [11]. In this attack, an adversary captures only a few of nodes, replicates them and then deploys arbitrary number of replicas throughout the network. Then, the adversary can carry out many internal attacks through these compromised nodes.

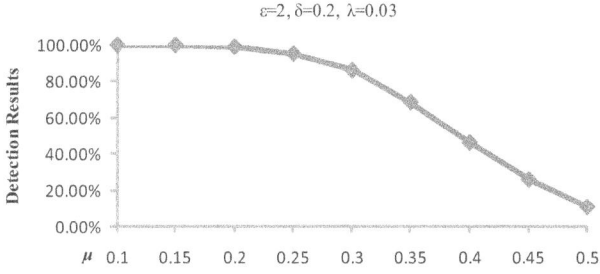

Figure 6. Sensitivity of μ and detection results

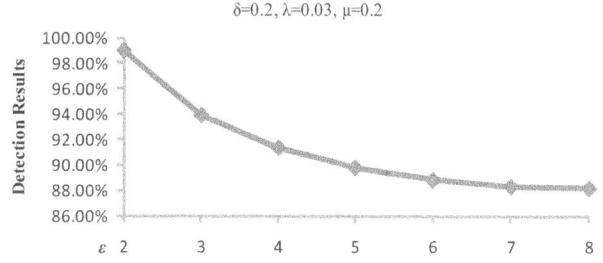

Figure 7. Sensitivity of ε and detection results

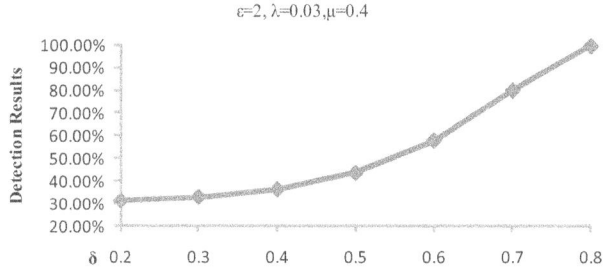

Figure 8. Sensitivity of δ and detection results

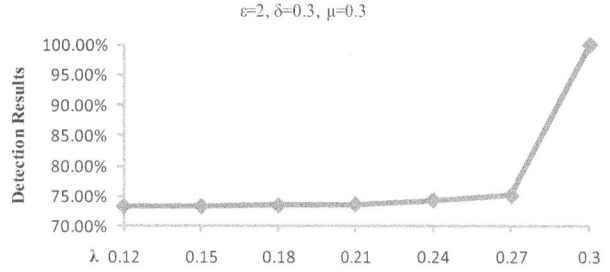

Figure 9. Sensitivity of λ and detection results

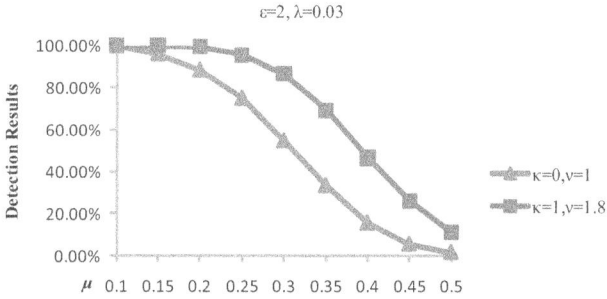

Figure 10. Comparisons of with and without counting attribute similarity

Table 2. Comparisons of BDM and MFDM

BDM(ε=2, δ=0.2, λ=0.03), MFDM(ε=2, δ=0.2, λ=0.03,η=1)									
μ	0.1	0.15	0.2	0.25	0.3	0.35	0.4	0.45	0.5
Detected ID (BDM)	3629	3627	3592	3455	3124	2492	1684	947	404
Detected ID (MFDM)	3629	3629	3599	3469	3149	2532	1742	1029	518
Differences	0	2	7	14	25	40	58	82	114

There are various approaches proposed to detect such clone attacks. One of the significant mechanisms is proposed by *Parno et.al* [11]. They propose two protocols to provide the globally-aware distributed node-replication detection systems. Their first protocol distributes location claims to a randomly selected set of witness nodes while the second protocol exploits the routing topology of the network to select witnesses for a node's location and utilizes geometric probability to detect replicated nodes. Another significant detection method is proposed by *Zeng et.al* [12]. They update the *Randomized Multicast* to propose two non-deterministic and fully distributed protocols to reduce the cost of communication based on random walk.

However, the detection process in sensor network is different from the detection of faked identities in OSNs. The nodes in sensor network are usually active in order to communicate with each other, while the identities in social networks may not be such active - an identity does not need to interact or cooperate with others all the time. For social network sites, the first step for detecting faked identities is to discover similar identities, while similarity discovering in sensor network may be negligible because the cloned nodes are same as the victim nodes. However, the detection approaches in sensor networks may inspire us to

design the validation process to verify faked identities in OSN sites, e.g. how to select users' friends for validation.

On the other hand, the approaches of searching and matching profiles in social networks may be similar with the detection of similar identities on social sites. In this scenario, *Bilge et.al* present an algorithm for matching individuals across social networks to conduct cross-site identity clone attack, based on attribute similarity, such as the similarities of name and education [1]. *Motoyama et.al* develop a system for searching and matching users on Facebook and MySpace via a boosting algorithm based on users' attributes [13]. *Markines et.al* summarize several folksonomy-based similarity measures and evaluate them in finding similar social tags [9]. *Xiao et.al* propose a *positional filtering* principle, which exploits the ordering of tokens in a record and leads to upper bound estimates of similarity scores, to achieve better qualities and improve the runtime efficiency in detecting near duplicate Web pages [15]. Compared to these approaches, our method is based on not only the similarities of attributes or items in entities but also the impact of friend network similarity when discovering the similar profiles.

Our proposed detection process may be extended by an algorithm proposed by *Bayardo et.al* [14]. In the beginning of detection process, we filter profiles by their similar names. However, we may overlook some ICAs where an adversary creates faked identity of the victims using their nicknames. It may be a more secure approach to calculate profile similarities of each profile with the victim and then select the profiles whose similarities with the victim is above the threshold. However, this is a time consuming task. Based on *Bayardo*'s novel indexing and optimization strategies that solve this problem without relying on approximation methods or extensive parameter tuning, we may achieve this goal in an acceptable time.

6. LIMITATIONS

In this section, we discuss some of the limitations of our proposed detection mechanisms:

- Some individuals never use the social network systems. When adversaries get enough personal information of these individuals, they can create faked identities without any misgiving to forge them and deceive their friends. Even, adversaries can create faked identities to forge the individuals who do not exist in the real world. After they successfully add some friends into the faked profiles and get their personal information, these friends probably become the victims in future. Our detection process cannot detect such attacks, as the victims do not register accounts on OSNs.

- Our detection framework can detect the existing faked identities on the OSNs but cannot defend against ICAs in future. This is because the smart adversary can first set up a genuine identity that never uses social networks or an identity that never exists in real world. After having achieved enough trust, he can alter attributes of this identity, such as name and gender, to forge a victim. But we argue that our framework can detect such attacks if OSN sites execute our detection process at the moment when a new profile is created or the sensitive attributes of an existing profile are updated.

- Although we validated our detection schemes by offline *Facebook* data, the detection schemes have not been tested on real world OSN systems. The main concern is that it is difficult to find known faked identities on OSN sites and use them to validate our models. In addition, creating some faked identities on OSNs for the validation will bring big damages to the sites. We plan to develop a Facebook application, implement our detection process and make it popular in *Facebook* users. After that, we can validate our models in the real system.

7. CONCLUSIONS

Identity clone attacks are becoming a significant threat in OSNs. It can severely affect the trust relationships among users in the OSN sites and expose users' personal information. In this paper, we have proposed two detection schemes to discover the potential faked identities. Through our experiments, we have demonstrated that our detection schemes are feasible and effective. We have also shown that our detection schemes can be easily adapted to other data with the different distributions by tuning various parameters. In addition, we have discussed several approaches to validating suspicious identities.

As future work, we plan to address the limitations and develop a *Facebook* or *Linkedin* third-party application to implement our proposed detection schemes in a more real OSN environment. We also plan to investigate the social authentication mechanism and the validation and the appeal mechanisms discussed earlier.

8. ACKNOWLEDGMENTS

This work has been supported by the US National Science Foundation award IIS-0545912. We would also like to thank *Alan Mislove* and his group for providing us the original *Facebook* data.

9. REFERENCES

[1] L. Bilge, T. Strufe, D. Balzarotti and E. Kirda, "All your contacts are belong to us: automated identity theft attacks on social networks", In Proceedings of the 18th international conference on World Wide Web, Madrid, Spain, 2009.

[2] Facebook Factsheet [Online]. http://www.facebook.com/press/info.php?statistics.

[3] Wikipedia. Social network [Online]. http://en.wikipedia.org/wiki/Social_network.

[4] Identity Badge [Online]. http://apps.facebook.com/identity_badge

[5] mysafeFriend [Online]. http://apps.facebook.com/mysafefriend

[6] FightIDTheft [Online]. http://www.facebook.com/FightIDTheft

[7] Facebook Identity Theft - Don't be a Victim! [Online]. http://www.facebook.com/group.php?gid=7086517815

[8] E. Spertus, M. Sahami and O. Buyukkokten, "Evaluating similarity measures: a large-scale study in the orkut social network", In Proceedings of the 11th ACM SIGKDD international conference on Knowledge discovery in data mining, pp. 678 – 684, Chicago, IL, USA, 2005.

[9] B. Markines, C. Cattuto, F. Menczer, D. Benz, A. Hotho, and G. Stumme, "Evaluating similarity measures for emergent semantics of social tagging", In Proceedings of the 18th international Conference on World Wide Web, pp. 641-650, Madrid, Spain, 2009.

[10] S. Schechter, S. Egelman, and R.W. Reeder, "It's not what you know, but who you know: a social approach to last-resort authentication", In Proceedings of the 27th international conference on Human factors in computing systems, pp. 1983-1992, Boston, MA, USA, 2009.

[11] B. Parno, A. Perrig, and V. Gligor, "Distributed detection of node replication attacks in sensor networks", In Proceedings of the IEEE Symposium on Security and Privacy, pp. 49–63, Oakland, CA, USA, 2005.

[12] Y.Zeng, J.Cao, S. Zhang, S.Guo, and L. Xie,"Random-walk based approach to detect clone attacks in wireless sensor network," IEEE Journal on Selected Areas in Conmmunications, Vol. 28, No. 5, pp. 677 – 691, 2010.

[13] M. Motoyama and G. Varghese, "I seek you: searching and matching individuals in social networks", In Proceeding of the 11th international workshop on Web information and data management, pp.67-75, Hong Kong, China, 2009.

[14] R. J. Bayardo, Y. Ma, and R. Srikant, "Scaling up all pairs similarity search", In Proceedings of the 16th international Conference on World Wide Web, pp. 131-140, Banff, Alberta, Canada, 2007.

[15] C. Xiao, W. Wang, X. Lin and J. X. Yu, " Efficient similarity joins for near duplicate detection", In Proceeding of the 17th international Conference on World Wide Web, pp. 131-140, Beijing, China, 2008.

[16] B. Viswanath, A. Mislove, M. Cha, and K. P. Gummadi, "On the evolution of user interaction in Facebook", In Proceedings of the 2nd ACM Workshop on online Social Networks, pp. 37-42, Barcelona, Spain, 2009.

Virtual Private Social Networks

Mauro Conti
CS Department
Vrije Universiteit Amsterdam
De Boelelaan 1081a
1081 HV Amsterdam, NL
m.conti@vu.nl

Arbnor Hasani
CS Department
Vrije Universiteit Amsterdam
De Boelelaan 1081a
1081 HV Amsterdam, NL
arbnor.hasani@student.vu.nl

Bruno Crispo
DISI
University of Trento
Via Sommarive 14
38123 Povo, Trento, IT
crispo@disi.unitn.it

ABSTRACT

Social Networking Sites (SNSs) are having a significant impact on the social life of many people—even beyond the millions of people that use them directly. These websites usually allow users to present a profile of themselves through a long list of very detailed information. However, even when such SNSs have advanced privacy policies, users are often not aware of their settings and, on top of that, users cannot abstain from sharing a minimum set of information (e.g. name and location). Such a small set of information has been proven to be enough to completely re-identify a user [22, 25].

In this work we introduce the concept of Virtual Private Social Networks (VPSNs), a concept inspired by the one of Virtual Private Networks in traditional computer networks. We argue that VPSNs can mitigate the privacy issues of SNSs, building private social networks that leverage architecture publicly available for SNSs. Furthermore, we propose FaceVPSN, which is an implementation of VPSNs for Facebook, one of the most used SNSs. FaceVPSN is the first privacy threats mitigation solution that has a light and completely distributed architecture—no coordinator is required. Furthermore, it can be implemented without any particular collaboration from the SNS platform. Finally, experimental evaluation shows that FaceVPSN adds a limited overhead, which, we argue, is acceptable for the user.

Categories and Subject Descriptors

K.4 [**Privacy**]: Abuse and crime involving computers. Intellectual property rights; K.6.5 [**Security**]: Protection

General Terms

Security

Keywords

Virtual Private Social Networks, Internet and Privacy, Social Networking Sites, Facebook Privacy

1. INTRODUCTION

Social Networking Sites (SNSs) are Internet-based applications that allow for user-generated content to be published and accessed easily by a global audience. Some of the SNSs are the most visited sites on the Internet. The biggest SNS, i.e. Facebook, which has more than 500 million users [9], allows users to create an account with an extensive choice of profile information fields (e.g. Basic Information, Interests, Profile Picture, Contact Information, etc.).

The ubiquity of social networks, present in an ever increasing number of people's life, has led to increasingly more private information being "leaked" online. In many cases (i) this is due to just carelessness of users. In many other cases, (ii) information is "leaked" because of the design of privacy controls of the SNSs. As an example, in Facebook, Name, Profile Picture, Gender, and Networks, are considered "publicly available information" (before a recent change [9], even Current City, Friend List and Pages one is a fan of were considered public). That is, such information, according to Facebook may *"be accessed by everyone on the Internet (including people not logged into Facebook), be indexed by third party search engines, and be imported, exported, distributed, and redistributed by Facebook and others without privacy limitations"* [9]. Furthermore, not only can anyone view these fields by simply knowing someone's user ID or username, but also they can be accessed by third party application developers and websites. In other words, a Facebook user cannot abstain from sharing certain information with other third parties. Finally, (iii) inference (of private attributes) can be accomplished by joining data of the profiles the user has in different SNSs (e.g. Facebook, LinkedIn, Twitter, Flickr)—while harder to get, information available from the real world could also be used. Consequently, the privacy related issues have raised the interests of security researchers.

The significance of the privacy issue is escalated by the fact that most of the profiles contain real information [12, 29]. According to [29], in Facebook 99.35% of the users use their real name, 92.2% reveal their birth date, 80.5% their current city, and 98.7% also display a profile picture of themselves. Furthermore, it is relatively easy to re-identify a user that has multiple (public) accounts in various SNSs [22].

There are countless reports on how this amount of data collected from SNSs are being (mis)used. For instance: marketing companies are getting community structure data [8]; identity thieves can perform identity thefts more easily [26]; students or employees are getting in trouble because of information that was found on social networks through de-anonymization techniques [28]; and even the robbers' life has been simplified [2]!

This work addresses these privacy issues by introducing the concept of Virtual Private Social Network to the Social Network environment; this is done in analogy to the concept of Virtual Private Network, VPN, used in computer networks. The main idea is to build private social networks between users leveraging the already existing architecture of SNSs. It is essential for a VPN to benefit from the existing infrastructure. Members of the VPN are network nodes, and they can communicate in a way that is confidential with regards to the nodes outside that VPN. Analogously, a VPSN leverages the infrastructure of an already existing social network, primarily because it is very unlikely for users to move away from popular social networks. Members of the VPSN are members of the social network they leverage. VPSN members can share information (specifically, the attributes of the profile) in a way that is confidential with regards to: i) the other members of the underlying social network; and ii) also against the social network administrator.

We underline that the concept of VPSN is not already present in current SNSs. That is, a user is not able to implement a VPSN with the available tools. While it is not clear whether privacy is a motivation strong enough to justify the implementation of a new SNS from the scratch, we believe the first SNS platform able to offer strong privacy will have a major competitive advantage [7]. However, our focus is on leveraging existing infrastructure, and mitigating the privacy problem for SNSs that already count millions of users.

We focus more specifically on Facebook—the most popular SNS—for which we implement our concept of Virtual Private Social Networks (VPSNs). We call this implementation FaceVPSN. The central problem being addressed is how to use Facebook as a VPSN to share real information only with whom the user intends to—without any other third party (including application developers) being able to see the real information.

Consequently, the aim of FaceVPSN is to implement VP-SNs in Facebook. The robustness of FaceVPSN lies in the fact that it is technically compatible with Facebook and it does not require its collaboration, while it completely leverages the already present and (freely) available Facebook architecture and systems—without requiring any additional infrastructure as other solutions do (e.g. FaceCloak [18] and NOYB [13]). In FaceVPSN, the required system resources are distributed among the VPSN members: each member is required to have a small storage and computation overhead that are proportional to the number of members in the VPSN the user belongs to.

Contribution. In this paper we propose and prototype, to the best of our knowledge, the new concept of Virtual Private Social Network with a distributed architecture. The solution does not rely upon the active collaboration of the SNS, i.e. Facebook. The contribution of this paper is threefold: 1) specification of the main security features and properties of a VPSN, and a description on how to realize them; 2) FaceVPSN, the design and implementation of an application, in the form of a Firefox extension, allowing users to implement VPSN in Facebook; 3) an evaluation of FaceVPSN.

Organization. The rest of the paper is organized as follows. Section 2 introduces related work in the field of privacy

issues in social networks. Section 3 introduces the new concept of Virtual Private Social Networks (VPSNs). Section 4 presents FaceVPSN, that is our implementation of VPSNs for Facebook. Section 5 contains the evaluation and discussions about the proposed solution. Finally, in Section 6 we present our concluding remarks.

2. RELATED WORK

Following the popularity of social networks, the issue of privacy in social networks has gained momentum in the last couple of years. Nonetheless, most of the published research deals primarily with general de-anonymization, and in few cases with anonymization techniques that are not designated for a specific SNS. We shall also bring to the reader's attention the fact that most of these works, referring to Facebook, have been made obsolete by the latest changes (in May 2010) of the Privacy Policy of Facebook [10].

Many papers investigate the different facets of privacy in SNSs. The authors in [19], [30], and [14] emphasize the issue of communities centered around attributes (i.e. female computer scientists in Amsterdam) when approaching privacy problems. They show the possibility to predict, with high probability, a user's attributes using the attributes of her friends and contacts. [15] presents a privacy protocol allowing anonymuous opinion exchanges over untrusted SNSs. In [16], the authors investigate the number of user accounts needed to be compromised to rebuild the entire social graph. This number is strictly dependent on the SNS's lookahead (a social network has lookahead l if a user can see all of the edges incident to the nodes within distance l from him). The paper recommends to limit the lookahead to 1 or 2, for any social network that wishes to decrease its vulnerability.

About solutions, in [3] the authors proposed a user privacy policy (in the form of a contract) to ensure the proper protection of private data. SNSs are supposed to implement such policies to improve the privacy of their users. Despite a prototype implementation being presented in [4], to have an impact the solution requires existing SNSs to adopt such a policy. Similarly, Persona [5] is a social network in which the user defines a privacy policy. This policy manages access to user information. Persona uses an application named Storage to allow users to store personal data, as well as share them through an API with others. The authors have integrated Persona with Facebook as an application to which users log-in through a Firefox extension, which interprets the special markup language used by Persona applications. Only users of Persona, with necessary keys and access rights, will be able to access the data from Storage, and view them in their browser. Nonetheless, it is only another Facebook application that can easily be removed by Facebook from the applications directory.

Another interesting recent thread of research is considering the possibility of new competitor social networks designed with privacy in mind [7, 27]. We expect those solutions, when supported by a good business model, to reach a wide consensus from users. However, differently from these solutions, our aim is to mitigate threats to the privacy of millions of users that are currently using existing SNSs. That is, we aim at leveraging (for free) the existing SNSs infrastructure to build on top of them Virtual Private Social Networks (VPSNs).

In [11], the authors propose the "privacy by proxy" API to allow Facebook to reveal users' private information only if this is explicitly allowed by the user. This is done by interpreting special FBML (Facebook Markup Language) tags (i.e. Facebook specific HTML-like tags) in the output of the applications. However, the solution in [11] requires the cooperation of Facebook. Similarly, another proposal, flyByNight application [17], requires the cooperation of Facebook. flyByNight provides secure messaging between Facebook friends, by encrypting and decrypting sensitive data using client-side JavaScript. However, it does not solve the privacy concerns with regards to publicly available information.

Another solution for privacy of communication in SNSs is the Secret Interest Groups (SIGs) framework [24]. Although, not a direct solution to privacy of public information, it offers an interesting new way to create self managed "secret groups" (about private topics), and control group memberships. The idea is integrated with Facebook as an implemented Java HTTP proxy. While the concept of SIGs is close to the one of VPSNs, we note that the solution suggested in [24]—even if not centralized or having a single authorization entity—envisages the presence of one or more managers that, for example, allow new users to join the SIG. Furthermore, even for the managers, any operation is "thresholdized". That is, more managers need to join and agree in order to make a decision (e.g. add a new member). We underline that such an approach is completely different from the one we propose in our work. That is, each single user is completely independent on defining who (and how) will be able to access his private information. Finally, for all the solutions implemented through a proxy, we argue that a user might not be willing to have a proxy filtering all of his browsing.

More similar to our approach, is the one of FaceCloak [18]. FaceCloak is a Firefox extension allowing users to specify which data in their profile, or Facebook activity, need to be kept private. The sensitive data are substituted with fake ones, while the encrypted version of the private data are published on a third party server. Users email keys to each other, so that their respective FaceCloak extensions can retrieve the real text from the third party server. Then, each time a user retrieves a friend's profile from Facebook, in order to substitute the fake data with the real ones FaceCloak must retrieve also the encrypted version of the sensitive data from the third party server. Hence, FaceCloak relies upon the availability of a "parallel" centralized infrastructure to store the encrypted data rather than leveraging on the existing Facebook platform. An obvious drawback of this solution is that users have to trust the security of the third party server. Also, the third party server represents a single point of failure.

NOYB ("None Of Your Business") [13] is another system for privacy protection on Facebook. Private profile information is divided into atoms (e.g. name and gender constitute one atom), and each atom is "replaced" with a corresponding atom from another randomly selected user who uses NOYB. Only authorized users can reverse the process of attributing the atoms of information to the real profile. NOYB is implemented as a browser add-on for the Firefox web browser. The problem with NOYB is that the anonymity depends on the number of its users.

None of the work in literature mention the concept of Virtual Private Social Networks (VPSNs). Furthermore, most of the reviewed literature does not address the problem of publicly available information on Facebook. The few proposed solutions that we mentioned above either (i) rely upon an additional centralized infrastructure or (ii) rely upon the collaboration of Facebook and add unnecessary encryption overhead in users' interaction with Facebook. In contrast, the solution proposed in this paper does not suffer from these limitations.

3. VIRTUAL PRIVATE SOCIAL NETWORKS

In this section, we introduce the concept of Virtual Private Social Networks (VPSNs), and describe their security features and properties. The concept of VPSNs is analogous to the concept of Virtual Private Networks (VPNs) applied to traditional computer networks. The mapping between VPN and VPSN can be seen as follows. First, both VPN and VPSN leverage an already pre-existing infrastructure: a real network in the case of VPN and a real social network in the case of VPSN. We will also refer to the already existing network as the host social network, in case of a VPSN. A network node in a VPN is mapped to a user in the VPSN. Nodes of a VPN can communicate in a way that is confidential with regards to other nodes outside the VPN. Similarly, in a VPSN, users can share information that are confidential with regards to other users which are not part of the VPSN. In particular, the information shared by users of a VPSN are those related to the user's profiles (e.g. Name, Profile Picture, and Current City).

We expect a VPSN to enjoy the following features:

- **Virtual.** A VPSN should not have its own infrastructure. Instead, a VPSN has to leverage the architecture and the infrastructure of an already existing social network.

- **Private.** The users that are not part of the VPSN should not be able to access profile information shared within the VPSN. This information must be confidential even with regard to the host social network manager (e.g. Facebook).

- **A social network.** The VPSN build on top of a real social network (e.g. Facebook) should remain a social network itself (as defined in [6] and extended in [7]). That is, it should have the same functionalities of the social network it leverages, even if the shared information is restricted to the VPSN member. In particular, we do not expect the host social network to be used only as a repository, just as we do not expect the VPSN actually being a complete social network infrastructure.

- **Hidden to users outside the VPSN.** The users that are not part of a VPSN should not be able to know about the existence of the VPSN (hence not even the VPSN members can be identified as so).

- **Hidden to the host social network manager.** SNSs managers might not encourage the use of VPSNs, because of the reasons exposed in the Introduction. For example, VPSNs would reduce the benefit of targeted advertisement (e.g. directed to profiles claiming a given current city). Hence, we envisage VPSNs to be hidden to the SNSs managers. In particular, VPSNs should not be identifiable by the SNSs, and of course they should not depend on the SNSs collaboration.

- **Transparent.** Once within the VPSN, the users should be able to use the service in a transparent way. That is, a user should be able to browse the real profile of a friend, as it would happen if they were both on the host social network, and sharing there the real profile information.

- **User might connect to more than one VPSN.** Similarly as it happens for VPNs, in VPSN we expect to be able to partake in several VPSNs. In particular, the user might: i) appear in two (or more) VPSNs with different profiles (e.g. appearing like currently being in Amsterdam in the first VPSN, while being in Rome in the second VPSN); ii) appear in different VPSNs with different levels of privacy (allowing friends in the first VPSN to see his current city, while retaining this information from friends in the second VPSN).

- **View.** We also extend the previous concept of a user being connected to different VPSNs, allowing even more fine tuning within the same network. In fact, the concept of appearing with different profiles to different sets of people can be generalized—a user might appear with a different profile (or with a different level of availability of information) to each single friend.

- **View evolution.** The view that one user has of another user's profile might evolve. That is, the amount and type of information shared might change over time.

- **Light.** The infrastructure required to let the VPSN work should be negligible and not be comparable to the one of the host social network. The induced overhead in terms of memory and computation should be as trivial as possible.

We observe that VPSNs cannot be easily implemented with the tools currently available in SNSs. One thing that might resemble a VPSN are the Facebook "groups" (or similar concept for other SNSs). However, a group is known to the SNS and it depends on the SNS collaboration. Even if we ignore this fact, there are other two major differences between a "group" and a VPSN. First, groups are centrally managed while VPSN management is completely distributed. Second, groups have a simple access control rule. Once part of the group, all the information within the group are available to the new member. On the other hand, with VPSN it is possible to create different "views" inside the same VPSN.

We underline that the focus of this work is about the privacy of (public) information shared as part of a social network profile. Other aspects connected to the users identification (e.g. traffic analysis), not based on this information, are orthogonal to the scope of this paper.

4. VPSNS IN FACEBOOK: FACEVPSN

In this section, we present FaceVPSN, which is our VPSN implementation for Facebook. To the best of our knowledge, this is also the first solution to address the problem of availability of public information—not only with respect to other users, but also against third party applications in Facebook. The concern for the availability of this information to third party application is confirmed by the fact that Facebook recently (May, 2010 [9]) gave the user the possibility to completely turn off the applications platform (before

these changes, third party applications were able to access by default user's "publicly available information" that consisted of Name, Profile Picture, Gender, Current City, Networks, Friend List, and Pages). Nevertheless, if a user has not turned off the applications platform, Name, Profile Picture, Gender, Networks, and User ID are still publicly available by default. The availability of this option is undermined by the evidence that *"every month, more than 70% of Facebook users engage with platform applications"* [9]. Hence, users do not just forget to turn off applications platform, rather they explicitly want and use applications. We consider 70% of Facebook users to be a high enough number for the privacy problem to be considered an unresolved issue. In addition, the availability of profile information to applications raises an even higher concern. In fact, applications can easily retrieve and process a big amount of profile information. Finally, we note that even if users choose to turn off applications platform, public pieces of information are still available just by browsing profiles, e.g. with USER_ID (www.facebook.com/index.php?profile=USER_ID), not mentioning the risk [23] of data stored by Facebook being hacked.

An overview of our solution, named FaceVPSN, is presented in Section 4.1. The architecture is presented in Section 4.2, whereas the implementation details are discussed in Section 4.3.

4.1 Overview

The simple solution of encrypting the attributes would not work, since Facebook does not allow publication of ciphertext or even scrambled text. Our approach is the following: we cannot stop the sharing of public information due to the design of Facebook, however we can publish pseudo information, which inevitably can be seen by third party applications. According to [29], this is one of the less frequently used privacy protection strategies by Facebook users. This behaviour is actually motivated by the following need: allowing the Facebook friends of a user to see his real Name, Profile Picture, Gender and Current City.

Given that User ID, Network names, Friend's names, and the names of the Pages a user is a fan of cannot be changed by the user in any way, the real concern is with regards to Name, Profile Picture, Gender and Current City. Hence, we propose that those fields are modified, through the Profile Editor of Facebook, in order not to contain the real values that correspond to Facebook account owner: we suggest to use pseudo values instead. This modification should be done by the user himself for three reasons:

1. The user can select the pseudo information to display (namely Name, Profile Picture and Current City), and thus still be in control of his published profile page (e.g. how his pseudo profile picture will look);

2. The user can choose not to share some of the real details with certain friends;

3. Users are already familiar with modifying profile information, hence doing this modification is not a barrier for using our proposed system.

Once pseudo information is stored on Facebook, the real information is sent only to friends allowed to see it. This information will be stored locally on the friends' machines, with a mechanism that is similar to how cookies work in browsing. However, differently from cookies, once this information is stored locally, it will not be sent back on a later occasion. Instead, it will be processed locally, when required. When a user browses a profile of another user in the VPSN, a FaceVPSN component is in charge to transparently show to the user the real information, instead of the one actually published on the host social network.

A possible variant to our current implementation might be the following. Instead of storing information locally, it might be stored steganographed within images attached in Facebook messages. FaceVPSN would take care of transparently managing this information when required. This approach would make the solution independent from the specific machine where the real information is stored. In this way, the user will be free to browse the VPSN from each machine where he is able to log-in on Facebook and install FaceVPSN.

4.2 Architecture

We implemented the replacement of pseudo information with real one through a Firefox extension. This is done whenever pseudo information is loaded on the user's Firefox browser. The Firefox extension we have implemented is called FaceVPSN and it replaces Name, Profile Picture, and Current City. The application is designed in such a way that it is also easily extendable to handle the replacement of other profile information. We use the notation in Figure 1(a) to illustrate the FaceVPSN architecture (Figure 1(b)).

After a Facebook page is requested (Step 1 in Figure 1(b)), Facebook replies with an HTML response that contains the content of the page to be displayed by the Firefox browser (Step 2). The functionality of FaceVPSN is implemented in JavaScript code, which is executed once certain events happen. In particular, when the document is loaded from Facebook, a "page load" event is fired (Step 3). Then, the JavaScript code of FaceVPSN searches to find pseudo names, cities, and profile pictures of the friends of the user. Afterwards, the JavaScript code replaces them with the real information stored in XML files. In the end, the Firefox browser displays the profile page with replaced pseudo information (Step 4).

In order to partake in the VPSN, the user needs to set up FaceVPSN, which currently works only with Mozilla Firefox web browser. A general overview of the required interaction for FaceVPSN set up is given in Figure 1(c) (using the notation in Figure 1(a)).

In Step 1, Facebook User 1 would modify his Name, Profile Picture, and Current City to some pseudo information through the profile editing interface of Facebook. Next, User 1 asks one of his friends, say, Facebook User 2, to install FaceVPSN and also emails him an XML file that contains details of pseudo and real information. User 2 would install FaceVPSN just like any other Firefox extension. It is as simple as dragging the downloaded XPI installation file to Firefox browser and a menu will pop up to confirm installation. User 2 has to add the XML file corresponding to User 1 to the list of preferences. This is done through the Graphical User Interface (GUI) of FaceVPSN. All that remains is for FaceVPSN to replace the pseudo information of Facebook User 1 whenever User 2 views User 1's profile, or a page that contains User 1's information (Step 5 and 6 in Figure 1(c)).

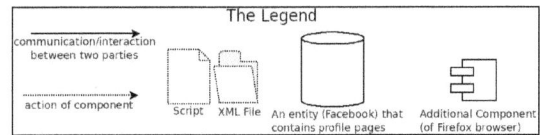

(a) Legend for figures 1(b) and 1(c).

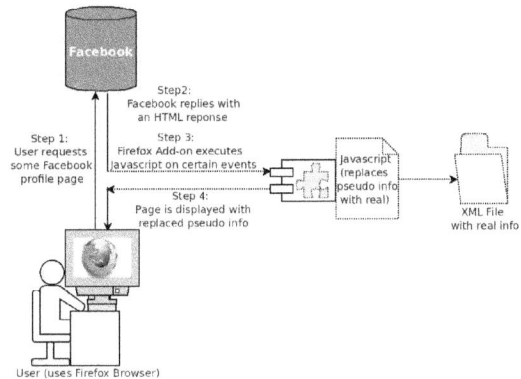

(b) Browsing

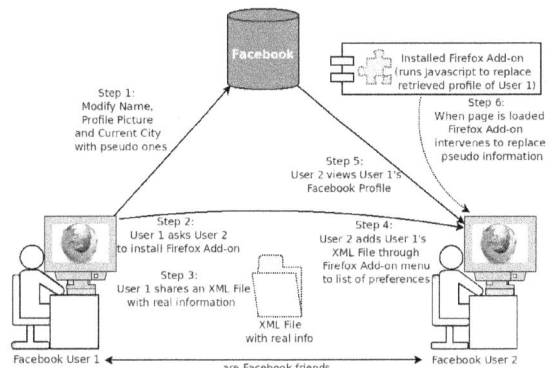

(c) Setup

Figure 1: FaceVPSN Architecture.

4.3 Implementation

FaceVPSN has been implemented as a Firefox extension and its functionality is written in JavaScript. The GUI has been written with XUL, the Firefox XML user interface markup language. In order to share real information in a structured way, that will be useful and easily accessible by the Firefox extension, we propose to use an XML file with the structure of the example shown in Figure 2. The user is not required to fill in every field. Nevertheless, he must specify at least his username and user ID. Then, for instance, he can choose to have only pseudo Name and City but no Profile Picture.

Essentially, everything is contained under the root tag `<FaceVPSN>`. We defined the current version to be "v0.1" in order to track future changes of structure of the file. In Figure 2 we show the typical case, that is, when a user shares only his information. Nonetheless, it is also possible that two or more users can share information in the same XML file; hence using more `<friend>` tags—the information of one person is contained inside those tags. We believe that the choice of using this implementation is convenient, for instance, when only one of close friends or siblings has to

```
<FaceVPSN version="0.1">
 <friend>
  <urls>
    <username>facebook.username</username>
    <id>user-ID-00000</id>
  </urls>
  <replacementinfo>
    <info>
      <pseudoname>"Pseudo Name"</pseudoname>
      <realname>"Real Name"</realname>
      <pseudocity>"Pseudo Current City"</pseudocity>
      <realcity>"Real Current City"</realcity>
      <pseudopicurl>"http://pseudoSmall.jpg"</pseudopicurl>
      <realpicurl>"http://realSmall.jpg"</realpicurl>
      <pseudosearchpicurl>"http://pseudoS.jpg"</pseudosearchpicurl>
      <realsearchpicurl>"http:/realS.jpg"</realsearchpicurl>
      <pseudobigpicurl>"http://pseudoBig.jpg"</pseudobigpicurl>
      <realbigpicurl>"http://realBig.jpg"</realbigpicurl>
    </info>
  </replacementinfo>
 </friend>
</FaceVPSN>
```

Figure 2: Example or XML File Structure.

take care of sharing the file for two or more people. Moving down the XML hierarchy, the reader can observe that we classified information into two categories:

- information contained inside `<urls>` tags, which will be used to check URLs to verify to whom the link or profile page corresponds to. This includes user's Facebook username (contained inside `<username>` tags) and user ID (contained inside `<id>` tags);

- information that will be used to replace pseudo information, and contained inside `<replacementinfo>` tags. This category of information contains the pseudo Name and Current City, and the corresponding real values. Additionally, there are three different Profile Picture URLs in Facebook. The most frequently used is the small boxed one, that appears for example in Wall posts. Yet, there is also a bigger profile picture that appears in a user's profile page with a different URL. Finally, there is another one that appears in search results.

Users add on FaceVPSN the XML files that refer to their friends—in order for FaceVPSN to know whose details to replace. FaceVPSN uses the preferences system of Mozilla [20] in order to save the user's preferences when the browser is started and closed. It also uses the input stream component of Mozilla [20] to actually open and read a file that the user has chosen from the dialog window. FaceVPSN handles replacement of pseudo names in text as well as links. Furthermore, it replaces the real name with a pseudo name when searching in Facebook (e.g. when tagging or in the search bar). Current City is replaced by checking the URL in the address bar to find whose profile is being viewed, to know to whom does a current city correspond to. The document's URL is checked to find either the friend's ID or username. The URL though, can contain a hash "#" that specifies a named anchor in the document. If that is the case, then there will be two different user IDs or usernames in the URL. Consequently, if the hash "#" is present in the URL, FaceVPSN always checks the part after it for each friend's username or user ID. On the other hand, profile pictures are replaced by changing image source to a different source link (remote or local).

To start the execution of replacement functions we add a Gecko (which is the Firefox rendering engine) specific event (i.e. DOMContentLoaded). This event is fired when the DOM Content of a page is loaded, albeit without any documents or images on it. Nonetheless, when the user navigates in Facebook, FaceVPSN has to re-perform replacements due to new content being displayed. For instance, the URL changes when a new picture of an album is being viewed or a different profile tab is opened. To get notified whenever the URL in the address bar changes, we added a progress listener to our code to re-apply replacements whenever location changes. Progress Listeners [20] allow Firefox extensions to be notified of events associated with documents loading on the browser and with tab switching events. More details on the implementation, are available on the project website [1].

In order to have the published (non real) information replaced on the browsed page, FaceVPSN has to match different regular expressions to find them. These are used primarily to find information that needs to be replaced, but also, for instance, if we consider the case of two friends with the same name then the replacements are to be performed based on some regular expression matching. This requirement can generally be fulfilled by distinguishing information based on usernames or user IDs, which are unique. Nevertheless, there is also a possibility to exactly match the places where information (i.e. we are referring to names here) is to be substituted. In this context, we could construct a number of regular expressions that would allow FaceVPSN to find and replace information in exact specified links (e.g. Name appearing in search list, Name appearing in View Photos of Friend link). In total we could come up with as far as 30 regular expressions (the list of regular expression used can be found in the Appendix).

Of course, the defined regular expressions are SNS dependent. That is, if the Facebook implementation change they must be adapted. For this, we envisage FaceVPSN to be continuously supported (e.g. by the open source community) and to automatically check for updates. Similarly, the regular expressions must be adapted if we aim at designing a VPSN implementation for other SNSs (e.g. Orkut), while the same general concept can be applied.

5. EVALUATION AND DISCUSSION

The implementation of FaceVPSN shows that it is indeed feasible to actualize the concept of VPSN. However, in this section we also give a thorough evaluation and discussion of FaceVPSN. First, we compare FaceVPSN with other solutions in literature (Section 5.1). Given that, to the best of our knowledge, the concept of Virtual Private Social Network is new to the literature (hence, there is no implementation of VPSN), we compare FaceVPSN with other solutions for mitigation of privacy threats in Facebook. Further on, in Section 5.2 we discuss the results of experimental evaluation we performed with FaceVPSN.

5.1 Comparison

Unlike other solutions, FaceVPSN is a decentralized solution that does not depend on the collaboration of Facebook. Moreover, handles the replacement of the "publicly available information" that the user can modify (i.e. Name, Profile Picture, and Current City). In particular, FaceVPSN enjoys all at once a set of features that no other current solution has. Table 1 summarizes the main points we highlighted with regards to the relevant solutions (about mitigating privacy threats in Facebook) in addition to FaceVPSN. The column headers shows five different features, while row headings indicate the considered solutions. In particular, we compare FaceVPSN with: FaceCloak [18], flyByNight [17], NOYB [13], Persona [5], and SIGs [24]. These are all solutions directly related to Facebook privacy issues. We remind the reader that our aim is to mitigate the privacy threat of the millions of users using SNSs like Facebook, and building VPSN without having an infrastructure comparable to those of SNSs. Hence, we do not consider solutions like Safebook [7] and PeerSoN [27]. In fact, these solutions do not mitigate privacy in Facebook but rather propose new competitor SNSs.

The first column of Table 1 (i.e. Facebook Collaboration) indicates if the solution requires the Facebook collaboration in order to work or exist. More specifically, we are interested to know whether Facebook can remove the application from the interaction cycle of users with Facebook. For instance, the solutions flyByNight, Persona, and SIGs require Facebook collaboration. That is, they can be removed by Facebook from the applications directory and consequently cannot be used by Facebook users. As such, the successful solution of the privacy problems by these applications is under direct threat from Facebook itself. However, considering that potentially every implementation aimed at solving privacy issues in Facebook depends on the Facebook implementation, we do not bring this second viewpoint into this column. For instance, if Facebook adds new profile information fields, NOYB has to be extended to support them or, when Facebook API changes, Persona and flyByNight have to be harmonized accordingly. Likewise, when Facebook changes the design of profile pages and how profile information is organized and displayed (e.g. different HTML tags) then FaceVPSN also needs to be adjusted to handle the changes. Nevertheless, we do not consider this aspect a barrier for the existence of a solution.

We also compared the architecture of the solutions (second column of Table 1). In particular, we observed whether the solution was implemented in a centralized or distributed architecture. In a centralized architecture there is one central component which is fundamental to the functionality of the whole system. This type of architecture suffers from the "single point of failure" problem. Conversely, a distributed architecture is one where there is no need for a central component or coordinator for the operation of the system. A third type, that is "thresholdized", applies to SIGs [24]. In particular, in SIGs a group is managed by a set of so-called managers that take decisions (e.g. admitting a new user in the group) using a threshold consensus. That is, before taking a decision, at least a given number (threshold) of managers have to agree on that decision. FaceCloak, that is implemented as a centralized architecture, requires an infrastructure that becomes comparable to that of Facebook (or even worse, when users belong to many VPSNs). Furthermore, in FaceCloak, if the third party server for storing encrypted private data is down, users' FaceCloak extension cannot decrypt information from Facebook. Similarly, if the flyByNight application server is down, users cannot see decrypted messages from their Facebook friends. In its current implementation, NOYB is also centralized in nature, given that the NOYB Firefox extension depends on external public dictionaries that it queries to retrieve and replace

"atoms". Persona as a social network proposal is a decentralized architecture: there is no central coordinator and users themselves define policies for sharing information through their "Storage". Nonetheless, the Persona Facebook application, just like flyByNight, depends on a third party server (i.e. the server where the application resides). In general, the centralized architectures with a single point of failure are potentially a barrier to widespread usage in social networks. On the contrary, FaceVPSN is implemented as a Firefox extension that revolves around its users. As it was specified in Section 4.2, the user himself is in charge of when and what information to share with others. Moreover, if the FaceVPSN Firefox extension of a user fails, this will not affect his friends.

The column labeled as "Overhead" shows the time overhead of the different solutions. To put it differently, if the data is available, it shows the additional time required for a user to see the benefits of the solution. As for previous solutions, the time overhead indicated in Table 1 is the one reported in the corresponding publication paper [18, 17, 13, 5, 24]. The overhead in flyByNight, which handles the encryption of private messages in Facebook rather than "publicly available information", depends on the size of the message. Both [24] and [13] do not provide information about their overhead, while we argue this is a relevant characteristic of these solutions. NOYB has an overhead that depends on the number of atoms to be replaced, as well as the number of different keys that need to be generated. In turn, this depends on the updates of profile fields and is upper bound by the number of fields. As a distinguishing factor of FaceVPSN from centralized solutions, we formally define the storage overhead of FaceVPSN (distributed) compared with the one of FaceCloak (centralized)—a similar comparison holds for other centralized solutions. Let us define: N as the total number of users; u_i the generic user ($1 \leq i \leq N$); the set of VPSNs the user u_i belongs as $V(u_i) = v_1, \ldots, v_j, \ldots v_V$; $Size(v_j)$ as the number of elements in VPSN v_j. We remind the reader that each user can give a different view (i.e. show a different profile) for every other user in the VPSNs he belongs to. FaceCloak [18] requires a storage that is $O(\sum_{i=0}^{N} \sum_{j=0}^{V(u_i)} Size(v_j))$. On the other hand, FaceVPSN (with decentralized architecture) requires a limited local storage (and computation) overhead that is $O(\sum_{j=1}^{V(u_i)} Size(v_j))$, for user u_i.

In the "Pre-requisites" column, we are mainly interested in potential barriers to the usage of the system. For instance, there is no noteworthy barrier in using FaceCloak, unless we take into account the future possibility to pay for a third party server. However, users have to email keys that are used by the system for decryption. With flyByNight though, users always have to use this Facebook application to view the decrypted text of their private messages. The same is true for Persona. Similarly, NOYB needs to be used not only by the user himself, but also by other users, in order to create a richer public dictionary, hence having more possibilities to substitute the atoms of his attributes. Finally, SIGs solution requires the user to browse through a proxy. On the contrary, with our solution the user does not depend on whether his friends choose to use FaceVPSN. However, the user still has to send by email to his friends the XML files with his details—and it is up to his friends to decide if they want to install the FaceVPSN extension and view his real details. We are aware that the need to email and manage XML

	Facebook Collaboration	Centralized/ Distributed	Overhead	Pre-requisites	Hide public info
FaceCloak [18]	No	Centralized	1 s (average) to view real text	Manage keys	Partially
flyByNight [17]	Yes	Centralized	depends on message size	Always need to use this Facebook app	Partially
NOYB [13]	No	Centralized	no data	Friends need to use this Facebook app	Partially
Persona [5]	Yes	Distributed	2.3 s (median; max 13.7 s)	Always need to use this Facebook app	No
SIGs [24]	Yes	"thresholdized"	no data	Browsing through the proposed proxy	No
FaceVPSN	**No**	**Distributed**	**<1 s (average) to view initial replacements**	**Manage XML files**	**Yes**

Table 1: Comparing FaceVPSN with state of the art solutions for privacy threat mitigation

files could hinder the usage of FaceVPSN. However, this is just how it works in the current implementation—ongoing work aims at automatizing these communications. For example, we could leverage the messaging system of Facebook itself (email and Jabber chat) to share XML info. Also, this could be done in a way that is private to Facebook, e.g. steganographed in pictures attached to emails.

Finally, and most significantly, we reviewed each solution to see if it addresses the problem of "publicly available information" (e.g. does it hide it from Facebook and third party applications?). This comparison is in the last column of Table 1, which indicates if the corresponding solution in the row is able to hide the information that Facebook classifies as public (Name, Profile Picture, and Current City), no matter the privacy configuration set by the user. FaceCloak, flyByNight and NOYB hide only partially those information. In particular, FaceCloak and NOYB are able to hide only text data and not pictures, while flyByNight can hide only message data. Persona does not handle profile information hiding at all. In contrast, FaceVPSN allows users to hide their real Name, Profile Picture, and Current City.

5.2 Experimental Evaluation

To illustrate the actual work of FaceVPSN, we used a test Facebook account, and created an XML file with the corresponding pseudo details and real details. The published profile resulting from this test account with pseudo information is shown in Figure 3(a). Having FaceVPSN working, and the proper XML file configured, we observed the proper replacement of information in news feeds, pop-ups, and profile pages. The resulting profile page shown to the user with FaceVPSN in action can be seen in Figure 3(b). Besides the profile page, other elements of Facebook are also handled by FaceVPSN. Figures 4(a), 4(c), 4(d), and 4(b) show example replacements in a chat window, notification window, pop-up window, and search bar, respectively.

Unfortunately, FaceVPSN (and privacy in general) comes at a price. To be more specific, the usage of FaceVPSN would deprive a user from some of the functionalitites of the Facebook platform. A user appearing with a pseudo name in Facebook might not get invited to particular events. In fact, this name is not accessible to third party applications through the APIs of Facebook (although this information is visible if an adversary opens the user page after knowing the published user ID). Thus, if users are concerned that their real friends will not be able to find them, they can also choose to display an alternate name in addition to the

(a) Test account before using FaceVPSN

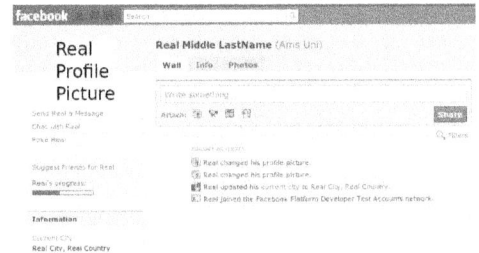

(b) Test account after using FaceVPSN

Figure 3: FaceVPSN in action. Profile Page.

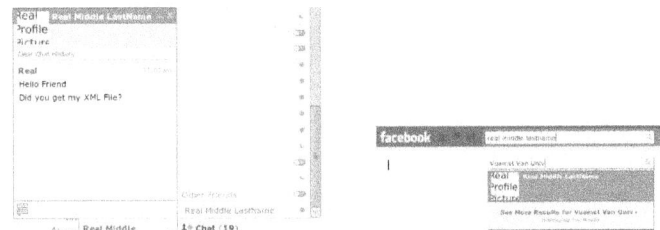

(a) Chat

(b) Search Bar

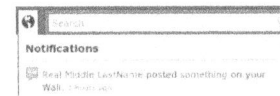

(c) Notification

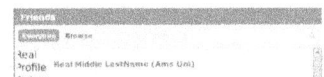

(d) Pop-up

Figure 4: FaceVPSN in action in different Facebook features. Name and Profile Picture always replaced as needed.

pseudo one. Furthermore, when a user wishes to change his real information (e.g. Current City), in our current implementation, the user has to re-send the XML file to his friends in order for them to view the updated real information. Ongoing work aims at making the sending and update of XML on the friend's machine more transparent, e.g. leveraging the Facebook messaging services themselves, as discussed in Section 4.1.

In our running FaceVPSN system, we observed that after managing the XML files, the other main issue was the time overhead for replacing the pseudo information with real one. In particular, we found two main variables influencing time performances: (i) the number of friends the user has; (ii) the required level of precision for the pseudo-to-real information replacement. In particular, this level corresponds to the number of regular expressions used (see Section 4.3).

Based on these observations, we ran a thorough set of experiments to investigate how this time overhead varies with the number of friends and considered regular expressions. For evaluation purposes, we used JavaScript Debugger (Venkman [21]) of Mozilla to get some profiling data of execution time of various functions of FaceVPSN. The experiments have been performed on a laptop with 1.86GHz Intel Pentium CPU and with Windows XP Professional with SP3 Operating System. Mozilla Firefox version 3.6.8 was used to conduct evaluation tests during which Firefox was ran with FaceVPSN and Venkman extensions. Besides Firefox, no other user applications were running.

First, we investigated the influence of the number of friends on the time overhead. We considered the browsing sequence path (e.g. browsing the Facebook home page, then the user profile page, and so on) described by the sequence in Table 4. In this experiment we assumed the worst case in terms of possible replacements. That is, we considered at the same time: (i) all the implemented regular expressions (refer to tables 2 and 3), and (ii) all the replacements running automatically (Table 4). We also assumed the worst case in terms of the number of user's friends that are within the VPSN of the user. That is, we assume FaceVPSN has to replace information for all the friends of the user. We measured the time overhead for the given browsing sequence path, for 1, 3, 5, 10, 15, 20, and 25 friends. For each number of friends, we run the browsing sequence 10 times (each sequence being made of the 20 steps described in Table 4), and generated the sample reports with data about execution times of FaceVPSN functions. The measured values represent the time when all the replacements are performed on a page, rather than how long afterwards will the first replacements be seen. The results obtained from this experiment are summarized in Figure 5(a). For each point on the x-axis (that is, for each given number of friends), the corresponding value on y-axis shows the average time overhead in a single step of the browsing sequence.

As expected, with the increase of the number of friends, whose details need to be replaced, there is an increase in the execution time. For example, the average replacing time overhead is 2,421 milliseconds for 5 friends in the user's VPSN, and 12,585 for 25 friends in the user's VPSN. This behaviour is understandable when considering the fact that replacements are performed many times for the various friends in the news feed, and also when HTTP requests are generated or URL changes in the address bar. We recall that FaceVPSN performs name replacement in various links (e.g. Friend's First and Last Name in profile page posts, someone's Photos, someone's Links etc.) through regular expres-

sions. In particular, this experiment was ran considering all the implemented regular expressions. We implemented these regular expressions in a way such that we were sure to handle each and every possible occurrence or required replacement, and also not to make any mistake. For example, to handle cases of friends with the same name, it is required to check with every friend's username and user ID.

Our first intention was to design a solution that, in terms of available features, was completely transparent if compared to the standard behaviour of Facebook. While the described full-featured implementation reached this aim, we now observe two issues. First, for a user even not handling all the cases might still be a reasonable behaviour. For instance, it is not essential to perform (automatic) replacement of pseudo information when user wants to view all comments in a post. This is because user has already seen the real information in some of the comments that are displayed initially. Furthermore, we observed that some of the browsing steps (steps 8, 13, and 16 in Table 4) differentiate from the others for the particular high time overhead they require. These operations are used to handle Ajax requests that, for example, implies continuous replacement while user is typing a name in a search bar. For example, let us assume the user wants to search for a friend with real name "Name". After user types just "N", a reply (for the Ajax request) with a suggestions list will show the list of all the friends that have a name starting with "N". After the user types "Na" the list will show all friends' names starting with "Na", and so on.

To investigate the influence of these two issues, we run further experiments. First, we wanted to study the influence that the number of considered regular expressions has on the time overhead. In particular, we re-ran the previous experiment only with two regular expressions being matched (i.e. the first two in the Table 3 in the Appendix). One is used to match a friend's username, whereas the other one is used to match user's ID. The results of this experiment are reported in Figure 5(b). Comparing this figure with the previous one (Figure 5(a), which shows results for all the implemented regular expressions), we can see that the time required for the replacement is significantly reduced. For example, considering 25 friends whose information need to be replaced, the replacing time overhead decreases from an average of 12,585 milliseconds to 5,145 milliseconds.

We can observe that the implementation of FaceVPSN with many regular expressions increases the overhead to an undesirable level. However, we shall point out that the reason we constructed all the regular expressions is that we wanted to be assured we are replacing names only in places we can undoubtedly say that they refer to a particular friend or user. The implementation with only two regular expressions (i.e. to match usernames and user IDs) is more efficient (refer to Figure 5(b)). Also, based on our tests, FaceVPSN (with two regular expressions) manages to match and replace all the names correctly. Hence, we argue that with two regular expressions we can get a reasonable level of experience with correctly substituted pseudo information.

After investigating the influence of the number of regular expressions, we also investigated the influence of the specific browsing operations that we observed being more time demanding—the ones that involve Ajax requests. Hence, we designed a more time efficient solution for such operations—at a price of a reduced transparency and reduced functionalities for these operations. In the alternative implementation,

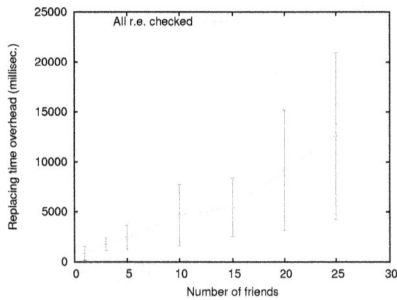

(a) All implemented regular expressions (r.e.) active.

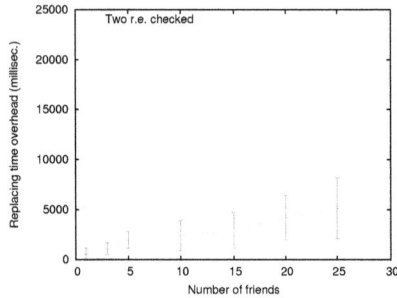

(b) Two regular expressions (r.e.) active.

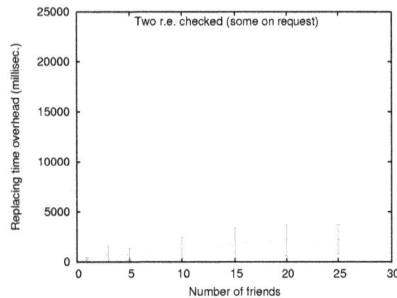

(c) Two regular expressions (r.e.) active. Some replacements made on request.

Figure 5: Replacing time overhead of FaceVPSN (average values, and standard deviation in bars).

we require the user to be aware of FaceVPSN for these operations. For example, when the user searches someone's profile in the search bar, we require the user to write the complete real name of the friend and then press F8. In this way, we remove the functionality of finding matching names while the user writes, but still the user is able to use the search bar and find the friend with his real name. Even if the results obtained in the previous experiments might be already satisfying, we argue that if the user is willing to sacrifice such described type of features, FaceVPSN can achieve even better performances. We run again the previous experiments of the setting with two regular expression, requiring an active user's participation for the replacements in browsing steps 8, 13, and 16 (Figure 4). The results are shown in Figure 5(c). From this figure, we can observe that the performances are significantly further improved when compared to the case of fully transparent behaviour (i.e. Figure 5(b)). Considering again the case of 25 friends in the user's VPSN, the replacement overhead decreases from 5,145 milliseconds

to 2,220 milliseconds, on average. The standard deviation of this overhead also decreases, as described by the bars in the graphs.

Based on our experience with FaceVPSN, when a user navigates to some page in Facebook, the first replacements can be seen in less than one second (on average) after the new page is shown. This varies according to what the user is viewing. In case of a profile page with only a few wall posts, then the replacements are performed in a few seconds. Conversely, if the user is viewing the home page of Facebook, and there happens to be a lot of news feeds with friends, whose information needs to be replaced, then it takes more time.

6. CONCLUSION

In this paper we introduced the concept of VPSNs—Virtual Private Social Networks (applied to the social networks), that is similar to the concept of Virtual Private Networks (applied to computer networks). VPSNs allow the building of private social networks, the information of which is not available outside, leveraging the infrastructure already present for Social Networks Sites (SNSs). We implemented our concept through FaceVPSN, a VPSNs system for Facebook, one of the most widely used SNSs. FaceVPSN is a completely distributed system that implements VPSNs and mitigates the privacy problem in Facebook. To the best of our knowledge FaceVPSN is the first privacy solution for Facebook that is all at once: i) completely distributed; ii) Facebook independent—cannot be removed by Facebook; iii) hides public information from users outside the VPSN, from Facebook, as well as from Facebook applications. The implementation shows the feasibility of the proposal, while experimental results confirm its efficiency and usability.

Future research aims to optimize FaceVPSN to further reduce the overhead and to make it more user friendly. That is, to make the way XML files are shared more transparent, e.g. transparently leveraging the messaging system of Facebook itself. To further protect the real information stored on the local machine (to which more than one user might have access), FaceVPSN could also store the real information in an encrypted way and decrypt them when needed, based on a per user access. Finally, the automatic evolution of the views, as defined in Section 4, is also subject to investigation. For example, a view that a user has of someone's profile might automatically evolve according to some trust rules, or depending on the type of relations between various VPSNs' members.

7. ACKNOWLEDGMENTS

This work is partly funded by the European Network of Excellence NESSoS contract no. FP7-256980.

8. REFERENCES

[1] Virtual private social networks website. http://sites.google.com/site/fbprivacy2010/.

[2] Please rob me, June 2010. http://pleaserobme.com/.

[3] E. Aimeur, S. Gambs, and A. Ho. Upp: User privacy policy for social networking sites. In *Proceedings of the Fourth International Conference on Internet and Web Applications and Services*, pages 267–272. IEEE Computer Society, 2009.

[4] E. Aimeur, S. Gambs, and A. Ho. Towards a privacy-enhanced social networking site. In *International Conference on Availability Reliability and Security*, volume 0, pages 172–179. IEEE Computer Society, 2010.

[5] R. Baden, A. Bender, N. Spring, B. Bhattacharjee, and D. Starin. Persona: an online social network with user-defined privacy. In *Proceedings of the ACM Conference on Data Communication*, pages 135–146. ACM Press, 2009.

[6] D. M. Boyd and N. B. Ellison. Social network sites: Definition, history, and scholarship. *Journal of Computer-Mediated Communication.*, 13(1):Article 11, 2007.

[7] L. A. Cutillo, R. Molva, and T. Strufe. Safebook: A privacy-preserving online social network leveraging on real-life trust. *IEEE Communicaions Magazine*, 47(12), December 2009.

[8] B. Dybwad. Facebook and others caught sending user data to advertisers, 2010. `http://mashable.com/2010/05/20/facebook-caught-sending-user-data-to-advertisers/`.

[9] Facebook. `http://www.facebook.com`.

[10] Facebook. Facebook's privacy policy. `http://www.facebook.com/policy.php`.

[11] A. Felt and D. Evans. Privacy protection for social networking apis. In *W2SP '08: in Conjunction with the 2008 IEEE Symposium on Security and Privacy.* IEEE Computer Society, 2008.

[12] R. Gross and A. Acquisti. Information revelation and privacy in online social networks. In *Proceedings of the 2005 ACM workshop on Privacy in the Electronic Society*, pages 71–80. ACM Press, 2005.

[13] S. Guha, K. Tang, and P. Francis. Noyb: Privacy in online social networks. In *Proceedings of the First Workshop on Online Social Networks*, pages 49–54. ACM Press, 2008.

[14] M. Hay, G. Miklau, D. Jensen, P. Weis, and S. Srivastava. Anonymizing social networks. Technical Report 07-19, University of Massachusetts Amherst, March 2007.

[15] M. Kacimi, S. Ortolani, and B. Crispo. Anonymous opinion exchange over untrusted social networks. In *SNS '09: Proceedings of the Second ACM EuroSys Workshop on Social Network Systems*, pages 26–32. ACM Press, 2009.

[16] A. Korolova, R. Motwani, S. U. Nabar, and Y. Xu. Link privacy in social networks. In *Proceeding of the 17th ACM conference on Information and Knowledge Management*, pages 289–298. ACM Press, 2008.

[17] M. M. Lucas and N. Borisov. Flybynight: Mitigating the privacy risks of social networking. In *Proceedings of the 7th ACM workshop on Privacy in the Electronic Society*, pages 1–8. ACM Press, 2008.

[18] W. Luo, Q. Xie, and U. Hengartner. Facecloak: An architecture for user privacy on social networking sites. In *Proceedings of the 2009 International Conference on Computational Science and Engineering*, pages 26–33. IEEE Computer Society, 2009.

[19] A. Mislove, B. Viswanath, K. P. Gummadi, and P. Druschel. You are who you know: Inferring user profiles in online social networks. In *Proceedings of the third ACM International Conference on Web Search and Data Mining*, pages 251–260. ACM Press, 2010.

[20] Mozilla. Observer notifications. `https://developer.mozilla.org/en/Observer_Notifications`.

[21] Mozilla. Venkman javascript debugger project page. `http://www.mozilla.org/projects/venkman/`.

[22] A. Narayanan and V. Shmatikov. De-anonymizing social networks. In *Proceedings of the 30th IEEE Symposium on Security and Privacy*, pages 173–187. IEEE Computer Society, 2009.

[23] A. of Exploits. Facebook's servers was hacked again by inj3ct0r team. `http://inj3ct0r.com/exploits/13403`.

[24] A. Sorniotti and R. Molva. Secret interest groups (sigs) in social networks with an implementation on facebook. In *Proceedings of the 2008 ACM Symposium on Applied Computing*, pages 621–628. ACM Press, 2010.

[25] L. A. Sweeney. `http://groups.csail.mit.edu/mac/classes/6.805/articles/privacy/sweeney-thesis-draft.pdf`.

[26] N. Tabakoff. Facebook users are sitting ducks for identity theft, 2009. `http://www.dailytelegraph.com.au/news/facebook-users-sitting-ducks-for-identity-theft/story-e6freuy9-122580713389/`.

[27] L.-H. Vu, K. Aberer, S. Buchegger, and A. , Datta. Enabling secure secret sharing in distributed online social networks. In *Proceedings of the Annual Computer Security Applications Conference*, pages 419–428, 2009.

[28] W. Wolfe-Wylie. The harm of facebook pictures, 2010. `http://www.torontosun.com/life/2010/08/10/14978476.html`.

[29] A. L. Young and A. Quan-Haase. Information revelation and internet privacy concerns on social network sites: a case study of facebook. In *Proceedings of the Fourth International Conference on Communities and Technologies*, pages 265–274. ACM Press, 2009.

[30] E. Zheleva and L. Getoor. To join or not to join: The illusion of privacy in social networks with mixed public and private user profiles. In *Proceedings of the 18th International Conference on World Wide Web*, pages 531–540. ACM Press, 2009.

APPENDIX

A. IMPLEMENTATION SETTINGS

This section gives further details on the implementation and the experimental settings. Table 2 summarizes the regular expressions we defined in order to match a friend name in several locations. Note that links to be matched might appear for the same scenario either with "?" or "&". Hence, we considered both cases in the defined regular expression. For example, regular expressions 3 and 4 consider these two possible alternatives while searching for a username in the search list. Also, note that "\\\" is used to match the character "&". Table 3 summarizes a set of regular expressions that are used in combination with User ID or Username. Finally, Table 4 describes the browsing sequence path used in the experiments.

Number	Regular Expression	Matches links with
1	afriend.username	username (e.g. name.surname)
2	afriend.id	id (e.g. 11111111)
3	afriend.username+"\\\?ref=search$"	username in search list ("?" case)
4	afriend.username+"&ref=search$"	username in search list ("&" case)
5	afriend.id+"\\\?ref=search$"	id in search list ("?" case)
6	afriend.id+"&ref=search$"	id in search list ("&" case)
7	afriend.username+"\\\?ref=sgm$"	username in pop-up windows ("?" case)
8	afriend.username+"&ref=sgm$"	username in pop-up windows ("&" case)
9	afriend.id+"\\\?ref=sgm$"	id in pop-up windows ("?" case)
10	afriend.id+"&ref=sgm$"	id in pop-up windows ("&" case)
11	afriend.username+"\\\?ref=ts$"	username in suggestions list ("?" case)
12	afriend.username+"&ref=ts$"	username in suggestions list ("&" case)
13	afriend.id+"\\\?ref=ts$"	id in suggestions list ("?" case)
14	afriend.id+"&ref=ts$"	id in suggestions list ("&" case)

Table 2: List of Regular Expressions to match the name in several places.

Number	Regular Expression	Matches with
1	buddy_list	same word to find users in chat list
2	Chat with	same word that appears in user's profile (it is used to replace user's first name in Chat with link in profile page)
3	messages	Message to link in profile page
4	MessageComposer	Send Friend a Message link in profile page
5	video	View Videos of Friend link in profile page
6	can_poke	Poke Friend link in profile page
7	friend_suggester_dialog	Suggest Friends to Friend link in profile page
8	notes	Subscribe to Friend's Notes link
9	share_posts	Subscribe to Friend's Links link
10	mutual$	"Mutual photos" link in photos profile section
11	profile.php\\\?id="+afriend.id+"$	Friend's Profile Link while in photos section
12	photo_search	Photos of Friend link while in photos section
13	photos&viewas	View Photos of Friend link in profile page
14	ref=mf	Friend's Name link when tagged in albums or videos
15	photo_comments.php	Friend's Photo Comments link
16	photo	Back to Friend's Photo link

Table 3: List of Regular Expressions used in combination with User ID or Username

Browsing Step	Browsing Operation	Automatic / On Request
1	Browsing home page	Always automatic
2	Browsing profile page	Always automatic
3	Browsing all comments in a wall post	Always automatic
4	Browsing info tab in profile page	Always automatic
5	Browsing photos tab	Always automatic
6	Browsing one picture	Always automatic
7	Browsing another picture	Always automatic
8	Replace name in search bar	Automatic or on request (pressing F8)
9	Browsing searched friend's profile page	Always automatic
10	Browsing home page	Always automatic
11	Browsing opened chat mini-window of friend's message	Always automatic
12	Browsing profile of friend who sent post	Always automatic
13	Replace name in search bar	Automatic or on request (pressing F8)
14	Browsing searched friend's profile	Always automatic
15	Browsing an event page which some friends attended	Always automatic
16	Browsing pop-up of attendands	Automatic or on request (pressing F9)
17	Browsing home page	Always automatic
18	Browsing message page	Always automatic
19	Browsing event page	Always automatic
20	Browsing photo page	Always automatic

Table 4: Test Browsing Sequence Path.

A Probability-based Approach to Modeling the Risk of Unauthorized Propagation of Information in On-line Social Networks

Barbara Carminati, Elena Ferrari, Sandro Morasca, Davide Taibi
Dipartimento di Informatica e Comunicazione
Università degli Studi dell'Insubria
Via Mazzini 5, I-21100, Varese, Italy
{barbara.carminati, elena.ferrari, sandro.morasca, davide.taibi}@uninsubria.it

ABSTRACT

The unauthorized propagation of information is an important problem in the Internet, especially because of the increasing popularity of On-line Social Networks. To address this issue, many access control mechanisms have been proposed so far, but there is still a lack of techniques to evaluate the risk of unauthorized flow of information within social networks. This paper introduces a probability-based approach to modeling the likelihood that information propagates from one social network user to users who are not authorized to access it. The approach is demonstrated via an example, to show how it can be applied in practical cases.

Categories and Subject Descriptors

H.2.0 [**Database Management**]: General—*Security, integrity and protection*; D.2.8 [**Software Engineering**]: Metrics—*complexity measures, performance measures*

General Terms

Security, Measurement

Keywords

Social Networks, Privacy, Access control, Information leakage

1. INTRODUCTION

The Web is no longer just a simple tool for publishing textual data or images, but it has now evolved into a complex collaborative knowledge management system. This evolution is mainly due to the rapid spread of social computing services, such as blogs, wikis, social bookmarking, collaborative filtering, and social networks [15]. On-line Social Networks (OSNs) represent one of the most relevant phenomena related to Web 2.0. OSNs are online communities that allow users to publish resources and record and/or establish relationships with other users, possibly of different type ("friend of," "colleague of," etc.), for purposes that may concern business, entertainment, religion, dating, etc. To have an idea of the relevance of the social networking phenomena, just think that Facebook counts more than 500 million users.[1]

Additionally, social networking services are today more and more used not only by single users, but at the enterprise level to communicate, share information, make decisions, and, in general, do business. This is in line with the emerging trend known as Enterprise 2.0 [14] — the use of Web 2.0 technologies within the Intranet, to allow for more spontaneous, knowledge-based collaboration. However, despite all the benefits of social network facilities in terms of knowledge-based collaboration and information sharing, there still exist important problems in the further diffusion of such technologies. One of the most serious obstacles is related to security, in terms of ensuring users that their privacy and access control requirements are preserved when sharing information within social networks. These needs have resulted in the development of several privacy preserving techniques and access control models (see, for example [5] for a survey) for OSNs. Almost all the defined access control mechanisms implement *topology-based* access control, which basically identifies authorized users by specifying constraints on the user social graph. As such, access control rules regulating information sharing are defined by specifying the relationships that users must have in order to have the right to access resources. For instance, by means of topology-based access control, it is possible to easily define rules to authorize "only direct friends," "only friends of friends," etc. Some of the access control models proposed so far also use trust and/or reputation as a further parameter on which access control is based. Additionally, a basic form of topology-based access control is also provided by existing commercial social networks. For example, in addition to allowing a user to mark a given resource as public, private, or accessible by direct contacts, Bebo (http://bebo.com), Facebook (http://facebook.com), and Multiply (http://multiply.com) support the option "selected friends" (selected contacts); Last.fm (http://last.fm) supports the option "profile neighbors" (i.e., the set of OSN members having musical preferences and tastes similar to mine); Facebook, Friendster (http://friendster.com), and Orkut (http://www.orkut.com) support the option "friends of friends"; Xing (http://xing.com) supports the options

---

[1]http://www.facebook.com/press/info.php?statistics.

"contacts of my contacts" (2nd degree contacts), and "3rd" and "4th degree contacts"; LinkedIn (http://www.linkedin.com) and Multiply support the option "my network" (n-th degree contacts, i.e., all the OSN members to whom a user is either directly or indirectly connected, independent of how distant they are).

The main benefit of topology-based access control is its flexibility in terms of policy specification, since authorized users can be simply specified by stating conditions on relationships, their depth, and trust levels. This flexibility, however, may potentially lead users to losing control of their data. Since access rules specify authorized users at an intensional level, i.e., as constraints on relationships in the OSN, the user specifying the rule might not be able to precisely identify who is authorized to access his/her resources. Even in small social networks, one can hardly understand which users are actually authorized even with simple access rules such as "friends of friends of my friends," due to the many relationships that users can establish. This possible loss of control generates serious potential *risks of unauthorized information flow*. A user does not directly know the set of users authorized by his/her policies, so he or she may not actually be aware of potentially malicious behaviors of these users in releasing accessed data to unauthorized users.

Therefore, there is a need for quantifying the *potential risks* that may result from the access rules specified in OSNs, so the users are fully aware of the possible effects of their decisions in specifying access rules. In this paper, we introduce a probability-based approach for quantifying the probability that user resources may become accessible to another user of the OSN. This probability is computed based on the probability of propagation of information associated with each direct relationship present in the OSN. Specifically, we show how to exactly compute the probability that a resource propagates from one user to another on the set of paths that link the two users. Also, because the exact computation of this probability may be computationally intensive, we show how an upper bound for this probability can be derived. Then, we quantify the *Unauthorized Access Risk* (UAR) as an upper bound to the probability that sensitive resources reach any unauthorized user in an OSN that enforces topology-based access control. The approach is demonstrated via an example having as target the Enterprise 2.0 domain, to show how it can be applied in practical cases. It is relevant to note that the probability-based approach for UAR estimation presented in this paper is just the core component of a more comprehensive framework for information flow management and prevention in OSNs. As it will be discussed in Section 5, the framework needs to be complemented with other important functionalities (e.g., automatic computation of probability of information propagation associated with a relationship, tailored GUI helping users to set up access control rules based on the UAR metric).

Assessing the implications of access control policies traditionally lies in the domain of safety/security analysis, which has been addressed for several different domains (e.g., operating systems [10], role-based access control [13], trust management [16]) but to the best of our knowledge not for OSNs. In contrast, in the field of OSN, literature offers several topology-based access control models and mechanisms for social networks (e.g., [1, 4, 6, 7, 8, 12]). However, to the best of our knowledge, this is the first work proposing a measure for the risk of information leakage due to unauthorized propagation. Inference problems in OSNs have been addressed by other work, but from a totally different perspective, mainly related to sensitive attribute inference. For instance, Zheleva and Ghetoor in [17] address the problem of inferences of private user attributes from public profile attributes, links, and group memberships in OSNs, whereas [11] investigates the effect of social relations on sensitive attribute inference. The work that is most related to the proposal in this paper is [2], where a privacy-preserving tool is proposed to enable a user to visualize the view that other users have of his or her Facebook profile, on the basis of the specified privacy policies. This means that a user should explicitly select one of his or her neighbors n in the OSN to see what n can see of his or her profile. However, due to the huge number of users in an OSN, it may be almost impossible by using this tool to understand the effect of a policy in terms of unauthorized information disclosure, which is the focus of our work.

The remainder of this paper is organized as follows. Section 2 introduces basic concepts on OSNs and topology-based access control. Section 3 presents the probability-based approach, whereas Section 4 shows some examples of its application. Finally, Section 5 concludes the paper and outlines future work.

2. BASIC CONCEPTS

In this section, we introduce the modeling approach we use to represent an OSN (Section 2.1), then, we illustrate the reference access control model we adopt to identify authorized users (Section 2.2).

2.1 The Underlying Model of OSNs

An OSN may be modeled as a directed labeled graph, where nodes correspond to users and arcs denote relationships between users. Given a relationship, the initial node of an arc denotes the user that has established the relationship and the terminal node the user that has accepted that relationship. For notational convenience, we use letters from the Greek alphabet to denote nodes.

The OSN model also supports different types of relationship (e.g., "friend of," "colleague of"), which are modeled as labels of the arcs. We say that two users α and β are in a *direct* relationship of a given type rt if there is an arc connecting α and β that bears the label rt. Also, two users α and β are in an *indirect* relationship of a given type rt if there is a directed path of more than one arc connecting α and β such that all of the arcs on the path bear the label rt.

A relationship of type rt from user α to user β may be characterized by a trust level, representing how trustworthy α considers β, as far as a relationship of kind rt is concerned. Thus, each arc is annotated with a value $t \in [0, 1]$ that quantifies the trust level associated with the relationship represented by the arc.

Information may be passed along the relationships of the OSN, and there is a risk that a confidential resource is illegally released to unauthorized users. As shown in Section 3.5, we introduce the *Unauthorized Access Risk* as an upper bound to the probability that a confidential resource reaches unauthorized users directly or via a path of relationships in the OSN. To this end, in our model, each arc is associated with the probability that information is propagated by means of the relationship represented by the arc. More precisely, given two users α and β, directly connected by an arc, $p(\alpha,\beta)$ quantifies the conditional probability that, if α knows a given resource rsc, then he or she propagates rsc to β, i.e.,

$$p(\alpha,\beta) = p(\alpha\_makes\_rsc\_known\_to\_\beta | \alpha\_knows\_rsc) \quad (1)$$

Thus, we assume that the probability of propagation of rsc from one node to another does not depend on the previous propagation history of rsc. So, even if α may receive rsc from multiple nodes, $p(\alpha,\beta)$ does not depend on the specific nodes that have propagated rsc to α, nor on the fact that α may have created rsc. Note that, in addition, $p(\alpha,\beta)$ is defined regardless of the fact that a resource rsc is legally or illegally propagated on the arc connecting α and β according to the access rules associated with rsc (see Section 2.2).

Summarizing, a social network OSN can be formally modeled as a tuple $OSN = <N, A, RT, TL, lab>$, where

- N represents the set of nodes (i.e., the users) of the social network;

- RT represents the set of relationship types existing in the social network;

- $A \subseteq N \times N \times RT$ is the set of arcs (i.e., the set of relationships between users in the social network) of the social network OSN;

- TL is the set of supported trust levels, which we assume to be the closed interval $[0,1]$ in this paper;

- $lab : A \rightarrow TL \times [0,1]$ is a labeling function that assigns to each relationship $r \in A$ a trust level $t \in TL$, and a probability $p \in [0,1]$ that information propagates along the arc.

Note that in what follows, for simplicity and notational convenience, we use graphs and not multigraphs, i.e., given any two nodes α and β, there is at most one arc connecting α to β. For instance, this means that it is not possible that α and β are connected by a "friend of" and "colleague of" direct relationship at the same time. So, the pair $<\alpha, \beta>$ uniquely denotes an arc connecting two nodes, where for simplicity we omit the relationship type.[2] Therefore, we can safely write $p(\alpha,\beta)$ to denote the probability associated with it. This will not affect the computation of the resource propagation probabilities of Section 3.

There may be several ways to compute probability $p(\alpha,\beta)$. Indeed, based on the social network context, it is easy to figure out different factors that impact this probability, like users' reputation, relationships semantics, etc. However, since this probability value is just a parameter of the proposed Unauthorized Access Risk measure, we do not address the issue of its computation in the current paper, but we plan to address this in our future work.

Figure 1 contains an example of a portion of an OSN for a financial domain. For instance, the arc from α to β shows that α is in relationship "MOf" (i.e., "manager of") with β, that this relationship has a 0.8 trust level, and that it has a 0.5 probability that information is propagated from α to β.

This example is explained in more details in Section 2.2 and used in Section 4 to show how our approach can be applied in practice.

2.2 Access Control

The access control mechanism allows us to identify the users that are authorized to access a confidential resource and those that are not authorized. As the reference access control model for OSNs, we now summarize the one proposed by us in [6]. The use of this access control model is motivated by the fact that it supports all properties of other access control models for OSNs proposed so far, i.e., constraints on type, depth and trust level of the relationships identifying authorized users. According to this model, each resource to be shared in the network is protected by a set of *access rules*, denoting the users authorized to access the resource in terms of the type, depth, and trust level of existing relationships in the network. Each access rule ar has the form $ar = <rsc, AC>$, where AC is a set of *access conditions*, all of which need to be satisfied in order to get access to resource rsc. Formally, an access condition is a tuple $ac = <v, rt, d\_max, t\_min>$, where v is the network user with whom the requestor of a given resource must have a direct or indirect relationship to obtain the access, whereas rt, d_max, and t_min are, respectively, the type, maximum depth, and minimum trust level that the relationship must have in order to get the access. The trust level of a direct relationship is provided by the annotation on the corresponding arc. The trust level of an indirect relationship, which is represented by a path linking two nodes of the graph, needs to be computed based on the trust levels associated with the arcs composing the path. The literature offers several algorithms to compute the trust of indirect relationships in OSNs [9]. At any rate, the specific algorithm for trust computation is not the focus of our paper, as it is used only to find the set of users that are or are not authorized to receive a confidential resource. So, the algorithm for trust computation does not impact the proposed probability-based approach shown in Section 3. In this paper, for simplicity, we suppose that the trust level of a path is obtained by multiplying the trust levels of all the arcs in the path. In addition, if users α and β are linked by a set of paths, we take the maximum value of trust along all these paths as the value for the trust that α has in β.

We exemplify the considered access control model by means of the OSN in Figure 1. The social network is designed to support agents working for a given financial company. By using the social networking functionalities, agents are able to find updated information on the company products and share a variety of information (e.g., opinions on new products, marketing strategies, data about the sales). Moreover, agents are able to establish relationships of different types.

Relationship types are defined according to the FOAF vocabulary [3], which has been extended to model the roles agents may play in the company. Thus, for instance, agent α has a relationship of type *ManagerOf* (MOf for short) with β and a relationship of type *ColleagueOf* (COf) with γ. In the example, social network relationships can be established also based on agents' personal relationships. As an example, β has established a *FriendOf* relationship (FOf) with γ.

Moreover, according to the company business strategies, agents can also form smaller networks or groups (for instance related to products of a particular type, or denot-

---

[2]Note that this assumption is in line with proposals in the social network analysis literature, where arcs are no labelled. Moreover, some of existing online social networks fit into a simply graph representation. As an example, in Facebook two users can establish only a unique friendship relationship.

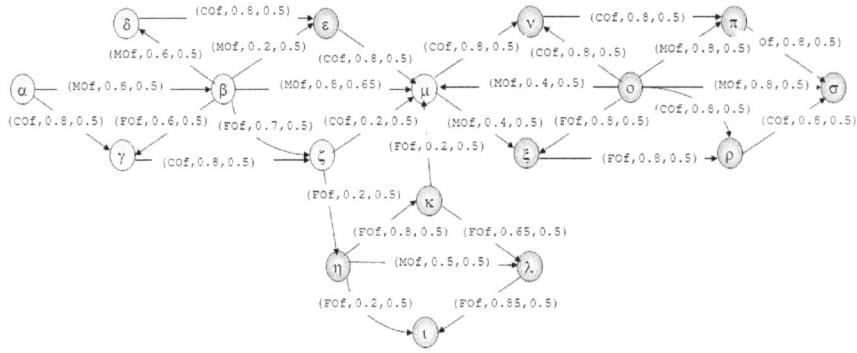

Figure 1: A portion of an OSN for a financial company

ing a partnership among some of the agents). As such, agents could have different requirements about resources sharing. For example, we can assume that agent α would like to share his/her opinions about a product (contained in the report $ProdX\_\alpha\_opinions$) with: *(1)* his/her colleagues and colleagues of his/her colleagues; *(2)* agents managed by him/her as well as agents managed by agents he/she manages. Moreover, α would like to share the report only with those nodes with whom the required relationship has a minimum trust value of 0.5. To enforce these requirements, α can specify the following access rule: $ar = <\ ProdX\_\alpha\_opinions,\ \{<\alpha, MOf, 2, 0.5>, <\alpha, COf, 2, 0.5>\}\ >$. Referring to Figure 1, the nodes that can access $ProdX\_\alpha\_opinions$ are β, γ, ζ, and μ. According to the specified access rule, ϵ is not allowed to access the report even if he or she satisfies the requirements on the relationship type, in that the trust level is 0.16, less than the 0.5 threshold required by the access rule in both access conditions.

3. PROPOSED APPROACH

We first show in Section 3.1 how we can compute the probability that a resource rsc propagates along a specific path from a specified node α to another node β. Then, in Section 3.2, we we discuss, through a few representative examples, how we can compute the probability that rsc propagates from α to β, *regardless of the specific path followed*. This leads to the explanation of the general formula and algorithm for computing this probability (3.3). Due to the computational complexity of the algorithm described in Section 3.3, we provide an upper bound to this probability in Section 3.4. Building on these concepts, Section 3.5 introduces the *Unauthorized Access Risk*, i.e., an upper bound to the probability that a resource is accessed by any unauthorized user.

3.1 Resource Propagation along a Path

We can define the probability that rsc propagates along a path in the graph denoting an OSN based on the probabilities associated with each arc. Given $path = <\alpha_1, \alpha_2, \ldots, \alpha_n>$, the probability $P(path)$ that rsc propagates from α_1 to α_n along $path$ is the conditional probability:

$$P(path) = P(\alpha_1\_makes\_rsc\_known\_to\_\alpha_n\_along\_path| \\ \alpha_1\_knows\_rsc) \quad (2)$$

That is also computed as

$$P(path) = P(\alpha_1\_makes\_rsc\_known\_to\_\alpha_2 \\ \wedge \alpha_2\_makes\_rsc\_known\_to\_\alpha_n\_along\_path| \\ \alpha_1\_knows\_rsc \wedge \alpha_1\_makes\_rsc\_directly\_known\_to\_\alpha_2) \\ P(\alpha_1\_makes\_rsc\_directly\_known\_to\_\alpha_2) \quad (3)$$

The first probability in the expression in the right-hand side of Formula (2) can be simplified as follows. The fact that $\alpha_1\_makes\_rsc\_directly\_known\_to\_\alpha_2$ is implied by the conditioning event $\alpha_1\_knows\_rsc \wedge \alpha_1\_makes\_rsc\_directly\_known\_to\_\alpha_2$, so we can remove $\alpha_1\_makes\_rsc\_known\_to\_\alpha_2$ from the conditional event and we have $P(\alpha_2\_makes\_rsc\_known\_to\_\alpha_n\_along\_path|\alpha_1\_knows\_rsc \wedge \alpha_1\_makes\_rsc\_directly\_known\_to\_\alpha_2)$. The conditioning event can be rewritten as $\alpha_1\_knows\_rsc \wedge \alpha_1\_makes\_rsc\_directly\_known\_to\_\alpha_2 \wedge \alpha_2\_knows\_rsc$. As the probability of propagation of rsc from α_2 does not depend on the previous history of rsc, $\alpha_1\_knows\_rsc \wedge \alpha_1\_makes\_rsc\_directly\_known\_to\_\alpha_2$ can be removed from the conditioning event. Also, by definition, $p(\alpha_1, \alpha_2) = p(\alpha_1\_makes\_rsc\_directly\_known\_to\_\alpha_2)$, where $p(\alpha_1, \alpha_2)$ is the probability given as an annotation of the arc from α_1 to α_2, as described in Section 2, so Formula (3) can be rewritten as

$$P(path) = P(\alpha_2\_makes\_rsc\_known\_to\_\alpha_n\_along\_path| \\ \alpha_2\_knows\_rsc) \\ P(\alpha_1\_makes\_rsc\_directly\_known\_to\_\alpha_2) \quad (4)$$

We can now recursively apply the same reasoning on this probability and we stop the recursion when $P(\alpha_{n-1}\_makes\_rsc\_known\_to\_\alpha_n\_along\_path|\alpha_{n-1}\_knows\_rsc)$, which is by definition equal to $P(\alpha_{n-1}, \alpha_n)$. So, $P(path)$ is actually the product of the individual probabilities of the arcs encountered along $path$, that is:

$$P(path) = \prod_{i \in 1..n-1} p(\alpha_i, \alpha_{i+1}) \quad (5)$$

3.2 Resource Propagation along a Set of Paths

Several different paths may connect two nodes α and β in an OSN. In what follows, we denote the *set of paths* that connect α to β as $\alpha \rightarrow \beta$. In this section, we show how we compute the probability $P(\alpha \rightarrow \beta)$ that rsc propagates from α to β along any path in $\alpha \rightarrow \beta$.

To this end, we use a few examples for illustration purposes. We start with the case of two paths that do not have any arc in common, even though they have the same start and end node. We then illustrate the more general case of two paths that have the same start and end node and that share at least one arc. Finally, we also discuss how to deal with paths with loops.

3.2.1 Two Paths with No Arcs in Common

In Figure 2, nodes α and γ are connected by means of two paths:[3] $path_1 = <\alpha, \beta, \gamma>$ and $path_2 = <\alpha, \gamma>$. So, we have $\alpha \rightarrow \beta = \{<\alpha, \beta, \gamma>, <\alpha, \gamma>\}$. Information may propagate from α to γ along both paths of even along one path and not the other. We assume that propagation of information along one arc is independent from propagation along any other arc. So, for instance, the propagation of rsc along $<\alpha, \gamma>$ is independent from the propagation of rsc along $<\alpha, \beta>$, and, therefore, along $<\alpha, \beta, \gamma>$.

Probability $P(\alpha \rightarrow \gamma) = P(path_1 \vee path_2)$, where $path_1 \vee path_2$ is the event that rsc propagates along $path_1$ or $path_2$, i.e., the event obtained as the disjunction of events $path_1$ and $path_2$. We can apply a general property of probabilities in the case of events built via disjunctions of events, which we rephrase for our case as follows:

$$P(path_1 \vee path_2) =$$
$$P(path_1) + P(path_2) - P(path_1 \wedge path_2) =$$
$$P(path_1) + P(path_2)(1 - P(path_1|path_2)) \quad (6)$$

This general property will be later applied to the more general example of two paths with arcs in common and used in the derivation of the general formula for the computation of the propagation probability (Formula (14)).

In Figure 2, we have $P(path_1) = p(\alpha,\beta)p(\beta,\gamma)$ and $P(path_2) = p(\alpha,\gamma)$. The two paths are independent, i.e., rsc's propagation along $path_1$ is independent of rsc's propagation along $path_2$, so we also have $P(path_1|path_2) = P(path_1)$ and

$$P(\alpha \rightarrow \gamma) = p(\alpha,\beta)p(\beta,\gamma) + p(\alpha,\gamma)(1 - p(\alpha,\beta)p(\beta,\gamma)) \quad (7)$$

As a further proof, we can also compute $P(\alpha \rightarrow \gamma)$ in a different way, which we use as the basis for computing the upper bound of $P(\alpha \rightarrow \gamma)$ in Section 3.4. $P(\alpha \rightarrow \gamma)$ can be computed as the complement of probability $Q(\alpha \rightarrow \gamma) = 1 - P(\alpha \rightarrow \gamma)$ that rsc does *not* propagate from α to γ on *either path*. Since the two paths are independent, $Q(\alpha \rightarrow \gamma)$ is the product of probability $1 - P(path_1) = 1 - p(\alpha,\beta)p(\beta,\gamma)$ and probability $1 - P(path_1) = 1 - p(\alpha,\gamma)$, i.e.,

$$P(\alpha \rightarrow \gamma) = 1 - (1 - p(\alpha,\beta)p(\beta,\gamma))(1 - p(\alpha,\gamma)) = \quad (8)$$
$$p(\alpha,\beta)p(\beta,\gamma) + p(\alpha,\gamma)(1 - p(\alpha,\beta)p(\beta,\gamma)) \quad (9)$$

3.2.2 Two Paths with Arcs in Common

However, it is not always the case that paths are independent. In the general case, two paths connecting α and β may very well have arcs in common, so they are not independent.

The two paths $path_1 = <\delta, \alpha, \beta, \gamma>$ and $path_2 = <\delta, \alpha, \gamma>$ from δ to γ share arc $<\delta, \alpha>$, so they are not independent. We can apply Formula (6), where $P(path_1) = p(\delta,\alpha)p(\alpha,\beta)p(\beta,\gamma)$ and $P(path_2) = p(\delta,\alpha)p(\alpha,\gamma)$. We now need to compute $P(path_1|path_2)$ to complete the formula. $P(path_1|path_2)$ is the probability that rsc propagates along $path_1$, once it is already known that rsc propagates along $path_2$. Thus, it is the probability that rsc propagates along

---
[3]Here and in the following figures, for simplicity we omitt the relationship type informationa associated with an arc.

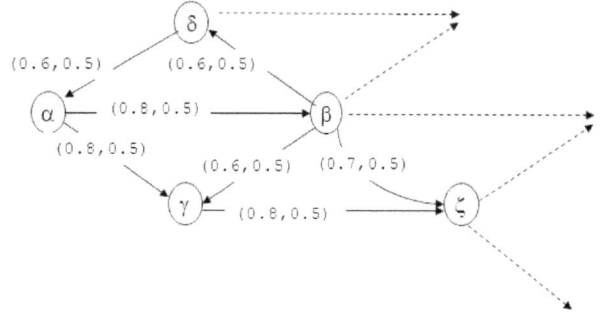

Figure 2: A fragment of an OSN

$<\delta, \alpha>$, $<\alpha, \beta>$, and $<\beta, \gamma>$, once it is known that it propagates along $<\delta, \alpha>$ and $<\alpha, \gamma>$. So it is the probability that rsc propagates along $<\alpha, \beta>$ and $<\beta, \gamma>$, since we already know rsc propagates along $<\delta, \alpha>$. Summarizing, we have:

$$P(\delta \rightarrow \gamma) =$$
$$p(\delta,\alpha)p(\alpha,\beta)p(\beta,\gamma) + p(\delta,\alpha)p(\alpha,\gamma)(1 - p(\alpha,\beta)p(\beta,\gamma)) =$$
$$p(\delta,\alpha)(p(\alpha,\beta)p(\beta,\gamma) + p(\alpha,\gamma)(1 - p(\alpha,\beta)p(\beta,\gamma))) =$$
$$p(\delta,\alpha)P(\alpha \rightarrow \gamma) \quad (10)$$

The right-hand part of the last equality in Formula (10) shows that Formula (6) gives results that are consistent with what one may already expect. $P(\delta \rightarrow \gamma)$ is the product of the probability $p(\delta,\alpha)$ that rsc propagates from δ to α and the probability $P(\alpha \rightarrow \gamma)$ that rsc propagates from α to γ.

3.2.3 Dealing with Loops

Some care needs to be exercised when cycles are present in the graph, but, as we now show with an example, the result will actually be a simplification of the graph. Suppose we have the graph in Figure 3 i.e., a graph with an "entry" node α, a loop $<\beta, \gamma, \delta, \beta>$, and an "exit" node ϵ. The computation of $P(\alpha \rightarrow \epsilon)$ can be broken down as the product of three probabilities:

$$P(\alpha \rightarrow \epsilon) = P(\alpha \rightarrow \beta)P(\beta \rightarrow \gamma)P(\gamma \rightarrow \epsilon) \quad (11)$$

Set $\beta \rightarrow \gamma$ contains an infinite number of paths, because of the presence of loop $<\beta, \gamma, \delta, \beta>$. However, no paths that contain a loop need to be taken into account for our goals. Suppose that rsc has reached node γ along path $<\alpha, \beta, \gamma>$. The probability that rsc reaches γ along that path is $P(<\alpha, \beta, \gamma>)$. The probability that rsc is known by γ after one iteration of the loop is:

$$P(\alpha, \beta, \gamma, \delta, \beta, \gamma) = P(\gamma, \delta, \beta, \gamma|\alpha, \beta, \gamma)P(\alpha, \beta, \gamma) =$$
$$P(\alpha, \beta, \gamma)P(\gamma, \delta, \beta, \gamma) \quad (12)$$

However, according to the meaning of our probabilities, $P(\alpha \rightarrow \beta)$ is the probability that, if rsc is known at node α, it also gets known at node β. So, $P(\alpha \rightarrow \alpha) = 1$. As a consequence, $P(<\gamma, \delta, \beta, \gamma>) = 1$, and:

$$P(<\alpha, \beta, \gamma, \delta, \beta, \gamma>) = P(<\alpha, \beta, \gamma>) \quad (13)$$

Thus, when computing $P(\alpha \rightarrow \beta)$, we can ignore all loops in $\alpha \rightarrow \beta$, and $\alpha \rightarrow \beta$ can be reduced to the paths in the hierarchy (i.e., the directed acyclic graph) in which α is not preceded by any other node and β is not followed by any

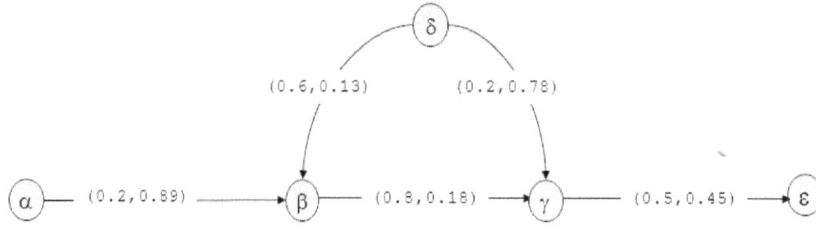

Figure 3: An example of graph with a loop

other node. Thus, we deal with a finite set of paths. Once the hierarchy from α to β is known, we can build $P(\alpha \to \beta)$ by starting from α and proceeding down the levels of the hierarchy.

3.3 Exact Computation of the Probability of Propagation along a Set of Paths

We can now show what happens in the general case, and how the probability of information propagating from one node to another node can be computed in a recursive manner. Given two nodes α and β, let us suppose that $\alpha \to \beta$ is composed of n paths $path_1, path_2, \ldots, path_n$. We compute $P(path_1 \vee path_2 \vee \ldots \vee path_n)$, where, from a logical point of view, $path_1 \vee path_2 \vee \ldots \vee path_n$ is a formula in Disjunctive Normal Form containing $n-1$ disjunction operators and each term $path_i$ is a conjunction of k_i predicates, each denoting the fact that rsc propagates along a specific arc of $path_i$. For instance, in Figure 1, $path_1$ can be also represented as the conjunction of the two predicates $prop_{<\alpha,\beta>}$, which denotes the fact that rsc propagates on arc $< \alpha, \beta >$, and $prop_{<\beta,\gamma>}$, which denotes the fact that rsc propagates on arc $< \beta, \gamma >$. So, we can write $path_1 = prop_{<\alpha,\beta>} \wedge prop_{<\beta,\gamma>}$. Likewise, $path_2 = prop_{<\alpha,\gamma>}$, and $path_1 \vee path_2 = prop_{<\alpha,\beta>} \wedge prop_{<\beta,\gamma>} \vee prop_{<\alpha,\gamma>}$. Because of the general property of probabilities of Formula (6), we can write:

$$P(path_1 \vee path_2 \vee \ldots \vee path_n) =$$
$$P(path_1 \vee path_2 \vee \ldots \vee path_{n-1}) +$$
$$P(path_n)(1 - P(path_1 \vee path_2 \vee \ldots \vee path_{n-1}|path_n)) \quad (14)$$

Let us examine the terms appearing in the formula.

- $P(path_n)$ can be computed directly as shown in Section 3.1.

- $P(path_1 \vee path_2 \vee \ldots \vee path_{n-1})$ can be computed recursively, by applying Formula (14) to the set of paths $\{path_1, path_2, \ldots, path_{n-1}\}$, which contains one less path than the initial set of paths, so recursion is guaranteed to end when the set of paths contains only one path.

- $P(path_1 \vee path_2 \vee \ldots \vee path_{n-1}|path_n)$ can be first simplified and then computed recursively. As for the simplification part, $P(path_1 \vee path_2 \vee \ldots \vee path_{n-1}|path_n)$ is the probability that rsc propagates along at least one path in $\{path_1, path_2, \ldots, path_{n-1}\}$ once it is known that rsc propagates along $path_n$. For instance, let us take the example in Figure 2 and let us show with logical arguments that $P(path_1|path_2) = p(\alpha,\beta) p(\beta,\gamma)$ in that case, as we have already shown when

we discussed Formula (10). The two paths from δ to γ can be rephrased in logical terms as $path_1 = prop_{\delta,\alpha} \wedge prop_{\alpha,\beta} \wedge prop_{\beta,\gamma}$ and $path_2 = prop_{\delta,\alpha} \wedge prop_{\alpha,\gamma}$. So, $P(path_1|path_2) = P(prop_{\delta,\alpha} \wedge prop_{\alpha,\beta} \wedge prop_{\beta,\gamma}|prop_{\delta,\alpha} \wedge prop_{\alpha,\gamma})$. The conditioning event $prop_{\delta,\alpha} \wedge prop_{\alpha,\gamma}$ is assumed to occur, so both $prop_{\delta,\alpha}$ and $prop_{\alpha,\gamma}$ are true. So, we can set $prop_{\delta,\alpha}$ and $prop_{\alpha,\gamma}$ to true in the conditional event (i.e., since only $prop_{\delta,\alpha}$ appears in the conditional event, we removed it from the conditional event) and the conditioning event, so $P(path_1|path_2) = P(prop_{\alpha,\beta} \wedge prop_{\beta,\gamma}) = p(\alpha,\beta)p(\beta,\gamma)$. From a logical point of view, we can replace $P(path_1 \vee path_2 \vee \ldots \vee path_{n-1}|path_n)$ with $P(path_1' \vee path_2' \vee \ldots \vee path_{n-1}')$, in which each single conjunction $path_i'$ is obtained by eliminating from the corresponding conjunction $path_i$ all those predicates that also appear in $path_n$, because it is assumed that those predicates are true, so they need not be evaluated when evaluating the truth value of $path_i$. As a consequence, the new probability $P(path_1' \vee path_2' \vee \ldots \vee path_{n-1}')$ is based on a predicate which is built as

- a formula in Disjunctive Normal Form containing $n-2$ disjunction operators, one less than the original formula

- and each term $path_i'$ is a conjunction of k_i' predicates, with $k_i' \leq k_i$, where k_i denotes the number of predicates in $path_n$ and k_i' the number of predicates in $path_n'$.

Thus, we can apply Formula (14) to $P(path_1' \vee path_2' \vee \ldots \vee path_{n-1}')$, and recursion is guaranteed to end.

Thus, we have found out a recursive algorithm for computing $P(\alpha \to \beta)$, regardless of the path along which rsc propagates from α to β. However, the computational complexity of the algorithm may be too high, as we now show. The number of recursions clearly depends on the number of paths. Suppose we have a hierarchy with $n+2$ nodes, i.e., with one initial node, one terminal node, and n intermediate nodes. Suppose that this hierarchy has $l+2$ levels and that each level has the same number of nodes, i.e., $n = a \cdot l$, except for the initial and the terminal levels. Suppose also that there is an arc from each node at level j to each node at level $j+1$. Then, it can be shown that the number of paths for this graph is $(\frac{n}{l})^l = a^{\frac{n}{a}}$. So, the number of paths grows exponentially with n, in this case.

3.4 An Upper Bound to the Probability of Propagation along a Set of Paths

Since the computational complexity for the exact computation of $P(\alpha \to \beta)$ may be too high, we here derive an upper bound for it. To this end, let us take $\alpha \to \beta = \{path_1, path_2, \ldots, path_n\}$ like we did in Section 3.2, so we can use $P(path_1 \lor path_2 \lor \ldots \lor path_n)$ in our derivation.

For notational convenience, let $Pre(\beta)$ be the set of nodes in the "preset" of β, i.e., the set of those nodes ζ that have a direct arc to β, i.e., $<\zeta, \beta> \in A$. We first show that:

$$P(\alpha \to \beta) \leq 1 - \prod_{\zeta \in Pre(\beta)} (1 - P(\alpha \to \zeta)p(\zeta,\beta)) \quad (15)$$

We can write $P(\alpha \to \beta)$ as follows:

$$P(\alpha \to \beta) = P(\alpha \to \zeta_1 \to \beta \lor \ldots \lor \alpha \to \zeta_n \to \beta) \quad (16)$$

Formula (16) shows that the probability that rsc propagates from α to β is the probability that it propagates on at least one path that goes from α to β through one of the $\zeta_i \in Pre(\beta)$. Based on the probability properties of disjunctions (that we already used in Formula (6)), we can also write that:

$$P(\alpha \to \beta) =$$
$$P(\alpha \to \zeta_1 \to \beta \lor \ldots \lor \alpha \to \zeta_{n-1} \to \beta) + P(\alpha \to \zeta_n \to \beta)$$
$$(1 - P(\alpha \to \zeta_1 \to \beta \lor \ldots \lor \alpha \to \zeta_{n-1} \to \beta | \alpha \to \zeta_n \to \beta)) \quad (17)$$

Now, we have:

$$P(\alpha \to \zeta_1 \to \beta \lor \ldots \lor \alpha \to \zeta_{n-1} \to \beta | \alpha \to \zeta_n \to \beta) \geq$$
$$P(\alpha \to \zeta_1 \to \beta \lor \ldots \lor \alpha \to \zeta_{n-1} \to \beta) \quad (18)$$

because knowing that rsc propagates from α to β via ζ_n will never decrease the probability of it propagating along any other paths. As we already discussed, knowing that rsc propagates from α to β via ζ_n means that some of the predicates in the paths in $\alpha \to \zeta_n \to \beta$ are true, so they can be removed from the conditional event $\alpha \to \zeta_1 \to \beta \lor \ldots \lor \alpha \to \zeta_{n-1} \to \beta$. This implies that the probability of propagation of rsc along the paths in $\alpha \to \zeta_1 \to \beta \bigcup \ldots \bigcup \alpha \to \zeta_{n-1} \to \beta$ may increase, but never decrease.

As a consequence, we can write:

$$P(\alpha \to \beta) \leq P(\alpha \to \zeta_1 \to \beta \lor \ldots \lor \alpha \to \zeta_{n-1} \to \beta) +$$
$$P(\alpha \to \zeta_n \to \beta)$$
$$(1 - P(\alpha \to \zeta_1 \to \beta \lor \ldots \lor \alpha \to \zeta_{n-1} \to \beta)) =$$
$$P(\alpha \to \zeta_n \to \beta) +$$
$$Q(\alpha \to \zeta_n \to \beta)P(\alpha \to \zeta_1 \to \beta \lor \ldots \lor \alpha \to \zeta_{n-1} \to \beta) =$$
$$1 - Q(\alpha \to \zeta_n \to \beta)Q(\alpha \to \zeta_1 \to \beta \lor \ldots \lor \alpha \to \zeta_{n-1} \to \beta) \quad (19)$$

which can be rewritten as:

$$Q(\alpha \to \beta) \geq$$
$$Q(\alpha \to \zeta_n \to \beta)Q(\alpha \to \zeta_1 \to \beta \lor \ldots \lor \alpha \to \zeta_{n-1} \to \beta) \quad (20)$$

We can now apply the same reasoning to $Q(\alpha \to \zeta_1 \to \beta \lor \ldots \lor \alpha \to \zeta_{n-1} \to \beta)$, so we obtain:

$$Q(\alpha \to \beta) \geq \prod_{\zeta \in Pre(\beta)} Q(\alpha \to \zeta \to \beta) \quad (21)$$

which can be rewritten as:

$$P(\alpha \to \beta) \leq 1 - \prod_{\zeta \in Pre(\beta)} (1 - P(\alpha \to \zeta)p(\zeta,\beta)) \quad (22)$$

since $Q(\alpha \to \zeta \to \beta) = 1 - P(\alpha \to \zeta)p(\zeta,\beta)$.

However, computing $P(\alpha \to \zeta)$ would imply enumerating all the paths in $\alpha \to \zeta$, whose computational complexity

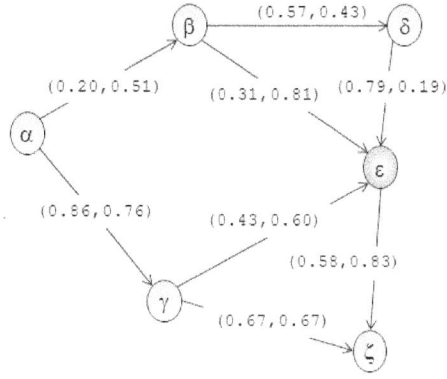

Figure 4: An example hierarchy

Table 1: Probability upper bounds and trust for the nodes in Figure 4

Node	UB	UB'	$Trust$
α	1.00	1.00	1.00
β	0.51	0.51	0.20
γ	0.76	0.76	0.86
δ	0.2193	N/A	0.114
ϵ	0.7435	0.456	0.3698
ζ	0.8121	0.5092	0.5762

may be too high. So, we introduce another approximation, based on the fact that, if we select $UB(\alpha \to \zeta) \geq P(\alpha \to \zeta)$ (UB as in Upper Bound) we have:

$$P(\alpha \to \beta) \leq 1 - \prod_{\zeta \in Pre(\beta)} (1 - P(\alpha \to \zeta)p(\zeta,\beta))$$
$$\leq 1 - \prod_{\zeta \in Pre(\beta)} (1 - UB(\alpha \to \zeta)p(\zeta,\beta)) \quad (23)$$

So, we need to build UB for all nodes. Here is one possibility:

$$UB(\alpha \to \beta) = 1 - \prod_{\zeta \in Pre(\beta)} (1 - UB(\alpha \to \zeta)p(\zeta,\beta)) \quad (24)$$

with $UB(\alpha \to \beta) = p(\alpha,\beta)$ for all those nodes β such that $Pre(\beta) = \{\alpha\}$, i.e., whose only node in the preset is α. Thus, we start from α and its successor nodes, and proceeding level by level in the hierarchy we can build function UB for all nodes. For instance, for the hierarchy in Figure 4, we obtain the values for UB reported in Table 1. (In this section, we only deal with column UB. The meaning of the other two columns will be illustrated in Section 3.5.)

Let us show how the computations of the values of UB were carried out for the nodes in Figure 1. Obviously, $UB(\alpha) = 1$, as α is the original owner of the resource. The values $UB(\beta) = 0.51 = p(\alpha,\beta)$ and $UB(\gamma) = 0.76 = p(\alpha,\gamma)$ can be computed directly as α is directly linked to β and to γ. At any rate, by using Formula (24), we also obtain $UB(\beta) = 1 - (1 - UB(\alpha) \cdot p(\alpha,\beta)) = p(\alpha,\beta)$ and $UB(\gamma) = 1 - (1 - UB(\alpha) \cdot p(\alpha,\gamma)) = p(\alpha,\gamma)$. Again, $UB(\delta) = 0.76 = p(\alpha,\beta) \cdot p(\beta,\delta)$ can be computed based on the probabilities associated with the arcs, because there is only one path from α to δ. Alternatively, via Formula (24), we also obtain $UB(\delta) = 1 - (1 - UB(\beta) \cdot p(\beta,\delta)) = p(\alpha,\beta) \cdot p(\beta,\delta)$. Let us now focus on $UB(\epsilon)$, which we compute based on

Formula (24), i.e., $UB(\epsilon) = 1 - (1 - UB(\beta)p(\beta,\epsilon))(1 - UB(\delta)p(\delta,\epsilon))(1 - UB(\gamma)p(\gamma,\epsilon))$. Likewise, $UB(\zeta) = 1 - (1 - UB(\gamma)p(\gamma,\zeta))(1 - UB(\epsilon)p(\epsilon,\zeta))$.

The value of $UB(\alpha \to \beta)$ obtained is a sharp approximation, as it does coincide with the real value of $P(\alpha \to \beta)$ whenever $\alpha \to \beta$ contains only independent paths, like the ones of the example of Section 3.2.1.

The computation of $UB(\alpha \to \beta)$ according to Formula (24) involves a number of multiplications that is quadratic with the number of nodes, as we now show. The computation of $UB(\alpha \to \beta)$ involves a number of multiplications equal to the number of incoming arcs of β, once the values of $UB(\alpha \to \zeta)$ are known for all ζ in $Pre(\beta)$. Likewise, the number of multiplications needed to compute the values of $UB(\alpha \to \zeta)$ for all of these ζ's is equal to the number of the incoming arcs of all of the ζ's, once the values of $UB(\alpha \to \tau)$ are known for all τ in their presets. By proceeding backwards from β to α, we obtain that the total number of multiplications needed to compute $UB(\alpha \to \beta)$ is equal to the sum of the number of the incoming arcs of all the nodes in $\alpha \to \beta$. Since the sets of incoming arcs of two different nodes are obviously disjoint, we have that the number of of multiplications needed to compute $UB(\alpha \to \beta)$ is equal to the number of arcs in $\alpha \to \beta$, which grows quadratically with the number of nodes.

3.5 Unauthorized Access Risk

We here introduce the *Unauthorized Access Risk* ($UAR(ar)$) as the probability that, given an access rule ar, a resource is passed to any unauthorized user. $UAR(ar)$ depends on the probability of propagation of the resource across the OSN, as defined in Section 3 and on the considered access rule (see Section 2). The intuition behind the definition of UAR is the following. An access rule identifies a set of authorized users and, consequently, a set of unauthorized users. An unauthorized release of a resource happens when a user not authorized by any access rules receives the resource. From that moment on, the resource can be always illegally propagated. Clearly, if an unauthorized user receives a resource, then there is at least an authorized user that passes the resource to him or her. This may happen only if there is a relationship in the OSN linking the authorized user to the unauthorized one. Therefore, we can quantify the UAR as the probability that any unauthorized user linked to at least one authorized user receives the resource from the latter.

Let $Auth(ar) \subseteq N$ be the set of authorized nodes and $UnAuth(ar) \subseteq N$ be the set of nodes not authorized by an access rule ar, given the set of nodes N and a resource rsc. Also, let $BorderUnAuth(ar) \subseteq UnAuth(ar)$ be the set of unauthorized nodes on the border with the authorized nodes, more precisely, $BorderUnAuth(ar)$ is the set of unauthorized nodes in whose preset there is at least one authorized node, i.e.,

$$BorderUnAuth(ar) = \{\alpha \in N | Pre(\alpha) \cap Auth(ar) \neq \emptyset\} \quad (25)$$

where, $Pre(\alpha) = \{\beta | < \beta, \alpha > \in A\}$. We define UAR as the probability that any node in $BorderUnAuth(ar)$ receives rsc. Once rsc is known to any of these nodes, it can be always propagated in an unauthorized way.

Based on these definitions, $UAR(ar)$ is defined as in Formula (26):

$$UAR(ar) = P\left(\bigvee_{\beta \in BorderUnAuth(ar)} \alpha \to \beta\right) \quad (26)$$

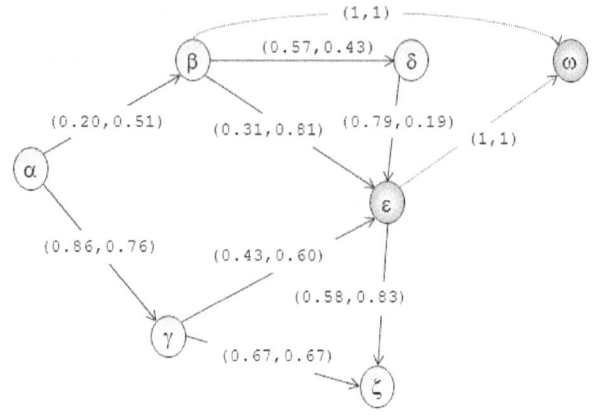

Figure 5: An example hierarchy with node ω

A first upper bound for $UAR(ar)$ can be computed as follows, by directly using the upper bound approximation derived in Section 3.4. Once the nodes in $BorderUnAuth(ar)$ have been identified, suppose we introduce an additional node ω and an arc from each node in $BorderUnAuth(ar)$ to node ω associated with a probability 1 of information propagation. We can compute UAR as the probability that rsc propagates from α to ω, according to the formulas in Section 3.1 and we can find an upper bound for it according to the procedure shown in Section 3.4.

For instance, take the example OSN in Figure 4 and suppose that the access rule specifies that authorized nodes need to have at least a level of trust of 0.5 and may have a maximum distance from α of 4. As the maximum distance between nodes in this hierarchy is 4, the nodes in $BorderUnAuth(ar)$ are those with a trust level lower than 0.5. As column *trust* in Table 1 shows, we have $BorderUnAuth(ar) = \{\beta, \epsilon\}$. Note that δ does not belong to $BorderUnAuth(ar)$ because none of the arcs in its preset is an authorized node, i.e., δ can only receive rsc from β, which is already an unauthorized node. Figure 5 is a modification of Figure 4, in which ω and the arcs that lead to it are represented with dashed lines, to pictorially denote the fact that they do not belong to the original graph. At any rate, if rsc is propagated to any node in $BorderUnAuth(ar)$, it is also propagated to ω with certainty, and, *vice versa*, if rsc is propagated to ω, then it must have been propagated to at least one node in $BorderUnAuth(ar)$.

We now show how we can compute an even stricter upper bound for the value of $UAR(ar)$, which, however, may require some additional computations. This is the upper bound we will use in the application example of Section 4. Since we are dealing with hierarchies, we may suppose that the nodes in the entire hierarchy are ordered, and we can index them in such a way that, given two values i and j, with $i < j$, then there may be a direct or indirect relationship from $node_i$ to node $node_j$, but no relationship from $node_j$ to node $node_i$. Therefore, we can extract the sub-ordering of the nodes in $BorderUnAuth(ar)$ from the general ordering of the nodes in the hierarchy and use a specific indexing from 1 to $bua = |BorderUnAuth(ar)|$ when dealing only with the nodes in $BorderUnAuth(ar)$. Thus, we can rewrite Formula

26 as follows:

$$UAR(ar) = P(\bigvee_{i \in \{1..bua\}} (\alpha \to \beta_i)) \qquad (27)$$

$UAR(ar)$ can also be computed as the complement of the probability that rsc does not propagate to any of the nodes in $BorderUnAuth(ar)$, i.e.,

$$UAR(ar) = 1 - P(\bigwedge_{i \in \{1..bua\}} \neg(\alpha \to \beta_i)) \qquad (28)$$

where $\neg(\alpha \to \beta_i)$ denotes the fact that the resource does not propagate from α to β_i. Based on the properties of conditional probabilities, we can also write:

$$UAR(ar) = 1 - P(\bigwedge_{i \in \{2..bua\}} \neg(\alpha \to \beta_i)|\neg(\alpha \to \beta_1))$$
$$P(\neg(\alpha \to \beta_1)) \quad (29)$$

As for the right-hand side of Formula 29, note that we can compute an upper bound for $P(\alpha \to \beta_1)$ based on the results of Section 3.4. So, we can compute a lower bound for $P(\neg(\alpha \to \beta_1)) = 1 - P(\alpha \to \beta_1)$, which leads to this first majorization of $UAR(ar)$:

$$UAR(ar) \le 1 - P(\bigwedge_{i \in \{2..bua\}} \neg(\alpha \to \beta_i)|\neg(\alpha \to \beta_1))$$
$$(1 - UB(\alpha \to \beta_1)) \quad (30)$$

We now show how a lower bound approximation can be found for $P(\bigwedge_{i \in \{2..bua\}} \neg(\alpha \to \beta_i)|\neg(\alpha \to \beta_1))$. This is the probability that none of the nodes β_i in $BorderUnAuth(ar)$ except β_1 receives rsc, conditioned on the fact that β_1 has not received rsc. Again, based on probability properties:

$$P(\bigwedge_{i \in \{2..bua\}} \neg(\alpha \to \beta_i)|\neg(\alpha \to \beta_1)) =$$
$$1 - P(\bigvee_{i \in \{2..bua\}} (\alpha \to \beta_i)|\neg(\alpha \to \beta_1)) \quad (31)$$

i.e., it is the complement of the probability that at least one of the nodes β_i in $BorderUnAuth(ar)$ (except β_1) receives rsc, conditioned by the fact that β_1 has not received rsc. The problem now becomes finding an upper bound approximation for $P(\bigvee_{i \in \{2..bua\}} (\alpha \to \beta_i)|\neg(\alpha \to \beta_1))$. This upper bound approximation can be found by "ignoring" the presence of β_1 in the graph, i.e., by computing $P(\bigvee_{i \in \{2..bua\}} (\alpha \to \beta_i))$ in a new graph obtained from the original one by removing β_1. To provide an intuitive justification for the fact that we obtain an upper bound, take the two sets of paths $\alpha \to \beta_1$ and $\alpha \to \beta_2$ and suppose that some paths in $\alpha \to \beta_1$ have arcs in common with at least one path $path_{\beta_2}$ in $\alpha \to \beta_2$. We know that rsc has not reached β_1 and that may have happened because rsc did not follow one of the arcs in $path_{\beta_2}$ in common with the paths in $\alpha \to \beta_1$. So the probability of $path_{\beta_2}$, once it is known that rsc has not reached β_1, is lower than the probability of $path_{\beta_2}$ if β_1 simply did not exist. This line of reasoning can be extended to all other paths in $\alpha \to \beta_2$ and to all other β_is, with $i \in 3..bua$. So, we can compute an upper bound approximation for $UAR(ar)$

as follows:

$$UAR(ar) \le 1 - P'(\bigwedge_{i \in \{2..bua\}} \neg(\alpha \to \beta_i))(1 - UB(\alpha \to \beta_1)$$
$$= 1 - (1 - P'(\bigvee_{i \in \{2..bua\}} (\alpha \to \beta_i)))(1 - UB(\alpha \to \beta_1) \ (32)$$

where $P'(\bigwedge_{i \in \{2..bua\}} \neg(\alpha \to \beta_i))$ and $P'(\bigvee_{i \in \{2..bua\}}(\alpha \to \beta_i))$ are computed as if β_1 did not exist. Note that $P'(\bigvee_{i \in \{2..bua\}}(\alpha \to \beta_i)) \le P(\bigvee_{i \in \{2..bua\}}(\alpha \to \beta_i))$, which would be the probability computed by taking into account β_1 as well. As Formula (32) shows, we now need to find an upper bound approximation for $P'(\bigvee_{i \in \{2..bua\}}(\alpha \to \beta_i))$, which we can obtain by recursively applying the same technique until all the nodes in $BorderUnAuth(ar)$ have been taken into account. We use $UB'(\alpha \to \beta_i)$ to denote the value of the upper bound obtained in this way.

For instance, take the OSN in Figure 4, for which we have $BorderUnAuth(ar) = \{\beta, \epsilon\}$. The resulting UB's are reported in Table 1. Note that, none of the values of UB' is greater than the corresponding UB value, and the difference appears to be significant in some cases. Also recall that node δ does not belong to $BorderUnAuth(ar)$, so we do not compute UB' for it. In this example, node β precedes node ϵ. We first compute the value of $UB'(\alpha \to \beta)$, which actually coincides with $UB(\alpha \to \beta)$, as β is not preceded by any node in $BorderUnAuth(ar)$. To compute the value of $UB'(\alpha \to \epsilon)$, we just need to remove β and all of its incoming and outgoing arcs from the graph.

We can also interpret this in a different way. Suppose we are computing an upper bound to the probability that rsc reaches β or ϵ and we are looking for an upper bound of the probability of rsc reaching ϵ. We should discard the possibility that ϵ receives rsc from β, because β is already an unauthorized node, so rsc would have already reached the unauthorized region of the graph.

4. A SIMULATION EXAMPLE

We have conducted several experiments in order to evaluate the effectiveness of UAR, and specifically its upper bound UB' that we derived in Section 3.4. As a dataset, we have considered a synthetic social network which has been generated by randomly creating relationships of 34 different types, among about 200 nodes.[4] The obtained OSN has the following features: 200 nodes, an average outdegree of 200 (note that this outdegree is for all the 34 relationship types), and 24.800 relationships. We limit the OSN at 200 nodes as we do not need a big graph to show the effectiveness of UAR, as this mainly depends on nodes authorized by the considered access control policies. We believe 200 nodes are enough to include such a set. Moreover, since the key reference scenario for our measures is Enterprise 2.0, we do not expect huge graphs as the ones of general purpose social networks, like Facebook. In the synthetic OSN, each arch has randomly associated a relationship type and a trust value. In contrast, the probabilities of propagation along the arcs have been set up on the basis of the experiments.

In what follows, we report the results of two experiments, in both of which we have considered an access control policy consisting of a single access condition of the form $<v$,

[4]We have exploited the RELATIONSHIP vocabulary available at http://purl.org/vocab/relationship.

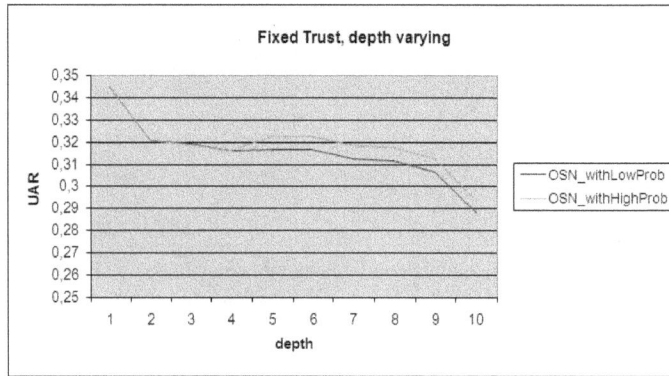

Figure 6: UAR values for ac=$<v, Fof, d\_max, 0.5>$

$Fof, d\_max, t\_min>$,[5] where v and t_min are fixed, whereas d_max varies. More precisely, in the experiment reported in Figure 6 we have fixed t_min to 0.5, i.e., $<v, Fof, d\_max, 0.5>$. The experiments have been conducted by considering two datasets. The first is a synthetic OSN, called $OSN\_withLowProb$, where relationships, nodes and trust values have been generated as described above and all the arcs have a low probability of propagation (i.e., less than 0.1), to simulate an OSN with a very low probability of passing information in an unauthorized way. Figure 6 confirms what we expect as the UAR general trend. In general, if a resource is publicly available, the obvious consequence is that no illegal propagation is enacted. As such, the corresponding UAR value is close to zero. Figure 6 gives us a proof of this. As the depth of the rule increases most of the 200 nodes of the OSN become authorized by the access condition, with always less users that are no authorized to access the resource. The decreasing of unauthorized users reflects in UAR, as this also reduces.

In the second dataset, called $OSN\_withHighProb$, we have set to an high level (i.e., a value greater than 0.9) the probability of propagation of about 10% of the nodes in the OSN. The aim of this experiment is to show how UAR detects this anomaly. As such, rather than randomly selecting the nodes whose probability have to be increased, we decided to select them in a particular area, to check if UAR shows this anomaly. In particular, we select 20 nodes among those with distance 5 to node v. As expected, the UAR measure detects these nodes, as confirmed by the jump between trends in Figure 6.

5. CONCLUSIONS AND FUTURE WORK

Access control for OSNs is becoming an urgent need and this has resulted in the definition of many access control models and mechanisms. Almost all of them exploit topology-based access control, according to which confidentiality requirements wrt resource release are defined in terms of the relationships in the network, their depth and trust level. Although topology-based access control is very powerful in terms of the access control requirements it can model, it is also true that, on the other hand, it may be difficult for the user specifying a policy to clearly understand its effects

---

[5]Note that, as the relationship types have been uniformly distributed, there exist an average of 730 arcs of Fof type.

and the potential risks of unauthorized information leakage it may cause. To address this issue, in this paper, we have proposed a probabilistic-based approach to estimate illegal leakage of resources in an OSN where access control is regulated according to the topology-based paradigm.

We believe this represents just the core component of a more comprehensive framework to handle illegal information flow in OSNs. As such, we plan to extend this work along several directions. A first direction regards the investigation of several functions to compute the probability of resource propagation, taking into account different dimensions of the social network graph (e.g., user reputation, relationship semantics) as well as resource properties (e.g., content, history) . Moreover, we plan to extend the probability model such to consider also multigraph where indirect relationships can be represented with paths consisting of edges having different relationship types.

6. ACKNOWLEDGMENTS

The research presented in this article was partially funded by the IST project QualiPSo, sponsored by the EU in the 6th FP (IST-034763); the FIRB project ARTDECO, sponsored by the Italian Ministry of Education and University; the project "La qualità nello sviluppo software," sponsored by the Università degli Studi dell'Insubria; and the PRIN project ANONIMO, sponsored by the Italian Ministry of Education and University. The work by Elena Ferrari was partially supported by a Google Research Award.

7. REFERENCES

[1] B. Ali, W. Villegas, and M. Maheswaran. A trust based approach for protecting user data in social networks. In *Proceedings of the 2007 Conference of the Center for Advanced Studies on Collaborative research (CASCON'07)*, pages 288–293, 2007.

[2] M. M. Anwar, P. W. L. Fong, X.-D. Yang, and H. J. Hamilton. Visualizing privacy implications of access control policies in social network systems. In *4th International Workshop, DPM 2009 and Second International Workshop, SETOP 2009*, pages 106–120, 2009.

[3] D. Brickley and L. Miller. FOAF vocabulary specification. RDF Vocabulary Specification, July 2005.

[4] B. Carminati, E. Ferrari, R. Heatherly, M. Kantarcioglu, and B. Thuraisingham. A semantic web based framework for social network access control. In *SACMAT '09: Proceedings of the 14th ACM symposium on Access control models and technologies*, pages 177–186, New York, NY, USA, 2009. ACM.

[5] B. Carminati, E. Ferrari, M. Kantarcioglu, and B. Thuraisingham. *Privacy-Aware Knowledge Discovery: Novel Applications and New Techniques*, chapter Privacy protection of personal data in social networks. Chapman & Hall/CRC Data Mining and Knowledge Discovery Series, 2010.

[6] B. Carminati, E. Ferrari, and A. Perego. Enforcing access control in web-based social networks. *ACM Transactions on Information & System Security*, 13(1):1–38, 2009.

[7] J. Domingo-Ferrer, A. Viejo, F. Sebé, and I. González-Nicolás. Privacy homomorphisms for social networks with private relationships. *Comput. Netw.*, 52(15):3007–3016, 2008.

[8] N. Elahi, M. Chowdhury, and J. Noll. Semantic access control in web based communities. In *ICCGI '08: Proceedings of the 2008 The Third International Multi-Conference on Computing in the Global Information Technology (iccgi 2008)*, pages 131–136, Washington, DC, USA, 2008. IEEE Computer Society.

[9] J. Golbeck. *Computing and applying trust in Web-based social networks*. PhD thesis, Graduate School of the University of Maryland, College Park, 2005. Available at: http://trust.mindswap.org/papers/GolbeckDissertation.pdf.

[10] M. A. Harrison, W. L. Ruzzo, and J. D. Ullman. Protection in operating systems. *Commun. ACM*, 19(8):461–471, 1976.

[11] J. He, W. W. Chu, and Z. Liu. Inferring privacy information from social networks. In *IEEE International Conference on Intelligence and Security Informatics*, 2006.

[12] S. R. Kruk, S. Grzonkowski, A. Gzella, T. Woroniecki, and H. Choi. D-foaf: Distributed identity management with access rights delegation. In *Proc. of the 1st Asian Semantic Web Conference*, volume 4185 of *Lecture Notes in Computer Science*, pages 140–154. Springer, 2006.

[13] N. Li and M. V. Tripunitara. Security analysis in role-based access control. *ACM Trans. Inf. Syst. Secur.*, 9(4):391–420, 2006.

[14] A. McAfee. Enterprise 2.0: the dawn of emergent collaboration. *MITSloan Management Review*, 47(3), 2006.

[15] Y. Tim Oreill. What is web 2.0: Design patterns and business models for the next generation of software. *Social Science Research Network Working Paper Series*, 2003.

[16] W. H. Winsborough and N. Li. Safety in automated trust negotiation. *ACM Trans. Inf. Syst. Secur.*, 9(3):352–390, 2006.

[17] E. Zheleva and L. Getoor. To join or not to join: the illusion of privacy in social networks with mixed public and private user profiles. In *Proc. of the WWW Conference*, pages 531–540. ACM, 2009.

Detection of Anomalous Insiders in Collaborative Environments via Relational Analysis of Access Logs

You Chen
Department of Biomedical Informatics
School of Medicine
Vanderbilt University
Nashville, TN, USA 37203
you.chen@vanderbilt.edu

Bradley Malin
Department of Biomedical Informatics
School of Medicine
Vanderbilt University
Nashville, TN, USA 37203
b.malin@vanderbilt.edu

ABSTRACT

Collaborative information systems (CIS) are deployed within a diverse array of environments, ranging from the Internet to intelligence agencies to healthcare. It is increasingly the case that such systems are applied to manage sensitive information, making them targets for malicious insiders. While sophisticated security mechanisms have been developed to detect insider threats in various file systems, they are neither designed to model nor to monitor collaborative environments in which users function in dynamic teams with complex behavior. In this paper, we introduce a *community-based anomaly detection system* (CADS), an unsupervised learning framework to detect insider threats based on information recorded in the access logs of collaborative environments. CADS is based on the observation that typical users tend to form community structures, such that users with low affinity to such communities are indicative of anomalous and potentially illicit behavior. The model consists of two primary components: relational pattern extraction and anomaly detection. For relational pattern extraction, CADS infers community structures from CIS access logs, and subsequently derives communities, which serve as the CADS pattern core. CADS then uses a formal statistical model to measure the deviation of users from the inferred communities to predict which users are anomalies. To empirically evaluate the threat detection model, we perform an analysis with six months of access logs from a real electronic health record system in a large medical center, as well as a publicly-available dataset for replication purposes. The results illustrate that CADS can distinguish simulated anomalous users in the context of real user behavior with a high degree of certainty and with significant performance gains in comparison to several competing anomaly detection models.

Categories and Subject Descriptors

H.2.8 [**DATABASE MANAGEMENT**]: Database Applications—*Data mining*; K.6.5 [**MANAGEMENT OF**

COMPUTING AND INFORMATION SYSTEMS]: Security and Protection—*Unauthorized access*

General Terms

Algorithms, Experimentation, Security

Keywords

Privacy, Social Network Analysis, Data Mining, Insider Threat Detection

1. INTRODUCTION

Collaborative information systems (CIS) allow groups of users to communicate and cooperate over common tasks in a virtual environment. They have long been called upon to support and coordinate activities related to the domain of "computer supported and cooperative work" [6], but, until recently, CIS were primarily limited to specialized groupware tools. Recent breakthroughs in networking, storage, and processing have facilitated an explosion in the development and deployment of CIS over a wide range of environments. Beyond computational support, the adoption of CIS has been spurred on by the observation that such systems can increase organizational efficiency through streamlined workflows (e.g., [5]), shave administrative costs (e.g., [10]), assist innovation through brainstorming sessions (e.g., [15]), and facilitate social engagement (e.g., [42]). On the Internet, for instance, the notion of CIS is typified in wikis, video conferencing, document sharing and editing, as well as dynamic bookmarking [13].

At the same time, CIS are increasingly relied upon to manage sensitive information [17]. For instance, various intelligence agencies have adopted CIS environments to enable timely access and collaboration between groups of agents and analysts [31]. These systems contain increasingly large amounts of information on foreign, as well as national, citizens, related to personal relationships, financial transactions, and surveillance activities. The unauthorized passing of information in such systems to emerging whistle-blowing publication organizations, such as WikiLeaks, could be catastrophic to both the managing agency and the individuals to whom the information corresponds. Yet, perhaps the most significant CIS in modern society is the electronic health record (EHR) system [43]. Evidence indicates that the management of patient data in electronic form can decrease healthcare costs, strengthen care provider productivity, and increase patient safety [26]. As a result, the Obama administration has pledged over \$50 billion dollars to develop, network, and promote the adoption of EHRs.

Given the detail and sensitive nature of the information in emerging CIS, they are a prime target for adversaries originating from beyond, as well as within, the organizations that manage them. Numerous technologies have been developed to mitigate risks originating from outside of the CIS (e.g., [3, 32, 37, 44]). However, less attention has been directed toward the detection of insider threats. While there are some technologies that have been developed to safeguard information from insiders, including the many variants of access control to prevent exposures [2, 7, 11] as well as behavior monitoring tools to discover exposures [23, 29, 30, 36, 38], these are insufficient for emerging CIS. In particular, there are several key limitations of existing insider threat detection and prevention models that we wish to highlight. First, existing models tend to manage each user (or group) as an independent entity, which neglects the fact that CIS are inherently designed to support team-based environments. Second, security models work under the expectation of a static environment, where a user's role or their relationship to a team is well-defined. Again, CIS violate this principle because teams are often constructed on-the-fly, based on the shifting needs of the operation and the availability of the users.

In a CIS, a user's role and relationship to other users is dynamic and changes over time. As a result, it is difficult to differentiate between "normal" and "abnormal" actions in a CIS based on roles alone. To detect insider threats in a CIS we need to focus on the behavior of the users. More specifically, if we shift the focus to behavior, we need to decide upon which models of behavior to pursue. And, once a prospective set of models is defined, we need to determine which allow for sufficient detection of steady behavior. For this work, we work under the hypothesis that typical users within a CIS are likely to form and function as communities. As such, the likelihood that a user acting in an unpredicatable (or unexpected) manner will be characterized by these communities is low. Based on this hypothesis, we focus on the access logs of a CIS to mine relations of users and to model behavioral patterns.

The goal of this paper is to introduce a framework to detect anomalous insiders from the access logs of a CIS in a manner that leverages the relational nature and behavior of system users. The framework is called the community-based anomaly detection system (CADS). CADS leverages the fact that, in collaborative environments, users tend to be team-oriented. As a result, a user should be similar to other users based on their co-access of similar objects in the CIS. For example, in an EHR system, an arbitrary user should accesses similar sets of patients' records as other users because of commonalities in care pathways (or business operations), such that we can infer which groups of users tend to collaborate by their co-access patterns. This, in turn, should enable the establishment of user communities as a core set of representative patterns for the CIS. Then, given such patterns, CADS can predict which users are anomalous by measuring their distance to such communities.

The main contributions of this paper can be summarized as follows:

- **Relational Patterns from Access Logs:** We introduce a process to transform the access logs of a CIS into community structures using a combination of graph-based modeling and dimensionality reduction techniques.

- **Anomaly Detection from Relational Patterns:** We propose a technique, rooted in statistical formalism, to measure the deviation of users within a CIS from the extracted community structures.

- **Empirical Evaluation:** We utilize several datasets to systematically evaluate the effectiveness of CADS. First, we study five months of real world access logs from the the EMR system of the Vanderbilt University Medical Center, a large system that is well integrated to the everday functions of healthcare. In addition, to facilitate replication of this work, we report on an evaluation of CADS with a publicly available dataset of editorial board memberships in various journals. In lieu of annotated data, we simulate user behavior, and empirically demonstrate that CADS is more effective than existing anomaly detection approaches (e.g., [23] and [36]). Our analysis provides evidence that the typical system user is likely to join a community with other users, whereas the likelihood that a simulated user will join a community is very low.

The remainder of this paper is organized as follows. In Section 2, we present prior research related to this work, with a particular focus on access control and anomaly detection. In Section 3, we introduce the CADS framework and describe the specific community extraction and anomaly detection methods that were developed for the framework. In Section 4, we provide a detailed experimental analysis of our methods with several datasets and illustrate how various facets of user behavior influence the likelihood of detection. Finally, we summarize the findings, discuss the limitations, and propose next steps for extensions of this work in Sections 5 and 6.

2. RELATED WORK

The focus of this work is on the detection of insider threats and the mitigation of risk in exposing sensitive information. In general, there are two types of related security mechanisms that have been designed to address this problem. The first is to model and/or mine access rules to manage recourses of the system and its users. The second is to learn patterns of user behavior to detect anomalous insiders. In this section, we review prior research in these areas and relate them to the needs and challenges of CIS.

2.1 Access Control

Formal access control schemas are designed to specify how resources in a system are made available to users. There are a variety of access control models that have been proposed in the literature, some of which have been integrated into real working systems. Here, we review several that are notable with respect to CIS.

The *access matrix model* (AMM) is a conceptual framework that specifies each user's permissions for each object in the system [37]. Though AMM permits fine-grained mapping of access rights, there are several weaknesses of this framework with respect to CIS. First, it does not scale well, which makes it difficult to apply to CIS, which can contain on the order of thousands of users and millions of objects (e.g., Kaiser Permanente covers over 8 million patients in its healthcare network [9]). Second, the AMM framework lacks the ability to support dynamic changes of access rights.

Role-based access control (RBAC) is designed to simplify the allocation of access rights, by mapping users to roles and then mapping permissions to the roles [2, 32]. While computationally more tractable, the roles created in RBAC tend to be static. As such, they are inflexible and not responsive to the shifting nature of roles, or the allocation of users to rules, in CIS. There are no clear ways to update or evolve RBAC over time. Recently, there have been investigations into *role mining* [20, 27, 41], which attempts to automatically group users based on the similarity of their permissions, but it is currently unknown how such approaches scale or could be managed dynamically.

The *Task-based access control* (TBAC) model extends the traditional user-object relationship through the inclusion of task-based and contextual information [29, 40]. TBAC, however, is limited to contexts that relate to activities, tasks, or workflow progress. Collaborative systems require a much broader definition of context, and the nature of collaboration cannot always be easily partitioned into tasks associated with usage counts.

Team-based access control (TeBAC) appears to provide a more natural way of grouping users in an enterprise or organization and associating a collaboration context with the activity to be performed [11]. Yet, at the present moment, these models have not yet been fully developed or implemented, and it remains unclear how to incorporate the team concept into a dynamic framework.

2.2 Anomaly Detection

Anomaly detection techniques are designed to utilize patterns of system use or behavior to determine if any particular user is sufficiently different than expected. These techniques can be roughly categorized into supervised and unsupervised learning approaches.

In a supervised anomaly detection approach, a set of labeled training instances are provided. The labels are usually of the form "anomaly" and "non-anomaly", though any number of labels can be applied. The instances are then supplied to learn or parameterize a classification model based on the variable features of the instances. The resulting models are then applied to classify new actions into one (or more) of the labels. Examples of such approaches include support vector machines and Bayesian networks [4, 38]. Supervised models have been shown to have relatively high rates of performance for anomaly detection, however, they are limited in the context of CIS. This is because the key prerequisite (i.e., a clearly labeled training dataset) is difficult to generate for a CIS, particularly in the context of a dynamic and evolving environment. Additionally, it may not be clear what the "features" are that can be used to represent the instances.

By contrast, unsupervised anomaly detection approaches are designed to make use of the inherent structure, or patterns, in a dataset to determine when a particular instance is sufficiently different. There are numerous variants of unsupervised learning that have been applied to insider thread detection. Three types of unsupervised approaches, in particular, specifically relate to our work: 1) nearest neighbors, 2) clustering, and 3) spectral projection.

Nearest neighbor anomaly detection techniques [23, 39, 30] have been widely used and are related to the approach proposed in this paper. These approaches are designed to measure the distances between instances using features such as social structures. They determine how similar an instance is to other "close" instances. If the instance is not sufficiently similar, then it can be classified as an anomaly. However, social structures in a CIS are not explicitly defined, and need to be inferred from the utilization of system resources. If distance measurement procedures are not tuned to the way in which social structures have been constructed, the distances will not represent the structures well. In our experiments, we compare our model to a state-of-the-art nearest neighbor-based method. The results demonstrate that the social structure is crucial to the design of a distance measure.

A second approach is *Clustering* [19, 14], which is invoked to integrate similar data instances into groups. Methods for clustering depend on a distance measurement similar to that utilized in nearest neighbor methods. The key difference between the two techniques, however, is that clustering techniques evaluate each instance with respect to the cluster it belongs to, while nearest neighbor techniques analyze each instance with respect to its local neighborhood. The performance of clustering-based techniques is highly dependent on the effectiveness of clustering algorithms in capturing the structure of normal instances. If the clustering technique requires computation of the pairwise distance for all data instances, then techniques, such as that described in [16], can be quadratic in complexity, which may not be reasonable for real world applications. In collaborative environment, such as EHR, the system can have a large number of users, and there is no obvious social structure, which makes distance measurement and cluster calculation both complex and inappropriate.

A third unsupervised approach is based on spectral projection of the data. Shyu et al. [36], for instance, present a spectral anomaly detection model to estimate the principal components from the covariance matrix of the training data of "normal" events. The testing phase involves comparing each point with the components and assigning an anomaly score based on the point's distance from the principal components. The model can reduce noise and redundancy, however, collaborative systems are team-oriented, which can deteriorate performance of the model as we demonstrate experimentally (See Section 4).

3. CADS FRAMEWORK

In this section, we present the community-based anomaly detection system (CADS). To formalize the problem studied in this work, we will use the following notation. Let U be the set of users who are authorized to access records in the CIS. Let S be the set of subjects whose records exist in the CIS. And, let T be a database of access transactions captured by the CIS, such that $t \in T$ is a 3-tuple of the form $< u, s, time >$, where $u \in U = \{u_1, u_2, \ldots, u_n\}$, $s \in S = \{s_1, s_2, \ldots, s_m\}$, and $time$ is the date the user accessed the subject's record. In this paper, m is the number of subjects in collection, and n is the number of users.

We begin this section with a high-level view of the CADS framework. This will be followed by the specific empirical methods applied within the framework.

3.1 Overview of Framework

The CADS framework consists of two general components, as depicted in Figure 1. We refer to the two components

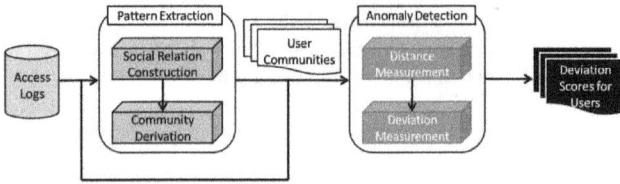

Figure 1: An overview of the community-based anomaly detection system (CADS).

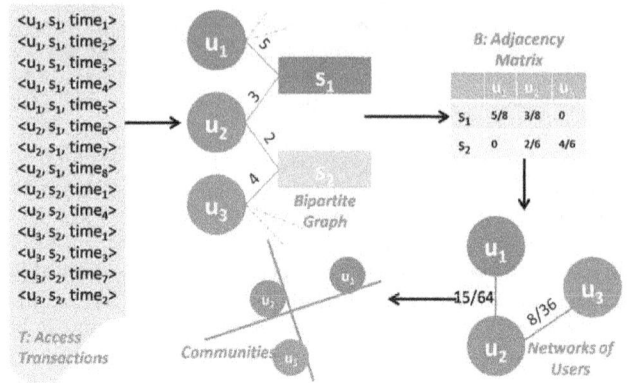

Figure 2: Process of community pattern extraction.

as 1) *Pattern Extraction* (CADS-PE), which feeds into 2) *Anomaly Detection* (CADS-AD).

In the CADS-PE component, the CIS access logs are mined for communities of users. One of the challenges of working with CIS access logs is their transactional nature. They do not report the social structure of the organization. Thus, it is necessary to transform the basic transactions into a data structure that facilitates the inference of social relations. The pattern extraction process in CADS-PE consists of a series of steps that result in a set of community patterns. First, the transactions are mapped onto a data structure that captures the relationships between users and subjects. Next, the structure is translated into a relational network of users. Then, the network is decomposed into a spectrum of patterns that models the user communities as probabilistic models.

In the CADS-AD component, the behaviors of the users in the CIS access logs are compared to the community patterns. Users that are found to deviate significantly from expected behavior, as prescribed by the patterns, are predicted as anomalous users. As in the CADS-PE component, the CADS-AD component consists of a process to translate access log transactions into scored events. First, each user is projected onto a subset of the resulting spectrum of communities. Next, the distance between the user and their closest neighbors in the communities is computed. In essence, the distance serves as the basis for a measure of deviance for each user from the derived community structures. The greater the deviance, the greater the likelihood that the user is an anomaly. The following section describes how each of these components is constructed in greater depth.

3.2 Community Pattern Extraction

The goal of the CADS-PE component is to model communities of users in the CIS. Since communities are not explicitly documented, CADS infers them from the relationships observed between users and subject's records in the CIS access logs. The community extraction process consists of three subcomponents: 1) user-subject network construction, 2) transformation to a user-user network, and 3) community inference.

3.2.1 Access Networks of Users and Subjects

The extraction process begins by mapping the transactions in T onto a bipartite graph. This graph is representative of the user-subject *access network*, such that users and subjects are modeled as vertices, and an edge represents the number of times that a user accessed the subject's record. Figure 2 depicts the translation of transactions into a bipartite graph of users and subjects.

We summarize the information in this graph in an adjacency matrix B of size $m \times n$ over an arbitrary time period

$[start, end]$, such that cell

$$B(i,j) = \frac{count(\langle u_j, s_i, time\rangle)}{\sum_{\forall u_k \in U} count(\langle u_k, s_i, time\rangle)} \quad (1)$$

where $count(\langle u_j, s_i, time\rangle)$ is the number of access transactions that appeared in the database during the $[start, end]$ period. The cells in this matrix are weighted according to inverse frequency; i.e., the importance of a subject's record is inversely proportionally to the number of users that access their record (e.g., subjects with 2 users contribute 0.5, and with 3 users contribute 0.33). In this way, subjects relate users proportionally to the rarity with which they are accessed [1].

3.2.2 Relational Networks of Users

The access network summarizes the frequency with which a user accesses a subject's record, but to infer communities we need to transform this data structure into one indicative of the relationships between the users. CADS achieves this by generating a user relationship network. This is represented by a matrix C of size $n \times n$, where cell $C(i,j)$ indicates the similarity of the access patterns of users u_i and u_j in B. To measure the similarity between users, we adopt an information retrieval metric $C = B^T B$, which was depicted in Figure 2. This matrix characterizes the magnitude of the distance between the sets of patients accessed by each pair of users. In general, this matrix represents the inferred relations of users in the CIS.

3.2.3 Community Inference via Spectral Analysis

While the C matrix contains the similarities between all pairs of users, it does not relate sets of users in the form of communities. Principal component analysis (PCA) has been used in earlier social network analysis studies to identify communities (e.g., [8, 28, 24, 33]). Most relevant to this work, [36] utilized PCA to build an intrusion detection model. Specifically, PCA was applied to "normal" training instances to build a model that was composed of the major and minor principal components. The model was then applied to measure the difference of an anomaly from normal instance via a distance measure based on the principal components. We will compare our model to [36], so we take a moment to illustrate how we do so. In terms of C, the goal is to find a basis P that is a linear combination of the n measurement types, such that $P \times C = Y$, where

$Y = [Y_1, Y_2, \ldots, Y_n]$. The rows of P are the principal components of C.[1]

In a collaborative environment, there are a large number of users and subjects, and, as our experiments illustrate (see Section 4), the C matrix tends to be extremely sparse. The general form of PCA does not scale well, so we use singular value decomposition (SVD), a special case of PCA, to infer communities of normal users. SVD is capable of handing large scale datasets and is particularly useful for sparse matrices [35]. Instead of capturing differences between users by via distances between all connected vertices in the network [36], we filter the network to retain only the nearest neighbors for each node. For an arbitrary node in the network, the nearest neighbors are discovered via a distance measure based on the principal component space.

For SVD, we define $Y' = (\sqrt{n-1})^{-1}C^T$. The covariance of Y' is calculated as $Y'Y'^T = ((\sqrt{n-1})^{-1}C^T)^T((\sqrt{n-1})^{-1}C^T)$, which is equal to $Cov = (n-1)^{-1}CC^T$. So, by applying SVD, C can be represented as $\omega \Lambda \upsilon^T$, where ω is an orthonormal matrix of size $n \times n$, Λ is a diagonal matrix of $n \times n$ with eigenvalues $\lambda_1, \lambda_2, ..., \lambda_n$ on the diagonal and values of zero elsewhere, and υ is an orthonormal matrix of size $n \times n$. The columns of υ are the principal components of C. The user relationship matrix C can be projected into the new space to generate a matrix $Z = \upsilon^T C$, where $Z_i = [Z_{i1}, Z_{i2}, ..., Z_{in}]$. This matrix can reveal the structure of the user communities. It is this set of communities that CADS uses as the basis of the anomaly detection.

Each row in matrix Z is the projection of all users on a principal component, or community. For example, the first row of Z corresponds to the projection of the users on the first principal component. We define the rate r as

$$\sum_{i=1}^{l} \lambda_i / \sum_{j=1}^{n} \lambda_j \ (l \prec n)$$

which demonstrates the degree that l principal components account for the original information. [35] showed that when r reaches a destination rate usually as 0.8, the selected l principal components can represent the original information with minimal information loss. Supposing selecting l components from n components r can be reached as a destination rate. In doing so, we truncate the set of communities, such that users are projected onto a subset $[Z_1, Z_2, ..., Z_l]$. The jth user can be presented as $(Z_{1j}, Z_{2j}, ..., Z_{lj})$.

The distance between a pair of users is calculated using a Euclidean distance function. Since each principal component Z_i in Z has a different "weight" in the form of the corresponding eigenvalue, λ_i should be applied to weight the components when computing the distance. We adopt a modified a Euclidean distance function to measure the distance

as follows.

$$Dis(u_i, u_j) = \sqrt{\sum_{q=1}^{l} ((Z_{qi} - Z_{qj})^2 \times \lambda_q / \lambda_{total})} \quad (2)$$

where

$$\lambda_{total} = \sum_{j=1}^{l} \lambda_j \quad (3)$$

. This measure provides more emphasis on the principal components that describe a greater amount of variance in the system. We use this distance measure to derive a matrix D of size $n \times n$. Cell $D(i, j)$ indicates the distance between u_i and u_j.

3.3 Community-Based Anomaly Detection

The goal of the CADS-AD component is to predict which users in the CIS are anomalous. We developed a process for CADS-AD that consists of two subcomponents 1) discover the nearest neighbors of each user via the CADS-PE community structures and 2) calculate the deviation of each user to their nearest neighbors.

3.3.1 Finding Nearest Neighbors

Let G_D be the graph described by matrix D. We need to find the k nearest neighbors for each user, but first we need determine the value of k. To do so, we used a measure known as *conductance*, which was designed for characterizing network quality [34, 18].

For this work, we define the *conductance* for a set of nodes A as $\psi(A) = N_A / min(Vol(A), Vol(V \setminus A))$, where N_A denotes the size of the edge boundary, $N_A = |(g, h) : g \in A, h \notin A|$, and $Vol(A) = \sum_{g \in A} d(g)$, where $d(g)$ is the degree of node g. Figure 3 depicts an example of a small cellular network. If we set the size of the cluster to 4 vertices, there are two clusters: α and β with *conductance* $\psi(\alpha) = 2/14, \psi(\beta) = 1/11$, respectively. Notice, $\psi(\alpha) > \psi(\beta)$, which implies that the set of vertices in β exhibits stronger community structure than the vertices in α.

To set k we use the network community profile (NCP), which is a measure of community quality. Building on the work in [22, 21], we define a NCP as a function of the community size. Specifically, for each value k, we compute $\phi(k) = min_{|A|=k}\psi(A)$. That is, for every possible community size k, NCP measures the score of the most community-like set of nodes of that size. When $\phi(k)$ reaches the minimum value, the correspond value of k will be assigned as the size of the communities.

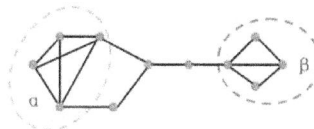

Figure 3: Example network with clusters α and β.

3.3.2 Measuring Deviation from Nearest Neighbors

The radius of a user d is defined as the distance to his k^{th} nearest neighbor. Every user can be assigned a radius value d by recording the distance to his k^{th} nearest neighbor. Users

---

[1] We define the covariance $Cov = (n-1)^{-1}CC^T$. The diagonal terms of Cov are the variance of particular measurement types. The off-diagonal terms of Cov are the covariance between measurement types. Cov captures the relationships between all possible pairs of measurements. The correlation values reflect the noise and redundancy in our measurements. In the diagonal terms, large values correspond to interesting communities; in the off diagonal terms, large values correspond to high redundancy. The principal components of C are the eigenvectors of CC^T, which are the rows of P.

can be characterized as a radius vector $d = [d_1, d_2, \ldots, d_n]$, and neighbors set knn_i. The smaller the radius, the higher the density of the user's network.

However, detecting anomalous users through radius is not sufficient. As shown in Figure 4, user q_2 and the users in cluster F are anomalous and can be detected via their radius. However, based on the radius of nodes, we cannot detect q_1 as an anomaly. Compared with nodes in area F, q_1 has a smaller radius, but it is anomalous. So we use deviation of the radius to calculate deviation of a node from its k nearest neighbors to detect q_1.

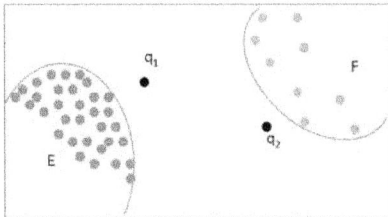

Figure 4: Illustration of different types of nodes in the neighborhood networks.

For a given user u_i, we calculate the deviation of the radius of the k nearest neighbors of the given user, including the user himself as follows:

$$Dev(u_i) = \sqrt{\sum_{u_j \in knn_i} (d_j - \bar{d})^2 / k} \qquad (4)$$

where

$$\bar{d} = \sum_{u_j \in knn_i} d_j / (k+1) \qquad (5)$$

Based on the measurement of radius deviation Dev, deviations of nodes in area E are nearly zero, and the deviation of node q_1 is larger. Normal users are likely to have smaller Dev, whereas anomalous users are likely to have higher Dev. Figure 5 is an example of deviation distribution on a real EHR data set (See Section 4). The figure shows that in a real system, most users have smaller deviations, such there are not many users with larger deviations.

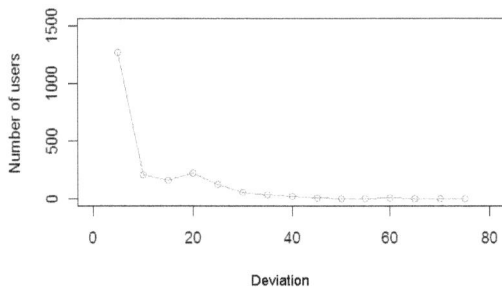

Figure 5: Distribution of user deviations on a real EHR data set

The deviation for every user can be assigned as $Dev = [Dev(u_1), Dev(u_2), \ldots, Dev(u_n)]$.

4. EXPERIMENTS

4.1 Anomaly Detection Models

As alluded to, there are alternative models to CADS that have been proposed in the literature. As such, we evaluate four models for anomaly detection.

- **High volume users:** This model serves as a baseline and uses a very simple rule to predict which user is anomalous. Fundamentally, this model ranks users based on the number of subjects accessed. The greater the number of subjects accessed, the higher the rank.

- **k-nearest neighbors (KNN):** [23] proposed an intrusion detection model based on the k-nearest neighbor principle. The approach first ranks a user's neighbors among the vectors of training users. It then uses the class labels of the k most similar neighbors to predict the class of the new user. The classes of these neighbors are weighted using the similarities of each neighbor to new user, which is measured by the cosine similarity of the vectors. For this work, we use the user vector in the B matrix in CADS. Each user is characterized by access records of m subjects. This model is then tested with a mix of real and simulated users as discussed below.

- **PCA:** [36] proposed an anomaly detection scheme based on a principal component classifier. The distance of a user is computed as the distance to known normal users in the system according to the weighted principal components. Again, we use B as the basis for training the system with the normal users and then evaluate the system with a mix of real and simulated users as discussed below.

- **CADS:** In essence, CADS is a hybrid of KNN and PCA. It utilizes SVD to infer communities from relational networks of users and KNN to establish sets of nearest neighbor. This model attempts to detect anomalous users by computing a users' deviation from their k nearest neighbors' networks.

4.2 Data Sets

We evaluate the anomaly detection models with two datasets. The first is a private dataset of real EHR access logs from a large academic medical center. The second is a public dataset and, though not representative of access logs, provides a dataset of social relationships for replication.

4.2.1 EHR Access Log Dataset

StarPanel is a longitudinal electronic patient chart developed and maintained by Department of Biomedical Informatics faculty working with staff in the Informatics Center of the Vanderbilt University Medical Center [12]. StarPanel is ideal for this study because it aggregates all patient data as fed into the system from any clinical domain and is the primary point of clinical information management. The user interfaces are Internet-accessible on the medical center's intranet and remotely accessible via the Internet. The system has been in operation for over a decade and is well-integrated into the daily patient care workflows and healthcare operations. In all, the EHR stores over 300,000,000 observations on over 1.5 million patient records.

We analyze the access logs of 6 months from the year 2006. The access network in this dataset is very sparse. For example, in an arbitrary week, there are $35,531$ patients, $2,377$ users and $66,441$ access transactions. In other words, only $66,441/(34,431 \times 2,377)$, or 0.07% of the possible user-patient edges were observed.[2]

For this dataset, we evaluate the anomaly detection models on a weekly basis, and report on the average performance. We refer to this as the EHR dataset.

4.2.2 Public Relational Network Dataset

We recognize that using a private dataset makes it difficult to replicate and validate our results. Thus, we supplement our study with an analysis on a publicly available dataset.

This dataset was initially studied in [25] and reports the editorial board memberships for a set of journals in a similar discipline (biomedical informatics) over the years 2000 to 2005.[3] It contains $1,245$ editors and 49 journals. In our experiments, we treated the editors as users, and the journals as subjects. For this dataset, we evaluate the anomaly detection models on the complete dataset and report on the performance. We refer to this as the Editor dataset.

4.3 Simulation of Users

One of the challenges of working with real data from an operational setting is that it is unknown if there are anomalies in the dataset. Thus, to test the performance of the anomaly detection models, we designed an evaluation process that mixes simulated users with the real users of the aforementioned datasets. We worked under the assumption that an anomalous user would not exhibit steady behavior. We believe that such behavior is indicative of the record access behavior committed by users that have accessed patient records for malicious purposes, such as identity theft.

The evaluation is divided into three types of settings:

Sensitivity to Number of Records Accessed: The first setting investigates how the number of subjects accessed by a simulated user influences the extent to which the user can be predicted as anomalous. In this case, we mix a lone simulated user into the set of real users. The simulated user accesses a set of randomly selected subjects, the size of which ranges from 1 to $1,000$ in the EHR dataset and from 1 to 20 in the Editor dataset.

Sensitivity to Number of Anomalous Users: The second setting investigates how the number of simulated users influences the rate of detection. In this case, we vary the number of simulated users from 0.5% to 5% of the total number of users, which we refer to as the mix rate(e.g. 5% implies 5 out of 100 users are simulated). Each of the simulated users access an equivalent-sized set of random subjects' records.

Sensitivity to Diversity: The third setting investigates a more diverse environment. In this case, we set the mix rate of simulated and the total number of users as 0.5% and 5%. And, in addition, we allow the number of patients accessed by the simulated users to range from 1 to $1,000$ in the EHR dataset and from 1 to 20 in Editor dataset.

---

[2]The sparseness enabled us to utilize an adjacency list to construct the user-patient and user-user matrices to reduce memory consumption and time calculation.
[3]This dataset can be downloaded from http://hiplab.mc.vanderbilt.edu/bmiEdBoards.

4.4 Tuning the Neighborhood Parameter

Both the KNN and CADS model incorporate a parameter that limits the number of users to compare to for an arbitrary user. We tuned this parameter for each of the datasets empirically.

In the EHR dataset, we calculate the network community profile (NCP) for the user networks. The result is depicted in Figure 6, where we observed that NCP is minimized at 50 neighbors. For illustrative purposes, we show the network in Figure 7 that results from a selection of 50 users from an arbitrary week of the study to their 50 nearest neighbors.

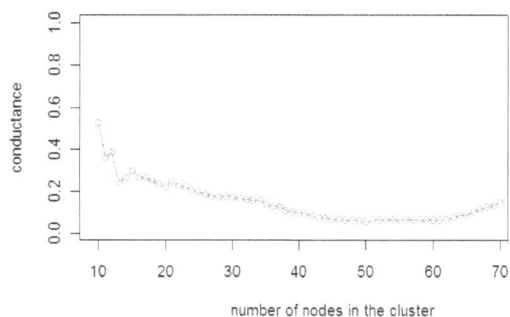

Figure 6: The NCP plot of network in the EHR dataset.

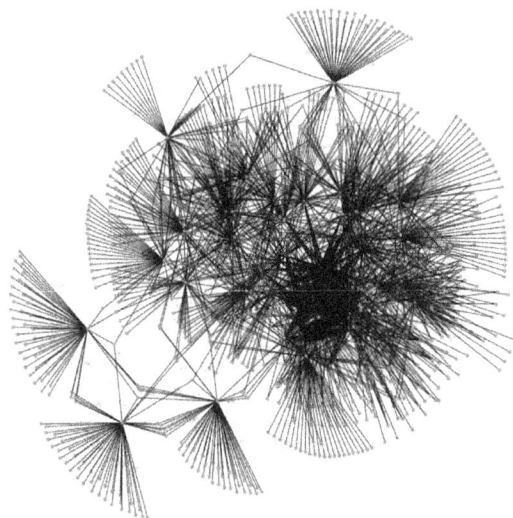

Figure 7: The 50-nearest neighbor network for fifty users in an arbitrary week of the EHR dataset.

In contrast, we find the NCP in the Editor dataset was minimized at 18 neighbors. This is smaller than the value for the Editor dataset and highlights its sensitivity to the network being studied. For instance, for the NCP dataset, we suspect this decrease in the value is because the number of users and size of the user network is smaller in the Editor dataset.

4.5 Results

4.5.1 Random Number of Accessed Patients

The first set of experiments focus on the sensitivity of CADS. To begin, we mixed a single simulated user with the real users. We varied the number of subjects accessed by the simulated user to investigate how volume impacts the CADS deviation score and the performance of the anomaly detection models in general. For illustration, the CADS deviation scores for the simulated users in the EHR and Editor datasets are summarized in Figure 8.

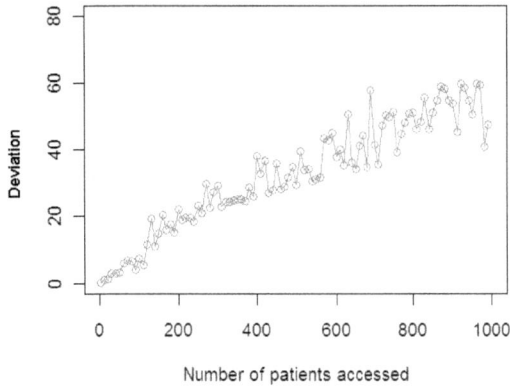

(a) EHR

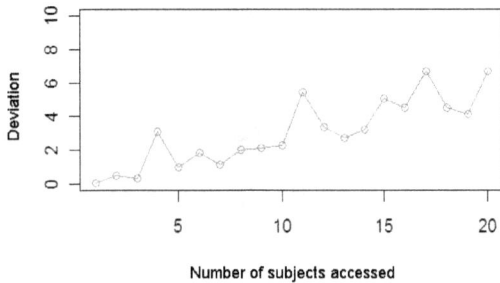

(b) Editor

Figure 8: CADS deviation score of the simulated user as a function of number of subjects accessed.

Notice that as the number of the subjects accessed by the users increases, so too does the deviation score. Note, the magnitude of the deviation score is significantly larger in the EHR dataset, which is because the number of subjects accessed by the simulated users is much greater (i.e., from 1 to 1,000 vs. 1 to 20). The observation that the deviation score tends to increases with the number of subjects accessed is what suggests why an organization might be tempted to utilize an anomaly detection model based on high volume accesses.

Next, we need to determine when the CADS deviation score is sufficiently large to detect the simulated user in the context of the real users. In Figure 9, we show how the

number of subjects accessed by a simulated user influences the performance of CADS. We find that when the number of accessed subjects for the simulated user is small, it is difficult for CADS to discover the user via the largest deviation score. This is not unexpected because CADS is an evidence-based framework. It needs to accumulate a certain amount of evidence before it can determine that the actions of the user are not the result of noise in the system. As the number of subjects accessed increases, however, so too does the performance of CADS. And, by the time number of accessed subjects is greater than 100 in the EHR dataset (Figure 9(a)) and 10 in the Editor dataset (Figure 9(b)), the simulated user can be detected with very high precision.

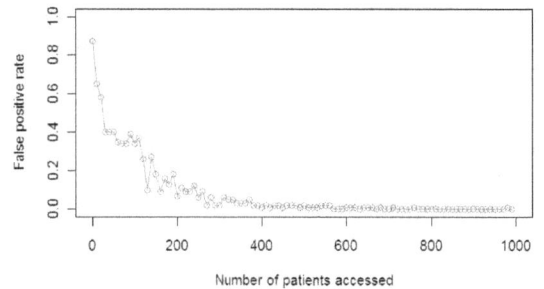

(a) EHR

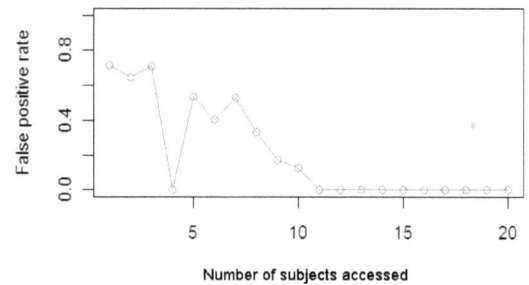

(b) Editor

Figure 9: Rate of detection of the simulated user via the largest CADS deviation score as a function of the number of patients accessed.

4.5.2 Random Number of Simulated Users

In order to verify how the number of simulated users influences the performance of CADS, we conducted several experiments when the number of simulated users was randomly generated. In these experiments, the number of subjects accessed by the simulated users was fixed at 100 in the EHR dataset and 5 in the Editor dataset. The mix rates of simulated users and the total number of users were set from 0.5% to 5%. The average true and false positive rates for CADS are depicted in Figure 10.

The figures show that when the number of simulated users increases, CADS achieves a higher area under the ROC curve (AUC). In the previous experiment, the number of simulated

(a) EHR

(b) Editor

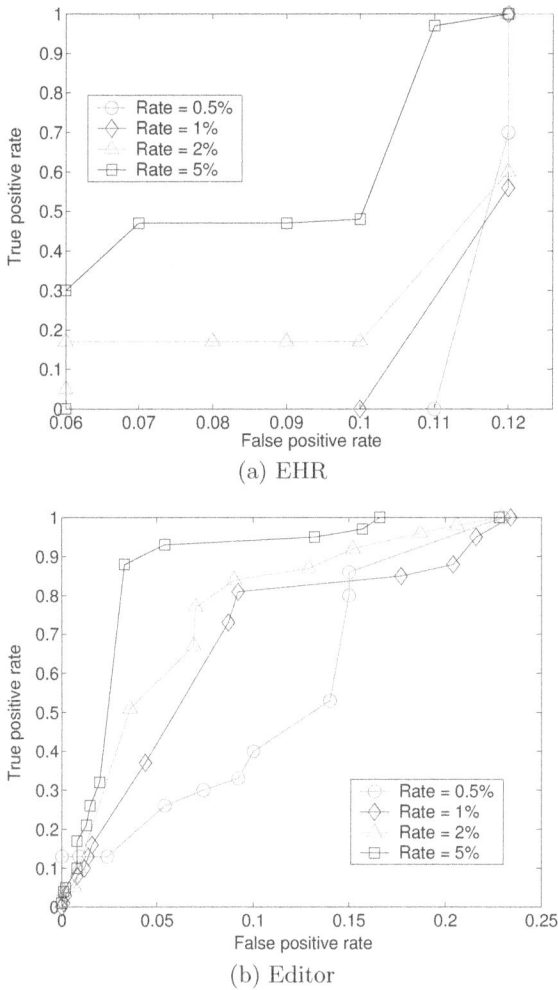

Figure 10: CADS performance with various mix rates of simulated and real users.

users is only one, so the false positive rates in Figure 9 is a little high.

4.5.3 Random Number of Simulated User and Accessed Patients

In this experiment, we simulated a more realistic environment to compare all four of the anomaly detection models. Specifically, we allowed both the number of simulated users and the number of patients accessed by the simulated users to vary. For each week, we constructed four test datasets. The mix rate between simulated users and the total number of users in each dataset was set as 0.5% and 5%. Additionally, the number of accessed subjects for each simulated user was selected at random.

The results are depicted in Figures 11 and 12. It can be seen that CADS exhibits the best performance of simulated user detection (according to AUC). At the lowest mix rate, CADS was almost two times more accurate at the most specific tuning level. Moreover, CADS is only marginally affected by the mix rate, whereas the other approaches are much more sensitive.

The results for the Editor dataset set are nearly the same as the EHR dataset, except for the high volume model. In

the Editor dataset, the high volume model achieves very high performance. We believe that the reason why high volume models achieve better in the Editor dataset is because the majority of real editors are related to only 1 or 2 journals each, whereas the majority of simulated editors are related to more than 2. Nonetheless, we find that the performance of CADS is competitive with the high volume model, while the PCA and KNN models are outperformed.

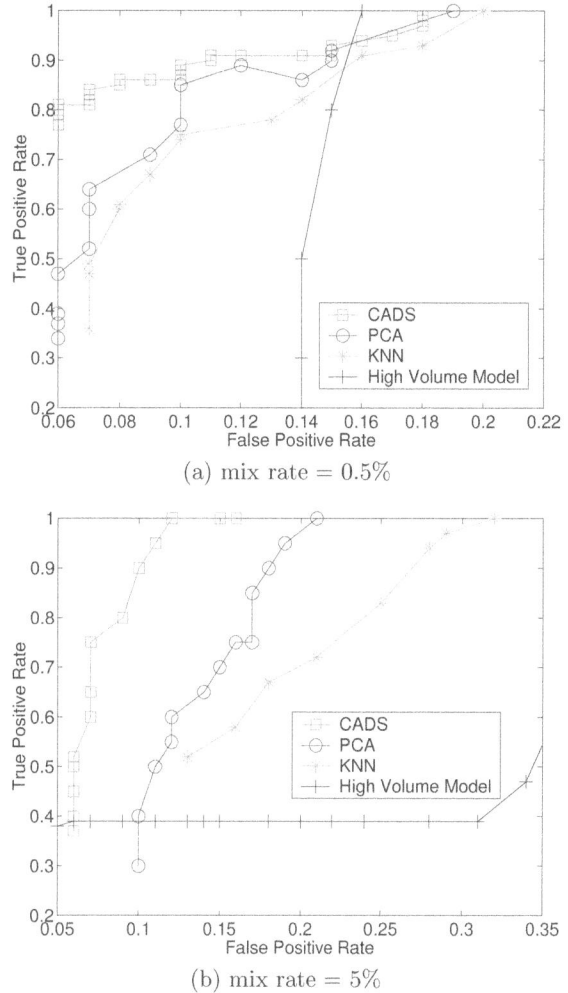

(a) mix rate = 0.5%

(b) mix rate = 5%

Figure 11: Comparison of different anomaly detection methods on the EHR dataset. The number of accessed subjects for simulated user is random.

Figure 13 depicts the CADS deviation score for simulated users as a function of the number of subjects accessed in the EHR dataset. The trend illustrates that the deviation score increases with the number of patients accessed. However, by returning to Figures 11, it can be seen that the performance of the high volume model in this setting is poor. This is because the CADS deviation score is small for many of the real users that accessed a large number of patients. As a result, if an administrator was to use a high volume model to detect anomalous insiders, it could lead to a very high false positive rate.

Figure 14 shows the distribution of subjects accessed per real user in an arbitrary week of the EHR dataset. Notice

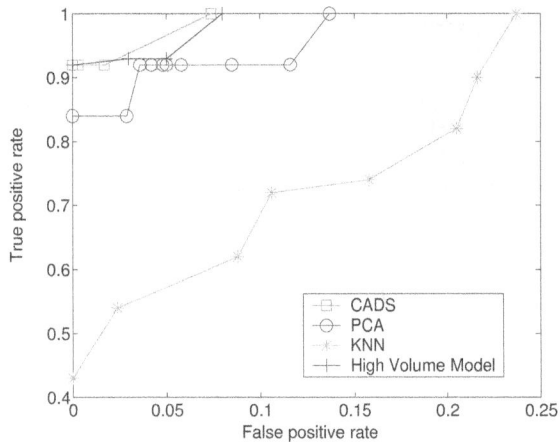

(a) mix rate = 0.5%

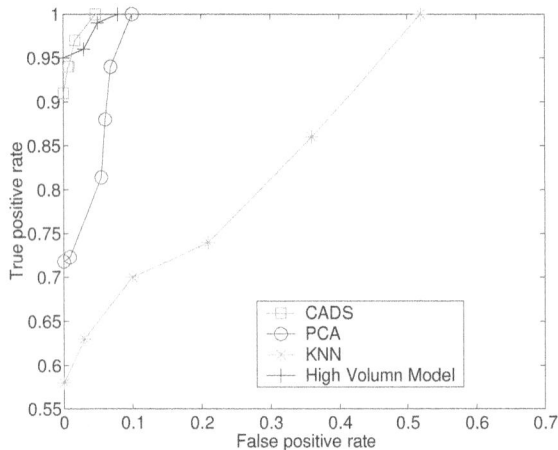

(b) mix rate = 5%

Figure 12: Comparison of different anomaly detection methods on the Editor dataset. The number of accessed subjects for simulated user is random.

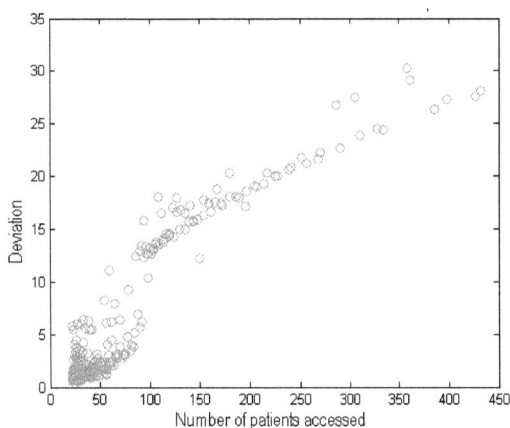

Figure 13: Deviation score of simulated users as a function of number of subjects accessed for the EHR dataset.

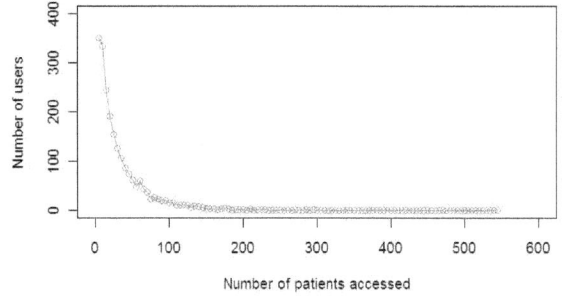

Figure 14: Number of patients accessed by real EHR users in an arbitrary week.

that the majority of users accessed less than 100 patients. However, there are also many simulated users that accessed less than 100 subjects' records (Figure 13). CADS can distinguish these simulated users from the real users with high performance. This is because, as we hypothesized, real users tend to form communities with a high probability, whereas the simulated users are more dispersed.

5. DISCUSSION

To detect anomalous insiders in a CIS, we proposed CADS, a community-based anomaly detection model that utilizes a relational analytic framework. CADS inferred communities from the relationships observed between users and subject's records in the CIS access logs. To predict which users are anomalous, CADS calculates deviation of users based on their nearest neighbor's networks. To investigate the flexibility and performances of CADS, we simulated anomalous users and performed evaluations with respect to the number of simulated users in the sysem and the number of records accessed by the user. Furthermore, we compared CADS with other three models: PCA, KNN and high volume users. The experimental findings suggest that when the number of users and complexity of the social networks in the CIS are low, very simple models of anomaly detection, such as high volume user detection, may be sufficient. But, as the complexity of the system grows tools that model complex behavior, tools such as CADS, are certainly necessary.

CADS blends the basis of both PCA and KNN and our empirical findings suggest that the former is significantly better at detecting anomalies than either of the latter. In part, this is because PCA and KNN capture different aspects of the problem. PCA is adept at reducing noise and revealing hidden (or latent) structure in a system, whereas KNN is for detecting overlapping neighborhoods with complex structure.

There are several limitations of this study that wish to point out, which we believe can serve as a guidebook for future research on this topic. First, our results are a lower bound on the performance of the anomaly detection methods evaluated in this paper. This is because in complex collaborative environments, such as EHR systems, we need to evaluate the false positives with real humans, such as the privacy and administrative officials of the medical center. It is possible that the false positives we reported were, in fact, malicious users. This is a process that we have initiated with officials and believe it will help tune the anomaly detection approach further via expert feedback.

Second, this work did not incorporate additional semantics that are often associated with users and subjects that could be useful in constructing more meaningful patterns. For instance, the anomaly detection framework could use the "role" or "departmental affiliation" of the EHR users to construct more specific models about the users. Similarly, we could use the "diagnoses" or "treatments performed" for the patients to determine if clinically-related groups of patients are accessed in similar ways. We intend to analyze the impact of such information in the future, but point out that the goal of the current work was to determine how the basic information in the access logs could assist in anomaly detection. We are encouraged by the results of our initial work and expect that such semantics will only improve the system.

Third, in this paper, we set the size of the communities to the users' k nearest neighbors, but we assumed that k was equivalent for each user in the system. However, it is known that the size of communities and local networks can be variable [22]. As such, in future work, we intend on parameterizing such models based on local, rather than global, observations.

Finally, the CADS model aims to detect anomalous insiders, but this is only one type of anomalous insiders. As a result, CADS may be susceptible to mimicry if an adversary has the ability to game the system by imitating group behavior or the behavior of another user. Moreover, there are many different types of anomalies in collaborative systems, each of which depends on the perspective and goals of the administrators. For instance, models could be developed to search for anomalies at the level of individual accesses or sequences of events. We aim to design models to detect various types of anomalies in the future.

6. CONCLUSIONS

In this paper, we proposed CADS, an unsupervised model based on social network analysis to detect anomalous insiders in collaborative environments. Our model assumed that "normal" users are likely to form clusters, while anomalous users are not. The model consists of two parts: pattern extraction and anomaly detection. In order to evaluate the performance of our model, we conducted a series of experiments and compared CADS with other established anomaly detection models In the experiments, we mixed simulated users with into systems of real users and evaluated the anomaly detection models on two types of access logs: 1) a real electronic health record system (EHR) and 2) a publicly-available set of editorial board memberships for various journals. Our results illustrate that CADS exhibited the highest performance at detecting simulated insider threats. Our empirical studies indicate that the CADS model performs best in complex collaborative environments, especially in EHR systems, in which users are team-oriented and dynamic. Since CADS is an unsupervised learning system, we believe it may be implemented in real time environments without training. There are limitations of the system; however, and in particular, we intend to validate and improve our system with adjudication through real human experts.

7. ACKNOWLEDGMENTS

The authors thank Dario Giuse for supplying the EHR access logs, and Steve Nyemba for preprocessing the logs, studied in this paper. The authors would also like to thank Erik Boczko, Josh Denny, Carl Gunter, David Liebovitz, and the members of the Vanderbilt Health Information Privacy Laboratory for thoughtful discussion on the topics addressed in this paper. This research was sponsored by grants CCF-0424422 and CNS-0964063 from the National Science Foundation and 1R01LM010207 from the National Library of Medicine, National Institutes of Health.

8. REFERENCES

[1] L. Adamic and E. Adar. Friends and neighbors on the web. *Social Networks*, 25:211–230, 2003.

[2] G. Ahn, D. Shin, and L. Zhang. Role-based privilege management using attribute certificates and delegation. In *Proceedings of the International Conference on Trust and Privacy in Digital Business*, pages 100–109, 2004.

[3] G. Ahn, L. Zhang, D. Shin, and B. Chu. Authorization management for role-based collaboration. In *Proceedings of IEEE International Conference on System, Man and Cybernetic*, pages 4128–4214, 2003.

[4] D. Barbara, N. Wu, and S. Jajodia. Detecting novel network intrusions using Bayes estimators. In *Proceedings of the 1st SIAM International Conference on Data Mining*, 2001.

[5] V. Bellotti and S. Bly. Walking away from the desktop computer: distributed collaboration and mobility in a product design team. In *Proceedings of the 1996 ACM Conference on Computer Supported Cooperative Work*, pages 209–218, 19996.

[6] F. Benaben, J. Touzi, V. Rajsiri, and H.Pingaud. Collaborative information system design. In *Proceedings of International Conference of the Association Information and Management*, pages 281–296, 2006.

[7] A. Bullock and S. Benford. An access control framework for multi-user collaborative environments. In *Proceedings of the ACM SIGGROUP Conference on Supporting Group Work*, pages 140–149, 1999.

[8] A. Chapanond, M. Krishnamoorthy, and B. Yener. Graph theoretic and spectral analysis of Enron email data. *Computational and Mathematical Organization Theory*, 11:265–281, 2005.

[9] R. Charette. Kaiser Permanente marks completion of its electronic health records implementation. *IEEE Spectrum*, March 8 2010.

[10] L. Eldenburg, N. Soderstrom, V. Willis, and A. Wu. Behavioral changes following the collaborative development of an accounting information system. *Accounting, Organizations and Society*, 35(2):222–237, 2010.

[11] C. Georgiadis, I. Mavridis, G. Pangalos, and R. Thomas. Flexible team-based access control using contexts. In *Proceedings of ACM Symposium on Access Control Model and Technology*, pages 21–27, 2001.

[12] D. Giuse. Supporting communication in an integrated patient record system. In *Proceedings of the 2003 American Medical Informatics Association Annual Symposium*, page 1065, 2003.

[13] T. Gruber. Collective knowledge systems: where the social web meets the semantic web. *Journal of Web Semantics*, 6(1):4–13, 2007.

[14] Z. He, X. Xu, and S. Deng. Discovering cluster-based local outliers. *Pattern Recognition Letters*, 24(9-10):1641 – 1650, 2003.

[15] C. Huang, T. Li, H. Wang, and C. Chang. A collaborative support tool for creativity learning: Idea storming cube. In *Proceedings of the 2007 IEEE International Conference on Advanced Learning Technologies*, pages 31–35, 2007.

[16] J.A.Hartigan and M.A.Wong. A k-means clustering algorithm. *Appl. Stat*, 28:104–108, 1979.

[17] S. Javanmardi and C. Lopes. Modeling trust in collaborative information systems. In *Proceedings of the 2007 International Conference on Collaborative Computing: Networking, Applications and Worksharing*, pages 299–302, 2007.

[18] R. Kannan, S. Vempala, and A. Vetta. On clusterings: Good, bad and spectral. *Journal of the ACM*, 51(3):497–515, 2004.

[19] T. Kohonen. Self-organizing maps. *Springer Series in Information Sciences*, 78(9):1464 – 1480, 1997.

[20] M. Kuhlmann, D. Shohat, and G. Schimpf. Role mining-revealing business roles for security administration using data mining technology. In *Proceedings of the 8th ACM Symposium on Access Control Models and Technologies*, pages 179–186, 2003.

[21] J. Leskovec, K. Lang, A. Dasgupta, and M. Mahoney. Statistical properties of community structure in large social and information networks. In *Proceedings of the 17th International Conference on World Wide Web*, pages 695–704, 2008.

[22] J. Leskovec, K. J. Lang, A. Dasgupta, and M. W. Mahoney. *Community Structure in Large Networks: Natural Cluster Sizes and the Absence of Large Well-Defined Clusters*. Computing Research Repository, abs/0810.1355, 2008.

[23] Y. Liao and V. R. Vemuri. Use of k-nearest neighbor classifier for intrusion detection. *Computer Security*, 21(5):439–448, 2002.

[24] H. Liu. Social network profiles as taste performances. *Journal of Computer-Mediated Communication*, 13:252–275, 2008.

[25] B. Malin and K. Carley. A longitudinal social network analysis of the editorial boards of medical informatics and bioinformatics journals. *Journal of the American Medical Informatics Association*, 14(3):340–347, 2007.

[26] N. Menachemi and R. Brooks. Reviewing the benefits and costs of electronic health records and associated patient safety technologies. *Journal of Medical Systems*, 30(3):159–168, 2008.

[27] I. Molloy, H. Chen, T. Li, Q. Wang, N. Li, E. Bertino, S. Calo, and J. Lobo. Mining roles with semantic meanings. In *Proceedings of the 13th ACM Symposium on Access Control Models and Technologies*, pages 21–30, 2008.

[28] J. Neville, M. Adler, and D. Jensen. Clustering relational data using attribute and link information. In *Proceedings of the IJCAI Text Mining and Link Analysis Workshop*, 2003.

[29] J. Park, R. Sandhu, and G. Ahn. Role-based access control on the web. *ACM Transactions on Information and System Security*, 4(1):37–71, 2001.

[30] D. Pokrajac, A. Lazarevic, and L. Latecki. Incremental local outlier detection for data streams. In *Proceedings of the IEEE Symposium on Computational Intelligence and Data Mining*, pages 504–515, 2007.

[31] R. Popp. Countering terrorism through information technology. *Communications of the ACM*, 47(3):36–43, 2004.

[32] R. Sandhu, E. Coyne, H. Feinstein, and C. Youman. Role-based access control models. *IEEE Computer*, 29(2):38–47, 1996.

[33] P. Sarkar and A. Moore. Dynamic social network analysis using latent space models. *ACM SIGKDD Explorations*, 7:31–40, 2005.

[34] J. Shi and J. Malik. Normalized cuts and image segmentation. *IEEE Transcations of Pattern Analysis and Machine Intelligence*, 22(8):888–905, 2002.

[35] J. Shlens. *A Tutorial on Principal Component Analysis*. Institute for Nonlinear Science, University of California at San Diego, 2005.

[36] M. Shyu, S. Chen, K. Sarinnapakorn, and L. Chang. A novel anomaly detection scheme based on principal component classifier. In *IEEE Foundations and New Directions of Data Mining Workshop*, pages 172–179, 2003.

[37] K. Sikkel. A group-based authorization model for cooperative systems. In *Proceedings of ACM Conference on Computer-Supported Cooperative Work*, pages 345–360, 1997.

[38] Q. Song, W. Hu, and W. Xie. Robust support vector machine with bullet hole image classification. *IEEE Transactions on Systems, Man, and Cybernetics*, 32(4):440–448, 2002.

[39] J. Tang, Z. Chen, A. Fu, and D. Cheung. Enhancing effectiveness of outlier detections for low density patterns. In *Proceedings of the Pacific-Asia Conference on Knowledge Discovery and Data Mining*, pages 535–7548, 2002.

[40] R. Thomas and S. Sandhu. Task-based authorization controls (tbac): A family of models for active and enterprise-oriented autorization management. In *Proceedings of the IFIP 11th International Conference on Database Security*, pages 166–181, 1997.

[41] J. Vaidya, V. Atluri, and J. Warner. Roleminer: mining roles using subset enumeration. In *Proceedings of the 13th ACM Conference on Computer and Communications Security*, pages 144–153, 2006.

[42] L. von Ahn. Games with a purpose. *IEEE Computer*, pages 96–98, 2006.

[43] M. von Korff, J. Gruman, J. Schaefer, S. Curry, and E. Wagner. Collaborative management of chronic illness. *Annals of Internal Medicine*, 127(12):1097–1102, 1997.

[44] L. Zhang, G. Ahn, and B. Chu. A rule-based framework for role-based delegation and revocation. *ACM Transactions on Information and System Security*, 6(3):404–441, 2003.

LeakProber: A Framework for Profiling Sensitive Data Leakage Paths

Junfeng Yu
College of computer science
and Technology, Huazhong
University of Science and
Technology, Wuhan, China
College of Information
Sciences and Technology
Pennsylvania State University
University Park
jfengyu@gmail.com

Shengzhi Zhang
Department of Computer
Science and Engineering
Pennsylvania State University
University Park
suz116@psu.edu

Peng Liu
College of Information
Sciences and Technology
Pennsylvania State University
University Park
pliu@ist.psu.edu

Zhitang Li
College of computer science
and Technology, Huazhong
University of Science and
Technology, Wuhan, China
leeying@mail.hust.edu.cn

ABSTRACT

In this paper, we present the design, implementation, and evaluation of LeakProber, a framework that leverages the whole system dynamic instrumentation and the inter-procedural analysis to enable data propagation path profiling in the production system. We integrate both the static analysis and runtime tracking to establish a holistic and practical approach to generating the sensitive data propagation graph (sDPG) with minimum runtime overhead. We evaluate our system on several data stealing attacks scenario for generating sDPG. The sDPG generated by our system captures multiple aspects of data accessing patterns and provides clear insights into the data leakage path. We also measure the performance of our system and find that it degrades the production system about 6% in the trace-on mode. When our prototype works in the trace-off mode, the runtime overhead is even lower, on an average of 1.5% across each benchmark we run. We believe that it is feasible to directly apply our prototype into production system environment.

Categories and Subject Descriptors

D.4.6 [**OPERATING SYSTEMS**]: Security and Protection—*Information flow controls*

General Terms

Reliability, Security

Keywords

Data Flow Analysis, Dynamic Instrumentation, Data Leakage

1. INTRODUCTION

Nowadays, enterprise data leakage or loss becomes an increasingly critical and challenging problem for system administrators to handle with. The reasons are at least threefold. First, data generally represents the most valuable asset for enterprise and organizations. Any leakage of the data or information may incur significant financial loss to the enterprise, and bring commercial benefits to the attackers. Second, as the bloom of the information sharing, data access is not only restricted to the legitimate customers and partners, but also allowed to some outsiders who might be potentially malicious. Last, the data stealing from outsiders and the abuse of insiders (either intentional or unintentional) have rendered most traditional security approaches (IDS, firewall) ineffective. With the further investigation of the data leakage problem, we believe that the key to tackle this issue is to audit how the sensitive data is processed on the production system, and distinguish legitimate processing flow with malicious processing flow. The auditing and differentiation of the sensitive data processing flow are always quite difficult, since the sensitive data are often processed by many different components, e.g., operating system kernel, device driver modules, system libraries, applications, etc.

To the authors' best knowledge, information flow auditing approach [24, 34, 20] has been proposed to solve the sensitive data leakage problem. RESIN [34] allows the programmer to specify application level data flow assertion explicitly and use language runtime to keep track of assertions as the data flow through the application. PQL (Program Query Language) [20] allows developers to describe a large class of application specific code patterns, and integrates both the static checker and dynamic checker to find and repair numerous security and resource management errors in open source applications. Although these approaches pioneer the information flow regulation policies for web applications with minimum runtime overhead, it is required that the web applications be written in special type-safe programming languages. Moreover, without tracing the whole system information flow across programs' boundary, these approaches could not catch some subtle stealing paths that an attacker might trigger at runtime.

Another alternative approach is to trace data flow information via dynamic instrumentation [26, 30, 15, 16, 33, 37]. TaintCheck [26] can dynamically trace the data propagation at the fine-grained granularity, but the runtime overhead introduced by binary instrumentation restricts it as an offline analysis system. Optimizations have been proposed in [28] to reduce the performance overheads of early dynamic tracking systems, but further performance improvement is still highly desired for the online deployment into the production systems. In contrast, hardware-based information tracking [29] can in most cases eliminate the runtime overhead related to the software-based information tracking with an almost acceptable overhead 23%. However, the required support on hardware hinders the wide deployment of such system.

In this paper, we present LeakProber, a system that allows us to track the propagation of sensitive data at the function granularity on the production system. LeakProber produces a systemic sensitive data propagation graph that pinpoints the profiles of the sensitive data leakage path. The sensitive data path profiles not only help the enterprise system administrators to find out the data leakage vectors but also are quite valuable for most anomaly detection algorithms that detect data stealing attacks against applications. For instance, existing anti-rootkit tools, e.g., [32, 27], can benefit with the prior knowledge of the attacked process provided by LeakProber.

To overcome the limitations of existing approaches, our prototype system integrates both static and runtime tracking to establish a holistic and practical approach to generating the sensitive data propagation graph (sDPG) with minimum runtime overhead. Our key idea is based on the observation that the sensitive data is processed by only a small portion of routines in system software stack and should follow certain accessing patterns. Thus, if we can extract sensitive data accessing patterns and sensitive data propagation paths at runtime, it is possible to highlight the abnormal data leakage path through a visualized data flow graph.

We develop a model to represent the sensitive data path with dynamic data and procedure as nodes, and dependency relations as routes between nodes. The path also indicates the information flow from one variable to the other due to the semantic effects of corresponding subroutine calls. We extend the kernel instrumentation infrastructure, kprobe [21] and uprobe [7], to achieve the whole system data flow tracking. Our prototype system can be easily loaded into kernel on demand without recompiling or restarting either kernel or applications. It does not require any changes to the application source code or binary code, thus the probe functionality is totally removed when the kernel module is disabled. This is particularly important in the production system because shutting down the system is not a viable option for removing the undesired functionality.

Our approach integrates a static preprocessing phase that identifies potential routine/data accessing summary relations and helps to achieve a semi-automatic probe points analysis. By combination of summary relation extracted by preprocessing phase and functional granularity trace events at runtime, the generated sensitive data propagation graph is more accurate than existing system-wide information flow tracking systems [30, 26, 28]. Furthermore, static preprocessing phase also provides an alternative instrumentation mechanism that allows user to specify sensitive data source and audits only relevant procedures possibly involved in the sensitive data accessing. With this optimization, we avoid inserting unnecessary instrumentation points among procedures without sensitive data accessing, which significantly reduces the runtime overhead.

To demonstrate the effectiveness of our approach, we evaluate LeakProber by generating the sensitive data propagation graph for real world applications. The sDPG generated by our prototype captures multiple aspects of data accessing patterns and provides clear insights into the data leakage path. We also measure the performance of our prototype and find that it degrades the production system about 6% in the trace-on mode. When our prototype works in the trace-off mode, the runtime overhead is even lower, on an average of 1.5% across each benchmark we run. Therefore, we believe it is feasible to directly apply our prototype to the production system environment.

The rest of the paper is organized as follows. Section 2 describes the problem scope and defines the terminologies used in this paper. The design and implementation issues of the system are presented in Section 3. In Section 4, we show the evaluation results. After discussing limitations of our LeakProber prototype in Section 5, We describe related work in Section 6. Finally, we conclude our paper in Section 7.

2. PROBLEM OVERVIEW

In this section, we first discuss the specific problem to be solved by LeakProber. Then we describe our model of the sensitive data propagation graph generation and present the definition and terminologies that will be used throughout the paper. Finally, we give an overview of our approach.

2.1 Problem Statement

Data leakage is the unauthorized data flow from within the legitimate enterprise/organizations to the external destination or recipient. It is not only restricted to the external intruders exploiting vulnerabilities in the code of software (e.g., web applications, database servers, OSes), installing data stealing malware, and launching an XSS, SQL Injection. As an insider, enterprise employees can also intentionally or accidentally leak sensitive information via e-mail, Web sites, FTP, instant messaging, databases, and etc.

Figure 1 shows the typical three-tiered web applications architecture: web service programs providing the user interface, application server programs managing the business logic, and database servers storing the persistent data. The left grey block represents the user interface through which the system administrator interacts with the management functionalities provided by the system. Input from untrusted channel is represented as red dashed line. Vulnerabilities in applications and kernel are marked as orange blocks. These are two common threats compromising the confidentiality. When computers execute vulnerable code or load data from

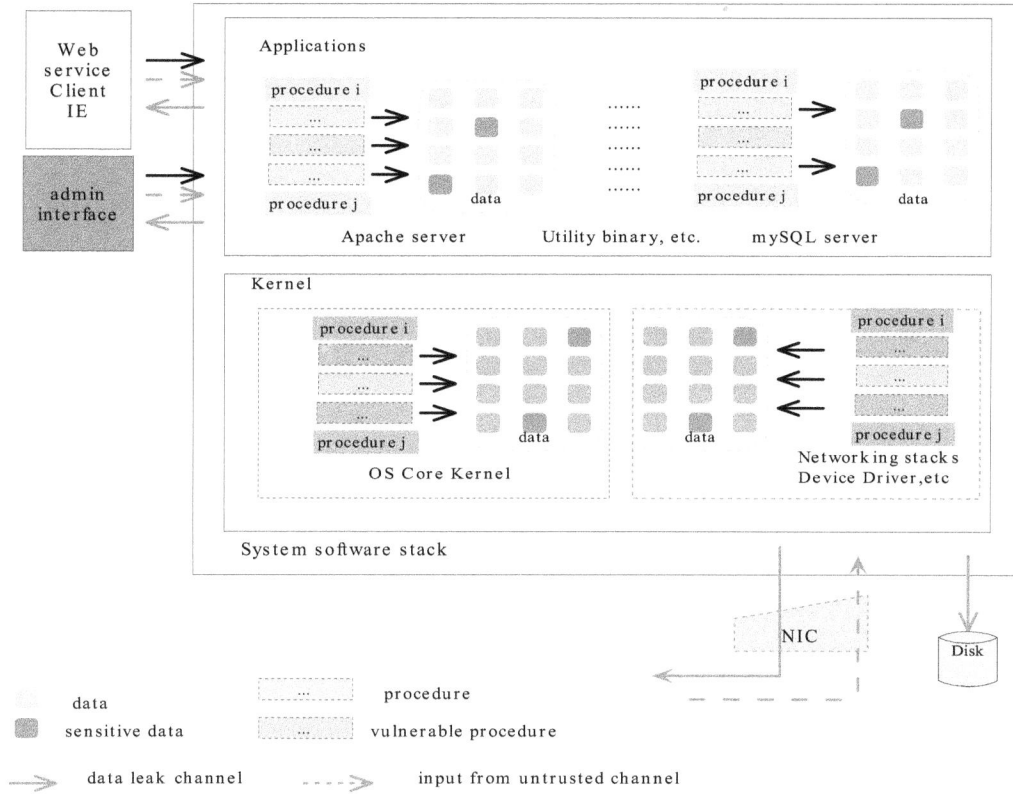

Figure 1: **Sensitive Data Flow in Typical Architecture of A Three-tiered Web Applications and System Software Stacks.**

untrusted channel, such as the Internet, the system may be compromised by malicious input and sensitive data might be exposed to attackers. The red lines denote the possible channels from which the sensitive data flows out of the system.

Figure 1 illustrates lots of vulnerable holes in current untrusted software stack: sensitive data is often handled by procedures from different components, including operating system kernel, device driver modules, system libraries, applications, and etc. Hence, sensitive data can be leaked through many ways. Any kind of data leakage involves two key processes: (1) data accessing routines (e.g., system call, function or procedure call, etc.) gain access to system memory or to persistent storage where sensitive data resides in; (2) target data will be transferred to potential sink routines. Intuitively, the goal that we set for our approach is to build a model and prototype system, which can extract a complete sensitive data accessing path with data and routine dependency relations. It stands as a basis for understanding the propagation of sensitive data throughout a running system and building a profile describing the sensitive data stealing path.

To facilitate the representation of procedures that cross user/kernel boundary in an unified manner, we classify software system stack's procedures into two categories: user space procedures and kernel space procedures. The former executes in less privilege mode. Thus, if an user space procedure wants to perform any action affecting the system state, it has to issue a request to the kernel with the help of system calls. The latter implements kernel services requests for applications that require privileged access of various resources: reading or writing data on disk, requesting more memory, interacting with other applications, making network connections, and so forth.

The sensitive data includes command line arguments, environmental variables, network sockets, files and *stdin* input, etc. Generally, the following can be potential source of the sensitive data: (1) hard-coded strings in applications; (2) disk files; (3) keyboard input; (4) specific memory locations; (5) Objects in database. Our prototype system requires users to explicitly specify the source of sensitive data in a configuration file.

2.2 Abstract Model for Data Flow Tracking

We model any execution of application or kernel by a triple $< P, V, R >$, with a set P of procedures, a set V of data variables, and a set R of binary relations between procedures and data variables. For instance, let P be the set of procedures and V be the set of variables to be analyzed. A binary relation R from a set P to a set V is a set of ordered pairs $< p, v >$, which is denoted as pRv, where $p \in P$, $v \in V$. Since we focus on learning relation set R through static analysis and runtime tracking, we first define possible relations as follows:

Propagation Relation: If there exists a data flow from $v \in V$ to procedure $p \in P$ through procedure arguments, return values, or indirect pointers and variables, the relation of $vR_{prop}p$ is defined as $V \times P$.

Taint Relation: If a procedure $p \in P$, or any subcalls of p transfers a sensitive data source or tainted data to a variable $v \in V$, the relation of $pR_{taint}v$ is defined as $P \times V$.

Call Relation: If a procedure $p \in P$ contains a call to another procedure $q \in P$, the relation of $pR_{call}q$ is defined as $P \times P$.

Alias Relation: Alias relation is between variables. For any $u \in V$, $v \in V$, if both of them refer to the same storage location, the relation of $uR_{alias}v$ is defined as $V \times V$.

Access Relation: Access relation is constructed when one invoked procedure accesses the memory of an variable. $pR_{access}v$ denotes that the invocation of procedure p will access the memory of the variable v.

Definition 1: The user-kernel boundary crossing dynamic trace (uk-BCDT) is represented in the form of a labelled graph defined by 3 tuples: $g_t = G(V, E, L_v)$, where a vertex $v \in V$ denotes one of the two types of vertices, namely, procedure vertices and variable vertices. Each $v \in V$ is labelled with vertex profile L_v, which is variable-length n-tuples. E is the set of directed edges, and an edge from p to q implies the relation $pR_{call}q$ or $pR_{access}q$. Note that in general all vertices profile at least has three elements $(T_{seq}, Proc_{id}, Addr)$, where procedure or variable was traced at the time sequence T_{seq}, $Addr$ denotes the virtual address, and the traced event belongs to $Proc_{id}$.

Definition 2: The sensitive data propagation graph (sDPG) is a directed graph $g_p = G(V, E, L_v)$, consisting of a set V of vertices and a set E of edges. A vertex $v \in V$ represents one of the three categories of vertices, namely, procedure vertices, variable vertices, and sensitive data source vertices. Each $v \in V$ is labelled with vertex profile L_v which is variable-length n-tuple. An edge $e \in E$ represents one of the two categories of edges, control dependence edge E_c, and summary relations edge E_s. The set of E_c denotes the call relations on procedure vertices $P \times P$, i.e., a directed $(p, q) \in E_c$ exists iff p calls q. The transitive flow of sensitive data between procedural and variable is represented by summary relations edge E_s, which are further deviced into two types: taint relation edge and propagation relation edge.

2.3 Approach Overview

The generation of sDPG involves three phases. Figure 2 illustrates the general workflow of LeakProber. First, we compute summary relations sets by performing a static inter-procedural analysis on the kernel and applications source code. This static preprocessing phase not only extracts procedure and data accessing summary relations, but also determines the instrumentation points in the software stacks, the probe handler types, and the arguments or variables to be traced. It takes the the user specified sensitive data source as input and identifies only relevant procedures involving sensitive data accessing.

This approach significantly reduces the unnecessary instrumentation points which enables the developing of uk-BCDT module in a semi-automatic way. Base on the list of the instrumentation points obtained from static preprocessing phase, we develop our systemic user-kernel boundary crossing trace module, which supports dynamic tracking sensitive data movement among local variables, global variables, subroutines throughout the whole system. It also stores additional information associated with each event, such as time sequence, the values of its source and target variables and

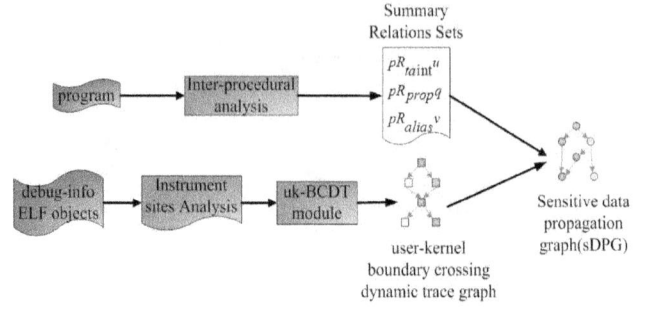

Figure 2: The General Workflow of LeakProber

the length of the data that denotes the amount of the propagated data. Finally, we generate sDPG by combining the results of summary relation sets and runtime tracking events by uk-BCDT.

3. DESIGN AND IMPLEMENTATION

In this section, we present how the sensitive data propagation graph is constructed based on summary relation sets and runtime tracking.

3.1 Extraction of Summary Relation Sets

A great deal of recent research has been devoted to developing algorithms for inter-procedural global flow analysis [9, 12, 14]. The aim of inter-procedural data flow analysis is to summarize the semantic effects of the subroutine calls that move sensitive data among variables. We implement our inter-procedural summary relation extraction module as an extension to the *GNU C* compiler, based on gdfa[5]. Gdfa is a generic data flow analyzer for per function data flow analysis in *GCC 4.3.0*. Gdfa relies on the support provided by *GCC* to traverse over CFGs (Control Flow Graph), and discover relevant features of procedure, variables, expressions etc.

According to the definition given in Section 2.2, inter-procedural taint analysis aims at finding the call sites where data moves from sensitive data source to tainted variables, and obtaining the relations defined in section 2.2, which are easy to construct from the analyzing program. Our system employs a context insensitive, flow-insensitive, Andersen-style analysis [9], and scales very well to the size of our applications. Moreover, popular compilers such as *GCC* use flow and context insensitive analysis, which simplifies the implementation of our system. We present Algorithm 1 to obtain taint relations from source code, and also determine the call sites where data is moved from sensitive data source to tainted variables. This is a forward data flow analysis and can be solved efficiently using an iterative algorithm.

We illustrate the inter-procedure summary relation sets with an example. Figure 3 shows a program fragment and the summary relation sets extracted by our inter-procedural analysis module. The pair (*get_passwd()*, *passwd*) means that variable *passwd* is tainted by procedure *get_passwd()*. We reduce the storage space required by inter-procedure analysis by creating a compact representation for each relations, then the extracted binary relation R_{taint} is given as R_{taint}:{(*get_passwd* (), *passwd*), (*get_passwd*(), *pw*), (*fread*(), *buf*), (*fopen*, *fp*), (*memcpy*(), *buf*)}.

Algorithm 1: ExtractTaintRelation

Input: Program and Sensitive Data source
Output: Taint Relation Set

---

1. initialize all variable as NOT TAINTED,
$V_{tainted} \leftarrow \emptyset, \{R_{tainted}\} \leftarrow \emptyset$.
2. search all calls to procedures $(p_1, p_2, ..., p_i)$ that read data from sensitive data source.
3. mark the variables tainted $(u_1, u_2, ..., u_i)$ by procedures $(p_1, p_2, ..., p_i)$ as TAINTED, update the set of $\{R_{tainted}\} \leftarrow \{p_1 R_{taint} u_1, ..., p_i R_{taint} u_i\}$.
4. check through the set of $\{R_{alias}\}$, if there exists a variable v, $u_i R_{alias} v$, and $q R_{taint} v$, update the set of $\{R_{tainted}\} \leftarrow \{q R_{taint} u_i\}$.
5. propagate the tainted variable throughout the program.
6. repeat Step 3 until a fixed point is reached.

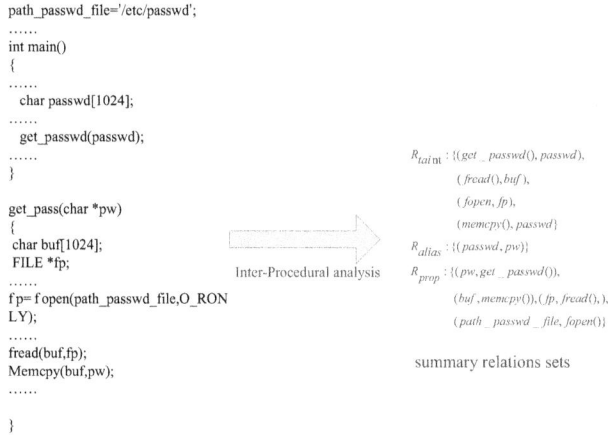

```
path_passwd_file='/etc/passwd';
......
int main()
{
......
  char passwd[1024];
......
  get_passwd(passwd);
......
}

get_pass(char *pw)
{
  char buf[1024];
  FILE *fp;
......
fp=fopen(path_passwd_file,O_RON
LY);
......
fread(buf,fp);
Memcpy(buf,pw);
......

}
```

Inter-Procedural analysis →

R_{taint} : {(get_passwd(), passwd),
(fread(),buf),
(fopen, fp),
(memcpy(), passwd}
R_{alias} : {(passwd, pw)}
R_{prop} : {(pw,get_passwd()),
(buf ,memcpy()),(fp, fread(),),
(path_passwd_file, fopen()}

summary relations sets

Figure 3: Example Program (left) and Its Summary Relations Sets Extracted by Inter-procedural analysis (right)

3.2 Systemic Runtime Tracking

To do a systemic dynamic trace in the production system, the trace facility needs to meet the following requirements: (1) to have a systemic scope, instrumentation points should cover the entire system, including applications, libraries, and the kernel itself; (2) to ensure full availability and continuity of all business and production critical processes during system tracing, the trace module need offer zero downtime and minimum overhead impact on the system; (3) to simplify the off-line analysis process, gathering and coalescing trace event should be done in an unified manner whereby both data and control flow can be followed across the user/kernel boundary.

User-kernel boundary crossing dynamic trace (uk-BCDT) module is built on top of kprobe(kernel space) [21] and uprobe(user space) [7] infrastructure. As a new feature in the Linux 2.6 kernel, Kprobe allows developer to dynamically break into any kernel routine and collect debugging and performance information non-disruptively. Similarly as kprobe creates and manages probe points in kernel code, uprobe creates and manages probe points in user applications. Uprobe allows user to write a kernel module, and specify each desired probe point where the process and virtual address

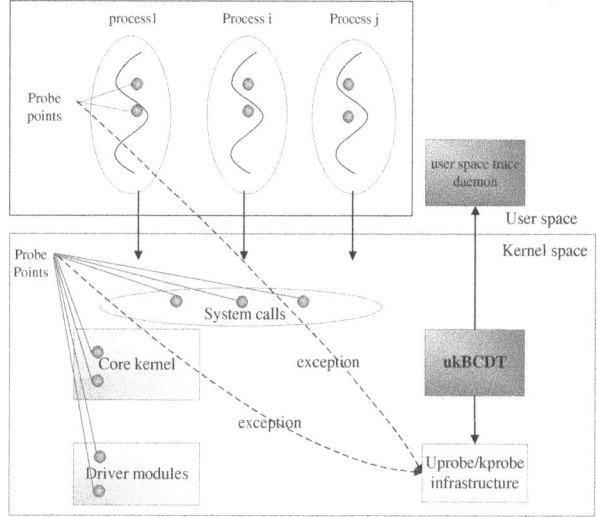

Figure 4: The Architecture of uk-BCDT Module

are probed. When any probe point is hit, the handler starts running. Since uprobe-based module can also use the kprobe APIs, thus a single uk-BCDT module can collect and correlate information from the user applications, shared libraries, the kernel/user interfaces and the kernel itself. It allows us to access events across different abstraction levels. By tracing events at both the kernel and user processes, and referring to the source code of them, uk-BCDT provides the complete view of the system required to understand systemic problems that span the user/kernel boundary.

As described in section 2.2, uk-BCDT module generates a custom trace event which encapsulates attributes like process id, time stamp and the virtual address of the routine. This event is then written to user space trace daemon through Replayfs [35], which provides an efficient way to move large blocks of data from the kernel to user space. Relayfs can be compiled into the kernel or built as a loadable module. Naturally, information flows are not the only aspect of program execution that is relevant to sensitive data leakage. According to Definition 2, it also should involve profiling and tracing a number of other aspects of program execution, including (1) tracing event time sequences, (2) variable values and attribute of variables (e.g., the length or type of variables). So every event logged to user space trace daemon contains some common attributes like the name of the event, type of event, id of the process that issued the event, time stamp. It also contains some specific fields allowing user defined data to be logged according to the trace event type.

We ensure that the timestamps of events across processes are generated using a single mechanism, which makes correlating these events easier. Note that the trace module uses the *do_gettimeofday()* kernel function call in Linux in order to obtain the absolute time at which an event occurs. Given the process id and timestamp, it is possible to correlate exactly the data access events that are executed within a particular invocation of a function. The single log corresponding to this session can subsequently be analyzed offline after the tracing phase has finished running.

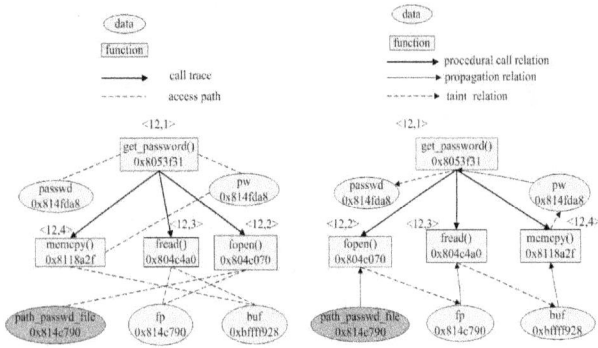

Figure 5: A Sample User-kernel Boundary Crossing Dynamic Trace of The Sample Program (*left*) and Its sDPG Constructed by Algorithm 2(*right*)

3.3 Sensitive Data Propagation Graph (sDPG) Construction

User-kernel boundary crossing dynamic trace(uk-BCDT) is an unified representation that holds full execution history including control flow, address, and dynamic profile information described in section 2. Moreover, summary relation sets contain sufficient information to support the sDPG construction. Below is the pseudo code for sDPG generation algorithm. Given an execution instance of uk-BCDT and summary relation sets, one can easily run this construction algorithm and combine them to build the sDPG. Initially, an initial $g_p = G(V, E, L_v)$ is duplicated from $g_t = G(V, E, L_v)$. Subsequently, R_{access} relation edges are replaced by R_{taint} or R_{prop}.

Algorithm 2: sDPG construction

Input: $g_t = G(V, E, L_v)$, summary relation sets
Output: $g_p = G(V, E, L_v)$

1. build an initial $g_p = G(V, E, L_v)$.
2. for each vertex in $g_t = G(V, E, L_v)$, duplicate sets V, E, L_v from $g_t = G(V, E, L_v)$.
3. for each vertex $g_p = G(V, E, L_v)$, where $p \in P, v \in V$, if there exists $pR_{taint}v$ or $pR_{prop}v$ in summary relation set, p and v correspond to a trace event relation $pR_{access}V$ in $g_t = G(V, E, L_v)$, replace $pR_{access}v$ with $pR_{taint}v$ or $pR_{prop}v$.
4. repeat Step 3 until all of the vertices have been traversed.

Figure 5 shows the sDPG obtained by applying construction algorithm to the execution instance of uk-BCDT and summary relation sets in Figure 3. The symbols used to represent the different types of vertices and edges in sDPG are shown in Figure 3. The vertices are labelled with vertex profiles which map different types of vertices to vertex profiles. Gray vertex *pass_word_file* represents the secret data, this kind of vertex is referred to as *sensitive data source*. Thick edges represent the runtime calling relationships among procedures. The thin and dash edges represent the summary relations which reflect data movement relations between procedures and variables.

4. EXPERIMENTAL EVALUATION

The aim of LeakProber is to profile sensitive data stealing path in the production system. We evaluate two aspects of our prototype system: its functionality of profiling and identifying data steal behaviors in real world system and the performance overhead introduced by uk-BCDT module. All experiments are conducted on a machine with AMD Athlon 64 X2 Dual core 3800+ processor and 2GB of RAM. The testbed machine runs the default configuration of Fedora 12 with Linux kernel version 2.6.31. The Linux kernel is patched and re-complied to support kprobe and uprobe infrastructure. In section 4.1 we describe the design of each of our experiments and analysis results in detail, in section 4.2 we concentrate on the study of the overhead caused by LeakProber.

4.1 Case Study

In order to experimentally demonstrate that data stealing path exhibits unusual profiles and can be tracked by our system, we setup a real world web server, including *apache*, *mysql*, *php* on Linux platform known as a LAMP system. They are the most widely deployed open source server applications for business application processing. Our prototype implementations are based on *MySQL 5.1.39*, *Apache HTTP Server 2.2.13* and *PHP 5.3.0*. We devise a set of data stealing attacks on real world server applications. When applying our approach, we concern ourselves with two primary issues: (1) does data steal path exhibit unusual profiles? (2) can sDPG capture complete sensitive data propagation path crossing user/kernel boundary with a systemic view?

In our first experiment we apply our prototype to generate sDPG during a password entering the server system by means of shell mode *adduser* command. We mimic an password steal attack by installing keylogger(vlogger [4]) in the test platform. Vlogger is a linux kernel level key logger, which is able to detect password prompt and automatically log user/password only.

Figure 6 shows the simplified sDPG generated in the experiment. In this scenario, we only focus on the data propagation path, so vertex labels which represent the traced vertex profiles are omitted. As shown in Figure 6, we define sensitive data source as user input and /etc/passwd, which are represented as dark eclipse. When adduser process prompts to get user input, it calls read() function on stdin of the adduser process. The sys_read() function will call tty_read() function of corresponding tty (e.g., /dev/tty0) to read input characters from end user and return it to the process. In Figure 6b, we can notice that function tty_read() has a different virtual address with the one in figure 6a, which indicates a system-call hijacking. Another important distinct difference is that a series of kernel space function calls e.g., sock_create() and udp_sendmsg(), have been traced in the experiment with keylogger installation. By comparing the difference between a normal process and a malicious one in a identical environment, it demonstrates that a complete keyboard input sensitive data stealing involves the following steps: (1) keylogger replaces the open system-call to hijack the tty buffer processing function and injects its code to gather keyboard data; (2) if keylogger has enough information collected, then it can send it periodically out to a remote machine via UDP protocol.

In our second experiment, we apply our prototype to generate sDPG when user connects to *mysql* database server

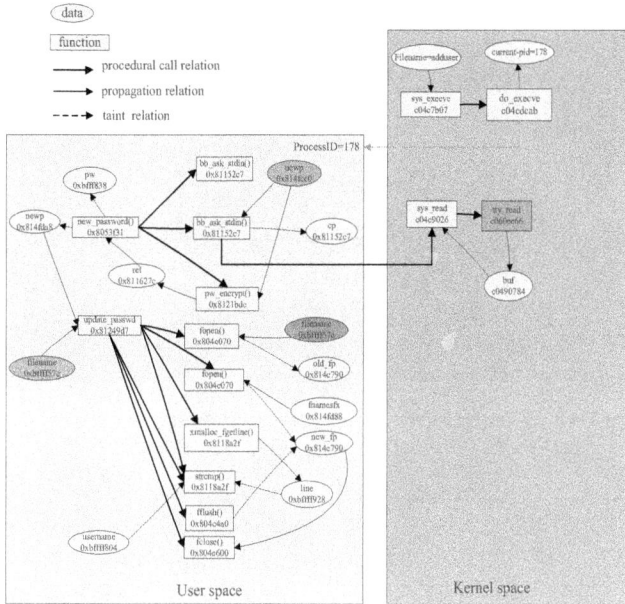

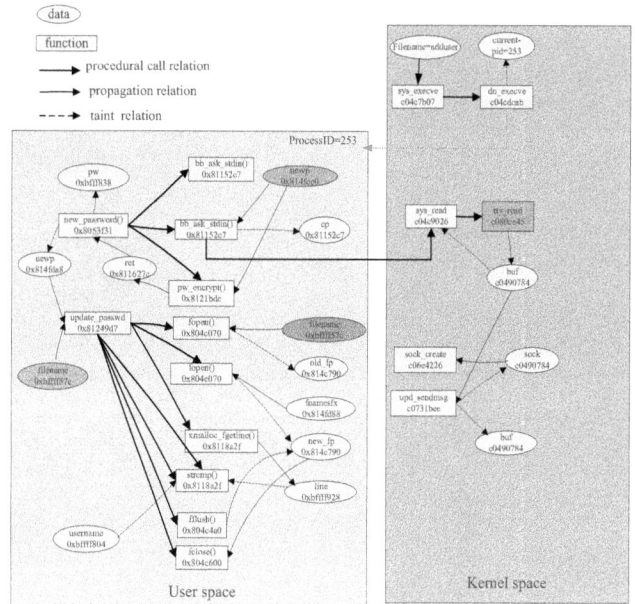

(a) A Simplified sDPG Generated while A Password Entered into Server System by Way of Shell Mode adduser Command

(b) A Simplified sDPG Generated while A Password Entered into Server System with Installation of vlogger.

Figure 6: A Simplified sDPG Generated while A Password Entered into Server System with Different Ways

and executes an *sql* query from the command line. By running *mysql -u root -p* command, *mysql* client will prompt user interactively for a password. Then we invoke a query *SELECT LOAD_FILE('/etc/passwd')*, which will display the contents of the /etc/passwd file revealing all user accounts on the system. As a common used SQL injection technique, it is possible to use a *UNION SELECT* with the built-in *mysql LOAD_FILE function*, to export the contents of any file on the system. Figure 7 shows a simplified sDPG generated in this experiment.

4.2 Performance

The overhead imposed during trace-on model is due to the additional instrumentation probe points and probe handler functions involved for collecting profile information in both user and kernel space. It ranges from recording call sites (timestamp, virtual address), specific variable type to data attributes. Figure 8 shows the different types of user-level probe points (uprobe, uretprobe) and kernel-level probe points (kprobe, kretprobe), and their distribution applied in our test platform's software stack. They consist of 341 probe points totally, and are distributed in different components of software stack: core kernel, device driver, system library, mysql-connector and utilities programs.

To investigate the slowdown due to our uk-BCDT module, we run two sets of experiments: native system and the one with our prototype system. We measure the overhead impact on real world application *MySQL*. We use version 2.2 of the Benchmark DBD suite [3], which is provided with MySQL source distributions. Figure 9 compares the native performance of benchmark to that of the same benchmark running in trace-on model and the trace-off mode. The times given are in seconds and represent the average over 13 runs. The native applications are compiled with *gcc 4.4.0* at optimization level *-o2*. As shown in Figure 9, when our proto-

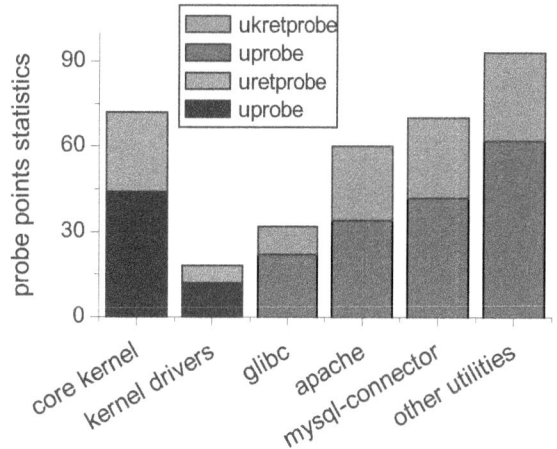

Figure 8: Statistics and Distribution of Different Types of Probe Points in Test Platform's Software Stack.

type system is working in the trace-on mode, the overhead imposed is very low, on an average of 7% across all benchmarks. To achieve the zero disabled probe effect required for production use, the uk-BCDT module can be unloaded from system kernel, so the system is just as if our prototype were not present at all. We measure the overhead imposed after turning off the uk-BCDT module. This overhead is pretty low, on an average of 1.5% across each benchmark we run. As future work, we will obtain more detailed results to help understand the individual uprobe and kprobe points contributions to the overall performance overhead.

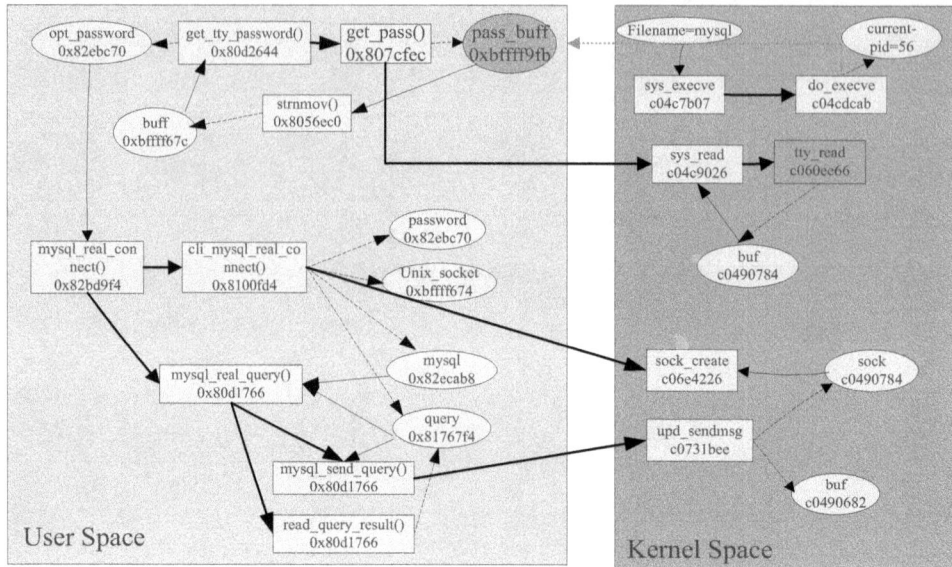

Figure 7: A Simplified sDPG Generated while Executing a SQL Query from The Command Line

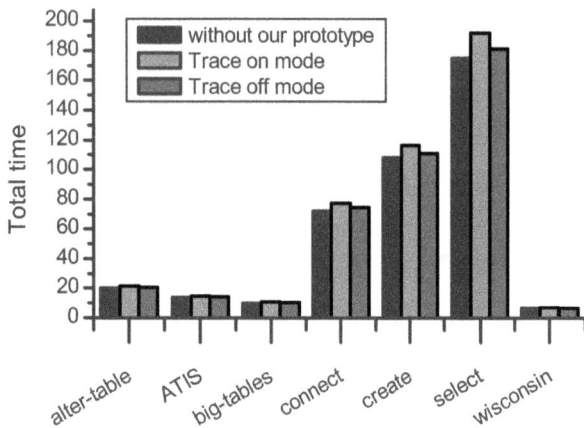

Figure 9: Performance Measurement for Different Running Modes

5. DISCUSSION

Despite the encouraging results obtained from our evaluation, there is much room to improve LeakProber.

Our static preprocessing phase uses the user-supplied sensitive data source definition to perform an inter-procedural data flow analysis on the target program to determine where dynamic instrumentation is actually required. In most cases, it prevents the system from inserting instrumentation everywhere by removing unnecessary tracking. However, the current static component only tells the developers where and which type of instrumentation should be added, and requires them to manually write a uk-BCDT module to perform a runtime tracking on interested data flow. Keeping track of and using such information are tedious and error-prone, if done by manual. Another limitation faced by our current prototype is that identification of sensitive data relies on user-supplied specification file and thus may be lack of simplicity. In ideal case, we expect our users to be data breaches experts who do not necessarily have expertise in compilers or formal specifications. The complexity of defining sensitive data source may hamper large-scale practical use.

We are currently exploring several approaches to eliminate the above limitations in our future work. The first one is to improve the simplicity of building uk-BCDT module. Recent effort such as systemtap [6] demonstrates techniques to automate the process of generating a tracing module. The novel feature allows user to leave the tedious task to the framework by specifying a description of instrumentation point. The systemtap script language is implemented by a translator that automatically creates C code, which is in turn compiled into a stand-alone kernel module. We expect to adopt a similar approach in our next implementation of LeakProber. It would allow user to focus on analyzing data leakage path without significantly complicating the job of developing a tracing module. Second, to simplify the process of identifying sensitive data, we plan to use a declarative annotation language, which has been previously used for static error checking, to replace the specification file currently used by our framework. Our final goal is to provide a simple-to-use interface for defining sensitive data source that is independent of the data input channel, thus enabling reuse across system software stack.

6. RELATED WORK

Our work builds upon many previous studies on data flow analysis. Due to lack of space, here we only provide a brief survey on related work that is most relevant thematically and technically to the design and implementation of our prototype.

Data flow tracking is used in many current systems to perceive sensitive data movement for confidentiality or integrity purpose [33, 26, 15]. TiantCheck is designed to detect previously unknown control-hijacking attacks, such as buffer overflow or application vulnerabilities. Panorama [33]

and HTH [22] perform system-wide information flow tracking to identify how sensitive data is stolen or manipulated by malware. Furthermore, a number of data flow tracking systems [30, 24, 28] allow user to build security policy and prevent unsafe application code to access confidential data. RIFLE [30] and JFlow [24] are capable of enforcing user-defined information-flow security policies for traced applications. Operating systems such as Flume [18] and HiStar [36] provide information flow control support. They permit users to define applications security policies which are then enforced by the underlying kernel.

These systems vary in numerous ways: instrumentation mechanisms, kinds of analysis approach supported, scope of data flow tracking, and runtime overhead. Static data flow analysis has been widely used for error checking and lightweight program verification. Data flow integrity projects compute a data flow graph for a vulnerable program using compile-time techniques, and insert extra guards to ensure that the flow of data at runtime is allowed by the data flow graph. However, static data flow analysis usually analyzes one single program and only predicts approximations of a program's runtime behaviors, which suffers from two major drawbacks: limit of tracking scope and accuracy.

Several works propose broad coverage attack detectors based on dynamic data flow tracking. LIFT [28] tracks data flow at runtime via dynamic binary translation to detect general security attacks. Similar to other dynamic data flow tracking systems, it relies on dynamic instrumentation mechanism to perform data tracking task. Generally, there are two approaches for dynamic instrumentation: probe based and (Just in time) jit-based. The probe-based approach works by dynamically replacing instructions in the original code with trampolines that branch to the instrumentation code. The probe can be either a breakpoint instruction or a software breakpoint instruction. In most cases, the probes can be inserted, enabled and disabled dynamically. Examples include LTT(Linux trace Toolkit) [31], DTrace [11], KProbes [21], and SystemTap [6]. These frameworks are usually meant for instrumentation at function boundaries. In contrast, the jit-based approach works by dynamically compiling the binary and can insert instrumentation code anywhere in the binary. Program shepherding [17] built on the DynamoRIO [13] infrastructure can enforce security policies on execution of untrusted binaries by monitoring control flow transfers. Similar systems such as Pin [19] and Valgrind [25], have been widely used in data flow tracking systems, and offer fine-grained instrumentation for application at the expense of higher overhead than ours.

There are several dynamic data flow tracking systems built on whole system emulation. Emulators typically mode low-level machine details and allow hardware level tracking. Emulators such as Bochs [1] and QEMU [2] provide a detailed emulation of a particular architecture with high performance penalty. Taint-Bochs [15] has been developed based on Bochs which allows one to track the propagation of sensitive data at instruction level, supporting to exam all places that sensitive data may reside. Ho et al [8], provide system-wide tracking with Xen virtual machine monitor and switch to a hardware emulator only when needed, to mitigate the performance penalty.

7. CONCLUSION

In this paper, we presented the design, implementation, and evaluation of LeakProber, a framework that leverages whole system dynamic instrumentation and inter-procedural analysis to enable data propagation path profiling in the production systems. We evaluate our system, LeakProber, by analyzing several representative data stealing attacks against real world web server applications. The results show that our system is able to extract detailed information about sensitive data flow. The sDPG generated by our system clearly highlights the malicious data accessing pattern through visualized data flow graph that will be very helpful for forensics or preventing leakage in an online manner by integrating access control system. The performance results show that the average overhead is 6% in the trace-on mode, which is low enough to make LeakProber practical to be applied in the production systems. We also discuss limitations of our current implementation and suggest how our system can be improved to be generally applicable to large-scale practical use.

8. ACKNOWLEDGEMENT

We would like to thank the anonymous reviewers for their constructive and insightful comments that helped improve the presentation of this paper. This work was supported by ARO W911NF-09-1-0525 (MURI), AFOSR FA9550-07-1-0527 (MURI), NSF CNS-0905131, and AFRL FA8750-08-C-0137. The work of Zhitang Li was supported by the National High Technology Research and Development Program of China (863 Program) under Grant No. 2007AA01Z420.

9. REFERENCES

[1] Bochs:the open source ia-32 emulation project. http://bochs.sourceforge.net/.

[2] Qemu. http://fabrice.bellard.free.fr/qemu/.

[3] The mysql benchmark suite. http://dev.mysql.com/doc/refman/5.0/en/mysql-benchmarks.html, 2002.

[4] Writing linux kernel key logger. http://www.phrack.org/phrack/59/p59-0x0e.txt, 2002.

[5] gdfa:a generic data flow analyzer for gcc. http://www.cse.iitb.ac.in/grc/software/gdfa-v1.1.pdf, 2009.

[6] Systemtap. http://sourceware.org/systemtap/, 2010.

[7] Uprobe. http://lkml.org/lkml/2010/7/27/121/, 2010.

[8] C. C. A. W. S. H. Alex Ho, Michael A. Fetterman. Practical taint-based protection using demand emulation. In *EuroSys*, pages 29–41, 2006.

[9] L. O. Andersen. *Program Analysis and Specialization for the C Programming Language*. PhD thesis, University of Copenhagen, 1994.

[10] D. Bruening, T. Garnett, and S. Amarasinghe. An infrastructure for adaptive dynamic optimization. In *CGO '03: Proceedings of the international symposium on Code generation and optimization*, pages 265–275, 2003.

[11] B. M. Cantrill, M. W. Shapiro, and A. H. Leventhal. Dynamic instrumentation of production systems. In *ATEC '04: Proceedings of the annual conference on USENIX Annual Technical Conference*, pages 2–2, 2004.

[12] B.-C. Cheng and W. mei W. Hwu. Modular interprocedural pointer analysis using access paths: design, implementation, and evaluation. In *PLDI*, pages 57–69, 2000.

[13] S. A. Derek Bruening, Evelyn Duesterwald. Design and implementation of a dynamic optimization framework for windows. In *In 4th ACM Workshop on Feedback-Directed and Dynamic Optimization*, 2000.

[14] N. Heintze and O. Tardieu. Ultra-fast aliasing analysis using cla: a million lines of c code in a second. In *PLDI '01: Proceedings of the ACM SIGPLAN 2001 conference on Programming language design and implementation*, pages 254–263, 2001.

[15] T. G. K. C. M. R. Jim Chow, Ben Pfaff. Understanding data lifetime via whole system simulation. In *Proc. 13th USENIX Security Symposium*, August 2004.

[16] T. G. M. R. Jim Chow, Ben Pfaff. Shredding your garbage: Reducing data lifetime through secure deallocation. In *Proc. 14th USENIX Security Symposium*, August 2005.

[17] V. Kiriansky, D. Bruening, and S. P. Amarasinghe. Secure execution via program shepherding. In *Proceedings of the 11th USENIX Security Symposium*, pages 191–206, 2002.

[18] M. Krohn, A. Yip, M. Brodsky, N. Cliffer, M. F. Kaashoek, E. Kohler, and R. Morris. Information flow control for standard os abstractions. In *SOSP '07: Proceedings of twenty-first ACM SIGOPS symposium on Operating systems principles*, pages 321–334, 2007.

[19] C.-K. Luk, R. Cohn, R. Muth, H. Patil, A. Klauser, G. Lowney, S. Wallace, V. J. Reddi, and K. Hazelwood. Pin: Building customized program analysis tools with dynamic instrumentation. In *Programming Language Design and Implementation*, pages 190–200, June 2005.

[20] M. Martin, B. Livshits, and M. S. Lam. Finding application errors and security flaws using pql: a program query language. In *OOPSLA '05: Proceedings of the 20th annual ACM SIGPLAN conference on Object-oriented programming, systems, languages, and applications*, pages 365–383, 2005.

[21] A. Mavinakayanahalli, P. Panchamukhi, and J. Keniston. Probing the guts of kprobes. In *Proceedings of the Ottawa Linux Symposium*, 2006.

[22] M. Moffie, W. Cheng, D. Kaeli, and Q. Zhao. Hunting trojan horses. In *ASID '06: Proceedings of the 1st workshop on Architectural and system support for improving software dependability*, pages 12–17, 2006.

[23] R. J. Moore. A universal dynamic trace for linux and other operating systems. In *Proceedings of the FREENIX Track: 2001 USENIX Annual Technical Conference*, pages 297–308, 2001.

[24] A. C. Myers. Jflow: Practical mostly-static information flow control. In *In Proc. 26th ACM Symp. on Principles of Programming Languages (POPL*, pages 228–241, 1999.

[25] N. Nethercote and J. Seward. Valgrind: a framework for heavyweight dynamic binary instrumentation. *SIGPLAN Not.*, 42(6):89–100, 2007.

[26] J. Newsome and D. Song. Dynamic taint analysis for automatic detection, analysis, and signature generation of exploits on commodity software. In *Proceedings of the Network and Distributed System Security Symposium (NDSS 2005)*, 2005.

[27] N. L. Petroni, Jr. and M. Hicks. Automated detection of persistent kernel control-flow attacks. In *CCS '07: Proceedings of the 14th ACM conference on Computer and communications security*, pages 103–115, 2007.

[28] F. Qin, C. Wang, Z. Li, H.-s. Kim, Y. Zhou, and Y. Wu. Lift: A low-overhead practical information flow tracking system for detecting security attacks. In *MICRO 39: Proceedings of the 39th Annual IEEE/ACM International Symposium on Microarchitecture*, pages 135–148, 2006.

[29] G. E. Suh, J. W. Lee, D. Zhang, and S. Devadas. Secure program execution via dynamic information flow tracking. In *ASPLOS-XI: Proceedings of the 11th international conference on Architectural support for programming languages and operating systems*, pages 85–96, 2004.

[30] N. Vachharajani, M. J. Bridges, J. Chang, R. Rangan, G. Ottoni, J. A. Blome, G. A. Reis, M. Vachharajani, and D. I. August. Rifle: An architectural framework for user-centric information-flow security. In *In MICRO 37: Proceedings of the 37th annual IEEE/ACM International Symposium on Microarchitecture*, pages 243–254. IEEE Computer Society, 2004.

[31] K. Yaghmour and M. R. Dagenais. Measuring and characterizing system behavior using kernel-level event logging. In *ATEC '00: Proceedings of the annual conference on USENIX Annual Technical Conference*, pages 2–2, 2000.

[32] H. Yin, Z. Liang, and D. Song. HookFinder: Identifying and understanding malware hooking behaviors. In *Proceedings of the 15th Annual Network and Distributed System Security Symposium (NDSS'08)*, February 2008.

[33] H. Yin, D. Song, M. Egele, C. Kruegel, and E. Kirda. Panorama: Capturing system-wide information flow for malware detection and analysis. In *Proceedings of ACM Conference on Computer and Communication Security*, Oct. 2007.

[34] A. Yip, X. Wang, N. Zeldovich, and M. F. Kaashoek. Improving application security with data flow assertions. In *SOSP '09: Proceedings of the ACM SIGOPS 22nd symposium on Operating systems principles*, pages 291–304, 2009.

[35] T. Zanussi, K. Yaghmour, and R. Wisniewski. relayfs: An efficient unified approach for transmitting data. In *In Proceedings of the Ottawa Linux Symposium 2003*, pages 494–507, 2003.

[36] N. Zeldovich, S. Boyd-Wickizer, E. Kohler, and D. Mazières. Making information flow explicit in histar. In *OSDI '06: Proceedings of the 7th USENIX Symposium on Operating Systems Design and Implementation*, pages 19–19, 2006.

[37] S. Zhang, X. Jia, P. Liu, and J. Jing. Cross-layer comprehensive intrusion harm analysis for production workload server systems. In *Annual Computer Security Applications Conference*, 2010.

Distributed Data Usage Control for Web Applications: A Social Network Implementation

Prachi Kumari, Alexander Pretschner[*]
Karlsruhe Institute of Technology
76131 Karlsruhe, Germany
{kumari,pretschner}@kit.edu

Jonas Peschla, Jens-Michael Kuhn
TU Kaiserslautern
67653 Kaiserslautern, Germany
{j_peschl,j_kuhn}@cs.uni-kl.de

ABSTRACT

Usage control is concerned with how data is used after access to it has been granted. Respective enforcement mechanisms need to be implemented at different layers of abstraction in order to monitor or control data at and across all these layers. We present a usage control enforcement mechanism at the application layer. It is implemented for a common web browser and, as an example, is used to control data in a social network application. With the help of the mechanism, a data owner can, on the grounds of assigned trust values, prevent data from being printed, saved, copied&pasted, etc., after this data has been downloaded by other users.

Categories and Subject Descriptors

H.4 [**Information Systems Applications**]: Miscellaneous

General Terms

Security

Keywords

Web based social networking, privacy policies enforcement, sticky policies, data usage control, Mozilla Firefox extension

1. INTRODUCTION

Usage control extends the concept of data protection beyond access control [1, 2]. That is, it influences the actions that can and have to be performed over data after access has been granted. In addition to access control requirements, usage control policies stipulate (i) what the recipient is allowed to do (rights) and (ii) what they must do (duties) with the data. Among other things, usage control requirements and the associated policies are relevant for privacy, the protection of intellectual property and/or secrets, digital rights management, and compliance with regulations such as HIPAA or SOX. The enforcement of usage control policies is particularly challenging in distributed environments where the data provider has no or only limited control over the IT infrastructure of the receiver.

Usage control policies can in general be enforced in two ways. *Detective enforcement* [3] aims at detecting violations of a policy. In case of a violation, usually a compensating, correcting, or notifying action is taken. In contrast, *preventive enforcement* aims at avoiding policy violations.

The subject of this paper is the preventive enforcement of usage control policies. These policies can and should be enforced at different layers of abstraction in the system. Among others, this has, for various policy languages [4–11], been done at the operating system level [12], at the X11 level [13], for Java [14, 15], the .NET CIL [16] and machine languages [17, 18]; at the level of an enterprise service bus [19]; for dedicated applications such as the Internet Explorer [20] or in the context of digital rights management [21–23]. The reason for this variety of enforcement mechanisms is that the *data* that has to be protected comes in different *representations*: as network packets, as attributes in an object, as window content, etc. In principle, all these representations eventually boil down to some representation in memory, but it turns out to be more convenient and simpler to perform protection at higher levels of abstraction. For instance, disabling the print command is easily done at the word processor level; taking screenshots is easily inhibited at the X11 level; prohibiting dissemination via a network is most conveniently performed at the operating system level; etc. The question of how data flows can be detected in-between different layers of abstraction is not the subject of this paper; see Section 5.

Instead, in this paper we present a usage control enforcement mechanism at the application layer, more specifically a web browser application. The context is privacy in web based social networks (WBSN) with use cases that have been taken from data protection requirements derived elsewhere [24]. One example use case that our system can handle is as follows: in a WBSN, Alice has a best friend Bob and an acquaintance Carol as her contacts. Alice wants Bob to be able to visit her profile and copy pictures from her album. Meanwhile, Carol should only be allowed to view Alice's profile and pictures but should not be able to copy her pictures. In today's WBSNs, it is not possible for Alice to enforce any such privacy controls where she can prohibit future usage of rendered data. We hence consider attacks on a user's privacy that emerge from *other users* rather than from the *provider of the WBSN*.

[*]This work was supported by the German National Science Foundation (DFG) under grant no. PR 1266/1-1.

Most of today's popular WBSNs offer access control mechanisms only. In these approaches, the user, in the role of a data provider, has no means to control the usage of the data once the social network's web server has delivered the respective web page. In particular, this means that all data that can be accessed by anyone *can also be used in any way*. We provide a mechanism to prevent this.

Few social networks provide some basic approaches to enforce usage control requirements. For instance, StudiVZ, a popular German social network for students, offers picture galleries where the context menu can be deactivated with JavaScript. This blocks the possibility to save a picture via a click on the right mouse button, or copy the selected content to the clipboard in this way. In general, it is also possible to use a feature of CSS that assigns different styles for each output media. If the user wants to print parts of a page with sensitive content, with this feature it is possible to hide the sensitive content or even the whole page. However, these techniques exhibit room for improvement. Among other things, suppressing the right click on pictures by JavaScript is only possible if JavaScript is enabled at all, and Javascript can be easily deactivated without much effort. Furthermore, this blocking prevents the user from accessing additional functionality in the context menu, which might not be intended to be deactivated.

Existing WBSNs also suffer from standard security problems, including social engineering, cross site scripting, hacking user accounts and breaking into the database or the system. Although these attack methodologies can be used by a sophisticated user to circumvent our mechanism, looking into these problems is outside the scope of this paper.

Problem. In sum, the problem that we tackle is the enforcement of usage control requirements in a web-based social network. We control events[1] such as print, copy&paste, save, etc. on *rendered data* like text and images. We hence consider privacy problems that are a consequence of other users rather than a WBSN provider misusing personal data.

Solution. Our solution is a system with three modules: the client (an extension for the browser of the user who accesses data from other users in a social network and which contains the policy enforcement point), the server (an augmentation of the social network system that generates and ships the policies that will be enforced by the client), and a policy decision point (a component that can be deployed anywhere and that evaluates user requests w.r.t. applicable policies). By means of a security analysis, we show that the policies are indeed enforced under specific assumptions.

Contribution. Our contribution is twofold: firstly, we are not aware of enforcement mechanisms for usage control policies at the application layer, achieved in the context of WBSN applications for a web browser. We present one here. Secondly, by means of the prototype, we provide insights into the limitations of solutions which are specific to one particular layer in the system. By the evaluation of the mechanism we also lay out the assumptions and conditions which need to hold true to provide guarantees in terms of security and effectiveness of the system.

Organization. Section 2 presents related work. Section 3, the core of this paper, introduces the proposed framework and the major terms used and describes the implemented mechanism both at the client and the server side. Section 4 evaluates the enforcement mechanism. The paper concludes by looking into possible refinements and planned future works in Section 5. Appendix A describes the architecture of the client-side enforcement mechanism.

2. RELATED WORK

Privacy and data protection problems in web based social networks have been outlined by a number of researchers [25–29]. One major issue is that WBSNs encourage users to share personal data without providing sufficient means to prevent the misuse of such data. Privacy settings in WBSNs generally offer only access control. They provide no means to control the usage of rendered data. This leaves users with the choice to publish data and lose complete control over the future use/abuse of it, or to refrain from publishing any data. The possibility of publishing data while maintaining usage control through policies has not been explored yet.

Research for privacy in social networks addresses two broad issues: (i) data protection from WBSN providers and (ii) data protection from other WBSN users. Solutions for the former tend to focus on decentralization of data storage in WBSN, while the latter focus on access control models for secure data sharing among users. Yeung et al. [30] have presented a decentralized WBSN architecture based on a friend-of-a-friend (FOAF) ontology [31]. Every user can upload his FOAF specification and profile data to his own trusted server. The friends/contacts of a user can access his data through his URI. Some other notable contributions in decentralization of data storage include Safebook, PeerSoN and MyNet. Safebook [32, 33] is a peer-to-peer WBSN which leverages trust relationships among users for data sharing. PeerSoN [34] is another such WBSN which uses peer-to-peer infrastructure coupled with encryption to enable users keep control of their data and use the social network offline. MyNet [35, 36] is an application that provides peer-to-peer social networking on mobile phones and other pervasive computing devices. In this paper, we consider WBSN providers as trusted parties and therefore do not look into this aspect of privacy protection.

The other category of solutions, directed towards securing user data against malicious WBSN users, propose access models for secure data sharing. These models are limited to providing differential access control and leave open the usage control aspect of data protection. We are aware of two models which use a similar approach as ours, but for access control. Gollu et al. [37, 38] have proposed Lockr, a model for access control in social networks based on social attestations and access control lists. Data access is granted based on social attestation which is a piece of metadata encapsulating a relationship between two users. However, Lockr does not provide any mechanism to prevent misuse of data once access has been granted. Another WBSN model has been proposed by Carminati et al. [39]. It is a decentralized rule based access control model which enforces access control at the client side. The access control rules are based on a trust model where users can rate their contacts as good friends, best friends, etc. This is similar to our approach for generating usage control policies but the cited model does not take into account the sensitivity of the data items (Section 3.3.1). The major difference, however, is that our system focuses on actually enforcing usage control requirements.

---

[1]In the remainder of this paper, we will call all user interactions *events* whereas the term *action* denotes the corresponding measure taken by the policy enforcement point, e.g., execution, inhibition, modification.

Other than these, the EU-funded research project Prime-Life has two applications for privacy in social networks [40–43]. Scramble! is a Firefox extension that stores encrypted data at the WBSN provider using the OpenPGP infrastructure. Clique is a WBSN that provides fine-grained access control based on *audience segregation*. According to this model, one user can have many *faces* (a profile with particular combination of information) according to different groups of his contacts. The groups represent social circles like family, colleagues etc. This work is not concerned with enforcing usage control requirements after data has been shipped.

Probably closest to our work in terms of usage control enforcement in web clients is that by Egele et al. [20]. They present a dynamic analysis method to identify if sensitive information flows out of the Internet Explorer. While their goal is entirely different from ours, this methodology can be used to identify user actions like copy&paste, save page etc. However, their dynamic analysis method identifies actions as illegitimate based on whether sensitive data flow was initiated by the browser or by its helper objects. It cannot identify an action as illegitimate if it was initiated by the browser, as in case of a usual copy&paste action.

To the best of our knowledge, there is no publicly available work that enforces usage control in WBSNs. However, quite some research has been conducted that focuses on usage control in other application domains and other levels of abstraction in the system [12–23], as explained in Section 1. All this work is specific to certain applications or levels of abstraction. They cannot directly be applied to the case of WBSNs as it requires enforcement of usage control policies in the server and the client applications.

At the server side, we have implemented a policy generation mechanism based on the trust model introduced by Kruk et al [44]. In their work, they have calculated trust to assess the relationship between two identities [45]. For this they introduce a *Friendship Level Metric* to assign a trust value between 0 and 1 to relationships. These trust values are multiplied on the paths between the resource owner and requester and the highest one is chosen. Depending on the *Social Network Access Control List* containing a maximum allowed relationship distance and the minimum trust, it is decided whether or not access is granted.

We use a similar approach, but we estimate exact trust values as we not only decide if data is accessible, but also to which degree it is usable, if access is granted to the requester. We want to stress that our implementation of the usage control mechanism is independent of the trust model used. It can be replaced by any other trust model as long as it can be used to generate usage control policies as we do.

At the client side, we have implemented a policy enforcement point in form of a Mozilla Firefox extension. There are many publicly available Firefox add-ons which provide some kind of privacy and security features, e.g., blocking advertisements and scripts, or hiding the user's IP address [46]. To the best of our knowledge, none of these add-ons can enforce data usage control requirements in the Firefox browser. In the context of privacy, a notable Firefox extension is the Tabulator which uses semantic web techniques to display the structure of web pages [47]. It can be used in the context of WBSNs to show a user how he is linked to other users and all the data displayed on his profile. This information can be used to increase awareness about data proliferation on the web. The extension does not enforce privacy policies.

Thus, to our knowledge, both in the context of WBSN and the web browser, we are the first to present an enforcement mechanism for usage control requirements.

3. USAGE CONTROL FRAMEWORK

3.1 User and System Requirements

Remember Alice's problem from Section 1. Alice wants to differentiate among people directly connected to her; and on this basis, she wants to control usage of her data. One solution to this problem is a policy-based usage control enforcement mechanism. The WBSN should enable Alice to specify usage control policies both for different contacts and for different kinds of data. At the same time, a policy enforcement mechanism for these policies is needed at the client side (web browser). There are hence two relevant sets of requirements, one set of requirements specific to policy generation mechanisms in WBSNs, and a second set for policy enforcement mechanisms in web browsers. (In principle, data can of course be accessed directly via the network, without passing through a browser. Many of today's social networks prohibit direct access via CAPTCHAs which solves the problem; the same is achieved, among other things, by authentication mechanisms of the kind discussed in Section 3.4.)

The user requirements that we implemented in our system have been derived elsewhere [24]. Typically, the user has requirements such as *only best friends can save my profile, only good friends can download sensitive pictures from my album* etc. Through such requirements, the owner controls three aspects of data usage: (i) Subject: "Who" (e.g., good friend, best friend) (ii) Object: "What" (e.g., pictures, profile) (iii) Events: "Usage" (e.g., save, download). The user requirements that we consider are given in Table 1.

Table 1: User requirements

Label	User requirements description
UR-1	User must be able to differentiate among contacts at the same degree of connection.
UR-2	User must be able to assign different sensitivities to different personal data.
UR-3	User must be able to define the set of allowed and inhibited actions.
UR-4	User preferences in requirements UR-1, UR-2 and UR-3 must be enforced together at the client side.
UR-5	Enforcement should not be client-specific.

We refine these requirements into a set of statements that, in the current implementation, refer to copy&paste, print, save, and view events, when user data is accessed by another user. Our policies are capable of expressing more complex requirements, including temporal and cardinal requirements [9], but for the sake of simplicity, we restrict ourselves to simple inhibition policies in this paper. The policy decision point (PDP), however, can interpret and monitor the entire expressiveness of the language.

To enforce these requirements, we derived a set of system requirements for the user requirements. These requirements detail the processes of policy generation and enforcement at the server's and the client's sides (Table 2).

While requirement SR-18 is relevant in practice, we are interested in a prototypical implementation and decided to implement our system solely for the Mozilla Firefox browser. This choice is motivated by three main reasons: firstly, it is possible to modify the functionality of the browser without

Table 2: System requirements for policy generation and enforcement

Label	User requirement description
SR-1	Contacts can be assigned to one of the following predefined categories: *best friends, good friends, friends, acquaintances, never met.*
SR-2	Categories in SR-1 are mapped to trust values 1.0, 0.8, 0.6, 0.4 and 0.2 respectively.
SR-3	New categories for contacts can be created by the user.
SR-4	A trust value ranging between 0.0 to 1.0 must be assigned to the new category at the time of creation.
SR-5	Personal data can be assigned one of the sensitivity levels: *private, high sensitive, medium sensitive, low sensitive, not sensitive.*
SR-6	Sensitivity levels in SR-5 are mapped to values 1.0, 0.8, 0.6, 0.4 and 0.2 respectively.
SR-7	Permission classes are *maximum permission, high permission, medium permission, low permission, minimum permission.*
SR-8	The user defines which of the four usage events viz. copy item, save page, print page and view page source are allowed/inhibited for each of the permission classes.[a]
SR-9	The controlled events in SR-8 apply *only* to text, images and the complete page excluding the content rendered by plug-ins.
SR-10	The policy is generated combining the requirements SR-(1-9).
SR-11	The WBSN sends the policy to the web browser on the client side.
SR-12	Before delivering content protected by usage control, the WBSN has to be sure, that there is a browser at the client side, which can enforce usage control and understands the information regarding usage control given by the server.
SR-13	The browser is able to provide authentication guarantees.
SR-14	The browser is able to enforce the received policy.
SR-15	The browser should differentiate between protected and unprotected pages[b] opened at the same time.[c]
SR-16	Policies delivered by WBSN have to be enforced by the browser until revocation.
SR-17	WBSN (and in turn the user) may revoke policies.
SR-18	Policies must not be browser/client specific.[d]

[a] At present, all other events than these four are out of the scope of our application.
[b] A protected page contains sensitive data protected by a usage control policy.
[c] This requirement distinguishes our solution from the Javascript fixes mentioned in the introduction section.
[d] This leaves scope for a more generic solution irrespective of the policy execution point.

modifying its core (add-ons, plug-ins); secondly, it is open source, has good SDK and developer network support and therefore is comparatively better suited for experiments than other browsers; thirdly, it is the second most used browser [48, 49], so offering a solution for it is likely to have more impact than other browsers.

3.2 High Level Interactions

We are now ready to describe the system which implements the system requirements given in Table 2. To translate these requirements to policies, we introduce a policy generation component in the social networking application. As policy generation requires modifying the source code of the social networking application, we could not use one of the existing popular applications like Facebook for our purpose. The instantiation of our social networking application is called SCUTA, an abbreviation for 'Social network with Control of Usage and Trust Assessment.' It is a modifica-

tion of the PHPizabi social networking platform [50]. The general idea is to use trust ratings for variable usage control. In our example, Alice can rate Bob and Carol for trust. The respective trust values are used to generate usage control policies for Bob and Carol. We would like to re-emphasize that although SCUTA works on trust assessments, it is independent of any particular concrete trust model. We are perfectly aware that trust is a challenging concept and that every single trust model is usually subject to a heated debate (which we do not want to enter in this paper). As a consequence, we simply assume an intuitive notion of trust to be given.

Figure 1 shows an overview sequence diagram of the usage control enforcement process. The policy enforcement point (PEP) resides at the client side in form of a Mozilla Firefox extension. We call it BRUCE, an acronym for 'Browser-side Usage Control Enforcement.' The server, SCUTA, generates policies and delivers both requested data and an associated policy to the client. The policy is then sent by BRUCE to the PDP and stored there. We chose to send the policy via BRUCE instead of sending it directly to PDP because we wanted to reuse the connection between BRUCE and the PDP (which is anyway required for enforcing the policy). In case of a usage event, BRUCE queries the PDP. The PDP allows or denies the attempt based on the policy.

Note that the PDP can be deployed at any of the three locations: the client, the server or a remote point. In our demonstrator, the PDP is run remotely. Moving the PDP out of the application-specific parts of usage control solution has the benefit that multiple PEPs which are application specific parts, can use the same PDP technology. This results in a greater knowledge base about occurring events for the PDP and avoids additional complexity for approaches to usage control at different levels of abstraction (see Section 5). Also, in the local network of a company, resource consumption could be reduced if the client machines of all employees were attached to one single PDP running on a central server. In our example, when Bob or Carol access Alice's data, irrespective of the client they use, they query the same PDP.

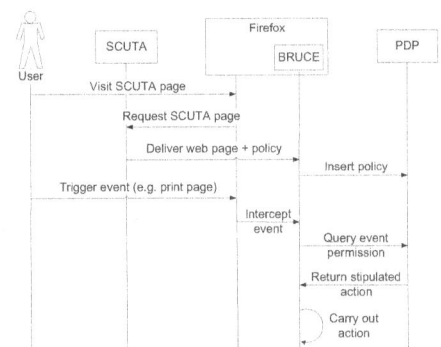

Figure 1: High level sequence diagram of the system

3.3 Policies

3.3.1 Permissions

In our policy generation model, we use three major terms: *trust*, the level of confidence one user has in the other user for not misusing his data; *sensitivity*, the intuitive degree of a data item being worth protection; and *permission*, the set of permitted user actions for a data item. We define permissions as a function of trust and sensitivity.

Trust. SCUTA provides functionality for a user to cluster his direct contacts into five predefined categories: best friend, good friend, friend, acquaintance and never met. There is a sixth class, not connected, that is automatically assigned by the system and that reflects the fact that the respective user is not in the friends' list of the other user. These six labels of contacts are mapped to trust levels on an equidistant scale of 0 to 1. 0 corresponds to not connected, .6 corresponds to friends, 1 to best friends, etc. Users can also create new categories for the contacts (e.g., colleagues) and assign trust values to them.

Sensitivity. Sensitivity is not global for all personal content of one user, but can differ for each data item. For example, in general an email address is more sensitive than the first or last names. SCUTA allows its users to rate their content according to five predefined sensitivity levels: minimum sensitive, low sensitive, medium sensitive, high sensitive and private. In addition, there is a sixth sensitivity level that implicitly labels all those data items that have not been rated for sensitivity by the user; their sensitivity is considered to be the lowest. Similar to trust assessments, these categories are mapped to equidistant sensitivity levels such that 0 corresponds to not labeled, .8 corresponds to highly sensitive, and 1 corresponds to private content.

Permissions. Trust and sensitivity are then combined to compute permissions $p(t,s) = t \cdot (1-s)$ where t is the trust rating of the recipient, and s is the data item's sensitivity value. SCUTA maps them to five predefined classes of permissions: minimum, low, medium, high and maximum that correspond to intervals of the same size (e.g., minimum permission iff $0 \leq p(s,t) \leq .2$ and high permission if $.6 < p(s,t) \leq .8$). Before these permission classes are computed, SCUTA verifies the existence of a PEP at the client side (Section 3.4). If the PEP does not exist, SCUTA nonetheless computes the permission class for each data element and delivers only the content for which all usage events are allowed. If there is no such permission class, no content is delivered. This is SCUTA's default behavior in absence of a PEP; it cannot be changed by the user.

Users can define what events are allowed for a particular category of permissions, as exemplified in Table 3.

Table 3: Mapping events to permission classes

Permission class	View item	Copy item	Save page	Print page	View page source
Minimum permission					
Low permission	x				
Medium permission	x	x			
High permission	x	x	x	x	
Maximum permission	x	x	x	x	x

The semantics of our policies is permit-override. This means that by default, everything is permitted. Explicitly stated prohibitions override this default.

3.3.2 Server-Side Policy Generation

Whenever a SCUTA-protected page is downloaded by a BRUCE-enabled Firefox browser (more precisely, in one tab of the browser), a new policy is created and sent to the PDP.

Each policy consists of a set of rules, one for each usage event and each permission class unless the default permissions apply. Usage is hence controlled identically for every data item within the same class, be this an image, a piece of text, etc. However, depending on the permission class, there can be different rules for different usage events. This design decision is motivated by efficiency and simplicity considerations—we could as well have chosen to have one rule per data item, resulting in possibly much larger policies.

If a web page is requested, SCUTA computes the permission class for every sensitive data item on the page. We then proceed in two steps.

Firstly, each sensitive data item is embedded into an HTML element which captures the computed permission class as shown in Listing 1. This augmented HTML code is shipped to the client.

```
<div>
 <table>
  <tr>
   <td><strong> E-mail </strong></td>
   <td><span class="lowPermission">
       alice@example.net </span></td>
  </tr>
  <tr>
   <td><img src="../images/Alice.jpeg"
       class="mediumPermission"/></td>
  </tr>
 </table>
</div>
```

Listing 1: HTML code with protection

Secondly, SCUTA generates a policy that associates a permission class with the set of allowed and prohibited actions for each of the permission classes. This is done w.r.t. the user's preferences, as stated in his WBSN profile. For instance, on the grounds of this information, it can be established that a *print* event is disallowed for all elements in the low permission class. We differentiate between data for which access is denied and data for which access is granted but usage is controlled. The idea is that for all data, for which access is denied (*view item* restricted in permission class), no usage control policies need to be generated, as access is a prerequisite for usage.

The policy is assigned an ID, the scope ID, that will be used by BRUCE to associate a specific browser tab (displaying the content governed by the policy) with the computed policy (there can be multiple tabs with different policies). The *scope* of a policy hence refers to one browsing session in one browser tab.

Finally, the HTML code that assigns permissions to data items as well as the policy that assigns permissions to allowed and prohibited usage events is shipped to the client.

3.3.3 Events

BRUCE controls events that correspond to usages of sensitive data items. In the policies, these are abstractly specified as, for instance, "copy" or "print." As an example, see Listing 2. These abstract events abstract from a specific browser technology: while copy&paste event is implemented differently in different browsers (and possibly in different implementations of the same browser), the main functionality is intuitively the same.

Viewed from the Firefox perspective, one abstract event can correspond to multiple internal events. Internal events ("cmd_copy," "context-copyimage-contents," "cmd_print,") are raised whenever user commands are executed. Usually, different user commands can trigger the same internal event. For instance, a copy to clipboard operation (one internal event) can be invoked from the edit menu, from a context menu, and by pressing the Ctrl-C keyboard shortcut (three different user commands).

While we specify policies at the level of abstract events (see above), our enforcement technology works at the level of internal events. This is explained in Section 3.5.

3.3.4 Concrete syntax: ECA Rules

Technically, policies come as sets of event-condition-action (ECA) rules [51, 52] with one rule per permission class per usage event, unless the default permission applies. The ECA rule describes what *action* has to be performed if a specific *event* is triggered and the *condition* has been evaluated to true. Trigger events are provided as abstract events in the above sense. Remember that they correspond to internal events (and respective user commands) executed on data, such as print, save as, etc., and that they are also used to define permission classes. As mentioned above, in the condition part, our policies can be specified for complex temporal logic conditions, but in this paper, we stick to conditions that always evaluate to true. Moreover, at present, the policy can contain only 'allow' or 'inhibit' in the action part. Other actions, including modification, execution, and delay [51], is the subject of current work.

An example ECA rule is given in Listing 2. It shows an ECA rule for a *copy* event, as defined by `<id>` element of the *triggerEvent* section. As mentioned above, the scope will be used by BRUCE to associate this policy with one specific browser tab. The PDP returns the action *inhibit* if the condition holds true; in this example, if the permission class of the content is either medium or low.

```
<controlMechanism>
        <id>copySelected(4bed490f465e5)</id>
    <description> prevents copying a content, if
        the content is marked by a specific class
    </description>
    <triggerEvent
        xmlns="http://www.master-fp7.eu/event">
      <id>copy</id>
      <parameter name="scope"
          value="4bed490f465e5"/>
    </triggerEvent>
    <condition
        xmlns="http://www.master-fp7.eu/pastOSL">
      <or>
        <XPathEval>
          /triggerEvent/parameter[@name='class']/
              @value='mediumPermission'
        </XPathEval>
        <XPathEval>
          /triggerEvent/parameter[@name='class']/
              @value='lowPermission'
        </XPathEval>
      </or>
    </condition>
    <actions>
      <inhibit/>
    </actions>
</controlMechanism>
```

Listing 2: Exemplary ECA rule

3.4 Policy Deployment

Before the generated policy can be deployed, SCUTA has to verify the existence of BRUCE on the client side. If BRUCE is not installed, the client should not render any

usage-protected data at all. The general idea is that server-side applications that support usage control would drive client users to obtain and install the extension because if no usage control enforcement mechanism is in place, access to usage-protected data would simply be denied. Once the existence of BRUCE has been established, SCUTA needs to send control information to BRUCE, including usage control policies and the scope IDs assigned to delivered pages. We implemented this with the help of custom HTTP headers. By doing so, it is also possible to use HTTPS communication without much effort to prevent some attack scenarios (Section 4).

Table 4: Header Field Commands

Header Field	Value	Semantics
x-auth_phrase	an arbitrary string	The extension send the x-auth_phrase value to the URL specified in x-auth_url.
x-auth_url	a valid URL	
x-policy_url	a URL pointing to a policy	The extension fetches the policy and inserts it into its responsible PDP.
x-set_scope	a unique identifier	The receiving tab is associated with the value. Usage commands will be checked for allowance with the scope as one parameter.
x-release_scope	a unique identifier	The scope associations for all tabs to the given value are removed and usage commands are blocked until a new URL is loaded.
x-revoke_policy	one or more identifiers separated by pipe symbols	The extensions informs the PDP about the mechanisms which shall be removed.

To the end of providing some basic authentication without relying on Public Key Infrastructures, we introduced two HTTP headers, *x-auth_phrase* and *x-auth_url* (see Table 4 for a list of header field commands, or HFCs). SCUTA starts by sending an authentication phrase (a nonce) to the client. By using HTTP headers, the server sends an authentication URL which is used by the client to send back the authentication phrase. A normal browser without a BRUCE PEP installed would simply not answer with an authentication response. Therefore, after a certain timespan, SCUTA can safely assume that the client is not equipped with BRUCE.

This very simple type of authentication is not intended to be secure against malicious attacks but only introduced as a placeholder for a more sophisticated solution. Such a solution could be based on the usage of public key cryptography. The above nonce can then be encrypted by SCUTA using the extension's public key. This will make sure that the nonce can only be decrypted by the extension using the private key. The extension then would compute the response to the received nonce and return it encrypted with the SCUTA's public key. Because this authentication mechanism would require the extension to have its own private key, we would of course need to secure it from being leaked or tampered with. For a more detailed security analysis, see Section 4.1.1.

Once the authentication has succeeded, SCUTA sends the header field command *x-policy_url*. BRUCE then fetches the respective policy and the scope ID (header field *x-set_scope*), and deploys the policy on the PDP via an XML-RPC message.

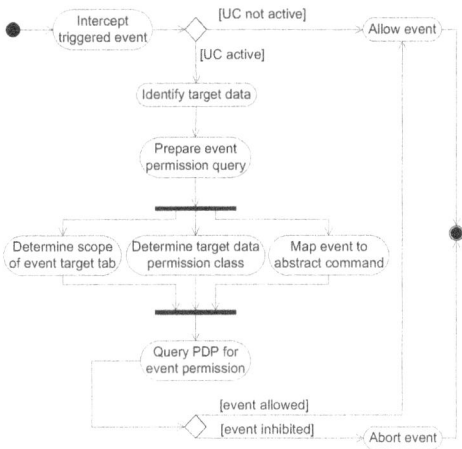

Figure 2: Client-side enforcement–the BRUCE perspective

If policies are to be revoked because a session ends, then SCUTA communicates this to BRUCE via the remaining two header fields, *x-release_scope* and *x-revoke_policy*. BRUCE then instructs the PDP accordingly.

3.5 Client-Side Policy Enforcement

Figure 2 provides a high level description of the usage control enforcement functionality of BRUCE.

Remember that user commands (e.g., Ctrl-C) trigger internal events (e.g., "cmd_copy"). In a nutshell, whenever such an internal event is raised, BRUCE retrieves the corresponding abstract event. This is because policies are specified in terms of abstract events. BRUCE then queries the PDP w.r.t. the abstract event that corresponds to the internal event. Depending on the decision of the PDP, it does or does not execute the code that corresponds to the internal event.

From BRUCE's viewpoint, each usage has three aspects: a scope, a target data item, and the abstract event that the usage is mapped to. Since our policies are based on permission classes (one rule per usage event per permission class unless default permissions apply) rather than on data items, BRUCE does not need to send a reference to the target data item to the PDP. Instead, queries sent to the PDP contain the abstract usage event and the scope as parameters.

The scope of an event corresponds to the scope ID of the policy that was generated for the protected page on which the event was triggered—that is, one specific session in a browser tab. The scope must be sent because there may be multiple tabs with different applicable policies. With this information from a query, the PDP knows which of the active policies applies.

The target of an event is either the entire protected page, a single DOM element or a set of DOM elements on the page (the Document Object Model, DOM, provides a structural representation of HTML documents which represents HTML elements as objects that can be accessed from arbitrary programming languages). This depends on which event the user triggered and whether or not multiple items are, for instance, selected on the page that is to be protected.

The extension sends a query to the PDP for each usage event. If the response is inhibition, then the intercepted event is aborted. The architecture and inner workings of BRUCE are described in Appendix A.

3.6 Example Revisited

Now we demonstrate how SCUTA and BRUCE help Alice grant different usage rights to Bob and Carol. We know that Alice has rated Bob as best friend and Carol as acquaintance. This assigns Bob and Carol the trust ratings of 1 and .4, respectively. Alice has a low sensitive picture with a sensitivity of .4. When Bob and Carol access this picture in Alice's profile, the picture is delivered to Bob's client with medium permission class ($p = 1 * (1 - .4) = .6$). A respective code snippet is shown in Listing 1. Carol's client gets the picture with low permission class ($p = .4 * (1 - .4) = .24$). The definition of actions in permission classes is as shown in Table 3. According to these settings in Alice's profile, Bob is allowed to copy the picture while Carol is only allowed to view it and cannot copy. The generated policy consists of a set of rules like the one in Listing 2. So when Carol tries to copy this picture, BRUCE queries the PDP for the allow/inhibit status of the event 'copy.' The PDP replies with 'inhibit' and the extension blocks the abstract command 'copy.' Thus Alice's picture is protected for copy by Carol.

4. EVALUATION

The goal of our system evaluation is twofold. On the one hand, we want to analyze and demonstrate the ability of our system to withstand deliberate attacks from malicious users. To this end, we explored possible ways in which the security of our system can be compromised by means of attack trees. On the other hand, we want to understand the limitations of our system. These were found out as a result of the security analysis. This helped us finalize the assumptions under which the system can provide guarantees about the enforcement of usage control (Section 4.2), the limitations of the system (Section 4.3) and future work in this direction.

4.1 Security analysis

Our evaluation is strictly limited to the application layer and does not cover vulnerabilities arising from the other layers. For example, the system can be circumvented by accessing usage controlled data directly in the cache folder via an external file browser, by inspecting the main memory with a memory spy, or by taking screenshots from the screen. We will get back to these issues in Section 5. Moreover, we do not consider attacks from WBSN providers since these are considered trustworthy in our context.

The attack tree for performing prohibited events on data is shown in Figure 3. The subtrees with the goals "get access to database" and "hijack user account" show attack scenarios for SCUTA.[2] We do not go into the details of them as they are classical security problems in themselves. However, we mention one standard attack in which resources such as pictures can be directly accessed by typing their URLs in the address bar. Luckily, there is a standard solution to this problem. The server generates a (random) token and

---

[2]*Login* shows the attack scenario where a malicious user can login as SCUTA administrator

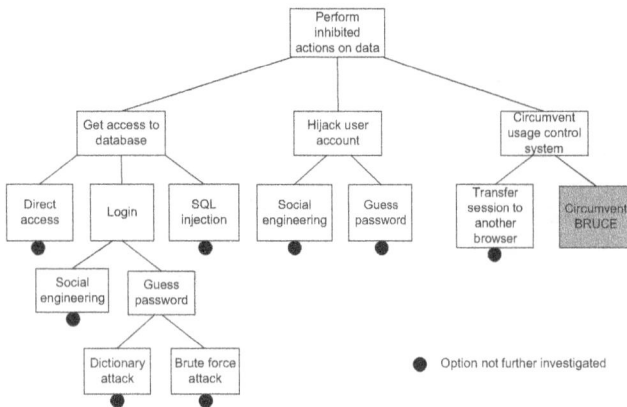

Figure 3: Attack tree for the system

a timestamp and includes them in the URL of the sensitive data item. The token is not bound to any user but is specific to a time interval which is used to invalidate the URL after a given timeout. In other words, before shipping the data item, the web server checks if a permitted time interval has not been exceeded; or it simply deletes the data item after the first download. In Listing 1, we show the unmodified URL of the image for simplicity's sake.

In the remainder of this section, we explore the subtree "circumvent BRUCE" in detail. For analyzing the circumvention of BRUCE, we treated SCUTA and the PDP module as black boxes and performed the security analysis under the assumption that they are secure with respect to the usage control system's specified functionality. Further security analysis covers three aspects of BRUCE: (i) Firefox's extension system; (ii) communication between SCUTA and the usage control extension; and (iii) communication between the PDP module and the usage control extension. The subtree is detailed in Figure 4.

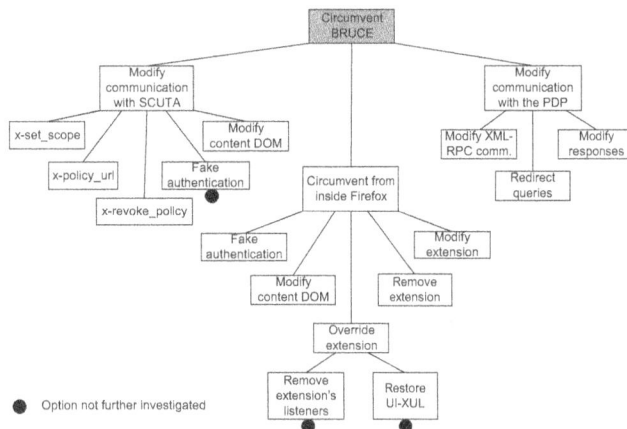

Figure 4: Attack tree for BRUCE

System vulnerabilities can be exploited in all the three submodules. As the server delivers sensitive content as soon as the client seems to be authentic, an attacker only needs to fake the authentication of the extension and leave the rest to the server itself. The extension only processes messages

and commands it receives. Whether they were manipulated before they arrived is not detectable. Also, the interception and dropping of messages is not detectable. At the PDP, as it only gets called by the extension and does not initiate any communication with other systems by itself, it is quite easy to overcome it. There is no chance that the PDP module gets to know about modification or omission of policies and permission queries. Also, if the PDP resides at a remote node additional points of attack in the system arise because the attacker could try to break in the traffic routed between the PDP and the client.

4.1.1 Modifying client-server communication

Both the message contents and its headers can be modified between SCUTA and BRUCE. As the provided solution uses information about HTML tags stored in the document, the system could be compromised by their modification. Policies refer to certain attributes of HTML elements to define usage restrictions. If the values of these attributes were changed, the extension would query for permission of commands with parameter values that differ from the original ones used in the policies. Thus the PDP module would allow those commands although they should have been inhibited.

This kind of attack could also be performed from the inside of Firefox by a malicious extension that modifies a web page after rendering, leading to the same result.

Instead of modifying HTML content, an attacker can also change the message headers. The header fields that can be used for this are 'x-policy_url', 'x-revoke_policy' and 'x-set_scope'.

Remember that 'x-policy_url' indicates the URL for the policy that has to be applied to the message's content. The extension will obtain and then insert it into the PDP module in order to make sure that it will be enforced. But as the URL's authenticity and integrity is not checkable, one could either replace the URL by another which points to a policy that grants all usage, or even easier: just delete this header.

Upon inspection of the HTTP messages that the browser receives, one is able to find out which policies were sent to it. Whenever a message with the header field 'x-policy_url' set arrives, the attacker can retrieve the specified policy. By investigating it, he could determine the IDs of the activated policies. This knowledge allows to insert 'x-revoke_policy' header fields with exactly these IDs into messages before they reach the browser. Due to these header fields, the extension would instruct the PDP module to discard the respective policies and from then on usage control for the messages mentioned in the beginning would be broken.

If a message contains a set_scope instruction, this means the server tells the extension to put the contents under usage control. So the simplest way to get around the system would be to remove this header field before the messages arrive at the browser. Although this would be sufficient, changing the value of this header to something that is not a known scope in the PDP module instead would have the same effect. The tab receiving the message would be taken under usage control and triggered commands checked for permission. But, as the PDP module would not know of the modified scope value, it would allow the commands.

Manipulation of messages and headers is a serious threat to the system. As the three involved subsystems do not exchange additional information to validate their intended actions and the integrity of emitted messages, one could easily compromise the system using a man-in-the-middle attack. The rather simple solution in this case is to use HTTPS instead of HTTP for the communication.

4.1.2 Modifying communication with the PDP

The usage control framework could also be circumvented by modification or redirection of messages exchanged between the extension and the PDP module. Due to the lack of integrity and authenticity checks in the system, such attacks would not be noticed. The XML-RPC interface provided by the PDP module offers methods for policy insertion, command permission checks and revocation of policies. An attacker can modify the request or response to circumvent the mechanism easily. For policy insertion calls, there are several kinds of changes that could be applied, but the easiest would be to replace the given policy with an empty one as this would lead to permission for all queried events. An attacker can also record the identifiers of the specified control mechanisms in the policy, instead of modifying them. These identifiers then can be put into a fake policy revocation call. The attacker can also redirect communication to another target server that supports the same interface as the PDP, but which handles incoming calls according to the attacker's wish.

A man-in-the-middle attack can easily compromise the usage control system just like it can by modifying the client-server communication. However, while the client and server have the possibility to use HTTPS in place of HTTP to exchange their messages, our current PDP module does not support HTTPS for communication (which is not a conceptual problem but a matter of maturity of our implementation). Hence, the unencrypted messages can be modified with no big effort. Therefore encryption and integrity checks should be considered in future work. For example, to discover if policies have been modified, the PDP module could compute a hash over received policies and send it to the originating web application. This way policy integrity could be checked, assuming authenticity of such messages could be assured. Tampered policy revocations could be prevented if the PDP module asked the respective web applications for authenticity of incoming revocation instructions.

4.1.3 Circumvention from within Firefox

Another vulnerability arises from interfering with BRUCE's behavior from within the Firefox browser. This can be done by modifying BRUCE's source code (which is written in Javascript) or deploying a nullifying extension. Some of the exploits are listed below:

- Reset usage command handling by changing back the overridden commands to their original definition;
- Revoke policies directly after they have been sent to the PDP module;
- Modify the scope mapping mechanism, e.g. discard all mappings;
- Alter usage command handling such that no queries are sent to the PDP module;
- Add internal events (and corresponding user commands, see Section 3.3.3) that exactly copy the behavior of usage-controlled internal events—since the name of the internal event is different, usage control requirements will not be enforced for these new events; or
- Fake the extension authentication.

Besides this, providing object orientation via prototyping-based programming is a special feature of Javascript that makes it easy to modify existing objects. This includes the possibility to replace methods by any arbitrary function definition. This complicates shielding the extension's code against malicious injections. Also, attempts to protect the extension against modifications of its source code would be futile as they could just be removed.

The aforementioned change can also be done by extracting the extension from its XPI archive[3], then modifying the corresponding source file and repacking it. After the next start of Firefox, usage control would not work anymore. To counter this, BRUCE's integrity should be checked right before it gets loaded. Another possibility to achieve this attack goal is by installing a malicious extension which can override the methods dynamically. In this case an integrity check at the start may prove useless. Detecting such changes during runtime appears to involve a considerable effort. The threat induced by a possible malicious extension is the bottleneck of the current system. Perhaps it is feasible to check other installed extensions if they modify BRUCE before the browser starts—a subject of future work.

4.2 Assumptions

Based on the evaluation of the system in the previous paragraphs, we draw the set of assumptions under which the system provides usage control according to the stipulated requirements and cannot be circumvented or forced to work in unexpected ways.

Our system guarantees client-side browser-level enforcement of usage control policies specified by the user and generated at the server side (user requirements given in Table 1) under the condition that the following requirements are met:

1. The communication between SCUTA and the Firefox extension is carried out over a secure channel.
2. The PDP module is extended by the capability to communicate over a secure channel.
3. The client must be able to guarantee that the Firefox extension is not modified before and after installation.
4. The client must be able to guarantee that no malicious extension is installed and if installed can be detected while running the extension.
5. A tamper-proof mechanism to authenticate the Firefox extension with SCUTA exists.
6. As every data that is delivered to the client is also stored in cache folders or displayed on a screen at the client side, usage control enforcement mechanisms exist to solve the problem at other levels of abstraction (see Section 5).

To meet the requirements 3 and 4, one could think of a client system which provides usage control on the levels below the application level. Then, the installation package of the Firefox extension could be shipped with a policy attached which implies satisfaction of these requirements.

Under the condition that the aforementioned requirements hold true, we consider our system to be secure at the client side and at the communication links level with respect to the attacker model presented in the security analysis. However, at the server side, attacks like social engineering, cross

---

[3]XPI is short for Cross-Platform Installer Module. It belongs to Mozilla's XPInstall technology, see https://developer.mozilla.org/en/XPI.

site scripting, hacking user accounts and breaking into the database or the system are classical problems and we cannot provide any guarantees against them in this paper. Looking into such more general security issues is not in the scope of this paper (Section 1).

4.3 Limitations

The developed system enforces usage control for data that is delivered by websites via web pages to the client. It implements the requirements given in Table 2. However, there is one limitation of our implementation in terms of functional completeness: The solution has been implemented only for native data. By native data we mean the content that Firefox can render by itself and this does not include contents handled by plug-ins [53], for example, Flash or PDF.

The limitations of the system, found during the evaluation, can be summarized as follows.

1. The system provides usage control guarantees only for the case of native data.
2. The system provides guarantees only if the assumptions in Section 4.2 are met.
3. The system provides usage control guarantees only for the *single user page* scenario (see below).
4. The system provides usage control guarantees only at the browser's level of abstraction. Data stored in cache folders is not protected; screenshots can also be taken.

In a *single user page* scenario, the page being rendered contains data only about one user, e.g., Alice's homepage. This can be contrasted to *multiple users page* scenario where the rendered page contains data about multiple users e.g. page displaying search results for "Alice" as there can be many users with the name Alice and their basic information like name, city, country are displayed on the webpage in a list. In the evaluation, we also found that implementing this does not seem to be a conceptual problem and is left as future work.

5. CONCLUSIONS AND FUTURE WORK

We have presented and evaluated a framework for enforcing usage control requirements at the application level for the particular case of web browsers. As an example, we have implemented our framework in the context of privacy protection in web based social networks. We use the case of WBSNs only for the demonstration of our proposed mechanism. The usefulness of our mechanism is of course not limited to WBSNs but extends to all the web applications that are accessed using a web browser. Referring to the use case in the introduction, when Alice specifies Bob and Carol as different kinds of contacts, they are assigned a trust level and based on the sensitivity of the data being accessed, Bob and Carol receive data with different policies. So while Bob can copy and print Alice's personal data and pictures, Carol can only view selected parts of the profile and cannot copy or print anything.

In the proposed framework, SCUTA acts as a policy generation point which can generate and render usage control policies in the form of ECA rules. The generated policy is communicated to the client through HTTP header fields. BRUCE provides usage control for Firefox's native data types to SCUTA. Policies that are bound to delivered content are fetched and then enforced by the framework. As

it only serves as policy enforcement point, it utilizes an external policy decision point via a fixed XML-RPC interface.

As the evaluation points out, our system guarantees client side data usage control enforcement at the browser level if certain assumptions hold true. This guarantee is with respect to the attacker model presented in the security analysis part of the evaluation. However, additional work has to be done in order to make sure that these assumptions are always met, e.g., for all clients and all content types. In this respect, our solution is not mature yet. To complete the set of manageable kinds of data, e.g., by Flash animations, additional effort has to be put into the examination of embedded data types, which are rendered in Firefox through plug-ins. The heterogeneity among them presents a challenge for a general solution which is independent of particular content types.

The guarantees provided by our mechanism depend on active security mechanisms implemented in other parts of the system. The security analysis investigated several possible types of circumvention. Intuitively, integrating encryption and certification into the system could improve security. Also, exchanging the header field commands by an interface that provides the same capabilities while being less prone to manipulations could contribute to better security. Another line of future work is to extend the implementation of usage control for pages that have data about multiple users.

The aforementioned challenges only mark the beginning of what future work has to cover in order to achieve relevant usage control systems. In this context, issues concerning usage control at different layers of abstraction also need to be addressed. For example, when a browser caches a picture which is protected by usage control at the browser level, in a file on the hard disk, usage control should be in place for the operating system level. Similarly, there must be a way to inhibit screenshots.

From the time when the picture "leaves the browser," the receiving layer should be capable of continuing usage control enforcement. For this we need a data-centric approach for usage control that transcends the traditional approach based on events: the flow of data through the different levels of abstraction has to be detected, and enforcement of data usage must take place at all these levels. We are currently working on such a framework. There already is usage control enforcement with data flow tracking for the operating system [12] and the X11 levels [13], and now we are working towards connecting them with the browser. We have already extended BRUCE to (1) identify protected pictures with files cached on the hard disk and to (2) pass on the information about the protected cached data along with the associated policies to the enforcement mechanism at the operating system level where the cache file can be usage-controlled. In a similar vein, we are working on a connection with the enforcement mechanism at the X11 level to inhibit screenshots.

Finally, we see another research challenge in the context of heterogeneous cyber-physical systems. In this direction we are working on connecting a smart metering system to SCUTA where the social network fetches energy usage data from the smart meter according to policies specified by the smart energy user. In this case, we are interested in looking into the issues of policy conflicts and evolution of obligations across system boundaries. Another point of interest is the delegation of rights and duties in such a system where usage control is not centralized but distributed.

6. REFERENCES

[1] A. Pretschner, M. Hilty, and D. Basin. Distributed usage control. *Commun. ACM*, 49(9):39–44, 2006.

[2] J. Park and R. Sandhu. The UCON ABC usage control model. *ACM Trans. Inf. Syst. Secur.*, 7(1):128–174, 2004.

[3] D. Povey. Optimistic security: a new access control paradigm. In *Proceedings of the 1999 workshop on New security paradigms*, NSPW '99, pages 40–45. ACM, 2000.

[4] R. Iannella (ed.). Open Digital Rights Language v1.1, 2008. http://odrl.net/1.1/ODRL-11.pdf.

[5] Multimedia framework (MPEG-21) – Part 5: Rights Expression Language, 2004. ISO/IEC standard 21000-5:2004.

[6] P. Ashley, S. Hada, G. Karjoth, C. Powers, and M. Schunter. Enterprise Privacy Authorization Language (EPAL 1.2). IBM Technical Report, 2003. http://www.zurich.ibm.com/security/enterprise-privacy/epal/Specification/.

[7] Open Mobile Alliance. DRM Rights Expression Language V2.1, 2008. http://www.openmobilealliance.org/Technical/release_program/drm_v2_1.aspx.

[8] X. Zhang, J. Park, F. Parisi-Presicce, and R. Sandhu. A logical specification for usage control. In *SACMAT '04: Proceedings of the ninth ACM symposium on Access control models and technologies*, pages 1–10. ACM, 2004.

[9] M. Hilty, A. Pretschner, D. Basin, C. Schaefer, and T. Walter. A policy language for distributed usage control. In *Proc. ESORICS*, pages 531–546, 2008.

[10] N. Damianou, N. Dulay, E. Lupu, and M. Sloman. The Ponder Policy Specification Language. In *Proc. Workshop on Policies for Distributed Systems and Networks*, pages 18–39, 1995.

[11] W3C. The Platform for Privacy Preferences 1.1 (P3P1.1) Specification, 2005. http://www.w3.org/TR/2005/WD-P3P11-20050104/.

[12] M. Harvan and A. Pretschner. State-based Usage Control Enforcement with Data Flow Tracking using System Call Interposition. In *Proc. 3rd Intl. Conf. on Network and System Security*, pages 373–380, 2009.

[13] A. Pretschner, M. Buechler, M. Harvan, C. Schaefer, and T. Walter. Usage control enforcement with data flow tracking for x11. In *Proc. 5th Intl. Workshop on Security and Trust Management*, pages 124–137, 2009.

[14] M. Dam, B. Jacobs, A. Lundblad, and F. Piessens. Security monitor inlining for multithreaded java. In *Proc. ECOOP*, pages pp. 546–569, 2009.

[15] I. Ion, B. Dragovic, and B. Crispo. Extending the Java Virtual Machine to Enforce Fine-Grained Security Policies in Mobile Devices. In *Proc. Annual Computer Security Applications Conference*, pages 233–242. IEEE Computer Society, 2007.

[16] L. Desmet, W. Joosen, F. Massacci, K. Naliuka, P. Philippaerts, F. Piessens, and D. Vanoverberghe. The S3MS.NET Run Time Monitor: Tool Demonstration. *ENTCS*, 253(5):153–159, 2009.

[17] U. Erlingsson and F. Schneider. SASI enforcement of security policies: A retrospective. In *Proc. New Security Paradigms Workshop*, pages 87–95, 1999.

[18] B. Yee, D. Sehr, G. Dardyk, J. Chen, R. Muth, T. Ormandy, S. Okasaka, N. Narula, and N. Fullagar. Native Client: A Sandbox for Portable, Untrusted x86 Native Code. In *Proc IEEE Symposium on Security and Privacy*, pages 79–93, 2009.

[19] G. Gheorghe, S. Neuhaus, and B. Crispo. xESB: An Enterprise Service Bus for Access and Usage Control Policy Enforcement. In *Proc. Annual IFIP WG 11.11 International Conference on Trust Management*, 2010.

[20] M. Egele, C. Kruegel, E. Kirda, H. Yin, and D. Song. Dynamic spyware analysis. In *Proceedings of USENIX Annual Technical Conference*, June 2007.

[21] Adobe livecycle rights management es. http://www.adobe.com/products/livecycle/rightsmanagement/indepth.html, August 2010.

[22] Microsoft. Windows Rights Management Services. http://www.microsoft.com/windowsserver2008/en/us/ad-rms-overview.aspx, 2010.

[23] A. Pretschner, M. Hilty, F. Schutz, C. Schaefer, and T. Walter. Usage control enforcement: Present and future. *Security & Privacy, IEEE*, 6(4):44–53, 2008.

[24] P. Kumari. Requirements analysis for privacy in social networks. 8th International Workshop for Technical, Economic and Legal Aspects of Business Models for Virtual Goods, Namur, 2010.

[25] A. Acquisti and R. Gross. Imagined Communities: Awareness, Information Sharing, and Privacy on the Facebook. In *Privacy Enhancing Technologies Workshop (PET)*, Robinson College, Cambridge, United Kingdom, June 2006.

[26] C. Dwyer and S. Hiltz. Trust and privacy concern within social networking sites: A comparison of Facebook and MySpace. In *Proceedings of the Thirteenth Americas Conference on Information Systems*, Keystone, Colorado, USA, August 2007.

[27] J. Grimmelmann. Facebook and the Social Dynamics of Privacy. *Legal Studies, New York Law School*, 7:33–34, 2008/2009.

[28] L. Edwards and I. Brown. Data Control and Social Networking: Irreconcilable Ideas? In A. Matwyshyn, editor, *Harboring data: Information security, law, and the corporation*. Stanford University Press, 2009.

[29] K. Williams, A. Boyd, S. Densten, R. Chin, D. Diamond, and C. Morgenthaler. Social Networking Privacy Behaviors and Risks. *Seidenberg School of CSIS, Pace University, USA*, 2009.

[30] C. Yeung, I. Liccardi, K. Lu, O. Seneviratne, and T. Berners-Lee. Decentralization: The future of online social networking. In *W3C Workshop on the Future of Social Networking Position Papers*, 2009.

[31] The friend of a friend (foaf) project. http://www.foaf-project.org/docs, September 2010.

[32] A. Cutillo, R. Molva, and T. Strufe. Privacy preserving social networking through decentralization. In *WONS'09: Proceedings of the Sixth international conference on Wireless On-Demand Network Systems and Services*, pages 133–140. IEEE Press, 2009.

[33] Safebook publications. http://www.safebook.us/publications.html, September 2010.

[34] Peerson: Privacy-preserving p2p social networks. http://www.peerson.net, September 2010.

[35] D. Kalofonos, Z. Antoniou, F. Reynolds, M. Van-Kleek, J. Strauss, and P. Wisner. MyNet: a Platform for Secure P2P Personal and Social Networking Services. In *6th IEEE International Conference on Pervasive Computing and Communications (PERCOM'08)*, Hong-Kong, China, March 2008.

[36] Z. Antoniou and D. Kalofonos. User-Centered Design of a Secure P2P Personal and Social Networking Platform. In *3rd IASTED International Conference on Human-Computer Interaction (IASTED-HCI'08)*, Innsbruck, Austria, March 2008.

[37] K. Gollu, S. Saroiu, and A. Wolman. A Social Networking-Based Access Control Scheme for Personal Content. In *21st ACM Symposium on Operating Systems Principles (SOSP '07)*, Stevenson, Washington, October 2007.

[38] A. Tootoonchian, K. Gollu, S. Saroiu, Y. Ganjali, and A. Wolman. Lockr: Social Access Control for Web 2.0. In *First ACM SIGCOMM Workshop on Online Social Networks (WOSN)*, Seattle, WA, August 2008.

[39] B. Carminati, E. Ferrari, and A. Perego. Enforcing access control in web-based social networks. *ACM Trans. Inf. Syst. Secur.*, 13(1):1–38, 2009.

[40] Website of the Scramble! project. http://www.primelife.eu/results/opensource/39-scramble, September 2010.

[41] Website of the clique project. http://clique.primelife.eu/, September 2010.

[42] F. Beato, M. Kohlweiss, and K. Wouters. Enforcing access control in social networks. In *Proc. HotPets*, 2009.

[43] B. Berg and R. Leenes. Audience segregation in social network sites. In *Proceedings for SocialCom2010/PASSAT2010.IEEE*, pages 1111–1117, 2010.

[44] S. Kruk, S. Grzonkowski, A. Gzella, T. Woroniecki, and H. Choi. D-foaf: Distributed identity management with access rights delegation. In *Proc. Asian Semantic Web Conference 2006*, 2006.

[45] FOAFRealm. Foafrealm project site. http://www.foafrealm.org/, Jul 2010.

[46] Mozilla's add-on repository AMO. https://addons.mozilla.org/, July 2010.

[47] The tabulator extension. http://dig.csail.mit.edu/2007/tab, September 2010.

[48] J. Peschla. Data usage control for a web application: The client. Bachelor's thesis, University of Kaiserslautern, July 2010.

[49] Browser market share. http://marketshare.hitslink.com/browser-market-share.aspx?qprid=0&qptimeframe=M&qpsp=138&qpnp=1, September 2010.

[50] Phpizabi homepage. http://www.phpizabi.net/, September 2010.

[51] A. Pretschner, M. Hilty, D. Basin, C. Schaefer, and T. Walter. Mechanisms for Usage Control. In *Proc. ACM Symposium on Information, Computer & Communication Security*, pages 240–245, 2008.

[52] MASTER consortium. MASTER Deliverable 5.1.1: Security Enforcement Language. http://www.master-fp7.eu/, April 2010.

[53] Mozilla's plugin documentation. https://developer.mozilla.org/en/Plugins, May 2010.

APPENDIX

A. COMPONENTS OF BRUCE

In this section we give a brief overview of the major components of the policy enforcement point. They appear in the order in which they are called throughout usage control setup and enforcement.

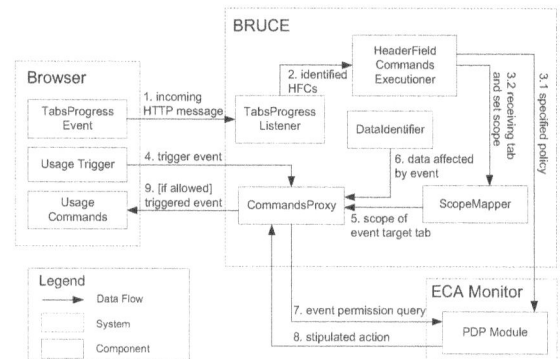

Figure 5: Architecture of BRUCE

TabsProgressListener is the component that is attached as event listener to the browser window so that it gets notified about all web-request and -response related events. This way it examines the HTTP headers of each incoming web-response for HFCs. Identified HFCs are forwarded to *HeaderFieldCommandsExecutioner* which carries them out. Besides, TabsProgressListener ensures that the browser cache cannot be accessed via Firefox itself.

HeaderFieldCommandsExecutioner carries out HFCs received from *TabsProgressListener*. Therefore it either communicates with the WBSN (authentication), the PDP (policy activation and revocation) or instructs *ScopeMapper* to update its mapping (scope assignment or release).

ScopeMapper is the component that maintains the associations between tabs and scopes.

CommandsProxy is the component that intercepts triggered usage events and decides about their progress. To determine whether an intercepted event has to be aborted, *CommandsProxy* queries *ScopeMapper* for the scope of the active tab and retrieves the event target from *DataIdentifier*. When a scope is set, then for each target element it queries the PDP with the parameter values for scope and abstract command. If for all queries the response is approval, the intercepted event is resumed, otherwise it is aborted. If no scope is set for the active tab it is either blocked and the event is aborted or the displayed page is not under usage control and the event is resumed.

DataIdentifier is an encapsulation of DOM element determination facilities. Given a usage related event and the target page it calculates the set of affected elements which is the target of the event as explained in Section 3.5.

MyABDAC: Compiling XACML Policies for Attribute-Based Database Access Control

Sonia Jahid
University of Illinois at
Urbana-Champaign
sjahid2@illinois.edu

Carl A. Gunter
University of Illinois at
Urbana-Champaign
cgunter@illinois.edu

Imranul Hoque
University of Illinois at
Urbana-Champaign
ihoque2@illinois.edu

Hamed Okhravi*
University of Illinois at
Urbana-Champaign
okhravi@mit.edu

ABSTRACT

Attribute-based Access Control (ABAC) based on XACML can substantially improve the security and management of access rights on databases. However, existing implementations rely on high-level policy interpretation and are not as efficient as mechanisms natively supported by commodity databases. In this paper we explore advantages and challenges arising from compiling XACML policies for database access into Access Control Lists (ACLs) natively supported by the database. The main contributions are an architecture and algorithms for efficiently addressing incremental changes in attributes that could trigger changes to the ACLs. We consider this in a context of reflective database access control where attributes used in access decisions are stored in the database itself. Our implementation and experiments demonstrate a significant improvement in access decision times compared to the best available optimizations for general XACML access engines.

Categories and Subject Descriptors

H.2.0 [**Database Management**]: General—*Security, integrity, and protection*

General Terms

Design, Experimentation, Security

Keywords

Access Control List, Database, XACML, MySQL, Attribute

---

*The author is currently with MIT Lincoln Laboratory.

1. INTRODUCTION

Databases are able to enforce access policies through low-level mechanisms like Access Control Lists (ACLs). A common approach is to implement Identity-based Access Control (IBAC) with ACLs. While very efficient, this approach has management disadvantages when policies are based on attributes. By contrast, Attribute-based Access Control (ABAC) policies, such as ones based on XACML [12], describe users and resources in terms of attributes and establish permissions using these attributes rather than identifiers. This provides more expressive and manageable access control. However, general ABAC policy implementations such as the Sun XACML Implementation (SunXACML) [31] are less efficient at deciding access rights on databases than ACLs, which are supported natively by common database systems.

In this paper we explore the idea of *policy compilation* to address this limitation and provide efficient implementation of ABAC over databases. The basic idea is to use attributes contained in the database itself, and compile high-level policies over these attributes into a collection of ACLs for the underlying database resources together with a collection of database-level mechanisms for their automated maintenance. This enables access rights to be described at a high level but implemented and maintained at a low level. For example, a high-level policy states 'give nurses of department infectious disease read and write access on patient records with infectious disease diagnoses' whereas an ACL says, 'give read and write permissions to principals a and b on objects o_1 and o_2'. We compile the former into the latter to provide the expressiveness of the high level policy as well as the efficiency of ACLs.

Existing policy decision point implementations such as SunXACML verify XACML policies on-the-fly to perform access control in general. A significant improvement in performance can be achieved by preprocessing specific policies to include optimizations. This is demonstrated by the XACML preprocessor XEngine [18]. XEngine maintains the generality of XACML while eliminating numerous inefficient decision-time processing steps by trading these improvements off against modest preprocessing costs. The goal of this paper is explore what further efficiency can be obtained by sacrificing some of this generality by specializing the optimizations to the case of *Reflective Database Access*

Control (RDBAC) [22]. RDBAC is concerned with ABAC access to a database where the database itself contains security attributes used by the decision engine. For example, the database contains a table that indicates who is a nurse, who is in the infectious disease department, and what constitutes an infectious disease diagnosis. This situation enables a step beyond optimizations that are specific to the policy, but not specific to the enforcement mechanism, to a situation in which compilation into the underlying enforcement mechanism is possible.

The trade off for RDBAC-specific optimization is the need for an efficient way to deal with changes not only in *policies* but also in *attributes*. Attribute value updates in the database require efficient, timely, and correct ACL recalculations. This needs a way to transform the ACLs to a correct and consistent state with minimal overhead by reconsidering a well-chosen subset of existing policies and permissions. An intuitive analogy here is to the way spreadsheets update values in cells as cells on which they depend are updated. In this context there is a trade off between updating the cells immediately (so up-to-date values can be seen in all cells) versus updating cells periodically (to save unnecessary recalculations if correct values are not needed immediately). Our goal here is to describe an architecture and algorithms that will do this on-demand for XACML over RDBAC. That is, the algorithm detects when a change to an attribute could affect an access right so that recompilation is triggered only when necessary and only affected ACLs require updates.

To test and validate ABAC policy compilation for databases, we implemented an engine named *MyABDAC* that compiles XACML policies into MySQL [16] ACLs. We compare our performance with that of SunXACML and XEngine to demonstrate non-trivial speed up in database access decision time with reasonable costs for compilation of thousands of policies and users. We choose a basic database system like MySQL for the demonstration because, if it can be done there, it will undoubtedly be easier and more efficient to do it for more full-featured commercial databases where the implementation could use support like the Oracle Virtual Private Database (VPD) [7] transformations.

The rest of the paper is organized as follows. Section 2 describes the problem and its challenges in details, Section 3 describes necessary background materials, Section 4 presents a system design, architecture, and approach for policy compilation, Section 5 describes updates and correctness, Section 6 analyzes MyABDAC performance in comparison with SunXACML and XEngine, Section 7 discusses the security and expressiveness, Section 8 discusses key related works, and Section 9 concludes.

2. CHALLENGES

Though compiling policies offers potential improvements in efficiency, it comes with several challenges. Policy compilation moves the decision point from high-level to low-level, that is, from application to database ACL. An ACL is a list of access rights attached to an object. It describes which users have what permission on the objects. In this case, objects are either tables or columns, and permissions are database operations such as 'SELECT', 'INSERT', and so on. The principals and resources reside in an organization database, and are used to construct the ACLs when they satisfy the attribute policies. Any update in their attribute values affects the permissions and may introduce inconsis-

tency in the database ACLs. Some permissions have to be revoked while some remain unchanged. A naïve approach is to recompile all the policies and build up the ACLs from scratch, but this is quite inefficient. Since ACLs are affected in different ways depending on the underlying data, the policy, and the combining algorithms in the policy [12], maintaining a consistent relationship between the high level attribute policy and the ACLs in the database is challenging. New attribute values may leave existing permissions unchanged, or they may add or eliminate permissions. What makes this determination challenging is the complexity of XACML policies in general, the potentially large number of the rules in a given database policy, and the number of users and resources that satisfy the rules.

An example in Figure 1 represents a high level XACML policy that illustrates some of the issues concretely. It consists of 2 policies P_1 and P_2 which consist of rules R_1, R_2, R_3, and R_4 respectively. Rules R_1 and R_2 permit read on $table_1$ to the nurses of department infectious disease and job experience greater than 5 years respectively. Rule R_3 denies read on $table_1$ to the nurses of qualification level less than 3. In case of conflict, a permit is prioritized for these rules in P_1. Rule R_4 denies the same permission to the $4th$ floor nurses. Suppose a nurse nrs_1 satisfies all these policies. Because of the 'permit overrides' combining algorithm in P_1 and P, nrs_1 gets read permission on $table_1$. If her department changes to 'medicine', her permission is unchanged because of R_2 within P_1. If no R_2 existed, then her permission would be revoked since there is no other rule in either P_1 or P_2 that permits this permission. If P_2 had 'permit overrides', R_2 did not exist, and another rule R_5 (*Permit, Dept=medicine, table_2*) existed in P_2, then, although $\langle table_1, nrs_1, select \rangle$ would be revoked, a new permission $\langle table_2, nrs_1, select \rangle$ would be added.

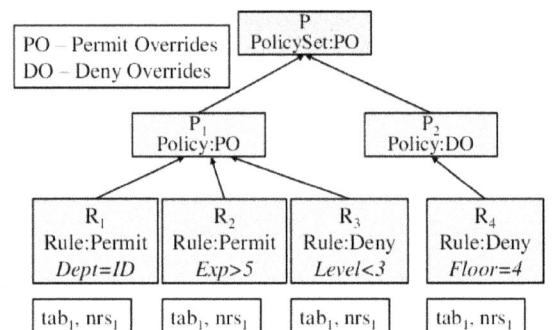

Figure 1: Representation of an XACML Policy

Though we discussed the challenges of updating a single user, there are cases when a large number of users are updated. For example, a company might give promotions to a range of employees who received favorable job reviews and thus trigger changes in permissions for all of these employees. This type of attribute update raises scalability issues. Besides, when a policy has a large number of rules that deal with different attributes, the primary challenge is to find out a subset of rules in the policy that have to be recompiled and reconsider the other existing permissions that all the updated users have in order to perform the minimum changes in database ACLs, and reduce expensive database operations. These issues challenge the correctness of permissions at low level database ACLs. Although compilation can improve efficiency at decision time, it also introduces the challenge of correct and efficient management.

3. BACKGROUND

In this section, we present some background on XACML and native database access control mechanisms.

At the core of an XACML policy are `Rules`. A `Rule` consists of a `Target`, an `Effect` (Permit or Deny), and, optionally, a `Condition`. The `Target` defines the access permissions between `Subject` and `Resource` elements using `Action`, and is used to decide whether a rule applies to a request. The `Condition` is used to further restrict the rule. Subjects and resources are expressed through attributes.

At the top of a policy exists a `PolicySet` or `Policy`. A `PolicySet` (`Policy`) consists of `PolicySet` or `Policy` (`Rule`), a policy-(rule)combining-algorithm, and a `Target`. The algorithms resolve an access decision in case of conflict or redundancy within a `Policy` or `PolicySet`. A `permit/deny-overrides` rule-combining algorithm permits/denies an access if at least one `Rule` results in permit/deny. `first-applicable` returns the effect of the first rule that applies to the request and ignores the rest. Policy-combining algorithm `only-one-applicable` returns *Indeterminate* if more than one `Policy` applies to a request. It returns the effect of the one applicable policy otherwise. If no match is found for a request, then *NotApplicable* is returned. Further information on XACML can be found in [12].

Most mainstream database systems maintain a list of permitted users along with their access rights on tables. Depending on the implementation, this can be either Access Control Matrix (a table with entries that indicate who can access what) or an ACL (for each object a list of who is allowed to access it). MySQL keeps ACLs in certain tables in a special database (`mysql`). Access control is performed in two stages: authentication, and privilege check for query execution. In the first stage the server consults tables `mysql.user` (which provides usernames, passwords, and global privileges), `mysql.db` and `mysql.host` (which provide privileges for specific databases tables) for user authentication. In the second stage it checks whether the user has the privileges needed to execute a given query. The server can also consult tables `mysql.tables_priv` and `mysql.columns_priv` and `mysql.procs_priv` for finer privileges at table, column, and stored routine levels respectively. These tables contain the ACLs for specific tables in the database. For example, if a user $user_0$ has `SELECT` access on $table_0$ and $table_1$, then there will be two entries in `tables_priv` with appropriate values. Details of MySQL access control mechanism can be found in [20].

4. SYSTEM ARCHITECTURE

Let us now consider how policy compilation for XACML into ACLs can be achieved with common database mechanisms. We describe a suitable architecture and show how to compile policies and analyze consistency. The system, which is illustrated in Figure 2, consists of three major components: 1) the database, in which the attributes, resources, and ACLs are all stored, 2) the high-level access policy, from which access enforcement is derived, and 3) the compilation

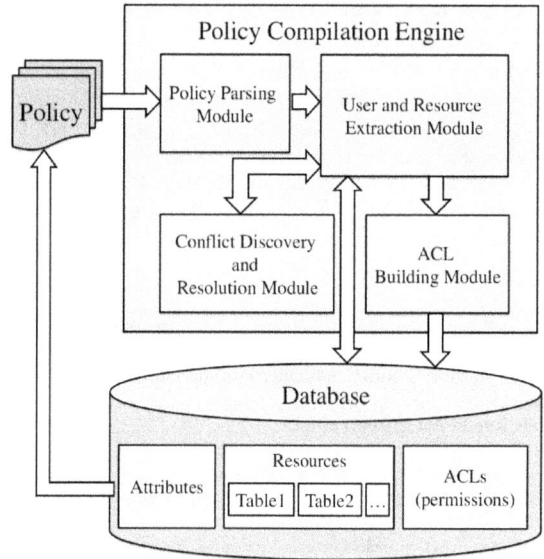

Figure 2: System Architecture

engine, which relates high-level policy to low-level policy and enforcement. We discuss each of these in turn.

4.1 Database

Database tables maintained, for example, by the human resources department of an organization contain information useful for access control decisions. This information includes user attributes such as department, job title, salary, birth date, email, mail, phone, and so on. Usually administrators have access to user information so that they can modify sensitive data like salary and job title. The frequency of change in these attributes varies, attributes such as birth date, joining date, and gender change rarely, while others, like various benefit plans, may change yearly, and still others, like short-term work assignments, might change quite frequently. Depending on the context, not all attributes are appropriate for access control. For instance, a phone number supplied by employee is less likely to be used in access control than, for instance, the job title of the employee. In a `hospital` database this attribute table can be of the form `employee(username, department, jobtitle, ...)` that stores all information about employees. An example record for a nurse is ⟨'alice','infectious disease department', 'nurse', ...⟩.

A database contains tables of records that define enterprise resources. For example, a resource table in a school might consist of a list of courses being offered in a given semester, including information like when and where the course meets, who is teaching it, and so on. Resource tables in a hospital might consist of patient information, administrative details, and so on. Various existing database mechanisms can be utilized in order to attach attributes to tables. For example, the information about a table or column in MySQL being marked as 'sensitive' in its comment field is stored as metadata in `information_schema.tables` table. Generally, databases maintain a special part to store the ACLs. In MySQL this is called `mysql`.

4.2 High-level Policy

The subjects and resources of our XACML policy are constructed using attributes extracted from the database. Resources are database tables or columns described through attributes or identifiers. Actions are database operations such as SELECT, INSERT, DELETE, which subjects can have on these resources. A 'Permit' allows and a 'Deny' prevents database access. Policies are generated using an interactive policy-builder that accesses the attribute database. A simplified XACML policy is shown in Figure 3.

```
<PolicySet PolicySetId=P PolicyCombiningAlgId=permit-overrides>
 <Target/>
 <Policy PolicyId=P1 RuleCombiningAlgId=permit-overrides>
  <Target/>
  <Rule RuleId=R1 Effect=Permit>
   <Target> <Subjects> <Subject><Id>position<Value>nurse
   <Id>department<Value>infectious disease</Subject> </Subjects>
   <Resources> <Resource>sensitive information</Resource>
   </Resources>
   <Actions> <Action>select,insert</Action> </Actions> </Target>
  </Rule>
  <Rule RuleId=R2 Effect=Permit>
   <Target> <Subjects> <Subject><Id>position<Value>nurse
   <Id>experience<Value>5</Subject> </Subjects>
   <Resources> <Resource>table1</Resource></Resources>
    <Actions><Action>select,delete</Action> </Actions> </Target>
  </Rule>
  <Rule RuleId=R3 Effect=Deny>
   <Target> <Subjects> <Subject><Id>position<Value>nurse
   <Id>level<Value>3</Subject> </Subjects>
   <Resources> <Resource>table1</Resource></Resources>
    <Actions><Action>select</Action> </Actions> </Target> </Rule>
  </Policy>
 <Policy PolicyId=P2 RuleCombiningAlgId=deny-overrides>
  <Target/>
  <Rule RuleId=R4 Effect=Deny>
   <Target> <Subjects> <Subject><Id>position<Value>nurse
   <Id>floor<Value>4</Subject> </Subjects>
   <Resources> <Resource>table1</Resource> </Resources>
   <Actions> <Action>select,insert</Action> </Actions> </Target>
  </Rule> </Policy>
</PolicySet>
```

Figure 3: An XACML Policy (Simplified)

At the root of the policy is a PolicySet P with policy-combining algorithm permit-overrides. P consists of two policies P_1 and P_2. P_1 consists of rules R_1, R_2, and R_3. R_1 permits 'nurses' of department 'infectious disease' to 'select' from and 'insert' into tables marked as 'sensitive information', R_2 permits 'nurses' with job experience greater that 5 years to 'select' and 'delete' from $table_1$, and R_3 denies 'nurses' of qualification level less than 3 (greater and less-than functions not shown in the policy) 'select' on $table_1$. P_1 has a permit-overrides rule combining algorithm. P_2 consists of R_4 that denies 'select' and 'insert' on $table_1$ to the $4th$ floor nurses. P_2's rule combining algorithm is 'deny-overrides'.

4.3 Compilation Engine

The Compilation Engine consists of four modules. We describe each of the components and their functions in turn and summarize their connections to the database.

The **Policy Parsing Module** (PPM) takes an XACML policy as input, extracts the rules out of it, and formulates a tuple for each of the rules. Parsing depends on the number of policies, the number of attributes each policy consists of, while it is independent of the underlying attribute data. It creates a tree structure of the XACML policy. Each Policy, PolicySet, and Rule element is a node in the tree. Rules are leaves, and the other elements are intermediate nodes. While parsing the rules of an XACML policy, the corresponding 'Policy' and 'PolicySet's are extracted and stored along with their combining algorithms in the process. For each Rule in the policy, it extracts a tuple ⟨policyID, ruleID, subject, resource, action, effect⟩. For instance, parsing R_1 of P_1 results in the following tuple. A

```
⟨ P1, R1, position='nurse' AND department = 'infec-
tious disease', resource = 'sensitive information',
'SELECT,INSERT', Permit⟩
```

pseudo-code of the described process is shown in Figure 8 in the appendix of the paper.

The **User and Resource Extraction Module** (UREM) interacts with the parsing module and gets the parsed policy. For each rule it formulates a subject query, and a resource query that extract the corresponding users and resources from the database respectively. For instance, the following queries are constructed for R_1 in P_1. If resources are expressed merely through their identifiers, the latter query is omitted. The tuple is saved in database with the attributes

```
1) SELECT username FROM hospital.employee
WHERE jobtitle='nurse' AND department='infectious dis-
ease';
2) SELECT table_name FROM information_schema.tables
WHERE table_comment='sensitive information';
```

replaced by the queries. The queries are cached to handle dynamic effects on the ACL in case any user attribute changes (a process described later). The queries are then executed, and a set of users (e.g. nrs_1, nrs_2) and tables (e.g. tab_1, tab_2) are obtained. Each of this is used to generate an access permission ⟨resource, user, action, effect⟩. Figure 4 shows the tree representation of the policy in Figure 3. Example access permissions for R_1, R_2, R_3, and R_4 are shown at leaves; s, i, and d stand for select, insert, and delete respectively.

Conflict Discovery and Resolution Module (CD-RM) checks for conflicts and redundancies in the policy. Since XACML policy has a hierarchical structure, conflict resolution is done recursively at each Policy and PolicySet level. In current approaches (as in SunXACML), these conflicts are detected and resolved on the fly when a user request comes, or are pre-processed (as in XEngine) for the combination of conditions in rules and policies. Since we are compiling XACML permissions into database ACLs, we need to do a data level conflict resolution during the compilation phase, that is, we have to do it for each extracted permission.

Policies consist of rules each of which extracts a set of permissions ⟨resource, user, action, effect⟩. We order the rules of each Policy according to the rule-combining algorithm, that is, if the rule-combining algorithm is permit-overrides, rules are sorted from permit to deny so that permit rules are executed first, and vice versa. This is not a necessary condition for conflict resolution, but enables us to finalize a

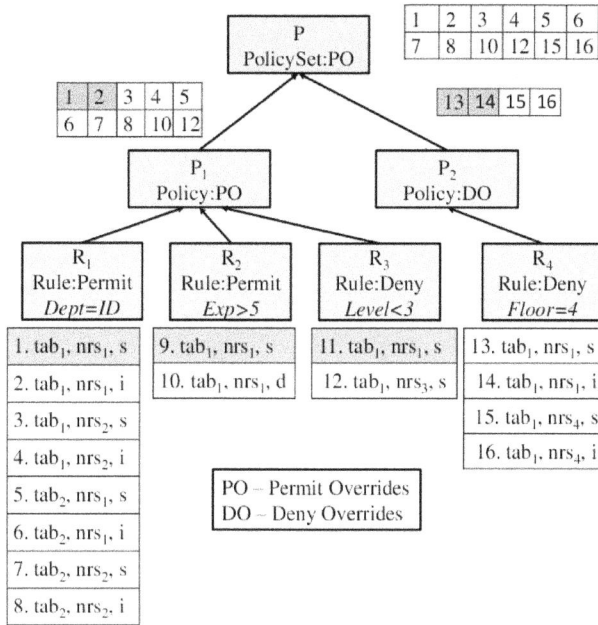

Figure 4: Tree Representation of a Policy, and Set of Permissions at Each Level

permission and determine its status, i.e., whether a permission is active, redundant, or conflict when it shows up for the first time in a Policy. For first-applicable algorithm, rule order is kept unchanged since if a permission shows up for the first time in any rule then that is the final permission. Suppose a combining algorithm is permit-overrides and the list of rules for this Policy is $R_1 : D, R_2 : D, R_3 : P$. Permission (r_0, u_0, s, D) shows up in R_1 and R_2 but (r_0, u_0, s, P) shows up in R_3. If the list is sorted, the last permission shows up first and can be finalized as soon as it shows up. With the unordered sequence, it is difficult to determine the status of (r_0, u_0, s, D) until the last rule is seen, since if no (r_0, u_0, s, P) shows up, the former should be 'active', otherwise it is a 'conflict'. This status information allows us to perform dynamic attribute update handling (described later). P and D represent permit and deny respectively.

At the Policy level, the permissions from the Rules are merged and combined to resolve conflict and remove redundancy. When a permission (r_0, u_0, s, D) shows up first, it is added to the final decision set at that level and marked as 'active'. If the same permission shows up from another rule in the same Policy later, it is marked as 'redundant'. If the same user, resource, and action shows up with a different effect, that is a 'conflict' for this permission. Since the rules are sorted, an existing permission complies with the rule-combining algorithm, and the latter permission is ignored. All the permissions are logged in the database along with their status.

At the PolicySet level, permissions are resolved using the same technique as at Policy level. The difference is, the children of PolicySet are not sorted since that does not help in finalizing permissions when they show up for the first time. This happens because though a policy-combining algorithm may be 'permit overrides', some Policies may extract permissions that 'deny' an access when no other permission

permits it and vice versa. This is not a flaw but a feature of XACML. Let us consider the policy-combining-algorithm to be 'permit-overrides'. A permission (r_0, u_0, s, D) received from one policy is added to the final decision list but replaced later if the same permission shows up with a permit effect from another Policy. Though the first permission would be marked 'active' at first, it would be remarked as 'conflict' when the latter shows up. The latter permission is marked 'active'. First-applicable combining algorithms don't need any permission replacement.

Considering the sample policy in Figure 4, permission 1 is active, 9 is redundant, and 11 is at conflict status. 11 is ignored because of 'permit-overrides' algorithm at P_1. Since P_2 contains only 1 rule, no conflict arises at P_2. Permissions from P_1 are $1, 2, 3, 4, 5, 6, 7, 8, 10$, and 12, and permissions from P_2 are $13, 14, 15$, and 16. At the PolicySet level, 13 and 14 from P_2 are ignored because of 1 and 2 respectively from P_1. The final permissions are $1, 2, 3, 4, 5, 6, 7, 8, 10, 12, 15$, and 16. The final decision list is free of any kind of redundancy or conflict. An 'Indeterminate' result from only-one-applicable is not a meaningful permission for databases. Since database permissions should be either Permit or Deny if a request matches a policy, we do not consider only-one-applicable in our system. A pseudo-code of the described conflict resolution is given in Figure 7 in Appendix.

The **ACL Building Module** (ACLBM) is responsible for updating database ACLs. It forms GRANT and REVOKE statements using the access decision lists received from CDRM. One GRANT/REVOKE statement is formulated per resource, per action. This is done by merging the users that have the same action on the same resource. In order to perform the minimum changes to the database ACLs, the permissions are checked against any existing permission in the database ACL. If a similar permission exists, it is not updated. If a

Table 1: Statements to Update ACL

GRANT select on tab_1 to nrs_1, nrs_2;
GRANT insert on tab_1 to nrs_1, nrs_2;
GRANT select on tab_2 to nrs_1, nrs_2;
GRANT insert on tab_2 to nrs_1, nrs_2;
GRANT delete on tab_1 to nrs_1;
REVOKE select on tab_1 from nrs_3, nrs_4;
REVOKE insert on tab_1 from nrs_4;

permission marked to be revoked does not exist, it is ignored, since 1) generally, databases deny access by default unless explicitly mentioned, and 2) revoking a nonexistent permission is not practical. Execution of these queries modifies the underlying database ACLs. A policy for which the UREM retrieves no user or resources from the database does not affect the database ACLs at all. Assuming MySQL to be the underlying database server, the statements in Table 1 are formulated to update the database ACL for the mentioned example.

5. UPDATES AND CORRECTNESS

The primary challenge of compiling policies into database ACL is to maintain consistency when user (or resource) attributes are updated. We will discuss user attribute updates; similar type of discussions apply to updates on resource attributes. When user attributes are changed, the affected users need reconsideration since some of their permissions may require revocation, new permissions may be granted, or both. Permissions may also remain unchanged. Naïve approaches include manual updates, or re-populating the database ACLs by recompiling all of the policies. We aim for automatic processing with the efficiency achieved by the use of incremental updating ideas employed in spreadsheets.

As in spreadsheets, the attribute update can be handled either in delayed fashion, or instantaneously. In delayed mode, any attribute value change is left for the next re-compilation of policies whereas in instantaneous mode, it is handled right away. Also, as the spreadsheet creates a dependency set of cells to perform recalculation, we create dependency relationships among attributes and rules to re-compile the necessary rules only. The compilation engine stores compilation information in the database for efficient ACL recalculation. This is done using two database tables, one to store the parsed rules, and another one to store the permission information. Parsed rules are stored in terms of subject and resource queries got from UREM, actions, and effects. Query caching enables us to omit policy parsing and start recompilation from user and resource extraction. The second table stores access information that describes which users have what permissions on which resources along with the status of each permission ('active', 'redundant', 'conflict') as discussed before. A summary of the tables in our design is shown in Table 2.

Table 2: Tables Storing Compilation Information

Table	Fields
ruledetails	ruleID, policyID, subjectQuery, resource, action, effect
log	username, resource, action, effect, status, ruleID

Updates are handled by recompiling the relevant subtree of the parsed policy that contains the rules dealing with the updated attributes. We get these rules from the **ruledetails** table. The update handling starts with getting the existing permissions of the affected users from the database ACL. After the user attributes are updated, we retrieve the rules that contain the changed attribute names. The challenge then is to comply with the policy and rule combining algorithms even by recompiling the related rules only. For each rule, we re-execute the subject retrieval query, and check if this rule contains any of the affected users. Updating permissions for the affected users is challenging since though a relevant rule might change an affected user's permission, there might exist some other rule irrelevant to the changed attributes that complies with the combining algorithm and expects no change in the permission.

We solve this in the following way: if a user's new permission complies with the rule-combining algorithm, it is accepted irrespective of her existing permission in the database ACL (e.g., a user's new permission is permit (deny) in a policy with permit-overrides (deny-overrides) rule-combining algorithm). If the new permission conflicts with the existing one, (existing permission is permit but the new one is deny in a policy with permit-overrides rule-combining algorithm), then we check for 'active' or 'redundant' rules (that are not related to the updated attributes) for this particular permission in this policy. These rules are retrieved from the

log table. If such a rule exists, it means that the existing permission should get priority and remain unchanged because of some other unchanged attributes of the user. Otherwise, the new permission is accepted. For first-applicable rule combining algorithm, a suggested change in permission finds out an 'active' or 'redundant' rule listed before the current executed-relevant rule from the **log** table to figure out which one is first-applicable. This is done for each Policy and the decision list is passed on to the parent PolicySet in the policy tree. The rest of the conflict resolution is done as discussed in CDRM (Section 4).

Let us consider the example policy in Figure 4. Permissions may change in several ways. We will discuss some example cases. Suppose nrs_1 is transferred to medicine department. The existing permission of nrs_1 is 1, 2, 5, 6, and 10 . At first the cached queries of R_1 are re-executed since it deals with the attribute 'department'. This does not extract nrs_1 any more and so 1, 2, 5, and 6 from R_1 need reconsideration. We look for the same permissions with 'redundant' status in other rules that don't deal with the changed attribute.

- 9 in R_2 is redundant for 1, and so 1 is not revoked. Since no other permissions exist that can keep the rest of the permissions unchanged (except 10), they are revoked. 10 is unchanged since it is not affected by the attribute change.
- If a rule R_5 with 'Permit' existed either in P_1 or P_2 that gives 'select' on tab_3 to the nurses of medicine department, then though permissions 2, 5, and 6 would be revoked, a new permission $\langle tab_3, nrs_1, select, Permit \rangle$ would be added to the ACLs.
- Suppose R_5 in P_1 gives the same permissions as 1, 2, 5, and 6, then none of the permissions is changed.
- Let us assume R_2 and R_5 don't exist. This requires all the permissions to be revoked.
- A change in an attribute that is not used in the policy does not affect the ACLs at all.

We call this dynamic update handling concept *logical trigger* since conceptually it is similar to database triggers. We could not use database triggers directly because of some limitations [20]. The logical trigger instantaneously re-executes relevant portion of the policy and updates MySQL ACLs when an attribute is updated. Generally high level policies rarely change, and hence recompiling the whole policy is more appropriate for this type of policy update.

6. EVALUATION

To evaluate policy compilation we implemented a prototype MyABDAC using Apache Struts [15], an open source web application framework. Since we are using MySQL ACL as the underlying access mechanism, we can provide column level granularity for resources. We designed a resource database (**hospital**) based on the schema from a local hospital and populated it with random data because of lack of enough information. The user attribute table consists of 50,000 users each with 100 attributes ($attr_0 - attr_{99}$). We constructed XACML policies with 100, 1000, 2000, ..., 5000 rules in 3 layers (PolicySet, Policy, Rule).

All the experiments were carried out on a 2.40GHz Intel Core2 Duo with 3GB memory, and running Ubuntu 8.10. The database server was MySQL version 5.0.67-community-nt.

6.1 Performance and Optimization

We measure space requirement, compilation time, and dynamic ACL update time. A few optimizations reduce the compile time to minutes. We do a comparison with two other approaches in the next section. We take the average in each experiment and round it to the nearest integer.

Space. To perform the worst case space requirement analysis, we grant 1, 2, or 3 privileges from SELECT, INSERT, and DELETE on the entire resource database, its tables, or columns to 50,000 users. For database-level privileges, users are given access on the entire hospital database. This requires only 30MB because it affects only user and db tables in mysql database. Each user is given access on $1-10$ tables for table privilege; this requires 212MB of space. For columns, each user gets access to $5-10$ columns of $1-10$ tables each. This requires the most disk space 1606MB, but this is still modest compared to the existing and future disk capacities. In general the space requirement increases lin-

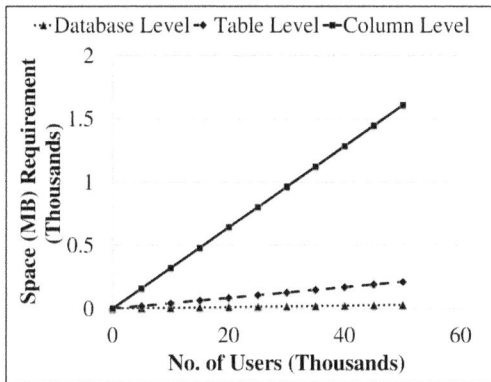

Figure 5: Space Requirement for MyABDAC

early with the number of users. Since it is scalable for such a large number of users, we believe that the approach fits applications within our scope where not all kinds of users need database accounts. Figure 5 shows the relationships among the space requirements for different levels of accesses.

Compilation Time. Policy compilation time includes parsing, user extraction from the database, and the population of ACLs by processing policies. We consider cases with 100, 1000, ..., 5000 rules over a test database. The results are illustrated in Figure 6.

Compiling a policy of 5000 Rules each with 10 subject attributes, 5 resources, and 2 actions takes 882sec with the following breakdown: parse-31sec, user extraction-720sec, and ACL population-131sec. Parse time (Figure 6a) is linearly proportional to the number of rules. User extraction (Table 6b) depends on the complexity in the WHERE clause of a SELECT statement for each Rule, and the underlying data type. ACL population is a series of GRANT statements. It depends on the number of GRANTs and the number of users per GRANT. For example, the 1000 rule policy generates 119 GRANTSs which add 36,142 permissions when no user has any permission on the database.

In another evaluation of this policy where the database already stored some random rights, and rights needed to be revoked in addition to GRANTs, the total compilation time

was 169sec with the following breakdown: parse-7sec, user extraction-148sec, ACL update-11sec. This includes 119 GRANTs and 21 REVOKEs with 36,059 addition and 1376 removal of rights respectively. If an administrator performs this task manually, she has to identify each user individually and update the ACL accordingly.

Optimization. In a naïve approach, one GRANT (REVOKE) statement for each resource in a rule adds (removes) the users extracted for that Rule into the database ACL. We optimize by updating the ACLs only after all the conflict resolution is done, and removing redundant permissions. For example, if a user has SELECT and INSERT permissions on $table_1$, then only a SELECT on $table_1$ in another rule is ignored. For the 3 types of permissions on a table, the total

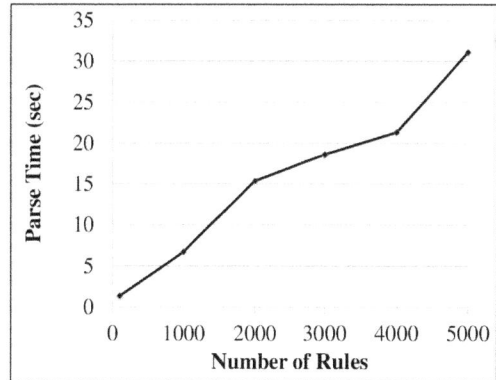

(a) Parse Time for Different numbers of Rules

No. of Rules	No. of Users Retrieved from DB	Retrieval Time (sec)	No. of GRANTs	Rights Granted	ACL Population Time (sec)
100	220	17	19	2180	0.16
1000	9569	150	119	36142	8
2000	23161	290	120	46982	12
3000	25432	431	120	109479	56
4000	24277	573	120	106196	52
5000	34558	720	120	170757	131

(b) Time to Extract Users from Database and Populate ACL

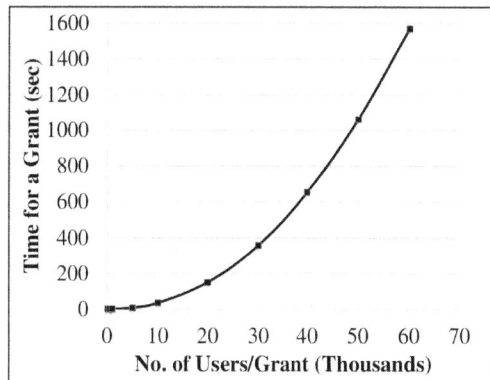

(c) ACL Population Time for Different No. of Users

Figure 6: Policy Compilation Time

combination of permissions is mapped to 120 for the 40 resource tables. This results in at most 120 GRANTs and 120

REVOKEs. Since grant and revoke statements are costly (Figure 6c), these optimizations reduce the compilation time to minutes. The results of this optimization are included in the values shown in the figures.

Update. A key performance issue is the cost of 'churn' on the attributes since this will trigger updates in the ACLs. We measured the cost of dynamic ACL update by updating $5, 10, ..., 20$ user-attributes. The update time depends on the updated attributes and the related rules, the number of users who are updated, and the obsolete and new permissions. The results of attribute updates are shown in Table 3. The structure of the update statements used is as follows:

```
UPDATE users SET attr_x = value_x, ..., attr_y = value_y
WHERE condition
```

Table 3: Update Analysis

Users Up-dated	Attributes Updated	Rules Recon-sidered	New Rights	Obsolete Rights	Total Time (sec)
1666	5	391	0	1	104
	10	662	10	1	143
	15	822	50	1	163
	20	900	50	1	161
5633	5	432	160	1	213
	10	682	1402	156	235
	15	813	1345	156	249
	20	888	1537	1	270
12384	5	391	41	1	369
	10	662	121	2	409
	15	822	261	2	433
	20	900	331	2	448

An entry such as row 6 of the table means the following: when 10 attributes of 5633 users are updated (number of users are determined by the condition part of the update statement), then 682 rules are reconsidered, 1402 new rights are added, and 156 rights are revoked. The total time for this is 235sec.

Since we insert random test data, we cannot predict the number of permission changes. But we perform two optimizations to: 1) remove redundant and overlapping permissions which reduces the number of GRANT and REVOKE statements, and 2) minimize the changes. For instance, if a user currently has SELECT and INSERT permissions, but SELECT and DELETE after update, we revoke INSERT and add DELETE. We believe that most of the time, few user attributes are changed and only a few users are affected, although there is no way to prove this for all circumstances, so optimizations are important.

6.2 Comparative Analysis

We compare MyABDAC with SunXACML and XEngine. Since we are compiling XACML to a database platform we expect some improvement in access decision times. These gains must be set against the costs we just described for ACL updates. We compare the access verification time a user faces when she submits a query. The request submitted is $\langle username, password, query \rangle$.

- In MyABDAC, access verification latency is just the time to establish a database connection. Credential verification is performed off line while creating the ACLs. Since it is done off line, users do not face this

time while accessing the database. As discussed, credential change is taken care of by the dynamic update handler.

- In SunXACML, the total time that a user faces includes database connection by the Policy Enforcement Point (PEP) as a super user, credential (username, password) verification, XACML request formation by retrieving user attributes from the database, and policy checking by the PDP, which checks all the policies against the retrieved attributes and returns the result back to PEP. If the result is Permit, the query is executed.

- In XEngine, the total time that a user faces includes database connection by the application as a super user, user credential verification, XACML request formation by retrieving user attributes from the database, request normalization, and finally policy checking.

Table 4: Comparison Results

Type	Explanation	Time (ms)
MyABDAC	Compilation (Offline Credential Check, ACL building)	417,610
	Database Connection	307
	Total (Online)	307
	Total (Offline)	417,610
SunXACML	Database Connection	307
	Credential Check	56
	XACML Request Construction	290
	XACML Request Verification	1221
	Total (Online)	1874
XEngine	Policy Conversion (Offline)	11340
	Database Connection	307
	Credential Check	56
	XACML Request Construction	290
	XACML Request Verification	32
	Total (Online)	685
	Total (Offline)	11340

Because of some limitations of current XEngine implementation, we could only test for equality in subject attributes in this comparison. This forced us to use fewer attributes in Subject elements since using more attributes does not retrieve enough users to populate database ACL. On the other hand, using too few attributes retrieves large number of users which is not practical for MyABDAC. So, we chose reasonable number of Subject attributes with a mixture of OR and AND conditions. Besides, there were some anomaly in the decisions returned by XEngine and SunXACML. Our returned decisions comply with those returned by SunXACML. A 'Not Applicable' is equivalent to 'Deny' since by default database denies any request if there is not explicit permission in the ACL.

Our results for 500 database requests are summarized in Table 4. We check a policy with 3000 Rules. The structure of the query is not important here since we are interested in the access check part rather than the time it takes to retrieve data by query execution. We used the same requests for both SunXACML and XEngine. The total online delay a user faces is 307ms in MyABDAC, 1874ms in SunXACML, AND 685ms in XEngine. A single request formation and verification requires over 4000ms in total in SunXACML, but since we take the average of request formation and verification time, the time faced is reduced.

MyABDAC runtime is 6 times faster than SunXACML and reasonably faster than XEngine. The MyABDAC offline compilation time is 418sec. This is reasonable when the window of vulnerability can accommodate it, which seems likely for many applications. For example, the time to change an employee job description on the HR database from the point that the employee is informed of the planned change may be hours or days so an hourly or daily recompilation may be sufficient.

We conclude that MyABDAC is a scalable and efficient policy compilation mechanism for attribute based database access control.

7. DISCUSSION

In this section, we analyze some security features and issues of compiling attribute-based policies for database access control, and discuss the expressiveness it provides.

7.1 Security Issues

Some security concerns with policy compilation include user modifiable attributes and the window of vulnerability when attributes change. On the other hand there are several ways in which policy compilation enhances security. We elaborate briefly on these issues.

User modifiable attributes, that is, attributes that users are allowed to update, should get careful consideration in ABAC. A concern in ABAC for databases is whether access information leakage vulnerability is created by using this type of attributes. Typically, in an organization, out of hundreds of attributes a user has, only some are used for access control. User modifiable attributes, such as email and mailing address usually are not used in access control. The other modifiable attributes are generally updated by an administrator, e.g., an assistant professor is promoted to associate professor. One possible approach is to limit the amount of information a user can access by updating attributes. This may be performed by creating an allowed attribute list for the sensitive data which explicitly mentions what user attributes can be used to access this data. Using other attributes to access this data will result in denial. This is almost similar to the idea where a data is labeled with a purpose for which it can be used [5].

A **window of access vulnerability** is the time between the change of privileges due to attribute updates and the next policy compilation. This generally is an issue in delayed mode. In instantaneous mode, this window duration is the time to update ACLs which we have tested to be in minutes for reasonable number of updates. For delayed policy compilation, how often the engine is executed depends on the organization requirements. Policy compilation needs to be done in a reasonable manner that neither makes the ACLs obsolete nor creates jitter by frequent compilations.

If the data that a user can access is not that important or attribute change is not that frequent, a window of vulnerability can be tolerated till the next compilation; e.g., when an assistant professor gets promoted to associate professor, the recompilation is not a first priority task, but when an employee is under investigation for some corruption, her access should be updated right away. From the performance analysis, we can see that policy compilation takes reasonable time and can be done several times a day reducing the duration of window of access vulnerability.

Policy compilation enhances the security of database access control in at least three ways.

1. First, because policy compilation alleviates the performance drawback of ABAC, it facilitates the usage of attributes instead of identities for access control decisions. Since ABAC policies describe the intent rather than the long list of access control entries, there is a smaller chance of accidental bugs in the policy which avoids unintentional access granting to unauthorized users.

2. Second, since policy compilation verifies a policy at the data level, it removes anomalies among conflicting permissions. Note that this is not possible when working with the high level policy since we do not know whether two sets of attribute-based rules intersect over the actual users or not. For example, it is not possible to tell whether the set of 'senior nurses' in the department of 'infectious disease' intersect with the set of 'NIH certified personnel' with 'more than 10 years of experience'. Policy compilation allows such anomalies to be identified without false positives/negatives.

3. Finally, MyABDAC complies with the principle of the least privileges and least common mechanism [26] by avoiding connecting to the database via superuser when users access some database resources. Since users connect through their own accounts, this approach significantly decreases the risks associated with a superuser database connection.

7.2 Expressiveness

There are several points about the expressiveness of policy compilation that merit discussion. These include the distinction between the extensional and intensional aspects of the policy and the ability of policy compilation to support other access control models such as Role-based Access Control (RBAC).

It is important to note that policies based on attributes can have unrealized contradictions. That is, some rules may grant permissions to individuals that other rules prohibit them from having, but there may, in fact, be no principals in the system that have the attributes in question so the policy conflict is not realized in any specific instance. While this situation can exist with the high-level policy, it is not an issue in the ACL since the ACL concretely describes permissions for specific principals. The underlying distinction here is between the *intensional* nature of the attribute rules compared to the *extensional* nature of the ACLs.

Policy compilation enables these two different types of access rules to live in a coherent common model. For example, we are able to go beyond attribute-policies by doing conflict resolution in the ACL. Consider an example; P_1: allow users of age> 25 to read $table_1$; P_2: revoke read access from users of age> 31 on $table_1$. If there is no user with age> 31 then there is no conflict. Therefore, though the policies are in conflict, actual data is not. Conflict arises when users u_1 and u_2 with ages 32 and 35 are added to the system. Depending on the resolution algorithm, one of these policies is activated and it updates the database ACL or the manager is warned of the conflict. This provides complete consistency checking regardless of the complexity of the rules in the high-level language and any challenges that might arise in checking consistency of these rules independent of the underlying extensional model they induce. Another advantage of this integrated perspective is the ability, irrespective of attributes and high-level policies based on them, the administrator could *manually* assign rights at the database level. This type of conflict resolution provides the flexibility of selective permission assignment, providing an option for explicit permissions in harmony with ABAC. This unifies ABAC and IBAC by allowing policies to be defined at high level but providing the flexibility to modify them at low level.

In **Role-based Access Control (RBAC)** [10, 27, 9], a set of users intended to have the same set of permissions are mapped to a role, which can be viewed as a kind of abstract user. Access rights over resources are defined for this abstract user so that changes in its permissions induce changes in the permissions of all of the users mapped to it. Applications can use RBAC to avoid over populating ACLs with users with same kind of permissions. Applications with such requirements can be benefited by MyABDAC with certain modifications. In this case MyABDAC should compile policies to map attributes to roles. A similar approach has been proposed in [2] for other languages. Compilation here needs to be performed on two sets of ABAC policies as in XACML interpretation. First a set of policies are compiled to map attributes to roles and this set is compiled to transform roles to ACLs. From the evaluation (Table 6b) we see that in one experiment 3000 rules add 109479 permissions to the database ACLs. This must contain a lot of common types of permissions. If large number of users have the same kind of access, then there is no reason to give each of them separate permission. MyABDAC should be used to map attributes to roles for those applications.

8. RELATED WORK

Three general areas of related work include policy verification for XACML, database access control techniques, and general attribute-based access control systems. We compare the current work with the most closely-related work in each of these areas.

To our knowledge, none of the existing works on XACML policy verification are specialized for database access control, and they solely focus on fast XACML policy evaluation. In these works, access verification is performed outside the database at application level. We specialize XACML policy verification for databases efficiently, and provide protection at the lowest level, i.e., within the database. Our concept of compiling high level policies to ACLs is analogous to SELinux [28] that uses user identity, domain, type, role, and levels attached to subjects (users, processes) and objects (files, sockets, etc) and compiles policies to binary formats for Linux kernel security server.

Sun has implemented an interpretation-based evaluation engine that verifies XACML policies [31] on-the-fly upon a request submission. A user submits a request to a Policy Enforcement Point (PEP) which authenticates the user, forms an XACML request consisting of related attributes, and submits it to a Policy Decision Point (PDP). The PDP checks all the stored XACML policies, verifies against the submitted request and sends a response back to the PEP.

Approaches have been proposed for fast XACML policy evaluation. Java XACML [13] uses traditional techniques such as indexing, decision caching, and caching policies to avoid evaluating all policies on each access. XEngine [18] preprocesses XACML policies by converting textual XACML to numerical policy (numericalization), transforming complex policy structures to a normalized structure (normalization), and converting normalized policy to tree data structures. It also transforms all types of conflict resolution rules to the 'first-applicable' rule in order to avoid evaluating all the rules each time. It creates a decision table from the policy which is consulted upon a request submission. Marouf *et. al.* [19] use statistical analysis to determine the frequently encountered rules inside an XACML policy. Then using rule reordering and clustering techniques they make the evaluation process faster and more efficient than Sun PDP. Finally, Karjoth *et. al.* [17] describe techniques to support IBM Tivoli Access Manager policies using XACML. The focus of this work is supporting legacy systems and preserving compatibility between XACML and IBM Tivoli policies rather than performance improvement.

Policy enforcement for database access control has been interpreted in several efforts. We did not find any literature on policy compilation over databases *per se*. Roichman *et. al.* [24] perform on-the-fly IBAC using parameterized view which is still not a part of current SQL servers. Olson *et. al.* transform transaction datalog policies into SQL view definitions for RDBAC [22]. Cook *et. al.* [6] use a middleware rule-engine to intercept user submitted query and change it if necessary to abide by rules. Stoller [30] extends SQL to support attribute-based access grant and revocation. It uses a modified SQL which is not supported by commodity databases. It uses special grant/revoke statements that limit the policy to a special form. Agrawal *et. al.* [1] propose a scheme to preserve privacy in a 'Hippocratic database'. Although Hippocratic databases use attributes and metadata stored in the database to make access decisions, they are specialized and not expressive enough for general security policies.

Another form of access control is Fine-Grained Access Control (FGAC), which provides row-level access granularity with a cost of query rewriting [11, 21] or view creation [23]. Oracle VPD [7], an example of FGAC defines policies as database functions attached to tables. Policies of this type require extra indirections in the form of tables or views. Query rewriting is problematic [8] in general. Using MyABDAC to perform FGAC by an appropriate form of policy compilation into database functions is a challenging next step.

Other than databases, ABAC has been applied to several areas. Bobba *et al.* [4] use user attributes in an enterprise database to send messages based on some attribute policies. Yu *et al.* [32] use attributes to establish mutual trust among parties. Stermsek *et al.* [29] perform Internet resource access control based on $\langle subject, operation, object \rangle$ triple along with attributes. Attributes define certain relationships (e.g., $subj_{attr1} = object_{attr1}$) to perform access control, or assign roles and permissions to the subject . Subject attributes are retrieved directly from the user (attribute documents and user public key certificate) or from a local database in the server.

Cryptosystems use attributes to enforce security in encryption and decryption in various ways. Sahai *et al.* [25] use biometric identities as attributes to provide a fuzzy, error tolerant identity-based encryption eliminating the necessity of public key certificates. They also propose attribute-based encryption (ABE) based on fuzzy-ibe. Bethencourt *et al.* [3] implements ABE by embedding attributes in keys, and Goyal *et al.* [14] uses attributes in the ciphertext. Both these approaches require cryptographically formed attributes to decrypt a ciphertext.

9. CONCLUSION

We introduced a model for efficient policy compilation for ABAC at database level using existing database access control mechanisms such as ACLs. The model describes how high level attribute-based policy can be efficiently converted into low-level ACLs for database resources. We described how to maintain ACL correctness in case of dynamic data. We implemented a prototype named MyABDAC as a proof of applicability of this idea and proved that the approach is scalable in terms of space and time. A comparison with SunXACML showed that policy compilation significantly improves attribute-based database access time with a price of reasonable offline compilation time. We also compared our approach with a pre-processed XACML engine and found out that for database access control, ACLs are faster than access verification at application level. We presented security enhancements provided by our approach in comparison with other approaches. A field that can be of further interest in this track is, how to support different roles a user has using the proposed technique.

Acknowledgements

This work was supported in part by HHS 90TR0003-01, NSF CNS 09-64392, NSF CNS 09-17218, NSF CNS 07-16626, NSF CNS 07-16421, NSF CNS 05-24695, and grants from the MacArthur Foundation, and Lockheed Martin Corporation. The authors would like to thank researchers involved in the project XEngine for providing their code. The views expressed are those of the authors only.

10. REFERENCES

[1] R. Agrawal, J. Kiernan, R. Srikant, and Y. Xu. Hippocratic databases. In *VLDB*, 2002.

[2] M. A. Al-Kahtani and R. Sandhu. A model for attribute-based user-role assignment. In *ACSAC*, 2002.

[3] J. Bethencourt, A. Sahai, and B. Waters. Ciphertext-policy attribute-based encryption. In *IEEE S & P*, 2007.

[4] R. Bobba, O. Fatemieh, F. Khan, C. A. Gunter, and H. Khurana. Using attribute-based access control to enable attribute-based messaging. In *ACSAC*, 2006.

[5] J.-W. Byun and N. Li. Purpose based access control for privacy protection in relational database systems. *VLDB J.*, 2008.

[6] W. R. Cook and M. R. Gannholm. Rule based database security system and method. http://www.freepatentsonline.com/6820082.html, November 2004.

[7] O. Corportation. Oracle virtual private database. Technical report, Oracle Corporation, 2005.

[8] C. Costa. A framework proposal for fine grained access control. *Informatica*, L1(2):99–108, 2006.

[9] D. Ferraiolo and R. Kuhn. Role-based access control. In *15th NIST-NCSC National Computer Security Conference*, 1992.

[10] D. F. Ferraiolo, D. R. Kuhn, and R. Chandramouli. *Role-Based Access Control.* Artech House, 2003.

[11] S. Franzoni, P. Mazzoleni, S. Valtolina, and E. Bertino. Towards a fine-grained access control model and mechanisms for semantic databases. In *ICWS*, 2007.

[12] S. Godik and T. Moses. eXtensible Access Control Markup Language (XACML). Technical Report v1.1, OASIS, August 2003.

[13] Google code enterprise java XACML implementation. http://code.google.com/p/enterprise-java-xacml.

[14] V. Goyal, O. Pandey, A. Sahai, and B. Water. Attribute-based encryption for fine-grained access control of encrypted data. In *ACM CCS*, 2006.

[15] Apache struts. http://struts.apache.org.

[16] MySQL. http://www.mysql.com.

[17] G. Karjoth, A. Schade, and E. V. Herreweghen. Implementing ACL-based policies in XACML. In *ACSAC*, 2008.

[18] A. X. Liu, F. Chen, J. Hwang, and T. Xie. XEngine: A fast and scalable xacml policy evaluation engine. In *ACM SIGMETRICS*, 2008.

[19] S. Marouf, M. Shehab, A. Squicciarini, and S. Sundareswaran. Statistics & clustering based framework for efficient XACML policy evaluation. *POLICY*, 2009.

[20] MySQL. *MySQL Reference Manual*, 2008.

[21] A. Nanda. *Fine Grained Access Control*. Proligence, 2003.

[22] L. E. Olson, C. A. Gunter, W. R. Cook, and M. Winslett. Implementing reflective access control in SQL. In *DBSec*, 2009.

[23] S. Rizvi, A. Mendelzon, S. Sudarshan, and P. Roy. Extending query rewriting techniques for fine-grained access control. In *ACM SIGMOD*, 2004.

[24] A. Roichman and E. Gudes. Fine-grained access control to web databases. In *SACMAT*, 2007.

[25] A. Sahai and B. Waters. Fuzzy identity based encryption. In *Eurocrypt*, 2005.

[26] J. H. Saltzer and M. D. Schroeder. The protection of information in computer systems. *Proceedings of the IEEE*, 63(9):1278–1308, 1975.

[27] R. S. Sandhu, E. J. Coyne, H. L. Feinstein, and C. E. Youman. Role-based access control models. *IEEE Computer*, 29(2), 1996.

[28] Security-enhanced linux. http://www.nsa.gov/research/selinux/index.shtml.

[29] G. Stermsek, M. Strembeck, and G. Neumann. Using subject- and object-specific attributes for access control in web-based knowledge management systems. In *SKM*, 2004.

[30] S. D. Stoller. Trust management and trust negotiation in an extension of SQL. In *TGC*, 2009.

[31] Sun Microsystems, Inc. *Sun's XACML Implementation*.

[32] T. Yu, M. Winslett, and K. E. Seamons. Supporting structured credentials and sensitive policies through interoperable strategies for automated trust negotiation. *ACM TISSEC*, 2003.

APPENDIX

This section contains pseudo-codes for Policy Parsing and Conflict Resolution. The pseudo-codes can be viewed as a summary of the processes described in Section 4.

```
1.  Input     : Parsed XACML Policy
2.  Output    : Final permissions
3.
4.  sortRulesByCombiningAlgorithm()
5.
6.  resolve(Element e)
7.    root = getRoot(e);
8.    if (root == Rule) then
9.      return root.access_listing;
10. else
11.   finals = null;
12.   for each child c of root do
13.     list = resolve(c);
14.     combine(finals, list, root.combining_algorithm, root.type);
15.   done
16.   return finals;
17. fi
18.
19. combine(AccessList finals, AccessList newList,
20. CombiningAlgorithm combining_algorithm, Element type)
21. if (type == 'Policy') then
22.   for each entry acl in newList do
23.     r = acl.resource;  u = acl.user;  a = acl.action;  e = acl.effect;
24.     status = null;
25.     if (finals.get(r,u,a)== null) then
26.       status = 'active';
27.       finals.add(acl);
28.     else if(finals.get(r,u,a).effect == e) then
29.       status = 'redundant';
30.     else
31.       status = 'conflict';
32.     fi
33.     saveAcl(acl,status);
34.   done
35.
36. else
37.   for each entry acl in newList do
38.     r = acl.resource;  u = acl.user;  a = acl.action;  e = acl.effect;
39.     if (finals.get(r,u,a)== null) then
40.       finals.add(acl);
41.     else if(finals.get(r,u,a).effect != e && combining-algorithm !=
            'first-applicable' && e == combining-algorithm ) then
42.       finals. updateEffect(r,u,a) = e;
43.     fi
44.     return finals;
45.   done
46. fi
```

Figure 7: Pseudo-code for Conflict Resolution

```
1.  Input   : An XACML policy
2.  Output: A tuple for each Rule
3.
4.  parse(Element e)
5.    root = getRoot(e);
6.    if (root == PolicySet) then
7.      for each child c of root do
8.        element = parse(c);
9.        policySet.add(element);
10.       return policySet;
11.   done
12.   else
13.     for each rule r in root do
14.       tuple = getTuple(r.id, r.subject, r.resource, r.action, r.effect);
15.       rules.add(tuple);
16.     done
17.     policy.add(rules);
18.     return policy;
19.   fi
```

Figure 8: Pseudo-code for Policy Parsing

Implementation and Performance Evaluation of Privacy-Preserving Fair Reconciliation Protocols on Ordered Sets

Daniel A. Mayer, Susanne Wetzel
Stevens Institute of Technology
Castle Point on Hudson
Hoboken, NJ 07030, USA
{mayer, swetzel}@stevens.edu

Dominik Teubert, Ulrike Meyer
RWTH Aachen
UMIC Research Center
Aachen, Germany
{dteubert, meyer}@itsec.rwth-aachen.de

ABSTRACT

Recently, new protocols were proposed which allow two parties to reconcile their ordered input sets in a fair and privacy-preserving manner. In this paper we present the design and implementation of these protocols on different platforms and extensively study their performance.

In particular, we present the design of a library for privacy-preserving reconciliation protocols and provide details on an efficient C++ implementation of this design. Furthermore, we present details on the implementation of a privacy-preserving iPhone application built on top of this library. The performance of both the library and the iPhone application are comprehensively analyzed. Our performance tests show that it is possible to efficiently implement private set intersection as a generic component on a desktop computer. Furthermore, the tests confirm the theoretically determined quadratic worst-case behavior of the privacy-preserving reconciliation protocols on the desktop as well as the iPhone platform. The main result of the performance analysis is that the protocols show linear runtime performance for average-case inputs. This is a significant improvement over the worst-case and is key for making these protocols highly viable for a wider range of applications in practice.

Categories and Subject Descriptors

C.2.0 [Computer-Communication Networks]: General—Security and protection; C.2.2 [Computer-Communication Networks]: Network Protocols—Applications; C.2.4 [Computer-Communication Networks]: Distributed Systems—Distributed Applications

General Terms

Design, Performance, Experimentation, Security

Keywords

Privacy, Ordered Sets, Private Set Intersection, Performance, Multi-Party Computation, Cryptographic Protocol, iPhone

1. INTRODUCTION

Secure multi-party protocols allow two or more parties to jointly compute a function of the inputs of each of the parties without requiring any of the parties to reveal their private input to anyone. Examples for such functions are computing the average of the inputs or determining the intersection of the input sets. In this context, Meyer et al. recently proposed protocols that allow two parties to reconcile their ordered input sets in a fair and privacy-preserving manner [24, 25]. In these protocols, the order of the private input set of a party is associated with the private preferences of that party with respect to the elements of its input sets. Fair reconciliation then means that the new protocols acknowledge the preferences of the parties in that they output only those common elements of the ordered input sets that maximize a common preference order. Applications of these protocols range from reconciling policies in Future Internet Architectures [29, 32] to determining common candidate time-slots while scheduling a meeting without involvement of a trusted server. In this paper we focus on the implementation and performance evaluation of these protocols. In particular, we describe the design and C++ implementation of a library for privacy-preserving reconciliation protocols on ordered sets. The library includes efficient implementations of the Paillier cryptosystem and the privacy-preserving set intersection protocol by Freedman et al. In addition, we describe the implementation of a proof-of-concept iPhone application *appoint* that is built on top of

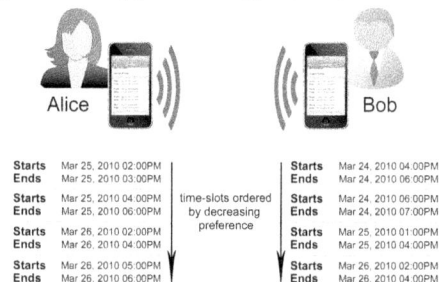

Figure 1: Illustration of *appoint*

the C++ library. *appoint* allows two parties to schedule a meeting, i.e., agree on a meeting time and date in a privacy-preserving manner. Each party has its own schedule which has a number of open time-slots available for potentially accommodating this meeting (see Figure 1). In addition, either party will typically prefer some time-slots over others. Using preference-maximizing reconciliation protocols for ordered sets, the two parties can agree on a time-slot which is open in both schedules and maximizes the parties' common preferences. In this context, it is in the interest of both parties to keep their individual schedules private while still being able to agree on a common meeting time. If one party published its entire schedule, it would allow the other party to possibly deduce sensitive information. Examples include work habits (e.g., the person never starts working before 10 am) or work load (evidenced by many open time-slots).

We provide a comprehensive performance evaluation of our protocols on a desktop computer as well as the iTouch[1]. The experiments on the desktop show that it is possible to efficiently implement private set intersection as a generic component. Furthermore, the tests confirm the theoretically determined quadratic worst-case behavior of the privacy-preserving reconciliation protocols [24]. The main result of the performance analysis on the desktop is that the protocols show linear runtime performance for average-case inputs. This is a significant improvement over the worst-case and is key for making these protocols highly viable for a wide range of applications in practice. The experiments on the iTouch further underline our protocols' practical relevance and show that smaller privacy-preserving applications are already viable on today's smartphones.

The remainder of this paper is organized as follows: Section 2 provides a brief overview on related work. In Section 3, the privacy-preserving tools and protocols are briefly reviewed. Section 4 presents the design and implementation of the library while Section 5.2 describes the implementation of application *appoint*. Finally, Section 6 focuses on the extensive performance evaluations. We close the paper with some remarks on future work.

2. RELATED WORK

Since Yao's seminal paper [35] on secure multi-party computation (SMPC), the field evolved from purely theoretical to practical. For example, recently, Pinkas et al. described the implementation of a two-party protocol using Yao's garbled circuits [30]. Other efforts of implementing general purpose SMPC protocols include [7–9, 22, 23].

Apart from general purpose SMPC, specialized protocols have been introduced to solve the multi-party computation problem for specific operations. One of these operations is private set intersection (PSI) which forms the foundation of the reconciliation protocols implemented and analyzed in this paper. Many PSI protocols have been suggested, e.g., [12–15, 19, 20]. For the performance analysis described in this paper we implemented the protocol suggested by Freedman et al. in [15], which is based on *oblivious polynomial evaluation*. Nevertheless, our overall implementation is designed to allow for a simple integration of any other PSI protocol in the future.

Voris et al. [34] previously performed an initial performance evaluation of the privacy-preserving reconciliation protocols introduced by Meyer et al. [24]. However, their work has shortcomings in that the analysis left open a number of crucial questions. In particular, the work in [34] does not provide explanations on the characteristics of the experimental results, e.g., why the experimental runtime is approaching a limit for larger set sizes. This especially is a problem since the experimental results are in disagreement with theoretical predictions. In addition, the experiments in [34] were not performed in a well-controlled test environment. That is, both, the length of the set elements as well as the number of elements in a set were changed at the same time. Furthermore, sets were generated at random (up to 1 million entries) but only 10 identical runs were averaged for each data point. Yet, the large number of possible set configurations would require significant averaging over different randomized sets in order to obtain a representative result. Overall, the experimental analysis done to date does not allow for any conclusions on the true practical behavior of the protocols introduced in [24].

The focus of this work is on analyzing the behavior of the recently revised protocols [25] in the worst and average case—with a particular focus on answering the open questions of [34] and presenting solid experimental evidence for the performance of the protocols. Furthermore, this work strives to provide a better understanding for the practical performance of the private reconciliation protocols and thus shows their suitability for a wide range of applications in practice. In particular, our proof-of-concept iPhone application underlines the protocols' practical relevance.

Today, SSL and PKI functions are part of any smartphone API (e.g., [2, 5]). Furthermore, the increased performance of mobile devices gives rise to more involved security- and privacy-related applications (e.g., [10, 16]). To the best of our knowledge, however, to date the field of secure multi-party computation on mobile devices is mostly unexplored. Our proof-of concept iPhone application is a first step to investigate whether or not privacy-preserving applications are already viable on smartphones.

3. PRELIMINARIES

3.1 Homomorphic Encryption

The privacy-preserving tools, which are at the core of the privacy-preserving reconciliation protocols by Meyer et al., require an additively homomorphic and semantically secure public key cryptosystem [15].

DEFINITION 1 (HOMOMORPHIC ENCRYPTION). *An encryption scheme is said to be homomorphic if for given encryptions* $E_k(m_1)$, $E_k(m_2)$ *it holds for all encryption keys* k *that* $E_k(m_1 \oplus m_2) = E_k(m_1) \otimes E_k(m_2)$ *for some operators* $\oplus$ *in the plaintext space and* $\otimes$ *in the ciphertext space.*

It is important to note that the operation $\otimes$ can be performed without prior decryption.

DEFINITION 2 (SEMANTIC SECURITY). *In a semantically secure setting an adversary does not learn anything about the plaintext (besides its length) from given ciphertexts [18].*[2]

---

[1] The 3rd generation iPod touch (iTouch) is used for development and testing. It is based on the same hardware as the iPhone 3GS.

[2] Semantic security is often referred to as *indistinguishability of encryptions*.

In the following, we will use the Paillier cryptosystem [28]. It is a semantically secure public key cryptosystem based on the composite residuosity assumption preserving the group homomorphism of addition. That is, given two ciphertexts $E(m_1)$, $E(m_2)$ one can efficiently compute $E(m_1 + m_2)$. Similarly, $E(m_1 \cdot c)$ can be obtained given only $E(m_1)$ and a constant c.

3.2 Adversary Model

Following the work in [25], this paper focuses on a passive adversary who is honest but curious and is generally referred to as *semi-honest*. This can informally be described as a person, algorithm, or program which follows the protocol and performs all required computations. Yet, it might store intermediate results and do additional polynomial time computations with the goal of learning as much as possible. A formal definition is given in [17]. A protocol is said to be privacy-preserving in the semi-honest model if no party learns anything but what can be derived from the output of the protocol and its own private input. In general, semi-honest adversaries are contrasted by a malicious adversary who can show arbitrary behavior.

3.3 Oblivious Polynomial Evaluation

Freedman et al. (FNP) developed a set of tools to facilitate privacy-preserving set intersections. Their scheme requires a semantically secure homomorphic cryptosystem such as Paillier's [15]. FNP's construction assumes a chooser C and a sender S and allows these two parties to compute the intersections $X_C \cap X_S$ of their private sets X_C and X_S (chosen from the same domain). At the end of the protocol, C only learns which elements C and S have in common and S learns nothing. The technique used by FNP is oblivious polynomial evaluation. Oblivious means that S only sees encrypted coefficients and evaluates the polynomial without having access to its actual coefficients.

The protocol works as follows: First, party C generates a polynomial containing all her set elements c_i as roots:

$$p_C(x) = (x - c_1) \cdot (x - c_2) \ldots (x - c_n) = \sum_{i=0}^{n} \alpha_i \cdot x^i \quad (1)$$

Then, C encrypts all α_i using her public key and sends them to S. S chooses a random r_i for each s_i in his set and obliviously computes $p_C^{s_i} := E_C\left(r_i \cdot p_C(s_i) + s_i\right)$. Party S then sends all $p_C^{s_i}$ back to C. C uses her private key to decrypt the result. Note that $p_C^{s_i}$ decrypts to $s_i \in X_C$ if s_i is in X_C and to a random number otherwise. Thus, C can tell which elements of S are also in her set. In order for S to be able to also determine the intersection, the protocol is executed in the opposite direction. The protocol is privacy-preserving in the semi-honest model.

3.4 Privacy-Preserving Reconciliation

In the following we assume that party A's (B's) private input is a set S_A (S_B) of size n with elements a_i (b_i) for $1 \le i \le n$.

The $3PR^C$ protocols [24] introduce fairness into the reconciliation process. Each set element is associated with a preference, i.e., its position within the set—also referred to as *rank* of an element. The respective set is referred to as *ordered set*. Given such an ordered set, the $3PR^C$ protocols allow two parties A and B to reconcile their ordered sets (assumed to be from the same domain and of equal length)

such that the result maximizes a *combined preference order* $\le_{AB}$ under a *preference order composition scheme* C.

The $3PR^C$ protocols by Meyer et al. do not inherently enforce a specific preference order composition scheme. Instead, a preference order composition scheme C may be chosen based on a particular application. In [24], two preference order composition schemes were introduced which implement common notions of fairness: *Sum of Ranks* and *Minimum of Ranks*:

DEFINITION 3 (SUM OF RANKS).

$$\forall x, y \in S_A \cap S_B : \quad x \le_{AB} y :\Leftrightarrow$$
$$rank_A(x) + rank_B(x) \le rank_A(y) + rank_B(y) \quad (2)$$

where $rank_A(x)$ and $rank_A(y)$ ($rank_B(x)$ and $rank_B(y)$) correspond to the preference of x and y in set S_A (S_B).

DEFINITION 4 (MINIMUM OF RANKS).

$$\forall x, y \in S_A \cap S_B : \quad x \le_{AB} y :\Leftrightarrow$$
$$min\left(rank_A(x), rank_B(x)\right) \le min\left(rank_A(y), rank_B(y)\right) \quad (3)$$

where $rank_A(x)$ and $rank_A(y)$ ($rank_B(x)$ and $rank_B(y)$) correspond to the preference of x and y in set S_A (S_B).

The $3PR^C$ protocols [25] encompass multiple rounds. In each round, pairs of set elements are compared according to the respective combined preference order $\le_{AB}$. For the sum of ranks composition scheme, the protocol includes up to $2n - 1$ rounds. In round $1 \le i \le 2n - 1$, all pairs of elements are compared where the sum of the ranks of these elements equals $2n + 1 - i$. For the minimum of ranks, the protocol includes at most n rounds. In round $1 \le i \le n$, the elements with rank i are compared with all elements having rank greater or equal to i. The comparisons in the $3PR^C$ protocols which were first introduced in [24] are based on the oblivious polynomial evaluation by Freedman et al. Specifically, comparing the two set elements a_i and b_j works as follows: Party A creates a polynomial $p_A(x) = (x - a_i) = \sum_{i=0}^{1} \alpha_i \cdot x^i$, encrypts the coefficients α_i with her public key and sends them to B. Party B obliviously evaluates the polynomial using b_j, i.e., computes $p_A^{b_j} := E_A\left(r_j \cdot p_A(b_j) + b_j\right)$ and sends the result to A. Party A now decrypts the result and checks whether it matches the corresponding a_i. If a match was found, she notifies B (through specific match confirmation operations), otherwise the protocol continues with a pair of set elements having an equal or lower combined preference. Note that this is a simplified description of the actual protocols [24]. In the following, we will refer to these protocols as $3PR^C$-*FNP-implicit* as the oblivious polynomial evaluation of the Freedman protocol is implicitly used in these protocols.

As described in [25], it is possible to generalize the original $3PR^C$ protocols in that the comparison may be carried out using an arbitrary PSI protocol. More specifically, it is possible to modularize the original protocols such that any PSI protocol may be explicitly used as a building block for the $3PR^C$ protocols. In the following, we distinguish between two variants of the modular protocols—$3PR^C$-*PSI-explicit-cached* and $3PR^C$-*PSI-explicit-non-cached*. These two protocols differ in that $3PR^C$-*PSI-explicit-cached* implements a caching mechanisms which allows the reusing of data. In particular, any set element may be part of comparisons at

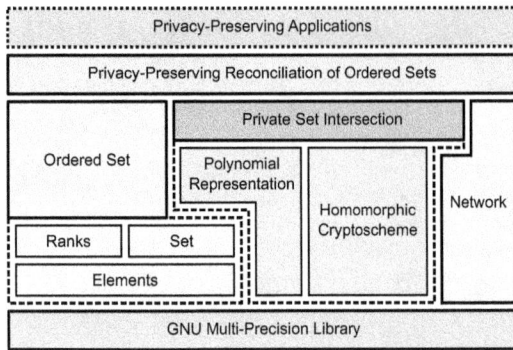

Figure 2: Building blocks of the PROS library.

various rounds. Instead of having to resend the corresponding data in each one of these rounds, the caching mechanism implemented in $3PR^C$-*PSI-explicit-cached* allows the eliminating of these additional data exchanges.

All the $3PR^C$ protocols (i.e., $3PR^C$-*FNP-implicit*, $3PR^C$-*PSI-explicit-non-cached*, and $3PR^C$-*PSI-explicit-cached*) were shown to be privacy-preserving in the semi-honest model [25], i.e., upon termination of the protocols, parties A and B have learned nothing but the set element that maximizes the combined preference order.

4. DESIGN AND IMPLEMENTATION OF THE PROS LIBRARY

The first main contribution of this paper is our new design of a modular library for *Privacy-Preserving Reconciliation of Ordered Sets* (PROS) which can be used to efficiently build privacy-preserving applications. Figure 2 illustrates the design of our PROS library. Each main component is coded in a different color and all interacting components use well-defined interfaces. Therefore, specific implementations for each component can be exchanged with other implementations–assuming they provide the same functionality—without requiring changes to any of the other components. The PROS protocols (blue) take ordered sets as inputs (yellow). An ordered set is a set combined with the ranks of its elements. Furthermore, the PROS protocols use PSI protocols (red). Currently, only Freedman's PSI, which operates on a polynomial representation of the data and uses a homomorphic cryptosystem, is implemented. The network layer (green) enables the communication between the different parties. All computations possibly involve long integers. This, in particular, applies to operations involving set elements, polynomials as well as cryptographic keys. The library builds on the well-known and efficient *GNU Multi-Precision Arithmetic Library* (GMP) [4]. In the following, we describe the different components in greater detail.

4.1 Ordered Sets

To allow for the flexibility of accommodating a multitude of sets containing different types of elements in the future, operations involving sets in our new library were implemented on an interface-defining virtual `ordered set` class. Internally, ordered sets are represented as a vector of integers and the position within the vector implicitly specifies the element's rank. The ordered set of integers is an implementation of the virtual `ordered set` class and provides all the necessary functions. New set element types, which are different from plain integers, can easily be integrated into

our library. In Section 5.2 this will be demonstrated for our iTouch application *appoint* which enables the scheduling of a meeting in a privacy-preserving manner.

4.2 Homomorphic Cryptosystem

The efficiency of the implementation of the homomorphic cryptosystem has great influence on the overall performance of privacy-preserving protocols. Each round of these protocols typically involves several encryption/decryption operations as well as homomorphic operations (e.g., homomorphic addition or homomorphic multiplication by a constant). It is therefore crucial to develop efficient implementations of these operations. The cryptosystem is implemented as an individual class and it provides algorithms for key management and exchange, encryption/decryption, as well as homomorphic operations.

In particular, the Paillier cryptosystem was implemented following the original description in [28]. It provides homomorphic operations for addition and multiplication by a constant. To determine primes p and q for the Paillier cryptosystem, the *key generation* uses the Mersenne-Twister pseudo random generator (PRG) provided by the GMP library to first generate a random number of desired length. The actual primes are determined as the next prime greater than the random number generated by the PRG. The UNIX `/dev/random` device provides the seed for the PRG. GMP provides basic functions to perform modular arithmetic. More involved constructions, as required by the cryptosystem, were implemented from scratch.

Whenever possible, *performance enhancements* were introduced in our implementation of the Paillier cryptosystem. For example, all constants used during encryption and decryption are precomputed at the time of key generation and stored for later use. Furthermore, the decryption process involves exponentiation modulo n^2 which can be significantly accelerated by first performing the calculations modulo the square of the two primes and then combining the result using the *Chinese Remainder Theorem (CRT)* modulo n^2 afterward [28].

The addition of other homomorphic cryptosystems to the PROS library is part of future work.

4.3 Polynomial Representation

Polynomials and operations on them are defined by a virtual `polynomial` class, which, in particular, provides functions to efficiently multiply polynomials (e.g., as required by Equation 1 in Freedman's PSI).

Two classes implementing the `polynomial` interface were developed: `vectorpolynomial` and `flintpolynomial`. The latter is based on *FLINT: Fast Library for Number Theory* [3] and was introduced to leverage the efficient algorithms provided by this library. Each class handles the representation of as well as all operations on the polynomials. In `vectorpolynomial`, polynomials are represented as vector of their coefficients. Since the coefficients represent large integers, they are stored as `mpz_class` objects, the native data type of GMP. `flintpolynomial` stores polynomials in the native data types of *FLINT*, which are based on *GMP* as well.

4.4 Network

In order to enable the execution of the reconciliation protocol, a communication interface between the (two) parties must be established. In our library, this was implemented through UNIX Sockets using the Transmission Control Protocol (TCP). Consequently, our protocols can be executed over basically any network used today.

A basic network interface was developed which allows sending and receiving integers as well as arbitrary byte-arrays over the network. This basic `network` class was extended to include a 32-bit header for all messages. This method allows for an efficient transmission of messages of arbitrary size.

In addition, the extended class provides functions to directly send `mpz_class` objects. GMP's export function is used to split long integers into blocks of 32 bits. These can be transmitted at once and re-imported into an `mpz_class` object, thus avoiding expensive string conversions.

When using FNP's PSI protocol, the individual amount of data transmitted in each round of the PROS protocols is small (bounded by n^2). To avoid transmission delays, the `TCP_NOWAIT` option is used when creating the TCP socket. This option disables *Nagle's algorithm*, a performance enhancement for TCP [21, pp. 815-816], and enables immediate transmission after each `send` system call.

4.5 Private Set Intersection

Freedman's PSI protocol (FNP-PSI) [15] forms the basis for the PROS protocols. Its main component is the *oblivious evaluation* of polynomials whose degree is equal to the size of the involved sets. A polynomial of degree n can be evaluated in $\Theta(n)$ using the *Horner Scheme* [11, p. 824]. Note that the evaluation has to be performed obliviously using the homomorphic operations of the Paillier cryptosystem. Using the homomorphic addition and multiplications by a constant, Horner's rule translates to $E(p(x_0)) = E\left(\sum_{i=0}^{n} a_i \cdot x_0^i\right) = E(a_0) \cdot (E(a_1) \cdot \ldots \cdot (E(a_{n-1}) \cdot E(a_n)^{x_0})^{x_0} \ldots)^{x_0}$

While Horner's scheme traditionally reduces the number of multiplications, the speed-up for the homomorphic operations is even greater since multiplications on plaintexts translate to (more expensive) exponentiations on ciphertexts.

In the implementation of the FNP protocol, the protocol obtains the basic polynomial root for each set element provided by the `set` class. *Alice* (in Freedman's protocol referred to as chooser C) multiplies all roots together using the functionality of the `polynomial` class such that they form the polynomial of Equation 1.

The coefficients of this polynomial are encrypted using Alice's public key. Then, they are sent from *Alice* to *Bob* (in Freedman's protocol referred to as server S) who uses Horner's rule to efficiently evaluate the polynomial in an oblivious fashion. The evaluation is repeated for all of Bob's set elements and the results are sent back to *Alice*. After decryption, *Alice* uses the `set` class to determine which of Bob's set elements are members of her own set.

Our PSI implementation is based on two new interface-defining virtual classes: `PSI` and *Private Matching* (`PM`). Concrete implementations of `PSI` provide two functionalities: one to `initialize` a set intersection and to learn the result and a second one to `respond` to a set intersection request. Each function takes the party's `set` as input. Our library uses *Standard Template Library* (STL) sets of `mpz_class` objects. `PM` was introduced into the library to handle degenerate sets of cardinality one. `PM` classes imple-

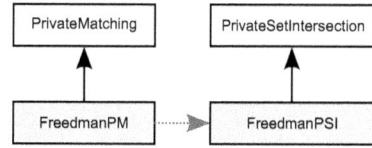

Figure 3: Class Hierarchy of the PSI and PM classes.

ment the same functions as `PSI` classes but take a single set element (`mpz_class`) as input.

Freedman's PSI was implemented based on this design along with the corresponding `PM` implementation which transforms the integer inputs into sets of cardinality one and executes Freedman's PSI on those. Figure 3 illustrates the (simplified) class hierarchy. The PROS library will be extended by other PSI protocols in the future.

4.6 Privacy-Preserving Reconciliation of Ordered Sets

We have developed implementations for all three protocols, $3PR^C$-*FNP-implicit* and $3PR^C$-*PSI-explicit cached/non-cached* (see Section 3.4). All protocols are implemented as separate C++ classes, which makes the management of the network connection, the key management as well as the generation of the sets independent of the protocols themselves. Each protocol class provides member functions which execute the protocol as either *Alice* or *Bob*. A basic key exchange protocol was developed which enables the exchange of the public keys of the two parties (executing the PROS protocol) as well as populating each `crypto` class with the appropriate keys. The performance of all variants will later be analyzed in Section 6.

4.6.1 The $3PR^C$-FNP-implicit Implementation

$3PR^C$ and the preference order composition schemes were analyzed in detail and the parts which are independent of the composition scheme C were isolated and placed in a base class from which all $3PR^C$ protocols are derived. This setup allows for easy addition of new preference order composition schemes. The current implementation contains both composition schemes which were introduced in Section 3.4. The concrete protocol classes for *Sum of Ranks* and *Minimum of Ranks* provide the order in which the set elements are to be compared. The structure of implementing a preference order composition scheme consists of several loops which construct and evaluate polynomials of the correct set elements according to the specifics of the respective preference order composition scheme.[3]

4.6.2 The $3PR^C$-PSI-explicit Implementation

In order to facilitate that an underlying PSI protocol can be substituted without having to modify the generic code defining the order in which the PSIs are carried out, $3PR^C$-*PSI-explicit* was implemented based on the `PM` interface introduced in Section 4.5. Note, that only `PM` functionality is required to implement $3PR^C$-*PSI-explicit*.

This approach of directly executing one `PM` per comparison adds additional overhead compared to $3PR^C$-*FNP-implicit*. This is because each comparison causes the initi-

---

[3]It shall be noted that $3PR^C$-*FNP-implicit* does not directly call the Freedman protocol which is implemented as part of the PSI layer of the PROS library. Instead, it accesses the polynomial representation and the homomorphic cryptosystem directly.

ating party to send some data (i.e., a polynomial in the case of FNP's PSI) corresponding to its set element to the other party. In particular, this may result in the repeated sending of data for the same element of the ordered set. In order to remedy this shortcoming, a caching mechanism was introduced into the PSI and PM class designs. The implementation of the caching mechanism depends on the used PSI, since different data need to be stored for different PSI schemes. In the case of Freedman's PSI, this cache keeps track of which polynomials have been sent to or received from the other party. Received polynomials are stored locally thus avoiding repeated transmission. Generally, an identifier id uniquely identifies each cache entry. Initialize and respond functions take the id as an additional parameter. Before the actual set intersection is executed, initialize checks its cache. If the id is in the cache then the data is not sent again. Instead the function only receives the evaluation results from the other party, decrypts them, and returns the result. If the id is not in the cache, the data is created, encrypted, and sent as usual. Also, the new id is added to the cache. Similarly, the respond function checks if certain data was received in the past. If this is the case, the cached data is processed and the results are sent to the other party. If the id is not in the cache, the data is received as usual, added to the cache (with its id), and then processed.

The party calling initialize passes as id parameter the rank of its set element used in the current step. For the respond function, the caller passes the rank of the other party's element which is to be compared against in this step as id. This is necessary to determine if the other party's data corresponding to the element of current rank was received before. Since the preference order composition schemes clearly define which two elements in the respective sets are to be compared in each step of the reconciliation process, the information on id is readily available to both parties and the explicit use does not violate any privacy guarantees.

Whenever a concrete PSI, such as FNP, was used, we will substitute the *PSI* portion of the name (e.g., $3PR^C$-*FNP-explicit*).

5. appoint - A PROS APPLICATION

We have developed a proof-of-concept application *appoint* on top of the PROS library which allows the privacy-preserving negotiation of a meeting time while taking user preferences into account. In particular, the $3PR^C$-*FNP-implicit* protocol is being used to facilitate the negotiation. Since more and more people are using their mobile devices to handle their calendars, our application was implemented on Apple's iTouch platform.

Since the iTouch API is exclusively provided for Objective-C, applications for the iTouch are usually written in Objective-C as well. Our existing library, however, is C++ based. To combine these languages, the application as a whole was compiled as Objective-C++, which is a proper superset of C++, thus enabling the use of C++ code. Combining C++ and Objective-C introduces the additional challenge of interfacing two different class concepts.

In developing the app we have compiled the *GMP* library for the iTouch platform. Due to the modular design of our PROS library it was possible to leverage most of the code. The network component was identified as the only component that was platform dependent and required modification. Further, an iTouch GUI was added as part of the

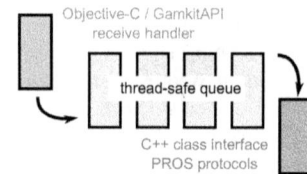

Figure 4: Flow of a received packet on the iTouch.

application to enable that a user user can transparently interact with the PROS library through a calendar-like interface. Since no modification to the rest of the library were required, the iTouch app can benefit directly from future improvements to the library. The existing C++ library interfaces with the new Objective-C code at two points: the network and the GUI. Both points will be discussed below. It is important to note, that our application runs on the genuine, i.e., non-*jail-breaked*, *iOS*.

5.1 Bluetooth Network

One major design decision was the choice of the network technology. The iTouch provides Internet connectivity via 802.11b/g and GSM/UMTS as well as peer-to-peer connectivity over Bluetooth 2.1. When accessing the Internet via wireless LANs, a device usually is behind some network address translation (NAT) device and cannot be contacted directly by another party [21, Ch. 28]. A similar situation holds for the Internet access via GSM/UMTS. To enable communication of two mobile devices under these circumstances requires some form of relay server. The use of such a semi-trusted third party, which relays data while ensuring its integrity, would weaken the privacy guarantee of *appoint*. Furthermore, the use case of *appoint* suggests that both parties are in the same physical location (conferences, meetings, business dinners etc.). Therefore, the network component was implemented using peer-to-peer networking via Bluetooth.

The Bluetooth networking on the iTouch is abstracted through the *GameKit API*, which was originally built to support multiplayer games and therefore follows an event-driven programming paradigm. When using the GameKit API, incoming data packets are dispatched to a receive handler for processing. This asynchronous form of communication provides a challenge when executing a protocol with a well-defined order of execution, based on static send and receive calls. Our solution is built on a thread-safe queue which serves as a global data structure (cf. Figure 4). Data is pushed into the queue by the event-based receive handler and read-access is provided by a C++ class which corresponds to the network component of Figure 2.

5.2 Time-Slot Representation

In order to apply the PROS protocols to the *appoint* setting, it was necessary to represent the time-slots and the preferences associated with them as an ordered set. We encode each time-slot as a 32-bit integer $Z = S||D$ (set element) which is the concatenation of two integers S (s bits long) and D (d bits long) where $32 = s + d$. We choose $s = 16$ bits to uniquely specify the start time of the time-slot as the number of minutes since midnight of the day on which the reconciliation is performed. With this setup we can plan up to 45 days ahead. D is 16 bits long and encodes the duration of the event in hours. This allows the encoding of a duration from 1 up to 65,535 hours. The ordered set,

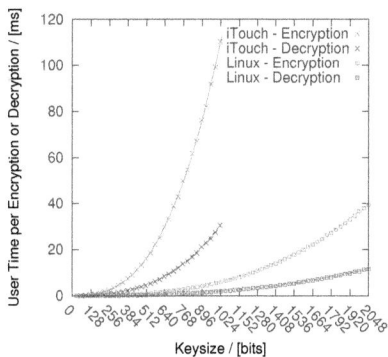

Figure 5: CPU time for encryption/decryption of 32-bit data.

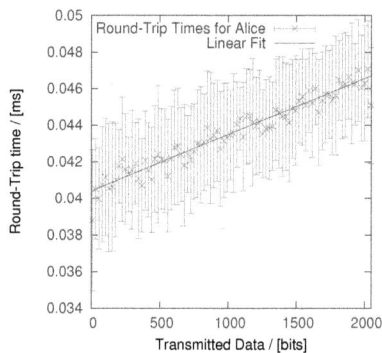

Figure 6: Network round-trip for data of reasonable size (Linux).

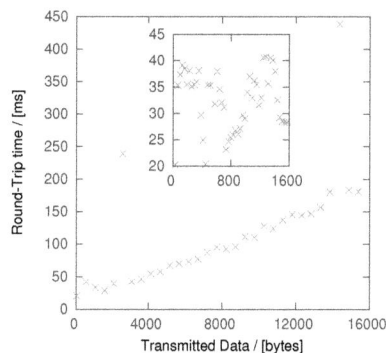

Figure 7: Network round-trip using Bluetooth on the iTouch.

which will be used by the PROS protocols, consists of these integers ordered by their preferences.

5.3 GUI Development

Interaction with smartphones using modern multi-touch displays is fundamentally different from that with desktop applications (e.g., [6, 26, 27]). In addition, the time an application remains open is very short. The user therefore expects a user interface (UI) which can be used quickly and intuitively.

We meet this challenge by not introducing new UI elements but instead using the ones provided natively through the *iOS SDK*. Furthermore, the look and feel of our application is built in the style of the native iTouch calendar application, thus simplifying the usage for iTouch users (see Appendix A for screenshots). For this, we leverage code provided by an open source project [1]. In addition, *appoint* uses the *Event Kit* framework, which was recently introduced in iOS 4, to access the local calendar on the iTouch and synchronize events with it.

When a user sets up his time-slots using the GUI, data is not directly passed to the protocols. Only once the negotiation is initiated, all time-slots are converted into integers with associated preferences as described in Section 5.2. The resulting ordered set is then passed to the PROS protocols. At the completion of the protocol, the one time-slot which maximizes the joint preference order is returned to the GUI. This value is then decoded and displayed to the user for acceptance and permanent storage in the calendar database.

6. PERFORMANCE EVALUATION

In the following, we provide a detailed analysis of our extensive performance tests. The tests were geared to gain a better understanding for the behavior of the protocols in practice and to explore their suitability for real-world applications. For this, we not only tested our Linux-based implementation of the PROS protocols and the FNP-PSI protocol, but also our proof-of-concept application *appoint*.

All Linux-based tests were performed on three dedicated machines having an identical configuration: AMD Athlon 64 Processor 3000+ at 1.8 GHz, 2 GB main memory, 64-bit Linux 2.6.32 (Ubuntu). For all experiments involving two parties the code for both parties was executed on the same host. While this does not represent the final setting in which the protocols might be utilized, it removes network latencies and simplifies the analysis and understanding of the data and the protocols. It is important to note that after one

party has finished its computations and has sent off its data to the other party, it only waits to receive back results but does not perform any additional computation. Thus, the two processes do not compete for the CPU or cause timing conflicts.

appoint was tested using two iTouch devices. The iTouches have an ARM Cortex-A8 at 600MHz CPU, 256 MB of DRAM and are running iPhone OS 3.1.3. During the tests, each party was run on a separate iTouch device. The purpose of this section was not to compare the iTouch platform with the Linux platform but rather to show the general performance of the PROS protocols using Linux and the viability of mobile applications based on these protocols using a resource-limited platform such as the iTouch.

We start by presenting the results of testing the cryptographic operations and the network operations. Then, we present the performance results of the PROS protocols.

6.1 Cryptographic Performance

The performance of a cryptosystem is mainly influenced by two parameters: the key size and the length of the plaintext. The behavior of our implementation of the Paillier cryptosystem with respect to both was analyzed experimentally by measuring the CPU time. The time for each pair of parameters was averaged over 10,000 randomly generated inputs by measuring the time required to first encrypt all 10,000 plaintexts and then the time to decrypt all these ciphertexts. For the tests on the Linux platform, the cryptographic keys were varied between 32 bits and 2,048 bits in steps of 32 bits. In addition, for each key size, the plaintext length was varied from 8 bits to 256 bits in steps of 8 bits. On the iTouch platform, plaintexts of size 32 bits were investigated for keys ranging from 32 bits to 1,024 bits in steps of 4 bits. In the following, we present two cuts through the parameter space: varying the plaintext length for a fixed key size and vice versa. We directly compare the timings for the iTouch with those for the Linux platform to demonstrate the difference in computational power and to allow the reader to better relate the results presented below. Figure 5 shows how the timings for one encryption (decryption) changes with the key size for a fixed plaintext of 32 bits. Fitting both data sets for the Linux and iTouch platforms yields a cubic upper bound on the runtime. The time for one decryption is significantly smaller than the time for an encryption. This is due to the highly optimized implementation of the decryption algorithm using pre-computations and CRT. In addition, the operations performed during a

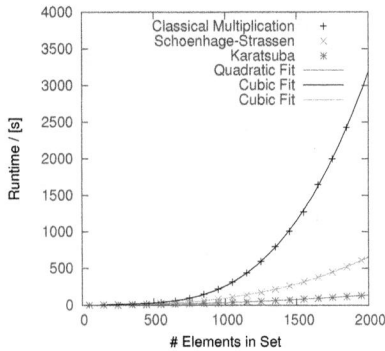

Figure 8: Wall time for the symmetric FNP-PSI protocol using 256-bit keys and 32-bit set elements.

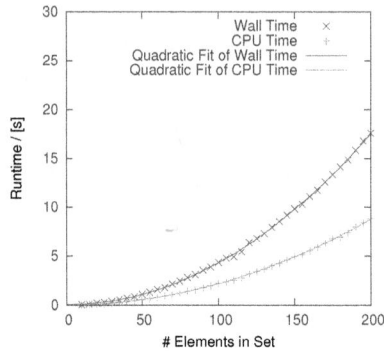

(a) $3PR^C$-FNP-implicit $3PR^C$ implementation. Wall and CPU time are shown.

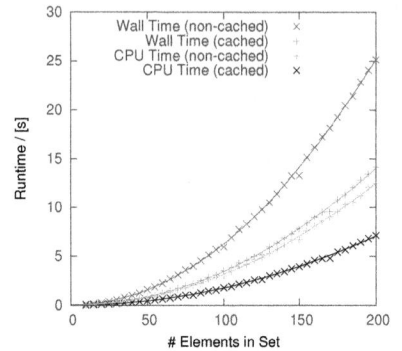

(b) $3PR^C$-PSI-explicit implementation. Wall and CPU time for the (non-) cached version are shown.

Figure 9: SOR worst-case runtime using 32-bit elements and 256-bit keys.

Paillier encryption are computationally more expensive than the operations as part of the decryption process. Due to a limit in space, the test results for varied plaintext sizes are presented in Appendix B.1.

6.2 Network Performance

To create a baseline for the network component used by the PROS and PSI protocols, the network implementation was tested for various sizes of the transmitted data. For the Linux platform, both the sender and the receiver were executed on the same machine. The data was transmitted internally using the loopback interface which almost completely eliminates network latency and thus allows an estimation of the overhead caused by the *send* and *receive* system calls.

Figure 6 shows the results for a series of tests. Each result was determined by first measuring the duration of 100,000 round-trip transmissions and then dividing the overall time by 100,000. This technique was necessary since the item for a single transmission is too short to be measured reliably. Each payload was randomly chosen and its size varied in steps of 8 bits between 8 bits and 2,048 bits. Since the data sent in each step of the protocol is bounded by the square of the modulus, the chosen range for the tests corresponds to reasonable key sizes. For each data size, the test was repeated 50 times and the average was plotted. The error bars show the standard deviation. The timing was performed using the wall time, i.e., the actual time which has passed—in contrast to CPU time, i.e., the time the process was actually allocated to the CPU. The broad scattering of the individual data can be explained by the process being preempted by the CPU during the measurement. The average behavior, however, is clearly linear. This was expected since—assuming constant overhead for executing the system call itself—doubling the data size results in double the transmission time.

Similar tests were performed for the Bluetooth network component for the iTouches. Figure 7 shows the results when varying the size of the data between 32 and 16,000 bytes in steps of 512 bytes averaging 100 round-trips. The inset shows an average of 32 ms per round-trip for data sizes which are commonly encountered during an execution of *appoint*.[4]

6.3 PROS and PSI Protocol Performance

6.3.1 Set Generation

In order to allow for the testing of all $3PR^C$ protocols as well as the FNP-PSI protocol such that the parameters can be adjusted precisely, the sets must be prepared in a controlled manner. A C++ program was written to pre-generate suitable sets. Pre-generating sets also has the benefit that different protocols can be tested with the exact same input.

Note that for both preference order composition schemes the *worst-case* behavior of the respective reconciliation protocols is caused by a pair of sets containing a single matching element located at the end of each set [25]. The generating algorithm for the worst-case scenario ensures that the remaining elements in both sets are unique and do not match. Thus, the protocols find the single match only in the last step, resulting in the worst-case runtime of the protocols. Since FNP-PSI works in a single round which includes the comparison of all set elements, the number of matching elements is not expected to have an impact on the runtime of FNP-PSI.

To create a pair of sets for the *average case*, one has to make assumptions on what the average input for the protocols is. In order to perform tests which are as general as possible, but can also be translated to real-world inputs, the number of matching elements was specified as a fraction of the total number of elements in each set. For the performance evaluation it is assumed that all matching set elements are distributed equally at random across all possible preferences. This is achieved by adding all common elements to both sets, padding them using non-matching elements until the total number of elements is reached, and then randomly ordering both sets.

6.3.2 Symmetric FNP-PSI Protocol

In this paper we focused on symmetric settings in which both parties learn the result of the computation. We therefore analyzed the performance of executing FNP-PSI twice: once initiated by each party respectively. Recall that FNP-PSI creates a polynomial which contains all of Alice's set elements as roots. Bob evaluates this polynomial at all his

---

[4]To illustrate the general performance of the iTouch's Blue-

tooth performance, the range of tested data sizes was chosen wider deliberately.

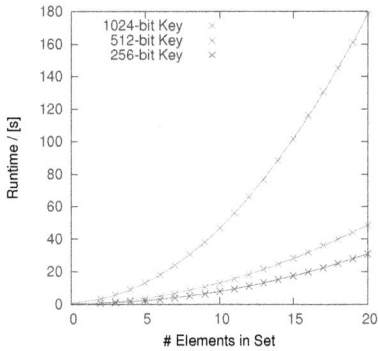

Figure 10: Runtime for the SOR scheme in the worst-case on the iTouch platform.

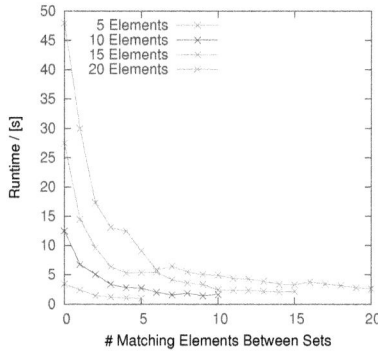

Figure 11: Runtime of the SOR scheme in the average case on the iTouch platform.

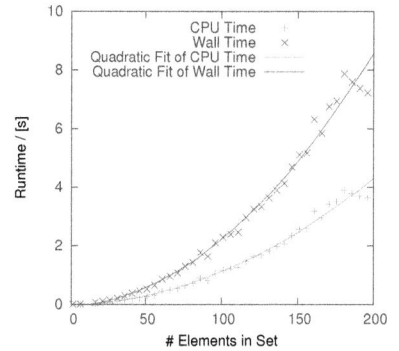

Figure 12: Runtime for the SOR scheme using $3PR^C$-*FNP-implicit* in the average-case (one match).

set elements and sends the results back. Since FNP-PSI computes the intersection of both sets and does not abort when a match is found, all steps need to be performed each time and the execution time is expected to be independent of the number and positions of the matching set elements.

The degree d of the polynomial introduced in Equation 1 grows linearly with the number of set elements resulting in a final degree of $O(n)$ [24]. Using classical multiplication (for polynomials), inserting an additional root requires $O(d)$ ring operations. Karatsuba's algorithm ($3d^{\log_2 3}$ operations) [33] and Schönhage and Strassen's FFT-based method ($O(d \log(d) \log \log(d))$ operations) [31,33] are two common and more efficient algorithms for multiplying polynomials. The runtime of FNP-PSI (as a function of the number of elements n) was analyzed using each multiplication algorithm. The tests were performed using the implementation provided by the FLINT library [3] for both advanced algorithms. For the tests, n was varied in steps of 100 between 50 elements and 2,000 elements averaging over 10 runs of the protocol. The key size was fixed at 256 bits and each set element had a length of 32 bits. Figure 8 shows the measured CPU time for one execution. While there is no significant difference in the runtime for small set sizes, the advantage of the advanced algorithms quickly becomes apparent for increasing n. For example for $n = 200$, using the advanced algorithms reduces the runtime by one third and for $n = 1,850$ the time required by Karatsuba's algorithm is only 5% of the classical implementation. In general, the complexity is reduced from $O(n^3)$ to $O(n^2)$.

6.3.3 Preference-Maximizing Protocols

Worst-Case.

In [24], the worst-case performance of the $3PR^C$ protocol for both preference order composition schemes sum of ranks (SOR) and minimum of ranks (MOR) was theoretically determined as $O(n^2)$ given sets of size $O(n)$ as input. Figure 9 shows the experimental results for $3PR^C$-*FNP-implicit* and both $3PR^C$-*FNP-explicit* protocols using the SOR preference order composition scheme on the Linux platform. The graphs were obtained by varying the number of set elements, using the worst-case setting described above, in steps of 5 between 5 and 200 averaging over 20 executions of the protocol. The key size was fixed at 256 bits and each set element was 32 bits in length. For each run, both wall time and CPU time were considered. Note that the CPU time is consistently 50% of the wall time which indicates

that the protocol is balanced amongst the parties. While one party is computing, the other one is waiting for the results. It is possible to fit the data points using a polynomial of degree two, which is in agreement with the quadratic behavior derived in [24]. Figure 9(a) shows the data for $3PR^C$-*FNP-implicit* and Figure 9(b) shows the $3PR^C$-*FNP-explicit* data. The positive effect of the caching mechanism is clearly visible. Both, wall time and CPU time are almost cut in half. The cached-variant of $3PR^C$-*FNP-explicit* is even more efficient than $3PR^C$-*FNP-implicit*. This is due to the fact that $3PR^C$-*FNP-implicit* uses the `vectorpolynomial` representation while $3PR^C$-*FNP-explicit* uses `flintpolynomial`. These results show, that the optimizations introduced by Meyer et al. are increasing the performance and that a naïve implementation as in $3PR^C$-*FNP-implicit-non-cached* suffers a significant performance loss. Using caching techniques, however, one can implement protocols that are both efficient and library.

appoint is solely based on $3PR^C$-*FNP-implicit*. Since the performance on the iTouches is significantly reduced with increasing key size, the worst-case tests were performed using 256-bit, 512-bit and 1,024-bit keys to investigate how the protocol performance develops. The number of set elements was varied between 2 and 20 in steps of 1. This corresponds to reasonable inputs for our application scenario, i.e., between two and twenty open time-slots. Figure 10 presents the results. For all key sizes the behavior is quadratic in the size of the set. However, as the tests of the cryptosystem indicated already, the performance is significantly reduced for large key sizes.

The results for the MOR preference order composition scheme are deferred to Appendix B.2.

Average-Case.

For the Linux platform, one set of experiments related to the average case was based on one matching element which was located at a random position in each ordered set. Given this random distribution, the average case is given by averaging the runtime over several independently chosen ordered sets. The cardinality was varied from 5 elements to 100 elements in steps of 5 elements and for each size the timings corresponding to 100 different ordered sets were averaged while using a fixed key. The resulting graph for $3PR^C$-*FNP-implicit* using the SOR scheme is shown in Figure 12. As in the worst-case scenario, the results show quadratic complexity with the CPU time being half of the wall time. However,

117

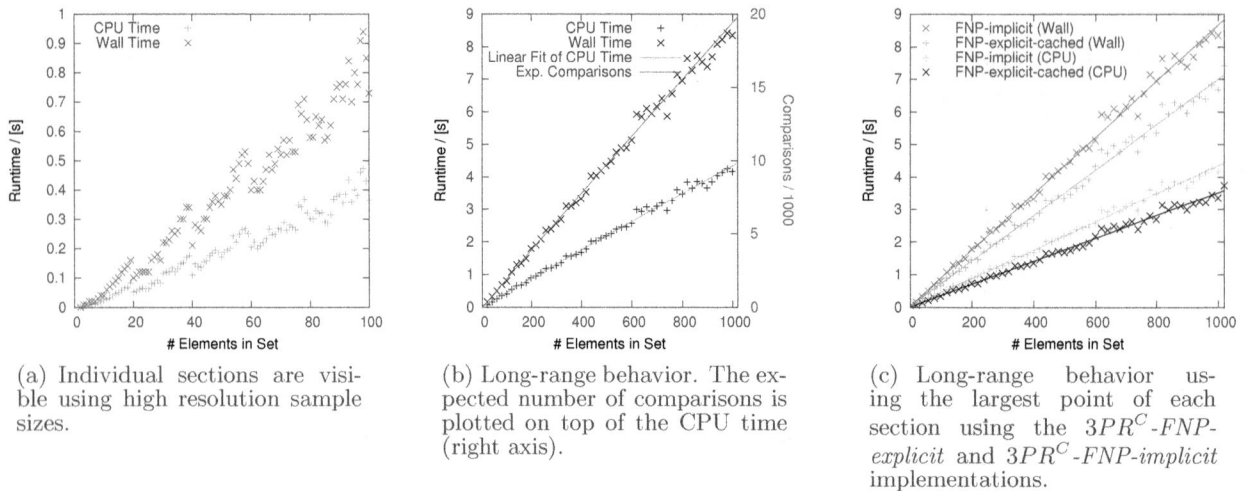

(a) Individual sections are visible using high resolution sample sizes.

(b) Long-range behavior. The expected number of comparisons is plotted on top of the CPU time (right axis).

(c) Long-range behavior using the largest point of each section using the $3PR^C$-FNP-explicit and $3PR^C$-FNP-implicit implementations.

Figure 13: Average-case runtime for the sum of ranks scheme using 32-bit set elements and 256-bit keys. Wall time and CPU time are shown. 100 runs were averaged and the fraction of matching elements is 5%.

the actual average runtime is about half of the one in the worst-case setting. This is due to the fact that a match, on average occurs after half the steps, i.e., when the elements in the middle of the ordered sets are being compared to each other.

Having only one matching set element is certainly a special case and thus additional experiments using multiple common elements were performed. Increasing the size of the ordered set while keeping the common elements constant does not constitute a good testing set. It is more representative to investigate how the runtime changes with ordered sets of different size where the sets have the same fraction of common elements. Figure 13(a) was obtained by creating ordered sets having 5% matching elements and varying their size n from 2 elements to 100 elements in steps of one element. The key size was kept constant at 256 bits and each set element had a length of 32 bits. For each data point, the timings corresponding to 100 different ordered sets were averaged while using a fixed key. Note that for $n < 20$ no single element matches since $0.05 \cdot 19 < 1$. Furthermore, an additional matching element is introduced for $n \in \{x \cdot 20 | x \in \mathbb{N}^+\}$. For the intervals in between, n increases but the number of matching elements remains constant. This structure is visible in Figure 13(a). The runtime drops down for $n = 20, 40, 60, \ldots$, i.e., whenever an additional matching element is introduced. The behavior in between appears quadratic for small n but cannot be clearly determined for the sections with larger n. This may be due to the fact that the number of possible combinations of matching elements increases with n and averaging 100 ordered sets may not be sufficient for reducing the error well-enough in order to obtain a clean graph.

For real-world applications, the overall behavior is often more important than the small-scale features described before. To remove the variations due to a new matching element, a set of tests was specifically crafted to only include the worst-case value of each section. For example, at $n = 20, 40, 60, \ldots$ a new matching element would be introduced and therefore ordered sets with $n = 19, 39, 59, \ldots$ were created. More precisely, the testing scenario varied n between 19 and 2,019 in steps of 20 and at each step 500 different ordered sets were considered to reduce the error

in the resulting average value. The key size was kept at 256 bits and each set element was 32 bits long. The resulting graph in Figure 13(b) clearly shows that the runtime increases only linearly. This is a significant reduction over the worst-case behavior and constitutes a major result w.r.t. practical applications based on these protocols. It is possible to confirm this linear behavior by modeling the expected number of comparisons statistically, using the average-case input described above. The probability of finding a match after exactly i comparisons is given by $p(i)_{i>1} = \prod_{j=0}^{i-2} \frac{n^2 - \alpha n - h}{n^2 - j} \cdot \frac{\alpha n}{n^2 - i + 1}$ where α is the fraction of matching elements. Evaluating the expected value numerically yields the blue curve (right axis) in Figure 13(b). The plot shows that our experimental runtime is proportional to the theoretically expected number of comparisons.[5]

The same experiment was carried out for both $3PR^C$-FNP-explicit protocols. Figure 13(c) compares the $3PR^C$-FNP-explicit-cached with the $3PR^C$-FNP-implicit. The relation between the runtime of the two implementations is similar to what it is in the tests for the worst-case scenario: $3PR^C$-FNP-explicit-cached has a runtime which is slightly less than that of $3PR^C$-FNP-implicit.

For the iTouch platform, tests were performed using 512-bit keys for sets of size 5, 10, 15, 20. For each set size, the number of matching elements was varied from 1 to the number of elements in the set. The set generation process is similar to the one described above. However, because of the low number of elements in the sets, it was feasible to test each possible set configuration, instead of testing only those for a fixed fraction. For each data point, 50 different sets were averaged. Figure 11 shows the results for SOR. The runtime rapidly decreases when the number of matches increases. For 1 to 15 elements, the application is very practical with turn-around times of at most 27 seconds.

Appendix B.2 details the results for the MOR composition scheme, which are very similar to those of SOR discussed here.

---

[5]Due to space limitations, the Linux results for the MOR scheme in the average case are not included in this paper. However, it is important to note that the results are very similar to those for the SOR scheme.

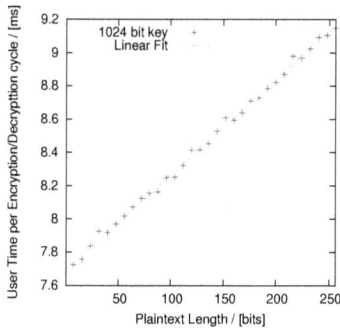

Figure 14: Time for encryption+decryption cycle as a function of plaintext size.

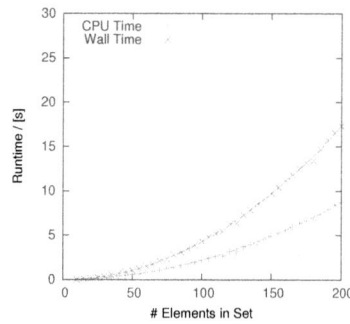

Figure 15: $3PR^C$-*FNP-implicit* $3PR^C$ implementation. MOR worst-case runtime using 32-bit set elements and 256-bit keys.

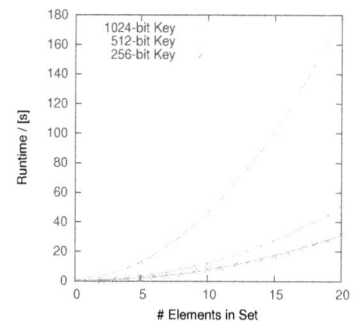

Figure 16: MOR worst-case runtime on the iTouch.

7. CURRENT AND FUTURE WORK

Directions for current and future work include the analysis of the protocols for LAN and WAN environments. In addition, we are investigating possible performance improvements for the encryption algorithm. We also plan to extend the library to include other homomorphic cryptosystems as well as leveraging our new, $3PR^C$-*PSI-explicit* implementation to evaluate the effect of using other privacy-preserving set intersection protocols.

Acknowledgment

In part, this work was supported by NSF Award CCF 1018616 and the UMIC Research Center, RWTH Aachen.

8. REFERENCES

[1] An Open-Source iPhone Calendar. http://github.com/klazuka/Kal/.

[2] Android API: java.security reference. http://developer.android.com/reference/java/security/package-summary.html.

[3] FLINT: Fast Library for Number Theory. http://flintlib.org/.

[4] GNU Multiple Precision Arithmetic Library. http://gmplib.org/.

[5] iPhone API: Certificate, Key, and Trust Services API. http://developer.apple.com/library/ios/#documentation/Security/Reference/certifkeytrustservices/Reference/.

[6] iPhone Human Interface Guidelines. http://developer.apple.com/library/ios/#documentation/UserExperience/Conceptual/MobileHIG/Introduction/Introduction.html.

[7] A. Ben-David, N. Nisan, and B. Pinkas. FairplayMP: A System for Secure Multi-Party Computation. In *15th ACM conference on Computer and communications security*, pages 257–266. ACM, 2008.

[8] P. Bogetoft, D. Christensen, I. Damgård, M. Geisler, T. Jakobsen, M. Krøigaard, J. Nielsen, J. Nielsen, K. Nielsen, J. Pagter, et al. Secure Multiparty Computation Goes Live. In *Financial Crypto. and Data Security*, volume 5628 of *LNCS*, pages 325–343. Springer, 2009.

[9] P. Bogetoft, I. Damgård, T. Jakobsen, K. Nielsen, J. Pagter, and T. Toft. A Practical Implementation of Secure Auctions Based on Multiparty Integer Computation. In *Financial Crypto. and Data Security*, volume 4107 of *LNCS*, pages 142–147. Springer, 2006.

[10] Y. Chen and W. Ku. Self-Encryption Scheme for Data Security in Mobile Devices. In *Consumer Comm. and Networking*, pages 850–854. IEEE, 2009.

[11] T. H. Cormen, C. E. Leiserson, R. R. L., and C. Stein. *Intro. to Algorithms*. MIT Press, third edition, 2010.

[12] E. D. Cristofaro, S. Jarecki, J. Kim, and G. Tsudik. Privacy-Preserving Policy-Based Information Transfer. In *Privacy Enhancing Technologies*, volume 5672 of *LNCS*, pages 164–184, 2009.

[13] D. Dachman-Soled, T. Malkin, M. Raykova, and M. Yung. Efficient Robust Private Set Intersection. In *Applied Cryptography and Network Security*, volume 5536 of *LNCS*, pages 125–142. Springer, 2009.

[14] E. De Cristofaro and G. Tsudik. Practical Private Set Intersection Protocols with Linear Complexity. In *Financial Cryptography'10*, volume 6052 of *LNCS*, pages 143–159, 2010.

[15] M. Freedman, K. Nissim, B. Pinkas, et al. Efficient Private Matching and Set Intersection. In *Advances in Cryptology - EUROCRYPT 2004*, volume 3027 of *LNCS*, pages 1–19. Springer, 2004.

[16] P. Gasti and Y. Chen. Breaking and Fixing the Self Encryption Scheme for Data Security in Mobile Devices. In *Euromicro on Parallel, Distributed and Network-based Processing*, pages 624–630. IEEE, 2010.

[17] O. Goldreich. *Foundations of Cryptography*, volume 2. Cambridge University Press, 2004.

[18] S. Goldwasser and S. Micali. Probabilistic Encryption. *JCSS*, 28(2):270–299, 1984.

[19] C. Hazay and Y. Lindell. Efficient Protocols for Set Intersection and Pattern Matching with Security Against Malicious and Covert Adversaries. *Journal of Cryptology*, 23(3):1–35, 2008.

[20] C. Hazay and K. Nissim. Efficient Set Operations in the Presence of Malicious Adversaries. In *PKC'10*, volume 6056 of *LNCS*, pages 312–331. Springer, 2010.

[21] C. M. Kozierok. *The TCP/IP Guide*. No Starch Press, 2005.

[22] Y. Lindell, B. Pinkas, and N. Smart. Implementing Two-Party Computation Efficiently With Security Against Malicious Adversaries. In *Security and*

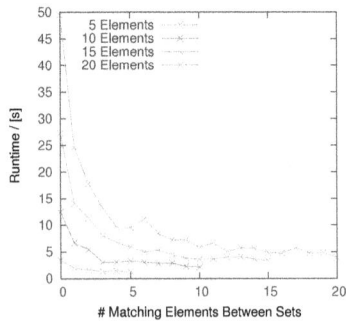

Figure 17: MOR average-case runtime on the iTouch.

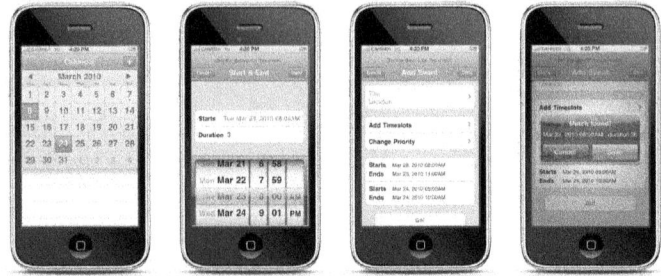

Figure 18: Screenshots of the *appoint* GUI.

Cryptography for Networks, volume 5229 of *LNCS*, pages 2–20. Springer, 2008.

[23] D. Malkhi, N. Nisan, B. Pinkas, and Y. Sella. Fairplay—A Secure Two-Party Computation System. In *USENIX Security Symposium-Volume 13*, page 20. USENIX Association, 2004.

[24] U. Meyer, S. Wetzel, and S. Ioannidis. Distributed Privacy-Preserving Policy Reconciliation. In *IEEE International Conference on Communications, 2007. ICC'07*, pages 1342–1349. IEEE, 2007.

[25] U. Meyer, S. Wetzel, and S. Ioannidis. New Advances on Privacy-Preserving Policy Reconciliation. Cryptology ePrint Archive, Report 2010/064, 2010. http://eprint.iacr.org/.

[26] T. Moscovich. Multi-touch interaction. In *CHI '06: Human Factors in Computing Systems*, pages 1775–1778. ACM, 2006.

[27] C. Müller-Tomfelde, H. Benko, and D. Wigdor. Imprecision, Inaccuracy, and Frustration: The Tale of Touch Input. In *Tabletops*, Human-Computer Interaction Series, pages 249–275. Springer, 2010.

[28] P. Paillier. Public-key Cryptosystems Based on Composite Degree Residuosity Classes. In *Advances in Cryptology — EUROCRYPT '99*, volume 1592 of *LNCS*, pages 223–238. Springer, 1999.

[29] J. Pan, R. Jain, M. Bowman, X. Xu, S. Chen, and C. BUPT. Enhanced MILSA Architecture for Naming, Addressing, Routing and Security Issues in the Next Generation Internet. In *IEEE ICC*, 2009.

[30] B. Pinkas, T. Schneider, N. Smart, and S. Williams. Secure Two-Party Computation is Practical. In *Advances in Cryptology–ASIACRYPT 2009*, volume 5912 of *LNCS*, pages 250–267. Springer, 2009.

[31] A. Schönhage and V. Strassen. Schnelle Multiplikation Grosser Zahlen. *Computing*, 7(3):281–292, 1971.

[32] A. Seehra, J. Naous, M. Walfish, D. Mazieres, A. Nicolosi, and S. Shenker. A Policy Framework for the Future Internet. In *HotNets-VIII*. ACM, 2009.

[33] J. Von Zur Gathen and J. Gerhard. *Modern Computer Algebra*. Cambridge University Press, 2 edition, 2003.

[34] J. Voris, S. Ioannidis, S. Wetzel, and U. Meyer. Performance Evaluation of Privacy-preserving Policy Reconciliation Protocols. In *Policy'07*. IEEE, 2007.

[35] A. Yao. Protocols for Secure Computations. In *23rd Annual IEEE Symposium on Foundations of Computer Science*, volume 23, pages 160–164. IEEE, 1982.

APPENDIX

A. appoint GUI

Figure 18 presents some screenshots of the *appoint* GUI. The leftmost one shows the main calendar screen which lists already scheduled appointments. Right next to it, the interface to enter a time-slot is illustrated. In the third screenshot one can see the list of time-slots—ordered by preference. Finally, the rightmost screenshot shows the result of the reconciliation process.

B. ADDITIONAL PERFORMANCE DATA

B.1 Crypto Performance as Function of Plaintext Size

Figure 14 shows that keeping the key size constant at 1,024 bits and varying plaintext sizes from 8 to 256 bits yields a linear runtime behavior.

B.2 MOR Worst-Case Performance

Figures 15 and 16 show the worst-case results for the MOR scheme on the Linux platform and on the iTouch respectively. The Linux timings were obtained by varying the number of set elements in steps of 5 between 5 and 200 averaging over 20 different sets. The key size was fixed at 256 bits and each set element was 32 bits in length. For the iTouch, keys of sizes 256-bit, 512-bit, and 1,024-bit were used. The number of set elements was varied between 2 and 20 in steps of 1 averaging timings for 50 different sets.

The timings for the MOR scheme are almost identical to the ones for SOR. This is due to the fact that in the worst-case the same number of comparisons is required in both cases. The tests show that the larger number of rounds required by SOR does not significantly impact the performance.

B.3 MOR Average-Case Performance

In Figure 17 the average-case performance using the MOR scheme on the iTouch platform is shown. The tests were performed based on the same parameters as the SOR tests: using 512-bit keys for sets of size 5, 10, 15, and 20. For each set size, the number of matching elements was varied from 1 to the number of elements in the set. The behavior is very similar to Figure 11.

An Empirical Assessment of Approaches to Distributed Enforcement in Role-Based Access Control (RBAC)

Marko Komlenovic
mkomlenovic@uwaterloo.ca

Mahesh Tripunitara
tripunit@uwaterloo.ca

Toufik Zitouni
tzitouni@engmail.uwaterloo.ca

Department of Electrical and Computer Engineering
University of Waterloo
Waterloo, Ontario, Canada

ABSTRACT

We consider the distributed access enforcement problem for Role-Based Access Control (RBAC) systems. Such enforcement has become important with RBAC's increasing adoption, and the proliferation of data that needs to be protected. We assess six approaches, each of which has either been proposed in the literature, or is a natural candidate for access enforcement. The approaches are: directed graph, access matrix, authorization recycling, CPOL, Bloom filter and cascade Bloom filter. We consider encodings of RBAC sessions in each, and propose and justify a benchmark for the assessment. We present our results from an empirical assessment of time, space and administrative efficiency based on the benchmark. We conclude with inferences we can make regarding the best approach to access enforcement for particular RBAC deployments based on our assessment.

Categories and Subject Descriptors

D.4.6 [**Operating Systems**]: Security and Protection—*Access Controls*; C.2.4 [**Computer-Communication Networks**]: Distributed Systems—*Distributed Applications*; D.4.8 [**Operating Systems**]: Performance—*Measurements*

General Terms

Security, Performance

Keywords

Role-Based Access Control, Access Enforcement, Efficiency, Empirical Assessment

1. INTRODUCTION

Modern enterprises generate and archive large amounts of data. Such data needs to be protected by access control systems. Access control deals with the provision of regulated accesses to resources by principals and is one of the most important aspects of security. The proliferation of data requires access control systems to scale to tens of thousands of resources and permissions [1].

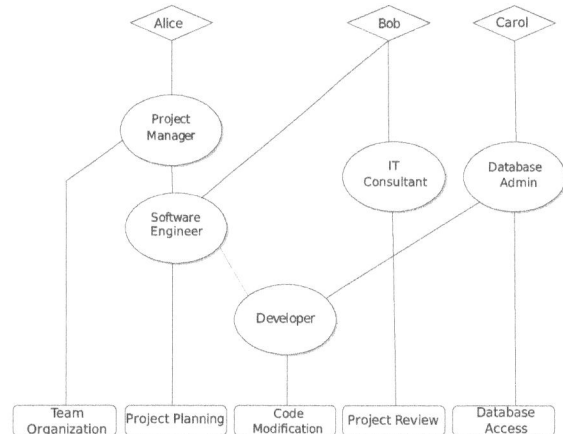

Figure 1: An Example RBAC policy. Users are shown in diamonds, roles in ovals and permissions in rectangles. Edges represent user-role, role-role and role-permission assignments. In the example, the user Alice is assigned to the role Project Manager and is therefore authorized to the permission Team Organization. She is also authorized to the role Developer, and therefore to Code Modification.

An important aspect of this scalability issue is the efficiency of access enforcement. Access enforcement is the process by which an entity called a reference monitor makes an 'allow' or 'deny' decision when a principal requests access to a resource. We consider access-enforcement in the context of Role-Based Access Control (RBAC) [2, 3], which is increasingly becoming the de-facto standard for access control in enterprise settings. In RBAC, rather than assigning a user directly to a permission, we assign a user to roles, and the roles to permissions. Also, the roles are associated with one another in a partial ordering called a role-hierarchy. An example of an RBAC policy is shown in Figure 1. There has been considerable research on RBAC. However, to our knowledge, there is very little work on efficient, scalable access-enforcement.

An approach to the problem is to distribute access enforcement across several reference monitors. With such an approach, a single, monolithic reference monitor is no longer a performance bottleneck. Such distributed enforcement, however, can be at odds with what is touted as one of the main benefits of RBAC – the ease of administration. Wei et al. [4] have proposed an architecture for distributed en-

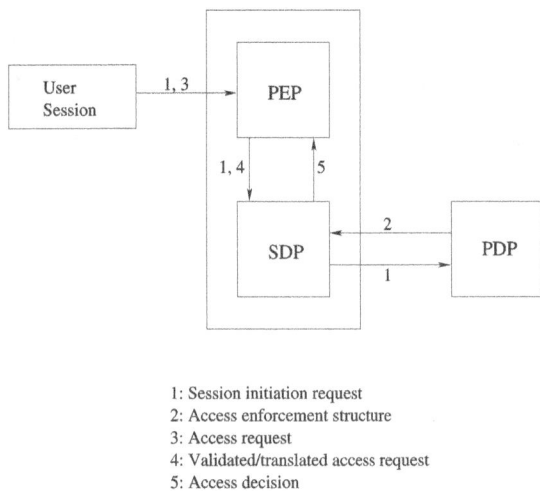

1: Session initiation request
2: Access enforcement structure
3: Access request
4: Validated/translated access request
5: Access decision

Figure 2: An architecture, reproduced from prior work [4, 5], for distributed access-enforcement in RBAC, and an associated process-flow. Our focus is on the Access enforcement (data) structure that is received by the SDP in Step 2, and that it uses to make access decisions.

forcement that attempts to reconcile these two issues (see Figure 2, which is a reproduction of corresponding figures from prior work [4, 5]).

In the architecture, the Policy Decision Point (PDP) is a centralized entity at which the RBAC policy is maintained. This centralization eases administration. Enforcement is performed at Policy Enforcement Points (PEPs). PEPs are aided by Secondary Decision Points (SDPs). An SDP can be seen as a cache of a portion of the RBAC policy from the PDP. In Figure 2 we show a typical chronological flow of events. In Step 1, a user activates a session at a PEP/SDP. In RBAC, users exercise permissions in sessions. A session is associated with a set of roles to which the user is authorized in the RBAC policy. In the example in Figure 1, users Alice and Bob may activate sessions s_a and s_b respectively. Alice may associate session s_a with the role Software Engineer, which authorizes s_a to the permissions Project Planning and Code Modification. Bob may associate s_b with the roles Software Engineer and IT Consultant, which authorizes s_b to the permissions Project Planning, Code Modification and Project Review.

The request to activate a session propagates to the PDP, which makes the decision on whether it is allowed. If it is, in Step 2, the PDP communicates a data structure to the SDP that the latter uses in Steps 3, 4 and 5 to make decisions on access requests that pertain to that session, that are communicated to it by the PEP.

The question we seek to answer is: what are the data structure and associated algorithms we should use in an SDP? There is evidence that "general purpose" approaches, such as storing an access control policy in a database and using the querying capabilities of the database, do not lend themselves to efficient access enforcement [6]. Consequently, it is necessary to carefully consider the approach that is used. In answering the question, we evaluate an approach along the following three axes.

Time efficiency – our primary goal is to make the SDP time efficient. An access check should be fast.

Space efficiency – we consider also the space that a particular data structure may take at the SDP. Space and time efficiency can be at odds; this is the classical time-space trade-off.

Administrative efficiency – with this, we ask whether a particular data structure at the SDP lends itself to easy administration in the propagation of administrative changes that are made at the PDP, to the SDP. We quantify this as the time it takes to update the SDP when an administrative change is made to the RBAC policy at the PDP.

Our approach to answering the question is to empirically assess six candidates. A challenge in conducting an empirical assessment is the lack of a meaningful benchmark. The establishment of meaningful benchmarks is seen as an important milestone in several settings in computing. We propose and adopt a benchmark in this paper (see Section 4). Our objective is for what we propose to serve as a macro-benchmark [7] – one that has RBAC policies and session profiles that are realistic.

In summary, our contribution is an assessment of six approaches to distributed access enforcement in the context of RBAC using a meaningful benchmark that we propose. In Section 3.1, we justify our choice of the six approaches.

The remainder of the paper is organized as follows. In the next section, we discuss related work. In Section 3, we describe the six approaches that we assess. In Section 4, we describe our benchmark and rationalize it. In Section 5, we present our assessment and results from it. We conclude in Section 6 with a "good," "fair" and "poor" rating of each of the six approaches along the three axes we mention above.

2. RELATED WORK

There is large amount of research in distributed access control, and in distributed RBAC in particular. However, there is relatively little work on efficient access enforcement in these contexts. To our knowledge, CPOL [6] is the state of the art in access enforcement in distributed settings. CPOL employs caching and a structure called an AccessToken that is application-specific to speed-up access enforcement. The work on CPOL points out also that simply using database querying does not suffice for fast access enforcement. Our work is close also to those of Wei et al. [4], Tripunitara and Carbunar [5] and Liu et al. [8], that address the access enforcement problem in RBAC. Wei et al. [4] propose the architecture that we adopt in this paper (see Figure 2). In that context, they propose authorization recycling which is one of the approaches that we assess. Tripunitara and Carbunar [5] adopt the architecture of Wei et al. [4] and propose an approach called the cascade Bloom filter for access checking. Their focus is fast and space efficient access checking for RBAC in low-capability devices. Liu et al. [8] propose a technique that they call transformations for access checking in RBAC. We see a transformation as encoding RBAC in an access matrix; it is one of the approaches that we assess.

3. THE APPROACHES

We compare six approaches in this work. They are: directed graph (Section 3.2), access matrix (Section 3.3), CPOL (Section 3.4), authorization recycling (Section 3.5) and the Bloom filter and the cascade Bloom filter (Section 3.6). For each approach, we discuss how we encode RBAC sessions in the particular data structure. We begin in Section 3.1 with a justification of the six choices.

3.1 Basis for the Choice of Approaches

Our primary objective is to compare four approaches from the research literature that have been proposed for distributed access enforcement. These are the access matrix [8], CPOL [6], authorization recycling [4] and the cascade Bloom filter [5]. Of these, the last two have been proposed specifically in the context of distributed access enforcement for RBAC. Their performance has been assessed only in isolation, and not relative to other approaches.

The access matrix [9, 10] is a well-established syntax for access control, with a long history. Liu et al. [8] propose its use (somewhat indirectly) for access control in RBAC. They do not consider RBAC sessions; we devise and adopt a particular encoding (see Section 3.3). In the work on CPOL [6], only an encoding of a trust management language in CPOL has been presented, and its performance has been assessed in that context only. The main elements of CPOL are sufficiently general that it can be used for RBAC (see Section 3.4 for our encoding). Consequently, we argue that it is an important candidate for access enforcement in RBAC.

The directed graph and the Bloom filter are two other candidates we consider. A natural representation of RBAC is as a directed graph. Consequently, it behooves us to consider it. The Bloom filter is also a meaningful candidate given that the cascade Bloom filter [5] is an extension to it, and an empirical argument over the use of the cascade Bloom filter over the "vanilla" Bloom filter has not been made before.

Certainly, one can think of other data structures that may be used for access-enforcement in RBAC. For example, one could encode RBAC sessions as Access Control Lists (ACLs) for the purpose of enforcement. However, we argue that our work gives a broad coverage of the possible approaches with valuable insights for other possible approaches as well. For example, an ACL is an encoding of an access matrix, which is one of the candidates we consider. There are also similarities between ACLs and the directed graph in the context of RBAC – both approaches are linear from the standpoint of time efficiency.

3.2 Directed Graph

An RBAC policy can be seen as a directed graph with a particular structure – it is acyclic, and its vertices can be partitioned into three sets (users, roles and permissions), with constraints on edges between the sets (e.g., the only outgoing edges from users are to roles). A natural data structure to use in the SDP, consequently, is a directed graph. When a session is activated, the PDP communicates to the SDP, in Step 2 of Figure 2, a directed graph, G.

Let $\widehat{G}$ be the complete RBAC policy at the PDP perceived as a directed graph. Let $S = \{s_1, \ldots, s_n\}$ be the set of sessions that are active at a PEP, and $R_i = \{r_1, \ldots, r_{m_i}\}$ be the set of roles that are associated with the session s_i. Let $P = \{p_1, \ldots, p_k\}$ be the set of permissions that are reachable

in $\widehat{G}$ from the roles in $\bigcup_i R_i$. Then the vertices of G are $S \cup P \cup R_1 \cup \ldots \cup R_n$. The edges of G are $\{\langle s_i, r_j \rangle : r_j \in R_i\} \cup E(I)$ where $E(I)$ is the set of edges of the subgraph I of $\widehat{G}$ that is induced by the vertices in $P \cup R_1 \cup \ldots \cup R_n$. That is, G is similar to a subgraph of $\widehat{G}$, except with sessions in place of users, and the edges induced by the vertices that are relevant to the sessions.

The access $\langle s, p \rangle$ is allowed if and only if the vertex p is reachable from s in G. We represent G as an adjacency list, which is a standard representation of a graph [11]. As an example, consider the sessions s_a and s_b from Section 1 for the RBAC policy in Figure 1. The session s_a is activated by Alice and is associated with the role Software Engineer. The session s_b is activated by Bob and is associated with the roles Software Engineer and IT Consultant. The resultant directed graph at the SDP is shown in Figure 3.

3.3 Access Matrix

The access matrix [9, 10] is a canonical and intuitively appealing representation for an access control policy. Consequently, we consider it a natural candidate as the data structure in an SDP. Our encoding of RBAC sessions in an access matrix is straightforward. Rows in the matrix are indexed by sessions, and columns are indexed by permissions. An entry in the matrix is a bit. An access request, $\langle s, p \rangle$ is an index into the matrix, and can be checked in constant-time. The access matrix that results at the SDP for our example sessions s_a and s_b from the previous section is shown in Figure 3.

3.4 CPOL

CPOL [6] is an approach to distributed access enforcement that has been proposed in the context of trust management. In trust management, the policy is distributed as well. Also, the syntax of policies is different from RBAC. Consequently, we need to provide an encoding of RBAC sessions in CPOL.

In CPOL, an AccessToken is used to determine whether access should be granted or not. In the original design [6], an AccessToken is opaque – its structure is specific to an application. A policy comprises Rules; each Rule contains an AccessToken. To check whether a particular access should be granted, we check the set of Rules and determine whether any of them contains an AccessToken that grants the access. For faster access enforcement, it is possible to aggregate AccessTokens in a Cache which is a keyed table.

Our encoding of RBAC in CPOL is as follows; we argue that this is the most natural encoding. We implement the SDP as a CPOL Cache. The key into the Cache is a session identifier. Each AccessToken is a set of permissions to which the session is authorized. Our study of the original implementation of CPOL suggests that there are two important aspect that affect the time efficiency of access checking: the manner in which the set of permissions is implemented within an AccessToken, and caching.

In our example of the sessions s_a and s_b for the RBAC policy from Figure 1 from the previous sections, we would have two CPOL Rules, $Rule_a$ and $Rule_b$, which contain $AccessToken_a$ and $AccessToken_b$ respectively. $AccessToken_a$ is {Project Planning, Code Modification}. $AccessToken_b$ is {Project Planning, Code Modification, Project Review}. The cache has keys s_a and s_b, for the two access tokens.

In our reimplementation of CPOL, we have adhered closely to the original implementation. In Section 5, we discuss

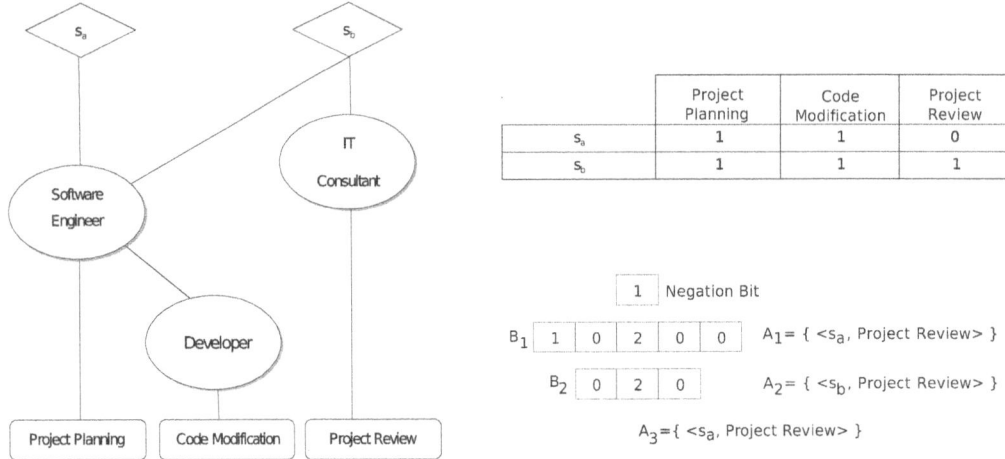

Figure 3: The directed graph, access matrix and cascade Bloom filter with 2 levels for our example sessions s_a and s_b that are discussed in the text, for the RBAC policy in Figure 1. (We discuss the encodings for CPOL and authorization recycling in Sections 3.4 and 3.5 respectively.) For the cascade Bloom filter, we assume that three indexing functions are used for Level 1, and two are used for Level 2. The Negation Bit is set, which indicates that A_1 is the set of authorizations that are disallowed. A_2 is the set of false positives in B_1, and $A_3 \subseteq A_1$ is the set of false positives in B_2.

why we have based our assessment on a new implementation. Our implementation compares in performance to the original (see Section 5). For ease of administration, we also maintain a set of Rules that are associated with an SDP, and a Condition for each entry of the Cache, as specified in the original design.

3.5 Authorization Recycling

Authorization recycling [4] is an approach to distributed access-enforcement in RBAC that was proposed in conjunction with the architecture in Figure 2. In this approach, two caches are maintained at the SDP, Cache$^+$ and Cache$^-$. The entries in Cache$^+$ indicate authorizations that are allowed, and the entries in Cache$^-$ indicate authorizations that are disallowed. An entry in a cache is $\langle R, p \rangle$, where R is a set of roles and p is a permission.

The access-enforcement algorithm is as follows. An access request $\langle s, p \rangle$ is mapped to $\langle R, p \rangle$, where R is the set of roles with which the session s is associated. We first check whether there exists an entry in Cache$^-$ of the form $\langle R', p \rangle$ such that $R \subseteq R'$. If there is, we deny the access request. This is because $R \subseteq R'$ implies that no role in R is authorized to p. Otherwise, we check whether there exists an entry in Cache$^+$ of the form $\langle R', p \rangle$ such that $R \supseteq R'$. If there is, we allow the request. This is because $R \supseteq R'$ implies that some role in R is authorized to p.

It is possible that neither of the above two conditions is met by $\langle R, p \rangle$ that corresponds to an access request $\langle s, p \rangle$. In this case, we need to consult the PDP. Unlike with the other approaches, in authorization recycling, no data structure is communicated from the PDP to the SDP in Step 2 of Figure 2. Rather, when an access request is made, if there is a match in neither Cache$^-$ nor Cache$^+$, the SDP communicates with the PDP and then updates its Cache$^-$ and/or Cache$^+$. We refer the reader to Wei et al. [4] for the algorithm that is used to update the two caches.

In our example of the two sessions, s_a and s_b for the RBAC policy from Figure 1 from the previous sections, both Cache$^+$ and Cache$^-$ are empty before a request for access takes place. Assume that Bob, in session s_b, requests permissions Project Planning and Database Access. The former succeeds and the latter fails, and for each attempt, the SDP acquires new state from the PDP. Cache$^+$ contains $\langle \{\text{Software Engineer}, \text{IT Consultant}\}, \text{Project Planning} \rangle$ after the request for Project Planning, and Cache$^-$ contains $\langle \{\text{Software Engineer}, \text{IT Consultant}\}, \text{Database Access} \rangle$ after the request for Database Access. Now, when Alice, in session s_a, requests permission Project Planning, the request succeeds based on the contents of Cache$^-$ and Cache$^+$.

3.6 (Cascade) Bloom Filter

A Bloom filter [12] is a probabilistic time- and space-efficient data structure for encoding a set A, and checking membership in A. We assume a universe, U of which A is a subset. A Bloom filter B is an array of m bits, with indices 0 through $m-1$. It is associated with k indexing functions $h_1, \ldots, h_k$ each of which maps every $e \in U$ to some integer between 0 and $m-1$. To represent that $e \in A$, we set the bit to which each h_i maps. To check whether $e \in A$, we check whether the bit to which every h_i maps is set. A counting Bloom filter [13] makes removal from a Bloom filter easier by associating a counter with each index rather than a bit.

As k and m are constants in the size of A (and U), B is represented in constant-space, and we can check whether $e \in A$ in constant-time. However, this check can result in a false positive; i.e., a check may return 'true' in some cases for which $e \notin A$. Consequently, a Bloom filter trades-off a probability of false positives for time- and space-efficiency.

The cascade Bloom filter [5] is an extension of the Bloom filter and has been proposed for the context with which we deal in this paper – distributed enforcement for RBAC. This approach uses several Bloom filters and associates each with a level, $l \geq 1$. Let the set encoded by the Bloom filter at level i, B_i, be called A_i. Then, $A_0 = U$, $A_1 = A$, and for $i > 1$, A_i comprises elements of A_{i-2} that are false positives in B_{i-1}. False positives of B_l are represented as a list.

The encoding of RBAC sessions in cascade Bloom filters that has been proposed [5] is as follows. Let $S = \{s_1, \ldots, s_n\}$ be the set of active sessions at a PEP-SDP, and P be the set of permissions such that $p \in P$ if any $s_i \in S$ is authorized to P. Then, U is $S \times P$, and A is the smaller (in cardinality) of $A_p = \{\langle s, p \rangle : s \text{ is authorized to } p\}$ and $A_n = \{\langle s, p \rangle : s \text{ is not authorized to } p\}$. A bit is maintained with the cascade Bloom filter to indicate which of A_p or A_n is encoded by it. The Bloom filter is a special case of the cascade Bloom filter, with the number of levels, $l = 1$. We adopt the same encoding of RBAC sessions for the Bloom filter as the cascade Bloom filter.

For the example of sessions s_a and s_b for the RBAC policy of Figure 1 from the previous sections, we show an example cascade Bloom filter with 2 levels in Figure 3.

4. A BENCHMARK

In this section, we discuss a benchmark for access-enforcement in RBAC that we have devised. The benchmark has two components: RBAC policies (Section 4.1) and session profiles (Section 4.2). We have designed and implemented programs to generate data sets for the benchmark. The programs are written in Java, and take as input arguments that correspond to the categorizations we discuss in Sections 4.1 and 4.2. We have made the programs available publicly [14].

4.1 RBAC Policies

The RBAC policies that comprise our benchmark are from prior research in RBAC, and experience with RBAC deployments that have been documented in books and the research literature. We present a summary in Table 1. We categorize RBAC policies along the following axes.

Source We have two sources, "Literature," and "Synthetic." By Literature, we mean that we have directly acquired particular kinds of policies from literature that documents research and experience with RBAC. Our sources for these can be classified into three. (1) top-down design of RBAC policies [3, 15, 16, 17], (2) role mining and engineering [18, 19, 20, 21, 22, 23, 24, 25], and, (3) evaluation of approaches to access-enforcement [4, 5, 8]. We also have created some new kinds of policies based on policies from the literature. We call these Synthetic policies.

Number of users, roles and permissions The numbers of users, roles and permissions are typically co-dependant in RBAC policies from the literature. In Table 1, we show the number of users, and the corresponding numbers of roles and permissions for policies from the literature, and for Synthetic policies. We point out that roles do not grow, for example, linearly, with users, but more as a step function.

We point out also that the number of permissions range from a fraction of the number of users, to a somewhat significant multiple. The reason for this range is that RBAC is deployed in one of two contexts. One is for high-level policies in which permissions are abstract. Another is at a much lower level, in which resources that are protected are individual files or email messages; in such systems, there can be a considerable number of permissions. (It is common for a permission to be a pair $\langle o, r \rangle$, where o is the object or resource that is protected, and r is a privilege or right.

Activation	Access checks
• Intra-session	• Number
– Number of roles	• Nature
– Number of permissions	
– Nature of roles	
– Nature of permissions	
• Inter-session	
– Number of sessions	
– Arrival rate	

Table 2: Session profile categories in our benchmark.

However, this is not the only encoding as a permission that is meaningful; see, for example, the work of Crampton [26].)

For our Synthetic policies, we consider numbers for typical enterprises that we have not already considered under Literature. The number of employees of an enterprise can be up to 1.6 million as of the writing of this paper [27]. If such enterprises deploy RBAC, we anticipate that they will want to model each employee as an RBAC user. For such policies, we anticipate that the number of roles will be in the same proportion to the number of users as for the largest range for users from the literature. We do not anticipate that the number of permissions will increase significantly. Consequently, we adopt for permissions similar numbers as the largest ranges from the literature.

Role Hierarchy (RH) and connectivity There are three categories we consider for the structure of RBAC policies. As Table 1 indicates, these are RH Depth, RH Model and Connectivity. By RH Depth, we mean the maximum path-length from a role to a permission. In our survey of the literature, the RH Depth does not exceed 5.

We consider two RH Models, Stanford and Hybrid. In the Stanford model [3], roles are layered, and a role at layer i directly inherits roles only in layer $i + 1$, and is inherited directly only by roles in layer $i - 1$ (or by users, for the topmost layer of roles). The Stanford model arises in the top-down design of RBAC policies. Realizing the Stanford model in an enterprise typically results in 4 or 5 layers of roles [3]. The hybrid model arises in both the top-down design of RBAC policies and in role mining. In the hybrid model, the role hierarchy is some partial ordering, and not layered as in the Stanford model. A special case of the two models is when there is no role-role relationship. This is called Core RBAC and arises in role mining [8, 21].

4.2 Session Profiles

There is some prior work which has datasets on session profiles [5, 8, 28]. We augment those datasets with our own. We categorize session profiles into two: activation and access checks; we summarize in Table 2.

Activation Under this category, we consider attributes associated with the activation of a session. We consider both intra- and inter-session attributes. An intra-session attribute is the *number of roles* in the session. For the number, we may specify a constant, or a range. Another attribute is the *nature of roles*. For this attribute, we may specify, for example, that only roles to which a user is directly assigned are activated. Another example is that only roles that do not violate some separation-of-duty condition may be activated [3]. The other two attributes are the *number* and *nature* of permissions.

Source	# Users	# Roles	# Permissions	RH Depth	RH Model	Connectivity
Literature	500-999 1000-1999 2000-2999 3000-3999 5000-6000 10000-40000	10-200 200 100 200-250 200 120-1300	10-3000 1000-3500 100-2000 1500-11000 1500-2000 100-11000	1–5	Stanford Hybrid Core	Constant (range) to roles, Constant (range) to permissions, Distributions (e.g., Zipf, uniform)
Synthetic	40001-400000 400001-1600000	1600-16000 16000-64000	1500-2000 1500-11000			

Table 1: A categorization of RBAC policies in the benchmark.

We have two inter-session attributes. One is the number of sessions that are activated. The other is the arrival rate of sessions. We consider two kinds of arrivals: bursty and uniform. By bursty arrival, we mean that session activations are interspersed with relatively long "quiet" periods in which we have no session activation. In the interim, we have access checks for the sessions that exist. In uniform session arrival, session activations are uniformly interspersed with access checks. We conjecture that bursty arrivals are likely with sessions that are directly used by humans, and uniform arrivals are possible if there are automated processes with which sessions are associated.

Access checks Our second category under session profiles relates to access checks. We have two broad attributes: the *number* and *nature* of access checks. Under number of access checks, we characterize how many access checks are made in the session. Under the nature of access checks, we characterize the permissions for which access checks needs to be made. For example, a session may exercise a large subset of the permissions to which it is authorized, and may do so multiple number of times.

5. ASSESSMENT

In this section, we discuss our assessment of the six approaches using the benchmark that we discuss in the previous section. In Section 5.1, we discuss our methodology for statistically sound data collection and evaluation. In Section 5.2, we discuss our assessment of time efficiency for inter-session attributes. In Section 5.3 we discuss our assessment for intra-session attributes. In Section 5.4, we assess the space efficiency of the approaches, and in Section 5.5, we assess how administratively efficient each approach is.

We have implemented all six approaches in Java; our implementations are available publicly [14]. For CPOL [6] and the (cascade) Bloom filter [5], we have acquired the original implementations. The code for the latter is already in Java, and we have made some minor modifications for our assessment. The original implementation of CPOL is in C++. We have reimplemented it in Java so we have "apples for apples" comparisons with the other approaches. In doing so, we have attempted to adhere to the original implementation as closely as possible. In particular, the manner in which the AccessToken (see Section 3.4) is implemented is crucial to the time-efficiency of CPOL. We observe that the timing measurements we obtain with our re-implementation (see Table 3) are close to those of Borders et al. [6].

5.1 Methodology

Meaningful empirical assessment is a significant challenge in computing [29]. For Java programs, non-determinism in making empirical observations can result from various factors, such as dynamic compilation and garbage collection. The methodology we adopt overcomes such non-determinism and is statistically rigorous. It is based on the work of Georges et al. [30].

Java programs run within an instance of a Virtual Machine (VM). We collect the average time across multiple VM invocations, as there can be variation across such invocations. Within a VM invocation, we need to avoid skew from the effects of starting up the VM and reach what is called steady-state [30]. For each VM invocation, we determine the number of benchmark iterations that we need to perform by finding at least k consecutive steady-state values for which the coefficient of variation (CoV) is less than some preset value (we have chosen 2%). The value of k starts at some value (4, in our case) and increases so long as the CoV decreases, upto the threshold. We record the mean of the k values for each VM invocation. Our final benchmark time is the mean across all VM invocations.

To minimize the effects from garbage collection, we keep the heap size constant across VM invocations. Apart from the mean, we also compute confidence intervals. Our objective is for the confidence intervals to not overlap, as then, with a certain confidence (95%, in our case), we can assert that the two values are statistically distinct. All the values we report and graph in this paper are statistically distinct from other values.

We have conducted our experiments on an isolated Intel dual core E8400 PC that runs at 3 GHz, has 3.5 Gbytes of RAM and runs the Ubuntu Linux operating system. Our Java version is 1.6.0_18, and we run the OpenJDK Runtime Environment.

5.2 Time Efficiency – Inter-Session

We have two inter-session attributes: the number of sessions, and the arrival rate. In Table 3 and Figure 4, we present our results for time efficiency, with the inter-session attributes as parameters. We also consider an intra-session attribute, the nature of RH. We discuss the results that pertain to that in the next section. In each dataset we have 25 users, each authorized to different numbers of roles and permissions. We have 100 roles in total, and 250 permissions. Our objective is to understand the behavior of each approach as the two inter-session attributes change. Conse-

		Direc. graph	Access matrix	Auth. recycl.	CPOL	Bloom filter	Cas. Bl. filter
Bursty	Stanford	32.70	0.79	2928.80	2.14	56.03	18.07
	Hybrid	9.41	0.80	94.07	3.12	60.15	32.40
	Core	5.17	0.74	10.18	2.87	50.41	29.94
Uniform	Stanford	29.47	0.62	1220.43	1.50	53.73	22.00
	Hybrid	8.45	0.62	49.73	1.44	55.57	25.54
	Core	5.93	0.60	4.44	1.51	55.62	26.16

Table 3: Average access check times in μs with the inter-session attributes, and one intra-session attribute (nature of RH), as parameters. The averages are across number of sessions from 2 through 15, for a given RBAC policy that comprises 25 users, 100 roles and 250 permissions. For the Stanford RBAC policy, we have adopted 5 layers, which is the maximum in Table 1. For the Hybrid RBAC policy, the depth varies between 1 to 5. We give the standard deviations for the bursty case in Figure 4.

quently, we consider from 2 through 15 sessions, and both bursty and uniform arrivals for the sessions. There are several observations we make from our results.

Arrival rates We observe from Table 3 that none of the approaches, except authorization recycling, is impacted by the session arrival rate (burst vs. uniform). The reason is that in authorization recycling, all the work is during access checking; session activation does not involve any exchange from the PDP to the SDP (except validation of the initiation). Consequently, authorization recycling can be impacted by bursty session arrival, which results in a number of access checks in a short periods.

Number of sessions The graphs in Figure 4 show the impact of the number of sessions on each approach. We observe that all six approaches are resilient to an increase in the number of sessions from the standpoint of time efficiency. That is, access check time does not necessarily grow with the number of sessions. We expect this to be the case, so long as the PEP/SDP is not stressed by adding too many sessions. None of the approaches has an access check algorithm whose time-complexity is parameterized by the number of sessions.

It is not our objective to stress a PEP/SDP by considering large numbers of sessions. Indeed, the number of sessions a PEP/SDP can support without significant impact on its performance depends on its resources such as hardware. Our objective is gain broader insights into the six approaches, notwithstanding the resources available to a PEP/SDP, assuming some realistic model of computation (the "Random-Access Machine" model, for example [11]).

Efficiency The access matrix is very time-efficient; in our tests, an access check takes less than 1 μs. This is unsurprising as an access check is done in constant time with minimal additional overhead. CPOL is only slightly less efficient; for this particular dataset, we can perceive the number of permissions to which a session is authorized as constant. Consequently, the manner in which a CPOL AccessToken is realized does not impact time-efficiency. The directed graph is highly efficient for Core RBAC. This is because a path from a session vertex to a permission vertex is exactly 2; consequently, it is highly efficient when we have only up to a few hundred roles. The cascade Bloom filter and the Bloom filter are also efficient. The major overhead with them are the computation of the indexing function (in our implementation, this is the cryptographic hash function, SHA-1 [31]), and searching a set in the worst case. Authorization recy-

cling is efficient for Core RBAC, but its performance degrades when we add a hierarchy. The reason is that the first time a permission is accessed, the SDP must communicate with the PDP; this must happen for every permission that is accessed. We study the impact on time efficiency from intra-session attributes (e.g., a large number of permissions in a session) in the next section.

Jitter By jitter, we mean the variation in access check times as the number of sessions changes. We can quantify this as the percentage error in the mean; that is, the ratio of the standard deviation to the mean. We observe from Figure 4 that this is quite small for the directed graph, access matrix and CPOL. It is higher for the cascade and Bloom filter, and very high for the Stanford RH for authorization recycling. The cascade and Bloom filter are affect by the heterogeneity of the permissions; if the union of permissions to which all sessions are authorized is larger, this can result in a deeper cascade or a larger set of false positives that must be maintained explicitly. Authorization recycling is affected by the heterogeneity of the roles that a user may activate in a session. In our datasets, a user is directly assigned to the same number of roles across each of the Stanford, Hybrid and Core policies. Consequently, there is more heterogeneity in the roles that a user may activate in the Stanford policy than in the other two.

5.3 Time-Efficiency – Intra-Session

We have studied the impact of intra-session attributes on time-efficiency. We vary three parameters in our experiments in this context: the number of roles per session, the number of permissions per session and the nature of RH (Stanford, Hybrid and Core). Figures 4 shows the impact of the last attribute on time efficiency, and 5 shows average access check times in μs for Core RBAC, for which the number of roles and permissions range from small (10) to large (10,000). Such numbers are consistent with Table 1.

Role hierarchy Table 3 and the graphs in Figure 4 show the impact of Stanford vs. Hybrid vs. Core as the choice for RH. Only for the directed graph and authorization recycling do we see an impact from the choice of RH. For the directed graph, a deeper RH results in an increased access check time as we need to traverse a longer path from a session vertex to a permission vertex. For authorization recycling, a deeper RH gives a user more choices of roles he may activate. This is reflective of our dataset – a user is directly assigned to the same number of roles for all three of the Stanford, Hybrid

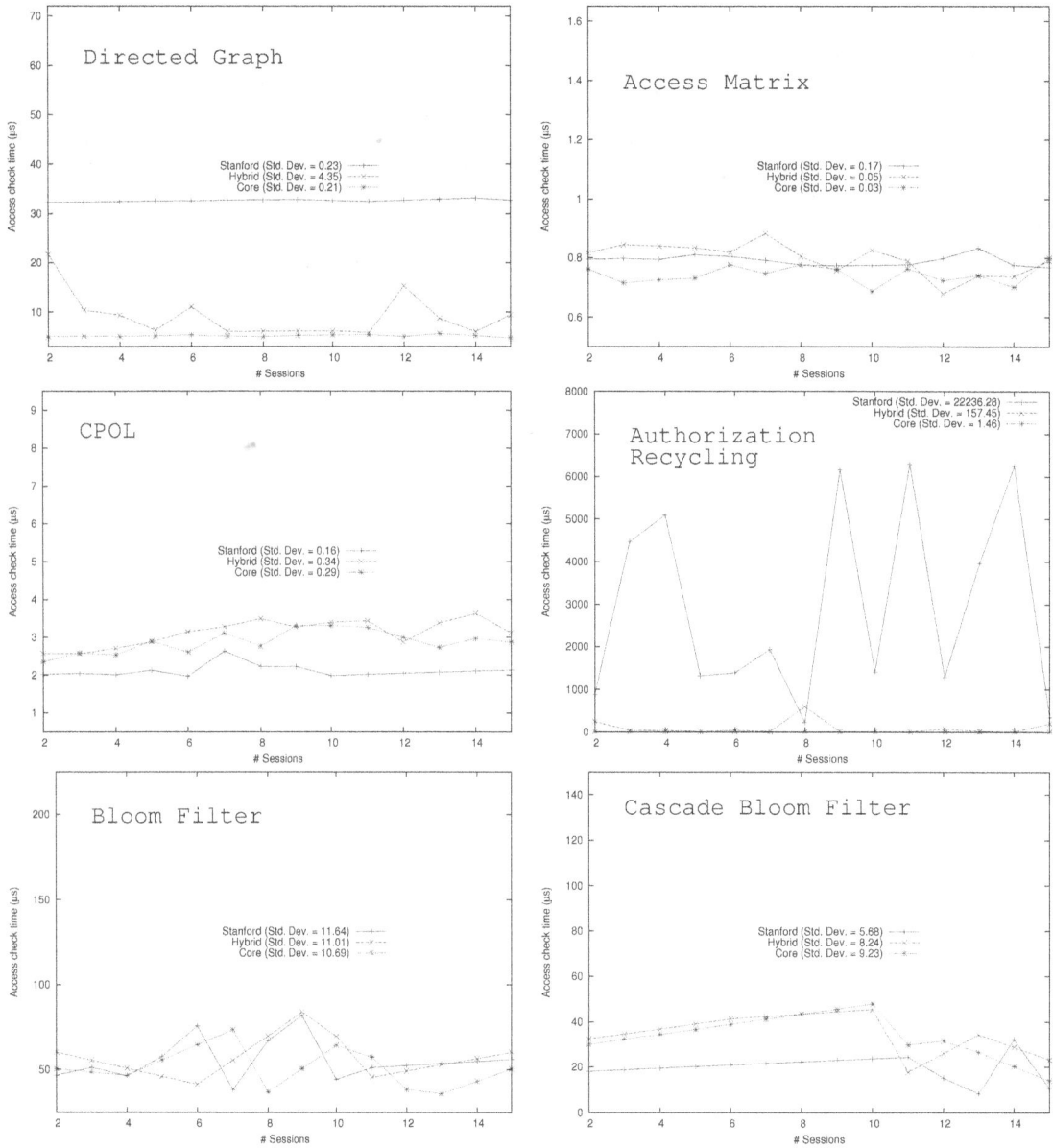

Figure 4: Average access check times in μs and the corresponding standard deviations for our six approaches as the number of sessions changes, for the three different kinds of role hierarchies.

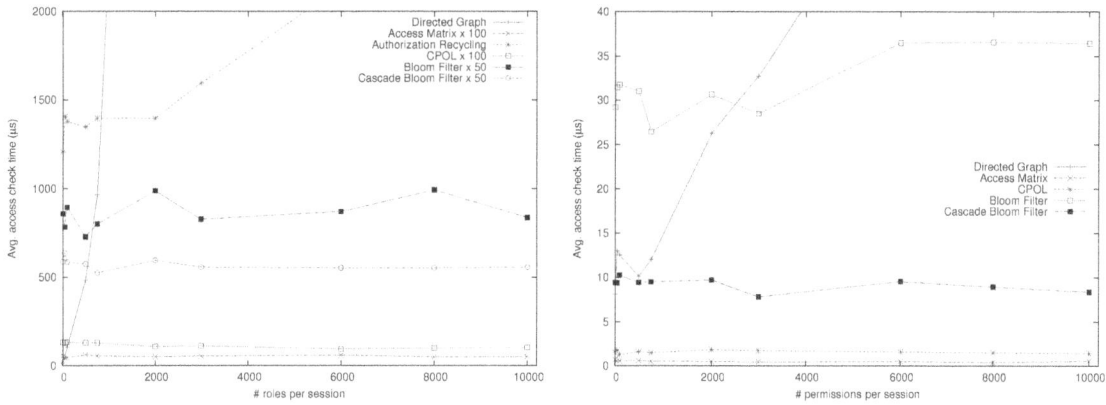

Figure 5: Time efficiency for small (10) to large (10,000) numbers of roles and permissions in a session. In the graph to the right, we do not plot authorization recycling as the numbers are much larger than the ones for the other approaches.

and Core RBAC policies. However, in the Stanford policy, he is authorized to more roles as a result of the deep RH. Consequently, the size of Cache$^-$ and Cache$^+$ is larger.

Scalability We observe from Figure 5 that the directed graph scales poorly as we increase the number of roles. The reason is that access checking for the directed graph is vertex reachability, which is linear in the size of the graph. Authorization recycling fairs somewhat poorly as we need to cache almost every role for each permission, and this results in it being linear in the number of roles, though with a smaller constant than for the directed graph. For the cascade and Bloom filter, access matrix and CPOL, the time for access checking is independent of the number of roles in a session. In this respect, they scale well with the number of roles.

The cascade and Bloom filter, access matrix and CPOL scale well also with the number of permissions, as Figure 5 indicates. This is somewhat surprising as an AccessToken in CPOL is linear in the number of permissions in a session. As we mention earlier, it is crucial to the time efficiency of CPOL that this encoding be efficient. Also, for the cascade and Bloom filters, the optimal values of the number of indices and the number of indexing functions changes with the number of permissions. (It may decrease for the cascade Bloom filter owing to the negation bit.) Notwithstanding this, upto 10,000 permissions, these issues appear to have no tangible impact on the time efficiency of these approaches. The directed graph fares poorly in this context as well. This is because the adjacency list approach often requires a linear search to find a vertex (permission, in this case). We do not plot authorization recycling in the graph for permissions in Figure 5 as the numbers for it are much higher than for the other approaches. It scales poorly with the number of permissions, as the number of entries in the two caches is linear in the number of permissions in a session.

5.4 Space-Efficiency

In this section, we analyze the space-efficiency of the six approaches. We base our assessment on what we have observed from our implementations, and an analysis of the data structures. The space needed for a directed graph grows linearly with the number of sessions. In the worst-case, it can also grow linearly with the number of permissions and roles

per session. However, on average, the size of the directed graph is constant in the number of permissions and roles. This is because we expect roles and permissions to be shared by several sessions.

The access matrix is highly space inefficient. The reason is that it grows quadratically with the number of sessions and the number of permissions to which any session is authorized. CPOL is linear in the number of sessions. It is linear also in the number of permissions per session, and therefore not as space efficient as the directed graph. It is agnostic to the number of roles in a session. Authorization recycling is linear in the number of sessions. However, it can be quadratic in the number of roles and permissions, in the worst case. The reason is that an entry in the Cache$^-$ or Cache$^+$ is a role set-permission pair.

The Bloom filter and the cascade Bloom filter are non-constant in space relative to the number of sessions and the number of permissions per session. The reason is that the optimal values for the number of indices and the number of indexing functions changes with the number of sessions and permissions. For the cascade Bloom filter, the number of indices may decrease with an increase in the number of session or permissions per session as a consequence of the negation bit (see Section 3.6 and Figure 3). Our code implements the algorithms for insertion and deletion that have been proposed by Tripunitara and Carbunar [5]. Consequently, the relationship between space and the number of sessions or permissions per session is a step function. The cascade and Bloom filter are agnostic to the number of roles per session.

In Figure 6, we present graphs that capture the above discussion. The graphs have been generated based on our implementations. The reason the access matrix is highly space-efficient for small numbers of sessions is that it is a bit matrix. However, as the number of sessions and permissions per sessions grow, its (quadratic) growth quickly negates the fact that each entry in the matrix is only a bit.

5.5 Administrative Efficiency

An administrative change is the addition or deletion of a user-role, role-role or permission-role relationship in an RBAC policy. The addition of a user at the PDP has no impact on an SDP. However, the removal of a user may im-

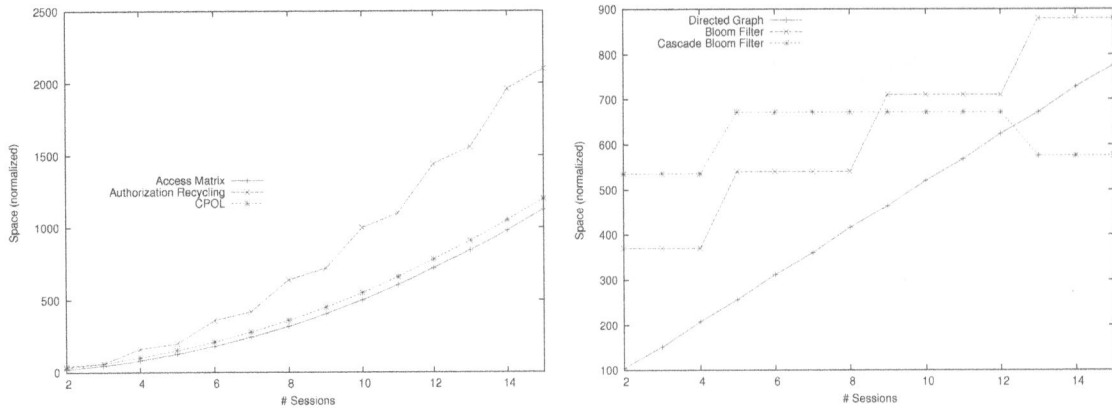

Figure 6: The space efficiency of our approaches. We show the three space inefficient approaches (access matrix, authorization recycling and CPOL) to the left, and the three space efficient approaches (directed graph, cascade and Bloom filter) to the right. In our dataset that we used to generate these graphs, The number of roles and permissions grows by a constant factor per session.

pact an SDP, as that user's sessions need to be removed. This impact is linear in the number of sessions in the worst case for the directed graph, quadratic in the number of sessions and permissions in the worst case for the access matrix, constant-time for authorization recycling, linear in the number of sessions in the worst case for CPOL, and quadratic in the number of sessions and permissions in the worst case for the cascade and Bloom filter.

The addition or removal of a permission can impact an SDP. The impact is constant-time for the directed graph, linear in the worst case in the number of sessions for the access matrix, quadratic in the number of sessions and roles in the worst case for authorization recycling, linear in the number of sessions for CPOL, and linear in the number of sessions in the worst case for the cascade and Bloom filter. The addition or removal of a role can authorize or forbid a session, respectively, to several permissions. We can infer the impact on the six approaches from our discussions on permissions.

In Table 4, we show the results of a proportional mix of administrative changes. The research literature on RBAC administration has focussed mostly on user-role changes, presumably because these are the most frequent in real-world deployments. We assume that 75% of the changes are to user-role relationships. We conjecture that permission-role changes are the next most frequent (20%) and changes to roles are infrequent (5%). In our experiments, sessions overlap with one another in terms of permissions and roles to a constant factor.

6. CONCLUSIONS

We summarize our conclusions in Table 5. For each approach, we rate it "good," "fair" or "poor" along the three axes that we adopt in this paper. For time efficiency, we split our rating into inter- and intra-session. The table allows us to choose the most appropriate approach for an RBAC deployment. For example, if the deployment is small in the size of the RBAC policy (e.g., only up to 100's of roles and permissions), then the access matrix is a good choice. If the deployment is larger, however, space considerations can dominate, and the cascade Bloom filter is a good choice. If

there is a need to balance reasonable space and access check time with ease of administration, then the directed graph is a good choice.

Summary We have assessed six approaches to distributed access enforcement in RBAC. Our approach is empirical, and we have proposed and used a benchmark as the basis. Based on our quantitative results, we are able to provide guidance on the best approach from the among the six for particular RBAC deployments.

Future work A validation of our conclusions in real-world RBAC deployments is an important piece of future work. Another issue is whether our approaches can apply to emergent access control models other than RBAC. We can also go back and ask this question in older contexts such as trust management. For example, it will be interesting to assess whether an encoding of trust management systems in the access matrix will give better performance than CPOL [6].

7. REFERENCES

[1] Personal Communication, Open Text Corporation, Aug. 2010.

[2] R. S. Sandhu, E. J. Coyne, H. L. Feinstein, and C. E. Youman, "Role-based access control models," *IEEE Computer*, vol. 29, pp. 38–47, February 1996.

[3] D. F. Ferraiolo, D. R. Kuhn, and R. Chandramouli, *Role-Based Access Control.* Artech House, Apr. 2003.

[4] Q. Wei, J. Crampton, K. Beznosov, and M. Ripeanu, "Authorization Recycling in RBAC Systems," in *Proceedings of the 13th ACM Symposium on Access Control, Models and Technologies (SACMAT'08)*, pp. 63–72, 2008.

[5] M. Tripunitara and B. Carbunar, "Efficient Access Enforcement in Distributed Role-Based Access Control (RBAC) Deployments," in *Proceedings of the 14th ACM Symposium on Access Control, Models and Technologies (SACMAT'09)*, pp. 155–164, 2009.

[6] K. Borders, X. Zhao, and A. Prakash, "Cpol: High-performance policy evaluation," in *Proceedings of the 12th ACM Conference on Computer and Communications Security (CCS'05)*, pp. 147–157, 2005.

	Direc. graph	Access matrix	Auth. recycl.	CPOL	Bloom filter	Cas. Bl. filter
100	13.45	2934.00	2294.20	321.75	1006.95	2530.05
200	22.20	9003.60	2757.00	1644.00	927.60	5559.30
300	39.15	1741.05	8085.60	5439.30	9760.50	2753.55
400	45.80	3748.80	524.00	5053.00	13755.00	4891.60
500	38.50	25097.25	8781.50	12567.25	3568.00	15980.00
600	87.30	20488.20	3272.10	3492.00	16399.50	7051.80
700	108.85	18676.70	19598.25	1737.05	7383.60	12406.45
800	142.00	33686.40	17520.40	7352.00	7076.80	1967320
900	151.65	17543.25	44167.05	17145.00	33234.30	41891.85
1000	158.50	31068.00	685.00	6800.00	19080.50	32351.50

Table 4: The administrative overhead on a Core RBAC policy. We assume a proportion of 75% changes to user-role relationships, 20% to role-permission relationships, and 5% to role-role relationships. The number of sessions is 1000, and every user has at least one session.

		Direc. graph	Access matrix	Auth. recycl.	CPOL	Bloom filter	Cas. Bl. filter
Time	Inter-session	fair	good	fair	good	fair	fair
	Intra-session	poor	good	poor	good	good	good
Space		fair	poor	poor	poor	fair	good
Admin		good	poor	poor	poor	poor	poor

Table 5: Our rating of "good," "fair" or "poor" for each approach that we assess. While we argue that these ratings follow from our quantitative observations, they are somewhat subjective.

[7] S. Wilson and J. Kesselman, *Java Platform Performance: Strategies and Tactics*. Prentice Hall, May 2000.

[8] Y. Liu, C. Wang, M. Gorbovitski, T. Rothamel, Y. Cheng, Y. Zhao, and J. Zhang., "Core role-based access control: efficient implementations by transformations," *PEPM'06: Proceedings of the 2006 ACM SIGPLAN symposium on Partial Evaluation and semantics-based Program Manipulation*, pp. 112–120, May 2006.

[9] G. S. Graham and P. J. Denning, "Protection — principles and practice," in *Proceedings of the AFIPS Spring Joint Computer Conference*, vol. 40, pp. 417–429, AFIPS Press, May 16–18 1972.

[10] M. A. Harrison, W. L. Ruzzo, and J. D. Ullman, "Protection in operating systems," *Communications of the ACM*, vol. 19, pp. 461–471, Aug. 1976.

[11] T. H. Cormen, C. E. Leiserson, R. L. Rivest, and C. Stein, *Introduction to Algorithms*. The MIT Press, 3 ed., Sept. 2009.

[12] B. Bloom, "Space/time trade-offs in hash coding with allowable errors," *Communications of the ACM*, vol. 13, no. 7, pp. 422–426, 1970.

[13] L. Fan, P. Cao, J. Almeida, and A. Broder, "Summary cache: A scalable wide-area web cache sharing protocol," *IEEE/ACM Transactions on Networking*, vol. 8, no. 3, pp. 281–293, 2000.

[14] Marko Komlenovic, Mahesh Tripunitara and Toufik Zitouni, "A platform for assessing approaches to distributed Role-Based Access Control (RBAC) enforcement," 2010. Available from `http://code.google.com/p/dist-rbac-eval/`.

[15] A. Kern, M. Kuhlmann, A. Schaad, and J. Moffett, "Observations on the role life-cycle in the context of enterprise security management," *7th ACM Symposium on Access Control Models and Technologies*, June 2002.

[16] A. Schaad, J. Moffett, and J. Jacob., "The role-based access control system of a european bank: A case study and discussion," *proceedings of ACM Symposisum on Access Control Models and Technologies*, pp. 3–9, May 2001.

[17] A. Kern, "Advanced features for enterprise-wide role-based access control," *Proceedings of the 18th Annual Computer Security Applications Conference*, pp. 333–343, December 2002.

[18] D. Zhang, K. Ramamohanarao, S. Versteeg, and R. Zhang., "Rolevat: Visual assessment of practical need for role based access control," *ACSAC*, pp. 13–22, 2009.

[19] J. Vaidya, V. Atluri, and J. Warner, "Roleminer: mining roles using subset enumeration," *Proceedings of the 13th ACM conference on Computer and communications security (CCS'06)*, pp. 144–153, 2006.

[20] D. Zhang, K. Ramamohanarao, T. Ebringer, and T. Yann, "Permission set mining: Discovering practical and useful roles," *ACSAC'08: Proceedings of the 2008 Annual Computer Security Applications Conference*, pp. 247–256, 2008.

[21] I. Molloy, N. Li, T. Li, Z. Mao, Q. Wang, and J. Lobo, "Evaluating role mining algorithms," *Proc. ACM Symposium on Access Control Models and Technologies (SACMAT)*, pp. 95–104, 2009.

[22] C. Blundo and S. Cimato, "A simple role mining algorithm," *Proceedings of the 2010 ACM Symposium on Applied Computing*, pp. 1958–1962, 2010.

[23] M. Frank, A. Streich, D. Basin, and J. Buhmann, "A probabilistic approach to hybrid role mining," *Proc. 16th ACM conference on Computer and Communications Security (CCS)*, pp. 101–111, 2009.

[24] I. Molloy, H. Chen, T. Li, Q. Wang, N. Li, E. Bertino, S. Calo, and J. Lobo, "Mining roles with semantic meanings," *Proc. ACM Symposium on Access Control Models and Technologies (SACMAT)*, 2008.

[25] M. Jafari, A. Chinaei, K. Barker, and M. Fathian, "Role mining in access history logs," *Journal of Information Assurance and Security*, 2009.

[26] J. Crampton, "On permissions, inheritance and role hierarchies," in *Proceedings of the Tenth ACM Conference on Computer and Communications Security (CCS-10)*, pp. 27–31, ACM Press, Oct. 2003.

[27] "Global 500." Fortune Magazine, 2010. Available from http://money.cnn.com/magazines/fortune/global500/2010/.

[28] Q. Yao, A. An, E. Terzi, and X. Huang, "Finding and analyzing database user sessions," *Proceedings of the 10th International Conference on Database Systems for Advanced Applications (DASFAA)*, 2005.

[29] T. Mytkowicz, A. Diwan, M. Hauswirth, and P. F. Sweeney, "Producing wrong data without doing anything obviously wrong!," in *Proceeding of the 14th international conference on Architectural Support for Programming Languages and Operating Systems (ASPLOS'09)*, pp. 265–276, 2009.

[30] A. Georges, D. Buytaert, and L. Eeckhout, "Statistically rigorous java performance evaluation," *Proceedings of OOPSLA'07*, pp. 57–76, May 2007.

[31] F. I. P. Standards, "Secure hash standard," 2002. Available from http://csrc.nist.gov/publications/fips/fips180-2/fips180-2withchangenotice.pdf.

A Language for Provenance Access Control *

Tyrone Cadenhead, Vaibhav Khadilkar, Murat Kantarcioglu and
Bhavani Thuraisingham
The University of Texas at Dallas
800 W. Campbell Road, Richardson, TX 75080
{thc071000, vvk072000, muratk, bxt043000}@utdallas.edu

ABSTRACT

Provenance is a directed acyclic graph that explains how a
resource came to be in its current form. Traditional access
control does not support provenance graphs. We cannot
achieve all the benefits of access control if the relationships
between the data and their sources are not protected. In
this paper, we propose a language that complements and
extends existing access control languages to support provenance. This language also provides access to data based on
integrity criteria. We have also built a prototype to show
that this language can be implemented effectively using Semantic Web technologies.

Categories and Subject Descriptors: D.4.6 [Operating
Systems]: Operating Systems —Access Control

General Terms: Languages, Security.

Keywords: Access Control, Provenance, RDF, SPARQL,
Regular Expressions, XML.

1. INTRODUCTION

Provenance is the lineage, pedigree and filiation of a resource (or data item) and is essential for various domains including healthcare and intelligence. Provenance can be used
to drill down to the source of a medical record or an intelligence report, to track the activities of a doctor or a field
agent, and to provide an audit trail that can be used later
for validation and verification tasks. Existing access control
specifications that define policies for resources do not easily support provenance [3]. Despite the current drawback of
provenance to divulge sensitive information, the security of
provenance has not been given a high priority in the research
community. It is clear that the protection of provenance is
required by laws and regulations to avoid the disclosure of

*This work was partially supported by Air Force Office
of Scientific Research MURI Grant FA9550-08-1-0265, National Institutes of Health Grant 1R01LM009989, National
Science Foundation Grants Career-0845803, CNS-0964350,
and CNS-1016343.

sensitive information [10]. For example, in a security intelligence agency, the improper disclosure of the source or the
ownership of a piece of classified information may result in
great and irreversible losses. Also, many compliance regulations require proper archives and audit logs for electronic
records, e.g. HIPAA mandates that we properly log accesses
and updates to the histories of medical records [10].

In order to define an access control policy for provenance,
it is imperative that we identify the parts of the provenance
graph that we want to protect. Therefore, we must have a
clear definition of the users, their actions and the resources
to be protected. Provenance takes the form of a directed
acyclic graph (DAG) that establishes causal relationships
between data items [15]. Traditional access control models
focus on individual data items whereas in provenance we are
concerned with protecting both, the data items and their relationships [3]. In this paper we refer to both, data items and
their relationships as resources, to be protected. In order to
protect a resource we need to first identify it in the provenance graph. This identification is one of the major distinguishing factors between a provenance access control model
and existing access control models. The provenance graph
structure not only poses challenges to access control models
but also to querying languages [11]. The various paths in
a provenance graph from a resource to all its sources are
important in proving the validity of that resource. Furthermore, these paths contain the pertinent information needed
to verify the integrity of the data and establish trust between
a user and the data; however, we do not want to divulge any
exclusive information in the path which could be used by an
adversary to gain advantages, for example in military intelligence.

We need appropriate access control mechanisms for provenance that prevent the improper disclosure of any sensitive
information along a path in the provenance graph. We need
to extend the traditional access control definition that protects a single data item to one where we now want to protect
any resources along a path of arbitrary length. In this paper,
we propose a policy language that extends the definition of
traditional access control languages to allow specification of
policies over data items and their relationships in a provenance graph. This language will allow a policy author to
write policies that specify who accesses these resources. The
language provides natural support for traditional access control policies over data items. We motivate this idea with the
following example. Consider a medical example where we
may want to give access to everything in a patient's record
that was updated by processes controlled only by the pa-

tient's physician and surgeon. For this example, the system would evaluate two policies. The first policy would check if the user has access to the medical record. This policy would be applied over all the medical records in the system with the traditional access control policies in place. The second policy would check if the patient's medical record has indeed only been modified by the patient's physician and surgeon. This second policy would be applied over the provenance graph associated with the given medical record. This example not only shows how existing access control policies can be integrated in our language, but also how traditional access control can be used to allow access to provenance.

The traditional definition of access control policies is extended in our policy language to include relationships over data items in the provenance graph by making use of regular expressions. The use of an existing access control language to build policies over the provenance graph would require enumerating all the possible paths that we want to protect in the graph as separate policies. The use of regular expressions in our language not only solves this problem, since many paths can be specified using the same regular expression, but also allows the same policy to be applied to multiple provenance graphs. In contrast to the first example these regular expressions can be used to first verify the quality of the data items and second, act as a "pseudo" access control mechanism for giving data access to the user. Again, we use the following example to motivate this idea. Consider a military scenario where access to an intelligence report can only be given to a user if the report was created by a particular field agent belonging to a specific agency in a particular country. In this example, the system would evaluate the regular expression in the policy over the provenance graph for the given intelligence report to check if that report was indeed created by the specified field agent belonging to the given agency in the specified country. If such a path exists in the provenance graph only then access is granted to the querying user for the report. This example emphasizes how provenance can be used to first determine integrity of the data in order to guarantee high quality information before access is given to the actual data items.

Our main contribution in this paper is the definition of an access control policy language for provenance. This language retains the properties of traditional access control to gain access to data. Furthermore, the language provides an additional advantage whereby provenance not only acts as an access control mechanism but also as an integrity mechanism for giving access to the data. We also build a prototype using Semantic Web technologies that allows a user to query for data and provenance based on access control polices defined using our policy language.

The rest of the paper is organized as follows. Section 2 gives a basic idea of access control and shows the drawbacks of using existing access control models for provenance. Section 3 provides a formalism to represent access control policies for provenance. In Section 4 we present existing storage mechanisms for provenance and we show how we can use regular expressions to support our policy language using Semantic Web technologies. In section 5 we show how the complexity changes from that of protecting single resources to that of protecting resources over relationships in a provenance graph. Section 6 presents an architecture which incorporates our policy language in an access control prototype system. Section 7 reviews previous work in the area of access

control for provenance. In closing, in Section 8 we provide our conclusions and future work.

2. ACCESS CONTROL

An access control system has three levels of abstraction [23]:

1. Policy. This is a high level requirement that specifies how access is managed and who, under what conditions, may access a resource.

2. Mechanism. This implements the regulations established by a policy.

3. Model. This is a formal representation of a policy. The model allows the verification of the security properties provided by the system.

An access control policy authorizes a set of *users* to perform a set of *actions* on a set of *resources* within an *environment*. Unless authorized through one or more access control policies, users have no access to any resource of the system. There are many access control policies defined in the literature. These can be grouped into three main classes [23], which differ by the constraints they place on the sets of *users*, *actions* and *objects* (access control models often refer to *resources* as *objects*). These classes are (1) RBAC, which restricts access based on roles; (2) DAC, which controls access based on the identity of the user; and (3) MAC, which controls access based on mandated regulations determined by a central authority. There are two major concerns with these policies. The first is the number of user to object assignments and the second is that these policies are defined over a single resource.

Role-Based Access Control (RBAC) models have enjoyed popularity by simplifying the management of security policies. These models depend on the definition of roles as an intermediary between users and permissions (which is a combination of actions and objects). The core model defines two assignments: a user-assignment that associates users to roles and a permission-assignment that associates roles with permissions. In [8], the authors argue that there is a direct relationship between the cost of administration and the number of mappings that must be managed. The drawbacks with using RBAC include, (i) each time a user does not have access to an object through an existing role, a new role is needed; and (ii) as the policies become more fine-grained, a role is needed for each combination of the different resources in the provenance graph [22]. Similar drawbacks apply to the DAC and MAC access control models since they both use mapping functions to associate users with objects.

Clearly, applying these traditional access control policies for fine-grained access control in provenance would result in prohibitive management costs. Moreover, their usage in provenance would be an arduous task for the administrator. In Section 5, we provide an analysis, which shows that the number of resources in a provenance graph is exponential in the number of nodes in the graph. We address these drawbacks in this paper and provide an implementation of a prototype mechanism, which shows that we can greatly reduce these mappings.

In summary, the general expectations of an access control language for provenance are (i) to be able to define policies over a directed acyclic graph; (ii) to support fine-grained access control on any component of the graph; and (iii) to seamlessly integrate existing organizational policies.

3. POLICY LANGUAGE

A generalized language that extends existing access control languages such as XACML [14] was proposed in [17]. We extend the syntax of this XML-based policy language in order to incorporate regular expressions in a policy. The existing provenance language in [17] was developed as a generalized model of access control for provenance, but did not address resources with arbitrary path lengths within the provenance graph. Therefore, this language suffers from the fact that a resource must be identified before hand, rather than be given as a string which is matched against the graph at execution time. An example of our adaptation of the lan-

```
<policy ID="1" >
  <target>
    <subject>anyuser</subject>
    <record>Doc1_2</record>
    <restriction>
      Doc1_2 [WasGeneratedBy] process AND
      process [WasControlledBy] physician|surgeon
    </restriction>
    <scope>non-transferable</scope>
  </target>
  <condition>purpose == research</condition>
  <effect>Permit</effect>
</policy>
```

Figure 1: Policy language

guage in [17] is given in Figure 1, which now allows the policy to be written using the regular expression syntax. We place an emphasis on the target, effect and condition elements given in [17], but make slight modifications to their meanings to incorporate regular expressions on a provenance graph. Since our focus in this paper is on specifying a policy for access control in provenance, we provide only the relevant XML elements in this paper. The interested reader can find other interesting elements of the language, such as obligation and originator preference, in [17].

The description of each element in Figure 1 is as follows: The **subject** element can be the name of a user or any collection of users, e.g. physician or surgeon, or a special user collection *anyuser* which represents all users. The **record** element is the name of a resource. The **restriction** element is an (optional) element which refines the applicability established by the subject or record. The **scope** element is an (optional) element which is used to indicate whether the target applies only to the record or its entire ancestry. The **condition** element is an (optional) element that describes under what conditions access is to be given or denied to a user. The **effect** element indicates the policy author's intended consequence for a true evaluation of a policy.

The scope element is useful, in particular, when we want to protect the record only if it is along a specified path in the provenance graph. This is achieved by using the predefined value "non-transferable". This element can also be used when we need to protect a path in the provenance graph if a particular record is along that path. This is achieved by the predefined value "transferable". The condition element is necessary when we want to specify system or context parameters for giving access, e.g. permitting access to provenance when it is being used for research. It is important

that we keep the number of policies to a minimum by combining them using regular expressions. This will improve the effectiveness of an access control system that protects the sensitive information from unauthorized users. It was also pointed out in [17] that when the policy size is not small, detecting abnormal policies is essentially a SAT problem. The reason is that the effects of different semantics for the predicates used in the condition and restriction elements may cause incorrect policy specifications, which may generate conflicting or redundant policies.

We achieve fine-grained access control by allowing a record value to be any (indivisible) part of a provenance graph. The regular expressions in the "restriction" element allow us to define policies over paths of arbitrary length in a provenance graph that apply to a subject or record. Also, since XML is an open and extensible language, our policy language is both customizable and readily supports integration of other policies.

3.1 The Grammar

In this section, we define a grammar for each of the tags in the language we propose.

```
<exp>  ::= <char>+ ("." <char>+)?
<char> ::= [a-z] | [A-Z] | "_" | "-" |
<reg>  ::= "*" | "+" | "?"
<bool> ::= " AND " | " OR " | "|"
<op>   ::=  " == " | " <= " | " >= " | " < " | " > "
<num>  ::= ([0-9])+
<sp>   ::= "[" <exp> "]"
```

We now define the set of strings accepted by each element in our language.

```
subject =  <char>+ | <num>

record  =  <exp>

restriction =  (<exp><num>?)+ (<op> | <sp><reg>?)
              (<exp><num>?)+
             (<bool> (<exp><num>?)+
             (<op> | <sp><reg>?)? (<exp><num>?)+)*

scope  =  <char>+

condition =  (<exp><num>?)+ (<op> | <sp><reg>?)
            (<exp><num>?)+
           (<bool> (<exp><num>?)+
           (<op> | <sp><reg>?)? (<exp><num>?)+)*

effect =  <char>+ | <num>
```

The grammar defined above allows us to evaluate the policy for correctness and secondly, allows a parser to unambiguously translate the policy into a form that can be used by the appropriate layer in our architecture.

4. DATA REPRESENTATION

We require a suitable data representation for storing provenance. Such a data representation must naturally support the directed graph structure of provenance and also allow path queries of arbitrary length. The Open Provenance Model (OPM) [15] does not specify protocols for storing or querying provenance information; but it does specify properties that any data model should have. One such property includes allowing provenance information to be shared among systems. Provenance data can be stored in the relational database model, the XML data model or the RDF data model [12]. Each of these in their current form has drawbacks with respect to provenance [11]. A relational model suffers from the fact that it needs expensive joins on relations (tables) for storing edges or paths. Also, current SQL languages that support transitive queries are complex and awkward to write. XML supports path queries, but the current query languages XQuery and XPath only support a tree structure. RDF naturally supports a graph structure, but the current W3C Recommendation for SPARQL (the standard query language for RDF) lacks many features needed for path queries. There are recent works on extending SPARQL with path expressions and variables. These include SPARQL Query 1.1 [9] which is now part of a proposal put forward by the W3C recently. The SPARQL 1.1 query language includes new features such as aggregates, subqueries, property paths, negation and regular expressions, but this is still a W3C Working draft as of this writing.

In the case of access control in provenance we may have two different sets of access control policies, one for traditional access control and one for provenance access control. This may result in the management of two different sets of policies if both, the traditional data items and provenance are placed in the same data store. If we allow this scenario, all requests from a user would be evaluated against both, the policies for the traditional access control and the policies for provenance. This would be the case even when the user is only working with the traditional data, and is not requesting the provenance information. In general, the lineage or ancestry of a data item may involve many sources and processes that influence a resource. Recording all these sources and paths may result in very large databases. Therefore, provenance may grow much faster than the actual data items and may be better served by a separate database. To this end, we will use a separate data store for provenance in our design of an architecture and prototype for provenance.

4.1 Graph Data Model

Of the many data models in the literature, we model our prototype based on a RDF data representation for provenance. This data model meets the specification of the OPM recommendation. RDF allows the integration of multiple databases describing the different pieces of the lineage of a resource; and naturally supports the directed structure of provenance.

The RDF terminology $\mathcal{T}$ is the union of three pairwise disjoint infinite sets of terms: the set $\mathcal{U}$ of URI references, the set $\mathcal{L}$ of literals (itself partitioned into two sets, the set $\mathcal{L}_p$ of plain literals and the set $\mathcal{L}_t$ of typed literals), and the set $\mathcal{B}$ of blanks. The set $\mathcal{U} \cup \mathcal{L}$ of names is called the vocabulary.

DEFINITION 1. (RDF Triple) A RDF triple (s, p, o) is an element of $(\mathcal{U} \cup \mathcal{B}) \times \mathcal{U} \times \mathcal{T}$. A RDF graph is a finite set of RDF triples.

A RDF triple can be viewed as an arc from s to o, where p is used to label the arc. This is represented as $s \xrightarrow{p} o$. Our provenance graph is constructed from a set of these RDF triples. RDF is intended to make assertions about a re-

source. This includes making multiple assertions about the same two resources; for example, a heart surgery h was controlled by a surgeon s, and the inverse relation: s performed a heart surgery h. This would be modeled as a directed loop in a RDF graph. In order to preserve the properties of a provenance graph, we need to place restrictions on the assertions made in a RDF graph. That is, we require a directed acyclic RDF graph to retain the causal dependencies among the nodes as needed in provenance.

DEFINITION 2. (Provenance Graph) Let $H = (V, E)$ be a RDF graph where V is a set of nodes with $|V| = n$, and $E \subseteq (V \times V)$ is a set of ordered pairs called edges. A provenance graph $G = (V_G, E_G)$ with n entities is defined as $G \subseteq H$, $V_G = V$ and $E_G \subseteq E$ such that G is a directed graph with no directed cycles.

We define a resource in a provenance graph recursively as follows.

- The sets V_G and E_G are resources.

- ϵ is a resource.

- The set of provenance graphs are closed under intersection, union and set difference. Let H_1 and H_2 be two provenance graphs, then $H_1 \cup H_2$, $H_1 \cap H_2$ and $H_1 - H_2$ are resources, such that if $t \in H_1 \cup H_2$ then $t \in H_1$ or $t \in H_2$; if $t \in H_1 \cap H_2$ then $t \in H_1$ and $t \in H_2$; or if $t \in H_1 - H_2$ then $t \in H_1$ and $t \notin H_2$.

4.2 Provenance Vocabulary

We define the nodes in the provenance graph using the nomenclature in [15]. This nomenclature defines three entities: artifacts, processes and agents. These entities form the nodes in V_G in our provenance graph G. An artifact is an immutable piece of state, which may have a physical embodiment in a physical object, or a digital representation in a computer system [15]. A process is an action or series of actions performed on or caused by artifacts and resulting in new artifacts [15]. An agent is a contextual entity acting as a catalyst of a process, enabling, facilitating, controlling, affecting its execution [15]. In RDF representation, an artifact, a process and an agent could be represented as,

```
<opm:Agent> <rdf:type> <opm:Entity>
<opm:Artifact> <rdf:type> <opm:Entity>
<opm:Process> <rdf:type> <opm:Entity>
```

The property rdf:type is used to indicate the class of a resource and the prefix opm: is reserved for the entities and relationships in the OPM nomenclature in [15].

Let $\mathcal{V}_G$ be the set of names appearing in a provenance graph G and $\mathcal{V}_G^P \subseteq \mathcal{V}_G$ be a set of names on the arcs in G. The label on each $e \in \mathcal{V}_G^P$ defines a relationship between the entities in G and also allows us to navigate across the different nodes by a single hop. A list of predicate names in $\mathcal{V}_G^P$ describing the causal relationships among the nodes in G are as follows:

```
<opm:Process> <opm:WasControlledBy> <opm:Agent>
<opm:Process> <opm:Used> <opm:Artifact>
<opm:Artifact> <opm:WasDerivedFrom> <opm:Artifact>
<opm:Artifact> <opm:WasGeneratedBy> <opm:Process>
<opm:Process> <opm:WasTriggeredBy> <opm:Process>
```

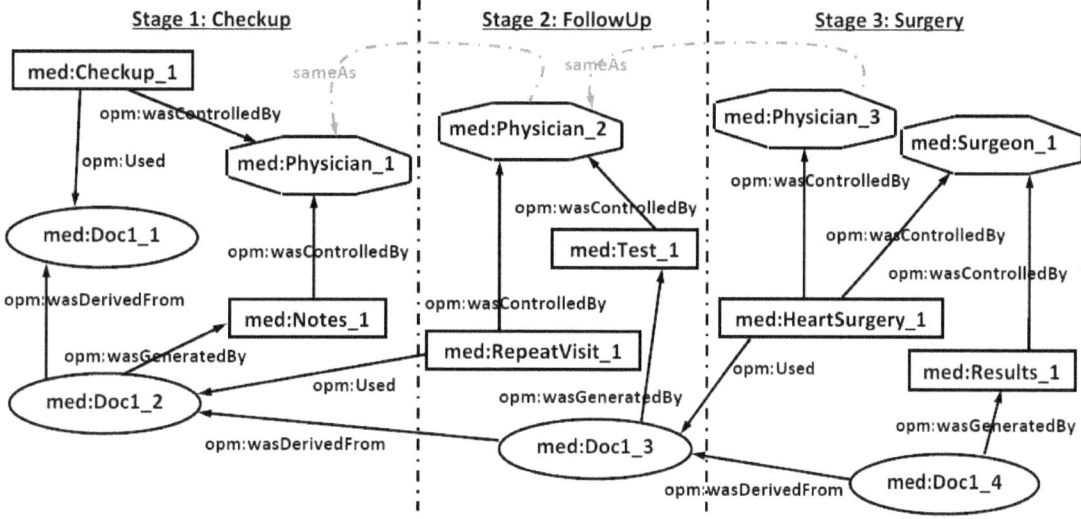

Figure 2: Provenance Graph

These predicates are the ones defined in [15] and they form the edges in our edge set, E_G, in our provenance graph G.

DEFINITION 3. *(Path) A path in a RDF graph is a sequence of RDF triples, where the object of each triple in the sequence coincides with the subject of its successor triple in the sequence.*

DEFINITION 4. *(Provenance Path) In G, a provenance path $(s \; \rho \; o)$ is a path $s(\xrightarrow{p})o$ that is defined over the provenance vocabulary $\mathcal{V}_G^P$ using regular expressions.*

DEFINITION 5. *(Regular Expressions) Let Σ be an alphabet of terms in $\mathcal{U} \cap \mathcal{V}_G^P$, then the set $RE(\Sigma)$ of regular expressions is inductively defined by:*

- $\forall x \in \Sigma, x \in RE(\Sigma)$;

- $\Sigma \in RE(\Sigma)$;

- $\epsilon \in RE(\Sigma)$;

- *If $A \in RE(\Sigma)$ and $B \in RE(\Sigma)$ then: $A|B, A/B, A^*, A^+, A? \in RE(\Sigma)$.*

The symbols | and / are interpreted as logical OR and composition respectively.

Our intention is to define paths between two nodes by edges equipped with * for paths of arbitrary length, including length 0 or + for paths that have at least length 1. Therefore, for two nodes x, y and predicate name p, $x(\xrightarrow{p})^*y$ and $x(\xrightarrow{p})^+y$ are paths in G.

The provenance graph in Figure 2 shows a workflow which updates a fictitious record for a patient who went though three medical stages at a hospital. In the first phase, the physician performed a checkup on the patient. At checkup, the physician consulted the history in the patient's record, med:Doc1_1 and performed the task of recording notes about the patient. At the end of the checkup, the physician then updated the patient's record, which resulted in a newer version, med:Doc1_2. In the second phase, the patient returned for a follow-up visit at the physician's request. During this visit, the physician consulted with the patient's record for a review of the patient's history and then performed a series of tests on the patient. At the end of this visit, the physician then updated the patient's record, which results in a newer version, med:Doc1_3. In the third phase, the patient returned to undergo heart surgery. This was ordered by the patient's physician and carried out by a resident surgeon. Before the surgeon started the surgery, a careful review of the patient's record was performed by both the patient's physician and surgeon. During the surgery process, the surgeon performed the task of recording the results at each stage of the heart surgery process. At the end of the surgery, the patient's record was updated by the surgeon, which resulted in a newer version, med:Doc1_4. The number in the suffix at the end of each process, agent and artifact is only meant to show an implicit condition whereby a larger number means that the provenance entity is at a later stage in the workflow process. The sameAs annotations on the light shaded arrows are meant to illustrate that the reference to physician is meant to be the same person in all the three phases. We use Figure 2 as a running example through the rest of the paper.

4.3 Path Queries

SPARQL is a RDF query language that is based around graph pattern matching [19].

DEFINITION 6. *(Graph pattern) a SPARQL graph pattern expression is defined recursively as follows:*

1. *A triple pattern is a graph pattern.*

2. *If P1 and P2 are graph patterns, then expressions (P1 AND P2), (P1 OPT P2), and (P1 UNION P2) are graph patterns.*

3. *If P is a graph pattern and R is a built-in SPARQL condition, then the expression (P FILTER R) is a graph pattern.*

4. *If P is a graph pattern, V a set of variables and $X \in \mathcal{U} \cup V$ then (X GRAPH P) is a graph pattern.*

The current W3C recommendation for SPARQL does not support paths of arbitrary length [7]; therefore, extensions are needed to answer the queries over the provenance graph. Many approaches to supporting paths of arbitrary length have been proposed in the literature, which include [7, 2, 13]. A W3C working draft for extending SPARQL to support property paths can be found in [9].

We use the following basic SELECT query structure to map a regular expression that is part of a policy or part of a user provenance query into a query over the provenance graph.

$$\text{SELECT } \vec{B} \text{ WHERE P,}$$

where P is a graph pattern and $\vec{B}$ is a tuple of variables appearing in P.

Using regular expressions as part of the SELECT query above we can answer our policy example that gives access to everything in a patient's record that was updated by processes controlled only by the patient's physician or surgeon. This would evaluate the following regular expression query on the provenance graph:

```
Select ?x
{
 med:Doc1_4 gleen:OnPath("([opm:WasDerivedFrom]*/
                [opm:WasGeneratedBy]/
                [opm:WasTriggeredBy]*/
                [opm:WasControlledBy])" ?x).
}
```

The gleen:OnPath function [7] is used to determine the set of nodes on the provenance path between med:Doc1_4 and ?x. We can think of s, ρ and o for the provenance path, $s(\xrightarrow{\rho})o$, as placeholders for med:Doc1_4, the expression given to the gleen:OnPath function and the variable ?x respectively.

4.4 Query Templates

We can use the set of names in $\mathcal{V}_G$ to answer common queries about provenance such as why-provenance, where-provenance and how-provenance [16]. To anticipate the varying number of queries a user could ask, we create templates which are parameterized for a specific type of user query. This simplifies the construction of queries by allowing us to map a user query to a suitable template. This in turn allows us to build an interface through which a user could interact with the system, as well as create an abstraction layer which hides the details of the graph from the user.

EXAMPLE 1. (*Why Query*)

```
med:Doc1_2 gleen:OnPath("([opm:WasDerivedFrom] |
        [opm:WasGeneratedBy] | [opm:WasTriggeredBy] |
        [opm:WasControlledBy] | [Used])*" ?x).
```

This allows us to specify all the resources reachable from med:Doc1_2 by issuing a query against the provenance graph. This query explains why med:Doc1_2 came to be in its current form. Figure 3(c) shows the part of the graph from Figure 2 that would result from executing this why-provenance query.

EXAMPLE 2. (*How Query*)

```
compute leaf-set for med:Doc1_3
for each XXX in leaf-set
    computeFreq(XXX)
```

The modified Gleen API [7] allows us to compute the leaf-set given the starting resource med:Doc1_3. Each leaf in the leaf-set {med:Physician_1, med:Physician_2, med:doc1_1} is the end of a unique path from med:Doc1_3 to that leaf. We then compute the frequency of each leaf in the leaf-set. This query would return the following polynomials:

```
med:Physician_2^1, med:Physician1_1^1, med:Doc1_1^1
```

A how-provenance query returns a polynomial representation of the structure of the proof explaining how the resource was derived. This normally involves counting the number of ways a provenance entity influences a resource.

EXAMPLE 3. (*Where Query*)

```
med:Doc1_4 gleen:OnPath("([opm:WasDerivedFrom] |
        [opm:WasGeneratedBy])" ?x).
```

This query would return the following triples:

```
(med:Doc1_4, opm:WasDerivedFrom, med:Doc1_3)
(med:Doc1_4, opm:WasGeneratedBy, med:Results_1)
```

A where query would be useful if we need to pinpoint where in the process a possible risk could occur as a result of performing a surgery on the patient. For example, a where-provenance could be used to identify at which phase in the flow any medication administered to the patient had a negative interaction with the ones the patient is already taking. By using this query, we could compare the information in med:Doc1_3 with those in med:Doc1_4 (which incorporates the recording of events during the surgery operation).

The Open Provenance Model [15] in general allows us to extend $\mathcal{V}_G$ to support annotations on the nodes and edges in our provenance graph. These annotations allow us to capture additional information relevant to provenance such as time and location that pertain to execution. The annotations are not part of the vocabulary provided by OPM. The idea of not providing annotations as part of the predicate vocabulary is to allow a user the flexibility of creating his/her own vocabulary for the nodes and edges. The annotations themselves can be added as RDF triples since RDF allows us to make assertions about any node in a RDF graph. This allows us to capture more contextual information about resources, which would allow us to model the provenance information to capture the semantics of the domain. While a particular causal relation, such as process P_2 was triggered by process P_1, may imply that P_1 occurs before P_2 on a single logical clock, it does not tell us the exact physical time both processes occur. Such additional information plays a critical role in the intelligence domain. These additional annotations allow us to build more templates, which give our prototype the ability to respond to queries like: when was a resource generated, what was a resource based on, which location a resource was created or modified at, etc. We show a simple example of a when query below,

EXAMPLE 4. (*When Query*)

```
Select ?x
{
    med:Doc1_4 med:modifiedOn ?x.
}
```

This query would return the timestamp value as a binding for the variable ?x, if the graph pattern in the where clause successfully matches a triple in the extended annotated provenance graph.

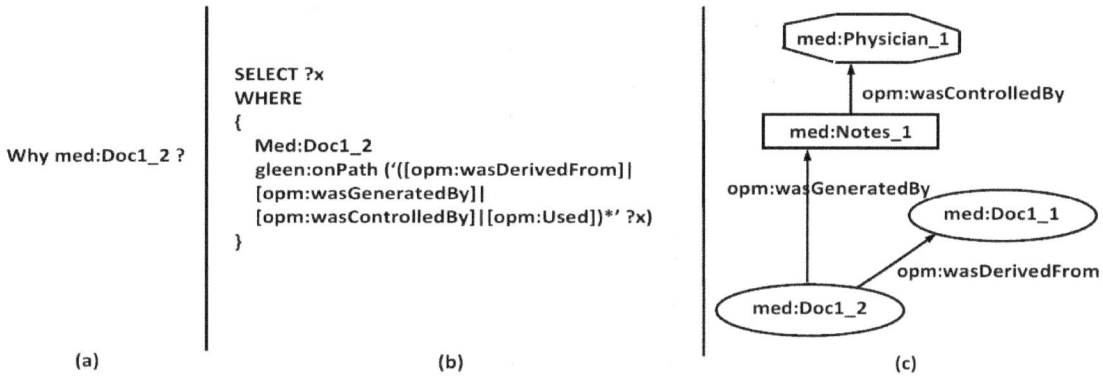

Figure 3: Why Query

5. GRAPH ANALYSIS

In this section, we will evaluate the impact of querying over a provenance graph with many subgraphs as resources. We will first address the complexity of protecting the resources in a provenance directed acyclic graph (digraph), then we will examine the case where two digraphs overlap, which may conflict with each other.

5.1 Analysis of Digraphs

We now provide a simple analysis addressing the concerns from Section 2 of traditional access control policies. We use the convention that a permission is a unique pair of (*action, resource*). Given n resources, m users and a set of only two actions (read, write), we have a maximum of $2 \times n$ possible permissions. This gives $m \times (2 \times n) = c_1 n$ mappings. To analyze RBAC, we assume the case where there is at least one role with two or more users assigned to it, from a possible set of r roles. Therefore, we have $r \times (2 \times n) = c_2 n$ mappings and we also assume that $c_2 \leq c_1$.

We continue our analysis by considering the varying number of relationships among the resources in a provenance graph. We assume that we have n nodes in our graph G. The first case is when the provenance paths are of length 0. This is similar to the case of access control policies over single resources. Next we consider the case where the provenance paths are of length 1. This is equivalent to counting the number of edges in E_G. We use the notion that a resource is a set of triples in G, and therefore; a resource is a directed acyclic graph (or digraph) from among all the allowed digraphs that can be formed from G. In general, the total number of ways of constructing a digraph from n nodes is given recursively as

$$a_n = \sum_{k=1}^{n}(-1)^{k-1}\binom{n}{k}2^{k(n-k)}a_{n-k} \qquad (5.1)$$

in [20, 21]. Given n nodes in a provenance graph G, a_n would represent the upper limit of resources to be protected in G. The work done in [20] shows that the number of ways of constructing a directed acyclic graph is exponential in the size of n single resources.

In general, a node in a digraph can have both, an in-degree and an out-degree. OPM restricts the relationships we can have among the nodes in a provenance graph (see [15] for a formal definition of a provenance graph). This restriction is on the dependency relationships involving agents; in simple terms the only relation involving an agent is a directed edge from a process to an agent. That is, agents in a provenance graph can only have an in-degree. Although, this restriction limits the maximum number of resources to be protected (as given in equation 5.1) by a factor, the upper bound for the maximum number of digraphs is still exponential. The OPM specification for a provenance graph describes how to trace an artifact or process back to their direct source (or cause), which could be a process, an artifact or an agent, using the edges in the graph. It does not however provide a standard arc name which explains the causes or sources for an agent in the graph. Therefore, a more useful definition of provenance according to OPM in the context of our analysis, would describe how an artifact or process came to be in their current form. This definition is still consistent with the ones in the literature. Hence, even in the cases where we only consider n' artifacts and processes in our provenance graph, where $2 \leq n' \leq n$, the number of digraphs is still exponential in n'."

A traditional access control policy would first require identifying a provenance path and then, expressing a policy for each of the resources on this path. The regular expressions presented in Section 4 allow us to specify a pattern for resources that need to be protected with an access control policy. Since a regular expression pattern can match many paths (each of arbitrary length), we can replace all policies that protect a resource on any of these paths with one policy.

5.2 Composition of Digraphs

Access control systems normally contain policies that are used to handle situations where two policies have opposite values for the *effect* element of a policy. This happens when one policy has a permit (or +ve authorization) effect whenever it evaluates to true, while another policy has a deny (or -ve authorization) whenever it evaluates to true and both of these policies protect the same digraph. The conflict could be as a result of two policies overlapping with each other to form a common digraph or when a digraph associated with a -ve authorization overlaps with a digraph that results from the execution of a user's query.

Different conflict resolution policies [23] have been proposed to resolve conflicts that result from opposite access authorizations on a resource. These policies include Denials-take-precedence, Most-specific-takes-precedence and Most-specific-along-a-path-takes-precedence.

There are three possibilities that could occur when two digraphs overlap with each other. We will discuss these possibilities when the Denials-take-precedence conflict resolution policy is applied.

1. $G1 \subseteq G2$: The digraph $G1$ is associated with a policy that denies viewing its contents and the digraph $G2$ is associated with a policy that permits viewing of its contents. In this situation, the system would have the effect of permitting viewing of the digraph $G2 - G1$.

2. $G1 \supseteq G2$: The digraph $G1$ is associated with a policy that denies viewing its contents and the digraph $G2$ is associated with a policy that permits viewing of its contents. In this situation, the user would be denied from viewing the contents of both, $G1$ and $G2$.

3. $G1 \cap G2$: The digraph $G1$ is associated with a policy that denies viewing its contents and the digraph $G2$ is associated with a policy that permits viewing its contents. In this situation, the system would have the effect of denying access to digraphs $G1$ and $G1 \cap G2$.

These three cases also apply when a user's query execution returns the digraph, $G2$, and the *effect* of the policy for $G1$ is "deny".

6. ARCHITECTURE

Our system architecture assumes that the available information is divided into two parts: the actual data and provenance. Both, the data and provenance are represented as RDF graphs. The reader should note that we do not make any assumptions about how the actual information is stored. A user may have stored data and provenance in two different triple stores or in the same store. Access control policies are defined in our XML-based language for both, the data and the provenance. These policies define access for users on resources in the data graph and on agents, artifacts, processes and paths in the provenance graph. A user application can submit a query for access to the data and its associated provenance or vice versa. In this discussion we first present the various modules in our prototype implementation. We then give an example of a scenario where the user already has access to the data item and is requesting additional information from the provenance. The same logic applies when we want to give high quality information to a user, where we would first verify the information against the provenance store before allowing access to the data item.

6.1 Modules in our Architecture

We now present a detailed description of the different layers in our architecture followed by an example.

User Interface Layer
The User Interface Layer is an abstraction layer that allows a user to interact with the system. A user can pose either a data query or a provenance query to this layer. This layer determines whether the query should be evaluated against the data or provenance. Our interface hides the use of regular expression queries (i.e., the actual internal representation of a provenance query) from a user by providing a simple question-answer mechanism. This mechanism allows the user to pose standard provenance queries such as why a data item was created, where in the provenance graph it was generated, how the data item was generated and when and what location it was created, etc. We show an example of a provenance query in Figure 3(a) that a user would pose to the system. This layer also returns results after they have been examined against the access control policies.

Access Control Policy Layer
The Access Control Policy Layer is responsible for ensuring that the querying user is authorized to use the system. It also enforces the access control policies against the user query and results to make sure that no sensitive information is released to unauthorized users. This layer also resolves any conflicts that resulted from executing the policies over the data stores. An example of a provenance policy that can be used in this layer is given in Figure 1.

Policy Parser Layer
The Policy Parser Layer is a program that takes as input a policy set and parses each policy to extract the information in each element. The parser verifies that the structure of the policy conforms to a predefined XML schema. Further, the parser also validates the value of each element in a policy using the grammar specified in Section 3.1.

Regular Expression-Query Translator
The Regular Expression-Query Translator takes a valid regular expression string and builds a corresponding graph pattern from these strings. This module works in two ways. First it associates a provenance query from a user to a corresponding template query, by invoking the necessary parameters associated with the user's provenance query, for example, Figure 3(a) shows a user query and the corresponding translation in Figure 3(b).

Data Controller
The Data Controller is a suite of software programs that store and manage access to data. The data could be stored in any format such as in a relational database, in XML files or in a RDF store. The controller accepts requests for information from the access control policy layer if a policy allows the requesting user access to a data item. This layer then executes the request over the stored data and returns results back to the access control policy layer where it is re-evaluated based on the access control policies.

Provenance Controller
The Provenance Controller is used to store and manage provenance information that is associated with data items that are present in the data controller. The provenance controller stores information in the form of logical graph structures in any appropriate data representation format. This controller also records the on-going activities associated with the data items stored in the data controller. This controller takes as input a regular expression query and evaluates it over the provenance information. This query evaluation returns a sub-graph back to the access control layer where it is re-examined using the access control policies.

We show an example of how a user query and a policy query are executed in our prototype system. The user query given in Figure 3(a) is submitted to the User Inter-

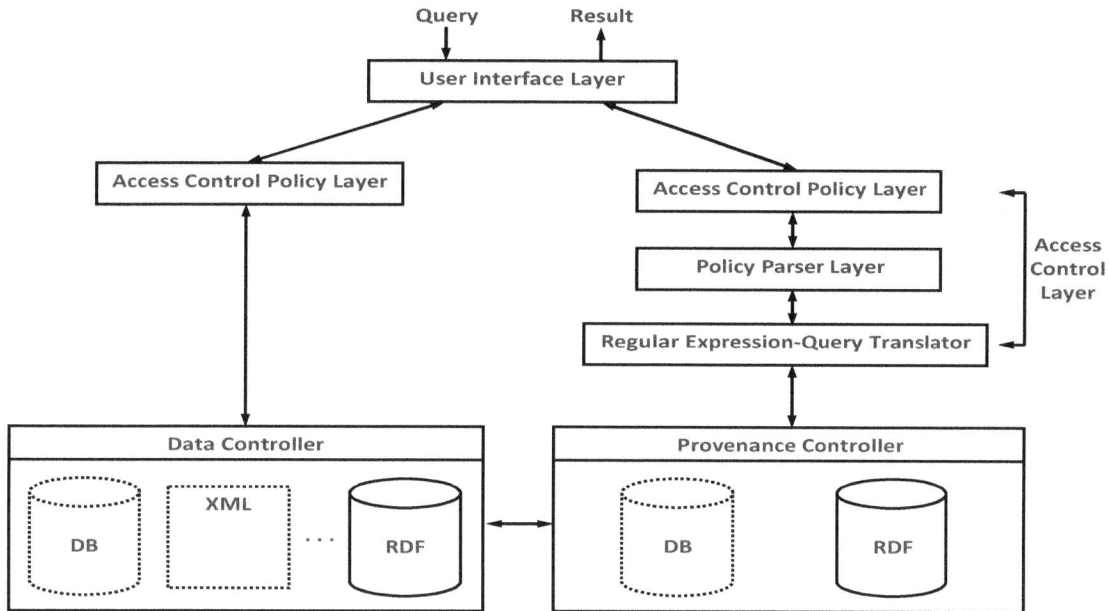

Figure 4: Architecture

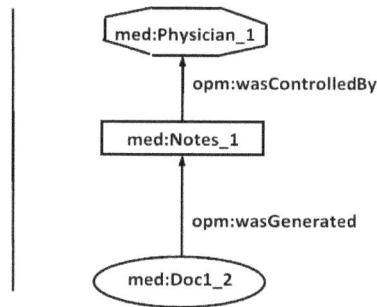

(a)

(b)

Figure 5: A resource protected by a policy

face Layer. This query asks for a complete explanation of why Doc1_2 came to be in existence. Doc1_2 is an internal node in the example provenance graph. This means that the user would have had access for the actual patient record in the traditional database before submitting a query about its provenance. Our Regular Expression-Query Translator in the Access Control Layer would transform this query into the query shown in Figure 3(b). The result of executing this query against the provenance graph shown in Figure 2 returns the results shown in Figure 3(c). This result is passed back to the Access Control Policy Layer. This layer also passes the policy given in Figure 1 to the Policy Parser Layer that parses the policy against a XML schema and the grammar given in Section 3.1. If the policy is well constructed, it is passed to the Regular Expression-Query Translator Layer that constructs the query given in Figure 5(a). This query is also evaluated against the provenance graph in Figure 2. The result of this query execution would return the digraph shown in Figure 5(b). This digraph represents the resource that the policy is protecting and is returned back to the Access Control Layer. The Access Control Layer would then

compare the resource from Figure 3(c) with the digraph in Figure 5(b). Since the digraph in Figure 3(c) contains the digraph in Figure 5(b), the Access Control Policy Layer would need to execute the *effect* that is given in the policy. Since in this case, the *effect* is Permit, the results in Figure 3(c) are passed to the User Interface Layer which in turn will return the results to the user. For the second case where we want to verify the integrity of the data, the process will be the same as described above, except that the user query would be about a leaf node stored in the traditional database and this leaf node is the last node of an ancestral chain in provenance.

6.2 Prototype

To implement the layers in our architecture we use various open-source tools. To implement the Access Control Layer, we use the policy files written in XML 1.0, and Java 1.6 to write the logic that enforces the policies. To implement the Policy Parser Layer, we use Java 1.6 and the XML schema specification. The XML schema allows us to verify the structure of our policy file. This layer was also pro-

Table 1: Workflows

Workflow #	1	2	3	4
Diameter(longest path)	13	13	13	13
no. of Artifacts	4	13	24	22
no. of Processes	6	41	23	58
no. of Agents	4	25	26	46
Annotated Graph(triples)	5347	7214	6743	8533

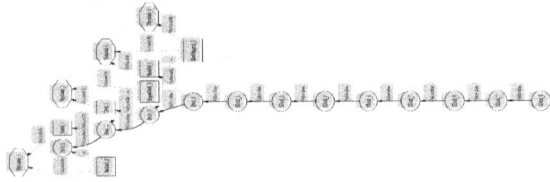

(a) Workflow 1 Structure

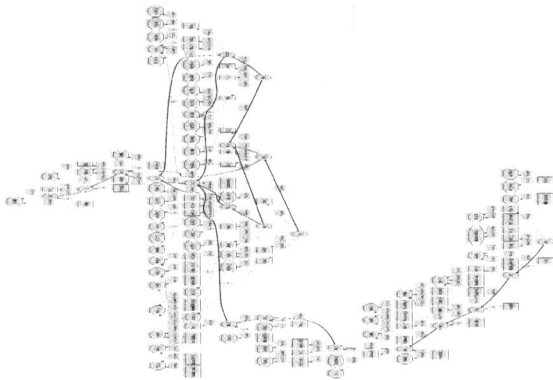

(b) Workflow 4 Structure

Figure 6: Workflow Topologies

grammed to apply the grammar in Section 3.1 against the values in the elements in the policies stored in the policy file. To implement the Regular Expression-Query Translator, we use the Gleen[1] regular expression library. This library extends SPARQL to support querying over a RDF graph using regular expressions [7]. To create the provenance store, we use the OPM toolbox[2]. This toolbox allows us to programmatically build workflows that use the OPM vocabulary and also allows us to generate RDF graphs corresponding to the workflow (with some tweaking to generate the RDF graphs for this prototype). There are other tools which support automatic provenance generation such as Taverna [18], but they are not as easy to use as the OPM toolbox. We use the OPM vocabulary which is based on RDF rather than existing vocabularies which have support for a more expressive representation of provenance, for example the vocabulary specification in [25]. Our aim in this paper is to demonstrate a general way of navigating a provenance graph, rather than capturing the semantics of the domain associated with the provenance paths.

We use synthetic data to build in-memory models, using the Jena API[3][5]. This tool allows us to add annotations

[1] http://sig.biostr.washington.edu/projects/ontviews/gleen/index.html
[2] http://openprovenance.org/
[3] http://jena.sourceforge.net/

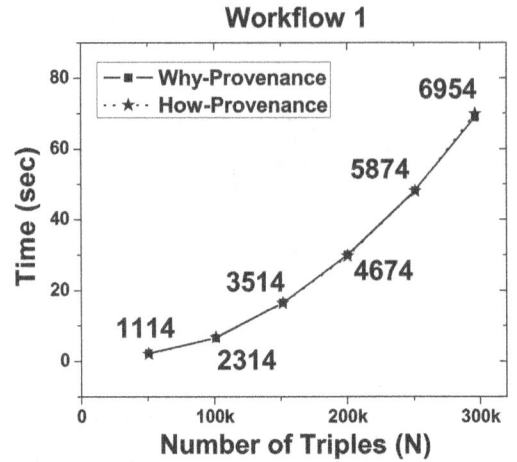

(a) Workflow 1 chain

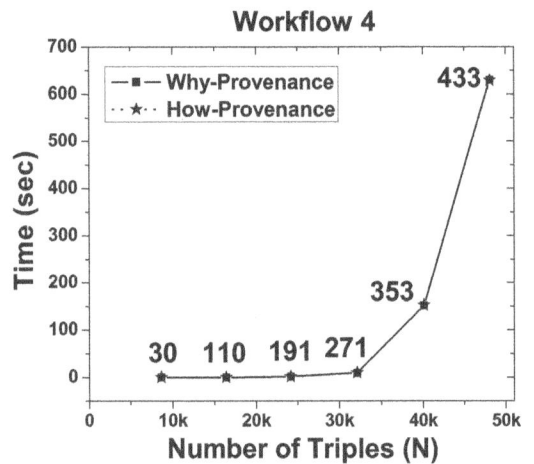

(b) Workflow 4 chain

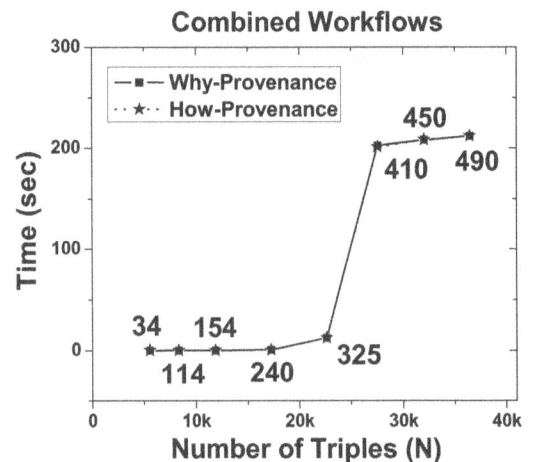

(c) Composite chain

Figure 7: Query Performance

to the existing RDF triples generated from executing the provenance workflows. We then issue different provenance queries, such as why, where, how, when and who against each of the provenance graphs in the in-memory Jena model. We have used in-memory models to simply show the feasibility of our prototype; however, in a real world scenario our prototype could query the provenance graphs stored in any disk-based storage.

6.3 Experiments

We generated four template workflow structures, each consisting of a varying number of provenance entities and RDF triples (as annotations). The composition of each workflow is shown in Table 1. Each workflow template has a different topology, with workflow 1 being the simplest and workflow 4 being the most intricate; Figure 6(a) and Figure 6(b) show the topology of workflow 1 and workflow 4 respectively.

We conducted three different experiments with our prototype using only workflow 1, only workflow 4 and a composite workflow consisting of all four workflows. For our experiments we varied the size of the in-memory models as shown in Figure 7. To vary the size of the experiment with workflow 1, we daisy chain a set of workflow 1's and record the time to perform each query. The results are shown in Figure 7(a). We similarly daisy chain a set of workflow 4's for our experiment involving only workflow 4 with the results shown in Figure 7(b). For our final experiment, we created one composite workflow, which is formed by daisy chaining six sets of workflow 1, followed by six sets of workflow 2, followed by six sets of workflow 3, followed by six sets of workflow 4. We then daisy chain these composite blocks and show the results of this final experiment in Figure 7(c).

Each point of the graph in Figure 7(a), Figure 7(b) and Figure 7(c) is labeled with the number of nodes in it's ancestry chain starting with the given node. This approximates the maximum number of hops needed to create a new digraph from the original provenance graph involving the starting resource. The execution times vary for each query template as well. A why-provenance query retrieves the transitive closure of the edges that justifies the existence of the resource, and so its execution time varies as the number of triples in its transitive closure grows. The structure of this query is given in Example 1. The how-provenance is like the why-provenance except that its execution time accounts for an additional step in computing the polynomials and therefore its execution time differs from the why-provenance execution time by 100-500 milliseconds. This difference is too small to be seen in Figure 7, therefore the how and why provenance query timings look very similar. The structure of this query is given in Example 2. As we increase the complexity of the workflows (from workflow 1 to workflow 4), the query execution time also increases (as shown in Figure 7). The other queries show almost constant execution times, ranging from 1-2 milliseconds. This is not surprising since these queries usually retrieve provenance information in the locality of the resource. For example, the when query just returns the RDF triple whose subject is the resource and whose predicate associates a time value with the resource and the where-provenance query finds the entities whose contents create the resource (i.e where the resource was copied from).

Our experiments were conducted on a IBM computer with 8 X 2.5GHz processors and 32GB RAM. For each pair of query and Jena model, we use the average execution time for the longest diameter in the graph. For a very simple topology (e.g. Figure 6(a)), our prototype is most efficient for both, finding the provenance resources (which involves single resources and their relationships) that an access control system is protecting and for finding the provenance resources a querying user is requesting.

7. RELATED WORK

A lot of research has been devoted to the study of access control in provenance. These include the work in [3], which emphasizes the need for a separate security model for provenance. This work also points out that existing access control models do not support the directed acyclic graph of provenance. The authors in reference [22] discuss the shortcomings of RBAC and instead propose ABAC which supports a fine-grained access control based on attributes rather than roles. In reference [24], the authors present an access control method for provenance over a directed acyclic graph. They build their access control model over a relational database which controls access to nodes and edges. They apply a grouping strategy to the provenance graph to create resources that need to be protected. We want to extend our access control model to support RDF triple stores in addition to relational databases. We support the idea of grouping by defining dynamic paths that are evaluated at query time based on incorporating regular expressions in our policies. In reference [6], the authors propose a grouping of provenance into blocks, and then applying a labeling strategy over these blocks. They also provide a language, SELinks, to encode their security policies. Reference [17] addresses the issues with existing access control models in provenance by proposing a general language. This language supports fine-grained policies and personal preferences and obligations, as well as decision aggregation from different applicable policies. We adapt the language given in [17] with support for regular expressions. Our language also incorporates other features of a general access control language such as support for fine-grained access control over the indivisible parts of a provenance graph, and integration of existing access control policies.

Research has also focused on general access control languages that are based on XML, logic and algebra. XACML [14] is an OASIS standard for an access control language that is based on XML. This language is very flexible and expressive. The work in [17] builds on XACML features to create a general access control language for provenance. Our language extends the XML-based policies in [17] for reasons such as, it is easy to write policies in XML and XML also provides a schema that can be used to verify the policies. Logic-based languages [1] offer features such as decidability and a formal proof of security policies. The work given in [4] shows how policies possibly expressed in different languages can be formulated in algebra. The algebra offers a formal semantics such as in logic-based languages.

8. CONCLUSION

In this paper we propose regular expressions as an extension to traditional access control policy specifications to protect not only traditional data items but also their relationships from unauthorized users. We presented our policy language, its XML-based structure and associated grammar for specifying policies over a provenance graph. We implemented a prototype based on our architecture that uses Semantic Web technologies (RDF, SPARQL) in order to evaluate the effectiveness of our policy language. We are exploring many directions for future research. We discuss some of them. (i) Our current research has focused on in-memory graphs. We plan to expand our experiments to include very large provenance graphs that use disk-based storage. (ii) The policies we have examined so far are those based on access control. We plan to investigate other types of policies including disclosure policies and release policies. This is necessary to further sanitize the resources that are being accessed. (iii) The applications we have been considering are in the areas of healthcare and intelligence. We plan to apply our language to other applications, especially in the area of e-science.

9. REFERENCES

[1] Abadi, M., "Logic in access control" *Proceedings of the 18th Annual Symposium on Logic in Computer Science (LICS03)*, pp. 228–233. Citeseer, 2003.

[2] Alkhateeb, F. and Baget, J.F. and Euzenat, J., "Extending SPARQL with regular expression patterns (for querying RDF)" *Web Semantics: Science, Services and Agents on the World Wide Web*, Vol. 7, No. 2, pp. 57–73, Elsevier, 2009.

[3] Braun, U. and Shinnar, A. and Seltzer, M., "Securing provenance" *Proceedings of the 3rd conference on Hot topics in security*, pp. 4, USENIX Association, 2008.

[4] Bonatti, P. and De Capitani di Vimercati, S. and Samarati, P., "An algebra for composing access control policies" *ACM Transactions on Information and System Security (TISSEC)*, Vol. 5, No. 1, pp. 1–35, ACM, 2002.

[5] Carroll, J.J. and Dickinson, I. and Dollin, C. and Reynolds, D. and Seaborne, A. and Wilkinson, K., "Jena: implementing the semantic web recommendations" *Proceedings of the 13th international World Wide Web conference on Alternate track papers & posters*, pp. 74–83, ACM, 2004.

[6] Corcoran, B.J. and Swamy, N. and Hicks, M., "Combining provenance and security policies in a web-based document management system" *On-line Proceedings of the Workshop on Principles of Provenance (PrOPr)*, Citeseer, 2007.

[7] Detwiler, L.T. and Suciu, D. and Brinkley, J.F., "Regular paths in SparQL: querying the NCI thesaurus" *AMIA Annual Symposium Proceedings*, Vol. 2008, pp. 161, American Medical Informatics Association, 2008.

[8] Ferraiolo, D. and Kuhn, D.R. and Chandramouli, R., "Role-based access control" *Artech House Publishers*, 2003.

[9] Harris, S. and Seaborne, A., "SPARQL 1.1 Query Language" *W3C Working Draft*, 2010.

[10] Hasan, R. and Sion, R. and Winslett, M., "Introducing secure provenance: problems and challenges" *Proceedings of the 2007 ACM workshop on Storage security and survivability*, pp. 18, ACM, 2007.

[11] Holland, D.A. and Braun, U. and Maclean, D. and Muniswamy-Reddy, K.K. and Seltzer, M., "Choosing a data model and query language for provenance" *Int. Provenance and Annotation Workshop*, Citeseer, 2008.

[12] Klyne, G. and Carroll, J.J. and McBride, B., "Resource description framework (RDF): Concepts and abstract syntax" *Changes*, 2004.

[13] Kochut, K. and Janik, M., "SPARQLeR: Extended SPARQL for semantic association discovery" *The Semantic Web: Research and Applications*, pp. 145–159, Springer, 2007.

[14] Lorch, M. and Proctor, S. and Lepro, R. and Kafura, D. and Shah, S., "First experiences using XACML for access control in distributed systems" *Proceedings of the 2003 ACM workshop on XML security*, pp. 25–37, ACM, 2003.

[15] Moreau, L. and Clifford, B. and Freire, J. and Gil, Y. and Groth, P. and Futrelle, J. and Kwasnikowska, N. and Miles, S. and Missier, P. and Myers, J. and others, "The Open Provenance Model—Core Specification (v1. 1)" *Future Generation Computer Systems, Elseview*, 2009.

[16] Moreau, L., "The Foundations for Provenance on the Web" *Foundations and Trends in Web Science*, Citeseer, 2009.

[17] Ni, Q. and Xu, S. and Bertino, E. and Sandhu, R. and Han, W., "An access control language for a general provenance model" *Secure Data Management*, pp. 68–88, Springer, 2009.

[18] Oinn, T. and Addis, M. and Ferris, J. and Marvin, D. and Greenwood, M. and Carver, T. and Pocock, M.R. and Wipat, A. and Li, P., "Taverna: a tool for the composition and enactment of bioinformatics workflows" *Bioinformatics*, Oxford Univ Press, 2004.

[19] Prud'hommeaux, E. and Seaborne, A. and others, "SPARQL query language for RDF" *W3C working draft*, Vol. 20, 2006.

[20] Robinson, R., "Counting unlabeled acyclic digraphs" *Combinatorial mathematics V*, pp. 28–43, Springer, 1977.

[21] Robinson, R.W., "Counting Labeled Acyclic Digraphs" *Proceedings of the Third Ann Arbor Conference on Graph Theory Held at the University of Michigan*, pp. 239-275, 1971.

[22] Rosenthal, A. and Seligman, L. and Chapman, A. and Blaustein, B., "Scalable access controls for lineage" *First workshop on on Theory and practice of provenance*, pp. 1–10, USENIX Association, 2009.

[23] Samarati, P. and de Vimercati, S., "Access control: Policies, models, and mechanisms" *Foundations of Security Analysis and Design*, pp. 137–196, Springer, 2001.

[24] Syalim, A. and Hori, Y. and Sakurai, K., "Grouping Provenance Information to Improve Efficiency of Access Control" *Advances in Information Security and Assurance*, pp. 51–59, Springer, 2009.

[25] Zhao, J., "Open Provenance Model Vocabulary Specification" *Latest version: http://purl.org/net/opmv/ns-20100827*, ACM, 2010.

Non-Interactive Editable Signatures for Assured Data Provenance

Haifeng Qian
Department of Computer Science
East China Normal University
haifeng.ecnu@gmail.com

Shouhuai Xu
Department of Computer Science
University of Texas at San Antonio
shxu@cs.utsa.edu

ABSTRACT

In order to make people truly benefit from data sharing, we need technical solutions to assuring the trustworthiness of data received from parties one may not have encountered in the past. Assured data provenance is an important means for this purpose because it (i) allows data providers to get credited for their contribution or sharing of data, (ii) is able to hold the data providers accountable for the data they contributed, and (iii) enables the data providers to supply high-quality data in a *self-healing* fashion. While the above (i) and (ii) have been investigated to some extent, the above (iii) is a new perspective that, to our knowledge, has not been investigated in the literature. In this paper, we introduce a novel cryptographic technique that can simultaneously offer these properties. Our technique is called *editable signatures*, which allow a user, Bob, to edit (e.g., replace, modify, and insert) some portions of the message that is contributed and signed by Alice such that the resulting edited message is jointly signed by Alice and Bob in some fashion. While it is easy to see that the above (i) and (ii) are achieved, the above (iii) is also achieved because Bob may have a better knowledge of the situation that allows him to provide more accurate/trustworthy information than Alice, who may intentionally or unintentionally enter inaccurate or even misleading data into an information network. This is useful because Alice's inaccurate or even misleading information will never be released into an information network if it can be "cleaned" or "healed" by Bob. Specifically, we propose two novel cryptographic constructions that can be used to realize the above functions in some practical settings.

Categories and Subject Descriptors

C.2.4 [**Computer-Communication Networks**]: Distributed Systems; D.4.6 [**Security and Protection**]: Authentication

General Terms

Security

Keywords

Digital signatures, editable signatures, multisignatures, aggregate signatures, data provenance, assured data provenance, data trustworthiness

1. INTRODUCTION

Because malicious attackers could intentionally enter inaccurate, misleading, or even malicious data into an information network with the aim to influence or manipulate honest people's decision-making, we need technical means to help end users (or data consumers) evaluate the trustworthiness of data received from other parties. Data provenance has a great potential for fulfilling this goal (see, for example, [6, 3, 19, 20, 11, 10]), as long as data provenance information (or provenance data) is adequately protected. Although protecting data provenance is especially important in settings where attacks are possible, it was not until very recently researchers started investigating the security issues related to data provenance [7, 12, 24, 23, 22].

1.1 Assured Data Provenance

While several kinds of data provenance can be relevant in real-life applications, the arguably most important type of provenance information is the so-called *source* provenance [8], which gives the origin of a piece of data. Existing studies on data provenance, such as those mentioned above, mainly focused on *passive data provenance*, meaning that data providers only need to associate the data they contributed with their digital signatures. However, this is not sufficient in many settings. For example, when the private signing key of a user has been compromised but without being promptly detected/revoked, the compromised key may be abused to sign messages that would be treated as trustworthy by receivers because the messages were digitally signed and the signatures can be verified using non-revoked public keys. Moreover, a dishonest user may intentionally abuse the fact — one's private signing key could have been compromised but without being detected — to inject inaccurate/misleading/malicious information into an information network possibly without being detected and punished. In addition, even an honest user, whose private signing key is adequately protected, may unintentionally inject inaccurate information into an information network just because she is unable to observe or produce more precise data.

The aforementioned potential threats against traditional passive data provenance approach inspires us of the following question: How can we achieve *proactive* or *assured* data provenance so that people can truly benefit from the large amount of data available to them? By assured data provenance, we informally mean the following: (i) Data providers can get credited for their contribution or sharing of data, which is important because the providers can have incentives for sharing, possibly higher quality, data. (ii) Data providers can be held accountable for the data they provide, which is important because such accountability can be seen as a deterrence against the introduction of malicious information. (iii) Data providers can jointly "clean" or "heal" the inaccurate, low-quality, misleading, or even malicious information before the relevant data items are released into an information network. Note that we are by-no-means advocating data censorship; in contrast, we believe that the users, who have some relevant data, together might be able to provide more trustworthy data than they individually do. To see the potential value of assured data provenance, let us look at the following example scenario (see also Figure 1).

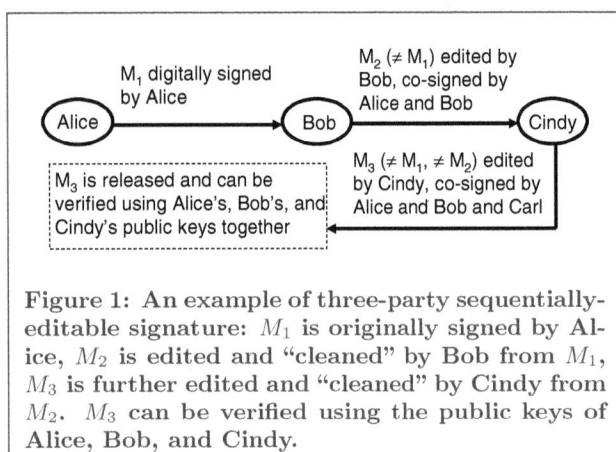

Figure 1: An example of three-party sequentially-editable signature: M_1 is originally signed by Alice, M_2 is edited and "cleaned" by Bob from M_1, M_3 is further edited and "cleaned" by Cindy from M_2. M_3 can be verified using the public keys of Alice, Bob, and Cindy.

Suppose a team of colleagues who need jointly write a report that must be appropriately signed (i.e., each one must be responsible for what he/she wrote in the report) because the report may be used as an input in a decision-making process. More specifically, suppose Alice drafted a message M_1, signed it with her private key, and sent Bob M_1 as well as her digital signature on M_1. Now, Bob may need to partially edit the message M_1 by adding new content and/or modifying some portions of M_1, simply because he has better or more accurate information about the message content (or semantics). Denote by M_2 the resulting new message, which consists of two parts M_{2A} and M_{2B}, where M_{2A} (which can be a proper portion of M_1) was contributed by Alice and M_{2B} is contributed by Bob. How should message M_2 be digitally signed so that the receiver of M_2 can verify that Bob is indeed responsible for the content of M_{2B} and Alice is responsible for the content of M_{2A}? This type of accountability is an important means for enhancing the trustworthiness of M_2. As shown in Figure 1, the above two-party editing chain, namely Alice→Bob, can be naturally extended to multi-party chains (e.g., Alice→Bob→Cindy→ ...).

Assuming that Alice, Bob, and Cindy are honest and that Bob and Cindy do not modify the respective contents of M_1 and M_2 unless he/she is certain about the modifications, M_3

would be more trustworthy than M_2, which in turn would be more trustworthy than M_1. Note that the above argument would be true even if Alice's private signing key has been compromised without being detected because M_1 will be edited by Bob and Cindy as shown in the example. This can be further enhanced by regulating that a message digitally signed by a single user, say M_1 signed by Alice alone, is not deemed as trustworthy as a message that is signed (after editing) by multiple users, correspondingly M_3 in the above example.

1.2 Discussion on Solution Space

Having introduced the usefulness of assured data provenance, let us explore how this problem may be resolved using existing techniques. The first attempt would be to let Bob sign, in addition to M_2, M_1 as well as Alice's signature on M_1. This would allow Cindy to know that M_2 is partially derived from M_1 and additionally contributed by Bob. This approach has several drawbacks and does not quite fulfill the aforementioned assured data provenance because of the following. (i) The resulting communication is the accumulation of the history of M_2. This can be very significant, for example, when M_1 and M_2 have (roughly) the same large size and when there are many signers since the communication cost is proportional to the number of signers. (ii) Cindy has to verify two digital signatures, one by Alice on M_1 and the other by Bob on M_2. In general, the number of digital signatures that need be verified is also proportional to the number of signers, which could be a heavy burden especially when M_1 and M_2 are large (even if they have much content in common). (iii) Even if Cindy may be allowed to known the modifications by Bob, it might be desired in many applications that only the resulting message M_3 is exposed to the outside receivers. The above approach cannot achieve this because the portions of message, which were originally written/signed by Alice and later modified/replaced by Bob and/or Cindy, are also exposed to the outside receivers. One may suggest to use encryption to hide the inner layers of messages and signatures, but this approach incurs extra key-management complexity, which as we will show is unnecessary.

The second attempt would be to let Alice and Bob sign M_2 together, namely that Alice signs M_{2A} and Bob signs M_{2B} because assured data provenance requires accountability. This would require *interaction* between Alice and Bob because Bob needs to inform Alice which part of her message M_1 has been modified by him. This approach would avoid the aforementioned drawbacks of the first attempt because of the following. (i) The resulting communication to Cindy is only M_2 plus its signature and the resulting communication to the outsider receivers is only M_3 plus its signature. (ii) Cryptographic aggregate techniques can "merge" Alice's, Bob's, and Cindy's signatures into a single one. (iii) The receiver cannot infer, for example, the content originally drafted by Alice but later modified by Bob or Cindy as long as the underlying communication channels are private, which is much easier to implement than a full-fledged key management. However, this approach has the very significant drawback that it requires interactions between the signers. For two-party scenarios, it requires one interaction between the two signers. However, for n-party scenarios, it could require $\frac{n(n-1)}{2}$ interactions in the worst case because the content of each signer may be edited/modified by later ones. The heavy interaction requirement may block the signing process unless all the signers always stay online. (Note that the above discussion also disqualifies the attempt to let the signers interactively edit messages without signing until the final message has been agreed upon. One burden of this naive approach is that the signers have to keep track of "who said what" and may cause disputes given that no one has really "committed" anything before he signs in the final phase.)

The above discussion raises the following question: Can we have a cryptographic mechanism that can avoid all of the drawbacks mentioned above? In this paper, we answer this question affirmatively by presenting a novel cryptographic tool for this purpose.

1.3 Our Contributions

The conceptual contribution of the present paper is the introduction of assured data provenance, which moves a step beyond the current paradigm of passive data provenance. The most important technical contribution of the present paper is the introduction of a new type of digital signatures called *editable signatures*. (Non-interactive) editable signatures are especially useful for assured data provenance when multiple signers need to jointly sign a message, which is the final outcome of some editing process (rather than in the much simpler case when the message is given as input in the beginning of the signing protocol), and might be of independent value.

We present two concrete non-interactive editable signature schemes. The first scheme gives the signers much freedom in the sense that any one can edit any message blocks. The resulting scheme is proven secure in the random oracle model, but it requires $O(n)$ pairing operations to verify such a signature. The second scheme gives the signers less freedom because it restricts which signer can edit which message blocks. Nevertheless, the resulting scheme is proven secure in the standard model (i.e., without using random oracle) while requiring only $O(1)$ pairing operations to verify such a signature.

Paper organization. Section 2 presents definitions of editable signatures. Section 3 describes the cryptographic preliminaries. Sections 4 and 5 present and analyze our two editable signature schemes, respectively. Section 6 briefly discusses previous related work. Section 7 concludes the paper with a discussion on future research directions.

2. DEFINITION AND SECURITY MODEL

2.1 High-level Ideas

Suppose that there are n (sequential) signers $\{A_i | i = 1, \ldots, n\}$, each having a pair of public and private keys (pk_i, sk_i), and that A_1 is the first signer (or the initiator), who drafts the first message M_1 and generates a signature σ_1 on M_1 using its private key sk_1. A_1 sends (M_1, σ_1) possibly through a secure channel to the next signer A_2. (Note that the secure channel can be realized using standard cryptosystems.) Then, A_2 will "edit" message M_1 to obtain a new message M_2 with an accompanying signature σ_2, which is partly based on σ_1. We also call the other signers the editors because they can edit both the messages and signatures provided by previous signers in some fashion. To facilitate message editing, we divide a message into ℓ blocks (chunks), namely $M_i = (m_1, \ldots, m_\ell)$, so that a block m_j

may be drafted by one signer and edited by other signers. For the sake of convenience, let us treat a message $M_i = (m_1, \ldots, m_\ell)$ as an ordered set of ℓ elements, with possibly some $m_j = \perp$ where $\perp$ is a placeholder and a special message block (but is not signed in a cryptographical sense as it will become clear later). In other words, M_i is treated as an ordered set $M_i = \{m_1, \ldots, m_\ell\}$ or equivalently $\{(1, m_1), \ldots, (\ell, m_\ell)\}$; these representations will be used interchangeably as it will become clear from the context. Nevertheless, there are three subtle issues.

First, who should decide which signer can sign/edit which message blocks? Note that in the most general case, a signer A_i $(1 \leq i \leq n - 1)$ does not have to restrict "which message blocks can be edited by which of the future signers A_j $(i < j \leq n)$." However, it may be desired sometimes that A_i can pre-determine which message blocks may be edited by which signers. This can only be achieved, of course, when the future signers do not sign messages from scratch (otherwise, for example, A_2 can simply disregard σ_1 on message M_1 while signing M_1 using sk_2). This does have practical meanings in assured data provenance because A_2 may not want to be held accountable for the message blocks in M_2 but was provided by M_1, namely the message blocks belonging to $M_1 \cap M_2$, while A_2 is responsible for the message blocks belonging to $M_2 \setminus M_1$. Moreover, in some cases it may be even desired that certain blocks of a final message must be signed by certain pre-defined signers (e.g., such predetermined attribution may be up to the first signer A_1). This allows to introduce some kind of access control that may be needed in some application scenarios.

Second, how should we represent and reflect the editing operations? Suppose the signers eventually generate a signature σ on a message $M_n = (m_1, \ldots, m_\ell)$. To reflect the editing operations, each message block m_i, $1 \leq i \leq \ell$, is associated with Γ_i, which bookkeeps the identities of its signers. In any case, the editing operation implies that each message block is signed at least by one signer, but it is not necessary that every message block is signed by the same set of signers.

Third, how are the (intermediate) signatures verified? The key issue here is, unlike σ_1 that can be verified using pk_1 alone, how σ_2 will be verified. In general, σ_2 might need be verified using both pk_1 and pk_2 because portion of M_2 was actually produced and thus signed by A_1 (and possibly by A_2 as well), and the other portion of M_2 was actually produced and thus signed by A_2 only. As we elaborate below, editable signatures are indeed general and accommodate the very useful notions of multisignatures, which allow multiple signers to endorse the same message (the concept was introduced by [13] and numerous elegant schemes have been proposed, including [4, 1]), and aggregate signatures, which allow to "absorb" multiple signers' signatures on multiple messages into a single one so as to reduce the length of signature tags (the concept was introduced by [4] and numerous elegant schemes have been proposed, including [15, 2, 16]). Specifically, we encounter the following interesting scenarios (using $n = 2$ as an example):

1) A_2 simply inherits whatever A_1 said in M_1. A_2 may sign (some message blocks of) M_2 using its private key sk_2. When A_2 signs M_2, σ_2 is a multisignature on message M_1.

2) A_2 deletes some actual (i.e., non-$\perp$) message blocks in M_1 and without adding actual message blocks (to

replace the deleted message blocks). In this case, the non-$\perp$ blocks of M_2 may be signed by both A_1 and A_2 (i.e., effectively a multisignature), or A_2 only signs some message blocks of M_2. It is challenging to technically allow this because we need to enable A_2 to "cancel" the portion of A_1's signature on $M_1 \setminus M_2$, without giving A_1's private key to A_2.

3) A_2 adds (but not necessarily appends) some actual message blocks to M_1. The resulting signature is an aggregate signature, where the message blocks belonging to M_1 may be signed by both A_1 and A_2 (i.e., effectively a multisignature) and the message blocks belonging to $M_2 \setminus M_1$ are signed by A_2 alone. It is also possible A_2 signs some message blocks of $M_1 \cap M_2$.

4) A_2 completely disagrees with what A_1 said in M_1. In this case, σ_2 is indeed a normal signature on M_2 that can be verified using public key pk_2 alone.

5) A_2 modifies (i.e., not adding or deleting) some message blocks. This is likely the most common scenario in practice, where the message blocks belonging to $M_1 \cap M_2$ are produced and signed by A_1 and possibly signed by A_2 as well (i.e., effectively a multisignature), the original message blocks belonging to $M_1 \setminus (M_1 \cap M_2)$ were produced and signed by A_1 and later edited by A_2, the message blocks belonging to $M_2 \setminus (M_1 \cap M_2)$ are newly produced and signed by A_2, and the resulting signature is an aggregate signature in spirit. Again, it is challenging because we need to enable A_2 to "cancel" the portion of A_1's signature on $M_1 \setminus (M_1 \cap M_2)$.

REMARK 2.1. *Non-interactive editable signatures may have an inherent drawback as we show in the following example. Suppose there are $n = 3$ signers, each message has $\ell = 2$ blocks, A_1 produces $M_1 = (m_1, m_2)$, A_2 edits M_1 to produce $M_2 = (m_1, \perp)$, and A_3 edits M_2 to produce $M_3 = (m_1, m_2)$, which is possible because A_2 thinks m_2 is wrong data but both A_1 and A_3 think m_2 is correct data. In the resulting signature on M_3, m_2 is only signed by A_3 while A_1 actually signed it as well. This may be seen as a kind of loss of information in applications such as evaluating the trustworthiness of M_3. This appears to be inherent to non-interactive editable signatures, and we leave it to future work to resolve this issue.*

2.2 Functional Definition

Suppose n signers $A_1, A_2, \ldots, A_n$ want to jointly edit and sign messages up to ℓ blocks in the fashion discussed above. For the sake of clarification, here we summarize the main notations used in the paper:

- A_i: The i-th signer (or editor if $i \neq 1$) and A_1 is the first signer (initiator), where $1 \leq i \leq n$.

- S: The set of all indices of message blocks (i.e., $S = \{1, \ldots, \ell\}$).

- $M = (m_1, \ldots, m_\ell)$ and $M' = (m'_1, \ldots, m'_\ell)$: M is the message A_i $(1 < i \leq n)$ received from signer A_{i-1}. M' is the message sent by signer A_i to signer A_{i+1} when $1 < i < n$, and is the final message when $i = n$ (in this case, the final message M' and its signature are released into an information network).

- Δ: The set of indices of message blocks that can be edited by an editor.

- $C \subseteq S$, $I \subseteq C$ and $\bar{I} \subseteq \Delta$: Suppose A_i $(1 < i \leq n)$ receives $M = (m_1, \ldots, m_\ell)$ and outputs $M' = (m'_1, \ldots, m'_\ell)$. Then C is the set of indices of message blocks that A_i does not edit, no matter A_i is allowed to edit or not. In other words, $C = \{i | m_i = m'_i, 1 \leq i \leq \ell\}$.

  I is the set of indices of message blocks that A_i does sign (because, for example, A_i is certain about the content of these message blocks). Note that it is possible that $I \setminus \Delta \neq \emptyset$, meaning that A_i can sign the message blocks A_i is not allowed to edit.

  $\bar{I}$ is the set of indices of message blocks that A_i indeed edited. Note that $\bar{I} = \Delta \setminus (C \cap \Delta) = \Delta \setminus C$.

- $\mathsf{edinfo}_{i-1} = (K_\Delta, \Delta)$ and $\mathsf{edinfo}_i = (K_{\Delta'}, \Delta')$, where $1 < i \leq n$: In the case $1 < i < n$, editor A_i uses the input auxiliary information $\mathsf{edinfo}_{i-1} = (K_\Delta, \Delta)$ to edit the message blocks in message M_{i-1} as specified by Δ, where K_Δ is the set of "editing keys" needed for editing signature σ_{i-1} provided by A_{i-1} with respect to Δ. Suppose A_i determines to allow the next editor A_{i+1} to edit message blocks as specified by Δ'. Then A_i will also prepare auxiliary information $\mathsf{edinfo}_i = (K_{\Delta'}, \Delta')$ for next editor A_{i+1}, who can then use $K_{\Delta'}$ to edit the message blocks in message M_i as specified by Δ'.

  In the case $i = n$, editor $A_i = A_n$ does the same as the above, except that it does not prepare edinfo_i as it is the last editor.

- Γ_i: The set of indices of message blocks (including possibly $\perp$ blocks) signed by A_i.

- L: The list of pairs (pk_i, Γ_i), which allows to correctly indicate "who signed which actual message blocks" and allows to verify signatures.

The functional definition of (sequential but) non-interactive editable signatures is described as follows.

DEFINITION 2.2. *A non-interactive editable signature scheme* $\mathsf{ES} = (\mathsf{Setup}, \mathsf{Gen}, \mathsf{FSign}, \mathsf{ESign}, \mathsf{Vf})$ *consists of the following algorithms or protocols:*

$\mathsf{Setup}(1^\lambda)$: *A randomized algorithm (possibly run by a central authority) that takes as input a security parameter λ, produces a set of global public parameters pp, and possibly specifies which signers have a final say on which message blocks (e.g., based on some policy).*

$\mathsf{Gen}(pp)$: *A probabilistic algorithm that, on input of public parameters pp, outputs an honest signer's pair of private and public keys (sk, pk).*

$\mathsf{FSign}(pp, sk_1, M_1)$: *Assume A_1 is the first signer with a pair of private and public keys (sk_1, pk_1). Given pp, $M_1 = (m_1, \ldots, m_\ell)$ with possibly some $m_i = \perp$, A_1 uses its private key sk_1 to generate a signature σ_1 on M_1, chooses a set $\Delta \subseteq S$, generates auxiliary information $\mathsf{edinfo}_1 = (K_\Delta, \Delta)$ which may be optional but otherwise allows the others to edit M_1 and σ_1 properly, and sets $L_1 = (pk_1, \Gamma_1)$ where $\Gamma_1 \subseteq S$ indicates the (actual) message blocks A_1 signed. Finally, it outputs $(M_1, \sigma_1, L_1, \mathsf{edinfo}_1)$, which will be sent to the second signer A_2 possibly over a private channel.*

ESign($pp, sk_i, M_i, M_{i-1}, \sigma_{i-1}, L_{i-1}, \mathsf{edinfo}_{i-1}$) **for** $1 < i \leq n$:
   Given the public parameters pp, M_{i-1}, the received σ_{i-1}, $L_{i-1} = [(pk_1, \Gamma_1), \ldots, (pk_{i-1}, \Gamma_{i-1})]$, and the resulting message M_i after A_i edits M_{i-1}, signer A_i first checks the validity of $(M_{i-1}, \sigma_{i-1}, L_{i-1})$ via the following algorithm $\mathsf{Vf}(pp, M_{i-1}, \sigma_{i-1}, L_{i-1})$. If invalid, A_i rejects and aborts; otherwise, A_i uses its private key sk_i and the received auxiliary information $\mathsf{edinfo}_{i-1} = (K_\Delta, \Delta)$ to edit the received signature σ_{i-1} to produce signature σ_i, prepares $(M_i, \sigma_i, L_i, \mathsf{edinfo}_i)$ where $L_i = [(pk_1, \Gamma_1'), \ldots, (pk_i, \Gamma_i')]$ and $\mathsf{edinfo}_i = \mathtt{null}$ if $i \geq n$ and $\mathsf{edinfo}_i = (K_{\Delta'}, \Delta')$ otherwise. If $i < n$, A_i sends $(M_i, \sigma_i, L_i, \mathsf{edinfo}_i)$ to signer A_{i+1}; otherwise, (M_i, σ_i, L_i) is the final message as well as its signature (that can be released to some information network). Note that Δ' may be determined by A_i according to some policy, and $K_{\Delta'}$ may be derived from edinfo_{i-1} and A_i's own private information. Note also that edinfo_i may be optional.

$\mathsf{Vf}(pp, M, \sigma, L)$: *Given parameters pp, L (the set of signers' public keys), a message M and an alleged signature σ, this deterministic algorithm outputs 0 (reject) or 1 (accept).*

We require an editable signature scheme to be *correct*, meaning that if all signers follow the protocols, then all of the resulting signatures will always be accepted as valid.

2.3 Security Model

Informally, security of non-interactive editable signature schemes requires that it is infeasible for an attacker to forge an editable signature involving at least one honest signer. Without loss of generality, we assume there is a single honest signer. The adversary can corrupt the other signers, and can choose their keys arbitrarily (but we require users to prove knowledge of their private keys during public-key registration with a Certification Authority or CA). More specifically, we require the adversary to hand all the private keys of the compromised signers to the CA, meaning that our scheme operates in the so-called Knowledge of Secret Key (KOSK) model [2]; we leave it to future work to weaken the operational model [17] as will be discussed in Section 7. Security definition will be split into two scenarios depending on who will be the target of attack: the first signer (called INITIATOR UNFORGEABILITY) or a future signer (called EDITOR UNFORGEABILITY). Both definitions are extensions to the classical security notion of digital signatures [9].

For INITIATOR UNFORGEABILITY, we require that no attacker can have a non-negligible advantage in the experiment specified in Figure 2, where the advantage of adversary $\mathcal{A}$ against $\mathsf{ES} = (\mathsf{Setup}, \mathsf{Gen}, \mathsf{FSign}, \mathsf{ESign}, \mathsf{Vf})$ is defined as the probability that experiment $\mathrm{Exp}_{\mathsf{iu.cma}}^{\mathsf{ES}}(\mathcal{A})$ outputs 1.

DEFINITION 2.3 (INITIATOR UNFORGEABILITY). *We say that an adversary can (t, ε_1)-break the* INITIATOR UNFORGEABILITY *of* ES, *if it in time t, has an advantage more than ε_1 (i.e., $\Pr[\mathrm{Exp}_{\mathsf{iu.cma}}^{\mathsf{ES}}(\mathcal{A}) = 1] \geq \varepsilon_1$). If there are no such adversaries, we say the scheme is (t, ε_1)-initiator-unforgeable.*

For EDITOR UNFORGEABILITY, we require that no attacker can gain a non-negligible advantage in the experiment specified in Figure 3, where the advantage of adversary $\mathcal{A}$ against $\mathsf{ES} = (\mathsf{Setup}, \mathsf{Gen}, \mathsf{FSign}, \mathsf{ESign}, \mathsf{Vf})$ is defined as the probability that experiment $\mathrm{Exp}_{\mathsf{eu.cma}}^{\mathsf{ES}}(\mathcal{A})$ outputs 1.

Experiment $\mathrm{Exp}_{\mathsf{iu.cma}}^{\mathsf{ES}}(\mathcal{A})$:

1. $pp \leftarrow \mathsf{Setup}(1^\lambda)$; $(pk^\star, sk^\star) \leftarrow \mathsf{Gen}(pp)$; $\mathcal{M} \leftarrow \phi$.

2. Run $\mathcal{A}(pp, pk^\star)$ with $pk_1 = pk^\star$ by handling oracle queries as follows:

   - To query key registration oracle, if a user wants to register pk with corresponding sk, the oracle requires sk. If sk is valid with respect to pk, the oracle returns (pk, c_{pk}), where c_{pk} is the public key certificate. We use a list consisting of $\mathsf{certList} = \{(pk, c_{pk}, sk)\}$ to record the registered keys.

   - To query the FSign oracle, $\mathcal{A}$ prepares $\Delta \subseteq S = \{1, \ldots, \ell\}$ and message M. $\mathcal{A}$ can initiate the FSign oracle concurrently and can interact with "clones" of the honest signer, where each clone maintains its own state, uses its own coins and the keys $(pk^\star, sk^\star)$ and then outputs $M, \sigma, \mathsf{edinfo} = (K_\Delta, \Delta)$ and $L = (pk_1, S)$. Bookkeep previously signed message blocks in $\mathcal{M}$.

   - To query the hash oracle, $\mathcal{A}$ submits a string and obtains its corresponding value from a random oracle (this oracle is optional if the scheme is constructed in the standard model).

   - Finally, $\mathcal{A}$ outputs a signature (M, σ, L), where $M = (m_1, \ldots, m_\ell)$.

3. If $(\mathsf{Vf}(pp, M, L) = 1) \wedge (pk^\star \in L[1]) \wedge m_i \notin \mathcal{M} = 1$ where $m_i \in M$ is signed by $sk^\star$ and $L[1] \setminus \{pk^\star\} \subset \mathsf{certList}[1]$, then return 1, otherwise return 0.

   Note that $L[1]$ and $\mathsf{certList}[1]$ represent the sets of the first coordinates of L and $\mathsf{certList}$, respectively.

Figure 2: INITIATOR-UNFORGEABILITY **Experiment**

DEFINITION 2.4 (EDITOR UNFORGEABILITY). *We say that an adversary can (t, ε_2)-break the* EDITOR UNFORGEABILITY *of* ES, *if it in time t, has an advantage more than ε_2 (i.e., $\Pr[\mathrm{Exp}_{\mathsf{eu.cma}}^{\mathsf{ES}}(\mathcal{A}) = 1] \geq \varepsilon_2$). If there are no such adversaries, we say the scheme is (t, ε_2)-editor-unforgeable.*

3. PRELIMINARIES

Cryptographic setting and assumption. In this section we briefly review some standard cryptographic setting [5]. Let $\mathbb{G}$ and $\mathbb{G}_T$ be two (multiplicative) cyclic groups of prime order p where the group actions on $\mathbb{G}$, $\mathbb{G}_T$ can be computed efficiently, g be a generator of $\mathbb{G}$, and $e : \mathbb{G} \times \mathbb{G} \to \mathbb{G}_T$ be an efficiently computable map with the following properties:

⋆ Bilinear: for all $u, v \in \mathbb{G}$ and $a, b \in \mathbb{Z}_p$, $e(u^a, v^b) = e(u, v)^{ab}$;

⋆ Non-degenerate: $e(g, g) \neq 1$.

We say $\mathbb{G}$ is a bilinear group if it satisfies these requirements.

DEFINITION 3.1. ([5]) *In a bilinear group $\mathbb{G}$, the Compu-*

Experiment $\mathrm{Exp}_{\mathsf{eu.cma}}^{\mathsf{ES}}(\mathcal{A})$:

1. $pp \leftarrow \mathsf{Setup}(1^\lambda)$; $(pk^\star, sk^\star) \leftarrow \mathsf{Gen}(pp)$; $\mathcal{M} \leftarrow \phi$. Without loss of generality, we assume $(pk^\star, sk^\star) = (pk_i, sk_i)$ where $i > 1$.

2. Run $\mathcal{A}(pp, pk^\star)$ by handling oracle queries as follows:

   - To query key registration oracle, if a user wants to register a public key pk corresponding to private key sk, the oracle requires sk. If sk is valid with respect to pk, the oracle returns (pk, c_{pk}) where c_{pk} is the public key certificate. We use a list consisting of $\mathsf{certList} = \{(pk, c_{pk}, sk)\}$ to record the registered keys.

   - To query the ESign oracle, $\mathcal{A}$ prepares M', (M, σ, L), and $\mathsf{edinfo} = (K_\Delta, \Delta)$. $\mathcal{A}$ can initiate the ESign oracle concurrently and can interact with "clones" of the honest signer, where each clone maintains its own state, uses its own coins and the keys $(pk^\star, sk^\star)$ and then outputs $(M', \sigma', L', \mathsf{edinfo}')$. Bookkeep previously signed blocks are included in $\mathcal{M}$.

   - To query the hash oracle, $\mathcal{A}$ submits a string and obtains its corresponding value from random oracle (this oracle is optional if the scheme operates in the standard model).

   - Finally, $\mathcal{A}$ outputs a signature (M, σ, L), where $M = (m_1, \ldots, m_\ell)$.

3. If $(\mathsf{Vf}(pp, M, L) = 1) \wedge (pk^\star \in L[1]) \wedge m_i \notin \mathcal{M}) = 1$ where $m_i \in M$ is signed by $sk^\star$ and $L[1] \setminus \{pk^\star\} \subset \mathsf{certList}[1]$, then return 1; otherwise, return 0.

Figure 3: EDITOR-UNFORGEABILITY **Experiment**

tational Diffie-Hellman (CDH) problem is: given $(g, g^a, g^b) \in \mathbb{G}^3$ for some $a, b \xleftarrow{R} \mathbb{Z}_p$, find $g^{ab} \in \mathbb{G}$.

Define the success probability of an algorithm $\mathcal{A}$ in solving the CDH problem on $\mathbb{G}$ as

$$\mathrm{Adv}_{\mathcal{A}}^{\mathsf{cdh}} \overset{\mathrm{def}}{=} \Pr\left[g^{ab} \leftarrow \mathcal{A}(g, g^a, g^b) : a, b \xleftarrow{R} \mathbb{Z}_p\right].$$

The probability is taken over the random choice of g from $\mathbb{G}$, of a, b from $\mathbb{Z}_p$, and the coin tosses of $\mathcal{A}$. We say an algorithm $\mathcal{A}$ (t, ε)-breaks the CDH problem on $\mathbb{G}$ if $\mathcal{A}$ runs in time at most t and $\mathrm{Adv}_{\mathcal{A}}^{\mathsf{cdh}} \geq \varepsilon$. If no adversary $\mathcal{A}$ can (t, ε)-break the CDH problem on $\mathbb{G}$, we say the CDH problem on $\mathbb{G}$ is (t, ε)-secure.

BLS signatures [5]. Since we will use the BLS signature scheme [5] as a starting point for our first scheme (presented in Section 4), we now review the BLS signature scheme $\mathcal{BLS} = (\mathsf{BLS.Gen}(1^\lambda), \mathsf{BLS.Sig}(sk, m), \mathsf{BLS.Ver}_{pk}(m, \sigma))$, which is specified in the afore-mentioned cryptographic setting.

$\mathsf{BLS.Gen}(1^\lambda)$: Pick random $x \xleftarrow{R} \mathbb{Z}_p$ and compute the public

key $pk = g^x$. The private key is $sk = x$. The scheme also needs a random oracle $H : \{0,1\}^* \to \mathbb{G}$.

$\mathsf{BLS.Sig}(sk, m)$: Given private key $sk = x$, and message m, compute and output $\sigma = H(m)^x$ as the signature.

$\mathsf{BLS.Ver}(pk, m, \sigma)$: On input public key $pk = g^x$, message M, and alleged signature σ, verify that

$$e(\sigma, g) \overset{?}{=} e(H(m), pk)$$

holds; if so, output 1 (accept), otherwise output 0 (reject).

It was proven in [5] that the scheme is existentially unforgeable under adaptive chosen-message attack [9] based on the hardness of the CDH problem in the random oracle model.

Waters signatures [21]. Since we will use the Waters signature scheme in [21] as a starting point for our second scheme presented in Section 5, we here briefly review it. Suppose a message is a bit string belonging to $\{0,1\}^k$ for some fixed k (in practice one may first apply a collision-resistant hash function $H' : \{0,1\}^* \to \{0,1\}^k$ to messages of arbitrary length). The scheme uses, in the afore-mentioned cryptographic setting, random generators $g, d \in \mathbb{G}$ and a vector of another $k+1$ random elements $\mu = (u', u_1, \ldots, u_k) \in \mathbb{G}^{k+1}$, where $u', u_1, \ldots, u_k$ define a function $H(\cdot)$ that given $m = (b_1, \ldots, b_k) \in \{0,1\}^k$, maps m to $H(m) = u' \prod_{i=1}^{k} u_i^{b_i} \in \mathbb{G}$.

The scheme $\mathcal{WS} = (\mathsf{W.Gen}(1^\lambda), \mathsf{W.Sig}(sk, m), \mathsf{W.Ver}(pk, m, \sigma))$ is specified as follows.

$\mathsf{W.Gen}(1^\lambda)$: Pick $x \xleftarrow{R} \mathbb{Z}_p$ and compute $B \leftarrow e(h, g^x)$. The public key is $pk = (\mu, B, d, g)$ and the private key is $sk = d^x$.

$\mathsf{W.Sig}(sk, m)$: Given sk and message $m = (b_1, \ldots, b_k) \in \{0,1\}^k$, pick a random $r \xleftarrow{R} \mathbb{Z}_p$ and compute

$$s \leftarrow d^x \cdot H(m)^r \quad \text{and} \quad t \leftarrow g^r.$$

The signature is $\sigma = (s, t) \in \mathbb{G}^2$.

$\mathsf{W.Ver}(pk, m, \sigma)$: Given public key pk, $m = (b_1, \ldots, b_k) \in \{0,1\}^k$, and $\sigma = (s, t) \in \mathbb{G}^2$, verify that

$$e(s, g) \overset{?}{=} A \cdot e(t, H(m))$$

holds; if so, output 1 (accept), otherwise output 0 (reject).

It was proven in [21] that the scheme is existentially unforgeable under adaptive chosen-message attack [9] based on the hardness of the CDH problem without using random oracles.

4. FULLY EDITABLE SIGNATURES

In this section we present a non-interactive fully-editable signature scheme, which gives the editors much freedom in terms of the message blocks they can edit. Specifically, in such a scheme an editor can edit the received message by itself and can assign to other editors the capability of further editing. Let $H : \{0,1\}^* \to \mathbb{G}$ be a hash function (random oracle). For $1 \leq i \leq \ell$, define

$$\mathsf{H}(i||m_i||pk_1) = \begin{cases} 1, & \text{if } m_i = \bot \\ H(i||m_i||pk_1), & \text{if } m_i \neq \bot. \end{cases}$$

The scheme is based on the afore-mentioned BLS signature scheme [5].

4.1 Construction

Recall that there are n signers $A_1, \ldots, A_n$; $S = \{1, \ldots, \ell\}$; $M = (m_1, \ldots, m_\ell)$; $\Gamma_i \subseteq S$ is the set of indices of message blocks that are signed by signer A_i. The scheme is described as follows.

$\underline{\mathsf{Setup}(1^\lambda)}$: On input a security parameter λ, it generates $\mathbb{G}$, $\mathbb{G}_T$, p, g, e, and random oracle H as specified above. Let $pp = (\mathbb{G}, \mathbb{G}_T, p, g, e, H)$, which is made public.

$\underline{\mathsf{Gen}(pp)}$: It takes pp as input, randomly chooses $x_i \xleftarrow{R} \mathbb{Z}_p$, outputs signer A_i's pair of private and public keys $(sk = x_i, pk = g^{x_i})$.

$\underline{\mathsf{FSign}(pp, sk_1, M_1)}$: On input $M_1 = (m_1, \ldots, m_\ell)$, A_1 determines a set $\Delta \subseteq S$ (the set of indices of blocks of M_1 that can be edited by signer A_2, including the $\perp$ blocks[1]), uses $sk_1 = x_1$ to compute

$$\sigma_1 = \left(\prod_{i=1}^{\ell} H(i || m_i || pk_1) \right)^{x_1},$$

sets $s_\alpha = H(\alpha || m_\alpha || pk_1)^{x_1}$ for $\alpha \in \Delta$, $K_\Delta = \{s_\alpha\}$, $\Gamma_1 = S$ (meaning that A_1 signed all the ℓ blocks, possibly including $\perp$ blocks), $\mathsf{edinfo}_1 = (K_\Delta, \Delta)$, and $L_1 = [(pk_1, \Gamma_1)]$. Finally A_1 sends $(M_1, \sigma_1, L_1, \mathsf{edinfo}_1)$ to signer A_2 over a private channel (which can be implemented using standard cryptosystems).

$\underline{\mathsf{ESign}(pp, sk_i, M', M, \sigma, L, \mathsf{edinfo})}$: Parse $M = (m_1, \ldots, m_\ell)$, $L = [(pk_1, \Gamma_1), \ldots, (pk_{i-1}, \Gamma_{i-1})]$ where Γ_j ($1 \leq j \leq i - 1$) is the set of the indices of the message blocks (including possibly $\perp$ blocks) signed by A_i, $M' = (m'_1, \ldots, m'_\ell)$ and $\mathsf{edinfo} = (K_\Delta, \Delta)$, where $K_\Delta = \{s_\alpha | \alpha \in \Delta\}$ (herein $\bigcup_{j=1}^{i-1} \Gamma_j = S$). If

$$e(\sigma, g) \neq \prod_{j=1}^{i-1} e\left(\prod_{\beta \in \Gamma_j} H(\beta || m_\beta || pk_j), pk_j \right),$$

abort; otherwise execute as follows:

- In the case $1 < i < n$, execute the following:
  1. Let $C = \{\alpha | m'_\alpha = m_\alpha, \alpha \in S\}$ be the set of indices of message blocks that A_i inherits (i.e., copy-and-paste) from A_{i-1}. Note that A_i does not have to sign those blocks with respect to C because, for example, A_i may be uncertain about the trustworthiness of these message blocks.
  2. Choose $I \subseteq C$ where I is the set of indices of messages blocks that A_i inherits and will sign as well. Let $\bar{I} = \Delta \setminus (C \cap \Delta) = \Delta \setminus C$, which is the set of indices of message blocks A_i will edit and sign.
  3. Compute

$$\sigma' = \sigma \cdot \left(\prod_{\alpha \in I \cup \bar{I}} H(\alpha || m'_\alpha || pk_i) \right)^{x_i} \cdot \prod_{\alpha \in \bar{I}} s_\alpha^{-1}.$$

4. Update $\Gamma_j = \Gamma_j \setminus \bar{I}$ for $j = 1, \ldots, i - 1$ and set $\Gamma_i = I \cup \bar{I}$.
5. Determine $\Delta' \subseteq \Delta$ according to some policy.
6. Update

$$s'_\alpha = \begin{cases} H(\alpha || m'_\alpha || pk_i)^{x_i}, & \text{for } \alpha \in \bar{I} \cap \Delta' \\ s_\alpha \cdot H(\alpha || m'_\alpha || pk_i)^{x_i}, & \text{for } \alpha \in I \cap \Delta' \\ s_\alpha, & \text{for } \alpha \in (C \setminus I) \cap \Delta' \end{cases}$$

and let

$$K_{\Delta'} = \{s'_\alpha | \alpha \in \Delta'\}.$$

7. Set $L' = [(pk_1, \Gamma_1), \ldots, (pk_i, \Gamma_i)]$ and return

$$(M', \sigma', L', \mathsf{edinfo}')$$

where $\mathsf{edinfo}' = (K_{\Delta'}, \Delta')$.

- In the case $i = n$, namely that the signer is the last one, the signer executes the same as A_j ($j \neq n$) does, except that it sets $\mathsf{edinfo}' = \texttt{null}$. The final signature output is (M', σ', L').

$\underline{\mathsf{Vf}(pp, M, \sigma, L)}$: Given parameters pp,

$$L = [(pk_1, \Gamma_1), \ldots, (pk_n, \Gamma_n)], \quad M = (m_1, \ldots, m_\ell)$$

and an alleged signature σ, the verifier accepts the signature if

$$e(\sigma, g) = \prod_{j=1}^{n} e\left(\prod_{\beta \in \Gamma_j} H(\beta || m_\beta || pk_j), pk_j \right), \quad (4.1)$$

and reject otherwise.

We stress that the channel between the signers are private, which is important because the auxiliary information edinfo should be kept secret to the respective pair of signers.

4.2 Security Analysis

Security of the above scheme is based on the security of the BLS scheme, which is proven in [5].

LEMMA 4.1. *If the BLS signature scheme is $(t, q_s, q_h, \varepsilon_1)$-unforgeable in the random oracle model, then our scheme is $(t', q'_s, q'_h, \varepsilon'_1)$-initiator-unforgeable in the random oracle model, where $t' = t - O((q_s + 1) \cdot \ell)T_e$, $q'_s \geq \frac{q_s}{\ell} - 1$, $q_h = q'_h$, $\varepsilon_1 = \varepsilon'_1$ and T_e is the time cost of one exponentiation in $\mathbb{G}$.*

PROOF. We prove that if there exists an adversary $\mathcal{A}_{\mathsf{iu.cma}}$ who can $(t', q'_s, q'_h, \varepsilon'_1)$-break the initiator unforgeability of our scheme, then we can construct an adversary $\mathcal{A}_{\mathsf{BLS}}$ that can $(t, q_s, q_h, \varepsilon_1)$-break the BLS signature scheme, where $t = t' + O((q'_s + 1) \cdot \ell)T_e$, $q_s \leq (q'_s + 1) \cdot \ell$, $q_h = q'_h$ and $\varepsilon_1 = \varepsilon'_1$.

Suppose adversary $\mathcal{A}_{\mathsf{BLS}}$ obtains from its BLS-signature environment denoted by $\mathcal{E}_{\mathsf{BLS}}$ the system parameter $pp_{\mathsf{BLS}} = (\mathbb{G}, \mathbb{G}_T, p, g, e, H)$ and the challenge public key pk^* of the BLS signature scheme. The environment $\mathcal{E}_{\mathsf{BLS}}$ provides oracle $\mathsf{BLS.Sign}$ that returns BLS signatures on requested messages. Then adversary $\mathcal{A}_{\mathsf{BLS}}$ starts to run adversary $\mathcal{A}_{\mathsf{iu.cma}}$ with public parameter $pp = pp_{\mathsf{BLS}}$ where the challenge public key $pk^* = pk_1$.

For the oracle queries made by the adversary $\mathcal{A}_{\mathsf{iu.cma}}$, $\mathcal{A}_{\mathsf{BLS}}$ operates as follows:

- If the adversary $\mathcal{A}_{\mathsf{iu.cma}}$ wants to register pk_j, it must submit its corresponding private key sk_j as well as pk_j to $\mathcal{A}_{\mathsf{BLS}}$. (pk_j, c_{pk_j}, sk_j) is inserted into list C.

---

[1] This is for the sake of convenience in specifying the scheme. Technically, A_2 can edit any $\perp$ block in M_1 without A_1's assistance. Note that this treatment has no side-effect in terms of security.

- For the FSign query on M, $\mathcal{A}_{\text{BLS}}$ does the following:

  1. Parse $M = (m_1, \ldots, m_\ell)$.
  2. If $m_i \neq \bot$, query for the signature σ_i from oracle BLS.Sig on messages $(i||m_i||pk_1)$; otherwise let $\sigma_i = 1$.
  3. Compute

  $$\sigma = \prod_{i=1}^{\ell} \sigma_i$$

  4. Pick up $\Delta \subseteq S$ and let

  $$K_\Delta = \{s_i = \sigma_i | i \in \Delta\}.$$

  5. Set $\text{edinfo} = (K_\Delta, \Delta)$ and $L = [(pk_1, \Gamma_1)]$ where $\Gamma_1 = S$.
  6. Output $(M, \sigma, \text{edinfo}, L)$.

- If $\mathcal{A}_{\text{iu.cma}}$ makes a query on H, $\mathcal{A}_{\text{BLS}}$ responds with the answer from its own random oracle H.

Adversary $\mathcal{A}_{\text{iu.cma}}$ finally outputs $M = (m_1, \ldots, m_\ell), \sigma, L = [(pk_1, \Gamma_1), \ldots, (pk_n, \Gamma_n)]$ to win the experiment $\text{Exp}_{\text{iu.cma}}^{\text{ES}}$. $\mathcal{A}_{\text{BLS}}$ does the following to output its own forgery.

1. Find the corresponding private key sk_j of pk_j ($2 \leq j \leq n$) in the list C and computes

$$\tilde{\sigma} = \sigma \cdot \prod_{2 \leq j \leq n} \left(\prod_{\alpha \in \Gamma_j \wedge m_\alpha \neq \bot} H(\alpha||m_\alpha||pk_j)^{-x_j} \right),$$

2. Let m_{α_0} be a message block s. t.

$$m_{\alpha_0} \notin \mathcal{M} \wedge \alpha_0 \in \Gamma_1 \wedge m_{\alpha_0} \neq \bot;$$

3. Query oracle BLS.Sig for signatures $\{\sigma_\alpha\}$ on messages $\{\alpha||m_\alpha||pk_1\}$ for α, s.t. $(\alpha \in \Gamma_1) \wedge (\alpha \neq \alpha_0) \wedge (m_\alpha \neq \bot) = 1$ (if not queried previously), output

$$\sigma_{\text{BLS}} = \tilde{\sigma} \cdot \left(\prod_{\alpha \in \Gamma_1 \wedge \alpha \neq \alpha_0 \wedge m_\alpha \neq \bot} \sigma_\alpha \right)^{-1}.$$

It is easy to verify that σ_{BLS} is a valid BLS signature on $\alpha_0||m_{\alpha_0}||pk_1$ under pk^*. For the time cost of reduction, we have $t = t' + O(q)T_e$, $q \leq (q'_s + 1) \cdot \ell$, $q_h = q'_h$ and $\varepsilon_1 = \varepsilon'_1$. $\square$

LEMMA 4.2. *If the BLS signature scheme is $(t, q_s \cdot \ell, q_h, \varepsilon_2)$-unforgeable in the random oracle model, then our scheme is $(t', q'_s, q'_h, \varepsilon'_2)$-editor-unforgeable in the random oracle model, where $t = t' + O(q_s)\mathsf{p}$, $q_s \approx q'_s \cdot \ell$, $q_h = q'_h$, $\varepsilon_2 = \varepsilon'_2$ and p is the time cost of one pairing.*

PROOF. We prove that if there exists an adversary $\mathcal{A}_{\text{eu.cma}}$ that can $(t', q'_s, q'_h, \varepsilon'_2)$-break the editor unforgeability of our scheme, then we can construct an adversary $\mathcal{A}_{\text{BLS}}$ that can $(t, q_s, q_h, \varepsilon_2)$-break the BLS signature scheme, where $t = t' + O(q_s)\mathsf{p}$, $q_s \leq q'_s \cdot \ell$, $q_h = q'_h$ and $\varepsilon_2 = \varepsilon'_2$.

At first the adversary $\mathcal{A}_{\text{BLS}}$ obtains from its environment $\mathcal{E}_{\text{BLS}}$ the system parameter $pp_{\text{BLS}} = (\mathbb{G}, \mathbb{G}_T, p, g, e, H)$ and challenge public key pk^* of the BLS signature scheme. The environment $\mathcal{E}_{\text{BLS}}$ provides oracle BLS.Sig that returns the BLS signature on requested message, similar to the proof for INITIATOR UNFORGEABILITY. Then adversary $\mathcal{A}_{\text{BLS}}$ starts

to run adversary $\mathcal{A}_{\text{eu.cma}}$ with public parameter $pp = pp_{\text{BLS}}$ where the challenge public key $pk^* = pk_i$.

For the oracle queries made by the adversary $\mathcal{A}_{\text{eu.cma}}$, $\mathcal{A}_{\text{BLS}}$ does as follows:

- If the adversary $\mathcal{A}_{\text{eu.cma}}$ wants to register pk_j for $j \neq i$, it must submit its corresponding private key sk_j as well as pk_j to $\mathcal{A}_{\text{BLS}}$. (pk_j, c_{pk_j}, sk_j) is inserted into list certList.

- If $\mathcal{A}_{\text{eu.cma}}$ makes a query on H, $\mathcal{A}_{\text{BLS}}$ responds with the answer from its own random oracle H.

- For ESign query on $(M', M, \sigma, \text{edinfo}, L)$, Parse $M = (m_1, \ldots, m_\ell)$, $L = [(pk_1, \Gamma_1), \ldots, (pk_{i-1}, \Gamma_{i-1})]$, $M' = (m'_1, \ldots, m'_\ell)$ and $\text{edinfo} = (K_\Delta, \Delta)$, where $K_\Delta = \{s_\alpha | \alpha \in \Delta\}$ and $\bigcup_{j=1}^{i-1} \Gamma_j = S$.

  Let

  $$H(\alpha||m_\alpha||pk_j) = \begin{cases} 1, & \text{if } m_\alpha = \bot \\ H(\alpha||m_\alpha||pk_i), & \text{if } m_\alpha \neq \bot \end{cases}$$

  for all $1 \leq j \leq n$ and $\alpha \in S$.

  If

  $$e(\sigma, g) \neq \prod_{j=1}^{i-1} e \left(\prod_{\beta \in \Gamma_j} H(\beta||m_\beta||pk_j), pk_j \right),$$

  abort; else execute as follows:

  - In the case $1 < i < n$, execute the following:

    1. Let $C = \{\alpha | m'_\alpha = m_\alpha, \alpha \in S\}$
    2. Choose $I \subseteq C$ where I is the set of indices of messages blocks that A_i will sign. Let $\bar{I} = \Delta \setminus C$, which is the set of indices of message blocks to be edited by A_i.
    3. Query its own oracle BLS.Sig for

    $$S_\alpha = H(\alpha||m'_\alpha||pk_i)^{x_i}$$

    where $\alpha \in (I \cup \bar{I}) \wedge m'_\alpha \neq \bot$.
    4. Define

    $$\sigma_\alpha = \begin{cases} S_\alpha, & \text{for } m'_\alpha \neq \bot; \\ 1, & \text{for } m'_\alpha = \bot. \end{cases}$$

    5. Compute

    $$\sigma' = \sigma \cdot \left(\prod_{\alpha \in I \cup \bar{I}} \sigma_\alpha \right) \cdot \left(\prod_{\alpha \in \bar{I}} s_\alpha^{-1} \right),$$

    6. Update $\Gamma_j = \Gamma_j \setminus (\bar{I})$ for $j = 1, \ldots, i-1$ and set $\Gamma_i = I \cup \bar{I}$;
    7. Pick up $\Delta' \subset \Delta$ and update

    $$s'_\alpha = \begin{cases} \sigma_\alpha, & \text{for } \alpha \in \bar{I} \bigcap \Delta' \\ s_\alpha \cdot \sigma_\alpha, & \text{for } \alpha \in I \bigcap \Delta' \\ s_\alpha, & \text{for } \alpha \in (C \setminus I) \bigcap \Delta' \end{cases}$$

    and let

    $$K_{\Delta'} = \{s'_\alpha | \alpha \in \Delta'\}.$$

    8. Set $L' = [(pk_1, \Gamma_1), \ldots, (pk_i, \Gamma_i)]$ and return

    $$(M', \sigma', \text{edinfo}', L')$$

    where $\text{edinfo}' = (K_{\Delta'}, \Delta')$.

– In the case $i = n$, namely that the signer is the last one, the signer does the same as A_j ($j \neq n$) does, except that it sets $\mathsf{edinfo}' = \mathtt{null}$. The final signature output is (M', σ', L').

Adversary $\mathcal{A}_{\mathsf{eu.cma}}$ finally outputs $M = (m_1, \ldots, m_\ell), \sigma, L = [(pk_1, \Gamma_1), \ldots, (pk_n, \Gamma_n)]$ to win the experiment $\mathsf{Exp}^{\mathsf{ES}}_{\mathsf{eu.cma}}$. $\mathcal{A}_{\mathsf{BLS}}$ does the following to output its own forgery.

1. Find the corresponding private key sk_j of pk_j ($1 \leq j \neq i \leq n$) in the list $\mathsf{certList}$ and computes

$$\tilde{\sigma} = \sigma \cdot \prod_{1 \leq j \neq i \leq n} \left(\prod_{\alpha \in \Gamma_j} \mathsf{H}(\alpha \| m_\alpha \| pk_j)^{-x_j} \right).$$

2. Let m_{α_0} be a message s. t.

$$m_{\alpha_0} \notin \mathcal{M} \wedge \alpha_0 \in \Gamma_i \wedge m_{\alpha_0} \neq \perp.$$

3. Query oracle $\mathsf{BLS.Sig}$ for signatures $\{\sigma_\alpha\}$ on messages $\{(\alpha \| m_\alpha \| pk_i)\}$ where

$$\left[(\alpha \in \Gamma_i) \bigwedge (\alpha \neq \alpha_0) \bigwedge (m_\alpha \neq \perp) \right] = \mathtt{true},$$

output

$$\sigma_{\mathsf{BLS}} = \tilde{\sigma} \cdot \left(\prod_{\alpha \in \Gamma_i \wedge \alpha \neq \alpha_0} \sigma_\alpha \right)^{-1}.$$

Therefore, it is easy to verify that σ_{BLS} is a valid BLS signature on $(\alpha_0 \| m_{\alpha_0} \| pk_i)$ under pk^*. For the time of reduction, we have $t = t' + O(q_s)\mathsf{p}$, $q_s \leq q'_s \cdot \ell$, $q_h = q'_h$ and $\varepsilon_2 = \varepsilon'_2$. $\square$

THEOREM 4.3. *Our scheme is secure in the random oracle model if the CDH problem is hard on bilinear groups.*

PROOF. Because it was proven in [5] that the BLS scheme is unforgeable in the random oracle model based on the CDH assumption, the above two lemmas show that our scheme achieves both INITIATOR UNFORGEABILITY and EDITOR UNFORGEABILITY in the random oracle model based on the CDH assumption as well. $\square$

Note that in the above scheme, the final editable signature of a message is just one group element of $\mathbb{G}$ (e.g., 160 bits if we use the parameters in [5]). However, the intermediate signatures should include the "editing keys" for the next editor, which could lead to $O(\ell)$ communication complexity. Verification also costs a linear number of pairings for a single signature. In summary, the resulting editable signatures are short, but their verification requires $\mathcal{O}(n)$ pairing operations. Next we will show a more efficient scheme that reduces the intermediate signature size and verification cost, but at the price of restricting the freedom of editors in terms of which message blocks they can edit.

5. NON-SWITCHABLE EDITABLE SIGNATURES

Now we present an editable signature scheme that allows the initiator (the first signer) assigns the blocks that can be edited by the respective editors, who however do not have such power. We call such a variant non-switchable editable signatures. This scheme is based on the Waters signatures

[21] and only requires a constant number of pairing operations in verifying a signature. Its security is proven in the standard model (i.e., without using random oracle). Furthermore, this scheme doesn't require private channels between the signers (because the information does not need to be kept secret).

5.1 Construction

Let $\mathbb{G}$, $\mathbb{G}_T$, p, g, e be the bilinear parameters reviewed above (and as in [5, 21]). In this scheme, the initiator A_1 determines that the i-th editor can at most edit the i-th block m_i, meaning that $\ell = n$ in this case. Moreover, if A_i does modify m_i provided by A_1 to obtain m'_i, then A_i must sign m'_i; if A_i does not modify m_i provided by A_1, then A_i must sign m_i as well (compared with the previous scheme where A_i does not have to sign m_i, here A_i must either sign m_i or modify m_i).[2] The scheme does not require private channels between the signers because the "editing keys" are somehow embedded into the private keys of the signers. As such, there is no need for the auxiliary information edinfo. Moreover, Γ_i is not needed because it is regulated that the i-th block m_i must be signed by A_i (and by A_1 when A_i does not modify m_i). Therefore, L only needs to indicate who has already processed and signed the message.

The scheme $\mathsf{ES} = (\mathsf{Setup}, \mathsf{Gen}, \mathsf{FSign}, \mathsf{ESign}, \mathsf{Vf})$ is described as follows:

$\underline{\mathsf{Setup}(1^\lambda)}$: On input a security parameter λ, it outputs

$$pp = (\mathbb{G}, \mathbb{G}_T, p, g, e).$$

$\underline{\mathsf{Gen}(pp)}$: It takes pp as input, randomly chooses

$$(x_i, y_{i0}, y_{i1}, \ldots, y_{ik}) \xleftarrow{R} \mathbb{Z}_p^{(k+2)},$$

computes $\mu_i = (u_{i0}, u_{i1}, \ldots, u_{ik})$ where $u_{ij} = g^{y_{ij}}$ for $j = 0, 1, \ldots, k$ and $B_i = e(d, g^{x_i})$, outputs the i-th signer's private and public key

$$sk_i = (d^{x_i}, y_{i0}, \ldots, y_{ik}), \quad pk_i = (\mu_i, B_i).$$

Note that μ_i defines $H_{\mu_i} : \{0,1\}^k \longrightarrow \mathbb{G}$ by setting

$$H_{\mu_i}(m) = u_{i0} \left(\prod_{j=1}^{k} u_{ij}^{m[j]} \right),$$

where $m[j]$ is the j-th bit of message m, which itself could be a hash value, say $m = h(a)$ of some message a where $h : \{0,1\}^* \rightarrow \{0,1\}^k$. We can define

$$H(M) = \prod_{j=1}^{\ell} H_{\mu_i}(m_i)$$

where $M = (m_1, \ldots, m_\ell)$.

$\underline{\mathsf{FSign}(pp, sk_1, M)}$: It takes $M = (m_1, m_2, \ldots, m_\ell)$ as input, picks up $L = [\phi, (pk_1, \ldots, pk_\ell)]$ and computes the following:

1. Randomly choose $r \xleftarrow{R} \mathbb{Z}_p$ and compute

$$s = d^{x_1} \cdot \left(\prod_{i=1}^{\ell} H_{\mu_i}(m_i) \right)^r, \quad t = g^r,$$

---

[2] In a future work, we will show that it is possible to eliminate this restriction. Nevertheless, the security proof will become more involved.

and set $\sigma' = (s, t)$ and $M' = M$.

2. Set $L' = [(pk_1), (pk_2, \ldots, pk_\ell)]$ meaning that A_1 has already signed M, but the others haven't, output (M', σ', L').

$\mathsf{ESign}(pp, sk_i, M', M, \sigma, L)$ for $1 < i \le n$: Parse input message $M = (m_1, \ldots, m_\ell)$, input signature $\sigma = (s, t)$, list $L = [(pk_1, \ldots, pk_{i-1}), (pk_i, pk_{i+1}, \ldots, pk_\ell)]$ meaning that $A_1, \ldots, A_{i-1}$ have processed. Abort the execution if

$$e(s, g) \ne \prod_{j=1}^{i-1} B_j \cdot e\left(\prod_{j=1}^{\ell} H_{\mu_j}(m_j), t\right);$$

otherwise execute as follows:

- In the case $1 < i < n$, execute the following:
  1. Randomly choose r' from $\mathbb{Z}_p$ and compute $t' = t \cdot g^{r'}$.
  2. Parse $M' = (m_1, \ldots, m_{i-1}, m_i', m_{i+1}, \ldots, m_\ell)$.
  3. If $m_i \ne m_i'$ (replacing m_i in M with m_i' in M'), compute

     $$s' = d^{x_i} \cdot s \cdot t^{\left[\sum_{j=1}^{k} y_{ij}(m_i'[j] - m_i[j])\right]} \cdot \left(H(M')\right)^{r'},$$

     where $m_i[j]$ and $m_i'[j]$ are the j-th bits of message m_i and m_i', respectively. Otherwise, ($m_i' = m_i$ and $M' = M$), compute $s' = d^{x_i} \cdot s \cdot H(M)^{r'}$.
  4. Let $L' = [(pk_1, \ldots, pk_i), (pk_{i+1}, \ldots, pk_\ell)]$, $\sigma' = (s', t')$ and send (M', σ', L') to the next signer.

- In the case $i = n$, execute the same as in the above except that (M', σ', L') is the final message and signature that can be released into an information network.

$\mathsf{Vf}(pp, M, \sigma, L)$: Given parameters pp, $L = [(pk_1, \ldots, pk_\ell), \phi]$, a message $M = (m_1, \ldots, m_\ell)$ and an alleged signature $\sigma = (s, t)$, the verifier accepts the signature if

$$e(s, g) = e(H(M), t) \prod_{i=1}^{\ell} B_i, \qquad (5.1)$$

and reject otherwise.

In order to further clarify the difference between the two schemes, we here reiterate that in the final signature, the first block m_1 is always signed by the initiator A_1 alone (i.e., not edited by any A_i with $i > 1$). Whereas, the i-th block m_i is first "drafted and signed" by A_1 and then processed by A_i in one of the following fashions: (i) A_i concurs with A_1 and thus signs m_i as well. In this case m_i is effectively signed with a multisignature by A_1 and A_i. (ii) A_i modifies m_i, which was provided by A_1, to obtain $m_i' \ne m_i$. In this case m_i' in the final message is only signed by A_i.

The non-switchable editable signature scheme is much more efficient than the fully editable signature scheme, in terms of both communication and computation since we do not require the initiator to transmit the auxiliary information. However, in addition to that the public keys are longer, a signature consists of two group elements that are longer than a signature in the previous scheme.

5.2 Security Results

LEMMA 5.1. *If the Waters signature scheme is (t, q, ε_1)-unforgeable, then our scheme is $(t - O(q), q, \varepsilon_1)$-initiator-unforgeable.*

PROOF. We prove that if there exists an adversary $\mathcal{A}$ that can (t', q', ε_1')-break the initiator unforgeability of our non-switchable editable signature scheme, then we can construct an adversary $\mathcal{B}$ that can (t, q, ε_1)-break the Waters signature scheme, where $t = t' - O(q)$, $q' = q$ and $\varepsilon_1' = \varepsilon_1$.

At the beginning we assume that adversary $\mathcal{B}$ obtains from its Waters signature environment denoted by $\mathcal{E}_{\mathsf{waters}}$ the system parameter $pp_{\mathsf{waters}} = (\mathbb{G}, \mathbb{G}_T, p, g, e, u_{10}, \{u_{1j}\}_{1 \le j \le k})$, and the challenge public key $pk_1 = pk_w^*$ of the Waters signature scheme. Here we assume that the message length of the underlying Waters signature scheme is k.

The environment $\mathcal{E}_{\mathsf{waters}}$ provides an oracle $\mathsf{W.Sig}$ that returns the Waters signature on requested message. Then adversary $\mathcal{B}$ starts adversary $\mathcal{A}$ with public parameter $pp = pp_{\mathsf{waters}}$ and the challenge public key $pk_1 = pk^* = pk_w^*$.

For the oracle queries made by the adversary $\mathcal{A}$, $\mathcal{B}$ executes as follows:

- If the adversary $\mathcal{A}$ wants to register $pk_v = (\mu_v, B_v)$ for $2 \le v \le \ell$ where $\mu_v = (u_{v0}, u_{v1}, \ldots, u_{vk})$ and $B_v = e(d, g^{x_v})$, it must submit its corresponding private key $sk_v = (d^{x_v}, y_{v0}, \ldots, y_{vk})$ where $u_{vj} = g^{y_{vj}}$ for $j = 0, 1, \ldots, k$, as well as pk_v to $\mathcal{B}$. Then (pk_v, c_{pk_v}, sk_v) is inserted into list $\mathsf{certList}$.

- For FSign query (M, L), $\mathcal{B}$ first parse $\sigma = (s, t)$, $L = [\phi, F]$ then does as follows:
  1. Parse $M = (m_1, m_2, \ldots, m_\ell)$;
  2. Make a $\mathsf{W.Sig}$ query from $\mathcal{E}_{\mathsf{waters}}$ and obtains the signature $\sigma_1 = (s_1, t_1)$ on message m_1 (if not queried) where

     $$s_1 = d^{x_1} \cdot H_{\mu_1}(m_1)^r,$$
     $$t_1 = g^r.$$
  3. Look for $sk_v = (d^{x_v}, y_{v0}, \ldots, y_{vk})$ from list $\mathsf{certList}$ for all $v \ne i$ and compute

     $$e = \sum_{v=2}^{\ell} y_{v0} + \sum_{v=2}^{\ell} \sum_{j=1}^{k} (m_v[j] \cdot y_{vj}),$$
     $$s' = s_1 \cdot t_1^e \cdot H(M')^{r'},$$
     $$t' = t_1 \cdot g^{r'}.$$

     where $m_v[j]$ is the j-th bit of the v-th block of message m_v and r' is a random number in $\mathbb{Z}_p$.
  4. Let $E = (pk_1)$ and $F = (pk_2, \ldots, pk_\ell)$.
  5. Set $\sigma' = (s', t')$, $L' = [E, F]$, and output $(M' = M, \sigma', L')$ as the response of $\mathcal{B}$ to such a query.

Adversary $\mathcal{A}$ finally outputs $(M, \sigma = (s, t), L = [E, F])$ to win the experiment $\mathsf{Exp}_{\mathsf{iu.cma}}^{\mathsf{ES}}$, where $F = \phi$. $\mathcal{B}$ parse $M = (m_1, \ldots, m_\ell)$, where $m_1 \notin \mathcal{M}$ since it is a valid forgery. Then, it executes the following to obtain a forgery of the Waters signature σ_w.

1. Look for $sk_v = (d^{x_v}, y_{v0}, \ldots, y_{vk})$ from list $\mathsf{certList}$ for all $v \ne 1$.

2. Compute

$$e = \sum_{v=2}^{\ell} y_{v0} + \sum_{v=2}^{\ell} \sum_{j=1}^{k} (m_v[j] \cdot y_{vj}),$$

$$s' = s \cdot t^{-e} \cdot \left(\prod_{v=2}^{\ell} d^{x_v} \right)^{-1},$$

$$t' = t.$$

where $m_v[j]$ is the j-th bit of the v-th block of message m_v.

3. Set $\sigma_w = (s', t')$.

Then, σ_w is a valid Waters signature on m_1. For time cost in reduction, we have $t = t' + O(q)$, $q' = q$ and $\varepsilon_1' = \varepsilon_1$. $\square$

LEMMA 5.2. *If the Waters signature scheme is (t, q, ε_2)-unforgeable, then the above non-switchable editable signature scheme is $(t - O(q), q, \varepsilon_2)$-editor-unforgeable.*

PROOF. We prove that if there exists an adversary $\mathcal{A}$ that can (t', q', ε_2')-break the editor unforgeability of our non-switchable editable signature scheme, then we can construct an adversary $\mathcal{B}$ that can (t, q, ε_2)-break the Waters signature scheme, where $t' = t - O(q)$, $q' = q$ and $\varepsilon_2' = \varepsilon_2$.

At the beginning we assume that adversary $\mathcal{B}$ obtains from its environment $\mathcal{E}_{\mathsf{waters}}$ the system parameter $pp_{\mathsf{waters}} = (\mathbb{G}, \mathbb{G}_T, p, g, e, u_{i0}, \{u_{ij}\}_{1 \le j \le k})$ for some fixed i, and challenge public key pk_w^* of the Waters signature scheme. Here we assume that the message length of the underlying Waters signature scheme is k.

The environment $\mathcal{E}_{\mathsf{waters}}$ provides an oracle W.Sig that returns the Waters signature on requested message. Then adversary $\mathcal{B}$ starts adversary $\mathcal{A}$ with public parameter $pp = pp_{\mathsf{waters}}$ and the challenge public key $pk_i = pk^* = pk_w^*$.

For the oracle queries made by the adversary $\mathcal{A}$, $\mathcal{B}$ executes the following:

- If the adversary $\mathcal{A}$ wants to register $pk_v = (\mu_v, B_v)$ for $1 \le v \ne i \le \ell$ where $\mu_v = (u_{v0}, u_{v1}, \ldots, u_{vk})$ and $B_v = e(d, g^{x_v})$, it must submit its corresponding private key $sk_v = (d^{x_v}, y_{v0}, \ldots, y_{vk})$ where $u_{vj} = g^{y_{vj}}$ for $j = 0, 1, \ldots, k$, as well as pk_v to $\mathcal{B}$. Then (pk_v, c_{pk_v}, sk_v) is inserted into list C.

- For ESign query (m_i', M, σ, L), $\mathcal{B}$ first parse $\sigma = (s, t)$, $L = [E, F]$ and check the validity by

$$e(s, g) \stackrel{?}{=} \prod_{pk_j \in E} B_j \cdot e(t, H(M)),$$

if invalid, abort; otherwise

1. Make a W.Sig query from $\mathcal{E}_{\mathsf{waters}}$ and obtains the signature (s_i, t_i) on message m_i' where

$$s_i = d^{x_i} \cdot H_{\mu_i}(m_i')^r,$$

$$t_i = g^r.$$

2. Let $M' = (m_1, m_2, \ldots, m_i', m_{i+1}, \ldots, m_\ell)$ (replacing m_i by m_i' in M) and compute

$$e = \sum_{v \ne i} y_{v0} + \sum_{v \ne i} \sum_{j=1}^{k} (m_v[j] \cdot y_{vj}),$$

$$s' = s_i \cdot t_i^e \cdot H(M')^{r'},$$

$$t' = t_i \cdot g^{r'}.$$

where $m_v[j]$ is the j-th bit of the v-th block of message m_v and r' is a random number in $\mathbb{Z}_p$.

3. Let $E = (pk_1, \ldots, pk_i)$, $F = (pk_{i+1}, \ldots, pk_\ell)$

4. Set $\sigma' = (s', t')$, $L' = [E, F]$, and output (M', σ', L') as the response of $\mathcal{B}$ to such a query.

Adversary $\mathcal{A}$ finally outputs $(M, \sigma = (s, t), L = [E, F])$ to win the experiment $\mathsf{Exp}_{\mathsf{eu.cma}}^{\mathsf{ES}}$, where $F = \phi$. $\mathcal{B}$ parse $M = (m_1, \ldots, m_\ell)$, where $m_i \notin \mathcal{M}$ since it is a valid forgery. Then, does the following to obtain a forgery of the Waters signature $\dot{\sigma}_w$

1. Look for $sk_v = (d^{x_v}, y_{v0}, \ldots, y_{vk})$ from list certList for all $v \ne i$.

2. Compute

$$e = \sum_{v \ne i} y_{v0} + \sum_{v \ne i} \sum_{j=1}^{k} (m_v[j] \cdot y_{vj}),$$

$$s' = s \cdot t^{-e} \cdot \left(\prod_{v \ne i} d^{x_v} \right)^{-1},$$

$$t' = t.$$

where $m_v[j]$ is the j-th bit of the v-th block of message m_v.

3. Set $\sigma_w = (s', t')$.

Then, σ_w is a valid Waters signature on m_i. For time cost in reduction, we have $t' = t - O(q)$, $q' = q$ and $\varepsilon_2' = \varepsilon_2$. $\square$

THEOREM 5.3. *Our scheme is secure if the CDH problem in bilinear groups is hard.*

PROOF. Since the Waters signature scheme is unforgeable under the CDH assumption, the above two lemmas show that our scheme is INITIATOR-UNFORGEABLE and EDITOR-UNFORGEABLE without using random oracles based on the CDH assumption. $\square$

6. RELATED WORK

While there have been many studies on data provenance [6, 19, 20, 11, 10, 3], the security aspect of data provenance has not been investigated until very recently [7, 12, 24, 23, 14, 22]. However, existing studies focused on what we called passive data provenance. In this paper, we introduced the novel concept of proactive or assured data provenance, which further guided us to propose the novel cryptographic technique we call editable signatures, which are a building-block for achieving assured data provenance management. Coincidentally, as shown in Section 2, the concept of editable signatures generalizes both multisignatures and aggregate signatures.

7. CONCLUSION

We introduced the novel concept of assured data provenance which, unlike existing passive data provenance approach, aims to "distill" less trustworthy data before they enter into an information network. This concept further guided us to propose a novel cryptographic tool, called editable signatures, which can be adopt to facilitate assured provenance management.

There are many questions for future research. In addition to those mentioned in the body of the paper, here we give more examples. On one hand, it would be very interesting to explore a full-fledged framework for characterizing the concept of assured data provenance. On the other hand, it is interesting to construct full-fledged editable signature schemes that operate in the weakest plain public-key (PPK) model [2] (where so-called "rogue key attack" is allowed) without random oracles. Our first scheme was proven secure in the KOSK model, but we believe that it can be proven secure in the weakest PPK model. However, this scheme is not as efficient as our second scheme, which is nevertheless difficult to be made secure in the PPK model. It is also interesting to construct practical editable signature models in the weaker operational models [17] such as the Proof of Possession (POP) of private key model [18].

Acknowledgements.

Haifeng Qian is partially supported by the National Natural Science General Foundation of China Grant No. 60703004, 60873217 and 61021004, the Research Fund for the Doctoral Program of Higher Education of China Grant No. 20070269005. Shouhuai Xu is supported in part by an AFOSR MURI grant and a State of Texas Emerging Technology Fund grant.

8. REFERENCES

[1] M. Bellare, C. Namprempre, and G. Neven. Unrestricted aggregate signatures. In *In ICALP, 2007.*, pages 9–13. Springer-Verlag, 2006.

[2] M. Bellare and G. Neven. Multisignatures in the plain public-key model and a general forking lemma. In *ACM Conference on Computer and Communications Security (CCS'06)*, pages 390–399, 2006.

[3] O. Benjelloun, A. Sarma, A. Halevy, and J. Widom. Uldbs: Databases with uncertainty and lineage. In *VLDB*, pages 953–964, 2006.

[4] D. Boneh, C. Gentry, B. Lynn, and H. Shacham. Aggregate and verifiably encrypted signatures. In *EUROCRYPT'03*, pages 416–432, 2003.

[5] D. Boneh, B. Lynn, and H. Shacham. Short signatures from the weil pairing. In *Asiacrypt'01*, pages 514–532, 2002.

[6] R. Bose and J. Frew. Lineage retrieval for scientific data processing: a survey. *ACM Comput. Surv.*, 37(1):1–28, 2005.

[7] U. Braun, A. Shinnar, and M. Seltzer. Securing provenance. In *HotSec'08*, 2008.

[8] P. Buneman, S. Khanna, and W. Tan. Why and where: A characterization of data provenance. In *Proceedings of the 8th International Conference on Database Theory (ICDT'01)*, pages 316–330, 2001.

[9] S. Goldwasser, S. Micali, and R. Rivest. A digital signature scheme secure against adaptive chosen-message attacks. *SIAM Journal of Computing*, 17(2).

[10] T. Green, G. Karvounarakis, Z. Ives, and V. Tannen. Update exchange with mappings and provenance. In *VLDB*, 2007.

[11] T. Green, G. Karvounarakis, N. Taylor, O. Biton, Z. Ives, and V. Tannen. Orchestra: facilitating collaborative data sharing. In *SIGMOD'07*, pages 1131–1133, 2007.

[12] R. Hasan, R. Sion, and M. Winslett. The case of the fake picasso: preventing history forgery with secure provenance. In *Proccedings of the 7th conference on File and storage technologies (FAST'09)*, pages 1–14, 2009.

[13] K. Itakura and K. Nakamura. A public key cryptosystem suitable for digital multisignatures. *NEC Research & Development*, 71:1–8, 1983.

[14] J. Lyle and A. Martin. Trusted computing and provenance: Better together. In *Proceedings of 2nd USENIX Workshop on the Theory and Practice of Provenance (TaPP'10)*, 2010.

[15] A. Lysyanskaya, S. Micali, L. Reyzin, and H. Shacham. Sequential aggregate signatures from trapdoor permutations. In *EUROCRYPT*, pages 74–90, 2004.

[16] G. Neven. Efficient sequential aggregate signed data. In *EUROCRYPT*, pages 52–69, 2008.

[17] H. Qian and S. Xu. Non-interactive multisignatures in the plain public-key model with efficient verification. *Inf. Process. Lett.*, 111(2):82–89, 2010.

[18] T. Ristenpart and S. Yilek. The power of proofs-of-possession: Securing multiparty signatures against rogue-key attacks. In *EUROCRYPT*, pages 228–245, 2007.

[19] W. Tan. Provenance in databases: Past, current, and future. *IEEE Data Eng. Bull.*, 30(4):3–12, 2007.

[20] N. Taylor and Z. Ives. Reconciling while tolerating disagreement in collaborative data sharing. In *SIGMOD'06*, pages 13–24, 2006.

[21] B. Waters. Efficient identity-based encryption without random oracles. In *EUROCRYPT'05*, pages 114–127.

[22] S. Xu, H. Qian, F. Wang, Z. Zhan, E. Bertino, and R. Sandhu. Trustworthy information: Concepts and mechanisms. In *Proceedings of 11th International Conference Web-Age Information Management (WAIM'10)*, pages 398–404, 2010.

[23] S. Xu, R. Sandhu, and E. Bertino. Tiupam: A framework for trustworthiness-centric information sharing. In *Proc. 2009 IFIP Trust Management Conference (TM'09)*, 2009.

[24] J. Zhang, A. Chapman, and K. Lefevre. Do you know where your data's been? — tamper-evident database provenance. In *Proceedings of the 6th VLDB Workshop on Secure Data Management (SDM'09)*, pages 17–32, 2009.

Identifying a Critical Threat to Privacy through Automatic Image Classification[*]

David Lorenzi
Rutgers University
1 Washington Park
Newark, NJ 07102
dlorenzi@cimic.rutgers.edu

Jaideep Vaidya
Rutgers University
1 Washington Park
Newark, NJ 07102
jsvaidya@business.rutgers.edu

ABSTRACT

Image classification, in general, is considered a hard problem, though it is necessary for many useful applications such as automatic target recognition. Indeed, no general methods exist that can work in varying scenarios and still achieve good performance across the board. In this paper, we actually identify a very interesting problem, where image classification is dangerously easy. We look at the problem of image classification, in the specific context of accurately classifying images containing highly sensitive data such as drivers licenses, credit cards and passports. Our key contribution is to build a Hierarchical Temporal Memory (HTM) network that is able to classify many sensitive images with over 90% accuracy, and use this to develop a system to automatically derive and transcribe sensitive information from image data. Our system classifies images into two groups – sensitive and non-sensitive. The group of sensitive images can then be further analyzed. This is a real world security issue that could easily lead to privacy problems such as identity theft, since scans of passports and drivers licenses are routinely emailed or kept in digital form, and many local documents are left unencrypted. Essentially, an attacker can use data mining and machine learning techniques very effectively to breach individual privacy. Thus, our main contribution is to demonstrate the efficacy of image classification for deriving sensitive information, which could also serve as a guide for other interesting applications such as document detection and analysis. Thus, it also serves as a warning against leaving data unencrypted and again proves that security through obscurity is simply not enough.

Categories and Subject Descriptors

I.4.8 [**Image Processing and Computer Vision**]: Scene Analysis—*Object Recognition*; K.4.4 [**Computers and Society**]: Electronic Commerce—*security*; I.5.1 [**Pattern Recognition**]: Models—*Neural nets*

---

[*]This work is supported in part by the National Science Foundation under Grant No. CNS-0746943.

General Terms

Security

Keywords

Privacy, Image Classification, Neural Networks

1. INTRODUCTION

Image classification, in its various forms, has a wide variety of useful applications. For example, automatic target recognition[2] can be considered one of the most sought after military goals in image exploitation. However, no general methods exist that can work in varying scenarios and still achieve good performance - for target recognition, this is due to the ambiguity in defining "target". Even in general, image classification can easily be considered to be a hard problem. Therefore, a lot of research has been done to achieve good performance on specific applications, and in limited contexts[9]. In this paper, we actually identify a very interesting sub-problem for which image classification turns out to be dangerously easy. This is interesting since in general, the fact that classification works well is a cause for celebration. However, in this particular case, this fact can be used in a rather destructive fashion. Specifically, the application we consider is that of accurately classifying images containing highly sensitive data such as drivers licenses, credit cards, and passports. From the perspective of an attacker, being able to accurately classify and extract data from such images could easily enable fraud such as identity theft, or even worse. Thus, a vast potential for a breach of privacy exists through this route.

One may question, whether this problem is real. However, this can be easily demonstrated from the following scenario of email interception / trojan attack. The ubiquity of email cannot be disputed today. Almost everyone has access to some form of email, either through their work, school, or even free email accounts widely available on the web. Data privacy becomes an important issue when personal data is routinely disclosed via email. People take the information they are sending to each other through email for granted, because most casual users of computers and email are ignorant of computer security issues. It is not difficult for an unscrupulous individual to intercept unencrypted email messages and read them, nor is it difficult to gain access to someone's inbox and comb through it, garnering sensitive information in the process. Even if you consider such interception to be difficult, more worryingly, in many cases, individuals now scan and send digital copies of documents (as TIFF images) to their colleagues or to officials. It is quite easy for people to become victims of trojan horse programs that are emailed to them. If an unscrupulous individual crafts an email mimicking the traits of a legitimate email and tricks the user into running a file that compromises their computer, the attacker now gets complete freedom of access, and is able to scan the local hard disk or other media for the sensitive images stored on it. Though this may be like searching for a needle in a haystack, when, as this paper shows, accurate and efficient detection and classification techniques exist, this becomes a huge problem. Other possible attack channels also include social networking and public file sharing (e.g., imageshack) websites, since sensitive images could automatically be shared without the user's knowledge.

Indeed, our main contribution in this paper is the observation that an attacker can apply data mining and machine learning techniques to detect and acquire sensitive data from images. This is a real world security issue, and shows that security through obscurity is simply not enough. In fact, we build a Hierarchical Temporal Memory (HTM) network that is able to classify many sensitive images with over 90% accuracy, and use this to develop a system to automatically derive sensitive information from image data. While the primary focus is on the ability to detect and classify images, not much more additional work is necessary for the attacker to derive sensitive textual information.

As stated above, the main classification technique used are Hierarchical Temporal Memory (HTM) Networks – a type of neural networks that are built according to biology and are well suited to image classification tasks. Our trained HTM network is able to classify many sensitive images with over 90% accuracy. As such, we identify a critical security and privacy problem since scanned images of driver's licenses and government issued passports can be picked up via the HTM, and the data contained within the image can be read and converted into textual form with an Optical Character Recognition program, ready to be cataloged in a database. While the paper primarily focuses on a proposed "attack" on a workstation using the trained HTM, we also discuss the security issues involved with an adversary using variations on the proposed method to attack on local computer systems, file servers, or the attacker building an identity theft network via trojan horses and botnets.

Thus, our contribution is two-fold. First, our system demonstrates the efficacy of image classification for deriving sensitive information, which could also serve as a guide for other interesting applications such as document detection and analysis. Secondly, it serves as a warning against unencrypted data and again proves that security through obscurity is simply not sufficient. The rest of the paper is organized as follows. Section 2 discusses Hierarchical Temporal Memory Networks, since the paper actively uses this technique. Section 3 looks at the related work. Section 4 presents the overall attack system that would be used by the attacker, and discusses the possible variants. Section 5 examines the actual images of interest, and looks at possible strong and weak features for identification. Section 6 presents the experimental analysis of the system. Finally, Section 7 concludes the paper and looks at future work.

2. PRELIMINARIES

In this section, we first discuss what are Hierarchical Tem-

poral Memory (HTM) Networks[7], then present the Numenta Toolkit[11], which is a freely available implementation that we use for building the actual network.

2.1 Numenta HTM's and Image Recognition

Since our problem is to differentiate between "sensitive" images and "non-sensitive" images, this can be considered as a standard classification problem. As such, once we decide how to generate / extract features from the underlying images, we could easily utilize any of the standard classification algorithms such as decision trees or k-nearest neighbor classification, etc. Indeed, since neural networks are also one of the most used techniques for this process[16, 4], these are quite suitable for our purpose as well.

In our case, we are particularly interested in the ability to generate a classifier that works like a human brain, for the express purpose of distinguishing certain types of images from each other. The recently developed Hierarchical Temporal Memory (HTM) actually fits the bill quite well. HTM networks are actually a type of neural network that try to approximate the vision cortex. The formalized mathematical model underlying this is based on the Memory-Prediction framework[10] developed by Jeff Hawkins.

An HTM network created for vision tasks is identical to the high level structure of a mammalian visual cortex. The network receives an image as input, performs a set of preprocessing operations on it, and passes the result through multiple levels of processing. As the image passes through each level, the HTM builds successively more abstract hierarchical representations, with the highest level representing global image properties and shape. These various levels of representations allow the network to be invariant to small changes in the input and increase the robustness of the system overall. For categorization tasks, these high-level representations are fed through a supervised classifier at the top of the network. The overall system performs static inference, that is, there is a single upward pass through the hierarchy. For example, Figure 1 shows an example HTM network for vision. The sensor (bottom level) receives the image, which is processed by the levels above. The selected node at level 4 (green) receives input from the blue nodes below it.

The Numenta Toolkit implements the HTM idea and makes it freely available for academic research. Therefore, we use this implementation, though other implementations could equally easily be used. However, unlike a full-fledged HTM network, the academic version used here for vision tasks has no feedback connections, temporal inference, or attention mechanisms. The version of the vision toolkit used in the experiments discussed in the paper operates on 200x200 pixel grayscale images. Larger images are down sampled to this resolution and converted to grayscale before they are fed into the HTM for classification, categorization etc. [11].

The structure of the hierarchy is very important in the case of recognizing "sensitive" images like passports and drivers licenses, and as such, lends itself to accomplishing the task of image recognition very well. For our task, we are looking for image data that is very regular in its structure, that is, it follows a set of rules/guidelines for its structure and does not deviate much from the prescribed format between instances. For example, a U.S. passport has a head and shoulders picture of the individual it belongs to on the upper left side, a machine readable code that is two lines long that extends the length of the bottom of the passport, and

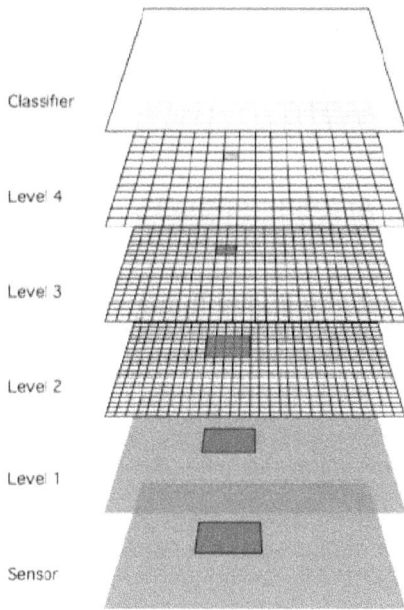

Figure 1: Example HTM Network for vision

a block of text containing the individual's information that is left justified bordering the headshot photograph. These are features that are inherent to all passports and vary negligibly between individual passports. Where the input data varies between images, things like: the textual data itself, personal facial features, different state seals etc. play a role in making the image unique, but do not affect the global structure of the image in a meaningful way. Due to this, the image can still be positively identified as a driver's license or a passport with a high degree of accuracy and few false positives.

2.2 HTM Network Implementation and Training

The HTM is useless to us unless we give it image data to train and test on, in order to understand how it is learning and to test if what we are teaching it is being used in an effective/efficient manner. Without restating the entire paper dedicated to the design and operation of HTM's, we need to understand the course that the input takes to generate the output.

The process of training an HTM model with spatio-temporal data is the process of knowing the state of the coincidence patterns and Markov-chains in each node at every level of the hierarchy. Although algorithms of varying levels of sophistication can be used to learn the states of an HTM node, the basic process can be understood using two operations, the first being memorization of coincidence patterns, and the second being a learning of a mixture of Markov chains over the space of coincidence patterns[7]. In the case of a simplified generative model, an HTM node remembers all the coincidence patterns that are generated by the generative model. In real world cases, where it is not possible to store all coincidences encountered during learning, storing a fixed number of a random selection of the coincidence patterns is sufficient as long as multiple coincidence patterns are allowed to be active at the same time[7].

The coincidence patterns enable the image identification algorithm to account for the inherent differences between each unique image, while still classifying it correctly. A 4 layer network, as shown in Figure 1 is sufficient for most image classification tasks, and additional layers do not significantly improve the classification[11]. The HTM networks are trained in a level-by-level manner, starting with the coincidence patterns and Markov chains at the first level and then moving up the hierarchy.

The specific network used is specialized to grayscale images. In this network, the first level of coincidences are replaced with Gabor filters of different orientations. At all levels, the coincidence patterns were restricted to have spatial receptive fields smaller than that of the Markov chains. In our paper, we build upon this replacement network, utilizing it to process images of driver's licenses, passports and any other images of interest we train for (e.g credit cards, student id's, social security cards) and discern them from other common images. This downward resolution resampling turns out to be helpful when processing a variety of images from different sources for the fact that no matter what resolution the image is fed into the model at, it will be shrunk down to a standardized size and then grayscaled by the preprocessor.

3. RELATED WORK

Within image classification, automatic target recognition[2] has been well studied over many years. Neural networks for automated target recognition have been experimented with for quite a while[14]. Different conceptual ideas we see implemented in one form or another in the HTM for vision tasks can be found in other papers published, like a coarse-to-fine strategy for multiclass shape detection[1], or using a Bayesian based hierarchical approach for target recognition[15]. As of late we have seen work specifically in the area of unsupervised learning of invariant feature hierarchies with applications to object recognition[13], and finally even direct work with HTM's via Content-based image retrieval of architectural drawings[3, 5]. One point that we would like to emphasize is the blending of disciplines involved in the formulation of the process proposed in this paper. We demonstrate the combination of techniques and research from a multitude of areas of study, especially in the areas of computer vision, image processing and machine learning. The paper also borrows ideas and concepts from the computer security community, using classifiers in intrusion detection systems for wireless networks[17] and using neural networks to detect system anomalies and system abuse[8]. Essentially, this paper really highlights the security issues inherent in digitizing personal information, specifically from the image processing sense, and shows how the power of classifiers can be utilized in a destructive way to breach privacy and security. We believe that this particular application of classifiers to security issues is a unique and original contribution to each of the communities respectively, and worthy of exploring as a legitimate new security threat.

4. ATTACK SYSTEM & EXPERIMENTAL DATA

Several types of image data can actually have sensitive personal information. As such, a wide variety of data was chosen to test the capabilities of HTM based neural networks, such as social security cards, passports, drivers' licenses, student IDs, and credit cards. These were selected due to the high probability that they would be stored on a computer in some form, as either strings of text, or as a scan in an image file. Disturbingly enough, a majority of this data has become searchable online, and all datasets for the experiments in this paper were garnered and compiled from a Microsoft Bing image search. As such, this paper also further illustrates the lack of importance people place on information security and ease of theft and resulting abuse that exists with this type of data.

4.1 Attack Algorithm Overview

The proposed attack begins with training and testing HTM neural networks to seek out and positively identify "sensitive images". These networks operate in a binary manner, determining whether a particular image can be classified as an instance of a particular type of "sensitive" image. Figure 2 gives an overview of the entire attack timeline. We discuss the details below.

4.1.1 Pre-Attack

The pre-attack phase consists of building the HTM networks for the types of data that are to be discovered and identified on the target machine. This requires the attacker to find training and testing images of the requisite type, then using them to build the relevant HTM network. The attacker must then package the HTM networks together, as each of these networks must run in parallel, because each image on the victim's machine needs to be run through each type of HTM to determine if it meets the specified criterion. The complete HTM Networks themselves are very small in size, approximately 2MB each. If an attacker was to launch the attack described in the paper, it would be approximately 10MB worth of data (for the 5 classification networks), as well as the space required for the actual classifier itself (which may vary based on how stripped down it is).

4.1.2 Attack

The attack phase begins with a gathering of images by a regex expression in a script or batch file that simply fetches each of a relevant type of image file format (e.g *.gif or *.jpg). These images are then fed into the HTM networks and processed. Positive hits are identified and pulled. Repeat these steps until every type of image file format desired has been searched or until the information desired is acquired.

When the attack is initiated, the attacker might want to run the HTM network with both the highest number of predicted total hits and probability of hits first. However, as positive identifications are made, the sample space of potential images shrinks accordingly. There exists the fact that images which are false positives of one group could in fact be an instance of another sensitive image category that are now removed from the sample space. If this is an issue, the attacker can simply rerun every image mutually exclusive of the outcomes from a particular HTM network and have no "filter down heuristic" running. If intrusion detection systems are not expected to be encountered, running the HTM's mutually exclusive will produce the most information, but result in the greatest use of system resources. The HTM's and regex expressions can be modified so as to

not trigger some types of intrusion detection systems that monitor CPU cycle use, memory usage, and disk I/O usage, by throttling the number of images the HTM is processing, or limiting the scope of the image search. The Trojan can even go so far as to attempt to fake a valid signature certificate signature to fool the operating system into thinking it is a legitimate signed process, if the process is not entirely stealth from the beginning. It is up to the attacker to determine this information and adjust accordingly before implementing the attack.

4.1.3 Post Processing & Database Creation

In the post processing step, an optical character recognition (OCR) program can be used to improve accuracy. The OCR program can translate the data garnered into text strings, and place them into a database, along with the original image from which they were extracted. For example, if an image of a credit card is targeted by the HTM, and is then found on the target system and selected for export to the OCR program, the number from the card can then be translated from the image into a text string and stored in a database along with the person's name on the card and any other relevant data needed to use the card. All of this can be done with off the shelf, open source programs that are widely available to the public for Windows or Unix.

4.2 Scope: Wide Area Attack vs. Personalized Attack

The type and style of attack on the target depends on how much prior knowledge the attacker has while compiling the attack package. For example, if the attacker knows his target is one person with an image of a passport on his computer, he can tailor the HTM package and the wordlists to only go after passport images and word search for passports. This makes the attack stealthier because the delivery package is smaller in terms of bytes and utilizes less system resources than a larger more generalized attack looking for more types of data. It also greatly decreases the time required for a successful attack, as fewer classifiers need to run.

On the other hand, attacking large, centralized stores of personal information can prove more fruitful for the attacker, as attacking something like a DMV would provide not only an implicit guarantee of "sensitive data" e.g. drivers license number, but also potentially other relevant information about the subject (age, sex, eye color, hair color, home address, etc) at which point an identity thief could begin scanning social networks for enough information to build an accurate personal profile and steal your identity. A company's HR database is also a prime target for attack, as it contains important information such as SSN's, bank account numbers (if the individual has direct deposit), home address, salary earned(only target employees' with a high salary), at which point the attacker has enough information to scan social networks for pictures of the individual, create a false driver's license with the attackers face allowing them to execute identity theft.

The true danger lies in that an attacker only needs certain pieces of the puzzle to be able to make highly probable guesses and/or turn to the Internet's social networks to flesh out the remaining information.

4.3 Styles of Attack

There are many methods by which an attacker could pack-

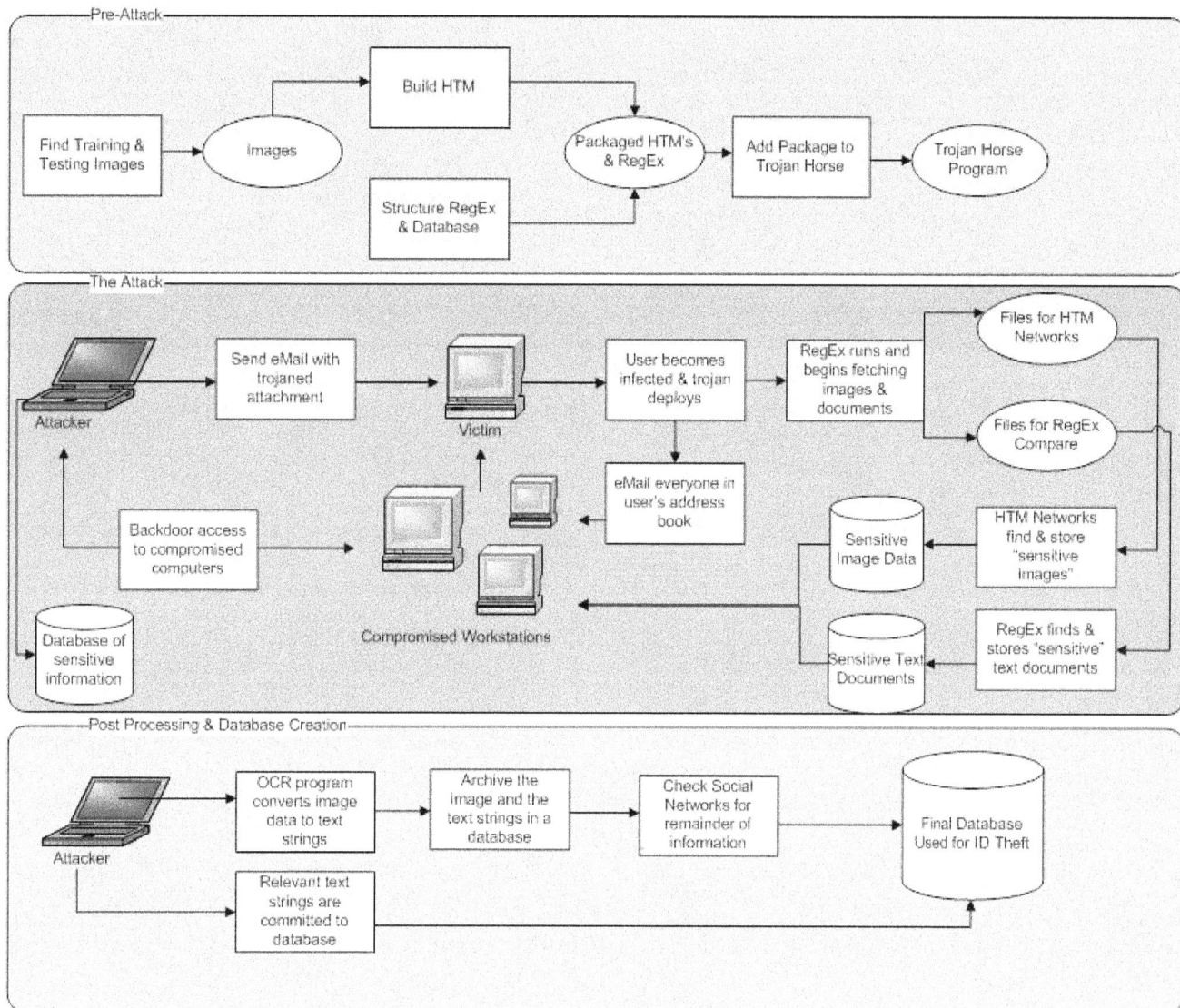

Figure 2: Flowchart for attack with HTM Networks

age and deploy these programs to garner information. One possibility, as described earlier, involves a Trojan horse program, in which a user downloads and runs a false program that actually contains the expressions and HTM's that run under the cover of the process of the fake program. This is the most effective method, because once a machine is successfully compromised, it is not much more work to install a backdoor at which point the machine can be added to a global botnet where its system resources can be utilized and commanded from a centralized attack server. The other advantage to this method is each of the other infected computers can act as intermediary drops points for the sensitive information, so that the loss of any one machine does not affect the ID theft network as a whole. This also helps to avoid the traditional centralized drop off server, which would be a target for other identity thieves as well as law enforcement and perhaps even some of the more sophisticated users that could backtrack from an infection. The best and most traditional method of distribution is via email using links to

redirect someone to a compromised site or embedding the trojan in some form of attachment (word processor document, spreadsheet, etc).

The Trojan can then have a worm component and begin emailing everyone in the infected machine's address book an infected file at which point they are added to the botnet and their machine is scanned for sensitive images. This attack very similar to other older, more traditional Trojan/worm combinations, however now the attacker has "intelligent agents" (the HTM's & regex) acting on his behalf to find sensitive information instead of having to comb through datafiles/images manually. This is essentially a sophisticated automation of such an attack, essentially a "fire and forget" Trojan. It is really up to the attacker to determine the best infection vectors, as these will be adapted according to the target and the constraints of the systems. The attacker can then periodically check the drop-off points for information to complete a profile for an identity theft.

161

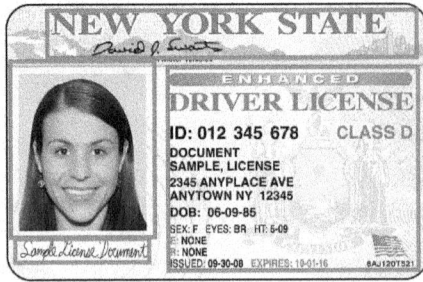

Figure 3: "Strong Features" of NY Drivers License

Figure 4: "Weak Features" of NY Drivers License

5. IMAGES OF INTEREST

We now examine the specific types of images of interest, from which sensitive information can be extracted. We discuss possible features of interest that might be useful in accurately classifying such images, though the HTM network may actually be finding and using other features. First, we look at Drivers licenses, followed by U.S. Passports. Other data types will also be discussed, though not at length, since it would be relatively redundant.

5.1 Drivers License

We first train HTMs to detect images of drivers' licenses. Both real and fake images are used to train and test the HTM's for the attack methods for finding and identifying "sensitive" images described earlier in the paper. There are two primary reasons for this. First, while the original goal was to use U.S. passports for the experiments, it was challenging to find a sufficient number of images of real passports for training and testing. Currently, there are simply not enough scans of passports available on the web, whereas there are plenty of scans and mockups of drivers licenses images that are freely available for gathering off of your search engine of choice. Additionally, it is more challenging to build a good classifier for classifying drivers licenses, since these show a wide degree of variability across states (each state has its own format for a drivers license). On the other hand, since the US Passport has a fixed format (and does not vary by state), it should be easier to detect it.

Privacy is also a concern when conducting experiments such as these that deal with sensitive data, so only images that were indexed in a search engine were considered for use. Microsoft's Bing search engine was used to gather the sets of drivers license images used in the training and testing of the HTM's for image recognition in our experiments. We now give examples of the strong and weak features typically found in the average drivers' license in the United States, using a new proposed drivers license to demonstrate these features.

5.1.1 Strong Features of Drivers License

In Figure 3, we see prominent features in a regular pattern that can easily be picked up by edge detection algorithms or other image recognition filters. The left justified headshot along with a handwritten signature make up the prominent left side features with the personal information left justified a few millimeters away from the headshot. The personal information is in a regular typeface that can be easily read by an OCR program and takes up a majority of the space of the license. In the lower right hand corner there is a promi-

nently featured American flag with some typeface characters underneath. Finally at the top the name of the state is in large font that can be OCR'ed. This image is meant to demonstrate traits that are common amongst all drivers licenses that will be picked up by the HTM when the image is processed.

5.1.2 Weak Features of Drivers License

This particular drivers license is very advanced from an anti-counterfeiting perspective, and thus, scanning it with an edge detection algorithm or applying a filter to it can yield some interesting results. Figure 4 shows some of the "weak features" of the drivers license. There are concentric ring designs that intersect with headshot picture on the left side of the license. There is a large state symbol watermark that features text and bold edges. There is a strong possibility that an OCR may pick up on the watermark text, depending on the thresholds set for detection upon scanning of the image. There is also very small "New York" printed repeatedly along the top length of the license, again perhaps causing some OCR programs some grief (although, the garbage text could easily be filtered out with some extra work). However, none of these features will hinder overall detection by the HTM (due to the hierarchy and the Gabor filter), but it will make the extraction of data step more difficult, and perhaps produce some foiled attempts when large scale image dumps are scanned and individual licenses cannot be checked by the attacker.

5.2 United States Passport

We are not concerned with all of the information on the passport, merely its "defining features"; more specifically, we are just concerned with identifying whether or not the image we are looking at is a U.S. passport based on these features.

5.2.1 Strong Features of U.S. Passport

Figure 5 illustrates these "strong features". The term "strong features" is used because these are the objects that will most likely be picked up by any edge detection algorithm. These features include the "unique" information of the individual's passport, the machine readable code at the bottom of the page, the facial features of the person, the three red nautical stars on the left edge of the photograph, and the letters printed at the top of the page. Most font typefaces are regular in their structure and edges, so it is easy to detect them and use optical character recognition methods to translate them from an image to textual data. Another important distinction is the location and layout of the passport. Specific information will always be in the same

Figure 5: "Strong Features" of U.S. Passport

Figure 6: Background Pattern of U.S. Passport

location, so looking for it is relatively easy and systematic, however, it can become difficult based on the number of pixels in the scanned image (e.g. the image resolution may be higher or lower).

5.2.2 U.S. Passport Background Pattern

The background pattern (shown in Figure 6) consists of a mesh of hexagons with five circles for edges, filled with 13 five sided stars and a diagonal line pattern. The red hexagons have lines slanting to the left, the blue hexagons have lines slanting to the right, and the white hexagons have lines slanting left. Some of the red hexagons will become a blend of red and blue toward the middle of the document, but the same rules as normal red hexagons apply. This pattern is a blend of strong and weak features.

5.2.3 Weak Features of U.S. Passport

The term "weak features" refers to features that are present in the passport, but are not as bold or straightforward as

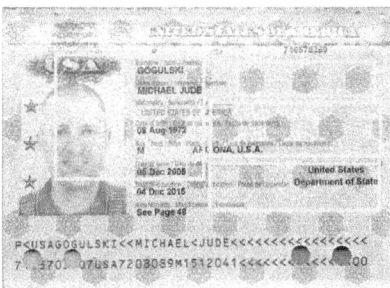

Figure 7: "Weak Features" of U.S. Passport

the strong features. These features are mainly designed to prevent counterfeiting, tampering, and alterations to the documents. The U.S. State department put these features into the document deliberately, and in our case, they do cause some interference with the strong features, making it more difficult to identify and extract the features of interest. These designs are very minute and intricate. For example, the blue waves placed over the image of the individual on the passport, obscuring the facial features and breaking up the lines of the face. The watermark of an eagle surrounded by a wreath of stars that overlaps the unique personal data and the image of the face, as well as the watermark wavy texts stating "The United States of America" and the three "seals" in the center right of the document. Our goal is to be able to stratify the strong features from the weak features, because both are vital for positive identification, yet both can interfere with the detection of each other. This can be achieved via image processing techniques, as discussed later.

6. EXPERIMENTAL ANALYSIS

We now discuss the specific experiments conducted to create and evaluate the classifier. As discussed earlier, while any image classification algorithm could be used, we actually train a neural network for classification. In specific, we use the Numenta software[1] to train a HTM Network for vision tasks designed to sort images into one of two bins, either sensitive images (bin1) or not sensitive images (bin2). The goal was to see at what point, in terms of number of training and testing images required, we could feasibly sort between the two with around 90% rate of success. Four experimental groups were created and named accordingly. As a control, the images from the experiment "puppies" included in the Vision Toolkit by Numenta were used to represent non-drivers license pictures in all four experiments. The images that were contained in the control group feature pictures such as that of landscapes and family photos, typical of common images found on users' systems.

6.1 Experimental Images

The images that were used to conduct these experiments are categorized into different groups based on what type of information is contained in the image. The groups are: documents with plain text, pure pictures, documents with pictures and plain text. Samples of these are shown in Figure 8. The networks were trained and tested by splitting the images into 4 groups, testing and training of drivers licenses, and testing and training of not drivers licenses. The drivers license group consists of documents with pictures and plain text, consistent with the layout and composition of a drivers license. The not drivers license group features pure images, containing no text of any kind, only objects, people or landscapes. The same experimental structure is used for all subsequent data styles (credit cards, social security cards, student ID's, passports). The deliberate focus on drivers' licenses is due to the fact that they have the highest rate of success amongst all the data types, and serve as a great example of structured images and textual data.

In each experiment, they were split 50/50 at random into training and testing groups from 1 large group of 197 images, with the extra image always going to the training group. The

---

[1]Numenta can be downloaded from http://www.numenta.com/vision/vision-toolkit.php.

Figure 8: Sample Images

(a) Image with Text

(b) Pure Image – Family Vacation

(c) Pure Image – Landscape

images used in the experiments were pulled from a common web search for drivers licenses. This is important for the fact that the pool of images contains drivers license from many different states, and some of the images are completely computer generated, while others are scans of real drivers licenses or are fake licenses altogether. The image quality, file format, compression algorithm used on the image, and pixel count varies wildly between each license. This is a benefit as it is indicative of real world possibilities encountered when searching for potential scans of "sensitive" information. There is no guarantee that it will be in a specific format or size. The specific details for each of the four datasets are given in Table 1 [2].

6.2 HTM Training and Test Results

Figures 9-12 shows the results from the experimental trials of each group of images. Each of the four sets was run through 4 tests, one train & test which trains the network on the training images, and then checks its accuracy on the test images. This was performed again with the training options turned on, these options include additional training to handle shifts, size changes, mirroring, and small rotations. Finally, two optimization runs were conducted, one with the training options on and one with the training options off. Optimization finds the best set of parameters for the network based on the features found in training images, and then tests the optimized network on the test images for accuracy. Table 2 gives the detailed set of system parameters used in each different run. The same set of parameters are used in each corresponding run over the different datasets. The networks were created by an Intel Core 2 Duo 2.26Ghz with 4 gigabytes of memory, and the times involved in creating each network are included in the tables.

---

[2] The actual compiled datasets can be found at http://cimic.rutgers.edu/~dlorenzi.

Table 1: Datasets(# of img in each category)

(a) Drivers License Image Data

Group	Category	Training	Testing
DL25	Drivers License	25	25
	Not Drivers License	99	98
DL50	Drivers License	50	50
	Not Drivers License	99	98
DL75	Drivers License	75	75
	Not Drivers License	99	98
DL100	Drivers License	100	100
	Not Drivers License	99	98

(b) Credit Card Image Data

Group	Category	Training	Testing
CC25	Credit Card	25	25
	Not Credit Card	99	98
CC50	Credit Card	50	50
	Not Credit Card	99	98
CC75	Credit Card	75	75
	Not Credit Card	99	98
CC100	Credit Card	100	100
	Not Credit Card	99	98

(c) Student ID Image Data

Group	Category	Training	Testing
SID25	Student ID	25	25
	Not Student ID	99	98
SID50	Student ID	50	50
	Not Student ID	99	98
SID75	Student ID	75	75
	Not Student ID	99	98
SID100	Student ID	100	100
	Not Student ID	99	98

(d) Social Security Card Image Data

Group	Category	Training	Testing
SSN25	Social Security Card	25	25
	Not Social Security Card	99	98

(e) Passport Image Data

Group	Category	Training	Testing
PP25	Passport	25	25
	Not Passport	99	98

6.3 Results Analysis

As discussed above, each experiment was performed with a set number of experimental images along with a control group of 197 images. Each experimental image block was run 4 times, with a train and test run followed by a train and test run with parameterization of the training set. The networks were then subsequently optimized based on standard optimization, and concluded with an optimization that took account for the parameterization of the experimental images (shift, size changes, mirroring, and small rotations). The number of images was increased by 25 each time, up to a maximum of 100, to see what detection rate could be achieved. The goal was to find a relative minimum number of images for this task to reliably detect and identify our "sensitive" image of interest. This is important for an adversary, as it makes it easier to target images of interest without

Figure 9: Drivers Licenses

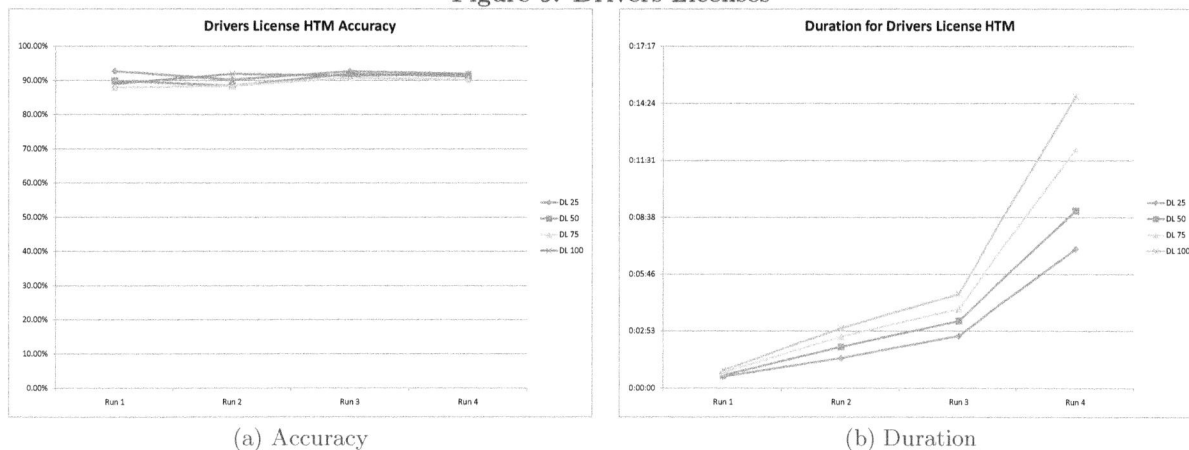

(a) Accuracy

(b) Duration

Figure 10: Credit Cards

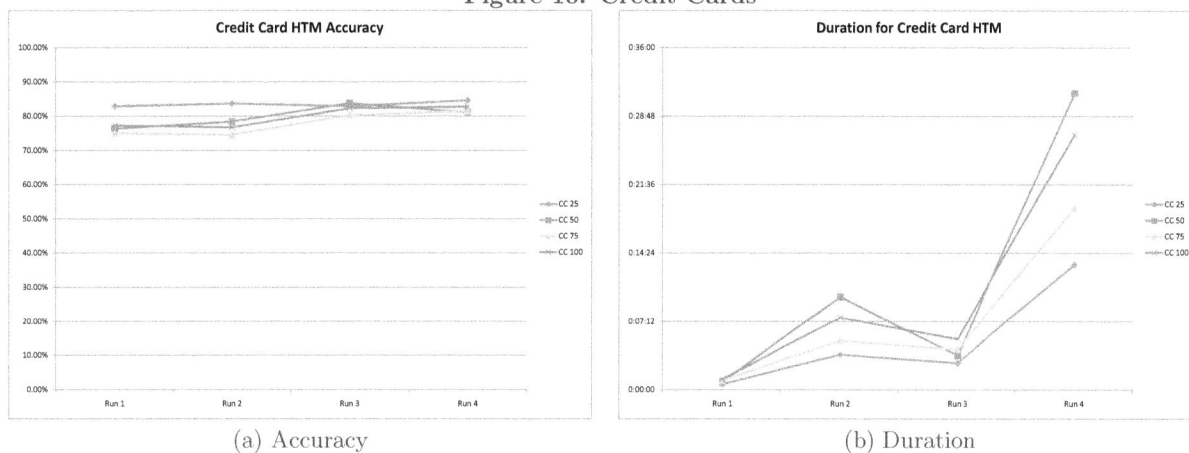

(a) Accuracy

(b) Duration

Table 2: System Parameters for Experimental Runs

	Run 1	Run 2	Run 3	Run 4
Action	Train and Test	Train and Test	Optimize	Optimize
Shift	n	y	n	y
Size Changes	n	y	n	y
Mirroring	n	y	n	y
Small Rotations	n	y	n	y

needing an overly large sample size of images to train the HTM as well as cutting down on the training time required for a high degree of positive identifications.

The data demonstrates that when you train the network to look for more subtle things like shifts, size changes, mirroring and small rotations, accuracy is sacrificed due to the additional requirements placed on the network, making it more difficult for a positive identification to occur. However, given a larger sample size, scanning for these nuances will aid in network robustness. It is also useful in gaining accuracy when you have numerous images of the same "ob-ject" from multiple angles and in varying sizes. However, in the case of our experiment, optimizing would seem to be more of a hindrance to improving accuracy due to the large variance among our image data, as the results demonstrate no particular trend towards improvement.

For an attacker, in cases where the total number of images scanned by the network is small, it is better to have false positives turn up in the list of image hits, because a quick visual confirmation of the image will determine if it contains sensitive information that has been obfuscated by anti-counterfeiting techniques implemented in the image or if it is an image of no value.

It is worth spending some time discussing the Gabor filter[6], as it does play an important role in image recognition. A Gabor filter is a linear filter used in image processing for edge detection[12]. Its impulse response is defined by a harmonic function multiplied by a Gaussian function. Because of the multiplication-convolution property (Convolution theorem), the Fourier transform of a Gabor filter's impulse response is the convolution of the Fourier transform of the harmonic function and the Fourier transform of the Gaussian function. Usually Gabor filters are used to detected edges at specific angles, i.e. a 90 degree filter will pick up all edges that run at that angle. A number of these

Figure 11: Students IDs

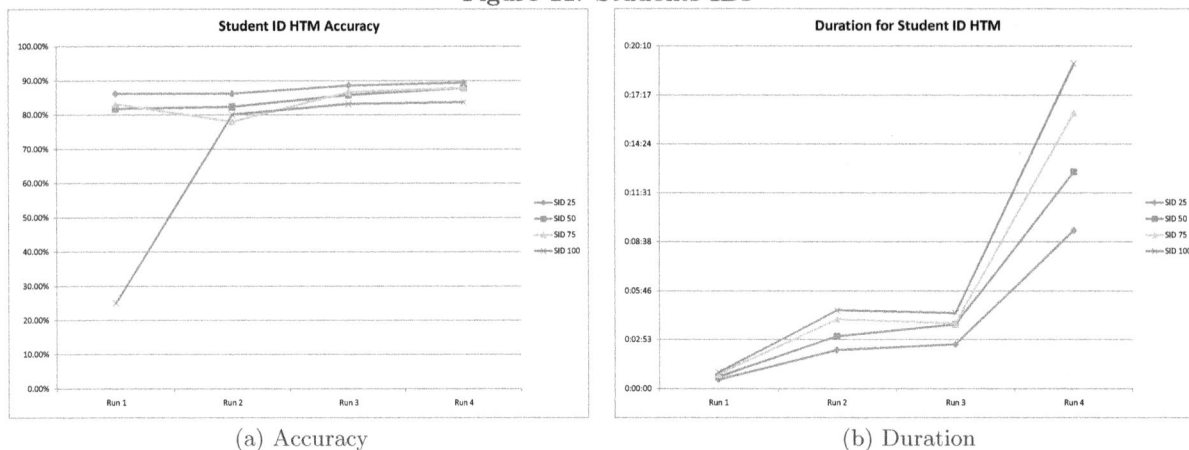

(a) Accuracy

(b) Duration

Figure 12: Passports and Social Security Cards

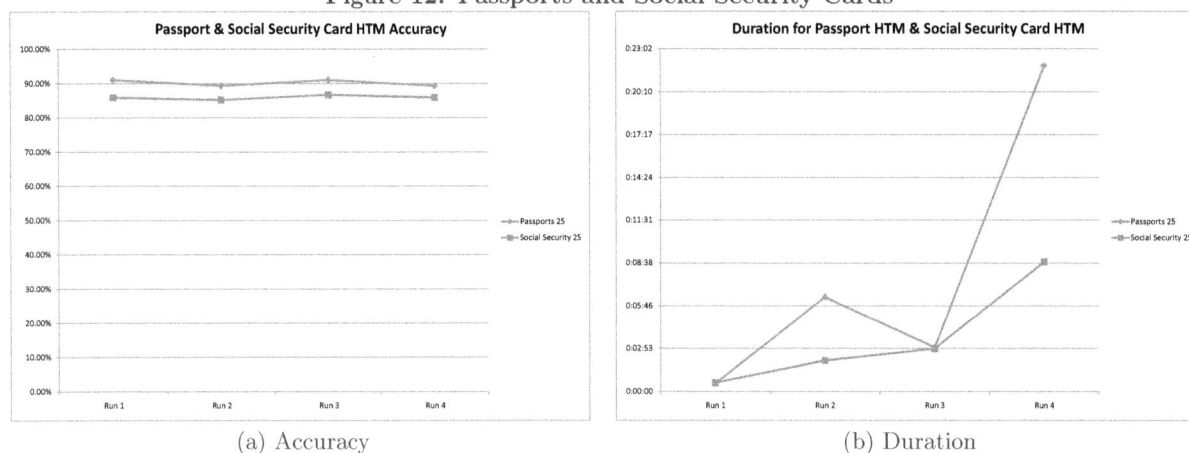

(a) Accuracy

(b) Duration

filters are created for different angles and each generates an image. Then resulting images are then put back together and closely represent the original image that was processed with the filters. While Numenta doesn't tell us what degree filters they use in their Vision Toolkit as it is proprietary software and they want to keep their trade techniques secret, they do tell you that the first level of coincidences in the HTM model are replaced with Gabor filters of different orientations. As the general global image properties migrate to the upper levels of the HTM, the model is built, and can handle the differences between each license while still being able to tell that it is a license.

The image data itself is worth discussing, due to the nature of the applications of sensitive personal data and the societal and personal costs involved with sensitive information disclosure. As a consequence of this, the image data used in the experiments to train these networks is of what could generally be considered low-grade images. Most of the image data is extremely heterogeneous, and as a consequence of this lack of standardization amongst the training data is a significantly more difficult to train network, because there are not as many common traits for the HTM to focus on. If legitimate scans of real drivers licenses were gathered and a "lossless" (one that does not produce artifacts when the im-

age is compressed) image file format was used to store these images, results in terms of accuracy would increase by a sizable margin. However, some of the robustness of the system comes from the generation of a generalized model. There is always a trade-off between accurate, specific models designed to capture one type of sensitive image and a generalized model that can grab many types of images. However, it is worth noting that approximately 85 to 90% accuracy can be achieved with this classifier. This serves to validate the fact that image classification algorithms are very effective at identifying such sensitive images. Since the emphasis of this paper was not really on creating new classification algorithms, and given that we have already achieved extremely good results, we did not go ahead and test the system with other classifiers. Based on our observations, we do expect that a focused attacker could achieve even better performance and that this is a very real significant threat.

One may ask at this point, that given this problem, is there any way of foiling such attacks. The HTM system proposed in this paper has a few weaknesses that can easily be exploited to foil the detection algorithm. Encrypting the files themselves or storing them in an encrypted container is the strongest and best security assurance that you can have against this type of attack. If the HTM (or indeed any other classifier) cannot read the file, then it cannot perform the preprocessing and edge detection algorithms required to discover the image properties to classify it correctly. You can use a masking program as well to alter the image data and prevent it from being recognized, but it will require such large scale alterations as to mask the global structure of the image that it becomes pointless, and significantly more time consuming on a per image basis than just encrypting the image files in an encrypted container. To test the encrypted files, a known image of a drivers license was encrypted and an attempt was made to run the file through the HTM for detection. The HTM simply crashed, as the file could not be read properly. Given that many tools exist for modern encryption and are freely and easily available, there is no justification for not encrypting such critical data. Indeed, this process can easily be automated, by simply setting up the scanner to automatically deposit the scanned images into a mounted encrypted folder (for example, simply ensure that the "\My Scans" folder on Windows based systems is encrypted).

Another possibility is to ensure that scanned sensitive images are somehow made self-destructing. Typically, the use of such images is often for a limited time, at the end of which they should be destroyed. This can also be easily done, simply by tagging the file to be securely erased by the system after a specific period of time has elapsed. Finally, if the system cannot be penetrated, it cannot be scanned. Thus, another way of foiling these attacks is to ensure that the system is never penetrated in the first place. However, in general, this is much more difficult to ensure, and also limits security to that particular system (i.e., if the data is backed up, it may still be vulnerable at a different site). All of these options should be explored.

7. CONCLUSION

In this paper, we have made two significant contributions. Our first contribution is more abstract – we posit that a modern attacker can use sophisticated image classification techniques to accurately filter out images containing sensitive data, and use data extraction tools to breach individual privacy. To validate this hypothesis, we have built a classification system based on Hierarchical Temporal Memory that is able to classify sensitive images with over 90% accuracy. We believe that this can also serve as a guide for other interesting applications such as document detection and analysis. Secondly, our work once again proves that proves that security through obscurity is simply not enough and robust countermeasures such as encryption must be utilized to protect security and privacy. In the future, we plan on expanding our search to other types of sensitive documents, and images, and build more advanced tools to automatically extract data – this may even be useful from a counter-intelligence perspective.

8. REFERENCES

[1] Y. Amit, D. Geman, and X. Fan. A coarse-to-fine strategy for multiclass shape detection. *IEEE Transactions on Pattern Analysis and Machine Intelligence*, 26:1606 – 1621, 2004.

[2] B. Bhanu. Automatic target recognition: State of the art survey. *IEEE Transactions on Aerospace and Electronic Systems*, 22:364 – 379, 1986.

[3] B. A. Bobier and M. Wirth. Content-based image retrieval using hierarchical temporal memory. In *MM '08: Proceeding of the 16th ACM international conference on Multimedia*, pages 925–928, New York, NY, USA, 2008. ACM.

[4] G. A. Carpenter. Large-scale neural systems for vision and cognition. In *IJCNN'09: Proceedings of the 2009 international joint conference on Neural Networks*, pages 3542–3547, Piscataway, NJ, USA, 2009. IEEE Press.

[5] R. Datta, J. Li, and J. Z. Wang. Content-based image retrieval: approaches and trends of the new age. In *MIR '05: Proceedings of the 7th ACM SIGMM international workshop on Multimedia information retrieval*, pages 253–262, New York, NY, USA, 2005. ACM.

[6] H. G. Frichtinger and T. Stroher. *Gabor analysis and algorithms, theory and applications*. Birkhauser, 1998.

[7] D. George and J. Hawkins. Towards a mathematical theory of cortical micro-circuits. *PLoS Comput Biol*, 5(10):e1000532+, October 2009.

[8] A. K. Ghosh and A. Schwartzbard. A study in using neural networks for anomaly and misuse detection. In *SSYM'99: Proceedings of the 8th conference on USENIX Security Symposium*, pages 12–12, Berkeley, CA, USA, 1999. USENIX Association.

[9] G. Griffin, A. Holub, and P. Perona. Caltech-256 object category dataset. Technical Report 7694, California Institute of Technology, 2007.

[10] J. Hawkins and S. Blakeslee. *On Intelligence*. Times Books, 2004.

[11] N. Inc. Numenta vision toolkit documentation tutorial.

[12] Y. Ji, K. H. Chang, and C.-C. Hung. Efficient edge detection and object segmentation using gabor filters. In *ACM-SE 42: Proceedings of the 42nd annual Southeast regional conference*, pages 454–459, New York, NY, USA, 2004. ACM.

[13] M. Ranzato, F. J. Huang, Y.-L. Boureau, and Y. LeCun. Unsupervised learning of invariant feature hierarchies with applications to object recognition. In *IEEE Conference on Computer Vision and Pattern Recognition*, pages 1–8, 2007.

[14] M. W. Roth. Survey of neural network technology for automatic target recognition. *IEEE Transactions on Neural Networks*, 1:28–43, 1990.

[15] B. Stenger, A. Thayananthan, P. H. Torr, and R. Cipolla. Model-based hand tracking using a hierarchical bayesian filter. *IEEE Transactions on Pattern Analysis and Machine Intelligence*, 28:1372 – 1384, 2006.

[16] C.-F. Tsai, K. McGarry, and J. Tait. Image classification using hybrid neural networks. In *SIGIR '03: Proceedings of the 26th annual international ACM SIGIR conference on Research and development in informaion retrieval*, pages 431–432, New York, NY, USA, 2003. ACM.

[17] Y. Zhang and W. Lee. Intrusion detection in wireless ad-hoc networks. In *MobiCom '00: Proceedings of the 6th annual international conference on Mobile computing and networking*, pages 275–283, New York, NY, USA, 2000. ACM.

k-out-of-n Oblivious Transfer based on Homomorphic Encryption and Solvability of Linear Equations

Mummoorthy Murugesan
Teradata Corporation
El Segundo, CA 90293, USA
mummoorthy@gmail.com

Wei Jiang
Dept. of Computer Science
Missouri University of Science
and Technology
Rolla, MO 65409, USA
wjiang@mst.edu

Ahmet Erhan Nergiz
Dept. of Computer Science
Purdue University
W. Lafayette, IN 47907, USA
anergiz@cs.purdue.edu

Serkan Uzunbaz
Dept. of Computer Science
Purdue University
W. Lafayette, IN 47907, USA
suzunbaz@cs.purdue.edu

ABSTRACT

Oblivious Transfer (OT) is an important cryptographic tool, which has found its usage in many crypto protocols, such as Secure Multiparty Computations [9], Certified E-mail [2] and Simultaneous Contract Signing [21]. In this paper, we propose three k-out-of-n OT (OT_k^n) protocols based on additive homomorphic encryption. Two of these protocols prohibit malicious behaviors from a receiver. We also achieve efficient communication complexity bounded by $O(l \cdot n)$ in bits, where l is the size of the encryption key. The computational complexity is comparable to the most efficient existing protocols. Due to the semantic security property, the sender cannot get receiver's selection. When the receiver tries to retrieve more than k values, the receiver is caught cheating with $1 - 1/m$ probability (Protocol II) or the receiver is unable to get any value at all (Protocol III). We introduce a novel technique based on the solvability of linear equations, which could find its way into other applications. We also provide an experimental analysis to compare the efficiency of the protocols.

Categories and Subject Descriptors

H.4.m [**Information Systems Applications**]: Miscellaneous; H.2.0 [**Database Management**]: Security, integrity, and protection

General Terms

Security, Algorithm

Keywords

Oblivious Transfer, Cryptographic Protocol

1. INTRODUCTION

In recent years, the tremendous amount of data collection has fueled concerns for information security and privacy. Many cryptographic schemes have been studied and proposed to accomplish tasks with minimal information disclosure. Protocols such as Secure Multiparty Computations [9], Certified E-mail [2] and Simultaneous Contract Signing [21] are some examples. Recent works on Digital Rights Management advocate privacy through oblivious transfer (OT) of digital contents to clients [14]. In such protocols, OT [20] is an important primitive cryptographic component.

A more concrete example utilizing the OT protocol is as follows. Suppose Bob, a researcher, wants to download some valuable cryptography research papers which are sold by an authority, Alice. Bob wants to get k out of n papers, which are very valuable for him. However, he does not want Alice to learn which research papers are retrieved in order to hide his topics of interest from Alice. In addition, Alice wants to ensure that Bob can get no more than the k number of papers he paid for. There comes the need for an OT protocol between Bob as the receiver and Alice as the sender.

There are two parties in an oblivious transfer protocol: a sender (e.g., Alice) who has a set of values and a receiver (e.g., Bob) who wants to get only certain values from Alice. Here, Alice wants Bob to obtain only a certain number of values, while Bob does not want to reveal to Alice any information about which values he chooses to get. The topic of OT has been extensively studied in many different forms using different cryptographic schemes. In this paper, we make use of homomorphic encryption that has the semantic security property (e.g., Paillier [18]) to propose efficient k-out-of-n OT (OT_k^n) protocols.

There are many types of OT protocols, each of which is based on different techniques and cryptographic schemes. Rabin's [20] first OT protocol was followed by other types of OT. In 1-out-of-n OT, the sender has n values and the receiver transfers one value. k-out-of-n OT is similar to 1-out-of-n OT where the receiver gets k of n values instead of one. In this paper, we focus on k-out-of-n OT. Although it can be achieved through k runs of 1-out-of-n OT, this increases time and communication complexity for most cases, and hence, it is costly.

We propose three efficient k-out-of-n OT protocols based on a probabilistic public key cryptosystem with additive homomorphic and semantic security properties. The semantic security property prevents the sender from getting the receiver's selections. The last two protocols (Protocol II and III) are designed in such a way that even a malicious receiver fails to get any advantage. Protocol II offers a high probability of detecting cheating receiver. Protocol III introduces a novel technique based on the feasibility of solving a system of k linear equations with more than k unknowns. Thus, any attempt to retrieve more than k values will prevent the receiver from getting any value at all.

The rest of the paper is organized as follows: Section 2 provides an overview on existing OT protocols and background information. Section 3 presents three efficient OT_k^n protocols. Protocol I is a simple scheme and provides a foundation for complex protocols II and III. Section 4 presents experimental results, and Section 5 concludes the paper with future research directions.

2. BACKGROUND AND RELATED WORK

In this section, we first present some early OT protocols, and then we introduce some background information on additive homomorphic encryption scheme and solving a system of linear equations. Rabin [20] first introduced OT_1^2, which is based on quadratic roots modulo a composite. After that, different versions of OT_1^2 were proposed in [7, 8]. Brassard et al. introduced OT_1^n named as all-or-nothing disclosure of secrets (ANDOS) inspired by OT_1^2 [3, 4]. This resulted in making the OT_1^n an open research problem in cryptographic protocol design.

The OT_k^n has become another open research problem following 1-out-of-n OT. Noting that these three problems can be reduced to each other, several works appeared based on this topic. In [22], Wu et al. stated that k-out-of-n t-bit string OT can be achieved applying Rabin's version of OT, $O(kt \log n)$ times. In another version, OT_k^n is achieved using a OT_1^n scheme $O(k)$ times [22]. Although there are efficient reduction protocols [16], there are numerous OT_k^n schemes [5] that do not rely on existing OT_1^2 or OT_1^n protocols, giving better complexity than the reduction versions of these protocols.

The OT_k^n scheme suggested by Noar and Pinkas [16] has a computation complexity $O(wk \log n)$ invocations of a basic OT_1^2, where w is a security parameter. The drawback of this scheme is that it works only when $k \leq n^{1/4}$. In [22], efficient homomorphic based OT_k^n was proposed for a condition when $k \geq n/\log n$. However, compared to our scheme, their protocols require interaction between sender and receiver, and a complex zero-knowledge paradigm is used to check that the receiver does not cheat to get more than k items. In a more recent work [5], efficient OT_k^n protocols were proposed based on the computational Diffie-Hellman Problem. The solution relies on the existence of a hash function such that $H : \{0,1\}^* \rightarrow G_q$, where G_q is group with prime order q. However, it is not clear how such a hash function is constructed.

The most efficient protocol based on homomorphic encryption is proposed in [13]. Let us denote this protocol as MM05-OT. This is an OT_1^n protocol that has $O(\log n)$ communication complexity and $O(n)$ computational complexity. This version of the protocol could be used to design an efficient OT_k^n with $O(k \log n)$ communication and $O(nk)$ computational complexity. However, a technical flaw in construction of this protocol (see Appendix A for more details) makes it produce wrong results.

2.1 Additive Homomorphic Encryption

In all three protocols, we use a probabilistic public key encryption scheme (Paillier's cryptosystem [18]) with the additive homomorphic property. Such an encryption function has *semantic security* (defined in [12]), and is additive homomorphic. Additive homomorphic property allows us to perform a specific algebraic operation on ciphertexts without decrypting them such that the plaintexts are also manipulated accordingly.

In our empirical study (Section 4), we adopt Paillier's cryptosystem [18] since it is efficient and commonly used in practice. Now we briefly present some of its key features (assuming that all the values are in appropriate domains). Let $E : R \times X \rightarrow Y$ represent such public key encryption scheme, where R, X and Y are finite domains identified with an initial subset of integers and $D : Y \rightarrow X$ be the decryption algorithm, such that $\forall (r, x) \in R \times X, D(E(r, x)) = x$. Initially, two large prime numbers p and q are chosen randomly and independently of each other. Let $N = pq$ and $g < N$ be a random integer. While (N, g) are public, the pair of randoms (p, q) remain private. The encryption scheme is defined as follows: Let the plaintext be $x < N$ and a random number be $r < N$. The encryption function $E(r, x) = c, c < N^2$, is probabilistic in nature because of the random number r, and the decryption function $D(c)$ results in the original plaintext $x < N$. The use of a random number r in the encryption provides the semantic security property so that encryptions of a same plaintext could result in different ciphertexts. Let $E : R \times X \rightarrow Y$ represent such public key encryption scheme, where R, X and Y are finite domains to represent $\mathbb{Z}_N^*, \mathbb{Z}_N$ and $\mathbb{Z}_{N^2}^*$ respectively. identified with an initial subset of integers and $D : Y \rightarrow X$ be the decryption algorithm, such that $\forall (r, x) \in R \times X, D(E(r, x)) = x$. Following are the important properties of the encryption scheme used in our protocol:

1. The encryption function is additive homomorphic, i.e., $\forall (r_1, x_1), (r_2, x_2) \in R \times X, E(r_1, x_1) +_h E(r_2, x_2) = E(r_3, x_1 + x_2)$, where r_3 can be computed from r_1, r_2, x_1 and x_2 in polynomial time. ($+_h$ indicates the operation to "add" two encrypted values).

2. The encryption function has *semantic security* as defined in [12]. Informally speaking, a set of ciphertexts do not provide additional information about the plaintext to an adversary with polynomial-bounded computing power.

3. The encryption function is probabilistic, i.e., if $r_1 \neq r_2$, then $E(r_1, x) \neq E(r_2, x)$ but $D(E(r_1, x)) = D(E(r_2, x))$, where D denote the decryption function. This property can be derived from the *semantic security* definition.

4. Given a constant k and a ciphertext $E(r_1, x)$, we can efficiently compute $k \times_h E(r_1, x) = E(r_2, k \cdot x)$ ($\times_h$

indicates the operation to multiply a ciphertext with a constant).

We use $E(x)$ and $D(c)$ to denote the encryption and decryption functions respectively, where x is a plaintext, c is a ciphertext. Note that our protocol is a generic in that any homomorphic probabilistic public key encryption systems, such as those proposed in [1, 15, 17], can be adopted in its implementation.

2.2 Solving Linear Equations

Since Protocol III (Section 3.3) uses the idea of solving linear equations, we now give a brief introduction to solving m equations with n unknowns. Let the system of equations be the following:

$$
\begin{aligned}
b_1 &= a_{11} \cdot x_1 + \cdots + a_{1n} \cdot x_n \\
&\vdots \\
b_m &= a_{m1} \cdot x_1 + \cdots + a_{mn} \cdot x_n
\end{aligned}
$$

The unknowns are $x_1, \ldots, x_n$, while $a_{11}, \ldots, a_{mn}$ are the coefficients and $b_1, \ldots, b_m$ are the constant values. The solution to this problem is an assignment of values to the unknowns $x_1, \ldots, x_n$. This system of equations have different solutions depending on the values of m and n:

1. $m < n$: If the number of equations is less than the number of unknowns, then there are infinitely many solutions. If we assume only positive values for the unknowns, then the solutions for each unknown x_i is in the range $(0, MIN(\frac{b_1}{a_{1i}}, \ldots, \frac{b_m}{a_{mi}}))$. An exhaustive search in this space will give all the possible assignments for the unknowns, resulting in many solutions. Thus the solution is not unique when $m < n$.

2. $m = n$: If the number of equations and unknowns are the same and the equations are linearly independent, then there is a single unique solution.

The complexity of solving n equations with n unknowns is typically $O(n^3)$. In the next section, we present three OT_k^n protocols.

3. PROTOCOLS FOR K-OUT-OF-N OT

The k-out-of-n OT is defined as follows: Suppose there are two parties, a sender and a receiver. The sender has a set of n values $v_1, \ldots, v_n$. The receiver retrieves k of these values without letting the sender know which values are retrieved. In other words, the transfer of k values is oblivious to the sender. Without privacy requirement, we can assume that the receiver sends a n-bit selection string to the sender. If $n = 5$, a selection string $X = \{0, 1, 0, 1, 0\}$ retrieves data values v_2 and v_4. The value 0 at positions 1, 3 and 5 means that the data values v_1, v_3 and v_5 are not selected. The sender can compute the component-wise product of X with data values, $Z_i = X_i * v_i$. Thus, $Z = \{0, v_2, 0, v_4, 0\}$ contains the data values retrieved by the receiver. We define a *well-formed selection string* with respect to n and k as follows:

DEFINITION 3.1. *(Well-formed Selection String X_n^k) Let X_n^k be a n-bit selection string from the receiver. X_n^k is considered well-formed with respect to a k-out-of-n protocol if the string X_n^k contains exactly k 1's and $n - k$ 0's.*

The simple protocol given above has two issues that need to be addressed to make it oblivious. First, the receiver's selection string X should not be revealed to the sender. Second, the receiver should not be able to get more than k values from the sender, i.e., X should be well-formed. This leads to two aspects of security in OT protocols:

1. **Sender's privacy/security** is about making sure that the receiver gets only the k values, and no more values are released. This results in a constraint that the selection string needs to be *well-formed*.

2. **Receiver's privacy/security** is based on hiding the k selections from the sender so that the sender does not know which values are selected by the receiver. This requirement results in transfer of values to the receiver in an oblivious manner.

There are two behavior patterns that the sender and receiver may adopt. A Semi-Honest party will strictly follow the steps of the protocol. He may also process the outputs and the messages exchanged to gain extra information. A malicious party may try to break the protocol by not following the prescribed steps, and deviating as necessary to gain advantage over the other party.

We now present three k-out-of-n protocols. Protocol I (Section 3.1) considers a semi-honest receiver and a malicious sender, and it mainly serves as a building block for the other two protocols. To prevent malicious receivers, Protocol II (Section 3.2) utilizes the cut-and-choose strategy [19] so that the sender's malicious behaviors can be detected with certain probability. Protocol II and Protocol III (Section 3.3) provide security in the presence of malicious receiver and sender. In addition, to maximize security, Protocol III uses a novel approach based on the solvability of equations. We believe this technique is a powerful tool, and in the future could be used in other settings.

3.1 Protocol I: Semi-honest Receiver and Malicious Sender

In this single-round protocol, we consider a semi-honest receiver and a malicious sender. There are three action phases in the protocol as given below.

Step 1. Receiver's Request: The receiver creates a public-private key pair (k_{pu}, k_{pr}) in probabilistic public key encryption scheme. While the private key k_{pr} is kept confidential with the receiver, the public key (k_{pu}) is revealed to the sender. We denote the number of bits to represent the keys as l (i.e., $|k_{pu}| = l$ and $k_{pu} < 2^l$). The receiver creates a n-bit selection string X as explained before, where bit $X_i = 1$ if the ith data value is to be retrieved from the sender. Otherwise, X_i is set to 0. Thus, k out of n bits of the string X are set to 1. To hide the selections from the sender, X is encrypted bit-wise using the public key k_{pu}: $\bar{X} = \{E(X_i), \ldots, E(X_n)\}$. The receiver sends the encrypted bits $\bar{X}_1, \ldots, \bar{X}_n$ to the sender.

Step 2. Sender's Reply: The data values $v_1, \ldots, v_n$ are stored at the sender. We denote the number of bits to represent any v_i as α (i.e., $v_i < 2^\alpha$). The sender receives $\bar{X}$ but cannot distinguish between $X_i = 1$ and $X_i = 0$ due to the semantic security of the encryption scheme [11]. The sender creates $\bar{Z}_1, \ldots, \bar{Z}_n$ from $\bar{X}$ and $v_1, \ldots, v_n$ as $\bar{Z}_i = \bar{X}_i \times_h v_i$, where $\times_h$ is the multiplication of constant against a ciphertext, allowed in the encryption scheme. Note that $\bar{Z}_1, \ldots, \bar{Z}_n$

are encryptions of either 0 or v_i values, and consequently, the sender has no way of knowing which k values are selected by the receiver. The sender sends $\bar{Z}_1, \ldots, \bar{Z}_n$ to the receiver.

Step 3. Unpacking at Receiver: The receiver decrypts the values of $\bar{Z}_1, \ldots, \bar{Z}_n$ to get $Z_1, \ldots, Z_n$ When $X_i = 1$, the corresponding Z_i is v_i. When $X_i = 0$, the corresponding $\bar{Z}_i$ is $E(0)$, and thus the receiver gets no information about the data values not selected by X. These values reveal the k data values for the indices when $X_i = 1$.

3.1.1 Security Analysis

We now analyze why this protocol is secure in the presense of a semi-honest receiver and a malicious sender. There are two possible effective malicious behaviors for the sender: 1) To discover receiver's selection of k values, and 2) To input the wrong data values (i.e., not the original data values of the sender).

The sender receives the following values from the receiver: $\bar{X}_1, \ldots, \bar{X}_n$, k and k_{pu}. While k is a public knowledge, k_{pu} is a random value to the sender. The n ciphertexts, $\bar{X}_1, \ldots, \bar{X}_n$ are generated using the key k_{pu} by the receiver. These are from a semantically secure encryption scheme. Let $C_1^*, \ldots, C_n^*$ be a set of randomly generated numbers containing same number of bits as $\bar{X}_i$s. Since the encryption scheme is semantically secure and the sender's computing power is polynomially bounded, it is impossible for the sender to distinguish between $\bar{X}_1, \ldots, \bar{X}_n$ and $C_1^*, \ldots, C_n^*$ without knowing k_{pr}. As a result, the sender will not gain any knowledge regarding the index values from $\bar{X}_1, \ldots, \bar{X}_n$.

Under the second malicious behavior, the sender refuses to properly execute the steps of the protocol, resulting in receiver getting wrong results. This is equivalent to input modification problem, where the sender purposefully modifies the data values. Zero-knowledge proofs [10] can be used to prevent the sender from changing data values once they are committed. However, that does not prevent the sender from committing wrong values to start with. Thus even zero-knowledge proofs cannot prevent such behavior. We consider the problem of input modification to be outside the scope of this problem.

A semi-honest receiver always sends a well-formed selection string X to the sender. Suppose the receiver tries to decrypt more than k values from $\bar{Z}_i, \ldots, \bar{Z}_n$ to obtain the corresponding data values. Since the server has multiplied the selection bit with the data values, only k of $\bar{Z}_i, \ldots, \bar{Z}_n$ will be non-zeros, and the remaining $\bar{Z}_i$ will contain 0. Thus the receiver will not gain any additional knowledge about the non-selected data values.

3.1.2 Complexity

We define the computational complexity as the number of encryptions/decryptions performed, since they are the most expensive operation in the protocol. To encrypt the selection string, the receiver performs n encryptions, and to get the results at the end, it performs n decryptions. At the sender's side, there are n homomorphic multiplications. Thus the overall computational complexity of the protocol is O(n).

Communication complexity is measured as the number of bits exchanged between the server and the receiver. The receiver transfers the selection string as n ciphertexts and the sender sends back n ciphertexts. As a result, the overall communication complexity of the protocol is O($l \cdot n$) in bits, where l is the number of bits of the encryption key.

3.2 Protocol II : Malicious Receiver and Malicious Sender

Protocol I is secure when the receiver is semi-honest, but fails when we consider a malicious receiver. If a receiver sets more than k bits in X to 1, it will reveal more than k data values to the receiver.

We now present a variation of Protocol I that works even in the presence of malicious receiver and malicious sender, utilizing the cut-and-choose strategy [19]. Instead of sending only one selection string, in Protocol II the receiver sends m encrypted selection strings. Out of these m strings, $m-1$ strings are revealed to the sender, and are verified by the sender to be well-formed. These strings are formed such that the opened selection strings do not reveal the actual user selection. The sender uses the remaining un-opened selection string for OT. This protocol prevents the receiver from getting more than k values with $\frac{m-1}{m}$ probability. Moreover, the receiver is caught if he tries to cheat. We now explain the steps of Protocol II in detail. The corresponding algorithm is given in Algorithm 1.

Step 1. Receiver's Request: The receiver first creates m public-private key pairs (k_{pu}^j, k_{pr}^j). It also generates random selection strings with n-bits each such that only k random bits are set to 1 and the remaining $n - k$ bits are set to 0 (i.e., well-formed w.r.t. n and k). There are $\frac{n!}{k!(n-k)!}$ possible n-bit strings with k 1's and $n-k$ 0's. When $n = 20$ and $k = 10$, the number of possible strings is 184,756. The receiver generates m such strings. Let these strings be $X^1, \ldots, X^m$, and we denote the i-th bit of string X^j as X_i^j. Note that these strings contain 1's in random positions and the ordering has no relation to the indices of the data values selected by the receiver. Let X^{real} be the actual selection string intended by the receiver. This string is kept secret at the receiver. Using the m public keys, the receiver encrypts the m random strings as follows:

$$\bar{X}^j = E_j(X_1^j), \ldots, E_j(X_n^j), j = 1, \ldots, m$$

E_j is the encryption using key k_{pu}^j. The receiver sends $\bar{X}^1, \ldots, \bar{X}^m$ to the sender, along with the individual cryptographic hashes (e.g., SHA-1, SHA-2) of the m private keys (step 1(e) of Algorithm 1).

EXAMPLE 1. *For $n = 5$ and $k = 2$, let $X^{real} = \{0, 1, 0, 1, 0\}$ be the actual user selection string. For $m = 2$, let us assume the receiver generates two random strings as $X^1 = \{1, 0, 0, 1, 0\}$ and $X^2 = \{0, 0, 1, 1, 0\}$.*

Step 2. Sender's Reply: The sender randomly picks $m-1$ encrypted strings from $\bar{X}^1, \ldots, \bar{X}^m$ and requests their decryption keys (step 2(a)) so that these encrypted strings can be decrypted and verified to be well-formed (to contain exactly k 1's and $n-k$ 0's).

Step 3. Receiver's reply: The receiver gets a request for $m - 1$ private keys from the sender. By sending these $m - 1$ private keys, the receiver can now prove to the sender that $m - 1$ (out of m) selection strings are well-formed. Let us assume u ($1 \leq u \leq m$) is the index of the only one selection string whose private key is not requested. This means that $\bar{X}^u = \bar{X}_1^u, \ldots, \bar{X}_n^u$ is the selection string that remains secret.

While $\bar{X}^u$ is not opened by the sender and subsequently used for the oblivious transfer, $\bar{X}^u$ is a random string that is well-formed for k. X^u contains k 1's and $n - k$ 0's but is not necessarily the equivalent of X^{real}, the actual selection string intended by the receiver. To make X^u and X^{real} equivalent, the receiver finds a permutation P that permutes the sequence $\bar{X}^u$ to get $\bar{X}'^u$ so that X'^u and X^{real} are equivalent. $\bar{X}'^u$ contains the same ciphertexts of $\bar{X}^u$ but re-arranged so that X^{real} and X'^u are the same, i.e., both retrieve same data values from the sender. Since the $\bar{X}'^u$ is still in encrypted form, the sender cannot get the real selection string. The receiver also sends the public key of u (k_{pu}^u) to the sender (steps 3(a)-(c)).

EXAMPLE 2. *From Example 1, assume the sender wants to open $\bar{X}^1$. The selection string $X^2 = \{0, 0, 1, 1, 0\}$ remains un-opened, and the sender has the encrypted $\bar{X}^2$ as $\{E_2(0),$ $E_2(0),\ E_2(1),\ E_2(1),\ E_2(0)\}$, Let these be $\{e_1,...,e_n\}$. The real user selection string X^{real} is $\{0, 1, 0, 1, 0\}$. The receiver now computes a permutation P so that entries of $\bar{X}^2$ will give X^{real}. One such possible permutation is $\{1 \rightarrow 3, 2 \rightarrow 5, 3 \rightarrow 2, 4 \rightarrow 4, 5 \rightarrow 1\}$ that produces $\bar{X}'^2$ as $\{e_5, e_3, e_1, e_4, e_2\}$, which is equivalent to $\{E_2(0),\ E_2(1),\ E_2(0),\ E_2(1),\ E_2(0)\}$. There are also other permutations that will result in X^{real}.*

Step 4. Sender's reply: After receiving the $m - 1$ keys, the sender first verifies whether the hash values of the keys match the hash values sent by the receiver at Step 1(e). If there is a mismatch, the sender stops the protocol as the receiver is attempting to send different keys than the ones used at Step 1(d). If the hash values match, the sender then verifies whether all $m - 1$ decrypted selection strings are well-formed. If any of the strings is not well-formed, the sender stops the protocol as the receiver is attempting to get more than k values. If all the $m - 1$ strings are well-formed, the sender is assured with $\frac{1}{m}$ probability that the un-opened string is also well-formed.

The sender uses the permutation P to re-order the un-opened string $\bar{X}^u$ to get a new sequence $\bar{X}'^u$. similar to Protocol I. It computes $\bar{Z}_1, \ldots, \bar{Z}_n$ from $\bar{X}'^u$ and $v_1, \ldots, v_n$, where $\bar{Z}_i = \bar{X}'^u_i \times_h v_i$. The sender sends $\bar{Z}$ values to the receiver.

Step 5. Unpacking at Receiver: The receiver decrypts the values of $\bar{Z}_1, \ldots, \bar{Z}_n$ to get the k data values for the indices when $X_i^{real} = 1$ (step 5(a)).

3.2.1 Security Analysis

The main difference between Protocol I and II is that the receiver could act malicious in Protocol II. Suppose the receiver is dishonest, then the only possible malicious behavior is to obtain more than k values from the sender. (Though it is possible for the receiver to obtain less than k values, it is not considered as an attack on the protocol.)

At step 4(d) of Algorithm 1, the sender computes the component-wise product of $\bar{X}'^u$ with the data values. To get more than k data values, it is imperative that $\bar{X}'^u$ must contain more than k non-zero values. To achieve this, the receiver needs to send more than k encryptions of non-zero values in one of the selection strings from $X^1, \ldots, X^m$ at Step 1(b). However, $\bar{X}'^u$ is used at step 4(d) only if all the remaining $m - 1$ selection strings are opened by the sender at step 4(b). For the receiver to succeed in cheating, the selection string that contains more than k non-zero values should not be selected at step 2(a) by the sender. This occurs with probability $\frac{1}{m}$. Moreover, this selection string is selected with $\frac{m-1}{m}$ probability, and if that happens, receiver is caught cheating by the sender at step 4(b).

Algorithm 1 Protocol II: k-out-of-n Oblivious Transfer

Require: Receiver's inputs: $X_1, \ldots, X_n$, k; Sender's inputs: $v_1, \ldots, v_n$.

1: Receiver:

  (a). Create n-bit selection string as X^{real}; Set $X_i^{real} = 1$ to retrieve value v_i; otherwise, set $X_i^{real} = 0$.

  (b). Create m random n-bit strings, $X^1, \ldots, X^m$, so that they contain exactly k 1's and $n - k$ 0's.

  (c). Create m public-private key pairs $(k_{pu}^1, k_{pr}^1), \ldots, (k_{pu}^m, k_{pr}^m)$.

  (d). **for** $j = 1$ **to** m **do**

    (d.1). Compute $\bar{X}_i^j \leftarrow E_j(X_i^j)$ for $i = 1, \ldots, n$.

    (d.2). Compute $h_j \leftarrow HASH(k_{pr}^j)$.

  (e). Send $\bar{X}^1, \ldots, \bar{X}^m$, k, $h_1, \ldots, h_m$ to the sender.

2: Sender:

  (a). Randomly select $m-1$ selection strings and request the private keys from receiver.

3: Receiver:

  (a). Let $\bar{X}^u$ be the selection string that is not selected by the sender.

  (b). Compute a permutation P that makes $\bar{X}^u$ and X^{real} equivalent.

  (c). Send the permutation P, $m - 1$ private keys requested and the public key k_{pu}^u

4: Sender:

  (a). Verify whether the hash values of the $m - 1$ keys match with $h_1, \ldots, h_m$. If not, stop the protocol.

  (b). Decrypt the $m - 1$ selection strings and verify whether all the $m - 1$ strings are well-formed. If not, stop the protocol.

  (c). Use the permutation P to compute $\bar{X}'^u$ from the only remaining selection string, $\bar{X}^u$.

  (d). Compute $\bar{Z}_i = \bar{X}'^u_i \times_h v_i$, for $i = 1, \ldots, n$.

  (e). Send $\bar{Z}_i, \ldots, \bar{Z}_n$ to the receiver.

5: Receiver:

  (a). Retrieve k data values by computing $v_i = D(\bar{Z}_i)$ for all i when $X_i^{real} = 1$.

Let us suppose a cheating receiver sends a selection string $\bar{X}'$ with more than k 1's to the sender at Step 1(e), and this string is selected by the sender at Step 2(a). At step 3(c), the receiver may try to send a different key (k'') than the one used (k') in the encryption of $\bar{X}'$. Since the sender has the hash of k', the receiver's attempt to successfully cheat will result in a key k'' that has the same hash as that of k'. This is same as successfully finding collision in the underlying hash function. However, collision in hash functions is extremely unlikely for SHA-1 or SHA-2. Thus the receiver cannot change the keys once the sender requests $m-1$ keys.

A malicious sender may try to learn the selections of the receiver. At step 1(e), the sender receives the encryptions of m random well-formed strings as $\bar{X}^1, \ldots, \bar{X}^m$, along with the hashes $h_1, \ldots, h_m$ of the private keys. Only one of these selection strings remains un-opened at step 4(b). So, the other $m-1$ sequences are random strings generated by the receiver with k 1's and $n-k$ 0's. As there are $\frac{n!}{k!(n-k)!}$ such combinations, these random strings do not reveal any information about X^{real}, the actual user selection. The sender itself could have generated such strings. The hash values are generated from one-way cryptographic hash functions. Thus, computing the actual strings (i.e., randomly generated private keys) from hashes $h_1, \ldots, h_m$, involve brute force attack on the key space (in the range of 2^{1024}), which is computationally impossible.

Let us now consider the selection string $\bar{X}^u$ that is not opened by the sender. This contains n ciphertexts, encryptions of 1's and 0's as $\{\bar{X}_1^u, \ldots, \bar{X}_n^u\}$. The sender learns nothing about the contents of these ciphertexts due to the semantic-security property of the encryption scheme. At step 4(c), the receiver uses the permutation P on $\bar{X}^u$ to get a new sequence, $\bar{X'}_1^u, \ldots, \bar{X'}_n^u$. Since the sender gains no knowledge about user's selection from $\bar{X}^u$, the re-ordered selection string $\bar{X'}^u$ also does not reveal any information. Thus a malicious sender will not gain any information about the receiver's selection in this protocol.

3.2.2 Complexity

At step 1(d) of Algorithm 1, the receiver performs $n \cdot m$ encryptions, and n decryptions at step 5(a). At the sender's side, there are $n \cdot (m-1)$ decryptions at step 4(b), and n homomorphic multiplications at step 4(d). Thus the overall computational complexity of the protocol is $O(n \cdot m)$.

At step 1(e), the receiver sends $n \cdot m$ encrypted values and m hash values. Since the ciphertexts have more bits than the hashes, the communication complexity is bounded by $O(l \cdot n \cdot m)$ bits. The sender sends back n ciphertexts to the receiver at step 1(e). As a result, the overall communication complexity of the protocol is $O(l \cdot n \cdot m)$ in bits. Protocol II needs an extra interaction between the sender and receiver as compared to Protocol I and III.

3.3 Protocol III - Hybrid Scheme

We now present a hybrid (based on encryption and algebra) protocol for OT_k^n. This scheme allows the receiver to construct k equations with k unknowns, where the unknowns are the data values from the sender. By solving the equations, the receiver gets the k data values it wants to retrieve. The equations are hidden (i.e., in encrypted form) from the sender such that the selected values are kept confidential from the sender. If the receiver attempts to retrieve more than k values, then the receiver is unable to even form the equations. Thus the greedy receivers will not get any data value at all. Algorithm 2 lists the steps of the protocol. We now describe the protocol in detail.

Step 1. Receiver's Request: Similar to Protocol I, the receiver creates a n-bit selection string X where bit $X_i = 1$ if the i-th value is to be retrieved from the sender. Otherwise, X_i is set to 0. To hide the selections from the sender, X is encrypted bit-wise using the public key k_{pr}: $\bar{X}_i = E(X_i)$. The

receiver sends the encrypted bits $\bar{X}_1, \ldots, \bar{X}_n$ to the sender (steps 1(a)-(b)). Refer to Table 1 that shows an example OT_2^5. As shown in Table 1(a), the receiver sets X_2 and X_4 to 1 so that v_2 (35) and v_4 (85) are retrieved.

Step 2. Sender's Reply: The sender generates two $k \times n$ random perturbations matrices, A and B. The matrix A is generated using a random number R_1^1 as the seed to the random number generator. Thus A consists of $k \cdot n$ random positive integer values. We denote the number of bits to represent any $A_{i,j}$ as β (i.e, $A_{i,j} < 2^\beta$). A can be completely re-generated given only the value of R_1^1.

The matrix B is generated from n random seeds $R_1^2, \ldots, R_n^2$. Each random seed (R_i^2) is used in generating k numbers which form the i-th column in matrix B. Thus B consists of $k \cdot n$ random positive integer values, generated through the random seeds, $R_1^2, \ldots, R_n^2$. Any i-th column of B can be completely re-generated given only the value of R_i^2. We also require that all the columns and rows are independent in A and B, i.e., their rank is k (assuming $k \leq n$). This property ensures that the resultant k equations are independent, which are then solved by the receiver. A randomly constructed matrix usually has this property with very high probability [6] (See Appendix B for more details). While A is revealed to the receiver (through R_1^1), B is kept secret at the sender.

In the first step, the sender uses the matrix A and $R_1^2, \ldots, R_n^2$ to compute a $k \times n$ matrix Y^1, where $Y_{i,j}^1 = R_j^2 * A_{i,j}$ for $i = 1, \ldots, k$ and $j = 1, \ldots, n$ (step 2(c)).

$$Y^1 = \begin{pmatrix} R_1^2 * A_{1,1} & , \ldots, & R_n^2 * A_{1,n} \\ & \cdots & \\ R_1^2 * A_{k,1} & , \ldots, & R_n^2 * A_{k,n} \end{pmatrix}$$

Using Y^1, the sender computes $\bar{Z}_1^1, \ldots, \bar{Z}_k^1$ from $\bar{X}$ and Y^1 as follows (step 2(e)):

$$\bar{Z}_1^1 = \bar{X}_1 \times_h Y_{1,1}^1 +_h \ldots +_h \bar{X}_n \times_h Y_{1,n}^1$$
$$\vdots$$
$$\bar{Z}_k^1 = \bar{X}_1 \times_h Y_{k,1}^1 +_h \ldots +_h \bar{X}_n \times_h Y_{k,n}^1$$

where $+_h$ is the homomorphic addition operation. Since $\bar{Z}_1, \ldots, \bar{Z}_k$ are in encrypted forms, the sender has no way of knowing which k values are selected by the receiver. These k values and the matrix A can be used by the receiver to construct k equations with k unknowns (assuming X is well-formed w.r.t n and k), where the unknowns are k of the n random seed values, $R_1^2, \ldots, R_n^2$.

In the second step, the sender uses the perturbation matrix B and $v_1, \ldots, v_n$ to compute a $k \times n$ matrix Y^2, where $Y_{i,j}^2 = v_j * B_{i,j}$ for $i = 1, \ldots, k$ and $j = 1, \ldots, n$ (step 2(d)).

$$Y^2 = \begin{pmatrix} v_1 * B_{1,1} & , \ldots, & v_n * B_{1,n} \\ & \cdots & \\ v_1 * B_{k,1} & , \ldots, & v_n * B_{k,n} \end{pmatrix}$$

Using Y^2, the sender creates $\bar{Z}_1^2, \ldots, \bar{Z}_k^2$ (step 2(f)):

$$\bar{Z}_1^2 = \bar{X}_1 \times_h Y_{1,1}^2 +_h \ldots +_h \bar{X}_n \times_h Y_{1,n}^2$$
$$\vdots$$
$$\bar{Z}_k^2 = \bar{X}_1 \times_h Y_{k,1}^2 +_h \ldots +_h \bar{X}_n \times_h Y_{k,n}^2$$

The sender sends $\bar{Z}_1^1, \ldots, \bar{Z}_k^1, \bar{Z}_1^2, \ldots, \bar{Z}_k^2$, and also the random seed R_1^1 (i.e., matrix A) to the receiver.

EXAMPLE 3. *In Table 1(b), we show a perturbation matrix A, the secret matrix B and the random seeds for B as R^2. Table 1(c) shows matrices Y^1 and Y^2. $\bar{Z}^1$ is computed as follows: $\bar{Z}_1^1 = E(0) \times_h 24 +_h E(1) \times_h 9 +_h E(0) \times_h 49 +_h E(1) \times_h 12$ and $\bar{Z}_2^1 = E(0) \times_h 120 +_h E(1) \times_h 12 +_h E(0) \times_h 14 +_h E(1) \times_h 14$. This results in $\bar{Z}_1^1 = E(21)$ and $\bar{Z}_2^1 = E(26)$. Similarly, $\bar{Z}_1^2 = E(456)$ and $\bar{Z}_2^2 = E(549)$ are computed and sent to the receiver.* □

the protocol is run multiple times, the sender generates new perturbation matrices for each run.

EXAMPLE 4. *As shown in Table 1(e), the receiver forms two equations, $3r_2 + 6r_4 = 21$ and $4r_2 + 7r_4 = 26$ after receiving $E(21)$ and $E(26)$ from the sender. Note that the co-efficients are directly from the perturbation matrix A. Since the receiver knows that $X_2 = 1$ and $X_4 = 1$, it uses only the 2nd and 4th column elements from A. The solution for these equations is $r_2 = 3$ and $r_4 = 2$. This matches with R^2 in Table 1(b). The receiver generates the elements of 2nd and 4th columns of B using 3 (r_2) and 2 (r_4) and forms another set of equations, $6v_2 + 3v_4 = 456$ and $11v_2 + 2v_4 = 549$ with data values v_2 and v_4 as unknowns. The receiver solves these equations to get the data values as $v_2 = 35$ and $v_4 = 82$.* □

i	X_i	v_i
1	0	50
2	1	35
3	0	46
4	1	82

(a)Inputs

$$A = \begin{pmatrix} 2 & 3 & 7 & 6 \\ 10 & 4 & 2 & 7 \end{pmatrix}$$
$$R^2 = \{12, 3, 7, 2\}$$
$$B = \begin{pmatrix} 4 & 6 & 1 & 3 \\ 5 & 11 & 2 & 2 \end{pmatrix}$$

(b) Random Matrices

$$Y^1 = \begin{pmatrix} 24 & 9 & 49 & 12 \\ 120 & 12 & 14 & 14 \end{pmatrix}$$
$$Y^2 = \begin{pmatrix} 200 & 210 & 46 & 246 \\ 250 & 385 & 92 & 164 \end{pmatrix}$$

(c) Matrices Y^1, Y^2

$$Z_1^1 = 9 + 12 = 21$$
$$Z_2^1 = 12 + 14 = 26$$

$$Z_1^2 = 210 + 246 = 456$$
$$Z_2^2 = 385 + 164 = 549$$

(d) Computing Z^1, Z^2

$$3r_2 + 6r_4 = 21$$
$$4r_2 + 7r_4 = 26$$

$$B = \begin{pmatrix} * & 6 & * & 3 \\ * & 11 & * & 2 \end{pmatrix}$$

Solve to get
$r_2 = 3,\ r_4 = 2$

$$6v_2 + 3v_4 = 456$$
$$11v_2 + 2v_4 = 549$$

3 generates {6, 11}
2 generates {3, 2}

(e) Solving for seeds

Solve to get
$v_2 = 35,\ v_4 = 82$

(f) Final steps in OT_2^4

Table 1: An Illustration OT_2^5 in Protocol III

Step 3. Unpacking at Receiver: The receiver decrypts the values of $\bar{Z}_1^1, \ldots, \bar{Z}_k^1$ to get $Z_1^1, \ldots, Z_k^1$. The decrypted values form k equations with k unknowns as follows.

$$Z_1^1 = X_1 * R_1^2 * A_{1,1} + \ldots + X_n * R_n^2 * A_{1,n}$$
$$\vdots$$
$$Z_k^1 = X_1 * R_1^2 * A_{k,1} + \ldots + X_n * R_n^2 * A_{k,n} \quad (1)$$

Since the receiver can re-generate the perturbation matrix A (constructed by using R_1^1), the random values $A_{i,j}$ are already known to the receiver. Assuming that X contains k 1s and $n-k$ 0s, the k equations from equation 1 will contain k unknowns which are the R_i^2's. By solving these k equations, the receiver gets the k random seeds from $R_1^2, \ldots, R_n^2$, for the columns selected by X.

Similarly, the receiver decrypts the values of $\bar{Z}_1^2, \ldots, \bar{Z}_k^2$ to get $Z_1^2, \ldots, Z_k^2$ and forms the following k equations.

$$Z_1^2 = X_1 * v_{i_1} * B_{1,1} + \ldots + X_n * v_{i_k} * B_{1,n}$$
$$\vdots$$
$$Z_k^2 = X_1 * v_{i_1} * B_{k,1} + \ldots + X_n * v_{i_k} * B_{k,n} \quad (2)$$

These k equations contain k unknowns which are the data values, and the co-efficients are matrix B elements from k columns. These co-efficients are known to the receiver from the previous step, by solving equation 1. Thus the receiver is able to solve equation 2 to obtain the k data values. If

---

Algorithm 2 k-out-of-n Oblivious Transfer

Require: Receiver's inputs: $X_1, \ldots, X_n$, k, k_{pu}, k_{pr}; Sender's inputs: $v_1, \ldots, v_n$, R_1^1, $R_1^2, \ldots, R_n^2$.

1: Receiver:

(a). Set $X_i = 1$ to retrieve value v_i; otherwise, set $X_i = 0$

(b). Encrypt each X_i separately as $\bar{X}_i = E(X_i)$, for $i = 1, \ldots, n$; Send $\bar{X}_1, \ldots, \bar{X}_n$, k, k_{pu} to the sender

2: Sender:

(a). Generate the $k \times n$ perturbation matrix A through R_1^1

(b). Generate the $k \times n$ perturbation matrix B, whose elements of i-th column are generated by R_i^2.

(c). Compute $k \times n$ matrix Y^1: $Y_{i,j}^1 = R_j^2 * A_{i,j}$, for $i = 1, \ldots, k$ and $j = 1, \ldots, n$

(d). Compute $k \times n$ matrix Y^2: $Y_{i,j}^2 = v_j * B_{i,j}$, for $i = 1, \ldots, k$ and $j = 1, \ldots, n$

(e). Compute $\bar{Z}_i^1 = \bar{X}_1 \times_h Y_{i,1}^1 +_h \ldots +_h \bar{X}_n \times_h Y_{i,n}^1$, for $i = 1, \ldots, k$

(f). Compute $\bar{Z}_i^2 = \bar{X}_1 \times_h Y_{i,1}^2 +_h \ldots +_h \bar{X}_n \times_h Y_{i,n}^2$, for $i = 1, \ldots, k$

(g). Send $\bar{Z}_1^1, \ldots, \bar{Z}_k^1$, $\bar{Z}_1^2, \ldots, \bar{Z}_k^2$ and R_1^1 to the receiver.

3: Receiver:

(a). Decrypt $Z_i^1 = D(\bar{Z}_i^1)$ and $Z_i^2 = D(\bar{Z}_i^2)$ for $i = 1, \ldots, k$

(b). Generate the perturbation matrix A using R_1^1

(c). Construct k equations with X, Z^1 and A; solve the equations to get k random seeds for matrix B

(d). Construct k equations with X, Z^2 and k random seeds from 3(c); solve the equations to get the k data values.

3.3.1 Security Analysis

Suppose the sender is dishonest and tries to discover receiver's selections. The only information the sender receives is the encrypted selection string, $\bar{X}_1, \ldots, \bar{X}_n$ at step 1(b). Since the encryption scheme is semantically secure and the sender's computing power is polynomially bounded, it is impossible for the sender to gain any knowledge from $\bar{X}$.

Suppose the receiver is dishonest and tries to obtain more than k values from the sender. To achieve this, the receiver first needs to send more than k encryptions of non-zero values at step 1(b). This will result in k equations (computed at steps 2(e)-(f)) with more than k unknowns. Let us consider the equations involving the random seeds at step 2(e), which the receiver solves at step 3(c). Since there are more unknowns than the equations, this will result in non-unique solutions for the random seeds. Thus the receiver will not be able to construct the equations for the data values at step 3(d) since only the unique random seeds can generate the co-efficients. Without the co-efficients, the k values $Z_1^2, \ldots, Z_k^2$ are just random values to the sender. Let us consider a scenario where the receiver generates all possible random seeds and tries to generate the co-efficients for the equation 2. Since X contains more than k 1's, for each co-efficient assignment, the receiver needs to solve k equations with more than k unknowns by performing $O(k^3)$ multiplications. For each case, there will be many non-unique solutions for the data values from equation 2. Thus a malicious receiver gets no data values at all if it attempts to cheat. Since we can use only positive integers (used in the homomorphic encryption) for constructing the equations, the server needs to make sure the domain is large enough to prevent any brute force attack.

EXAMPLE 5. *In Table 1(a), suppose the receiver wants to retrieve v_1 also in OT_2^5. This will result in the following assignment of X and $\bar{X}$: $X = \{1, 1, 0, 1, 0\}$ and $\bar{X} = \{E(1), E(1), E(0), E(1), E(0)\}$. The sender will generate only two equations as follows: $\bar{Z}_1^1 = E(1) \times_h 24 +_h E(1) \times_h 9 +_h E(0) \times_h 49 +_h E(1) \times_h 12 +_h E(0) \times_h 4$ and $\bar{Z}_2^1 = E(1) \times_h 120 +_h E(1) \times_h 12 +_h E(0) \times_h 14 +_h E(1) \times_h 14 +_h E(0) \times_h 36$. The corresponding equations are: $2r_1 + 3r_2 + 6r_4 = 45$ and $10r_1 + 4r_2 + 7r_4 = 146$. With three unknowns, the receiver will be unable to solve these equations to get the unique values in R^2 to generate the columns of B. This means that the equations for the data values cannot be constructed. Thus the system is secure even in the presence of greedy receivers.* $\square$

3.3.2 Complexity Analysis

At step 1(b) of Algorithm 2, the receiver performs n encryptions, and $2k$ decryptions at step 3(a). Also, at steps 3(c)-(d), the receiver solves k equations which results in a complexity of $O(k^3)$ ordinary multiplications. However, the expensive encryptions dominate the $O(k^3)$ operations to result in $O(n)$ as the complexity for the receiver. At the sender's side, there are $n \cdot k$ homomorphic additions and $n \cdot k$ multiplications at steps 2(e)-(f). Thus the computational complexity of the protocol is $O(n \cdot k)$.

At step 1(b), the receiver sends n encrypted values. At step 2(g), the sender sends back $2k$ ciphertexts to the receiver. Since $n > k$, the overall communication complexity of the protocol is $O(l \cdot n)$ in bits.

3.4 Selection of the Key Size (l)

We now present a systematic approach to selecting a proper key size for the encryption scheme used in protocol II. The encryption function of the paillier scheme requires that the plaintext x is less than 2^l, where l is the key size. The data values v_i's are assumed to be less than 2^α, and the perturbation matrix entries are less than 2^β. In the randomization step (step (d) of Algorithm 2), the data values are multiplied with the perturbation matrix to produce matrices, Y^2. This results in the entries of Y^2 to be less than $2^{\alpha+\beta}$. In Step 3 (Unpacking at Receiver) of the protocol, the receiver decrypts $\bar{Z}_i^2$ to get Z_i^2. Suppose $\alpha + \beta > l$, then it would result in a $v_i * B_{ji}$ that is greater than 2^l. This results in wrong solutions to be computed at the receiver. Thus, the essential condition for the protocol to succeed is $\alpha + \beta < l$. With this condition, the entries $Y_{i,j}^2$'s are less than 2^l. Based on the values of α and β, the receiver selects the key size.

Let us consider Z_1^2 as $z_1 + .. + z_k$ where $z_1 = v_{i_1} * B_{1,i_1}$. It is possible that while each z_i is less than 2^l, the sum Z_1 may be larger than 2^l. Though this is very unlikely to happen, we can alleviate this problem by selecting the key size (l) such that $\alpha + \beta + k < l$, where k is the number of data values transferred. This condition is sufficient for the protocol to succeed all the time. The protocols in Certified E-mail [2] and Simultaneous Contract Signing [21] use OT for transferring keys of symmetric key encryption schemes such as DES and AES. The generally accepted key size for AES is 128 bits (α). For random numbers in matrix A and B, 32 is a sufficient β value. This leaves the key size(l) for the Paillier scheme in our protocol to be greater than 160 bits. Thus the key size of 1,024 is sufficient for the practical purposes of running our protocol.

4. EXPERIMENTAL ANALYSIS

We now report the performance of the protocols, implemented in C and executed on Ubuntu 8.10 with a Intel dual core 2.33 GHz processor and 4 GB RAM. Since computational complexity is the major bottleneck, we show the performance results in terms of time taken at the sender side, since the receiver's computation is a constant number of decryptions. The sender's data values are generated randomly, with the maximum being $2^{32} - 1$ (integer values). Similarly, the random matrix elements are also random integers. We use Paillier encryption scheme for all the three protocols.

Figure 1 shows the effect of k on the running time for a fixed $n = 100$. For this experiment, the key size in the Paillier encryption is set to 1024 bits (sufficiently large for practice as shown in Section 3.4). The Y-axis shows the running time in seconds for k ranging from 5 to 25, while n is fixed at 100. Protocol I is the most efficient, taking a constant time of .03 seconds. Protocol II with $m = 10$ and $m = 20$ take 6 and 12.5 seconds respectively. Protocol III's running time increases sub-linearly as k increases, but remains well under Protocol II ($m = 20$).

At step 3(c)-(d) of Algorithm 2 (Protocol III), the receiver solves equations to get the k values from the sender. In this experiment, we measure the time taken for solving the equations. We used the Matlab software to solve the linear systems by varying the number of equations, which is kept same as the number of unknowns. Figure 2 shows how the running time changes sub-linearly as the number of equations increases. For solving 50 equations (with 50 unknowns) it takes approximately 3.5 milliseconds, and for 100 equations the running time is 7.7 milliseconds. Compared to the time spent on encryptions and decryptions from Figure 1, the time taken for this step is negligible.

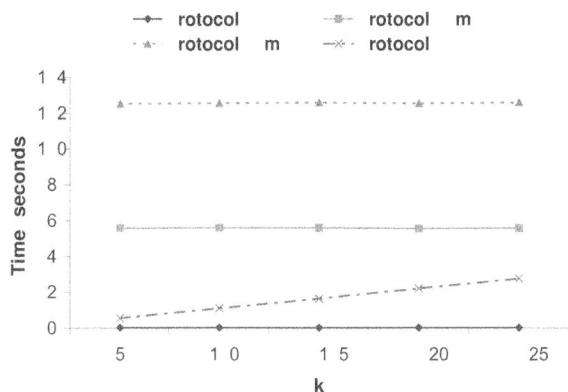

Figure 1: OT_k^{100}: Effect of k for a fixed $n = 100$

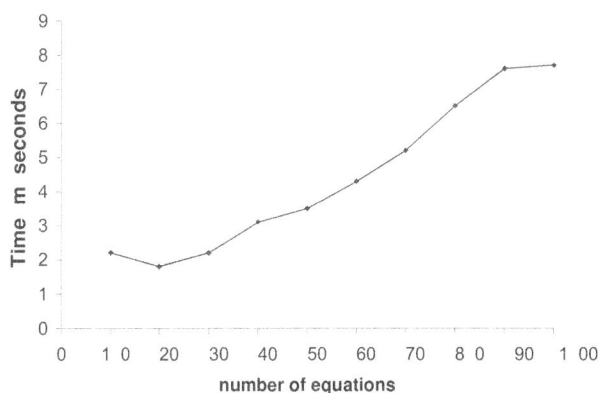

Figure 2: Time taken for solving equations

5. CONCLUSION AND FUTURE WORK

In this paper, we present three efficient k-out-of-n OT protocols that take advantage of additive homomorphic crypto system. While Protocol I is simple and efficient, it does not protect the sender from malicious receiver. Protocol II withstands malicious behaviors from sender and receiver. Moreover, the receiver is caught with $1/m$ probability if it attempts to retrieve more than k values. Protocol III presents a novel technique based on the solvability of linear equations. A malicious receiver will be unable to solve k equations with more than k unknowns. Protocols I and III are very efficient in terms of communication cost since they require only one round and exchange of $O(n)$ messages from the receiver to the sender. As a future work, we shall improve the complexity of communication from the receiver to sender. In case of retrieving small number of items obliviously from a large database, there will be a big network overhead while sending the encrypted index values to the sender. A more efficient protocol could be less dependent on the size of the database.

6. ACKNOWLEDGMENTS

Support for this work was partially provided by MURI award FA9550-08-1-0265 from the Air Force Office of Scientific Research.

7. REFERENCES

[1] J. C. Benaloh. Secret sharing homomorphisms: Keeping shares of a secret secret. In A. Odlyzko, editor, *Advances in Cryptography, CRYPTO86: Proceedings*, volume 263, pages 251–260. Springer-Verlag, Lecture Notes in Computer Science, 1986.

[2] M. Blum. Three application of oblivious transfer: Part i: Coin flipping by telephone; part ii: How to exchange secrets; part iii: How to send certified electronic mail. 1981.

[3] G. Brassard, C. Crépeau, and J.-M. Robert. Information theoretic reductions among disclosure problems. In *FOCS*, pages 168–173, 1986.

[4] G. Brassard, C. Crépeau, and J.-M. Robert. All-or-nothing disclosure of secrets. In *Proceedings on Advances in cryptology—CRYPTO '86*, pages 234–238, London, UK, 1987. Springer-Verlag.

[5] C.-K. Chu and W.-G. Tzeng. Efficient k-out-of-n oblivious transfer schemes. *Journal of Universal Computer Science*, 14(3):397–415, 2008.

[6] C. Cooper. On the distribution of rank of a random matrix over a finite field, June 2000.

[7] C. Crépeau. Equivalence between two flavours of oblivious transfers. In *CRYPTO '87: A Conference on the Theory and Applications of Cryptographic Techniques on Advances in Cryptology*, pages 350–354, London, UK, 1988. Springer-Verlag.

[8] C. Crépeau and J. Kilian. Weakening security assumptions and oblivious transfer. In *CRYPTO '88: Proceedings on Advances in cryptology*, pages 2–7, New York, NY, USA, 1990.

[9] O. Goldreich. *The Foundations of Cryptography*, volume 2, chapter General Cryptographic Protocols. Cambridge University Press, 2004.

[10] O. Goldreich, S. Micali, and A. Wigderson. Proofs that yield nothing but their validity or all languages in np have zero-knowledge proof systems. *Journal of ACM*, 38:690–728, 1991.

[11] S. Goldwasser and S. Micali. Probabilistic encryption. *Journal of Computer and System Sciences*, 28(2):270–299, 1984.

[12] S. Goldwasser, S. Micali, and C. Rackoff. The knowledge complexity of interactive proof systems. In *Proceedings of the 17th Annual ACM Symposium on Theory of Computing (STOC'85)*, pages 291–304, Providence, Rhode Island, U.S.A., May 6-8 1985.

[13] B. Malek and A. Miri. Optimal secure data retrieval using an oblivious transfer scheme. In *IEEE International Conference on Wireless And Mobile Computing, Networking And Communications*, volume 2, pages 25–31, 2005.

[14] H. min Sun, K. hang Wang, and C. fu Hung. Towards privacy preserving digital rights management using oblivious transfer, 2006.

[15] D. Naccache and J. Stern. A new public key cryptosystem based on higher residues. In *Proceedings of the 5th ACM conference on Computer and communications security*, pages 59–66, San Francisco, California, United States, 1998. ACM Press.

[16] M. Naor and B. Pinkas. Oblivious transfer and polynomial evaluation. In *STOC '99: Proceedings of the thirty-first annual ACM symposium on Theory of computing*, pages 245–254, 1999.

[17] T. Okamoto and S. Uchiyama. A new public-key cryptosystem as secure as factoring. In *Advances in Cryptology - Eurocrypt '98, LNCS 1403*, pages 308–318. Springer-Verlag, 1998.

[18] P. Paillier. Public key cryptosystems based on composite degree residuosity classes. In *Advances in Cryptology - Eurocrypt '99 Proceedings, LNCS 1592*. Springer-Verlag, 1999.

[19] B. Pinkas. Fair secure two-party computation. In *Advances in Cryptology – EUROCRYPT)*, pages 87–105, Warsaw, Poland, May 4-8 2003.

[20] M. O. Rabin. How to exchange secrets by oblivious transfer. Technical report, Aiken Computation Laboratory, Harvard University, 1981.

[21] M. Stanek. M.: Efficient simultaneous contract signing. In *In 19th International Conference on Information Security (SEC 2004)*, pages 441–455. Kluwer Academic Publishers, 2004.

[22] Q. Wu, B. Qin, C. Wang, X. Chen, and Y. Wang. t-out-of-n string/bit oblivious transfers revisited. In *ISPEC*, pages 410–421, 2005.

APPENDIX

A. DEFICIENCY OF MM05-OT PROTOCOL

As we mentioned before, there is a flaw related to the MM05-OT protocol that makes it to produce incorrect results. One of the key steps in the MM05-OT protocol is to encrypt a *ciphertext* using Paillier's scheme. However, as we show below, encrypting a ciphertext under Paillier's scheme will "almost always" result in incorrect result.

The main idea behind the MM05-OT protocol is to submit the encrypted index bits of the selection to sender. For example, to select the 3rd entry out of 8 values, the receiver sends $[E(0), E(1), E(1)]$ and $[E(1), E(0), E(0)]$ to the sender. The following construction is an example commonly used in the MM05-OT protocol.

$$E(\bar{x}_1 \cdot E(\bar{x}_0 v_0 + x_0 v_1)) = E(\bar{x}_1)^{E(\bar{x}_0 v_0 + x_0 v_1)}$$

Thus the MM05-OT protocol relies on using ciphertexts in the multiplicative operation of the Paillier. However, this step "almost always" causes the MM05-OT protocol to produce incorrect results. We have the following claim:

CLAIM 1. *The probability for MM05-OT to produce correct results is negligible.*

PROOF. Let P denote the probability that the MM05-OT protocol produces the correct result, l be the size of the encryption key in bits, and M be a plaintext According to Paillier's scheme, $E(M)$ is uniformly distributed in $[0, 2^{2l} - 1]$, for any M in $[0, 2^l - 1]$. Since the MM05-OT protocol requires encrypting a ciphertext, the protocol generates correct results only when $E(M)$ is in $[0, 2^l - 1]$. Therefore, we have the following analysis:

$$\begin{aligned} P &= Prob\left(E(M) \in \left[0, 2^l - 1\right]\right) \\ &= \frac{2^l}{(2^l)^2} = \frac{1}{2^l} \end{aligned}$$

In practice, l is generally greater than 1024. Thus, $P \leq \frac{1}{2^{1024}} \to 0$. As a consequence, the MM05-OT protocol almost never generates correct results. $\square$

B. PROBABILITY OF RANDOM MATRICES BEING SINGULAR

Here we provide more details on the probability that a randomly constructed $k \times k$ matrix has full rank or non-singular. Suppose $A_{k,k}$ is a random matrix, and each value $A_{i,j}$ is bounded by 2^s, where s denotes the number of bits. From [6], we have:

$$Pr(Rank(A) = k) = \Pi_{l=1}^{k}\left(1 - \frac{1}{2^{sl}}\right)$$

A lower bound on this probability can be derived as:

$$Pr(Rank(A) = k) \geq \left(1 - \frac{1}{2^s}\right)^k$$

When k is fixed, the limit of this lower bound goes to 1 as $s \to \infty$. Therefore, we can control this probability by selecting appropriate values for s. For $k = 10$ and $s = 32$, the probability is 0.9999999997671694. In other words, the probability of a 10×10 matrix containing randomly chosen integers being singular (not full rank) is about $1/10^{10}$.

Mixture of Gaussian Models and Bayes Error under Differential Privacy

Bowei Xi
Department of Statistics
Purdue University
xbw@purdue.edu

Murat Kantarcıoğlu
Dept. of Computer Science
University of Texas at Dallas
muratk@utdallas.edu

Ali Inan
Dept. of Computer Eng.
Isik University
Istanbul, Turkey
ali.inan@isikun.edu.tr

ABSTRACT

Gaussian mixture models are an important tool in Bayesian decision theory. In this study, we focus on building such models over statistical database protected under differential privacy. Our approach involves querying necessary statistics from a database and building a Bayesian classifier over the noise added responses generated according to differential privacy. We formally analyze the sensitivity of our query set. Since there are multiple methods to query a statistic, either directly or indirectly, we analyze the sensitivities for different querying methods. Furthermore we establish theoretical bounds for the Bayes error for the univariate (one dimensional) case. We study the Bayes error for the multivariate (high dimensional) case in experiments with both simulated data and real life data. We discover that adding Laplace noise to a statistic under certain constraint is problematic. For example variance-covariance matrix is no longer positive definite after noise addition. We propose a heuristic method to fix the noise added variance-covariance matrix.

Categories and Subject Descriptors

G.3 [**Probability and Statistics**]: Multivariate statistics; H.2.7 [**Database Management**]: Database Administration—*Security, integrity, and protection*; H.2.8 [**Database Management**]: Database Applications—*Statistical databases*

General Terms

Algorithms, Experimentation, Security

Keywords

Differential Privacy, Statistical Databases, Mixture Models, Classification

1. INTRODUCTION

Mixture models are widely used, theoretically mature tools in statistical pattern recognition and pattern classification

[2, 7]. The basic assumption behind mixture models is that the data are obtained by sampling a population consisting of several distinct sub-populations with their own distributions. Gaussian mixture models refer to the case where each model follows multivariate normal (Gaussian) distribution.

Mixture models are suitable for both unsupervised learning (e.g., clustering using the Expectation Maximization algorithm) and supervised learning (e.g., classification using the Bayes' decision rule). In this study, we assume that the records of an input data set belongs to different categories and focus on the classification task. Various studies have established tight bounds on Bayes classification error such as the Chernoff and Bhattacharyya bounds. We investigate the problem of building Gaussian mixture models in a privacy-preserving environment and try to establish similar bounds under differential privacy as the privacy protection mechanism.

Building Gaussian mixture models over a specific data set requires obtaining the mean vector and the covariance matrix for each class/category. This is often a straightforward task. However, when the data set in question contains sensitive information, special care has to be taken. Consider the following motivating scenario. A medical researcher believes that a certain disease (e.g., diabetes mellitus) can be diagnosed based on a series of attributes (e.g., blood pressure, weight, height, blood sugar, etc.) that is assumed to follow multivariate normal distribution and is recorded for every patient admitted to a hospital. The researcher would like to build a Gaussian mixture model and empirically test this belief using the resulting classifier. Yet, the hospital database contains highly sensitive information (e.g., disease history of the patient) and should prevent direct access to the data, even for research purposes.

Instead of granting direct access, the data users (i.e., the researcher in our example) are provided with a sanitized view of the database containing private information[1]. Various alternative privacy protection mechanisms have been suggested for producing a sanitized view. Among the first were anonymization methods such as k-anonymity [14], ℓ-diversity [12], and t-closeness [11]. Anonymization methods try to break the association between data records and individuals by grouping together similar records. Once the groups are formed, through generalization, suppression or partitioning [15] a sanitized version of the data set is released to the data user. Most definitions of anonymity (e.g.,

---

[1]Unless the data are distributed across multiple parties, methods based on Secure Multi-party Computation (SMC) do not apply here.

k-anonymity, ℓ-diversity, etc.) differ in the way the groups are formed.

Anonymization methods protect privacy only against adversaries with certain background information. Dwork proves in [3] that every privacy protection mechanism is vulnerable to some kind of background knowledge and "bad disclosures" might occur regardless of participation into the attacked database. Therefore, Dwork suggests that instead of tailoring privacy definitions against different types of background knowledge, one should minimize the risk of disclosure that arises from participation into a database. This notion is captured by the *differential privacy* protection mechanism [3]. Differential privacy restricts the access to a statistical interface, where users can only issue aggregate statistical queries to the database and the responses are perturbed with random noise. The magnitude of the noise depends on the privacy parameter (e.g., ϵ in ϵ-differential privacy) and sensitivity of the set of queries. Sensitivity is a function of the query set and not the database. As shown in [16], computing the sensitivity is NP-hard.

In this paper, we develop a privacy preserving method of building a Bayesian classifier for the mixture of Gaussian models. This is achieved by modeling the underlying database as a statistical database protected with differential privacy against disclosures, and querying necessary statistics from the database to build the classifier over the noisy responses. Main contributions of this work are as follows:

1. Sensitivity of statistical queries are formally analyzed. More accurate or exact bounds for sensitivity are established.

2. For the univariate (one dimensional) Gaussian case, we establish theoretical bounds on Bayes error under differential privacy based on the Bhattacharyya bound [2].

3. We show the applicability of our methods and examine the Bayes error for the multivariate (high dimensional) Gaussian case through experiments, using both simulated data and real-world data.

4. We propose a heuristic method to fix the noise added variance-covariance matrix, which is no longer positive definite and cannot be directly used in building a Bayesian classifier.

The rest of the paper is organized as follows. We formally define the problem in Section 1.1 and provide a brief overview of differential privacy as a protection mechanism in Section 1.2. Related work in the area is discussed in Section 2. In Section 3, we calculate the sensitivity of various query sets that retrieve necessary statistics from the database. Since the exact value of sensitivity depends on the number of records, our calculation is in terms of the database size. Then, in Section 4, we establish theoretical bounds on the Bayes error under differential privacy as the privacy protection mechanism. Section 5 gives experimental results and finally Section 6 concludes our discussion and presents future directions of research.

1.1 Problem Definition

Let $D = \{A_1, \cdots, A_d\}$ be a *d*-dimensional database such that the domain $Dom(A_i)$ of each attribute A_i, $i = 1, ..., d$, is continuous and bounded. For the analysis of sensitivity in

Section 3, we assume that each domain is normalized to the range $[0, 1]$ to simplify the expression of sensitivity. Assume the database D is comprised of *n* records. Without loss of generality, we assume that D is represented as a relation. Then the value of attribute A_i of record x_k, $k = 1, ..., n$, is denoted by $x_k[A_i]$.

We are interested in building mixture of Gaussian models over databases D that fit the above description. When privacy is not a concern, this is a straightforward task. Without delving into too much details of Gaussian mixture models, let us restrict the discussion to the following: one only needs to compute the expected values of each attribute A_i and the variance-covariance matrix Σ:

$$\Sigma_{ij} = cov(A_i, A_j) = E[(A_i - \mu_i)(A_j - \mu_j)],$$

where $\mu_i = E(A_i)$. More details follow in Section 4.

In our definition of the problem, we consider a database D that contains privacy-sensitive information that is protected through differential privacy. This provides us with a statistical database interface. The interface answers aggregate queries only (e.g. count, sum etc.) and to each response adds random noise [3, 5]. In what follows, we briefly review differential privacy and analyze the sensitivities of certain queries.

1.2 Differential Privacy

Given a set of queries $Q = \{Q_1, ..., Q_q\}$, differential privacy adds Laplace noise with λ magnitude to the true response. Magnitude λ is determined by two parameters: privacy parameter ϵ and query set sensitivity $S(Q)$. Here, ϵ is assumed to be set by the data curator (i.e. the party that holds the database D). Sensitivity $S(Q)$, on the other hand, is a function of the query set Q.

Sensitivity of a query set is defined over all possible pairs of databases that differ in only one record, referred to as sibling databases.

$$S(Q) = \max_{\forall \text{ sibling databases } D_1, D_2} \sum_{i=1}^{q} |Q_i^{D_1} - Q_i^{D_2}| \quad (1)$$

That is, sensitivity of Q is the maximum difference in the total L_1 norm that a single record update can possibly cause in the query responses. Notice that the definition is independent of the original database D.

Once ϵ and $S(Q)$ are known, λ can be set such that $\lambda \geq S(Q)/\epsilon$ to facilitate uninterrupted querying[2]. The rest is straightforward. In response to each query Q_i, the database first computes the result Q_i^D over all records in D and then adds Laplace noise to obtain the noisy response R_i^D:

$$R_i^D = Q_i^D + r, \quad (2)$$

where $r \sim \text{Laplace}(\lambda)$. Obviously, the key to designing accurate differential privacy mechanism is to minimize the sensitivity $S(Q)$. In our problem definition, the query set Q is already fixed. However, there are multiple methods to query a statistic. Therefore we examine the sensitivities for different query approaches separately.

---

[2]If Q is not available ahead of the time and therefore $S(Q)$ cannot be computed, λ will be fixed heuristically. In such scenarios, the database must keep track of the sensitivity of the queries answered so far. If the pre-specified sensitivity threshold λ is exceeded, the database simply stops responding.

2. RELATED WORK

Gaussian mixture models are classical models that are widely used in practice [2, 7]. Despite their popularity in practice, so far, privacy issues related to building mixture models have received little attention. Merugu et al. propose in [13] that instead of perturbing original data to protect privacy, in distributed settings, statistical information describing mixture models can be released. The basic idea is to generate data samples based on mixture models and run data mining tasks over the samples. However, as discussed by Kantarcioglu et al. in [9], releasing (non-perturbed) two-class mixture models might violate individual privacy. Our approach is motivated by the results of [9].

Privacy preserving data mining has been studied extensively in recent years. Initial works in the area consisted mostly of two approaches: 1) perturbation methods (e.g., random noise addition method by Agrawal et al.[1]); 2) anonymization methods (e.g., k-anonymity method proposed by Sweeney [14]) that yield a *sanitized* version of the original data set. However, successful attack strategies against proposed solutions in both directions necessitated new definitions of privacy and anonymity. For example, Kargupta et al. shows in [10] that the random noise added according to [1] could be problematic since "in many cases the original data can be accurately estimated from the perturbed data". Similarly, ℓ-diversity [12] presents an attack scenario against k-anonymity definition of [14] based on lack of diversity over sensitive attributes. Such vulnerabilities have lead to the definition of differential privacy [3]. Dwork proves in [3] that for every privacy definition, there exists some background knowledge that results in disclosure of sensitive information and therefore violation of individual privacy. Consequently, a new and much stronger privacy definition that minimizes the risk of disclosure irrespective of attendance to a database is proposed, namely, differential privacy.

Differential privacy [3] models the database as a statistical database that only responds to statistical queries and adds to the responses random noise, whose magnitude is proportional to the privacy parameter ϵ and the sensitivity of the query set. Here, sensitivity is a function of the query set and not the database in question.

Various different formulations of differential privacy have been suggested. Initial definitions of sensitivity operate over sibling data sets that have the same size but differ in only record (i.e., one data set can be mapped to another by updating only one record) [3, 5]. Some later studies consider insertion of a new record when defining sibling data sets [4]. The distinction between the two approaches might appear minor. However, for most query sets, the prior definition asks for sensitivity computations twice that of the later. We follow [3] in our sensitivity computations.

Sensitivity calculations of many important functions are analyzed in [5], including some statistics used in this paper as well. However, the bounds achieved by [5] are admittedly crude. Dwork et al. calculate the sensitivity of querying the mean vector as $2\gamma/n$, where n is the number of records in the database and $\gamma = \max_x ||v(x)||_1$ (i.e., the maximum L_1 norm of any record). We establish the exact sensitivity on the same query, which equals to one half of the previously established bound: d/n, where d represents the dimensionality (i.e., the number of attributes)[3]. Similarly, [5] crudely

calculates the sensitivity of the variance-covariance matrix Σ. Here, we provide a complete, more formal analysis of the sensitivity of the query retrieving Σ, and establish much tighter bounds.

Privacy preserving classification with differential privacy as the underlying privacy protection mechanism has received little attention so far. In [6], Friedman et al. presented a method of ID3 classification that builds a decision tree through recursive queries retrieving the information gain across an attribute and the partitioning mechanism. A different solution to ID3 classification by Jagannathan et al. [8] builds multiple random decision trees using sum queries. In this study, we present a Bayes classifier based on Gaussian mixture models by querying the mean vector and the covariance matrix for each class category. To the best of our knowledge, we are the first to explore Bayes error for Gaussian mixture models in detail under differential privacy as the protection mechanism.

3. SENSITIVITY AS FUNCTIONS OF SAMPLE SIZE AND DIMENSIONALITY

Assume two sibling databases D_1 and D_2 have n records each, and they differ by one record. Next we establish the sensitivity of queries given sample size n and d attributes. [5] provided upper bounds for the sensitivity of querying mean and variance-covariance matrix. [5] defined $\gamma = max||x'||_1$. Since all the attributes are normalized to $[0, 1]$, $\gamma = d$ in our setting. [5] showed that the sensitivity of directly querying the mean is smaller than or equal to $2d/n$, and the sensitivity of querying the variance-covariance matrix is smaller than or equal to $8d^2/n$. In this section we obtain the exact sensitivity of directly querying the mean, and indirectly through querying sum and sample size, or indirectly querying the median, which is the mean for symmetric distributions. We also obtain a much tighter upper bound for querying the variance-covariance matrix.

We notice there are multiple ways to query a statistic. For example, the value of sample mean can be obtained indirectly through the sample median for any symmetric distribution. The sample mean can also be obtained through the sum divided by the sample size. Users can attempt various methods to query a statistic and to reduce sensitivity. We discuss the different sensitivities associated with the different methods to query a statistic in this section. The following summarize the findings in this section:

1. The sensitivity of directly querying mean is d/n, which decreases with increasing sample size n.

2. The sensitivity of directly querying sum is d, not affected by the sample size n, so is the sensitivity of directly querying median.

3. Notice mean can be obtained indirectly through querying median for symmetric distributions, or through querying sum and sample size. These two indirect query methods for mean have sensitivity not affected by sample size.

---

[3]We assume that all domains are normalized to the range

[0,1], therefore having the value of γ to be fixed, $\gamma = d$. This is a trivial task if the domains are bounded, which has to be the case since differential privacy requires a bounded domain.

4. Directly querying variance has sensitivity between $\frac{1}{n} - \frac{1}{n^2}$ and $\frac{3}{n} - \frac{3}{n^2}$, so does directly querying covariance. Directly querying variance-covariance matrix (upper triangle only) has sensitivity between $(\frac{1}{n} - \frac{1}{n^2})d(d+1)/2$ and $(\frac{3}{n} - \frac{3}{n^2})d(d+1)/2$.

3.1 Directly Querying Mean and Sum

We examine the sensitivity of directly querying the mean and the sum. These two statistics are closely related. One can be solved from another. Yet the sensitivity for querying these two statistics are quite different.

THEOREM 3.1. *Assume we have two sibling databases and each has n records, i.e. $|D_1| = |D_2| = n$, where sample size $n \geq 1$. Let $Q = \{Mean_1, ..., Mean_d\}$, where $d \geq 1$. Hence*

$$S(Q) = d/n.$$

Proof: Let $Mean_i^{(n-1)}$ be the mean of A_i over the common $n-1$ records shared by D_1 and D_2. Let the unique record in D_1 be x_1 and the unique record in D_2 be x_2. Then the mean values of A_i in D_1 and D_2 are

$$Mean_i^{(n),1} = \frac{(n-1) \times Mean_i^{(n-1)} + x_1[A_i]}{n},$$

$$Mean_i^{(n),2} = \frac{(n-1) \times Mean_i^{(n-1)} + x_2[A_i]}{n}.$$

We have

$$|Mean_i^{(n),1} - Mean_i^{(n),2}| = \frac{|x_1[A_i] - x_2[A_i]|}{n}.$$

Then we have

$$max_{\{D_1,D_2\}} \sum_1^d |Mean_i^{(n),1} - Mean_i^{(n),2}|$$
$$= \left(max_{\{D_1,D_2\}} \sum_{i=1}^d |x_1[A_i] - x_2[A_i]| \right)/n$$
$$= \quad d/n \quad = \quad S(Q).$$

When all the d attributes in the x_1 and x_2 differ by 1, we reach the maximum, which determines the sensitivity. ■

THEOREM 3.2. *Assume we have two sibling databases and each has n records, i.e. $|D_1| = |D_2| = n$, where sample size $n \geq 1$. Let $Q = \{Sum_1, ..., Sum_d\}$, where $d \geq 1$. Hence*

$$S(Q) = d.$$

Proof: Let $Sum_i^{(n-1)}$ be the sum of attribute A_i over the common $n-1$ records shared by D_1 and D_2. Again let the unique record in D_1 be x_1 and the unique record in D_2 be x_2. Then the sum of A_i in D_1 and D_2 are

$$Sum_i^{(n),1} = Sum_i^{(n-1)} + x_1[A_i],$$

$$Sum_i^{(n),2} = Sum_i^{(n-1)} + x_2[A_i].$$

When all the d attributes in the x_1 and x_2 differ by 1, we have

$$max_{\{D_1,D_2\}} \sum_1^d |Sum_i^{(n),1} - Sum_i^{(n),2}|$$
$$= \quad max_{\{D_1,D_2\}} \sum_{i=1}^d |x_1[A_i] - x_2[A_i]|$$
$$= \quad d \quad = \quad S(Q).$$

The two theorems do not rely on the distribution of A_i over the interval $[0,1]$. The sensitivity of $Q = \{Mean_1, ..., Mean_d\}$ improves linearly as the sample size n increases given a fixed d. It requires the sample size to be much larger than the dimensionality, $n >> d$, to have a small sensitivity. On the other hand increasing the sample size n will not improve the sensitivity of $Q = \{Sum_1, ..., Sum_d\}$, which is determined solely by dimensionality.

Since sensitivity is defined over all possible sibling databases with all possible sample sizes, the following corollary establishes the overall sensitivity of directly querying the mean.

COROLLARY 3.1. *Let $Q = \{Mean_1, ..., Mean_d\}$, where $d \geq 1$. $S(Q) = d$, for all possible pairs of sibling databases.*

Proof: Following Theorem 3.1, when we set n=1, we obtain the maximum change of L_1 norm over all possible sibling databases. The problem can be solved in a more straightforward fashion. Note $Mean_i$ has minimum value 0 and maximum value 1. Let D_1 and D_2 each contains 1 record. $x_1 = \vec{0}$ and $x_2 = \vec{1}$. Then D_1 has the minimum $Mean_i$ $\forall i = 1, ..., d$ and D_2 has the maximum $Mean_i$ $\forall i = 1, ..., d$. The maximum L_1 difference is $d = S(Q)$. ■

3.2 Directly Querying Median

For Gaussian distribution, or in general any symmetric distribution, median equals to mean. However the sensitivity of directly querying the median is quite different than that of directly querying the mean. The sensitivity of directly querying the median of d attributes is a constant d, same as directly querying the sum, regardless of sample size n.

THEOREM 3.3. *Let $Q = \{Median_1, ..., Median_d\}$, such that $Median_i$ retrieves the median of attribute A_i. Hence the overall sensitivity for for all possible pairs of sibling databases is:*

$$S(Q) = d.$$

Proof: First consider one attribute A_i. Since attribute A_i is normalized to interval $[0,1]$, the minimum value of the median is 0 and the maximum is 1. Therefore, it is sufficient to show that there is a pair of sibling databases (D_1, D_2) such that the response to $Median_i$ shifts by 1.

Let database D_1 have $2m+1$ records, $m \geq 0$, where

$$x_j[A_i] = \begin{cases} 0, & if \ 1 \leq j \leq m+1 \\ 1, & otherwise. \end{cases}$$

Construct database D_2 by changing the value of $x_m[A_i]$ from 0 to 1. Notice the response to $Median_i$ over D_1 is 0, while it is 1 over D_2, which achieves the maximum L_1 difference.

For $Q = \{Median_1, ..., Median_d\}$, similarly we let D_1 have

$$x_j = \begin{cases} \vec{0}, & if \ 1 \leq j \leq m+1 \\ \vec{1}, & otherwise. \end{cases}$$

Construct database D_2 by changing the value of x_{m+1} from $\vec{0}$ to $\vec{1}$. Hence the responses to the query over D_1 and D_2 achieve the maximum difference in L_1 norm. We conclude $S(Q) = d$, $\forall n \geq 1$. ■

3.3 Indirectly Querying Mean

There are multiple ways of estimating a statistic. For example, querying the median is equivalent to querying the mean for any symmetric distribution. Another choice is to issue two queries, one for sum and the other for sample size.

THEOREM 3.4. *Assume we have two sibling databases and each has n records, i.e. $|D_1| = |D_2| = n$, where sample size $n \geq 1$. Let $Q = \{Sum_1, ..., Sum_d, SampleSize\}$, where $d \geq 1$. Hence $S(Q) = d$.*

Proof: The query for sample size has sensitivity 0, since both D_1 and D_2 have the same sample size. Then we only need to consider the sensitivity of Sum_i. Similar to the proof of Theorem 3.2, we obtain $S(Q) = d$. ∎

3.4 Directly Querying Variance and Covariance

Next we examine the sensitivity of directly querying variance, covariance, and the whole variance-covariance matrix. We establish much tighter bounds for the sensitivity in this section.

THEOREM 3.5. *Assume we have two sibling databases and each has n records, i.e. $|D_1| = |D_2| = n$, where sample size $n \geq 2$. Without loss of generality let $Q = \{Var_1\}$ for attribute A_1. Then*

$$\frac{1}{n} - \frac{1}{n^2} \leq S(Q) \leq \frac{3}{n} - \frac{3}{n^2}.$$

Proof: Assume $x_3, ..., x_{n+1}$ are the $n-1$ common records shared by the two databases D_1 and D_2. Let x_1 be the unique record in D_1 and x_2 be the unique record in D_2. Here we estimate the sample variance as the following:

$$Var_1 = \frac{1}{n}\sum_{i=1}^{n}(x_i[A_1] - \bar{x}[A_1])^2 = \frac{\sum_{i=1}^{n}x_i^2[A_1]}{n} - \bar{x}^2[A_1].$$

Let Var_1^i be the sample variance of database D_i, $i = 1, 2$. Then we have

$$
\begin{aligned}
&Var_1^1 - Var_1^2\\
=&\left[\frac{\sum_{i=3}^{n+1}x_i^2[A_1] + x_1^2[A_1]}{n} - \left(\frac{\sum_{i=3}^{n+1}x_i[A_1] + x_1[A_1]}{n}\right)^2\right]\\
&-\left[\frac{\sum_{i=3}^{n+1}x_i^2[A_1] + x_2^2[A_1]}{n} - \left(\frac{\sum_{i=3}^{n+1}x_i[A_1] + x_2[A_1]}{n}\right)^2\right]\\
=&(x_1^2[A_1] - x_2^2[A_1])(\frac{1}{n} - \frac{1}{n^2})\\
&+\frac{2(x_2[A_1] - x_1[A_1])(\sum_{i=3}^{n+1}x_i[A_1])}{n^2}
\end{aligned}
$$

When $x_i[A_1] = 0$, $i = 3, ..., n+1$, $x_1[A_1] = 1$, and $x_2[A_1] = 0$, we have

$$Var_1^1 - Var_1^2 = \frac{1}{n} - \frac{1}{n^2}.$$

This is a lower bound for $S(Q)$.

On the other hand we have

$$
\begin{aligned}
|Var_1^1 - Var_1^2| &\leq \left|(x_1^2[A_1] - x_2^2[A_1])(\frac{1}{n} - \frac{1}{n^2})\right|\\
&+\left|\frac{2(x_2[A_1] - x_1[A_1])(\sum_{i=3}^{n+1}x_i[A_1])}{n^2}\right|
\end{aligned}
$$

We obtain an upper bound by letting every component on the right hand side of the above inequality reach their maximum individually.

$$
\begin{aligned}
max|Var_1^1 - Var_1^2| &\leq 1 \times (\frac{1}{n} - \frac{1}{n^2}) + \frac{2 \times 1 \times (n-1)}{n^2}\\
&= \frac{3}{n} - \frac{3}{n^2}
\end{aligned}
$$

Therefore we have

$$\frac{1}{n} - \frac{1}{n^2} \leq S(Q) \leq \frac{3}{n} - \frac{3}{n^2}.$$

∎

THEOREM 3.6. *Assume we have two sibling databases and each has n records, i.e. $|D_1| = |D_2| = n$, where sample size $n \geq 2$. Without loss of generality let $Q = \{Cov_{1,2}\}$ for attributes A_1 and A_2. Then*

$$\frac{1}{n} - \frac{1}{n^2} \leq S(Q) \leq \frac{3}{n} - \frac{3}{n^2}.$$

Proof: Again assume $x_3, ..., x_{n+1}$ are the $n-1$ common records shared by the two databases D_1 and D_2. Let x_1 be the unique record in D_1 and x_2 be the unique record in D_2. The sample covariance is the following:

$$
\begin{aligned}
Cov_{1,2} &= \frac{1}{n}\sum_{i=1}^{n}(x_i[A_1] - \bar{x}[A_1])(x_i[A_2] - \bar{x}[A_2])\\
&= \frac{\sum_{i=1}^{n}x_i[A_1]x_i[A_2]}{n} - \bar{x}[A_1]\bar{x}[A_2].
\end{aligned}
$$

We have the difference as

$$
\begin{aligned}
&Cov_{1,2}^1 - Cov_{1,2}^2\\
=&\frac{\sum_{i=3}^{n+1}x_i[A_1]x_i[A_2] + x_1[A_1]x_1[A_2]}{n}\\
&-(\frac{\sum_{i=3}^{n+1}x_i[A_1] + x_1[A_1]}{n}) \times (\frac{\sum_{i=3}^{n+1}x_i[A_2] + x_1[A_2]}{n})\\
&-\frac{\sum_{i=3}^{n+1}x_i[A_1]x_i[A_2] + x_2[A_1]x_2[A_2]}{n}\\
&+(\frac{\sum_{i=3}^{n+1}x_i[A_1] + x_2[A_1]}{n}) \times (\frac{\sum_{i=3}^{n+1}x_i[A_2] + x_2[A_2]}{n})
\end{aligned}
$$

Cleaning up the above expression we have

$$
\begin{aligned}
&Cov_{1,2}^1 - Cov_{1,2}^2\\
=&(x_1[A_1]x_1[A_2] - x_2[A_1]x_2[A_2])\left(\frac{1}{n} - \frac{1}{n^2}\right)\\
&-(x_1[A_1] - x_2[A_1])\left(\frac{\sum_{i=3}^{n+1}x_i[A_2]}{n^2}\right)\\
&-(x_1[A_2] - x_2[A_2])\left(\frac{\sum_{i=3}^{n+1}x_i[A_1]}{n^2}\right)
\end{aligned}
$$

Let $x_i[A_1] = x_i[A_2] = 0$ for $i = 3, ..., n+1$, $x_1[A_1] = x_1[A_2] = 1$, and $x_2[A_1] = x_2[A_2] = 0$. We have $Cov_{1,2}^1 - Cov_{1,2}^2 = 1/n - 1/n^2$. Hence this is a lower bound of $S(Q)$.

We also have

$$
\begin{aligned}
&|Cov_{1,2}^1 - Cov_{1,2}^2| \\
\leq\ & |x_1[A_1]x_1[A_2] - x_2[A_1]x_2[A_2]| \left(\frac{1}{n} - \frac{1}{n^2}\right) \\
+\ & |x_1[A_1] - x_2[A_1]| \left|\frac{\sum_{i=3}^{n+1} x_i[A_2]}{n^2}\right| \\
+\ & |x_1[A_2] - x_2[A_2]| \left|\frac{\sum_{i=3}^{n+1} x_i[A_1]}{n^2}\right|
\end{aligned}
$$

Let every component reach their maximum values, we have

$$
\begin{aligned}
max|Cov_{1,2}^1 - Cov_{1,2}^2| &\leq \left(\frac{1}{n} - \frac{1}{n^2}\right) + \frac{n-1}{n^2} + \frac{n-1}{n^2} \\
&= \frac{3}{n} - \frac{3}{n^2}.
\end{aligned}
$$

Therefore we have

$$
\frac{1}{n} - \frac{1}{n^2} \leq S(Q) \leq \frac{3}{n} - \frac{3}{n^2}.
$$

For large sample size n, the above result shows the sensitivity of a single variance or a single covariance decreases as $O(1/n)$. Next we consider querying the whole variance-covariance matrix.

THEOREM 3.7. *Assume we have two sibling databases and each has n records, i.e. $|D_1| = |D_2| = n$, where sample size $n \geq 2$. Without loss of generality let $Q = \{\Sigma\}$ for d attributes. We consider only the upper triangle. Then*

$$
\left(\frac{1}{n} - \frac{1}{n^2}\right)\frac{d(d+1)}{2} \leq S(Q) \leq \left(\frac{3}{n} - \frac{3}{n^2}\right)\frac{d(d+1)}{2}.
$$

Proof: Again assume $x_3, ..., x_{n+1}$ are the $n-1$ common records shared by the two databases D_1 and D_2. Let x_1 be the unique record in D_1 and x_2 be the unique record in D_2. We follow the thread in the above two theorems. Then we have

$$
\begin{aligned}
&|Q^1 - Q^2| \\
=\ & \sum_{k=1}^{d-1}\sum_{l=k+1}^{d} |(x_1[A_k]x_1[A_l] - x_2[A_k]x_2[A_l])(\frac{1}{n} - \frac{1}{n^2}) \\
&- (x_1[A_k] - x_2[A_k])\left(\frac{\sum_{i=3}^{n+1} x_i[A_l]}{n^2}\right) \\
&- (x_1[A_l] - x_2[A_l])\left(\frac{\sum_{i=3}^{n+1} x_i[A_k]}{n^2}\right)| \\
+\ & \sum_{k=1}^{d} |(x_1^2[A_k] - x_2^2[A_k])(\frac{1}{n} - \frac{1}{n^2}) \\
&- 2(x_1[A_k] - x_2[A_k])\left(\frac{\sum_{i=3}^{n+1} x_i[A_k]}{n^2}\right)|
\end{aligned}
$$

When $x_3 = ... = x_{n+1} = \vec{0}$, $x_2 = \vec{0}$, and $x_1 = \vec{1}$, we have the above sum equal to $(\frac{1}{n} - \frac{1}{n^2})\frac{d(d+1)}{2}$. This forms a lower

bound of $S(Q)$. We also have

$$
\begin{aligned}
&|Q^1 - Q^2| \\
\leq\ & \sum_{k=1}^{d-1}\sum_{l=k+1}^{d} \{\ |x_1[A_k]x_1[A_l] - x_2[A_k]x_2[A_l]| \times (\frac{1}{n} - \frac{1}{n^2}) \\
+\ & |x_1[A_k] - x_2[A_k]| \times \left|\frac{\sum_{i=3}^{n+1} x_i[A_l]}{n^2}\right| \\
+\ & |x_1[A_l] - x_2[A_l]| \times \left|\frac{\sum_{i=3}^{n+1} x_i[A_k]}{n^2}\right|\ \} \\
+\ & \sum_{k=1}^{d} \{\ |x_1^2[A_k] - x_2^2[A_k]| \times (\frac{1}{n} - \frac{1}{n^2}) \\
+\ & 2|x_1[A_k] - x_2[A_k]| \times |\frac{\sum_{i=3}^{n+1} x_i[A_k]}{n^2}|\ \}
\end{aligned}
$$

Let each component reach their maximum values (i.e. $x_3 = ... = x_{n+1} = \vec{1}$), we have

$$
max|Q^1 - Q^2| \leq (\frac{3}{n} - \frac{3}{n^2})\frac{d(d+1)}{2}.
$$

Hence we establish an upper bound for $S(Q)$ too. Combining the lower and upper bounds we have:

$$
(\frac{1}{n} - \frac{1}{n^2})\frac{d(d+1)}{2} \leq S(Q) \leq (\frac{3}{n} - \frac{3}{n^2})\frac{d(d+1)}{2}.
$$

We obtain a much tighter bound for querying the variance-covariance matrix. The above result indicates that in order to reduce sensitivity for querying the whole variance-covariance matrix, we need the sample size to be much larger than d^2, $n >> d^2$. Next as what we do for directly querying the mean, we can obtain an upper bound for the maximum change in L_1 norm for querying the variance-covariance matrix for all possible sibling databases with all possible sample sizes. The following establishes an upper bound for the overall sensitivity of directly querying the variance-covariance matrix.

COROLLARY 3.2. *Let $Q = \{\Sigma\}$, where Σ retrieves the variance-covariance matrix. $S(Q) \leq 3d(d+1)/8$.*

Proof: We let $n = 2$ in the upper bound specified by Theorem 3.7. We then obtain the overall upper bound for all possible sample size: $S(Q) \leq 3d(d+1)/8$. ∎

The primary reason behind high overall sensitivity in Corollaries 3.1 and 3.2 calculations is the small sample size of the databases. Even though any databases that will be used to build Gaussian mixture models would contain thousands if not millions of records, by definition sensitivity is calculated over all possible sibling databases.

3.5 Multiple Querying Methods for A Statistic and The Effect on Sensitivity

Different methods to issue the queries for the same statistic are associated with very different sensitivity values. To obtain the sample mean, we can query the median instead if the attribute is from a symmetric distribution, or we can query the sum and the sample size. Based on the above theorems, we discover that querying the median or the sum together with sample size has sensitivity d, which is not affected by sample size n. Directly querying the mean has sensitivity d/n, fast approaching 0 as sample size increases. Some indirect queries can result in high sensitivity.

There are also alternative methods to issues a set of queries to construct variance, covariance, and a variance-covariance matrix, instead of directly querying the statistics. For example, for attribute A_1, we can query the sums and the sample size, i.e. $\sum_{i=1}^n x_i[A_1]$, $\sum_{i=1}^n x_i^2[A_1]$, and n. Another method is to query the means, i.e. $(\sum_{i=1}^n x_i[A_1])/n$ and $(\sum_{i=1}^n x_i^2[A_1])/n$. We then construct the variance from the sums or the means. However querying the sums and querying the means have very different sensitivity values.

While working with differential privacy, we usually try to come up with query methods that will perturb the results as little as possible. However, most accurate results need not be computed with query sets of smaller sensitivities. Comparing the direct query for mean in Corollary 3.1 and the indirect query in Theorem 3.4, we observe the indirect query is more resilient to noise. Any positive or negative noise with magnitude larger than 1 completely disguise the mean value retrieved by direct querying (as in Corollary 3.1). Yet Laplace distribution has support over $(-\infty, \infty)$. The conclusion we would like to draw is that, directly querying a statistic may not always be the best idea, especially for databases with small sample size.

Later in simulation we assume databases have relatively large sample size and we apply sensitivity values of directly querying the mean and variance-covariance matrix, after adjusting for the range.

4. BAYES ERROR OF GAUSSIAN MIXTURE MODELS UNDER DIFFERENTIAL PRIVACY

Let $D = \{A_1, \ldots, A_d, W\}$ be a database of n records, where W represents a binary class attribute with the domain

$$Dom(W) = \{w_1, w_2\},$$

and each attribute A_i, $1 \leq i \leq d$ represents a continuous attribute with the domain $Dom(A_i) = \mathbf{R}$.

Our purpose is to build a classifier using D that, given a non-classified record in terms of a d-dimensional feature vector $\mathbf{x} \in \mathbf{R}^d$, assigns a class value to $\mathbf{x}$ such that the probability of mis-classification

$$P(error|\mathbf{x}) = \begin{cases} P(w_1|\mathbf{x}) & \text{if } \mathbf{x} \in w_2 \\ P(w_2|\mathbf{x}) & \text{if } \mathbf{x} \in w_1 \end{cases}$$

is minimized. The following Bayes' decision rule describes one such classifier:

Assign w_1 if $P(w_1|\mathbf{x}) > P(w_2|\mathbf{x})$; otherwise assign w_2.
(3)

Here, the probabilities $P(w_i|\mathbf{x})$ can easily be calculated based on Bayes' theorem:

$$P(w_i|\mathbf{x}) = \frac{p(\mathbf{x}|w_i)P(w_i)}{p(\mathbf{x})}.$$

The specific case where $p(\mathbf{x}|w_i)$ has multivariate normal (Gaussian) density is known as the "mixture of Gaussian models" problem and it has been studied extensively due to its tractability [2]. For each class value w_i, the mean μ_i and the covariance matrix Σ_i of the distribution of $p(\mathbf{x}|w_i) \sim N(\mu_i, \Sigma_i)$ are estimated from the data set D. Based on the parameters of these distributions, the feature space $\mathbf{R}^d$ can

be partitioned into possibly disconnected decision regions $\mathcal{R}_i$ such that $\mathbf{x} \in \mathcal{R}_i$ implies $\mathbf{x}$ will be classified as w_i.

The Bayes error is calculated by integrating the probability of incorrect decision(s) over decision regions. For binary classification, this implies [2]:

$$\begin{aligned} \text{Bayes Error} &= P(\mathbf{x} \in R_1, w_2) + P(\mathbf{x} \in R_2, w_1) \\ &= P(\mathbf{x} \in R_1|w_2)P(w_2) + P(\mathbf{x} \in R_2|w_1)P(w_1) \\ &= \int_{\mathcal{R}_1} p(\mathbf{x}|w_2)P(w_2)d\mathbf{x} + \int_{\mathcal{R}_2} p(\mathbf{x}|w_1)P(w_1)d\mathbf{x} \end{aligned}$$

In mixture of Gaussian models, such error can be bounded from above using the *Chernoff* bound or the *Bhattacharyya* bound as explained in [2]. Among these two approaches, the Chernoff bound is never looser than the Bhattacharyya but computationally more complex.

Our purpose is to calculate similar error bounds for privacy preserving Gaussian mixture models. Specifically, data set D will act as a statistical database that only responds to aggregate queries about the records. Using differential privacy as the underlying privacy protection mechanism, all responses to the queries will be perturbed with independent Laplace noise $\mathcal{L}(0, \lambda)$, where $\lambda \geq S(Q)/\epsilon$ is the magnitude of the added noise, $S(Q)$ is the sensitivity of the query set issued to the database (as defined in [3]) and ϵ is the privacy parameter.

In order to build a Gaussian mixture model, the query set Q including the following statistical information has to be issued to the database D:

- The number of records in D (sensitivity of this query is 0),

- The distribution of class values / categories (i.e., $P(w_1)$ and $P(w_2)$),

- For each category, parameters of the multivariate Gaussian distribution (i.e., $p(\mathbf{x}|w_i)$) in terms of μ_i and Σ_i.

4.1 Truncated Gaussian Distribution

Differential privacy works well for bounded variables. For unbounded variables one extremely large or small record has the ability to cause an extremely large change in any statistic queried and inflate the sensitivity. However Gaussian distribution has support over the entire real line. Assume we truncate a Gaussian variable to interval $[\mu - k\sigma, \mu + k\sigma]$ and the original Gaussian variable $X \sim N(\mu, \sigma^2)$ has density $f(x)$. The truncated Gaussian variable has density:

$$I_{\{\mu - k\sigma \leq x \leq \mu + k\sigma\}}(x) \frac{f(x)}{Z(k) - Z(-k)},$$

where $Z(\cdot)$ is the cumulative distribution function of the standard normal variable, and $I_{\mu - k\sigma \leq x \leq \mu + k\sigma}(x)$ is an indicator function. If we choose sufficiently large k, $Z(k) - Z(-k)$ is almost 1, and the truncated Gaussian variable and the genuine Gaussian variable have almost identical properties, such as density, mean, variance etc. We notice a Gaussian variable has probability 0.999999998 to fall into the bounded interval $[\mu - 6\sigma, \mu + 6\sigma]$. Therefore in the simulation study we choose $k = 6$.

4.2 One Dimensional Bayes Error Bound

We can obtain an upper bound for the one dimensional Bayes error with Gaussian mixture models under differential privacy for binary classes. Assume class $\omega_1 \sim N(\mu_1, \sigma_1^2)$ and class $\omega_2 \sim N(\mu_2, \sigma_2^2)$. Further assume class ω_1 has n_1 records and class ω_2 has n_2 records. First note the *Bhattacharyya* bound [2] states that

$$\text{Bayes Error} \leq \sqrt{P(\omega_1)P(\omega_2)}e^{-K}, \qquad (4)$$

where

$$K = \frac{1}{4}\frac{\mu_1^2 + \mu_2^2 - 2\mu_1\mu_2}{\sigma_1^2 + \sigma_2^2} + \frac{\log(\sigma_1^2 + \sigma_2^2)}{2} - \frac{\log(4\sigma_1^2\sigma_2^2)}{4}. \quad (5)$$

Considering the Laplace noises added to the queries of mean and variances in each class, we have the following theorem.

THEOREM 4.1. *The Gaussian mixture models are as specified above. Assume under differential privacy the query responses are the sample means and the sample variances plus independent Laplace noises:*

$$\hat{\mu}_1 = \bar{x}_1 + r_1, \ \hat{\mu}_2 = \bar{x}_2 + r_2, \ \hat{\sigma}_1^2 = S_1^2 + r_3, \ \hat{\sigma}_2^2 = S_2^2 + r_4.$$

Since there are multiple ways to query a statistic, we simply assume the independent Laplace noises $r_i \sim L(0, \lambda_i)$ for a general result. We have for $0 < p < 1$,

$$P(K^L(p) < K < K^U(p)) = p^8,$$

and

$$Pr(\text{Bayes Error} < \sqrt{P(\omega_1)P(\omega_2)}e^{-K^L(p)}) \geq p^8,$$

where

$$K^U(p) =$$

$$\frac{\sum_{i=1}^2 \{\mu_i + \sqrt{\frac{\sigma_i^2}{n_i}}Z(1-\frac{p}{2}) - \lambda_i\log(1-2|\frac{1-p}{2}|)\}^2}{4\{\sum_{i=1}^2 \frac{\sigma_i^2}{n_i}\chi_{n_i-1}^2(\frac{p}{2}) + \sum_{i=3}^4 \lambda_i\log(1-2|\frac{1-p}{2}|)\}}$$

$$- \frac{\prod_{i=1}^2 \{\mu_i - \sqrt{\frac{\sigma_i^2}{n_i}}Z(1-\frac{p}{2}) + \lambda_i\log(1-2|\frac{1-p}{2}|)\}^2}{2\{\sum_{i=1}^2 \frac{\sigma_i^2}{n_i}\chi_{n_i-1}^2(1-\frac{p}{2}) - \sum_{i=3}^4 \lambda_i\log(1-2|\frac{1-p}{2}|)\}}$$

$$+ \frac{\log\{\sum_{i=1}^2 \frac{\sigma_i^2}{n_i}\chi_{n_i-1}^2(1-\frac{p}{2}) - \sum_{i=3}^4 \lambda_i\log(1-2|\frac{1-p}{2}|)\}}{2}$$

$$- \frac{\log\{4\prod_{i=1}^2 [\frac{\sigma_i^2}{n_i}\chi_{n_i-1}^2(\frac{p}{2}) + \lambda_{i+2}\log(1-2|\frac{1-p}{2}|)]\}}{4},$$

and

$$K^L(p) =$$

$$\frac{\sum_{i=1}^2 \{\mu_i - \sqrt{\frac{\sigma_i^2}{n_i}}Z(1-\frac{p}{2}) + \lambda_i\log(1-2|\frac{1-p}{2}|)\}^2}{4\{\sum_{i=1}^2 \frac{\sigma_i^2}{n_i}\chi_{n_i-1}^2(1-\frac{p}{2}) - \sum_{i=3}^4 \lambda_i\log(1-2|\frac{1-p}{2}|)\}}$$

$$- \frac{\prod_{i=1}^2 \{\mu_i + \sqrt{\frac{\sigma_i^2}{n_i}}Z(1-\frac{p}{2}) - \lambda_i\log(1-2|\frac{1-p}{2}|)\}^2}{2\{\sum_{i=1}^2 \frac{\sigma_i^2}{n_i}\chi_{n_i-1}^2(\frac{p}{2}) + \sum_{i=3}^4 \lambda_i\log(1-2|\frac{1-p}{2}|)\}}$$

$$+ \frac{\log\{\sum_{i=1}^2 \frac{\sigma_i^2}{n_i}\chi_{n_i-1}^2(\frac{p}{2}) + \sum_{i=3}^4 \lambda_i\log(1-2|\frac{1-p}{2}|)\}}{2}$$

$$- \frac{\log\{4\prod_{i=1}^2 [\frac{\sigma_i^2}{n_i}\chi_{n_i-1}^2(1-\frac{p}{2}) - \lambda_{i+2}\log(1-2|\frac{1-p}{2}|)]\}}{4}.$$

$Z(r)$ *is the r quantile of the standard normal distribution. $\chi_{n-1}^2(r)$ is the r quantile of χ_{n-1}^2. $\lambda\log(1-2|\frac{1-p}{2}|)$ and $-\lambda\log(1-2|\frac{1-p}{2}|)$ are $p/2$ and $(1-p/2)$ quantile of Laplace distribution $L(0, \lambda)$.*

Proof: Since both classes follow Gaussian distribution, we have the following distribution for the sample means and the sample variances:

$$\bar{x}_1 \sim N(\mu_1, \frac{\sigma_1^2}{n_1}),$$

$$\bar{x}_2 \sim N(\mu_2, \frac{\sigma_2^2}{n_2}),$$

$$\frac{n_1 S_1^2}{\sigma_1^2} = \frac{\sum_{i=1}^{n_1}(x_{1,i} - \bar{x}_1)^2}{\sigma_1^2} \sim \chi_{n_1-1}^2,$$

$$\frac{n_2 S_2^2}{\sigma_2^2} = \frac{\sum_{i=1}^{n_2}(x_{2,i} - \bar{x}_2)^2}{\sigma_2^2} \sim \chi_{n_2-1}^2.$$

Note the sample means and the sample variances are independent. Also note we add independent Laplace noises $r_i \sim L(0, \lambda_i)$,

$$\hat{\mu}_1 = \bar{x}_1 + r_1, \ \hat{\mu}_2 = \bar{x}_2 + r_2, \ \hat{\sigma}_1^2 = S_1^2 + r_3, \ \hat{\sigma}_2^2 = S_2^2 + r_4.$$

With probability p (for example $p = 0.90, 0.95$, etc.), we have:

$$\mu_i - \sqrt{\frac{\sigma_i^2}{n_i}} \times Z(1-\frac{p}{2}) < \bar{x}_i < \mu_i + \sqrt{\frac{\sigma_i^2}{n_i}} \times Z(1-\frac{p}{2}), \ i = 1, 2,$$

$$\frac{\sigma_i^2}{n_i} \times \chi_{n_i-1}^2(\frac{p}{2}) < S_i^2 < \frac{\sigma_i^2}{n_i} \times \chi_{n_i-1}^2(1-\frac{p}{2}), \ i = 1, 2,$$

$$\lambda_i \log(1-2|\frac{1-p}{2}|) < r_i < -\lambda_i \log(1-2|\frac{1-p}{2}|), \ i = 1 - 4,$$

where $Z(1 - p/2)$ is the $(1 - p/2)$ quantile of the standard normal distribution, $\chi_{n_i-1}^2(r)$ is the r quantile of $\chi_{n_i-1}^2$ ($r = p/2$ or $1-p/2$), and $\lambda_i \log(1-2|\frac{1-p}{2}|)$ and $-\lambda_i\log(1-2|\frac{1-p}{2}|)$ are $p/2$ and $(1-p/2)$ quantile of Laplace distribution $L(0, \lambda_i)$.

In Equation 5, plugging in the bounds of the sample means, the sample variances, and the Laplace noises, we have:

$$Pr(K^L(p) < K < K^U(p)) = p^8,$$

where $K^L(p)$ and $K^U(p)$ are specified in the main theorem. Because $Pr(K^L(p) < K) \geq p^8$, we have

$$Pr(\text{Bayes Error} < \sqrt{P(\omega_1)P(\omega_2)}e^{-K^L(p)}) \geq p^8.$$

∎

The proof is based on genuine Gaussian distributions. Bhattacharyya bound can be applied to truncated Gaussian distribution [2] and we can obtain useful information if k is sufficiently large. We are not able to develop theoretical results for multivariate Gaussian distribution. We obtain information for high dimensional Bayes error through experiments in the next section.

5. EXPERIMENTAL EVALUATION

In order to evaluate the performance of Gaussian mixture models learned from data under differential privacy, we have conducted extensive experiments. Since our goal is to understand how differential privacy affects the Bayes error of Gaussian mixture models, we try to avoid introducing other types of errors. Clearly, one of the issues with using Gaussian mixture models in practice is that such models may not represent the underlying data accurately. To sidestep this issue, and make sure that we do not have additional errors due to modeling real data distribution inaccurately, we generated data sets from known Gaussian mixture parameters. The parameters are estimated from real life data in one experiment, and synthetic in the rest. Later on, we use these data sets for our experiments. By using such generated data sets, we ensure that we do not introduce errors due to wrong model selection.

Each reported experiment is repeated five times using the following steps:

1. Given the parameters of the Gaussian mixture models, we generate training sets of increasing sample sizes.

2. Since differential privacy requires bounded attribute values, we truncate the generated training samples using $\mu \pm 6\sigma$ confidence intervals for every attribute.

3. Using the truncated training data set, pre-specified ϵ value, and the sensitivity values computed after adjusting for the actual range of every attribute, we add Laplace noise to the mean and variance-covariance matrix of each Gaussian component. One issue we have to deal with in our experiments is the fact that after noise addition, the variance-covariance matrix cease to be a positive definite matrix. In order to make sure that the privacy properties of the Laplace noise addition are protected, we employ the following heuristic processing on the *noise added variance-covariance matrix* M:

   (a) Copy the noise added upper triangle of the matrix M to lower triangle to make M symmetric.

   (b) Using eigenvalue decomposition, represent M as $V \times D \times V'$ where V is an orthogonal matrix of eigenvectors and D is a diagonal matrix of eigenvalues. If any of the values in D is negative, replace it with the minimum positive eigenvalue of the matrix. [4]

   (c) Repeat step (b) until we obtain a positive definite matrix. [5]

4. We generate a separate test data set of size 50,000 using the original parameters without the noises, and report the effectiveness of the Gaussian mixture models using the Laplace noise added parameters. Meanwhile, we report the effectiveness of the regular Gaussian mixture models based on the parameters learned from the truncated training data sets. Test data set of size 50,000 is chosen to make sure that the estimated Bayes errors are as accurate as possible.

5.1 Experimental Results

In our first set of experiments, the Gaussian mixture distributions have the following parameter values.

---

[4]Please note that a symmetric matrix is positive definite iff all the eigenvalues are positive.

[5]This problem could be represented as the following optimization problem: Given M, find M' such that M' is symmetric positive definite and $s(M, M')$ is minimum for some distance metric s. We leave the exploration of such optimization problem as a future work.

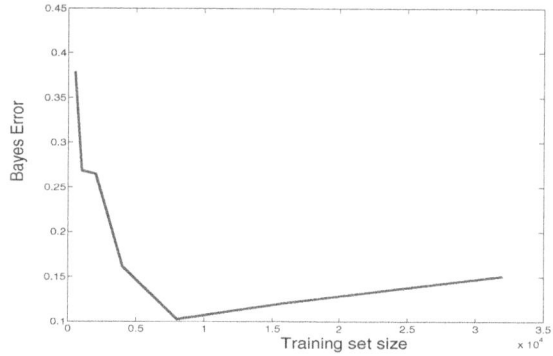

Figure 1: Bayes error versus training set size for $\epsilon = 0.1$.

$$\mu_1 = [1.8, 3.2, 3.8, 6, 5.5],$$
$$\Sigma_1 = \text{diag}\{0.36, 1.21, 3.24, 5, 76, 0.64\},$$
$$\mu_2 = [0.5, 1, 1.5, 2.5, 3.5],$$
$$\Sigma_2 = \text{diag}\{2.56, 0.64, 4.00, 1.44, 0.16\}.$$

The mixing probability is 0.7. We tested different ϵ values ranging from 0.01 to 0.1. For the training data set size, we have conducted experiments with 500, 1000, 2000, 4000, 8000, 16000, and 32000. For this Gaussian mixture, *all the models built with ϵ less than 0.1 resulted in Bayes errors more than 0.3.* Please note that predicting everything as class one has a Bayes error 0.3. For these reasons, we do not report the experiments with ϵ values less than 0.1. In all of our experiments with different training data sets, Bayes error without noise addition was less than 0.01. In Figure 1, we show the Bayes error rates for different training set sizes for fixed $\epsilon = 0.1$. As the results indicate, even for large training set sizes the Bayes error is more than 0.1. If we compare this with 0.01, the Bayes error from estimated parameters without noise addition, this result indicates that directly adding noise to variance-covariance matrix may cause significantly larger Bayes error.

In another set of experiments, we want to understand the joint effect of correlated attributes, dimensionality, and the training set size. In each of these experiments, the first Gaussian component has the identity covariance matrix with mean $\vec{0}$. For the second Gaussian component, we fixed the mean vector to $\vec{1}$. For covariance matrix Σ, we set $\Sigma_{i,i} = \sigma$ and $\Sigma_{i,j} = \Sigma_{j,i} = 0.5 \times \sigma$ for various σ values. As a reference, we report the Bayes error rates without the noise addition for different σ values for training set size 500 in Table 1. We would like to stress that this is the worst case for the scenarios without noise addition, since Bayes error will be smaller as the training set size increases. The results for Gaussian Mixture models under differential privacy are reported in Figures 2, 3, 4, and 5. The results indicate that for training samples of sizes less than 16000, the Bayes error caused by differential privacy is prohibitively high. Again these results suggest that differential privacy needs to be applied to large data sets with large ϵ values to provide useful results.

Finally, we used the Parkinson data set from the UCI Machine learning repository. We computed the mean and

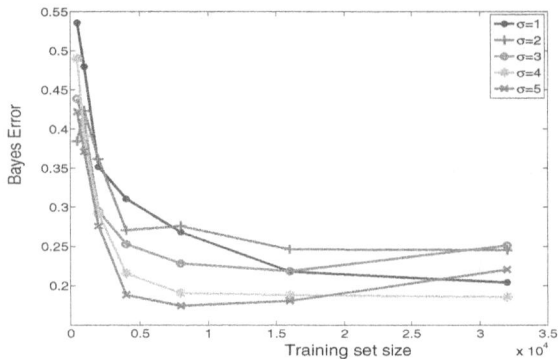

Figure 2: Bayes error versus training set size for $\epsilon = 0.1$, **5 dimensional Gaussian mixture.**

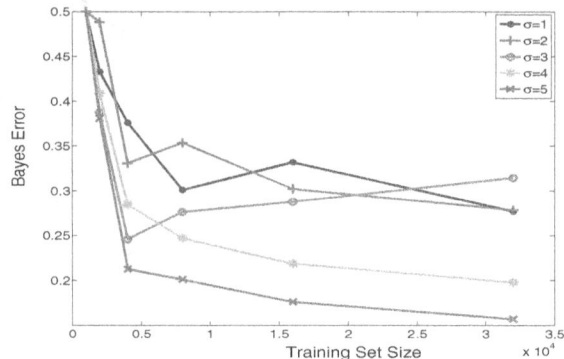

Figure 4: Bayes error versus training set size for $\epsilon = 0.1$, **15 dimensional Gaussian mixture.**

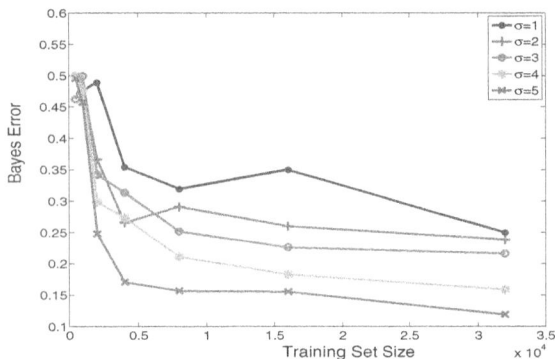

Figure 3: Bayes error versus training set size for $\epsilon = 0.1$, **10 dimensional Gaussian mixture.**

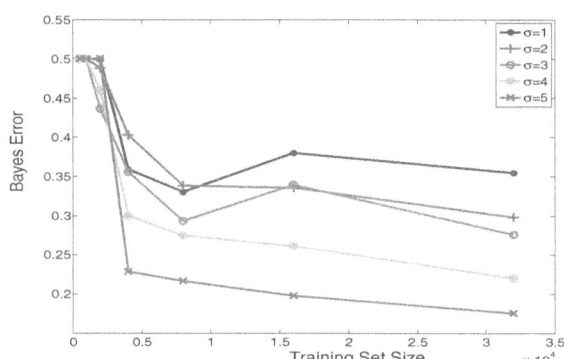

Figure 5: Bayes error versus training set size for $\epsilon = 0.1$, **20 dimensional Gaussian mixture.**

covariance matrix of each class in the Parkinson data set and used these parameters in our experiments. In all of the experiments, we set $\epsilon = 0.1$. For the Parkinson data set, a classifier that put all the records into the majority class has Bayes error 0.2462. Unfortunately, all the Gaussian mixture models with different sample sizes under differential privacy have Bayes error around 0.24. On the other hand, in non-differentially private case, the Bayes error is less than 0.01. The above results suggest that direct noise addition to Gaussian mixture parameters could cause significant distortion.

6. SUMMARY

In this article we examine sensitivities of various statistics queried from a statistical database, and the performance of Bayesian classifier using the noise added mean and variance-covariance matrix. In the process we identify an interesting

issue associated with random noise addition: The variance-covariance matrix without the added noise is positive definite. However simply adding noise can only return a symmetric matrix, which is no longer positive definite. Consequently the query result cannot be used to construct a Bayesian classifier. We implement a heuristic method to repair the noise added matrix to achieve positive definiteness in the experiments.

This is a general issue for random noise addition. Adding noise to a statistic under certain constraint may return query results that no longer satisfy the constraint. The query results need to be further modified in order to be used in subsequent studies. An interesting question is how to provide query results that are helpful for subsequent studies while safely protecting database participant's privacy. Each constrained statistic may need an algorithm to achieve its original properties after noise addition.

7. ACKNOWLEDGMENTS

This work was partially supported by Air Force Office of Scientific Research MURI Grant FA9550-08-1-0265, Army Research Office MURI Grant W911NF-08-1-0238, National Institutes of Health Grant 1R01LM009989, National Science Foundation Grants Career-0845803, CNS- 0964350, CNS-1016343, and DMS-0904548.

dimension v.s. σ	1	2	3	4	5
5	0.18	0.22	0.20	0.17	0.14
10	0.12	0.19	0.16	0.12	0.09
15	0.10	0.18	0.15	0.09	0.06
20	0.08	0.18	0.14	0.08	0.05

Table 1: **Bayes Error for increasing dimensionality and σ values for fixed training set size 500.**

8. REFERENCES

[1] R. Agrawal and R. Srikant. Privacy-preserving data mining. *SIGMOD Rec.*, 29(2):439–450, 2000.

[2] R. O. Duda, P. E. Hart, and D. G. Stork. *Pattern Classification.* Wiley, New York, 2. edition, 2001.

[3] C. Dwork. Differential privacy. In *ICALP (2)*, pages 1–12. Springer, 2006.

[4] C. Dwork. Differential privacy: A survey of results. In *Theory and Applications of Models of Computation*, pages 1–19. Springer Berlin / Heidelberg, 2008.

[5] C. Dwork, F. Mcsherry, K. Nissim, and A. Smith. Calibrating noise to sensitivity in private data analysis. In *In Proceedings of the 3rd Theory of Cryptography Conference*, pages 265–284. Springer, 2006.

[6] A. Friedman and A. Schuster. Data mining with differential privacy. In *KDD '10: Proceedings of the 16th ACM SIGKDD international conference on Knowledge discovery and data mining*, pages 493–502, New York, NY, USA, 2010. ACM.

[7] K. Fukunaga. *Introduction to statistical pattern recognition (2nd ed.).* Academic Press Professional, Inc., San Diego, CA, USA, 1990.

[8] G. Jagannathan, K. Pillaipakkamnatt, and R. N. Wright. A practical differentially private random decision tree classifier. In *ICDM Workshops*, pages 114–121, 2009.

[9] M. Kantarcıoğlu, J. Jin, and C. Clifton. When do data mining results violate privacy? In *KDD '04: Proceedings of the tenth ACM SIGKDD international conference on Knowledge discovery and data mining*, pages 599–604, New York, NY, USA, 2004. ACM.

[10] H. Kargupta, S. Datta, Q. Wang, and K. Sivakumar. On the privacy preserving properties of random data perturbation techniques. In *ICDM '03: Proceedings of the Third IEEE International Conference on Data Mining*, page 99, Washington, DC, USA, 2003. IEEE Computer Society.

[11] N. Li, T. Li, and S. Venkatasubramanian. t-closeness: Privacy beyond k-anonymity and l-diversity. In *ICDE '07*, pages 106–115, Istanbul, Turkey, 2007. IEEE.

[12] A. Machanavajjhala, J. Gehrke, D. Kifer, and M. Venkitasubramaniam. l-diversity: Privacy beyond k-anonymity. In *ICDE '06*, page 24, Atlanta, GA, USA, 2006. IEEE Computer Society.

[13] S. Merugu and J. Ghosh. Privacy-preserving distributed clustering using generative models. In *ICDM '03: Proceedings of the Third IEEE International Conference on Data Mining*, page 211, Washington, DC, USA, 2003. IEEE Computer Society.

[14] L. Sweeney. k-anonymity: a model for protecting privacy. *International Journal on Uncertainty, Fuzziness and Knowledge-based Systems*, 10(5):557–570, 2002.

[15] X. Xiao and Y. Tao. Anatomy: simple and effective privacy preservation. In *VLDB '06: Proceedings of the 32nd international conference on Very large data bases*, pages 139–150, Seoul, Korea, 2006. VLDB Endowment.

[16] X. Xiao and Y. Tao. Output perturbation with query relaxation. *PVLDB*, 1(1):857–869, 2008.

Relationship-Based Access Control: Protection Model and Policy Language

Philip W. L. Fong
Department of Computer Science
University of Calgary
Calgary, Alberta, Canada T2N 1N4
pwlfong@ucalgary.ca

ABSTRACT

Social Network Systems pioneer a paradigm of access control that is distinct from traditional approaches to access control. Gates coined the term Relationship-Based Access Control (ReBAC) to refer to this paradigm. ReBAC is characterized by the explicit tracking of interpersonal relationships between users, and the expression of access control policies in terms of these relationships. This work explores what it takes to widen the applicability of ReBAC to application domains other than social computing. To this end, we formulate an archetypical ReBAC model to capture the essence of the paradigm, that is, authorization decisions are based on the relationship between the resource owner and the resource accessor in a social network maintained by the protection system. A novelty of the model is that it captures the contextual nature of relationships. We devise a policy language, based on modal logic, for composing access control policies that support delegation of trust. We use a case study in the domain of Electronic Health Records to demonstrate the utility of our model and its policy language. This work provides initial evidence to the feasibility and utility of ReBAC as a general-purpose paradigm of access control.

Categories and Subject Descriptors

D.4.6 [**Security and Protection**]: Access Controls

General Terms

Security, Design, Language, Theory

Keywords

Contexts, electronic health records, modal logic, policy language, relationship-based access control, social networks

1. INTRODUCTION

A social network is a collection of assertions regarding the relationships between individuals in a given population.

Each assertion says something about the nature of the underlying relationship. For example, an assertion "`father(john, peter)`" specifies that the father of John is Peter.

Recent years have witnessed the growing popularity of Social Network Systems (SNSs). An SNS is essentially an information sharing system that explicitly tracks the social network of its users. Where the relationship assertions come from depends on the domain of application. In some applications (e.g., Facebook), each assertion represents a consensus reached by the participants of that relationship: i.e., each assertion is jointly articulated by those participants[1]. In other applications (e.g., Google Buzz), the assertions may be mined from user data without the consensus of those users. It is also conceivable that the assertions are maintained as part of the on-going operation of a system (e.g., professional relationships between health service providers and their clients).

An SNS maintains a social network for at least two reasons. First, it is used by the users to navigate the information space of the system (i.e., by "traversing" the "edges" of the social network). Second, the social network is used as a basis for formulating the access control policies of user-contributed resources (e.g., "this photo album is accessible only by my friends-of-friends"). It is this second use of social networks that this work focuses on.

Although SNSs have a humble beginning in social computing, we believe that they pioneer a paradigm of access control that has much wider applications. This paradigm is characterized by (1) the explicit tracking of one or more social networks by the protection system, and (2) the expression of access control policies in terms of the relationship between the resource owner and the resource accessor in these social networks. Such an access control paradigm is particularly suited for application domains in which those relationships on which authorization decisions are based arise not from the subjective assessment of the users, but from the structure of trust that is inherent in the application domain. Examples of such relationships include professional relationships as well as relationships induced by organizational structures. Following Gates [18], we call this paradigm of access con-

---

[1]In the case of Facebook, a built-in protocol allows one of the participants of a relationship to extend an invitation to the other participants, requesting that a relationship assertion be added into the social network. If the invitation is accepted, then the relationship is said to have been articulated with the **joint consent** of the two participants. Alternatively, we also say that the relationship is **jointly articulated** by the two participants.

trol *Relationship-Based Access Control (ReBAC)*. This work advocates the adoption of ReBAC for application-level security and privacy, and provides initial evidence for the feasibility and utility of this access control paradigm.

1.1 Motivations

Relationships as Basis of Authorization.

Many traditional access control systems base their authorization decisions on unary predicates of users. For example, the accessor must have a certain identity, or a certain role. In many emerging application domains, such as healthcare and education domains, it is more natural to base authorization decisions on whether the resource owner and accessor are in a particular kind of relationship (e.g., professional relationship). This need is evident when we examine how Role-Based Access Control (RBAC) models [31, 15, 14] have been pushed to the limit to cope with this demand. For example, some previous work defines *parameterized roles* [30, 27] (also called *role templates* [20]), such as manager(john), to represent the role assumed by the manager of John. Such a parameterized role is merely a way of encoding a binary relation manager(u, v) between user u and her manager v. We believe that in some application domains, it is more natural to simply model binary relations rather than unary predicates that are further parameterized. Section 3 presents a formal access control model that features a relationship-based authorization scheme.

Composing Relations.

In a standard RBAC system, when a permission p is assigned to a role R, we are essentially formulating the following policy: *"grant p to user u if $R(u)$".* Here we interpret R as a unary predicate on users (more precisely, R is induced by the user-role assignment). A natural question to ask is whether we can use combinators to compose R from simpler unary predicates. It turns out, except for boolean combinations, there is really not much one can do with unary predicates. These boolean combinations can usually be encoded by the role hierarchy with ease. Binary relations, however, are an entirely different breed of animal. In particular, binary relations are *composable*. Given binary relations R_1 and R_2, one may compose the relation $R_1 \circ R_2$. This means complex binary relations can be composed from primitive building blocks. As an example, consider the relation friends. We can derive the friends-of-friends relation by the composition friends ∘ friends. Relation composition is but one way of building complex binary relations from simple ones. In Section 4, we propose a policy language, based on modal logic, for supporting the specification and composition of complex binary relations.

Delegation of Trust.

Composite relations are interesting because they can be employed to express delegation of trust [5, 13, 36, 27, 26, 3]. For example, by granting access to friends-of-friends, we are essentially delegating to our friends to decide who may access. Section 5 presents a case study to demonstrate this use of ReBAC policies.

Context-specific Relationships.

Another consideration is the contextual nature of relationships. Many existing SNSs features a single social network

as the basis of all authorization decisions. Yet one size truly does not fit all. Many relationships we encounter are contextual. A physician who is my treating physician in one medical case may very well be a consulting expert in a different medical case of mine. As a result, the physician may enjoy a different level of access in each case. This contextual nature of relationships motivates the need for a ReBAC system to track multiple access contexts. Relationships can be articulated or dissolved separately in each access context. The result is that authorization decisions may be different in each context even though the access request remains the same.

Sharing of Relationships Across Contexts.

The need of tracking a distinct social network for each access context shall be balanced by the equally important need for distinct contexts to share relationships. Some relationships have a wide scope of effectiveness. The fact that Alice is a parent of Bob is significant in multiple contexts: in diagnosis for uncovering hereditary connections, in institutional registration for billing purposes, etc. There is thus a need for the access control system to support the sharing of wide-scope relationships across multiple access contexts, and to do so in a rational manner.

1.2 Contributions

This work provides initial evidence for the feasibility and utility of using ReBAC as a general-purpose protection model. Specifically, contributions of this work are the following:

1. A ReBAC model is formulated to capture the core idea of employing social networks as the basis of authorization decisions. Contrary to Facebook-style SNSs, this model tracks social networks that are poly-relational (e.g., child-parent relationships are distinct from patient-physician relationships) and directed (i.e., child-parent relationships are distinct from parent-child relationships). These features allow the model to capture rich domain concepts.

2. The model captures the context-dependent nature of relationships. Relationships are articulated in contexts, and accesses are authorized also in contexts. Sharing of relationships among contexts are achieved in a rational manner through a context hierarchy.

3. A policy language based on modal logic is proposed for expressing ReBAC policies. The language provides means for composing complex policies from simple ones.

4. A case study in the domain of Electronic Health Records (EHR) systems is conducted to demonstrate the utility of the proposed ReBAC model. The case study highlights features such as delegation of trust and scoping of relationships.

2. RELATED WORK

The term Relationship-Based Access Control and the acronym ReBAC were previously coined by Gates [18] as she articulated the protection requirements of Web 2.0 applications. According to her, "a paradigm of access control needs to be developed that is based on interpersonal relationships."

Our model is one approach to meet this requirement. Other authors who coined similar terms include [23, 19, 7].

There exists a number of parallels between RBAC [31, 15, 14] and ReBAC, such as those highlighted in Section 1.1 (user-role assignment vs inter-user relationships, permission-role assignment vs policies) and Section 6 (sessions vs contexts, role hierarchy vs context hierarchy, separation-of-duty constraints vs well-formed contexts). In these two sections, we attempt to underline the fact that ReBAC is not entirely distinct from RBAC. Instead, it is a natural generalization through the use of binary relations over users rather than unary relations (i.e., roles) for capturing domain knowledge. The concrete benefits brought about by this generalization is the flexibility to compose complex policies from primitive ones, and the support of trust delegation.

Trust delegation is one of the main features of Trust Management Systems and other distributed authorization systems [5, 13, 36, 27, 26, 3]. In these systems, authorization decisions are based on declarative policy statements, the satisfaction of which is based in turn on assertions made by multiple principals. By using declarative policies and articulating user relationships, our formulation of ReBAC is highly related to trust management, allowing it to support trust delegation. Note that, however, we envision the model being used for application-level security and privacy in the same manner RBAC is used, rather than in situations necessitating distributed authorization. The model is also different from trust management in that we constrain the compatibility of assertions (i.e., relationships) through the use of a well-formed context hierarchy (see Section 6, cf. [2]), and we employ a modal logic as the policy language.

Recent years have seen the proposal of a number of access control systems or models for SNSs. We begin with the work of Kruk *et al.* [24]. D-FOAF is a distributed identity management system that employs a social network to enable trust delegation. The social network is mono-relational, with relationships that are directed and weighted (i.e., to represent the strength of relationships). Access control policies are expressed as distance and strength thresholds (e.g., allow access if owner and accessor are connected by a path of length no more than k and the aggregate strength of that path is at least δ). As the social network is essentially a weighted directed graph, authorization decisions are computed by a variant of Dijkstra algorithm. Our model tracks poly-relational social networks, and the policy language can be pushed to express distance-based policies. Support for relationship strength is rudimentary (see Section 6).

Carminati *et al.* developed a decentralized social network system that tracks poly-relational social networks in which relationships are weighted by trust levels [9, 10, 6, 11, 12]. In an early proposal [9, 11], a typical access control policy grants access when there exists a path between the owner and the accessor, consisting of relationships of a particular type, of length below a certain bound, and with aggregate trust level above a certain threshold. The final system [12] eventually adopts a distributed trust metrics, in which the trust between the owner and the accessor is obtained by the weighted average trust levels between the accessor and the "trustworthy" neighbours of the owner. In our work, access control policies are declarative and qualitative. Relationship paths may be composed of multiple types of relationships.

In [8], Carminati *et al.* proposed an access control system for social computing, in which semantic web technolo-

gies, including the Resource Description Framework (RDF) and the Web Ontology Language (OWL), are adopted to describe user profiles, relationships among users, resources, relationship between users and resources, and actions. Doing so allows them to see a social network as a knowledge base of user-user and user-resource relationships, and based on which access control policies are formulated. Our work has been partly influenced by this knowledge-based perspective, though our proposed model is agnostic to implementation and representation issues. In addition, although our model captures only user-user relationships, our work offers a declarative policy language and a context hierarchy to scope the effectiveness of relationships.

Fong *et al.* proposed an access control model that formalizes and generalizes the access control mechanism implemented in Facebook [17]. The model admits arbitrary policy vocabulary that are based on graph-theoretic properties (e.g., allow access if owner and accessor participate in the same k-clique, if owner and accessor share k common neighbours, etc). The present work differs from theirs in three ways. First, [17] models capability-like entities called search listings, the reachability of which is a necessary condition for access. In the present work, access control policies are the only condition of access. Second, the present model captures relationship types and contexts, which are not modelled in [17]. Third, in a subsequent work [1], Fong *et al.* employ bi-rooted graphs as a policy language. Here we employ modal logic for specifying policies.

PriMa [32] is another recently proposed privacy protection mechanism for SNSs. The premise of the work is the observation that, because of the growing complexity of the social network and the proliferation of user content categories, it is perhaps wise not to rely on regular users to manually set up their access control policies. PriMa is a scheme by which access control policies are automatically constructed for users. The policy construction algorithm considers factors such as the following: average privacy preference of similar and related users, popularity of the owner (i.e., the more connected is the owner, the more sensitive its profile items), accessibility of similar items in similar and related users (i.e., if my peers do not grant me access, then I better do not grant access easily), closeness of owner and accessor (measured by the number of common friends), etc. These factors are then combined to generate access control rules for profile items. The proposed ReBAC model does not preclude the use of automatic policy inference engines such as [32]

Squicciarini *et al.* [33] considered access control policies of data that is co-owned by multiple parties in an SNS setting, such that each co-owner may separately specify her own privacy preference for the shared data. A voting algorithm was adopted to enable the collective enforcement of shared data. Game theory was applied to evaluate the scheme. In our model, we assume that there is exactly one stakeholder (i.e., owner) for each resource. Generalizing the model to cope with co-ownership is an interesting future direction.

3. A REBAC MODEL

A thesis of this work is that an SNS can be adopted as the access control system of an information sharing platform. We describe here an archetypical ReBAC model, which offers two main features.

First, the social networks tracked by this model are poly-relational, in the sense that the model tracks not only *whether* a relationship exists beween two individuals, but also the *type* of that relationship (e.g., patient-physician, parent-child, etc). This is a generalization of mono-relational networks, such as those found in Facebook-style SNSs [17]. This generalization can be exploited to support the rich relational concepts found in many application domains. The model further captures the idea that an authorization decision is based solely on the relationship between the resource owner and the resource accessor in a certain social network.

Second, the model tracks multiple access contexts. Relationships may be articulated in separate contexts. To facilitate the sharing of relationship across contexts, the access contexts are organized into a tree-shaped hierarchy (see Figure 1). The hierarchy facilitates a sharing mechanism known as relationship inheritance. When an access is requested in an access context, the relationships articulated in all the ancestor contexts are combined with the relationships in the target access context to form a single social network. This social network is the one on which authorization decisions are made. Lastly, the creation and destruction of access contexts follow a stack discipline: new contexts are introduced as leaves, and only leaves can be removed from the tree. This features supports the scoping of the effectiveness of relationships.

An access control system is traditionally modelled as a state transition system [22, 28]. State transitions capture the management aspects of the system, including various forms of system reconfigurations. Actual accesses are performed with respect to a given state of the system [28]. In this section, we describe the global parameters to an ReBAC protection system, delineate its state space as well as state transitions, and specify the authorization procedure.

3.1 Notations

Consider a function $f : X \rightarrow Y$ and individuals x_0 and y_0, where $y_0 \in Y$, but x_0 may or may not be in X. We write $f[x_0 \mapsto y_0]$ to denote the function $f' : X \cup \{x_0\} \rightarrow Y$ defined as follows: $f'(x) = y_0$ if $x = x_0$, but $f'(x) = f(x)$ if $x \neq x_0$. Suppose further $X' \subseteq X$. We write $f \mid X'$ for the restriction of f to the domain X'. Given a binary relation $R \subseteq X \times X$ and individuals $x, y \in X$, we write $x \, R \, y$ iff $(x, y) \in R$. We also write R^* to denote the reflexive transitive closure of R.

3.2 Social Networks and Relation Identifiers

We assume that an SNS defines a countable set $\mathcal{I}$ of *relation identifiers*. Each identifier denotes a type of relationships that is tracked by the system (e.g., parent-child, patient-physician, etc). A typical member of $\mathcal{I}$ is denoted by i.

A social network is essentially a directed graph with multiple kinds of edges. While individuals are represented by vertices, each kind of directed edges represents a distinct type of relationship between users. Formally, a *social network* G is a relational structure [4] of the form $\langle V, \{R_i\}_{i \in \mathcal{I}} \rangle$, where:

- V is a finite set of vertices, each representing an individual in the social network.

- $\{R_i\}_{i \in \mathcal{I}}$ is a family of binary relations. The binary relation $R_i \subseteq V \times V$ specifies the pairs of individuals participating in relationship type i.

In the definition above, the binary relations need not be irreflexive or symmetric: i.e., the graph may contain circles,

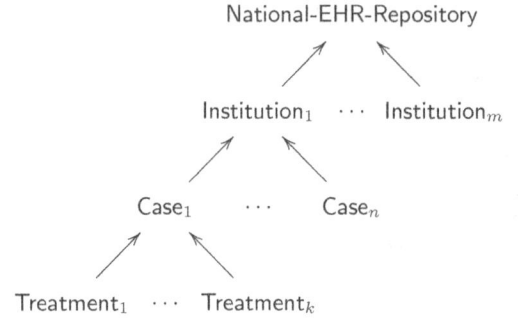

Figure 1: A sample hierarchy of access contexts in an EHR application.

and the relationships may not be reciprocal. This is more general than Facebook-style SNSs, in which the social network is a simple graph [17].

We denote by $\mathcal{G}(V, \mathcal{I})$ the set of all social networks defined over vertex set V and relation index set $\mathcal{I}$. That is, members of $\mathcal{G}(V, \mathcal{I})$ share the same vertex set V, but differ only in the edges.

We introduce some additional conventions and notations related to relation identifiers and social networks before we move on to discuss access control policies.

We adopt the following convention to name relation identifiers. We assume that, with every binary relation, there are named roles for each of the two participants. For example, in a parent-child relationship, the parent and the child are the two roles. We will use the receiving role to name the relation. That is, the relation identifier child names the parent-child relation, while the identifier parent names the inverse relation (i.e., the child-parent relation).

A social network is *inverse-closed* whenever the following holds: for every $i \in \mathcal{I}$, there is an identifier $-i \in \mathcal{I}$ such that $R_{-i} = (R_i)^{-1}$. That is, the inverse of a relation is always defined in the social network. For example, if, for a given social network, $\mathcal{I} = \{\text{parent}, \text{child}, \text{physician}, \text{patient}\}$, and the identifiers denote respectively the child-parent, parent-child, patient-physician and physician-patient relations, then the social network is inverse-closed. Unless stated otherwise, we consider only inverse-closed social networks. In such a case, we omit the inverses when we enumerate $\mathcal{I}$, using the following notational convention: $\mathcal{I} = \{\text{parent}, \text{physician}, -\ldots\}$.

Suppose $G = \langle V, \{R_i\}_{i \in \mathcal{I}} \rangle$ is a social network, and $\Delta = \{R'_i\}_{i \in \mathcal{I}}$ is a family of binary relations defined over the vertex set V. Intuitively, Δ represents edges for a social network defined over V. We write $G + \Delta$ to denote the social network $\langle V, \{R_i \cup R'_i\}_{i \in \mathcal{I}} \rangle$, that is, the social network obtained from G by adding the edges in Δ. Similarly, we write $G - \Delta$ to denote $\langle V, \{R_i \setminus R'_i\}_{i \in \mathcal{I}} \rangle$ (i.e., the social network obtained from G by deleting the edges in Δ).

Given two social networks $G = \langle V, \{R_i\}_{i \in \mathcal{I}} \rangle$ and $G' = \langle V', \{R'_i\}_{i \in \mathcal{I}} \rangle$, we write $G \cup G'$ to denote the social network $\langle V \cup V', \{R_i \cup R'_i\}_{i \in \mathcal{I}} \rangle$. This social network, called the *union* of G and G', is obtained by superimposing G and G' on one another. The binary operation $\cup$ is obviously commutative and associative. Suppose $\mathcal{G} = \{G_1, \ldots, G_k\}$ is a finite set of social networks. We write $\bigcup \mathcal{G}$ to denote $G_1 \cup \ldots \cup G_k$.

3.3 Access Control Policies

An SNS controls accesses initiated by **users**. Let $\mathcal{U}$ be the set of all **user identifiers** (or simply **users**) in the system. We denote typical members of $\mathcal{U}$ by u and v. Accesses are directed against **resource identifiers** (or simply **resources**). A resource may represent one or more objects or certain system operations[2]. Let $\mathcal{R}$ be the set of resources protected by the SNS. A typical member of $\mathcal{R}$ is denoted by r.

Associated with every access request are therefore the following: (a) a protected resource $r \in \mathcal{R}$ that is being accessed, (b) the **owner** $u \in \mathcal{U}$ of that resource, and (c) the **accessor** $v \in \mathcal{U}$ who requests the access. Note that we use the term "owner" in a sense different from how it is used in Discretionary Access Control (DAC) [21, 28]. In DAC, the owner of an object may explicitly grant access of the object to other users in the system. This sense of controlling to whom access shall be granted is not the main focus of our usage (although it is entire possible that the system allows the owner of a resource to specify the policy of access at her own discretion, as we shall point out in Section 3.4). On the contrary, when we say that a user is the owner of a resource, we mean that an accessor must be in a specific kind of relationship with the owner (with respect to a certain social network) in order to be granted access. The marking of an individual as the anchoring end of such a relationship-based authorization procedure is the primary sense of our usage of the term "owner".

Associated with every resource is an **access control policy**. Such a policy is modelled as a ternary predicate of the following signature: $\mathcal{U} \times \mathcal{U} \times \mathcal{G}(\mathcal{U}, \mathcal{I}) \to \{0, 1\}$. Specifically, given an owner, an accessor, and a social network, the predicate returns a boolean value to indicate whether access shall be granted. We write $\mathcal{PP}(\mathcal{U}, \mathcal{I})$ to denote the set of all policy predicates with the above signature.

3.4 Protection System

A **protection system** (or simply a **system**) N is a 7-tuple $\langle \mathcal{I}, \mathcal{U}, \mathcal{R}, \mathcal{C}, c_0, policy, owner \rangle$, where:

- $\mathcal{I}$ is the set of relation identifiers, as discussed above.

- $\mathcal{U}$ is a finite set of users in the system.

- $\mathcal{R}$ is a finite set of resources to be protected by the system. We assume that the universe of user and resource identifiers remain constant throughout system lifetime (e.g., with fixed bit length), as creation and destruction of users and resources are not the focus of this modelling exercise. Note that this does not pose a real restriction to the system, as user creation can be readily modelled by a dormant user turning active.

- $\mathcal{C}$ is a *countably infinite* universe of **access contexts** (or simply **contexts**). An access is requested in the backdrop of a specific access context. Each context may give a different authorization decision even if the owner, accessor and resource involved in the access are the same. As we shall see in the sequel, contexts can be created or destroyed during system execution.

- The **root context** $c_0 \in \mathcal{C}$ is a distinguished context. When we introduce the context hierarchy below, we shall see that c_0 is the root of the context hierarchy.

- The function $policy : \mathcal{R} \to \mathcal{PP}(\mathcal{U}, \mathcal{I})$ assigns a policy predicate to every resource in the system. As policy revision is not a focus of the present modelling exercise, we assume that policy settings remain constant throughout system lifetime, and model the settings as a static parameter of the system. For an example of how policy revision could have been incorporated into the modelling of an SNS, see [17].

- There is a function $owner : \mathcal{R} \to \mathcal{U}$ that assigns an owner to every resource in the system.

In the definition above, we do not speculate on where the access control policy of a resource comes from. There are at least three possibilities:

Mandatory. Some of the resources may have policies mandated by the system administrator.

Discretionary. For other resources, the resource owners are responsible for specifying their access control policies.

Policy Vocabulary. A moderate position, which is adopted by many existing SNSs, is for the system to mandate a **policy vocabulary**, that is, a set of "canned" policy predicates (e.g., friends, friends-of-friends), from which users take their picks.

3.5 Protection State

Given a protection system $N = \langle \mathcal{I}, \mathcal{U}, \mathcal{R}, \mathcal{C}, c_0, policy, owner \rangle$, a **protection state** (or simply a **state**) γ is a triple $\langle C, sn, extends \rangle$ composed of the following elements:

- $C \subseteq \mathcal{C}$ is the set of **active contexts** in the state. It is required that this set is finite and non-empty, containing at least the element c_0. Each active context defines a scope of effectiveness for some articulated relationships.

- There is a function $sn : C \to \mathcal{G}(\mathcal{U}, \mathcal{I})$ that maps each context of the state to a social network. Specifically, the social network $sn(c)$ records the relationships that have been articulated in context c. By articulating a relationship in a context, one is placing the relationship in the scope of effectiveness represented by that context.

- $extends \subseteq C \times C$ is a binary relation defined over $\mathcal{C}$, such that (a) the directed graph $(C, extends)$ is a tree, (b) c_0 is the root of the tree, and (c) if $(c_1, c_2) \in extends$ then c_1 is the child of c_2 in the tree. States satisfying these three conditions are said to be **well-formed**. The *extends* relation defines a **context hierarchy**. A tree-shaped context hierarchy corresponds to the nested structure of relationship scopes. Relationships articulated in c will be visible to the authorization decisions made in c and all the descendent contexts of c.

  Using the notational conventions in Section 3.1, we also write "c_1 *extends* c_2" iff c_1 is a child of c_2, and "c_1 *extends** c_2" iff c_1 is either c_2 or one of the descendants of c_2.

We denote the set of all well-formed states for N by $\mathcal{ST}(N)$.

---

[2]In standard RBAC literature, what we call a resource is called a permission [31, 15, 14]. We avoid the term "permission" because "permission owner" is not natural in English.

3.6 Authorization

Authorization is achieved by consulting relationships in a social network. In the following, we will specify the social network on which authorization decisions are based.

Given a state $\gamma = \langle C, sn, extends \rangle$, the **effective social network** of an access context $c \in C$ is defined as the following social network:

$$esn_\gamma(c) = \bigcup \{ sn(c') \mid c' \in C, \ c \ extends^* \ c' \}$$

Specifically, $esn_\gamma(c)$ is obtained by taking the union of all social networks $sn(c')$, where c' is either the context c or one of the ancestors of c in the context hierarchy. In essence, G contains not only the relationships of $sn(c)$, but also the relationships of the social networks associated with the ancestor access contexts. The effective social network of a context is the social network that will be used as the basis of authorization decisions made in that context.

Accesses are modelled as queries over states. Specifically, a query has the following syntax:

$$q ::= v \ \textbf{accesses} \ r \ \textbf{in} \ c$$

Let $\mathcal{Q}(N)$ be the set of all queries for system N.

The sequent "$\gamma \vdash_N q$" asserts the successful authorization of access q in state γ of system N [3]:

$$
\frac{
\begin{array}{c}
N = \langle \_,\_,\_,\_,\_, policy, owner \rangle \qquad \gamma = \langle C, \_, \_ \rangle \\
c \in C \\
P = policy(r) \qquad u = owner(r) \qquad G = esn_\gamma(c) \\
P(u, v, G)
\end{array}
}{
\gamma \vdash_N v \ \textbf{accesses} \ r \ \textbf{in} \ c
} \text{ (AUTH)}
$$

When accessor v requests to access resource r in access context c, the system will look up the policy predicate $P = policy(r)$ associated with the resource, as well as the resource owner $u = owner(r)$. The effective social network G for context c is then derived. The system applies the predicate P to the owner u, the accessor v, and the social network G in order to arrive at an authorization decision.

The rule above captures two important ideas of this model. First, it captures the idea that authorization decisions are made primarily by consulting the relationship between the accessor and the owner. In other words, only the social network aspect of the system state is significant in authorization decisions. In a real implementations, relationships may not be the sole basis for authorization decisions. It is entirely possible for the system to have a hybrid authorization scheme that is both relationship based and, for instance, role based. In this work we consider a pure form of ReBAC.

Second, the rule above also captures the notion of relationship inheritance, allowing relationships articulated in ancestor contexts to be inherited by the effective social network of a descendent context. An important consequence of this particular design is the monotonic nature of relationship inheritance. Suppose $c \ extends \ c'$. Let social networks $G = \langle \mathcal{U}, \{R_i\}_{i \in \mathcal{I}} \rangle$ and $G' = \langle \mathcal{U}, \{R'_i\}_{i \in \mathcal{I}} \rangle$ be $esn_\gamma(c)$ and $esn_\gamma(c')$ respectively. Then $R'_i \subseteq R_i$ for all $i \in \mathcal{I}$. That is, the effective social network of a child context contains no less relationships than that of a parent context.

---

[3] We adopt a Prolog-style convention and write an underscore "_" in place of a variable whenever that variable is not significant.

3.7 State Transition

State transitions capture the evolution of the context hierarchy, as well as the mutation of social networks. Intuitively, the creation and destruction of access contexts follow a stack discipline, thereby allowing users to model the nested scopes of social relationships.

We proceed to define a state transition relation to specify the dynamic behaviour of a system. In fact, what we define is an *upper bound* of the actual transition relation, in the following sense. An instantiation of this access control model will *refine* the transition relation specified below, in such a way that (a) certain transitions described below may not be allowed, but (b) the refined relation will never allow transitions that are not allowed by the following specification. The additional restrictions imposed by an instantiation are usually motivated by the access control requirements of a specific application domain. We will return to this matter in the sequel.

Given a system $N = \langle \mathcal{I}, \mathcal{U}, \mathcal{R}, \mathcal{C}, c_0, policy, owner \rangle$, we define the transition relation $\cdot \xrightarrow{\ \cdot \ }_N \cdot \ \subseteq \mathcal{ST}(N) \times \mathcal{T}(N) \times \mathcal{ST}(N)$, where $\mathcal{T}(N)$ is a set of **transition identifiers** with the following syntax:

$$t ::= \mathsf{push}(c, c, \Delta) \mid \mathsf{pop}(c) \mid \mathsf{edge}(c, \Delta, \Delta)$$

where c is a context and Δ is a family of binary relations.

The transition relation is specified via three rules, the first of which models the creation of contexts:

$$
\frac{
\begin{array}{c}
c_1 \in \mathcal{C} \setminus C \qquad c_2 \in C \\
C' = C \cup \{c_1\} \\
sn' = sn[c_1 \mapsto \langle \mathcal{U}, \Delta \rangle] \\
extends' = extends \cup \{(c_1, c_2)\}
\end{array}
}{
\langle C, sn, extends \rangle \xrightarrow{\ \mathsf{push}(c_1, c_2, \Delta) \ }_N \langle C', sn', extends' \rangle
} \text{ (PUSH)}
$$

The PUSH rule specifies the semantics of the operation $\mathsf{push}(c_1, c_2, \Delta)$, which adds a new leaf c_1 to the context hierarchy. The new context is a child of the existing context c_2. We are also given the option of initializing the new context with relationships in the relation family Δ.

The POP rule below models the destruction of contexts.

$$
\frac{
\begin{array}{c}
c \in C \setminus \{c_0\} \qquad \neg \exists c' \in C \,.\, c' \ extends \ c \\
C' = C \setminus \{c\} \\
sn' = sn \mid C' \\
extends' = extends \cap (C' \times C')
\end{array}
}{
\langle C, sn, extends \rangle \xrightarrow{\ \mathsf{pop}(c) \ }_N \langle C', sn', extends' \rangle
} \text{ (POP)}
$$

The operation $\mathsf{pop}(c)$ removes a leaf context c from the context hierarchy. Relationships articulated in a context are dissolved when the context is removed, marking the end of the scope of those relationships. Note that the root context c_0 cannot be removed, nor can one remove a context that is not a leaf. The latter restriction ensures a last-in-first-out discipline.

The EDGE rule models the revision of social networks.

$$
\frac{
sn' = sn[c \mapsto (sn(c) + \Delta_1) - \Delta_2]
}{
\langle C, sn, extends \rangle \xrightarrow{\ \mathsf{edge}(c, \Delta_1, \Delta_2) \ }_N \langle C, sn', extends \rangle
} \text{ (EDGE)}
$$

The operation $\mathsf{edge}(c, \Delta_1, \Delta_2)$ adds relation family Δ_1 to, and removes relation family Δ_2 from, the social network associated with the context c.

196

As we pointed out, an instantiation of this model shall define a transition relation that is a refinement of the one specified above. Additional restrictions may arise from the following needs. First, there may be domain-specific constraints to the shape of the context hierarchy. For example, the hierarchy in Figure 1 is constrained to have a maximum height of four. These constraints cause certain transitions allowed by the PUSH and POP rules to become illegitimate. Second, there may be restrictions on what relationships may be articulated in each context. In the example of Figure 1, supervisory relationships shall only be articulated in an Institution context. Such restrictions cause certain transitions allowed by the EDGE and PUSH rules to become illegitimate.

We do not explicitly track the initiator of each transition, because the authorization of transitions is not a focus of this work. In principle, the transitions can be considered resources and thus protected by the same protection system.

Lastly, the transition relation defined above (or any of its refinements) preserves the three well-formedness conditions specified in Section 3.5.

4. A MODAL APPROACH TO REBAC POLICY SPECIFICATION

Section 3.4 outlines a number of ways by which access control policies originate in a ReBAC system. In many situations, it is desirable to have a policy language for specifying ReBAC policies. First, a policy language facilitates the specification of composite policies, which in turn forms the basis of trust delegation. Second, a policy language facilitates the static analysis of policies and system configuration [16], an agenda we plan to pursue as future work. Our goal in this section is to devise a policy language for expressing ReBAC policies, and we propose to adopt a modal logic for this purpose.

A ReBAC policy predicate describes the relationship between an owner and an accessor in a social network, which in turn can be naturally captured by a relational structure. A modal logic is essentially a language for describing the topological properties of a relational structure. Specifically, a modal logic provides "an internal, local perspective on relational structures" [4]. That is, a modal formula specifies topological properties from the perspective of a specific vertex in a relational structure, by describing how the relational structure appears to a "crawler" locating at that vertex. Such a perspective is particularly useful for the specification of ReBAC policies: a modal formula could be employed to specify how an owner relates to potential accessors in a social network. We back up this claim by introducing a basic modal language for specifying ReBAC policies.

4.1 Syntax and Semantics

A formula in our basic modal language expresses a desired relationship between an owner and an accessor in a given social network. The syntax of the language is given below.

$$\phi, \psi ::= \top \mid a \mid \neg\phi \mid \phi \vee \psi \mid \langle i \rangle \phi$$

where $i \in \mathcal{I}$ is a relation identifier. The formula $\top$ is the constant true, and is satisfied by any pair of owner and accessor. The atomic formula a asserts that the accessor is the owner herself. The connectives $\neg$ and $\vee$ are the usual boolean negation and disjunction. For example, $\neg\phi$ asserts

that the owner and the accessor do not participate in the relationship specified by ϕ. The formula $\langle i \rangle \phi$ asserts that the owner is related to a vertex via an i relationship, and that vertex is in turn related to the accessor in a manner specified by the formula ϕ.

The formal semantics of formulas are captured by the satisfaction relation $(G, u, v \models \phi)$, which asserts that, in social network $G = \langle V, \{R_i\}_{i \in \mathcal{I}} \rangle$, owner $u \in V$ and accessor $v \in V$ are related in a manner specified by formula ϕ:

- $G, u, v \models \top$

- $G, u, v \models a$ iff $u = v$.

- $G, u, v \models \neg\phi$ iff it is not the case that $G, u, v \models \phi$

- $G, u, v \models \phi \vee \psi$ iff either $G, u, v \models \phi$ or $G, u, v \models \psi$

- $G, u, v \models \langle i \rangle \phi$ iff there exists $u' \in V$ such that $(u, u') \in R_i$ and $G, u', v \models \phi$

We also introduce derived forms to capture the duals of the above constructs.

$$\bot = \neg\top \quad \bar{a} = \neg a \quad \phi \wedge \psi = \neg(\neg\phi \vee \neg\psi) \quad [i]\phi = \neg\langle i \rangle \neg\phi$$

Intuitively, $\bar{a}$ means that the accessor is not the owner, and $[i]\phi$ means that every individual related to the owner via an i relationship is also related to the accessor in a manner specified by ϕ.

The language above deviates from a typical basic modal language in two ways. Firstly, there are only two propositional symbols, namely, a and $\bar{a}$. Other basic modal languages generally support multiple propositional symbols. Secondly, our satisfaction relation relates two individuals in a relational structure. On the contrary, the satisfaction relation of a standard modal language asserts a property of one individual in the context of a relational structure.

We write $[\![\phi]\!]$ to denote the predicate $P(u, v, G)$ that returns true iff $G, u, v \models \phi$. One can now use modal formulas to specify policy predicates, for example, by setting $policy(r) := [\![\phi]\!]$.

4.2 Examples

We illustrate how our modal language can be used for specifying ReBAC policies. Consider an SNS with relation identifiers $\mathcal{I} = \{\text{parent}, \text{sibling}, \text{spouse}, -\ldots\}$ and inverse-closed social networks. Suppose further we are to specify a ReBAC policy $[\![\phi]\!]$ for a resource r. In the following, we will state a number of policies first in English, and then provide a choice of ϕ that captures the English specification.

"Grant access to the owner's spouse." The policy can be expressed by the formula "$\langle \text{spouse} \rangle$ a". Essentially, the idiom "$\langle i \rangle$ a" asserts that successful accessors must be related to the owner directly via an i relationship.

"Grant access to the owner's child." The policy can be expressed by the formula "$\langle$-parent$\rangle$ a". This example demonstrates how one can name the inverse of a relation in an inverse-closed environment.

"Grant access to grand parents." The formula that expresses this policy is "$\langle \text{parent} \rangle \langle \text{parent} \rangle$ a". This example illustrates how composite relationships can be expressed.

"Grant access to parents, aunts and uncles." A possible formula is:

$$\langle \text{parent} \rangle \text{a} \vee \langle \text{parent} \rangle \langle \text{sibling} \rangle \text{a} \vee$$
$$\langle \text{parent} \rangle \langle \text{sibling} \rangle \langle \text{spouse} \rangle \text{a}$$

This example illustrates the use of boolean connectives.

"Grant access unless the accessor is a parent of the owner." A possible formula is:

$$\neg \langle parent \rangle \, a$$

Another possible formula is:

$$[parent] \, \bar{a}$$

This example illustrates the duality of $[i]$ and $\langle i \rangle$.

"Grant access to a sibling who is not married." A formula to express the policy is:

$$\langle sibling \rangle (a \wedge [spouse] \perp)$$

Note that the idiomatic phrase "$[spouse] \perp$" asserts that the matching sibling "has no spouse".

"Grant access to a married sibling." A formula to express this policy is:

$$\langle sibling \rangle (a \wedge \langle spouse \rangle \top)$$

The idiomatic phrase "$\langle spouse \rangle \top$" asserts that the matching sibling "has a spouse".

"Grant access if accessor is the only child of the owner." A formula to express the policy is:

$$\langle \text{-}parent \rangle \, a \wedge [\text{-}parent] \, a$$

4.3 Model Checking

Suppose $policy(r) = \llbracket \phi \rrbracket$. Then the authorization of the request "v **accesses** r **in** c" in state γ involves testing "$G, u, v \models \phi$", where $G = esn_\gamma(c)$ and $u = owner(r)$. This test is known in the literature as local model checking [34]. The definition of the satisfaction relation can be interpreted procedurally as a recursive algorithm for model checking. Whenever a modal operator "$\langle i \rangle$" or "$[i]$" is encountered in the process, a query of the form "$(u, ?x) \in R_i$" will be directed against the social network $esn_\gamma(c)$, where "$?x$" is an uninstantiated variable. The result of the query is a (possibly empty) list of compatible bindings for $?x$. The time complexity of the algorithm, measured in terms of the number of queries made, is essentially that of depth-first search, the search tree of which has a height bounded by the maximum level of nesting of modal operators in ϕ. Due to the small world phenomenon [35], we believe the nesting of modal operators will be moderate.

To apply the above recursive procedure, one needs to have access to $esn_\gamma(c)$. Fortunately, it is not necessary for the system to explicitly construct $esn_\gamma(c)$. Specifically, a query "$(u, ?x) \in R_i$" against $esn_\gamma(c)$ can be compiled into queries against social networks $sn(c')$, for all ancestor contexts c' for which $c \ extends^* \ c'$. Because well-formed context hierarchies are trees, the number of relevant contexts is linear to the height h of the context hierarchy. This adds a factor of $O(h)$ to the time complexity of model checking. In our running example, as we also anticipate to be the case in many application domains, h is bounded by a constant.

5. A CASE STUDY: ELECTRONIC HEALTH RECORDS

To demonstrate the utility of the proposed model, this section presents a case study in the domain of Electronic Health Records (EHR) systems. Specifically, we adapt the

EHR case study originally proposed in [3] to illustrate the use of the proposed model[4].

Consider an EHR system owned by some National Health Authority. The proposed ReBAC model is instantiated for this EHR system. Specifically, there are four kinds of contexts in our instantiation (see Figure 1). At the root of the context hierarchy is the National-EHR-Repository context, which tracks relationships of high degree of permanence, and of global significance. The children of the root are Institution contexts. They track relationships specific to clinical institutions. An Institution context is created when that institution comes into existence. The children of an Institution context are Case contexts, one for each medical case. The relationships tracked in such a context describe responsibilities of clinicians attending to that case. Lastly, each Case context may have children that are Treatment contexts. These contexts track relationships that are specific to the administration of a particular treatment. The hierarchy has a maximum depth of four.

5.1 Treating Clinicians

Suppose the National Health Authority is to mandate a default access control policy for patient records. That is, for each patient record r, we are to come up with a reasonable policy formula ϕ so that we can set $policy(r)$ to $\llbracket \phi \rrbracket$.

The crux of the problem is to characterize the relation between a patient and her ***treating clinicians***. The treating clinicians of a patient are those clinicians responsible for treating the patient. They should be granted the right to examine the patient's records. Our goal is therefore to produce a formula *treating-clinician* that captures this relation. We build this formula incrementally.

General Practitioner.

Bob visits Zoe, his General Practitioner (GP), about his heart problem. Zoe needs to be able to access Bob's records.

The first candidate of a treating clinician is the GP of a patient. When Zoe first became the GP of Bob, she requested Bob to give his consent to treatment. This was achieved by adding the pair (Bob, Zoe) to the binary relation R_{gp} of the social network $sn(\text{National-EHR-Repository})$. In essence, an edge of type gp is added to the social network in the National-EHR-Repository context to link Bob to Zoe. This can be achieved by an EDGE transition.

Given this set-up, the formula *treating-clinician* can be defined as follows:

$$treating\text{-}clinician = \langle gp \rangle \, a$$

The formula identifies the GP to be a treating clinician of a patient.

Referral.

Zoe refers Bob to a local hospital's cardiologist, Hannah. This referral shall enable Hannah to access Bob's records. Bob's express consent shall not be needed.

Hannah creates a new case for Bob's heart problem. This is achieved by using the PUSH rule to create a new Case context as a child of the hospital's Institution context. The intention is that all relationships applicable only to this case

---

[4] Two elements of the original study have been left out in our adaptation: (a) handling of exceptions and "break-the-seal" policies, and (b) policies regulating the disclosure of third-party contributed information regarding a patient.

are articulated in this context. When the case closes, all such relationships will dissolve.

Zoe and Hannah then jointly articulate the referral relationship by adding a referrer type edge (Hannah, Zoe) to the social network in the Case context of Bob's heart problem.

With this set-up in mind, the formula *treating-clinician* will be revised as follows:

$$treating\text{-}clinician = \langle gp \rangle\, a \vee \langle gp \rangle\, \langle \text{-referrer} \rangle\, a$$

When Hannah attempts to access Bob's records in the appropriate Case context, she will succeed. The express consent of Bob is not required. Delegation of trust occurs through the joint consent of Zoe and Hannah. Also, this delegation will be revoked when the heart problem case closes.

Surgical Team.

Hannah prescribes a heart bypass operation. A surgical team is assembled, with Lily as the lead of the team, which is further composed of other clinicians. The team needs access to Bob's records.

Hannah uses the PUSH rule to create a Treatment context for the heart bypass operation. This Treatment context is a child of the Case context corresponding to Bob's heart problem. An appoint-team type edge (Hannah, Lily) will be added to the social network of this Treatment context. Also, a member type edge (Lily, v) will be added to the Treatment social network for each member v of the surgical team. In essence, Lily acts as a representative of the surgical team.

The above set-up leads to the following revision of the *treating-clinician* formula:

$$treating\text{-}clinician = \langle gp \rangle\, a \vee \langle gp \rangle\, \langle \text{-referrer} \rangle\, a$$
$$\vee\ \langle gp \rangle\, \langle \text{-referrer} \rangle\, \langle \text{appoint-team} \rangle (a \vee \langle \text{member} \rangle\, a)$$

Such a policy gives access to the entire surgical team, including both Lily and other team members. Note that this access will be revoked when the Treatment context is destroyed.

Ward Nurses.

While Bob is recovering in his ward, the ward nurses need access to his records. Bob's ward is under the supervision of the head nurse Nancy.

In the Institution context, the hospital articulates a ward-nurse type edge (Nancy, v) for each nurse v under the supervision of Nancy. When Bob first registered into the hospital, a register-ward edge (Bob, Nancy) is articulated in the Institution context.

The set-up above allows us to add another disjunct to the *treating-clinician* formula (for brevity we do not repeat the other disjuncts):

$$treating\text{-}clinician = \ldots \vee$$
$$\langle \text{register-ward} \rangle (a \vee \langle \text{ward-nurse} \rangle\, a)$$

The policy grants access to Nancy and the nurses in her ward so long as Bob stays in that ward.

5.2 Agent

Another resource to be protected is agency. Specifically, a patient needs to declare who will act for her when she is incapacitated. (Note that this policy is formulated under the discretion of the patient, rather than mandated by the system.) We want to formulate a policy formula *agent* that captures the relation between a patient and her agent.

During Bob's operation, complications arise. Bob needs to be kept in artificial coma. Zoe appoints Bob's wife, Carol, to be his agent.

Prior to the incident, Bob formulated the following policy for agency:

$$a \vee \langle agent \rangle\, a$$

The policy allows either Bob or his agent to act for him.

When Bob is in comma, Zoe adds an edge (Bob, Carol) of type agent into the root context National-EHR-Repository, thereby allowing Carol to act for Bob. Because of the global nature of the root context, the agent edge needs to be explicitly removed when Bob recovers and deems the agency relationship no longer applicable.

6. DISCUSSIONS

Throughout this work we have assumed that there exists a standard taxonomy of relationship types specific to the domain of application. The taxonomy is represented by the set $\mathcal{I}$. This assumption is shared by previous work [12, 8]. We believe this assumption is reasonable, as the taxonomy can be developed as part of the requirement engineering process, just like the role hierarchy requires careful engineering.

Relationship identifiers can provide qualitative representation of relationship strength: e.g., $\mathcal{I} = \{$acquaintance, friend, bff[5]$\}$. With some clumsiness, some policies that are based on relationship strength can be expressed in our policy language: e.g., $\langle friend \rangle\, \langle bff \rangle\, a$. In application domains in which accessibility is based on professional relationships, we do not anticipate there is a need for strength-based policies.

Contexts and context inheritance could be used for modelling various domain concepts, including the following: (1) administrative units and organizational structures, such as institutions, departments, teams, etc; (2) task-like entities, such as cases, treatments, transactions, etc; (3) episodic entities such as stages, periods, etc.

In RBAC, every access is performed in a session, in which roles are activated. An analogous arrangement in our model is that every access must be performed in a context. Doing so "activates" the relationships that are articulated in either that context or one of the ancestor contexts. The activated relationships are then used for authorizing the requested access. Thus, contexts capture sets of relationships that can be legitimately "activated" at the same time. The requirement that the context hierarchy must be well-formed (i.e., in tree shape) specifies the compatibility of relationships: relationships residing in different branches of the hierarchy cannot be "activated" at once. This is analogous to RBAC constraints over what roles can be activated simultaneously in the same session (e.g., separation of duty [29]).

7. LIMITATIONS AND FUTURE WORK

The context hierarchy assumes a tree shape: i.e., only single inheritance is permitted. Multiple inheritance corresponds to a more flexible means of constraining when relationships can be "activated" simultaneously. In principle, multiple inheritance can be incorporated into the model with ease. The only problem is that model checking could become intractable, as the number of social networks that must be

---

[5] Bff is a popular shorthand for "best friend forever."

consulted to evaluate a policy formula could be exponential to the height of the hierarchy. A research problem is to identify a controlled form of multiple inheritance that could lead to efficient model checking.

This work relies on the user to select an appropriate context to initiate access. Context identification mechanisms can be designed to suggest appropriate contexts to users. Such a mechanism may involve the translation of location, time, proximity, device and network information into one or more plausible contexts [25]. Alternatively, one may embed ReBAC in a Workflow Management System, and map workflow tasks to contexts. We leave the detailed design of these mappings to future work.

An outstanding issue is whether the modal language can express all the ReBAC policies one desires to express. This is the problem of *representational completeness*. Modal languages capture the idea of bisimulation [4, Chapter 2], but [1] found that some useful relational policies are characterized by graph isomorphism instead of bisimulation. Can the modal language be extended to make it representationally complete? Besides modal languages, what are other linguistic devices that can be exploited to facilitate relation composition?

In this work we focus on binary relations because they can be readily composed. It is conceivable that our model can be generalized to incorporate relations of higher-arity. A question is whether doing so really brings additional benefits in terms of expressiveness (as every relation can be encoded by one or more binary relations). Another challenge is to fashion appropriate modal operators in the policy language when relations of arbitrary arity are involved (in principle this can be done [4]).

It is conceivable that contexts may correspond to geographically separated administrative domains. This means model checking must be conducted by consulting social networks that are stored in a distributed manner. How do we design efficient model checking algorithms when distributed storage is taken into account?

8. SUMMARY

This work advocates the use of Relationship-Based Access Control in application domains in which binary relations are more natural for expressing authorization decisions than unary relations (e.g., roles). To demonstrate the feasibility of this approach, we proposed an access control model that bases authorization decisions on the relationships between the resource owner and the resource accessor in a social network. The model features the notion of access contexts for capturing the contextual nature of relationships, and employs a context hierarchy to facilitate the rational sharing of relationships between contexts. A modal language has been proposed to facilitate the specification and composition of ReBAC policies. A case study in the domain of EHR systems has been presented to demonstrate the utility of this approach. We have thus provided initial evidence on the feasibility and utility of ReBAC as a general-purpose protection approach for application security and privacy.

Acknowledgments

This work is supported in part by an NSERC Strategic Project Grant. The author would like to thank Jason Crampton for some early discussions, and Ida Siahaan for her careful reading of a draft of this work.

9. REFERENCES

[1] Mohd Anwar, Zhen Zhao, and Philip W. L. Fong. An access control model for Facebook-style social network systems. Technical Report 2010-959-08, Department of Computer Science, University of Calgary, Calgary, Alberta, Canada, July 2010. Submitted for review.

[2] Lujo Bauer, Limin Jia, and Divya Sharma. Constraining credential usage in logic-based access control. In *Proceedings of the 23rd IEEE Computer Security Foundations Symposium (CSF'10)*, pages 154–168, Edinburgh, UK, July 2010.

[3] Moritz Y. Becker and Peter Sewell. Cassandra: Flexible trust management, applied to electronic health records. In *Proceedings of the 17th IEEE Computer Security Foundations Workshop (CSFW'04)*, Pacific Grove, California, USA, June 2004.

[4] Patrick Blackburn, Maarten de Rijke, and Yde Venema. *Modal Logic*. Cambridge, 2001.

[5] Matt Blaze, Joan Feigenbaum, and Jack Lacy. Decentralized trust management. In *Proceedings of the 1996 IEEE Symposium on Security and Privacy (S&P'96)*, pages 164–173, Oakland, California, USA, May 1996.

[6] Barbara Carminati and Elena Ferrari. Privacy-aware collaborative access control in web-based social networks. In *Proceedings of the 22nd Annual IFIP WG 11.3 Working Conference on Data and Applications Security (DAS'08)*, volume 5094 of *Lecture Notes in Computer Science*, pages 81–96, London, UK, July 2008. Springer.

[7] Barbara Carminati and Elena Ferrari. Enforcing relationships privacy through collaborative access control in web-based social networks. In *Proceedings of the 5th International Conference on Collaborative Computing: Networking, Applications and Worksharing (CollaborateCom'09)*, Washington DC, USA, November 2009.

[8] Barbara Carminati, Elena Ferrari, Raymond Heatherly, Murat Kantarcioglu, and Bhavani Thurainsingham. A semantic web based framework for social network access control. In *Proceedings of the 14th ACM Symposium on Access Control Models and Technologies (SACMAT'09)*, pages 177–186, Stresa, Italy, June 2009.

[9] Barbara Carminati, Elena Ferrari, and Andrea Perego. Rule-based access control for social networks. In *Proceedings of the OTM 2006 Workshops*, volume 4278 of *Lecture Notes in Computer Science*, pages 1734–1744. Springer, October 2006.

[10] Barbara Carminati, Elena Ferrari, and Andrea Perego. Private relationships in social networks. In *Proceedings of Workshops in Conjunction with the International Conference on Data Engineering – ICDE'07*, pages 163–171, Istanbul, Turkey, April 2007. Springer.

[11] Barbara Carminati, Elena Ferrari, and Andrea Perego. A decentralized security framework for web-based social networks. *International Journal of Information Security and Privacy*, 2(4):22–53, October 2008.

[12] Barbara Carminati, Elena Ferrari, and Andrea Perego. Enforcing access control in web-based social networks. *ACM Transactions on Information and System Security*, 13(1), October 2009.

[13] Dwaine Clarke, Jean-Emile Elien Carl Ellison, Matt Fredette, Alexander Morcos, and Ronald L. Rivest. Certificate chain discovery in SPKI/SDSI. *Journal of Computer Security*, 9(4):285–322, 2001.

[14] David F. Ferraiolo, D. Richard Kuhn, and Ramaswamy Chandramouli. *Role-Based Access Control*. Artech House, 2nd edition, 2007.

[15] David F. Ferraiolo, Ravi Sandhu, Serban Gavrila, D. Richard Kuhn, and Ramaswamy Chandramouli. Proposed NIST standard for role-based access control. *ACM Transactions on Information and System Security*, 4(3):224–274, August 2001.

[16] Philip W. L. Fong. Preventing Sybil attacks by privilege attenuation: A design principle for social network systems. Technical Report 2010-984-33, Department of Computer Science, University of Calgary, Calgary, Alberta, Canada, December 2010. Submitted for review.

[17] Philip W. L. Fong, Mohd Anwar, and Zhen Zhao. A privacy preservation model for Facebook-style social network systems. In *Proceedings of the 14th European Symposium on Research In Computer Security (ESORICS'09)*, volume 5789 of *Lecture Notes in Computer Science*, pages 303–320, Saint Malo, France, September. Springer.

[18] Carrie E. Gates. Access control requirements for Web 2.0 security and privacy. In *IEEE Web 2.0 privacy and security workship (W2SP'07)*, Oakland, California, USA, May 2007.

[19] Fausto Giunchiglia, Rui Zhang, and Bruno Crispo. RelBAC: Relation based access control. In *Proceedings of the Fourth International Conference on Semantics, Knowledge and Grid (SKG'08)*, pages 3–11, Beijing, China, December 2008.

[20] Luigi Giuri and Pietro Iglio. Role templates for content-based access control. In *Proceedings of the Second ACM Workshop on Role-Based Access Control (RBAC'97)*, pages 153–159, Fairfax, Virginia, USA, November 1997.

[21] G. Scott Graham and Peter J. Denning. Protection: Principles and practices. In *Proceedings of the 1972 AFIPS Spring Joint Computer Conference*, volume 40, pages 417–429, Alantic City, New Jersey, USA, May 1972.

[22] Michael A. Harrison, Walter L. Ruzzo, and Jeffrey D. Ullman. Protection in operating systems. *Communications of the ACM*, 19(8):461–471, August 1976.

[23] Song hwa Chae and Wonil Kim. Semantic representation of RTBAC: Relationship-based access control model. In *Advances in Web and Network Technologies, and Information Management: Proceedings of APWeb/WAIM 2007 International Workshops: DBMAN 2007, WebETrends 2007, PAIS 2007 and ASWAN 2007*, volume 4537 of *Lecture Notes in Computer Science*, Huang Shan, China, June 2007. Springer.

[24] Sebastian Ryszard Kruk, Slawomir Grzonkowski, Adam Gzella, Tomasz Woroniecki, and Hee-Chul Choi. D-FOAF: Distributed identity management with access rights delegation. In *Proceedings of the First Asian Semantic Web Conference (ASWC'06)*, volume 4185 of *Lecture Notes in Computer Science*, pages 140–154, Beijing, China, September 2006. Springer.

[25] Devdatta Kulkarni and Anand Tripathi. Context-aware role-based access control in pervasive computing systems. In *Proceedings of the 13th ACM Symposium on Access Control Models and Technologies (SACMAT'08)*, pages 113–122, Estes Park, CO, USA, June 2008.

[26] Ninghui Li, Benjamin N. Grosof, and Joan Feigenbaum. Delegation logic: A logic-based approach to distributed authorization. *ACM Transactions on Information and System Security*, 6(1):128–171, February 2003.

[27] Ninghui Li, John C. Mitchell, and William H. Winsborough. Design of a role-based trust-management framework. In *Proceedings of the 2002 IEEE Symposium on Security and Privacy (S&P'02)*, pages 114–130, Berkeley, California, USA, May 2002.

[28] Ninghui Li and Mahesh V. Tripunitara. On safety in discretionary access control. In *Proceedings of the 2005 IEEE Symposium on Security and Privacy (S&P'05)*, pages 96–109, Oakland, California, USA, May 2005.

[29] Ninghui Li, Mahesh V. Tripunitara, and Ziad Bizri. On mutually exclusive roles and separation-of-duty. *ACM Transactions on Information and System Security*, 10(2), 2007.

[30] Emil Lupu and Morris Sloman. Reconciling role based management and role based access control. In *Proceedings of the Second ACM Workshop on Role-Based Access Control (RBAC'97)*, pages 135–141, Fairfax, Virginia, USA, November 1997.

[31] Ravi S. Sandhu, Edward J. Coyne, Hal L. Feinstein, and Charles E. Youman. Role-based access control models. *IEEE Computer*, 19(2):38–47, February 1996.

[32] Anna Squicciarini, Federica Paci, and Smitha Sundareswaran. PriMa: An effective privacy protection mechanism for social networks. In *Proceedings of the 5th ACM Symposium on Information, Computer and Communications Security (ASIACCS'10)*, pages 320–323, Beijing, China, April 2010.

[33] Anna C. Squicciarini, Mohamed Shehab, and Joshua Wede. Privacy policies for shared content in social network sites. *The VLDB Journal*, 2010. To appear.

[34] Colin Stirling and David Walker. Local model checking in the modal mu-calculus. *Theoretical Computer Science*, 89:161–177, 1991.

[35] Duncan J. Watts. *Small Worlds*. Princeton University Press, 1999.

[36] Stephen Weeks. Understanding trust management systems. In *Proceedings of the 2001 IEEE Symposium on Security and Privacy (S&P'01)*, pages 94–105, Oakland, California, USA, May 2001.

Enforcing Physically Restricted Access Control for Remote Data

Michael S. Kirkpatrick
Department of Computer Science
Purdue University
West Lafayette, IN 47907
mkirkpat@cs.purdue.edu

Sam Kerr
Department of Computer Science
Purdue University
West Lafayette, IN 47907
stkerr@cs.purdue.edu

ABSTRACT

In a distributed computing environment, remote devices must often be granted access to sensitive information. In such settings, it is desirable to restrict access only to known, trusted devices. While approaches based on public key infrastructure and trusted hardware can be used in many cases, there are settings for which these solutions are not practical. In this work, we define physically restricted access control to reflect the practice of binding access to devices based on their intrinsic properties. Our approach is based on the application of physically unclonable functions. We define and formally analyze protocols enforcing this policy, and present experimental results observed from developing a prototype implementation. Our results show that non-deterministic physical properties of devices can be used as a reliable authentication and access control factor.

Categories and Subject Descriptors

K.6.5 [**MANAGEMENT OF COMPUTING AND INFORMATION SYSTEMS**]: Security and Protection—*authentication*

General Terms

Security

Keywords

physically unclonable functions, applied cryptography, access control

1. INTRODUCTION

Controlled remote access to protected resources is a critical element in security for distributed computing systems. Often, some resources are considered more sensitive than others, and require greater levels of protection. Recent advances in access control [6, 1, 21] provide means to tighten the security controls by considering users' contextual factors. While these techniques offer more fine-grained control than traditional identity-based approaches, we desire an even stronger guarantee: Our goal is to provide a means by which access is granted only to known, trusted devices.

To achieve our aim, we had to address two separate issues. First, we required the ability to identify a device uniquely. That is, our scheme must be able to distinguish between two devices with software that is configured identically. Second, we had to establish a mechanism for encrypting the data for access by only the identified device.

A naïve approach to this problem would be to apply authentication mechanisms at the network and transport layers, for instance Challenge-Handshake Authentication Protocol (CHAP), Transport Layer Security (TLS), or Internet Protocol Security (IPsec). However, these solutions fail to provide our desired security guarantees in three ways. First, they differentiate based on stored data, *e.g.,* cryptographic keys. If this data is leaked, these solutions can be broken. Our approach, however, does not rely on the security of data stored on the client.

Second, these approaches are too coarse-grained, granting or denying access below the application layer. That is, our solution allows a server program to selectively grant access to subsets of data based on the unique hardware of the remote device. Existing approaches cannot provide this flexibility.

The third and final shortcoming of these basic approaches is that they can be completely bypassed by improper management and insider threats. In a recent report [35], the most common cause (48%) of data breaches was privilege misuse, which includes improper network configuration and malicious insider threats. In our approach, access control decisions are based on the physical properties of the remote devices themselves. While this does not completely eliminate insider threats, our solution does offer a higher level of defense against such insider threats.

Alternatively, one could rely on a public key infrastructure (PKI) using trusted platform modules (TPMs). While these approaches will work in traditional computing environments, our interests extend to environments for which TPMs are not available or PKI is considered to be too expensive. Specifically, we desire a solution that could also be deployed in low-power embedded systems. In these scenarios, the computing power required for modular exponentiation can quickly exhaust the device's resources. Our approach relies on a cryptographic scheme that offers similar guarantees as PKI, but with less computation required.

Our solution is based on the use of physically unclonable functions (PUFs) [14, 15]. PUFs rely on the fact that it is physically impossible to manufacture two identical devices. For example, two application-specific integrated circuits (ASICs) can be manufactured on the same silicon wafer, using the same design. However, a circuit in one ASIC may execute faster than the equivalent circuit in the other, because the wire length in the first is a nanometer shorter than the second. Such variations are too small to control and can only be observed during execution. PUFs quantify these variations as challenge-response pairs, denoted (C, R), that are unique to each particular hardware instance. A robust PUF is unpredictable, yet consistent for a single device. It is also unforgeable, as the physical variations that determine the PUF are too small to control.

Previous works on PUFs have focused on two areas. First, PUFs can be used to store cryptographic keys in a secure manner. Given a PUF pairing (C, R) and a key K, the device stores $X = R \oplus K$. In this case, R acts as a one-time pad, and X is a meaningless string of bits that can be stored in plaintext on a hard-drive. When the key is needed at a later time, the device again executes the PUF to get R and recovers the key as $K = R \oplus X$. The second use of PUFs is to generate cryptographic keys directly by mapping R to, for example, a point on an elliptic curve. In such a usage, the PUF does not have to store any data.

The advantages of employing PUFs for key generation and storage are subtle, and may be missed at first glance. First, note that no cryptographic keys are explicitly stored; the only data above that is ever stored is the value X, which is a random, meaningless bit string that reveals no information regarding the key K. A second advantage, which follows from the first, is that any key exists only at run-time. Furthermore, if the PUF is integrated into the processor itself, then the keys never even exist in main memory. Thus, PUFs offer very strong protections of cryptographic keys.

While these previous works assume a traditional cryptographic scheme is in place, we propose a new and unique direction for PUF research. That is, we propose incorporating the randomness of the PUF directly into an application-layer access request protocol. Our light-weight multifactor authentication mechanism, coupled with a dynamic key generation scheme, provides a novel technique for enforcing access control restrictions based on the device used.

The main contributions of our work can be summarized as follows.

- We propose the notion of physically restricted access control. That is, we propose integrating a device's distinct characteristics directly into an access request.

- We define protocols for registering a device and making an access request, and present formal analyses of the security guarantees.

- We present a prototype implementation of our client-server architecture, which includes the creation of a PUF on a field-programmable gate array (FPGA) for experimental evaluation. Our implementation provides several insights concerning the adoption of PUF technology in security protocols.

- We provide empirical results that validate our use of a PUF to create a light-weight multifactor authentication system.

The rest of this paper is organized as follows. Section 2 details our threat model and deployment assumptions. Section 3 describes related work in the area of trusted computing, authentication, and access control. Section 4 provides an overview of how PUFs are created and controlled. In Section 5, we define our notion of *physically restricted access control*, specify protocols for enforcing this goal, and provide a formal analysis of our security guarantees. Section 6 provides details of our implementation, including our choices of cryptographic primitives for our protocol and our PUF FPGA implementation. Section 7 presents empirical results of our experiments. In Section 8, we discuss additional issues relevant to future implementations of our scheme. We then conclude in Section 9.

2. THREAT MODEL

In describing our threat model, we start with the central server S. We first note that the adversary's goal is to gain access to sensitive data stored on S. We place no restrictions on what constitutes this data; we simply note that a server application running on S is responsible for the access control decisions. Next, we assume that S is trusted and secure. While this may seem like a strong assumption to make, we stress that it is the *data* stored on S that is important. That is, if an adversary can compromise S, there is no need to attack our protocols, as he has already "won."

Regarding the client devices C, we assume that the organization has the authority to tightly control the software running on each device. While this is a daunting task for traditional computing, recall that we are also highly motivated by the concerns of embedded distributed applications. Embedded devices do not require the complex code base that exists in a traditional workstation; thus, satisfying this requirement is easier. Furthermore, our protocols will still apply in traditional schemes, too. Specifically, remote attestation techniques can be used to ensure that only known, trusted software is running.

Our main adversaries, then, are the users. We consider two classes of users as threats. First, client users have full access to the device, with the exception of installing software. That is, these users can read any data stored on the device. However, they cannot extract the data from memory to external storage. Also note, in the case of embedded systems, there might not actually be a user, as the devices may be executing autonomously. If there is a human user, he will have a password, and we assume it is protected.

The other class of users that pose a threat, whether malicious or not, are administrators. While administrators may have access to the data on S directly, our assumption is that the goal of a malicious administrator is to enable access to an untrusted device, thereby bypassing the physical restrictions. This adversary has access to all secret data stored on S.

Finally, we also consider network-based attackers, such as eavesdroppers. In all cases, we apply standard cryptographic assumptions. Specifically, we assume that adversaries are limited to probabilistic, polynomial-time attacks.

3. RELATED WORK

The literature of computer security contains a long history of identification schemes and authentication protocols [24, 23, 11, 12]. Modern research in this area has become more focused on addressing issues concerning digital identity management under specialized circumstances, such as internet banking [10], secure roaming with ID metasystems [20], digital identity in federation systems [5], authentication for location-based services [18], and location-based encryption [2]. These works rely on knowledge or possession of a secret, and do not bind the authentication request to a particular piece of hardware.

The origin of PUFs can be traced to attempts to identify hardware devices by mismatches in their behavior [22]. The use of PUFs for generating or storing cryptographic keys has been proposed in a number of works [31, 17, 16, 15, 14]. AEGIS [32, 33], a new design for a secure RISC processor, incorporates a PUF for cryptographic operations. Biometrics have also been used to generate secure keys [19]. We will contrast our approach with this scheme in Section 6.1. Our work contrasts with these, as we aim to integrate the unique PUF behavior directly into an authentication protocol, rather than simply providing secure key storage.

In a previous work, we presented a very rudimentary sketch of incorporating PUFs into an authentication system (reference omit-

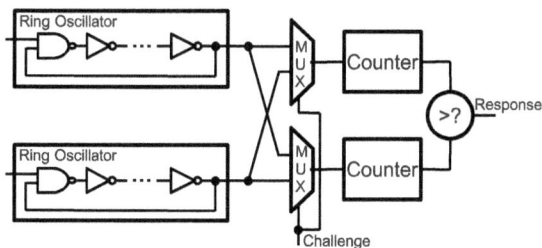

Figure 1: A sample 1-bit PUF based on ring oscillators

ted for purposes of anonymity). However, the focus of that paper was on joint installation of PUF challenges to combat insider threats. Additionally, that work did not present any formal protocol definition or implementation. In contrast, our current work presents substantial more significant results. We present formal definitions of our approach, protocols, and security proofs of our design. Also, our current work addresses the technical details involved with such an implementation, including the necessity of error-correcting codes, and presents empirical results of our prototype implementation.

Besides our previous work, [3] and [13] are perhaps the most similar to our current work. However, the former focuses on binding software in a virtual machine environment, whereas the latter focuses on authenticating banking transactions. Our protocols focus on light-weight multifactor authentication for distributed settings to bind remote file access to trusted systems.

Other types of trusted hardware exist for various purposes. TPMs can provide secure key storage and remote attestation [34, 4, 30, 28]. In many cases, the secure storage of TPMs can be used to bind authentication to a piece of hardware. However, we are interested in solutions for distributed computing that do not rely on TPMs, as TPMs may not be available for the devices used.

Finally, a new direction for hardware identification has emerged to identify unique characteristics of RFID devices [8, 7, 29]. These works are similar to previous work on PUFs, where they focus on identifying the device. These works do not propose new protocols that incorporate the unique behavior directly.

4. PUFS

The fundamental idea of PUFs is to create a random pairing between a challenge input C and a response R. The random behavior is based on the premise that no two instances of a hardware design can be identical. That is, one can create a PUF by designing a piece of hardware such that the design is intentionally non-deterministic. The physical properties of the actual hardware instance resolve the non-determinism when it is manufactured. For example, the length of a wire in one device may be a couple of nanometers longer than the corresponding wire in another device; such differences are too small to be controlled and arise as natural by-products of the physical world.

While there are several types of PUFs, in this work we focus on PUFs derived from ring oscillators (ROs). Figure 1 shows a sample 1-bit RO PUF. A RO consists of a circular circuit containing an odd number of not-gates; this produces a circuit that oscillates between producing a 1 and 0 as output. In a 1-bit PUF, the output of two ROs pass through a pair of multiplexors (MUX) into a pair of counters that count the number of fluctuations between the 0 and 1 output. The PUF result is 1 if the counter on top holds a greater value, and

0 otherwise. The role of the challenge in a 1-bit RO PUF is to flip the MUX.

Clearly, it is not desirable to have such a one-to-one correspondence for larger PUFs. As such, for larger output bit strings it is better to have a pool of ROs, and randomly select pairs for comparison based on the challenge. In [33], the authors evaluate the entropy resulting from random pairings of ROs, and show that N ROs can be used to produce $\log_2(N!)$ bits. For example, 35 ROs can be used to create 133 bits. Thus, a small number of ROs can be used to exhibit good random behavior. Another way to introduce entropy into the PUF behavior is to apply a cryptographic hash to the output. Given a strong hash function, changing a single bit of the PUF challenge, which yields a single flipped PUF bit, will produce a very different output.

The interesting properties of PUFs arise from the fact that it is virtually impossible for two ROs to operate at the same frequency. Specifically, miniscule variations in the wire width or length can cause one RO to oscillate at a faster speed than the other. As these variations are persistent, one of the oscillators will *consistently* be faster. Thus, the behavior of PUFs based on ROs depends on the physical instance of the device. Also, if the PUF is large enough, the behavior is unique. Furthermore, as these variations can be neither predicted nor controlled, they cannot be cloned.

With the exception of our implementation description in Section 6, we will assume an *idealized PUF* in our protocol design. That is, given a challenge-response pair $< C_i, R_i >$ and another challenge $C_j \neq C_i$, one cannot predict the value of R_j. Consequently, our results apply to any PUF that meets this ideal, rather than just RO-based PUFs.

5. PHYSICALLY RESTRICTED ACCESS CONTROL

In this section, we start by defining our notion of physically restricted access control. Next, we offer a high-level protocol and formal analysis for achieving this goal. We then present a more concrete example of this protocol that is derived from the Feige-Fiat-Shamir identification scheme.

We assume that the protected resources consist of files on a central server and subjects request access to these files remotely. For a file access request by a subject from a given device, the access control system checks whether the subject is allowed to access the file from the device; if this is the case, the server encrypts the file with a dynamically generated key and sends the resulting data to the device.

We thus assume an access control model based on a number of sets. Let $\mathcal{S}$ denote the set of subjects, $\mathcal{D}$ the set of trusted devices, $\mathcal{F}$ the set of protected files, and $\mathcal{R}$ the set of privileges. For simplicity, we assume $\mathcal{R} = \{read, write\}$. A permission can be written as the tuple $< s, f, r >$, such that $s \in \mathcal{S}, f \in \mathcal{F}$, and $r \in \mathcal{R}$. Thus $\mathcal{P} \subseteq \mathcal{S} \times \mathcal{F} \times \mathcal{R}$ defines the set of authorized permissions subject to the physical restrictions. Let $PUF_d : C \rightarrow R$ be the PUF for a trusted device $d \in \mathcal{D}$.

We define **physically restricted access control** to be the restriction of an access request $< s, d, f, r >$, subject to the following conditions:

- The identity of s is authenticated.

- $< s, f, r > \in \mathcal{P}$.

- $d \in \mathcal{D}$, and the authentication is performed implicitly by the ability of d to demonstrate a one-time proof of knowledge of PUF_d.

- A dynamic encryption key k_{PUF} based on the proof of PUF_d is used to bind the request to the device.

An important element of this definition is the notion of *hardware binding* of the cryptographic key. That is, the key k_{PUF} is generated dynamically and relies on the physical properties of the hardware itself (*i.e.*, the PUF). Consequently, k_{PUF} is never explicitly stored on the requesting device. This dynamic key generation is in contrast to traditional key management, in which keys are generated *a priori*. This approach simplifies the administration work, while reducing the threat of a rogue administrator transferring keys to an untrusted device.

One possible criticism to our definition is that it does not consider what happens to the contents of the file after decryption. That is, if the device d is malicious (or is infected with malicious software), it could simply broadcast the contents after decryption. We counter this objection by noting that remote attestation techniques could be applied to ensure that only trusted applications are running on the device. Hence, we assume either the device is free of malware, or the server can detect the malware and abort.

In addition to such software attacks, an attacker with physical access and sufficient technical skill could read the contents directly from the device's memory. However, such an attack exists regardless of the access control methodology applied. As such, we consider such threats beyond the scope of our work.

5.1 Protocols

Our protocols rely on a number of cryptographic primitives. Let H denote a collision-resistant hash function, while $\mathsf{Enc}_k(m)$ denotes the symmetric key encryption of a message m with the key k, using a cipher that is secure against *probabilistic polynomial time* (PPT) known ciphertext attacks. Define $\mathsf{Auth}(\cdot)$ to be a robust authentication scheme that is resilient against PPT adversaries. $\mathsf{Gen}(\cdot)$ denotes a pseudorandom key generator based on the provided seed value.

Let $\mathsf{Commit}(\cdot)$ denote a commitment scheme that ensures confidentiality against PPT adversaries. $\mathsf{Chal}(\cdot)$ and $\mathsf{Prove}(\cdot)$, then, indicate a random challenge and the corresponding zero-knowledge proof of the secret value bound to the commitment. Furthermore, we assume that any PPT adversary $\mathcal{A}$ has negligible probability of guessing $\mathsf{Prove}(\cdot)$ without access to the committed secret value. Assuming C denotes the PUF-enabled client (also called the device) and S indicates the server, the table in Table 1 gives the formal definition of our protocols.

Given these formalisms, we now explain the intuition behind each protocol. In $\mathsf{Request}(adm, m)$, an administrator adm requests a set of m challenges to be used with a new (unspecified) device.[1] S authenticates adm and creates a database entry of the form $< adm, n, C_1, \ldots, C_m >$, binding those challenges and the nonce to that administrator. Hence, only that administrator is authorized to use that particular set of challenges. We use $prms$ to indicate any parameters needed for the commitment and proof scheme. For instance, in our implementation $prms$ consists of a modulus.

For $\mathsf{Enroll}(adm, pwd, C_1, \ldots, C_m, prms)$, we are assuming a trusted path from adm to C. That is, no eavesdropper learns the administrator's password, and all data are entered correctly. Based on this assumption, adm provides the inputs to C, which initiates an enrollment protocol that starts with authenticating adm. C uses a

pseudorandom generator to produce a one-time-use key otk derived from the administrator's password pwd, the nonce n, and the challenges. S can retrieve the nonce and challenges from its database, thus recreating the key on its end. C uses otk to encrypt a commitment of the PUF challenge-response pairs. S acknowledges receipt of the values with a hash of the commitment.

Finally, $\mathsf{Access}(user, file, action)$ defines the access request protocol. As before, S authenticates the user making the request, and selects a random set T of the challenges $C_1, \ldots, C_m$. After receiving $\mathsf{Chal}(T)$, C executes the PUF to get the responses R_i for each $C_i \in T$. The corresponding zero-knowledge proof $p \leftarrow \mathsf{Prove}(T)$ is derived from these responses. S uses p and the user's password pwd as inputs to a pseudorandom generator to produce a one-time-use key k. S encrypts the file contents c with this key, returning the encrypted file to C. Hence, the intuition behind this protocol is that the file can only be decrypted by that user with that particular PUF-enabled device.

We note that there is one important consideration regarding our definition of $\mathsf{Access}(user, file, action)$. Unlike the previous protocols, this protocol will be executed repeatedly. However, there are only 2^m subsets of $\mathscr{P}(C_1, \ldots, C_m)$. After all subsets are exhausted for a single user, the necessary proof will be reused. However, this repetition is acceptable, as the proof is never made public. Instead, the proof is used as an input to the key generation. Furthermore, assuming the nonce z is never repeated, the keys generated will always be different, even if $p \leftarrow \mathsf{Prove}(T)$ is reused.

In designing our protocols, we envisioned both traditional computing and embedded applications. In the embedded scenario, there may not be a human *user* making the request $\mathsf{Access}(user, file, action)$. A straightforward variant of our protocol could accommodate this situation by eliminating $\mathsf{Auth}(user)$ from that protocol. Then, S must make the access control decision based on the device making the request, not the *user* doing so. Though this flexibility is a nice feature of our design, we will not investigate the security claims of this variant in this paper.

5.2 Security Analysis

Here, we present our formal analysis of the security properties of our protocols. We start with three lemmas, and complete our analysis with a theorem that our approach satisfies our definition of physically restricted access control.

Lemma 1.

A PPT adversary $\mathcal{A}$ can enable an untrusted device with only negligible probability.

Proof: Based on our assumption that $\mathsf{Auth}(\cdot)$ is resilient against PPT adversaries, S will abort the $\mathsf{Request}(\cdot)$ and $\mathsf{Enroll}(\cdot)$ protocols, except with negligible probability. Even with a transcript of $\mathsf{Request}(\cdot)$, $\mathcal{A}$ must be able to forge the $\mathsf{Enc}_{otk}(\cdot)$ message to enable an untrusted device. However, with no knowledge of pwd, this feat is also infeasible, by our assumptions of $\mathsf{Enc}_k(\cdot)$. Therefore, $\mathcal{A}$ has only negligible probability of completing the $\mathsf{Enroll}(\cdot)$ protocol and enabling an untrusted device. $\square$

Lemma 2.

An honest client C can validate its enrollment with the legitimate S, except with negligible probability.

Proof: Similar to Lemma 1, a PPT adversary $\mathcal{A}$ has negligible probability of forging $\mathsf{H}(\mathsf{Commit}(< C_1, R_1 >, \ldots, < C_m, R_m >))$. Hence, if C receives such a hash, it has high assurance that the hash originated from the legitimate S and the enrollment succeeded. $\square$

---

[1] In general, we assume $C_i \leftarrow \mathsf{Gen}(1^n) \; \forall \; 1 \leq i \leq m$; that is, each challenge is the result of a pseudorandom generator with a security parameter 1^n. However, in some applications, it may be desirable for S to define the challenges predictably. As such, we are intentionally vague on the selection of $C_1, \ldots, C_m$.

Request(adm, m) – Administrator adm requests m challenges to enable a new device.
– S performs Auth(adm)
– S responds with $C_1, \ldots, C_m$, parameters $prms$, and a nonce n
Enroll($adm, pwd, C_1, \ldots, C_m, prms$) – C (after receiving data provided by adm) sends a commitment of the PUF to S.
– S performs Auth(adm)
– C generates $otk \leftarrow$ Gen($pwd, n, C_1, \ldots, C_m$)
– C provides Enc$_{otk}$(Commit($< C_1, R_1 >, \ldots, < C_m, R_m >$))
– S responds with H(Commit($< C_1, R_1 >, \ldots, < C_m, R_m >$))
Access($user, file, action$) – Subject $user$ requests $action$ for $file$, which is encrypted with key $chal$ and transferred. If $action = read$, S sends the file. Otherwise, C sends it.
– S performs Auth($user$) and issues Chal (T), where $T \subset \mathscr{P}(C_1, \ldots, C_m)$
– S responds with a nonce z
– S verifies that $user$ is permitted to perform $action$ on $file$
–   Generate and transfer Enc$_{chal}$(c), where $p \leftarrow$ Prove(T) and $chal \leftarrow$ Gen(p, z, pwd)

Table 1: Protocols for enforcing physically restricted access control

Lemma 3.

A PPT adversary $\mathcal{A}$ with transcripts of Request($\cdot$) *and* Enroll($\cdot$) *can model the PUF with only negligible probability.*

Proof: In order for $\mathcal{A}$ to learn the commitments of the PUF behavior, $\mathcal{A}$ must either decrypt Enc$_{otk}$(Commit($< C_1, R_1 >, \ldots, < C_m, R_m >$)) or find a preimage of H(Commit($< C_1, R_1 >, \ldots, < C_m, R_m >$)). However, based on our assumptions regarding Enc$_k$($\cdot$) and H($\cdot$), both actions are infeasible. Thus, these protocols do not leak enough information for a PPT adversary $\mathcal{A}$ to model the PUF. $\square$

Informally, these lemmas demonstrate that the Request($\cdot$) and Enroll($\cdot$) protocols guarantee integrity and confidentiality against PPT adversaries. That is, by viewing a transcript of both protocols, $\mathcal{A}$ fails to learn the administrator's pwd or the PUF challenge-response pairs. Furthermore, any tampering by $\mathcal{A}$ will be detected by either S or C. Also, $\mathcal{A}$ cannot launch a man-in-the-middle attack against Enroll($\cdot$), as doing so requires knowledge pwd. Applying these lemmas, we propose the following theorem.

Theorem 1.

The Access($\cdot$) *protocol enforces physically restricted access control under the PPT adversarial model.*

Proof: By Lemma 1, we are guaranteed that only trusted devices will be able to produce $p \leftarrow$ Prove(T). Lemma 2 ensures that trusted devices receive confirmation if their enrollment is successful; as such, if the confirmation is not received, proper mitigation can be performed. By Lemma 3, we are guaranteed that PPT adversaries cannot possess a model of the PUF behavior by observing a transcript of the Request($\cdot$) and Enroll($\cdot$) protocols. We explicitly model the authentication of $user$, check that $user$ is authorized to perform $action$ on $file$, and the device is implicitly authenticated by generating a one-time proof of knowledge of the PUF behavior. Furthermore, the one-time key $chal \leftarrow$ Gen(p, z, pwd) exists only at run-time, is never transmitted, is bound to the hardware of the requesting (trusted) device (by the use of the PUF), and is used to encrypt data transferred between C and S. The probability of a PPT adversary generating $chal$ is negligible, so the encryption successfully enforces the access control policy. Therefore, by definition, the Access($\cdot$) protocol enforces physically restricted access control under the PPT adversarial model. $\square$

6. IMPLEMENTATION

In this section, we describe our implementation of a PUF-based access control mechanism based on our protocols described above. We start by describing our protocol instantiation and our implemen-

tation of a PUF using ring oscillators, which is the same method used in [32]. We also describe the use of Reed-Solomon codes to ensure the PUF produces a consistent result that can be used for authentication, and detail our minimal storage requirements.

6.1 Protocol Instantiation

The underlying premise of our protocol instantiation is the Feige-Fiat-Shamir identification scheme. Our choice of hash function was SHA-1, although a better choice would be SHA-256, which offers more protection against preimage attacks and is collision-resistant. Our choice of symmetric key cryptography was AES which also provides the security against PPT adversaries that we require.

Our Auth($\cdot$) primitive uses the hash function and a nonce n in a challenge-response protocol. Specifically, S generates n, and the user must respond with H(H(pwd), n). Note that both hashes are necessary, as our implementation of S protects the secrecy of user passwords by storing H(pwd), not the passwords themselves. Furthermore, as the response requires knowledge of both n and the password (in the form of H(pwd)), this challenge-response pair preserves the secrecy of pwd from PPT adversaries. Figure 2(a) shows our implementation of Request(adm, m), in which an administrator A requests a new set of challenges from the server S. The parameter N returned in step 4 is used as a modulus in the other protocols.

Our Enroll($adm, pwd, C_1, \ldots, C_m, prms$) implementation is shown in Figure 2(b). Our Commit($\cdot$) primitive consists of the pairs (C_1, R_1^2), $\ldots$, (C_m, R_m^2), where the multiplication is modulus N. The security of this commitment relies on the intractability of computing R_i by observing R_i^2 (mod N). That is, even if a PPT adversary gains access to the committed values stored on S, he can compute the modular square roots with only negligible probability, and the confidentiality of the PUF is assured. As we will explain in Subsection 6.4, we used the `mcrypt` utility to generate the cryptographic keys, thus providing the functionality of the Gen($\cdot$) primitive.

Our instantiation of Access($user, file, action$) is shown in Figure 2(c). As we mentioned previously, our choice of Chal($\cdot$) and Prove($\cdot$) is based on the Feige-Fiat-Shamir identification scheme. The first step of this scheme is for the prover (C) to generate a random r and send $x \equiv +/- r^2$ (mod N).[2] The user is then authenticated using a nonce and a cryptographic hash. Given the challenge set $T \subset \mathscr{P}(C_1, \ldots, C_m)$ (where $\mathscr{P}$ denotes the power set), C executes the PUF for each $C_i \in T$. That is, C computes $y \equiv r \cdot \prod R_i^{p_i}$ (mod N), where $p_i = 1$ if $C_i \in T$ and $p_i = 0$

---

[2]Randomly flipping the sign of r^2 (mod N) ensures that the scheme is a zero-knowledge proof of knowledge.

(a) Request(adm, m): Requesting a set of m challenges

(b) Enroll($adm, pwd, C_1, \ldots, C_m, prms$): Generating the Feige-Fiat-Shamir PUF commitments.

(c) Access($user, file, action$): Using Feige-Fiat-Shamir and the PUF to generate a one-time-use key to encrypt the file.

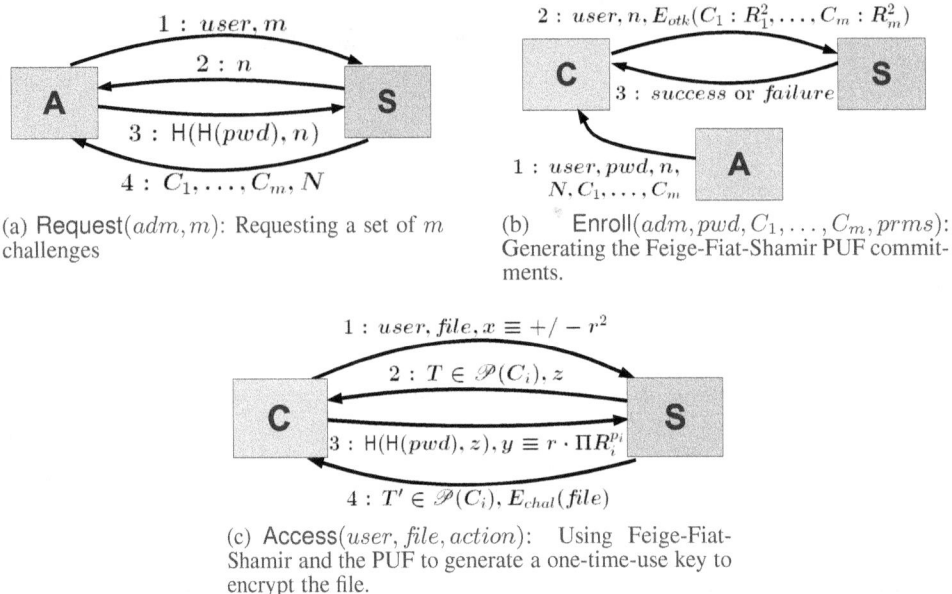

Figure 2: Physically restricted access control protocols. All multiplications are modulo N.

otherwise. Thus, the proof $p \leftarrow \mathsf{Prove}(T)$ is the value +/- y^2 (mod N). As both parties also know $\mathsf{H}(pwd)$ and the nonce z, and they can compute +/- y^2 (mod N), they can use the proof to generate $chal \leftarrow \mathsf{Gen}(p, z, pwd)$ as required by the protocol.

There is an important subtlety here that should be noted. Under the traditional Feige-Fiat-Shamir scheme, the prover sends y and the verifier must compare both y^2 (mod N) and $-y^2$ (mod N) with the product of x and the committed values. That is, it would seem that C and S would have to attempt the encryption and/or decryption twice. However, this is not the case. S always uses $x \cdot \prod R_i^{p_i}$ (which includes the correct sign). As the decision of whether or not to flip the sign of x was made by C, C clearly knows whether the proof should be y^2 (mod N) or $-y^2$ (mod N). Hence, the encryption and decryption only need to be attempted once by each party.

In addition, readers who are familiar with existing work in generating cryptographic keys from biometrics [19] may object to our use of the responses as the secrets. In that work, the authors create a secure key $\mathcal{K}$ and compute $\Theta_{lock} = \mathcal{K} \oplus \Theta_{ref}$, where Θ_{ref} denotes the reference biometric sample. To authenticate a sample Θ_{sam} at a later point, the system applies the bit mask Θ_{lock} in an attempt to recover the key $\mathcal{K}$.

In our approach, this bit mask is unnecessary for two reasons. First, unlike biometric data, the PUF responses exist only at runtime and are never made public. In contrast, biometric data, such as fingerprints, are always present and can be harvested. Thus, PUF responses are more private and, consequently, more protected. Second, revoking a biometric is impossible; however, it must be possible to revoke the associated key. The bit mask makes this possible. In our scheme, though, revocation of a PUF response R_i is simple: S stops using the associated challenge C_i. Hence, applying the bit mask to the PUF response is unnecessary for our scheme.

6.2 PUF Creation

We used the Xilinx Spartan-3 FPGA to implement a PUF. To simplify the circuitry, we created independent pairs of ROs, each forming a 1-bit PUF. To ensure that we could count a high number of oscillations, we implemented a 64-bit counter to receive the data

from each multiplexor. Each oscillator consisted of a series of nine inverter gates. Our experiments with fewer gates resulted in the oscillator running at too high of a frequency, but nine gates offered good, consistent behavior.

We controlled the PUF execution time by incrementing a small counter until it overflowed. The Spartan-3 uses a 50 MHz clock, so a 16-bit counter overflows in approximately 1 ms. We also increased the counter size to 20 bits, which required 21 ms to overflow. We did not notice any observable difference in the consistency; hence, a 16-bit counter offers sufficient time for the oscillators to demonstrate quantifiably different behavior.

Our design is based on a 128-bit PUF. However, in our experiments, we needed to create a state machine to write the PUF result out to a serial port. The extra space for the state machine would not fit on the Spartan-3. As such, we reduced the PUF size to 64 bits for experimental evaluation. In future designs, all work will be performed on the device itself, the state machine will not be needed, and accommodating 128-bit PUFs (and larger) will certainly be feasible.

From the perspective of space on the device, the limiting factor is the usage of the look-up tables (LUTs). Implementing a 128-bit PUF on the Spartan-3 occupies 39% of the available input LUTs and 78% of slices. However, as more ROs are added, the number of slices grows only slightly, while the usage of the LUTs increases more quickly. Implementing two independent 128-bit PUFs on the same device would occupy 78% of the LUTs and 99% of slices. Note, though, that these numbers are based on our simplistic PUF design, which consists of 128 pairs of independent 1-bit ROs. More advanced designs [33] select random pairs from a pool of ROs; in such an approach, a 128-bit output can be produced from 35 ROs, whereas our approach would use 256 (128 pairs).

By implementing the full PUF as independent 1-bit PUFs, there is a direct correlation between each bit of the challenge and each bit of the response. That is, flipping only a single bit of input would result in only a single bit difference in the output. To counteract this correlation, we take a hash of the PUF output. As a result of the properties of cryptographic hash functions, a single bit difference in the PUF output will produce a very different hash result. This hash step prevents an attacker from using the one-to-one mapping to model the PUF.

6.3 Error Correction

PUFs are designed to be generally non-deterministic in their behavior. The physical properties of the device itself resolves this non-determinism to create a consistent and predictable challenge-response pattern. However, variations in the response are inevitable. For instance, if two ring oscillators operate at nearly identical frequencies, the PUF may alternate between identifying each as the "faster" oscillator. Reed-Solomon codes [26] correct these variations up to a pre-defined threshold.

Reed-Solomon codes are linear block codes that append blocks of data with parity bits that can be used to detect and correct errors in the block. To guarantee that we can correct up to 16 bits of output for a 128-bit PUF, we use a RS(255,223) code. Note that this code operates on an array of *bytes*, rather than bits. To accommodate this, we encode each PUF output bit into a separate byte. Alternatively, we could have compacted eight bits at a time into a single byte for a more compact representation. In fact, doing so is necessary for implementations that use larger sizes of PUF output. For our current work, though, we find this encoding to be acceptable, even if it is not optimal.

RS(255,223) reads a block of 223 input symbols and can correct up to 16 errors. After converting the PUF output to a string of bytes, we pad the end of the string with 0s. The encoding produces a *syndrome* of 32 bytes that must be stored. When the PUF is executed at a later point, the response is again converted to a string of bytes and padded, and these 32 bytes are appended. The array of bytes is then decoded, correcting up to 16 errors introduced by the noisy output of the PUF.

While Reed-Solomon codes can correct errors in a data block, they operate under the assumption that the original data is correct. In the case of PUFs, it is also possible that the original data varies from the normal behavior observed at later times. To counteract this initial bias, during the enrollment process, we execute the PUF three times, not once. For each bit, we do a simple majority vote. That is, the "official" PUF result is the result of the consensus of the three executions.

6.4 Client-Server Implementation

We implemented our protocols as a custom client-server prototype. Both applications use a custom-built package for performing arbitrary-length arithmetic operations for large numbers. All hash operations use the SHA-1 implementation by Devine [9]. We incorporated the Reed-Solomon code library created by Rockliff [27]. Recall that, in our protocols, we use symmetric key encryption in a number of steps; the symmetric keys are generated from a shared secret. In all cases, we wrote the secret to a file, used the Linux utility `mcrypt` (which reads the file and generates a strong key from the data), and immediately destroyed the file using `shred`. The cryptographic algorithm used was 128-bit AES (Rijndael). To minimize the possibility of leaking the key by writing the shared secret to a file, we used `setuid` to run server under a dedicated uid, and restricted read access to the file before writing the secret.

6.5 Storage Requirements

The storage requirements of our solution for both C and S are minimal. C must store N, the challenges C_i, and an error-correcting syndrome for each challenge. As we detailed above, N and C_i are each 128 bits, or 16 bytes in length. Each syndrome (one per challenge) is 32 bytes in length. Thus, the total storage for C in our

prototype is $48m + 16$ bytes. For 16 challenges, then, the storage requirement is under 1 KB.

S also must store a minimal amount of data. S stores N and the $R_i^2 \pmod{N}$ commitments, each of which are 128 bits (16 bytes) in size. In addition, S stores a hash of each user's password. If SHA-1 is used, that hash is 20 bytes. If a denotes the number of devices enabled and b denotes the number of authorized users, the total storage requirement for our system is $(16m+16)a+20b$ bytes of data. *E.g.*, given 100 users, S can enable 1000 devices with 16 challenges each for less than 268 KB of storage.

7. EXPERIMENTAL EVALUATION

We now present the experimental evaluation of of our prototype. Our evaluation goals focused on two areas. First, we strove to demonstrate that RO-based PUFs are both non-deterministic and consistent. That is, different physical instantiations of the same PUF design produce different behavior, but repeating the PUF execution on the same input and hardware produce results that can be reliably quantified as the same binary string. Our second area of evaluation was on the performance of our client-server prototype. In that portion, we show that our design offers better performance than using traditional PKI to distribute symmetric encryption keys.

The output from the PUF, implemented using a Xilinx Spartan-3 FPGA, is transferred to a client application via serial cable, although in deployed settings all operations would occur on the same device. All client and server operations were executed on a system with a 2.26GHz Intel® Core™ 2 Duo CPU with 3GB of 667MHz memory. The OS used was Ubuntu 9.04, with version 2.6.28-15 of the Linux kernel.

7.1 PUF Consistency

As noted in Section 6, we implemented a 64-bit PUF and wrote the serialized output to a workstation via cable. In our experiments, we observed an average of 0.2 bits that differed from the "official" PUF result. The maximum difference that we observed was 5 bits. Clearly, the use of Reed-Solomon codes that can correct up to 16 error bits at each iteration will be able to provide consistent output from the PUF, even if we double the size of the PUF to 128 bits. Furthermore, note that changes in environmental conditions, such as different temperatures, will affect the absolute speeds at which the ROs oscillate. However, the PUF result is based on the *relative* speeds; that is, increasing the temperature will slow both ROs in a pair down, but is unlikely to change which of the two oscillates faster. Consequently, the PUF shows very consistent behavior that can be used to build a reliable authentication mechanism.

7.2 Client/Server Performance

To evaluate the performance of our client and server implementations, we executed a series of automated file requests, given several different files sizes. In these experiments, we emulated the PUF in software. As noted in Section 6.2, we can control the PUF execution time; overflowing a 16-bit counter adds only 1 ms to the client computation time. Figures 3 and 4 report the amount of time for computing key portions of the Access protocol for some of the file sizes that we measured.

In these figures, "Generate Proof" (shown in blue) refers to the time to authenticate the user by generating or checking the hash $H(H(pwd), z)$ and the proof y sent in step 3. "Generate Key" (shown in green) refers to the amount of time required to create the 128-bit AES key needed to encrypt or decrypt the file, $E_{chal}(file)$. The AES computation is shown in orange.

Figures 3 and 4 are shown on both a (truncated) linear scale and a logarithmic scale. The key observation of these figures is that the

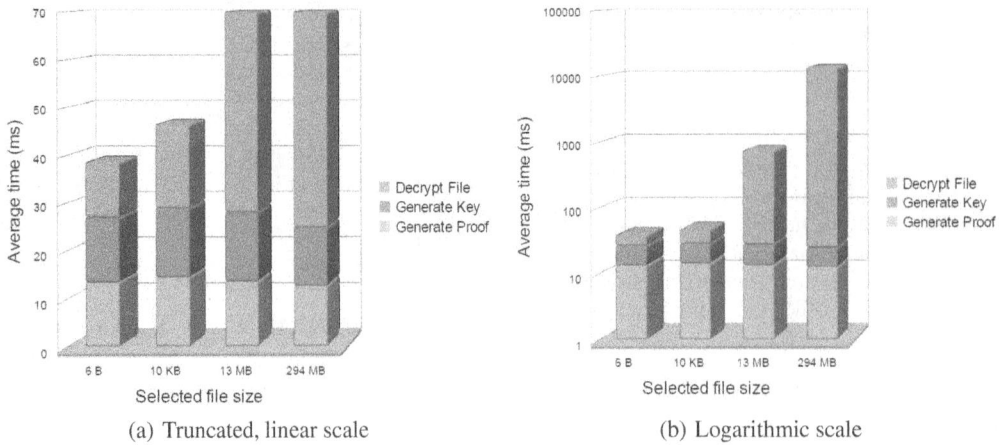

(a) Truncated, linear scale   (b) Logarithmic scale

Figure 3: Average client-side computation time for steps 3 and 4 of the Access protocol.

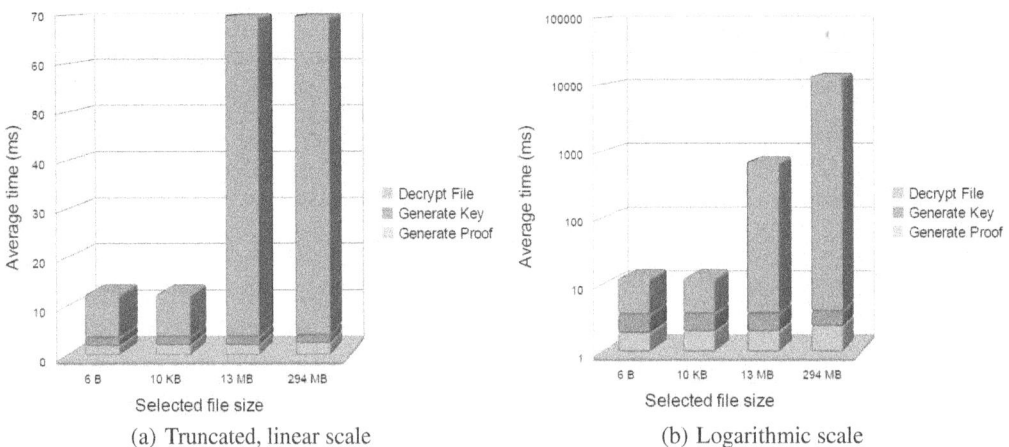

(a) Truncated, linear scale   (b) Logarithmic scale

Figure 4: Average server-side computation time for steps 3 and 4 of the Access protocol.

two primary functions of our protocol, plotted as "Generate Key" and "Generate Proof," are fairly constant and minimal. The client side operations take approximately 14 ms on average, which is the same length of time as decrypting a 6-byte piece of data with AES (12 ms on average). The server burden is even less, requiring approximately 2 ms for each protocol stage and 9 ms to encrypt the file. As the file size increases, the AES encryption clearly becomes the limiting factor, as it increases approximately linearly with the file size, while our protocol overhead remains constant.

Comparing the performance of our approach with traditional PKI (specifically, RSA) required addressing a number of factors. First, the intractability assumption behind our approach (as described in the next section) states that finding the modular square root is at least as hard as factoring the product of primes, *assuming the product and the modular square are the same size.* That is, computing R_i from a 128-bit R_i^2 is only as difficult as breaking a *128-bit* RSA key, which is quite a weak claim. Thus, we needed to increase the size of the PUF output. Note, though, that the PUF execution time does not change. The only additional performance overhead is the extra time required to do the modular multiplication on larger numbers.

The other disparity between our approach and RSA is that the result of an RSA decryption would give you the key itself. In our approach, we would be left with a 1024-, 2048-, or 4096-bit value that

would have to be converted into an AES key. However, based on our experiments with `mcrypt`, we observed only negligible overhead to convert this PUF output value into a key. Thus, this extra work had no measurable impact on our performance.

Figure 5 shows the difference in performance between our PUF-based key generation and using RSA to encrypt an AES key. The RSA modular exponentiation requires approximately four times the computation time as our client-side PUF-based key generation. Thus, our approach offers a clear performance advantage, which may be very beneficial for low-power embedded devices.

8. DISCUSSION

We start this section with a brief discussion on PUF and RSA key sizes. We then focus on possible attack models for our design.

8.1 On Key Sizes

In the previous section, we showed the performance difference between our 128-bit PUF-based client-server architecture and various sizes of RSA keys. However, comparing the security guarantees of our system with the use of PKI to distribute symmetric keys is somewhat challenging. Revealing R_i^2 while assuming R_i to be secure relies on the assumption that computing modular square roots is intractable. [25] shows that this computation is at least as difficult as factoring the product of primes, *provided the num-*

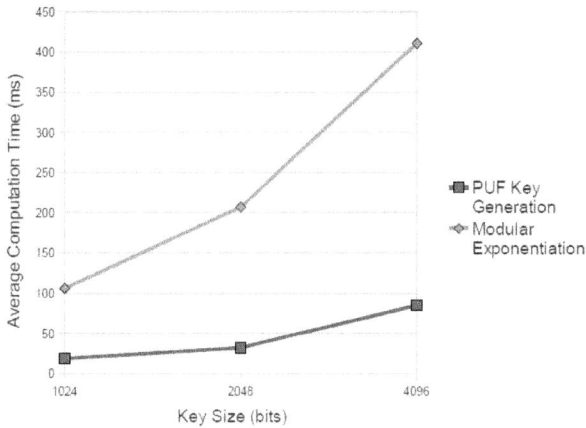

Figure 5: Large PUF computation compared with RSA-based modular exponentiation

bers are all large. Intuitively, though, computing a 128-bit modular square root is only as hard as factoring a 128-bit RSA key, which is quite a weak claim. We counter this criticism of our design with the following justifications.

First, attacking the R_i values in this manner can only occur at S. That is, the R_i^2 values are never transmitted in the clear where an attacker can eavesdrop. In RSA, though, public keys are used to encrypt the symmetric keys before transmitting them across the network. Transmitting keys in this manner creates an attack surface that our approach avoids.

Second, the PUF could be repeatedly polled to produce a larger output bit string. That is, appending 8 responses for a 128-bit PUF will create a 1024-bit bit string. Additionally, we showed that increasing the size yields a minimal performance cost when compared with common RSA key sizes. Consequently, we do not consider criticisms based on the key size to detract from the soundness of our overall design.

8.2 Additional Threats & Attacks

In Section 5.2, we provided a formal analysis of our protocol. Here, we expand on this analysis with an informal discussion of the remaining threats to our design. First, recall that our protocol is built on the assumption that C is a trusted device. As such, we do not consider attacks in which C leaks secure data received through a legitimate access request. The presence of malware on C makes this a very realistic concern. However, we consider this threat beyond the scope of our work, and focus on what can be accomplished under the assumption that the C is trusted.

A common flaw in authentication protocols is vulnerability to a replay attack. Consider a PPT adversary $\mathcal{A}$ with a transcript of of Access($user, file, action$), as shown in Figure 2(c). If either z or T were different, the replay attempt would fail. Additionally, even if both z and T are the same, $\mathcal{A}$ would learn nothing new. That is, under the PPT assumption, $\mathcal{A}$ cannot decrypt $E_{chal}(file)$. The only threat in this scenario would be if the session involved *uploading* the file from C to S. In this case, $\mathcal{A}$ could force S to revert the status of *file* to an earlier version. However, this can only happen if both z and T are identical. Assuming a large range of values for these variables, this attack can succeed with only negligible probability.

Now consider a stronger adversary $\mathcal{A}$ that has learned the pairs (C_i, R_i^2) for a particular device. Under the PPT model, such an adversary can only have learned these values by successfully attacking S. Clearly, if $\mathcal{A}$ can bypass S's protection of the pairs, he can also directly access all of the files on the system. Hence, the only remaining motivation of such an attacker is to try to model the PUF by learning the PUF responses.

The defenses against such an adversary rely on a number of factors. First, even if we set aside the PPT model and assume that the adversary has somehow learned the key used to encrypt $E_{chal}(file)$ *and* the inputs to Gen(p, z, pwd). Note that this p is exactly the proof generated in the Feige-Fiat-Shamir identification scheme, which is known to be zero-knowledge. Hence, observing additional sessions provides no new information regarding the values of R_i.

Thus, $\mathcal{A}$ can only model the PUF by computing the modular square roots. Returning to the PPT model, such an attack can succeed with only negligible probability, as computing modular square roots is at least as difficult as factoring a large product of primes for composite values of N [25]. Admittedly, in our prototype, we used only 128-bit values (which is quite weak), but we demonstrated that it would be straightforward to increase the PUF output to larger sizes with minimal overhead. Hence, a PPT adversary could not model the PUF, even with possession of the pairs (C_i, R_i^2).

Finally, consider the case of a malicious administrator. Insider threats are very difficult to prevent in general, as these attackers have been granted permissions because they were deemed trustworthy. In our approach, there is no inherent mechanism for preventing a malicious administrator from enabling untrusted devices. One simple defense would be to apply separation-of-duty, thus requiring multiple administrators to input the same challenges to each device.[3] Another approach would be to require a supervisor to approve the enrollment request. Incorporating such defense-in-depth techniques would strengthen our scheme against these threats.

9. CONCLUSIONS

In this work, we have proposed a novel mechanism that uses PUFs to bind an access request to a trusted physical device. In contrast to previous work, we do not use the PUF to generate or store a cryptographic key. Rather, we incorporate the PUF challenge-response mechanism directly into our authentication and access request protocols. Furthermore, our approach avoids expensive computation, such as the modular exponentiation used in public key cryptography. As a result, our PUF-based mechanism can be used in settings where PKI or TPMs are either not available or require too much performance overhead. We have presented the details of our implementation. Our empirical results show that PUFs can be used to create a light-weight multifactor authentication that successfully binds an access request to a physical device.

10. ACKNOWLEDGEMENTS

The work reported in this paper has been partially funded by Sypris Electronics.

11. REFERENCES

[1] S. Aich, S. Sural, and A. K. Majumdar. STARBAC: Spatiotemporal role based access control. In *OTM Conferences*, 2007.

[2] J. Al-Muhtadi, R. Hill, R. Campbell, and M. D. Mickunas. Context and location-aware encryption for pervasive computing environments. In *Proceedings of the 4th IEEE Conference on Security in Pervasive Computing and Communications*, March 2006.

---

[3] Of course, this does nothing against colluding administrators!

[3] M. J. Atallah, E. D. Bryant, J. T. Korb, and J. R. Rice. Binding software to specific native hardware in a VM environment: The PUF challenge and opportunity. In *VMSEC '08*. ACM, 2008.

[4] S. Berger, R. Cáceres, K. A. Goldman, R. Perez, R. Sailer, and L. van Doorn. vtpm: virtualizing the trusted platform module. In *USENIX-SS'06: Proceedings of the 15th conference on USENIX Security Symposium*, Berkeley, CA, USA, 2006. USENIX Association.

[5] A. Bhargav-Spantzel, A. C. Squicciarini, and E. Bertino. Establishing and protecting digital identity in federation systems. In *Proceedings of the 2005 ACM Workshop on Digital Identity Management*, pages 11–19. ACM, 2005.

[6] M. L. Damiani, E. Bertino, B. Catania, and P. Perlasca. GEO-RBAC: A spatially aware RBAC. *ACM Transactions on Information Systems and Security*, 2006.

[7] B. Danev, T. S. Heydt-Benjamin, and S. Čapkun. Physical-layer identification of RFID devices. In *Proceedings of the USENIX Security Symposium*, 2009.

[8] S. Devadas, E. Suh, S. Paral, R. Sowell, T. Ziola, and V. Khandelwal. Design and implementation of PUF-based "unclonable" RFID ICs for anti-counterfeiting and security applications. In *2008 IEEE International Conference on RFID*, pages 58–64, 2008.

[9] C. Devine. FIPS-180-1 compliant SHA-1 implementation. http://csourcesearch.net/c/fid1A3BFA49A2F9E1FFB3147B7238E287C22E7ED0A3.aspx, 2006.

[10] Federal Financial Institutions Examination Council. *Authentication in an Internet Banking Environment*, October 2005.

[11] U. Feige, A. Fiat, and A. Shamir. Zero knowledge proofs of identity. In *Proceedings of the 19th Annual ACM Symposium on Theory of Computing*, pages 210–217, 1987.

[12] A. Fiat and A. Shamir. How to prove yourself: Practical solutions to identification and signature problems. In *Proceedings on Advances in Cryptology (CRYPTO '86)*, pages 186–194. Springer-Verlag, 1987.

[13] K. B. Frikken, M. Blanton, and M. J. Atallah. Robust authentication using physically unclonable functions. In *Information Security Conference (ISC)*, September 2009.

[14] B. Gassend, D. Clarke, M. van Dijk, and S. Devadas. Controlled physical random functions. In *Proceedings of the 18th Annual Computer Security Applications Conference (ACSAC)*, 2002.

[15] B. Gassend, D. Clarke, M. van Dijk, and S. Devadas. Silicon physical random functions. In *Proceedings of the 9th ACM Conference on Computer and Communications Security (CCS '02)*, 2002.

[16] J. Guajardo, S. S. Kumar, G.-J. Schrijen, and P. Tuyls. FPGA intrinsic PUFs and their use for IP protection. In *Proceedings of the 9th Cryptographic Hardware and Embedded Systems Workshop (CHES)*, pages 63–80, 2007.

[17] J. Guajardo, S. S. Kumar, G.-J. Schrijen, and P. Tuyls. Physical unclonable functions and public-key crypto for FPGA IP protection. In *International Conference on Field Programmable Logic and Applications*, pages 189–195, 2007.

[18] K. Han and K. Kim. Enhancing privacy and authentication for location based service using trusted authority. In *2nd Joint Workshop on Information Security*. Information and Communication System Security, 2007.

[19] F. Hao, R. Anderson, and J. Daugman. Combining crypto with biometrics effectively. *IEEE Trans. Comput.*, 55(9):1081–1088, 2006.

[20] L. N. Hoang, P. Laitinen, and N. Asokan. Secure roaming with identity metasystems. In *IDtrust '08*. ACM, March 2008.

[21] D. Kulkarni and A. Tripathi. Context-aware role-based access control in pervasive computing systems. In *Proceedings of the 14th Symposium on Access Control Models and Technologies (SACMAT)*, 2008.

[22] K. Lofstrom, W. Daasch, and D. Taylor. IC identification circuit using device mismatch. In *Solid-State Circuits Conference, 2000. Digest of Technical Papers. ISSCC. 2000 IEEE International*, pages 372–373, 2000.

[23] S. P. Miller, B. C. Neuman, J. I. Schiller, and J. H. Saltzer. Kerberos authentication and authorization system. In *Project Athena Technical Plan*, 1987.

[24] R. M. Needham and M. D. Schroeder. Using encryption for authentication in large networks of computers. *Communications of the ACM*, 21(12):993–999, December 1978.

[25] M. O. Rabin. Digitalized signatures and public-key functions as intractable as factorization. Technical Report MIT/LCS/TR-212, MIT Laboratory for Computer Science, January 1979.

[26] M. Riley and I. Richardson. Reed-solomon codes. http://www.cs.cmu.edu/afs/cs.cmu.edu/project/pscico-guyb/realworld/www/reedsolomon/reed_solomon_codes.html, 1998.

[27] S. Rockliff. The error correcting codes (ecc) page. http://www.eccpage.com/, 2008.

[28] R. Sailer, T. Jaeger, X. Zhang, and L. van Doorn. Attestation-based policy enforcement for remote access. In *Proceedings of the 11th ACM Conference on Computer and Communications Security (CCS '04)*, pages 308–317. ACM Press, 2004.

[29] N. Saparkhojayev and D. R. Thompson. Matching electronic fingerprints of RFID tags using the hotelling's algorithm. In *IEEE Sensors Applications Symposium (SAS)*, February 2009.

[30] D. Schellekens, B. Wyseur, and B. Preneel. Remote attestation on legacy operating systems with trusted platform modules. In *Science of Computer Programming*, pages 13–22, 2008.

[31] G. E. Suh and S. Devadas. Physcal unclonable functions for device authentication and secret key generation. In *Proceedings of the 44th IEEE Design Automation Conference (DAC)*, pages 9–14. IEEE Press, 2007.

[32] G. E. Suh, C. W. O'Donnell, and S. Devadas. AEGIS: A single-chip secure processor. In *Elsevier Information Security Technical Report*, volume 10, pages 63–73, 2005.

[33] G. E. Suh, C. W. O'Donnell, and S. Devadas. Aegis: A single-chip secure processor. *IEEE Design and Test of Computers*, 24(6):570–580, 2007.

[34] Trusted Computing Group. Trusted Platform Module Main Specification. http://www.trustedcomputinggroup.org/, October 2003.

[35] Verizon RISK Team. 2010 data breach investigations report. Technical report, 2010.

Towards Defining Semantic Foundations for Purpose-Based Privacy Policies

Mohammad Jafari, Philip W.L. Fong, Reihaneh Safavi-Naini, Ken Barker
Department of Computer Science
Univ of Calgary
2500 University DR NW, Calgary, AB, Canada, T2N-1N4
{jafarm,pwlfong,rei,kbarker}@ucalgary.ca

Nicholas Paul Sheppard
Library eServices,
Queensland Univ of
Technology
GPO Box 2434, Brisbane
Australia, QLD 4001
nicholas.sheppard@ieee.org

ABSTRACT

We define a semantic model for *purpose*, based on which purpose-based privacy policies can be meaningfully expressed and enforced in a business system. The model is based on the intuition that the purpose of an action is determined by its situation among other inter-related actions. Actions and their relationships can be modeled in the form of an *action graph* which is based on the business processes in a system. Accordingly, a modal logic and the corresponding model checking algorithm are developed for formal expression of purpose-based policies and verifying whether a particular system complies with them. It is also shown through various examples, how various typical purpose-based policies as well as some new policy types can be expressed and checked using our model.

Categories and Subject Descriptors

K.6.5 [**Management of Computing and Information Systems**]: Security and Protection

General Terms

Security

Keywords

Purpose, Privacy Policy, Access Control, Modal Logic

1. INTRODUCTION

Privacy policies and enforcement technologies are crucial for mitigating risks involved in storage and processing of data in digital form and making such systems safe and reliable. *Purpose of access* is one of the core concepts in privacy which considers the data user's intent as a factor in making access control decisions. This enables differentiating between access to the same piece of data, even by the same person, when it is for a different purpose. For example, a patient may want to allow a physician to see the blood-test results for the purpose of *medical treatment*; but deny access to the same data by the same person for a purposes such as *research*.

Purpose has been considered in major privacy legislations, such as the U.S. Privacy Act (1974) and Canada's Federal Privacy Act (1983). These laws and similar ones in other countries stipulate that personal information must be used only for the purpose that was declared at collection time. More recent research considers *purpose* a decision factor in privacy-oriented access control models [5, 2, 19] and in policy languages [27, 25, 20].

One major issue is that in nearly all existing models, purposes are treated as opaque labels (i.e. a character string) with little or no semantics. This leads to ambiguity and arbitrary interpretation of purposes in privacy policies, often contrary to the interests of data owners. For example, if the privacy policy of a company states that data collected from customers may be used for the purpose of *service improvement*, this is likely to be very unclear to the customers who do not get to have a clear understanding of what exactly this entails, under what conditions it is violated, and how it is enforced.

Besides, and in our opinion as a consequence of such a lack of semantics, enforcing purpose-based policies continues to be a challenging problem. The main difficulty in purpose enforcement is how to identify the purpose of an agent when it requests to perform an action. Some common proposed mechanisms are *self-declaration* in which the agent explicitly announces the purpose of data access (e.g. [16]), and *role-based* enforcement in which the purpose is identified based on the agent's role in the system (e.g. [5]). The first method obviously cannot stop a malicious agent from claiming false purposes. The second method has been criticized to be inefficient in capturing purpose of an action since roles and purposes are not always aligned and members of the same organizational role may practice different purposes in their actions [15]. Therefore, identifying the purpose of an action, or verifying a claimed purpose remains an open question, partly because enough attention has not been paid to the link between actions and their purposes.

This paper addresses these problems by: (a) developing a formalism with which *purpose*, and its relationship to actions is clearly defined, and (b) designing a corresponding mechanism using which the purpose of an action can be identified and thereby adherence to purpose-based policies can be verified and enforced.

Section 1.1 gives an overview of our work by discussing the concept of purpose and how it relates to actions in Section 1.1.1, sketching our formal framework in Section 1.1.2, and showing how our proposed framework will be used in a practical scenario in Section 1.1.3. Section 1.2 goes over some related work and Section 2 formalizes the basics for definition of purpose. Section 3 develops a modal logic to articulate actions and their teleological relationships which is the foundation for formally defining purpose-based policies. Section 4 defines the form of a purpose-based policy in our model and illustrates how various examples of common purpose-based policies can be expressed using the developed language. This section also demonstrates how our model is capable of expressing new types of policies that are not considered in the current literature. Compliance checking for policies is discussed in Section 5 by giving a model checking algorithm that tests whether a given system adheres to some given policy. Section 6 provides a further elaboration of several key points about the framework, leaving Section 7 to make some concluding remarks.

1.1 Our Work

This section briefly describes our conceptual framework, the formal tools that we have developed on its basis, and a walk-through of how it can be used in practice.

1.1.1 Conceptual Framework

Intentional actions are often assigned a *purpose* that refers to the aim and rationale to perform them. One may ask or talk about the purpose of reading a book, increasing salaries, or collecting information. Hence, everyday usages of *purpose* presume a sense of teleology (or final aim) concerning the goal behind executing an action and its ultimate consequences. Thus, the purpose of *reading* a book may be to entertain, or by increasing salaries the ultimate intention may be to attract high-quality workforce, and information may be collected to do medical research.

Observing how *purpose* is used in the natural language reveals that purposes often refer to an action or a set of actions. A web search for *"for the purpose of"* yields top results such as: disseminating information, pricing, promoting, language verification, *etc.* all of which are names of some abstract actions. Typical purpose names mentioned in privacy standards and guidelines also refer to actions; for example, *completion and support of activity* and *website and system administration* in P3P [27], or *treatment* and *research* in Healthcare XSPA [21] and Dimitropoulos's report [8]. The correspondence of purposes and actions has also been observed by others in the literature as it will be mentioned in Section 1.2.

In the first place, purpose of an action is something that only exists in the mind of the agent performing the action. However, an agent's purpose for an action affects other actions performed, so, the set of actions that precede or follow the action are affected by the agent's purpose. Thus, related actions can be indicative of the purpose and the purpose of the action may be revealed by looking at the actions that precede or follow it. For example, when someone borrows money and later uses the money to pay a phone bill, it can be inferred that the purpose of borrowing money has been to pay the bill. Conversely, it is possible to *enforce* a purpose by restricting the surrounding actions. Thus, the purpose of *paying the bill* can be enforced by forbidding the agent from doing anything but making the payment as a consequence of borrowing the money.

Thus, purpose can be defined by the situation of an action within a larger context containing other actions and the relationships among them. This context can be defined as a network of relationships that capture the intention, or more precisely, the purpose of the action. Accordingly, we can define the purpose of an action as *its placement in a collection of other related actions*; we call such network of inter-related actions a *plan*. This is the fundamental assumption that forms the basis of our purpose model in this paper.

Intuitively, a *plan* is a collection of interrelated actions together with various relationships among them. Later in Section 2, we define *action graph* as an abstract model to capture such plans with only two types of relationships. These two types of relationships are based on the following observations of two types of purposes:

Purpose as a High-Level Action.

In some contexts, *purpose* refers to a more abstract, or semantically higher-level action in a plan. Thus, doing something for some purpose, actually means doing it as a part, or a sub-action, for that higher-level action. For example, when Alice checks some patient's blood pressure *for the purpose of surgery*, it means that checking the blood pressure is a part of a more complex and abstract action of *surgery*. Similarly, when it is said the a surgery is performed *for the purpose of treatment*, it is because the high-level action of *medical treatment* includes *surgery* as a part.

In some contexts purpose refers to a desired state of affairs, such as doing some action for the purpose of *happiness*. In such cases we assume that the purpose refers to the abstract action of *reaching* that state. Thus, doing something for the purpose of *happiness*, can be interpreted as doing something as part of the abstract action of *pursuing happiness*, which is the higher-level action.

Purpose as a Future Action.

In some contexts, purpose is used to indicate that an action is performed as a prerequisite of another action in future. For example, when Bob withdraws money from a bank account for the purpose of *paying the bills*, it means the former action is done as a prerequisite to performing the latter.

1.1.2 Formal Framework

We develop formal tools for expressing and verifying purpose-based policies. A formal model is developed for the business processes in the system. This can be used to formalize the relationships between different high-level and low-level actions in a business system in the form of a graph. Correspondingly, a formal language is also developed using which purpose-based policies can be expressed about such business processes. The model checking algorithm can be used to check whether the business processes in a particular system comply with the policies.

1.1.3 Walk-Through

We motivate our framework by explaining how it can be used in practice. Suppose there is an organizations with well-defined business processes. The aim is to check whether the business processes in this organization comply with a set of purpose-based privacy rules.

Step 1: Vocabulary.

A common terminology is necessary for referring to system's actions so that business processes and policies can use the same vocabulary. Low-level actions such as *read, write, etc.* are well-known and common across many domains with clear and standard meanings. More complex and abstract actions like *surgery, marketing, etc.* can be taken from standard vocabularies that exist in many domains such as clinical systems in healthcare (e.g. [22]). In this paper, we do not discuss how such a vocabulary is developed and assume it exists.

Step 2: Abstract Model of Actions in the System.

The next step is to make a formal model of actions in the system and their relationships. The action names in such a model are taken from the common vocabulary and their relationships can be extracted based on the business processes in the system. This model reflects how the system works and is used to evaluate whether it complies with the purpose-based policy. Definition and explanation of this model is given in Section 2.

Step 3: Policy.

Purpose-based policy is a set of rules about the purposes of actions in the system. For example, one may want to make sure some data is not used for the purpose of *marketing*, or patient files are not modified when used for the purpose of *research*. Such rules come from different origins; there are global system-wide rules that apply to an entire organization or even multiple organizations, and are usually authored by a management authority. For example, a jurisdictional policy may stipulate that employee ethnicity data must not be used for the purpose of *promotions* in any organization in the country. On the other hand, there are data-dependent policies, such as patient consents, that are specific to treatment of a particular piece of data and are effective only if that piece of data is being processed. Such policies are usually defined by the data owner.

Policy rules should be formalized using a language we develop in Section 3. The atomic propositions in the language (e.g. *marketing, research*, and *promotion* in the previous examples) are taken from the common vocabulary described above. The semantics of the language is defined based on the formal model of the actions in the system, and therefore, what is expressed in the language has a clear meaning about the actions in the system and their relationships.

Step 4: Model Checking and Policy Enforcement.

Our final goal is to test whether the system complies with the policies. Having a formal model of the actions in the system and after formalizing the policy rules using the developed language, a model checking algorithm is used to check whether the model satisfied the rules. The model checking algorithm can also be used to enforce the policy at run-time by blocking access if the model did not comply with it. For example, if Alice's consent requires that her blood test results cannot be *read* for the purpose of *research*, the model checking algorithm can be run when a read access is requested to her file and test whether the purpose-based rule is satisfied.

1.2 Related Work

The conceptual link between purposes and actions has been observed by a number of others in the literature and can be considered supportive to our approach of defining purpose using related actions.

van Sataden *et. al.* suggest that purpose names can be taken from the verbs in a standard dictionary [26]. Similarly, Powers *et. al.* mention that business purposes are a form of high-level action and argue that in high-level privacy policies instead of referring to low-level actions such as *read* or *write*, high-level business purposes such as *treatment* or *diagnosis* are used [23].

In the context of an object-oriented system, Yasuda *et al.* associate purpose with the caller method [28]. For example, if the *housekeeping* method of a person object calls the *withdraw* method of a bank account object, the implication is that money is withdrawn for the purpose of *housekeeping*. This is consistent with our definition of purpose in its first meaning that refers to a higher-level, more abstract action.

In their development of a formal semantics for privacy policies, Breaux and Antón propose to model purpose as an auxiliary related action [4]. For example, the policy that *data is collected for the purpose of marketing* is taken to mean the primary action of *data collection* is related to the auxiliary action of *marketing* that happens later. This is very similar to our notion of purpose as a future action.

HL7 Reference Information Model ("RIM") specifications, a data model used as the basis for designing many healthcare systems, mentions the *has reason* relation between two actions for specifying that one is the *reason* for the other [11]. In this design, *reason* is similar to *purpose* of an action, especially in its sense as as future action.

There are some proposals [9, 10, 6, 15] that suggest associating purpose with the units of work in a system. They argue that *tasks* or *workflows*, can be used to identify the purpose of an action by looking at the higher-level unit of work in which it takes place. The higher-level unit of work is basically equivalent to our definition of more abstract actions, so this approach is consistent with the first type of purpose as defined above. Our proposed model is more general and can encompass these approaches as very simple special cases. Moreover, our work extends earlier approaches by considering both meanings of purpose as future event and more abstract action. Also, it allows multiple purposes to be present for a single action which is a feature that is not considered in any other works on purpose-based models as far as we are aware (see Section 6.6).

A different line of research on *obligations* in access control systems is also concerned about actions and how they relate to future actions (e.g. [12, 13]). The part of our model that considers future actions has some similarities to this line of work, but we are also concerned about other relationships among actions which are not of interest in the study of obligations. Also, even in the study of future actions we do not follow a strict linear notion of time and our model allows multiple future actions whose order is immaterial (see Section 2).

As the formal language, we use modal logic to articulate the relationships among actions. Temporal logic, which is a special type of modal logic, has been used previously to formalize different relationships between actions; for example, control flow [17] or obligations policies [12].

We introduce action graphs as an abstract model of different actions in the system and their order. Our model of action graph is similar to *control flow graph* used to assess programs in programming languages [1] and hierarchical planning in the artificial intelligence literature [24].

2. MODELING PLANS: ACTION GRAPH

Based on the discussion in Section 1.1.1, we define a formalism for a *plan* that captures the actions and two types of relationships among them. The action graph can be thought of as an abstract model based of the business processes in a system. We define an *action graph* as a directed graph in which nodes correspond to actions (both high-level and low-level) and edges denote the relationships among them.

There are two types of edges each corresponding to one type of relationship mentioned in Section 1.1.1: *prerequisite-of* and *part-of*. The prerequisite-of relationship signifies that one action is performed as an antecedent for another action, and the part-of relationship indicates that one action is performed as part of a higher-level more abstract action. For brevity, we will refer to the prerequisite-of and part-of relationships, respectively as the F- and A-relationships, short for *future* and *abstract*.

An example of such a graph is shown in Figure 1 where various purposes can be identified based on F- and A-edges. For example, the purpose of *opening the file* (node g), is to *read* its contents (node h), which is manifested by the F-relationship between the two that says opening the file is a prerequisite for reading its content. Moreover, both *opening* and *reading* the file are for the purpose of *loading the patient's information* (node f). This means that *opening* and *reading* the file are part of the realization of the *load patient's file* action. Similarly, *loading the patient's file* is in turn for the purpose of *checking blood pressure history* (node e), and so on. Eventually, as the graph shows, all of the actions in the graph are for the purpose of *cancer treatment* (node a) as they are all part of the realization of this action.

Note that an action can be assigned numerous purposes. For example, the action of *opening the file* can at the same time be associated with the purpose of *reading the file, surgery preparation, cancer treatment, etc.*

2.1 Defining the Model

The action graph is a directed graph with two sets of edges, each corresponding to one type of relationship as discussed above. It is defined as $AG = (V, A, F)$ in which V is the set of vertices each of which corresponds to an action, and A and F are subsets of $V \times V$, and respectively correspond to A- and F-relationships. We will use the shorter

form uu' instead of the more common (u, u') to denote pairs throughout this paper. The action graph satisfies the following conditions:

(a) $A \cap F = \emptyset$,

(b) (V, A) is a tree with its root being the only sink vertex,

(c) $uu' \in F \rightarrow \exists v. \{uv, u'v\} \subseteq A$, and

(d) $(V, A \cup F)$ is a directed acyclic graph.

Intuitively, an action graph is a hierarchical workflow, with nodes representing actions. Condition (a) says that the A- and F- relations cannot co-occur between the same pair of nodes. Condition (b) requires that an action can only be part of a single higher-level action, and there exists a single highest-level action. Condition (c) settles that the prerequisite of an action should be part of the same higher-level action. Finally, condition (d) forbids circularity in the graph.

Based on the intuition that F- and A- relationships cannot be circular, we assume that the action graph does not have a cycle, and hence property (d). Real workflows and business processes may however contain cycles which makes it difficult to build an action graph based on them. We leave solving this problem as a future work and assume the action graphs is acyclic for the moment.

Theorem 1 extends property (c) to the reflexive transitive closure of the F-relationship. The proof is given in Appendix A.

Theorem 1.
$uu' \in F^* \Rightarrow \exists v. \{uv, u'v\} \subseteq A$ where F^* is the transitive closure of F. ∎

In order to accommodate action attributes into the model, we define the labeling function L. Suppose P is the set of all atomic propositions defined by the vocabulary. These propositions can refer to different facts about the actions, such as their names, locations, *etc.* The labeling function $L : V \mapsto 2^P$ maps each action to the set of all atomic propositions that hold true for that action, i.e. all of its attributes. The simplest of such attributes is the name of the action; for example the node representing the surgery action is mapped to a *surgery* proposition which belongs to the vocabulary. See Section 6.1 for a discussion of other attributes such as authorized roles, location, *etc.* and how they can be used to model more complex policies.

3. A MODAL LOGIC FOR FORMALIZING PURPOSE-BASED POLICIES

Since purpose is captured in the form of A- and F-edges in an action graph, defining purpose-based rules requires a language capable of expressing constraints on these relationships. For instance, if the purpose of *marketing* is forbidden for action a, this is interpreted in the action graph as the restriction that action a should not lead to *marketing* along F- and A-edges in the graph; in other words, it must not be a prerequisite, nor be a part of, a *marketing* action.

In this section, we define a modal logic with different modal operators useful to capture such restrictions. There are four basic modal operators and two derived forms. The

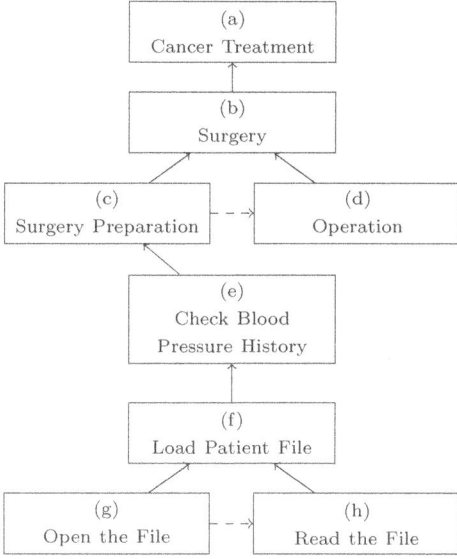

Figure 1: An example of an action graph as defined in Section 2. The F– and A–edges are shown with dashed and solid arrows respectively. Actions are labeled with letters for convenient later reference.

six modal operators are analogous to the conventional temporal logic operators, i.e. $\Diamond$, $\Box$, and $\bigcirc$, that are particularized for F– and A–relationships. We will first give the formal definition of the syntax and semantics of the language, and then, explain the meaning of the operators using some examples.

The syntax of the language is presented in Backus-Naur Form as follows:

$$\phi ::= \top \mid p \mid \neg\phi \mid \phi \wedge \phi \mid (\mathcal{A})\phi \mid (\mathcal{F})\phi \mid [\mathcal{A}]\phi \mid [\mathcal{F}]\phi \quad (1)$$

where p is any atomic proposition.

The semantics of the language is defined by a satisfaction relation ($\models$) in the context of a certain vertex v in the action graph $AG = (V, F, A)$, and a labeling function L. We write $AG, L, v \models \phi$, or more simply $v \models \phi$ where the context is clear; we also write $v \not\models \phi$ when it is not the case that $v \models \phi$. The satisfaction relation $\models$ is defined as follows:

- $v \models \top$ always holds.

- $v \models p$ holds iff $p \in L(v)$.

- $v \models \neg\phi$ holds iff $v \not\models \phi$.

- $v \models \phi_1 \wedge \phi_2$ holds iff $v \models \phi_1$ and $v \models \phi_2$.

- $v \models (\mathcal{A})\phi$ holds iff $\exists vv' \in A, v' \models \phi$.

- $v \models (\mathcal{F})\phi$ holds iff $\exists vv' \in F, v' \models \phi$.

- $v \models \langle\mathcal{A}\rangle\phi$ holds iff $\exists vv' \in A^*, v' \models \phi$.

- $v \models \langle\mathcal{F}\rangle\phi$ holds iff $\exists vv' \in F^*, v' \models \phi$.

A^* and F^* are the reflexive transitive closures of respectively A and F.

We also define the following derived forms to facilitate expressing more complex formulas:

$$\bot \stackrel{def}{=} \neg\top$$

$$\phi_1 \vee \phi_2 \stackrel{def}{=} \neg(\neg\phi_1 \wedge \neg\phi_2)$$

$$\phi_1 \rightarrow \phi_2 \stackrel{def}{=} \neg(\phi_1 \wedge \neg\phi_2)$$

$$[\mathcal{A}]\phi \stackrel{def}{=} \neg\langle\mathcal{A}\rangle(\neg\phi)$$

$$[\mathcal{F}]\phi \stackrel{def}{=} \neg\langle\mathcal{F}\rangle(\neg\phi)$$

Based on the action graph of Figure 1, several examples are presented to clarify the operators' meanings. To keep the examples simple, we assume that the set of atomic propositions is the same as the set of vertices and the labeling function is an identity in that each vertex maps to its name. In other words: $P = V$ and $\forall v \in V. L(v) = v$.

F–Next and A–Next.

$(\mathcal{F})\phi$ and $(\mathcal{A})\phi$ mean that ϕ is true at least in one of the immediately following nodes along the F– or A–edges respectively. For example, in the graph of Figure 1, we have $c \models (\mathcal{F})d$, since d is a next node of c according to the F–relation (i.e. $(c, d) \in F$), and $d \models d$. Similarly, we have $e \models (\mathcal{A})(\mathcal{F})d$, since c is a next node of e according to the A–relation (i.e. $(e, c) \in A$), and $c \models (\mathcal{F})d$ as discussed above.

F–Diamond and A–Diamond.

$\langle\mathcal{F}\rangle\phi$ and $\langle\mathcal{A}\rangle\phi$ mean that in the paths of F–, or respectively, A–edges beginning inclusively from the current node, there exists at least one node for which ϕ is true. For example, in the graph of Figure 1, we have $g \models \langle\mathcal{F}\rangle(\mathcal{A})f$ because along the path of F–edges beginning from g, there is a node, namely h, satisfying $(\mathcal{A})f$. Similarly, $e \models \langle\mathcal{A}\rangle(\mathcal{F})d$, because along the path of A–edges beginning inclusively from e, there is a node, namely c, that satisfies $(\mathcal{F})d$.

F–Box and A–Box.

$[\mathcal{F}]\phi$ and $[\mathcal{A}]\phi$ mean that along the paths of F–, or respectively, A–edges beginning inclusively from the current node, all of the nodes satisfy ϕ. For example, in the graph of Figure 1 we have $g \models [\mathcal{F}](\mathcal{A})f$, since along the only path of F–edges beginning inclusively from g, all of the nodes (i.e. g and h) satisfy $(\mathcal{A})f$. Similarly, we also have $g \models [\mathcal{A}](c \rightarrow \langle\mathcal{F}\rangle d)$, because along the path of A–edges beginning from g, the formula $c \rightarrow \langle\mathcal{F}\rangle d$ is true for all nodes. Note that since A–edges by definition form a directed tree there is only one such path.

Theorem 2 is crucial in simplifying policy formulas (see the proof in Appendix A).

Theorem 2.

Any formula of the form $\langle*\rangle...\langle*\rangle\phi$ in which $*$ can be either of $\mathcal{A}$ or $\mathcal{F}$ is equivalent to:

- $\langle\mathcal{A}\rangle\phi$ if it has the form $\langle\mathcal{A}\rangle^n\phi$,

- $\langle\mathcal{F}\rangle\phi$ if it has the form $\langle\mathcal{F}\rangle^n\phi$,

- $\langle\mathcal{F}\rangle\langle\mathcal{A}\rangle\phi$ if it has the form $\langle\mathcal{F}\rangle^n\langle\mathcal{A}\rangle^m\phi$ $(m, n \in \mathbb{N})$,

- and $\langle\mathcal{A}\rangle\langle\mathcal{F}\rangle\phi$ otherwise.

Similarly, $[*]...[*]\phi$ in which $*$ can be either of $\mathcal{A}$ or $\mathcal{F}$, is equivalent to:

- $[\mathcal{A}]\phi$ if it has the form $[\mathcal{A}]^n\phi$,

- $[\mathcal{F}]\phi$ if it has the form $[\mathcal{F}]^n\phi$,

- $[\mathcal{F}][\mathcal{A}]\phi$ if it has the form $[\mathcal{F}]^n[\mathcal{A}]^m\phi$ $(m, n \in \mathbb{N})$,

- and $[\mathcal{A}][\mathcal{F}]\phi$ otherwise. ∎

4. PURPOSE-BASED POLICY

A purpose-based policy is a set of rules based on the purposes of actions. A simple example of such rules is to forbid reading a some piece of information for the purpose of *marketing*. In this paper, we only consider purpose-based authorization policies, i.e. those policies that allow or forbid some actions in the system based on their purposes. More complex types of policies that go beyond a yes-or-no decision about an action are left as future work but briefly glanced at in Section 6.3.

Based on our conceptual framework (Section 1.1.1), we assume that a purpose-based policy can be expressed in the form of a set of restrictions on an action graph. For instance, the simple policy that a file should not be read for the purpose of *marketing*, can be interpreted as a restriction that the action of *reading the file* should neither be part of *marketing* action, nor be a prerequisite for a future *marketing* action. The modal logic defined in Section 3 provides a language to express such restrictions, so, we can define the purpose-based policy by assigning formulas of that language to actions. A purpose-based policy will be a set of such rules.

On this basis, we define the purpose-based policy *POLICY* as a set of formulas of the form $a_i \rightarrow \phi_i$ in which a_i's are action names (i.e. atomic propositions belonging to the vocabulary), and ϕ_i's are formulas belonging to the modal logic language defined in Section 3. Each such rule states that the purpose-based formula ϕ_i should hold when action a_i is to be performed. If this is not the case, the action graph in question (and hence the corresponding business process) is deemed as non-compliant, or a reference monitor blocks the action.

An action graph $AG = (V, A, F)$ satisfies a policy if all the rules of the policy hold in all of its nodes:

$$\forall v \in V. \forall r \in POLICY. v \models r$$

4.1 Types of Policy Rules

This section describes several types of rules in purpose-based policies that can be expressed using the developed language. The current purpose-based policies found in the literature fall into the first three types discussed here. The rest are new types that are a contribution of this paper.

4.1.1 Required Purposes

One type of rule is to require that some action be for some particular purpose; for example, "action a must be for the purpose of *treatment*". To formulate this, one should essentially say that the *treatment* purpose should be visited at some point by traversing along F– or A–edges. According to Theorem 2 any formula of such a form can be reduced to either $\langle\mathcal{A}\rangle\langle\mathcal{F}\rangle$treatment, or one of: $\langle\mathcal{A}\rangle$treatment, $\langle\mathcal{F}\rangle$treatment, or $\langle\mathcal{F}\rangle\langle\mathcal{A}\rangle$treatment. Since the latter three cases all imply the former, the disjunction of the four is

equivalent to the former, and hence, the rule can be written in the following form:

$$POLICY \ni (a \rightarrow \langle\mathcal{A}\rangle\langle\mathcal{F}\rangle\text{treatment})$$

Since in our model, it is possible that an action be associated multiple purposes (see Section 6.6), a rule can require more than one purpose. For example, an action may be required to be both for the purpose of *order-processing* and *delivery*. Using the logical conjunction, this can be formulated as:

$$(\langle\mathcal{A}\rangle\langle\mathcal{F}\rangle\text{order-processing}) \wedge (\langle\mathcal{A}\rangle\langle\mathcal{F}\rangle\text{delivery})$$

4.1.2 Forbidden Purposes

There are cases where a purpose must be forbidden for an action; for example, "action a should not be for the purpose of *marketing*". This is actually the negation of the type discussed in Section 4.1.1 and can be formulated as:

$$POLICY \ni a \rightarrow (\neg\langle\mathcal{A}\rangle\langle\mathcal{F}\rangle\text{marketing})$$

or equivalently, as:

$$POLICY \ni a \rightarrow ([\mathcal{A}][\mathcal{F}]\neg\text{marketing})$$

4.1.3 Compound Forbidden and Required Purposes

A rule may arbitrarily forbid or allow purposes. For example, a rule may forbid performing action a for the purpose of *marketing* unless the *treatment* purpose is also involved. In other words, it should either be that the *marketing* purpose is not involved, or both *marketing* and *treatment* are present. Using the types of rules already discussed in Sections 4.1.1 and 4.1.2, we can write this as:

$$POLICY \ni a \rightarrow (\langle\mathcal{A}\rangle\langle\mathcal{F}\rangle\text{marketing} \rightarrow \langle\mathcal{A}\rangle\langle\mathcal{F}\rangle\text{treatment})$$

4.1.4 Order-Based Rules

There are cases where the order of purposes matters; for example, suppose that an insurance company covers the costs of the activities performed for the purpose of *surgery*, but it also wants to make sure that the *surgery* is in turn for the purpose of *treatment*, and not for other purposes such as *cosmetics*, or *birth control*. In such cases, not only the presence of certain purposes, but also their order is important. The above rule, for instance, requires that the *surgery* purpose appear and also be in sequence with the *treatment* purpose. The first part (existence of the *surgery* purpose) is a simple rule of the type discussed in Section 4.1.1. The latter part dealing with the order is a new type with which we are concerned here.

As shown in Section 4.1.1, the requirement that the *treatment* purpose should appear is formulated as $\langle\mathcal{A}\rangle\langle\mathcal{F}\rangle$treatment and this should hold for the *surgery* node, hence:

$$\phi = (\text{surgery} \rightarrow \langle\mathcal{A}\rangle\langle\mathcal{F}\rangle\text{treatment})$$

Now, we want to say that ϕ should hold at all of the nodes accessible from the current node, that is the right-hand side of the implication must hold for any *surgery* node visitable by traversing along the A– and F–edges. This can be stated using a formula of the form discussed in Theorem 2, which is eventually reduced to the following simple form according to that theorem:

$$POLICY \ni a \rightarrow ([\mathcal{A}][\mathcal{F}] (\text{surgery} \rightarrow \langle\mathcal{A}\rangle\langle\mathcal{F}\rangle\text{treatment}))$$

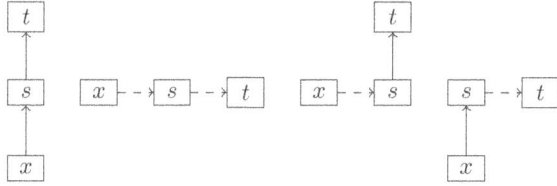

Figure 2: Four cases for a *treatment* (*t*) purpose at the distance of two.

Note that a simpler rule that requires both *surgery* and *treatment* purposes does not necessarily describe the same requirement. Imagine a scenario where someone wants to perform a cosmetic surgery but has a blood pressure problem that makes such a surgery dangerous and therefore needs to go through a treatment process to cure that problem first. In such a case, both *treatment* and *surgery* purposes are involved, but the order is contrary to what is desired, that is, the *treatment* is for the purpose of *surgery*.

It is possible to simplify order-based rules by assigning them to a different node in the action graph. For instance, the above rule can be simplified by finding all the *surgery* nodes (accessible from *a*) and requiring them to be for the purpose of *treatment* by a simpler rule of the type discussed in Section 4.1.1:

$$POLICY \ni \text{surgery} \rightarrow (\langle \mathcal{A} \rangle \langle \mathcal{F} \rangle \text{treatment})$$

This can help an organization to simplify such rules by converting them into a simpler form and assigning them to different nodes of the action graph.

4.1.5 Distance-Based Rules

Another possible type of rules limits the distance between the purpose and the action in order to forbid access even for valid purposes, when they are very indirect and rendered irrelevant due to the degree of indirectness. For example, a rule may allow access for *treatment* purpose only within a distance of 3, or in other words, when the *treatment* purpose is involved but there are at most two other intervening purposes.

Distance-based policies are a bit more complex to formulate. First, we consider exact (rather than maximum) distances. For example, a distance of 2 for *treatment* can be formulated with the following which captures different cases of a distance of 2. These cases are shown in Figure 2.

$$(\mathcal{A})^2 \text{treatment} \vee (\mathcal{F})^2 \text{treatment}$$
$$\vee (\mathcal{F})(\mathcal{A}) \text{treatment} \vee (\mathcal{A})(\mathcal{F}) \text{treatment}$$

Higher distances can be formulated similarly, with longer formulas. A maximum distance rule then, can be formulated by the disjunction of all distances lower than the maximum; for example, 3, or 2, or 1, for the maximum distance of 3. The following notation [3] can facilitate formalizing distance-based rules. Note that * is used to represent either of $\mathcal{F}$ or $\mathcal{A}$:

$$\langle * \rangle^{\leq d} \phi \stackrel{def}{=} \bigvee_{0 \leq i \leq d} (*)^i \phi$$

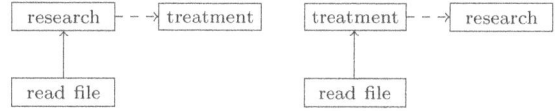

Figure 3: An example showing how the difference between *purpose as prerequisite-of* and *purpose as part-of* can affect the policy.

4.1.6 Other Miscellaneous Rules

In all rule types discussed so far, we have treated A– and F–relationships similarly and did not distinguish between purposes resulting from these two relationships. However, there are cases where the rule is based on such a distinction. As an example, consider the following two scenarios:

- A patient's data is used in some research project, and the results of the research will eventually be used to improve the treatment of some disease.

- The patient's data is used in the course of treatment, but the results of the treatment will later be used for research purposes.

In both cases the data is used for the purpose of *research* and *treatment*, but the difference between *purpose as part-of* and *purpose as prerequisite-of* distinguishes them. Figure 3 shows these two scenarios. Thus, the patients can be more precise in their consent to allow the data be used only as part of a treatment process and not as part of some research that will subsequently be used in treatment. Such a rule can be formulated as:

$$\langle \mathcal{A} \rangle \text{treatment}$$

Figure 3 illustrates how this rule allows the first case, but denies the latter. Note that a simpler rule of the type discussed in Section 4.1.1 that require *treatment* purpose, would be satisfied by both cases, contrary to what is desired.

As another example, consider a case where a customer is giving contact information to a company and does not like this information to be used for *marketing* purposes with the exception of receiving free promotion product samples. Thus, the rule is that access is not allowed for *marketing* unless there is also a *delivery* purpose involved as *part of* the marketing. Note that a delivery that *leads to* marketing, that is, done as a prerequisite for a marketing action in future, is not allowed because it may, for example, correspond to the case where an item is delivered and the address is kept for later use when sending marketing mails, which is unacceptable to the customer. Such a case can be formulated as:

$$\langle \mathcal{A} \rangle \langle \mathcal{F} \rangle \text{marketing} \rightarrow$$
$$(\langle \mathcal{A} \rangle \langle \mathcal{F} \rangle \text{delivery} \wedge [\mathcal{A}][\mathcal{F}] (\text{delivery} \rightarrow \langle \mathcal{A} \rangle \text{marketing}))$$

This rule says that if the *marketing* purpose is present, the *delivery* purpose must also be present and it must be *part of* a *marketing* purpose.

5. MODEL CHECKING

Model checking is the problem of deciding whether or not a node in a given action graph satisfies a formula. The input to the algorithm is the formula ϕ, an action graph AG,

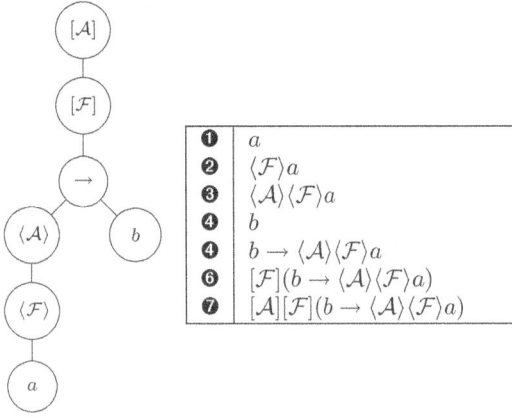

Figure 4: The abstract syntax tree of the formula $[\mathcal{A}][\mathcal{F}](b \to \langle\mathcal{A}\rangle\langle\mathcal{F}\rangle a)$ and the ordered set of its subformulas based on its post-order traversal.

a certain node v, and the labeling function L; the output is a yes-or-no answer that indicates whether $AG, L, v \models \phi$ holds. In other words, model checking is the process of testing whether a plan adheres to a policy rule.

Figure 5 outlines a model checking algorithm. This algorithm is based on the standard model checking algorithm for CTL [7] and the model checking algorithm for history-based access control policies [18], so we only give a brief discussion here.

The main idea of the algorithm is that evaluating a formula at a certain node can be performed recursively by (a) evaluating its subformulas on that node, and (b) evaluating it on the current and immediately proceeding nodes along the F– and A–edges in the action graph. For example, checking $\langle\mathcal{A}\rangle\phi$ can be performed recursively by checking whether ϕ holds in the current node, and $\langle\mathcal{A}\rangle\phi$ holds in any of the immediately next nodes along A-edges.

Using dynamic programming, the result of this recursive algorithm can be built bottom-up. For this purpose, a mechanism is needed for ordering both subformulas and the nodes of the action graph so that the two-dimensional array of the dynamic programming can be formed. For ordering the subformulas, we use the post-order traversal of the abstract syntax tree of the formula. Figure 4 shows an example of such a tree. This guarantees that the subformulas of a complex formula are evaluated first and allows evaluating a formula in a bottom-up manner, beginning from the atomic propositions. The algorithm for post-order traversal is straightforward. For ordering the nodes of the action graph, we rely on a topological sort based on A– and then F–edges, beginning from the sink. As an example, the order of nodes for the action graph of Figure 1 is: a, b, d, c, e, f, h, and g.

The algorithm fills a two-dimensional array, like the one of Figure 6, in which each cell indicates whether or not the corresponding sub-formula holds true at the corresponding node. It begins by evaluating the first sub-formula (an atomic proposition) on the first node of the action graph (the sink node) and continues to fill the array using the following rules:

- Evaluation of an atomic proposition on a node n is simply checking whether it is a member of $L(n)$.

Input: $AG = (V, A, F)$, L, ϕ
Output: Res: evaluation of ϕ on every node in AG.

```
1  Subformulas= post-order traversal of φ's abstract syntax tree
2  Nodes = Topological sort of AG.V
3  Res //stores the results
4  foreach (n in Nodes)
5    foreach (f in Subformulas)
6      if (f.isAtomic())
7        Res[f,n]=(f ∈ L(n))
8      else if (f.operator== ¬)
9        Res[f,n]=¬(Res[f.operand,n])
10     else if (f.operator== ∧)
11       Res[f,n]=Res[f.operand1,n]∧ Res[f.operand2,n]
12     else if (f.operator== (A))
13       Res[f,n]=false
14       foreach (a so that (n,a) ∈ AG.A)
15         if (Res[f.operand,a]==true)
16           Res[f,n]=true
17     else if (f.operator== (F))
18       Res[f,n]=false
19       foreach (a so that (n,a) ∈ AG.F)
20         if (Res[f.operand,a]==true)
21           Res[f,n]=true
22     else if (f.operator== ⟨A⟩)
23       Res[f,n]=false
24       if (Res[f.operand,n]==true)
25         Res[f,n]=true
26       else
27         foreach (a so that (n,a) ∈ AG.A)
28           if (Res[f,a]==true)
29             Res[f,n]=true
30     else if (f.operator== ⟨F⟩)
31       Res[f,n]=false
32       if (Res[f.operand,n]==true)
33         Res[f,n]=true
34       else
35         foreach (a so that (n,a) ∈ AG.F)
36           if (Res[f,a]==true)
37             Res[f,n]=true
38  return Res
```

Figure 5: The pseudo-code of the model checking algorithm.

- Evaluation of logical operators are done based to the rules of logic. Note that because of the post-order traversal, the operand subformulas are already evaluated.

- Formulas of the form $(\mathcal{A})\phi$ and $(\mathcal{F})\phi$ are evaluated by checking whether ϕ is evaluated as true at least in one of the nodes immediately following the current node along the A– and F–edges respectively. Note that because of the topological sort, proceeding nodes are already evaluated and the results already exist in the table.

- Formulas of the form $\langle\mathcal{A}\rangle\phi$ and $\langle\mathcal{F}\rangle\phi$ are evaluated to true if they are true for one of the immediately proceeding nodes along the A– and F–edges respectively, or if ϕ has been evaluated to true for the current node.

- Formulas of the form $[\mathcal{A}]\phi$ and $[\mathcal{F}]\phi$ are evaluated to true if they are true in all immediately proceeding nodes, respectively along the A– and F–edges, and also ϕ has been evaluated to true at the current node.

Figure 6 shows the dynamic programming array evaluated for the formula of Figure 4 on the action graph of Figure 1. We have assumed a simple labeling function that maps nodes to their names as a proposition. Note that this algorithm

		a	b	d	c	e	f	h	g
❶	a	1	0	0	0	0	0	0	0
❷	$\langle\mathcal{F}\rangle$❶	1	0	0	0	0	0	0	0
❸	$\langle\mathcal{A}\rangle$❷	1	1	1	1	1	1	1	1
❹	b	0	1	0	0	0	0	0	0
❺	❹→❸	1	1	1	1	1	1	1	1
❻	$[\mathcal{F}]$❺	1	1	1	1	1	1	1	1
❼	$[\mathcal{A}]$❻	1	1	1	1	1	1	1	1

Figure 6: The dynamic-programming array for evaluating the formula of Figure 4 on the action graph of Figure 1.

will end up evaluating the formula for all nodes in the action graph; it can be changed to halt as soon as it evaluates the formula on the particular node of interest. It is also noteworthy that for evaluating multiple formulas it will be more efficient to extract all the subformulas and then evaluate all formulas in a single pass.

The correctness of the algorithm can be checked by noticing that the recursive part of the dynamic programming calculation matches the definition of the operators. The complexity of the algorithm is $O(|\phi|(e+n))$ in which $|\phi|$ is the size of the formula (i.e. the total number of atomic propositions and operators), e is the number of edges in the action graph, and n is the number of its nodes. Note that based on the loops of line 4 and 5 of Figure 5, all subformulas (with a total number of $|\phi|$) are evaluated at each node. The evaluation in the worst case needs examining that node and all of its outgoing edges. If d_i shows the out-degree of the ith node, the complexity is $O(|\phi|((1+d_1)+...+(1+d_n)))$ which in turn yields $O(|\phi|(e+n))$.

6. DISCUSSION

Several additional aspects of this work should be considered:

6.1 Modeling More Complex Policies

The labeling function L maps actions to the set of propositions that hold true for that node (see Section 3). So far, we have only used very simple labeling functions that map each node to its name as a proposition. However, the labeling function can model other attributes of actions, such as the authorized roles, input data types, time and location constraints, *etc.* This enables defining more complex policies, particularly those that combine purpose constraints with other types of constraints, e.g. role-based, or time- and location-based. For example, a policy that settles *any action for the purpose of research must be limited to business hours* can be formulated as the following, assuming that *biz-hours* is a proposition that holds true for actions that are restricted to business hours:

$$[\mathcal{A}][\mathcal{F}](\langle\mathcal{A}\rangle\langle\mathcal{F}\rangle\text{treatment} \rightarrow \text{biz-hours})$$

Another interesting example is the case of an action's location which can be important in privacy policies. Suppose that *third-party* is a proposition that is true for actions performed by collaborator organization, and false for actions that are performed within the organization. Using such a scheme, an inter-organizational workflow can be modeled as a single unified action graph in which the location of actions is captured using this *third-party* attribute. A policy rule

such as "reading for the purpose of research is not allowed by third parties" can then be modeled as:

$$[\mathcal{A}][\mathcal{F}](\text{reading} \land \langle\mathcal{A}\rangle\langle\mathcal{F}\rangle\text{research} \rightarrow \neg \text{ third-party})$$

Note that these formulas do not consider the semantics of the *biz-hours* or *third-party* propositions; but, given that the evaluation of this proposition is otherwise taken care of, they regulate the relationships between purpose-based rules and other types of constraints in a system. We leave further exploration of this extension as a future work.

6.2 Setting Distance-Based Policies

Since the granularity of an action graph depends on how the system is designed, distance-based policies (recall Section 4.1.5) are very system-dependent. For example, a maximum distance of three may be very far in one system and very close in another, based on the granularity of the action graph. Therefore, the policy maker should be aware of the internal structure of the system to build meaningful distance-based policies. This can be true in case of organizational policies where the policy maker is aware of the details of the organization and the systems in use, but in cases such as the ethics consent in healthcare, the policy maker is an outsider to the organization and such policies cannot be meaningfully settled.

Distance can also be defined between two purposes and make the ground for a new type of policy. For example, one scenario may require that the *surgery* purpose be within 3 steps of the *treatment* purpose. We did not discuss such policies here, as we could not imagine a pragmatic case for them.

6.3 Purpose-Based Obligations

Obligations are commitments that should be incurred after an agent performs an action [12]. Currently our model only considers allowing or blocking an action based on the purpose-based policy. A further step would be to enable assigning obligations to agents as a result of performing an action. For example, the billing system in a hospital may charge a patient's or insurer's account with different amounts, depending whether the *surgery* is for the purpose of *treatment* or *cosmetics*. Or, different fees may be charged when a movie is played for the purpose of *entertainment* or *education*. We did not discuss purpose-based obligations in this paper but believe it is an interesting topic of future work.

6.4 Obligations and the F-Relationship

Suppose action a is related to a_F by an F- relationship. At run-time, if the reference monitor allows an agent to perform a based on a purpose-based policy that relies on the performance of a_F, it can be said that it is under the condition that the action a_F is performed in future. In fact, if a_F is not performed the policy would be violated. This matches the classic notion of obligation and the reference monitor can issue an obligation in such cases.

This observation points out the relationship between obligation policies and purpose-based policies which is another interesting topic for future work.

6.5 Use of First-Order Predicate Logic

The logic we have built for formalizing purposes is a modal logic over a propositional logic. However, using propositional logic has a scalability problem. For example, if there are one million health records in a system, atomic propositions should be used to express the policy regarding each of them which will make the system very complex. In other words, lack of quantifiers and predicates may lead to scalability issues in formalizing policies. On the other hand, first-order predicate will make the verification of policies undecidable in the general case. One direction of future work could be to extend the logic to first-order logic and then study the conditions under which an efficient algorithm for policy evaluation can be developed.

6.6 Multiple and Nested Purposes

The current literature generally assumes that a single purpose is associated with an action. In practice, however, a single action may have multiple purposes that are independent or tangentially related. For example, the purpose of reading a book may be both to enjoy the literature and to prepare for an exam. In turn, the purpose of preparing for the exam may be to pass the course and subsequently to get a degree. One can observe that a single action may be associated with a chain of multiple nested purposes and/or multiple independent purposes. Capturing this broader aspect of purposes is one contribution of our model.

6.7 Simplified Version of the Logic

If we simplify the logic to only contain the A–relationships, the action graph will be reduced to a directed tree. In such a tree, the purposes of an action can be captured as a *chain* of *nested purposes* and a simplified version of our logic, resembling a simple temporal logic, would be adequate to express the restrictions on such a chain. This simpler case of the model allows the chain of nested purposes to be associated with the stack context in a programming language, or a workflow as it shows the hierarchy of nested actions each of which is being performed as part of the other. Therefore, a reference monitor can be implemented very straightforwardly by watching the stack. This result has not appeared in the literature yet but is available through our tech report series [14].

6.8 Other Types of Relationships

In our current model of action graph, we only consider two types of relationships between actions. These two have obviously an implication of purpose as we discussed in Section 1.1.1. Other types of relationships such as temporal precedence or causality exist between actions and they may also be captured in an extended model of the action graph. Deciding whether or not to include other types of relationships in the action graph and how they may or may not imply a purpose is a topic of future work.

7. CONCLUSION

We developed a framework for expressing and enforcing purpose-based privacy policies. We defined the semantics of an action's purpose in terms of its situation among other related actions. A modal logic was developed to enable expressing restrictions about the relationships among actions; thereby expressing purpose-based policies. Finally, a model checking algorithm was described to check the compliance of a system with such policies. We also showed how our framework is capable of formalizing common purpose-based policy rules and also introduced some new types of such rules.

The main future work is to evaluate the model by studying a practical case of formalizing and enforcing purpose-based policies in a business system.

8. REFERENCES

[1] A. V. Aho, M. S. Lam, R. Sethi, and J. D. Ullman. *Compilers: Principles, Techniques, and Tools, 2nd Edition*. Addison-Wesley, 2006.

[2] C. A. Ardagna, S. De Capitani di Vimercati, and P. Samarati. Enhancing user privacy through data handling policies. In *Data and Applications Security*, pages 224–236, Sophia Antipolis, France, 2006.

[3] C. Baier and J.-P. Katoen. *Principles of Model Checking*. MIT Press, 2008.

[4] T. D. Breaux and A. I. Antón. Deriving semantic models from privacy policies. In *IEEE POLICY'05*, pages 67–76, Stockholm, Sweden.

[5] J.-W. Byun, E. Bertino, and N. Li. Purpose based access control of complex data for privacy protection. In *SACMAT '05: Proceedings of the tenth ACM symposium on Access control models and technologies*, pages 102–110, New York, NY, USA, 2005. ACM.

[6] W. Cheung and Y. Gil. Towards privacy aware data analysis workflows for e-science. In *Proceedings of the 2007 Workshop on Semantic e-Science (SeS2007)*, Vancouver, Canada, pages 17–25, July 2007.

[7] E. M. Clarke and E. A. Emerson. Design and synthesis of synchronization skeletons using branching-time temporal logic. In *Logic of Programs, Workshop*, pages 52–71, London, UK, 1982. Springer-Verlag.

[8] L. L. Dimitropoulos. Privacy and Security Solutions for Interoperable Health Information Exchange. http://healthit.ahrq.gov/portal/server.pt/gateway/PTARGS_0_241358_0_0_18/IAVR_ExecSumm.pdf, 2006.

[9] S. Fischer-Hübner. *IT-Security and Privacy: Design and Use of Privacy-Enhancing Security Mechanisms*. Springer, Berlin, Germany, 2001.

[10] Q. He. Privacy enforcement with an extended role-based access control model. Technical Report TR-2003-09, North Carolina State University, 2003.

[11] Health Level Seven Inc. HL7 Reference Information Model, ANSI/HL7 V3 RIM, R1-2003, 2003.

[12] M. Hilty, D. Basin, and A. Pretschner. On obligations. In *ESORICS 2005: Proceedings of the 10th European Symposium On Research in Computer Security*.

[13] K. Irwin, T. Yu, and W. H. Winsborough. On the modeling and analysis of obligations. In *CCS '06: Proceedings of the 13th ACM conference on Computer and communications security*, pages 134–143, Alexandria, Virginia, USA, 2006.

[14] M. Jafari. Nested purposes. Technical report, (unpublished), December 2009.

[15] M. Jafari, R. Safavi-Naini, and N. P. Sheppard. Enforcing purpose of use via workflows. In *WPES '09: Proceedings of the 8th ACM workshop on Privacy in the electronic society*, pages 113–116, 2009.

[16] M. Jawad, P. S. Alvaredo, and P. Valduriez. Design of PriServ, a privacy service for DHTs. In *International Workshop on Privacy and Anonymity in the Information Society*, pages 21–26, Nantes, France, 2008.

[17] T. Jensen, D. Le Metayer, and T. Thorn. Verification of control flow based security properties. pages 89 –103, Oakland, CA, USA, May 1999.

[18] K. Krukow, M. Nielsen, and V. Sassone. A logical framework for history-based access control and reputation systems. *J. Comput. Secur.*, 16(1):63–101, 2008.

[19] Q. Ni, E. Bertino, J. Lobo, and S. B. Calo. Privacy-aware role-based access control. *IEEE Security and Privacy*, 7(4):35–43, 2009.

[20] Organisation for the Advancement of Structured Information Standards. Privacy policy profile of XACML v2.0. http://docs.oasis-open.org/xacml/2.0/access_control-xacml-2.0-privacy_profile-spec-os.pdf, 2005.

[21] Organisation for the Advancement of Structured Information Standards. Cross-Enterprise Security and Privacy Authorization (XSPA) Profile of Security Assertion Markup Language (SAML) for Healthcare Version 1.0, 2009.

[22] I. H. T. S. D. Organization. SNOMED CT, Systematized Nomenclature of Medicine-Clinical Terms. http://www.ihtsdo.org/snomed-ct/.

[23] C. S. Powers, P. Ashley, and M. Schunter. Privacy promises, access control, and privacy management. In *ISEC '02: Proceedings of the Third International Symposium on Electronic Commerce*, pages 13–21, Research Triangle Park, North Carolina, US, 2002. IEEE Computer Society.

[24] S. J. Russell and P. Norvig. *Artificial Intelligence: A Modern Approach (3rd Edition)*. Prentice Hall, 2009.

[25] M. Schunter and C. Powers. The Enterprise Privacy Authorization Language (EPAL 1.1). http://www.zurich.ibm.com/security/enterprise-privacy/epal, 2003.

[26] W. van Staden and M. S. Olivier. Purpose organisation. In *ISSA2005: Proceedings of the Fifth Annual Information Security South Africa Conference*, Sandton, South Africa, 2005.

[27] World-Wide Web Consortium. The Platform for Privacy Preferences 1.1 (P3P1.1) Specification, 2006.

[28] M. Yasuda, T. Tachikawa, and M. Takizawa. A purpose-oriented access control model. In *Proceedings of Twelfth International Conference on Information Networking*, pages 168–173, Jan. 1998.

APPENDIX

A. PROOFS

THEOREM 1. $uu' \in F^* \Rightarrow \exists v \ \{uv, u'v\} \subseteq A$ where F^* is the transitive closure of F.

PROOF. $uu' \in F^*$ implies either $uu' \in F$, in which case $\exists v \ \{uv, u'v\} \subseteq A$ holds based on the property (c), or there exist $u_1, ..., u_n$, so that:

$$uu_1 \in F \wedge u_1 u_2 \in F \wedge ... \wedge u_n u' \in F$$

Applying property (c) for each of the terms yields
$\exists v_1 \ \{uv_1, u_1 v_1\} \subseteq A$, $\exists v_2 \ \{u_1 v_2, u_2 v_2\} \subseteq A$, and so on.

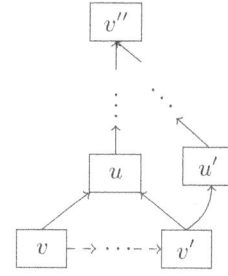

Figure 7: Proof of Lemma 1.

And since according to the property (b) (V, A) is a tree, $u_1 v_1 \in A \wedge u_1 v_2$ implies $v_1 = v_2$. Similarly it follows that all v_i's are the same and hence Q.E.D. □

LEMMA 1. *The following is a valid formula:*

$$\langle \mathcal{F} \rangle \langle \mathcal{A} \rangle \phi \leftrightarrow \langle \mathcal{F} \rangle \phi \vee \langle \mathcal{A} \rangle \phi$$

PROOF. Assuming that v satisfies the left-hand side, and based on the definition of $\langle \mathcal{F} \rangle$, it follows that $\exists v' \in V.vv' \in F^* \wedge v' \models \langle \mathcal{A} \rangle \phi$. Extending the definition of $\langle \mathcal{A} \rangle$, it follows that:

$\exists v' \in V. \exists v'' \in V.vv' \in F^* \wedge v'v'' \in A^* \wedge v'' \models \phi$

If $v' = v''$ it follows that $\exists v' \in V.vv' \in F^* \wedge v' \models \phi$ which in turn leads to: $v \models \langle \mathcal{F} \rangle \phi$.

Now suppose that $v' \neq v''$. The fact that $vv' \in F^*$ implies that $\exists u.\{vu, v'u\} \subseteq A$ according the Theorem 1. On the other hand, $v'v'' \in A^*$ implies one of the following cases when $v' \neq v''$: (A.1) $v'v'' \in A$
(A.2) $\exists v', v'u' \in A \wedge u'v'' \in A^*$.

In case (A.1), $v'v'' \in A$, and since we already had $v'u \in A$ it follows that $u = v''$ as (V, A) is a tree. Then, since $v'' \models \phi$, it follows that $u \models \phi$, and as $vu \in A$, it follows that $v \models \langle \mathcal{A} \rangle \phi$ which implies the right-hand side.

Now consider Figure 7 for case (A.2). since we have already proved that $v'u \in A$, the fact that $v'u' \in A$ implies $u = u'$ as (V, A) is a tree, which leads to the conclusion that $vv'' \in A^*$, since we already proved that $vu \in A$ above, and have $u'v'' \in A^*$ from the assumption of case (A.2). And as $v'' \models \phi$, we have $v \models \langle \mathcal{A} \rangle \phi$ which implies the right-hand side.

Proving the converse is easy since it straightforwardly follows from the semantic definitions that each of the terms in the right-hand side imply the left-hand side. □

LEMMA 2. *The box and diamond operators are idempotent, i.e. the following are valid formulas for all $n \in \mathbb{N}$:*

$$\langle \mathcal{F} \rangle^n \phi \leftrightarrow \langle \mathcal{F} \rangle \phi$$
$$\langle \mathcal{A} \rangle^n \phi \leftrightarrow \langle \mathcal{A} \rangle \phi$$
$$[\mathcal{F}]^n \phi \leftrightarrow [\mathcal{F}] \phi$$
$$[\mathcal{A}]^n \phi \leftrightarrow [\mathcal{A}] \phi$$

PROOF. For the diamond operators, we only prove the case for $\langle \mathcal{A} \rangle$ as the proof for $\langle \mathcal{F} \rangle$ is straightforwardly similar. Also, we only need to prove the case $\langle \mathcal{A} \rangle \langle \mathcal{A} \rangle \phi \leftrightarrow \langle \mathcal{A} \rangle \phi$ and the general case for n follows inductively.

According to the definition of $\langle \mathcal{A} \rangle$, $v \models \langle \mathcal{A} \rangle \langle \mathcal{A} \rangle \phi$ implies $\exists v' \in V.vv' \in A^* \wedge \exists v'' \in v.v'v'' \in A^* \wedge v'' \models \phi$. But then, it follows by transitivity that $vv'' \in A^*$. Therefore, $v \models \langle \mathcal{A} \rangle \phi$.

Now, suppose $v \models \langle\mathcal{A}\rangle\phi$. Then, $\exists v' \in A.vv' \in A^* \wedge v' \in \phi$. Note that $vv \in A^*$. Thus, $v \models \langle\mathcal{A}\rangle\langle\mathcal{A}\rangle\phi$.

For the box operators, we can prove that $[\mathcal{F}]^2\phi \equiv [\mathcal{F}]\phi$ as follows, using the first part of the theorem:

$$[\mathcal{F}][\mathcal{F}]\phi \leftrightarrow \neg\neg[\mathcal{F}][\mathcal{F}]\phi \leftrightarrow \neg\langle\mathcal{F}\rangle\neg[\mathcal{F}]\phi \leftrightarrow \neg\langle\mathcal{F}\rangle\langle\mathcal{F}\rangle\neg\phi$$
$$\leftrightarrow \neg\langle\mathcal{F}\rangle\neg\phi \leftrightarrow [\mathcal{F}]\phi.$$

$\square$

THEOREM 2. *Any formula of the form $\langle*\rangle...\langle*\rangle\phi$ in which $*$ can be either of $\mathcal{A}$ or $\mathcal{F}$ is equivalent to:*

- $\langle\mathcal{A}\rangle\phi$ *if it has the form $\langle\mathcal{A}\rangle^n\phi$,*
- $\langle\mathcal{F}\rangle\phi$ *if it has the form $\langle\mathcal{F}\rangle^n\phi$,*
- $\langle\mathcal{F}\rangle\langle\mathcal{A}\rangle\phi$ *if it has the form $\langle\mathcal{F}\rangle^n\langle\mathcal{A}\rangle^m\phi$ $(m,n \in \mathbb{N})$,*
- *and $\langle\mathcal{A}\rangle\langle\mathcal{F}\rangle\phi$ otherwise.*

Similarly, $[*]...[*]\phi$ in which $*$ can be either of $\mathcal{A}$ or $\mathcal{F}$, is equivalent to:

- $[\mathcal{A}]\phi$ *if it has the form $[\mathcal{A}]^n\phi$,*
- $[\mathcal{F}]\phi$ *if it has the form $[\mathcal{F}]^n\phi$,*
- $[\mathcal{F}][\mathcal{A}]\phi$ *if it has the form $[\mathcal{F}]^n[\mathcal{A}]^m\phi$ $(m,n \in \mathbb{N})$,*
- *and $[\mathcal{A}][\mathcal{F}]\phi$ otherwise.*

PROOF. We begin by the first part about diamond operators. Applying Lemma 2 to remove all consecutive repetitions of $\langle\mathcal{A}\rangle$ and $\langle\mathcal{F}\rangle$ will reduce the formula either to one of the trivial cases, or to one of the following forms ($n \geq 2$):
(A.1)$(\langle\mathcal{A}\rangle\langle\mathcal{F}\rangle)^n\phi$
(A.2)$(\langle\mathcal{A}\rangle\langle\mathcal{F}\rangle)^n\langle\mathcal{A}\rangle\phi$
(A.3)$(\langle\mathcal{F}\rangle\langle\mathcal{A}\rangle)^n\phi$
(A.4)$(\langle\mathcal{F}\rangle\langle\mathcal{A}\rangle)^n\langle\mathcal{F}\rangle\phi$

Case (A.1):

$$(\langle\mathcal{A}\rangle\langle\mathcal{F}\rangle)^n\phi \leftrightarrow \langle\mathcal{A}\rangle\langle\mathcal{F}\rangle\langle\mathcal{A}\rangle\langle\mathcal{F}\rangle(\langle\mathcal{A}\rangle\langle\mathcal{F}\rangle)^{n-2}\phi$$
$$\leftrightarrow \langle\mathcal{A}\rangle\langle\mathcal{F}\rangle\langle\mathcal{A}\rangle\phi'$$

where $\phi' = \langle\mathcal{F}\rangle(\langle\mathcal{A}\rangle\langle\mathcal{F}\rangle)^{n-2}\phi$. Applying the Lemma 1 we will have $\langle\mathcal{A}\rangle(\langle\mathcal{F}\rangle\phi' \vee \langle\mathcal{A}\rangle\phi')$ and since diamond operators can be distributed over disjunctions, it follows that $\langle\mathcal{A}\rangle\langle\mathcal{F}\rangle\phi' \vee \langle\mathcal{A}\rangle\langle\mathcal{A}\rangle\phi'$ and then $\langle\mathcal{A}\rangle\langle\mathcal{F}\rangle\phi' \vee \langle\mathcal{A}\rangle\phi'$. But this yields to $\langle\mathcal{A}\rangle\langle\mathcal{F}\rangle\phi'$ since $\langle\mathcal{A}\rangle\phi' \rightarrow \langle\mathcal{A}\rangle\langle\mathcal{F}\rangle\phi'$. Replacing ϕ' and applying Lemma 2 we will have:

$$\langle\mathcal{A}\rangle\langle\mathcal{F}\rangle\langle\mathcal{F}\rangle(\langle\mathcal{A}\rangle\langle\mathcal{F}\rangle)^{n-2}\phi \leftrightarrow \langle\mathcal{A}\rangle\langle\mathcal{F}\rangle(\langle\mathcal{A}\rangle\langle\mathcal{F}\rangle)^{n-2}\phi$$
$$\leftrightarrow (\langle\mathcal{A}\rangle\langle\mathcal{F}\rangle)^{n-1}\phi$$

This will recursively lead to $\langle\mathcal{A}\rangle\langle\mathcal{F}\rangle\phi$.

Case (A.2): Applying case (A.1) we will get $\langle\mathcal{A}\rangle\langle\mathcal{F}\rangle\langle\mathcal{A}\rangle\phi$ and then by applying Lemma 1:

$$\langle\mathcal{A}\rangle(\langle\mathcal{F}\rangle\phi \vee \langle\mathcal{A}\rangle\phi) \leftrightarrow \langle\mathcal{A}\rangle\langle\mathcal{F}\rangle\phi \vee \langle\mathcal{A}\rangle\langle\mathcal{A}\rangle\phi$$
$$\leftrightarrow \langle\mathcal{A}\rangle\langle\mathcal{F}\rangle\phi \vee \langle\mathcal{A}\rangle\phi$$

And since $\langle\mathcal{A}\rangle\phi \rightarrow \langle\mathcal{A}\rangle\langle\mathcal{F}\rangle\phi$, if will follow that $\langle\mathcal{A}\rangle\langle\mathcal{F}\rangle\phi$.

Case (A.3): Rewriting the formula as $\langle\mathcal{F}\rangle(\langle\mathcal{A}\rangle\langle\mathcal{F}\rangle)^{n-1}\langle\mathcal{A}\rangle\phi$ and applying the result of case (A.1) we will get to $\langle\mathcal{F}\rangle\langle\mathcal{A}\rangle\langle\mathcal{F}\rangle\langle\mathcal{A}\rangle$ And then using Lemma 1:

$$\langle\mathcal{F}\rangle\langle\mathcal{A}\rangle\langle\mathcal{F}\rangle\langle\mathcal{A}\rangle\phi \leftrightarrow \langle\mathcal{F}\rangle\langle\mathcal{F}\rangle\langle\mathcal{A}\rangle\phi \vee \langle\mathcal{A}\rangle\langle\mathcal{F}\rangle\langle\mathcal{A}\rangle\phi$$
$$\leftrightarrow \langle\mathcal{F}\rangle\langle\mathcal{A}\rangle\phi \vee \langle\mathcal{A}\rangle\langle\mathcal{F}\rangle\langle\mathcal{A}\rangle\phi$$
$$\leftrightarrow \langle\mathcal{F}\rangle\phi \vee \langle\mathcal{A}\rangle\phi \vee \langle\mathcal{A}\rangle(\langle\mathcal{F}\rangle\phi \vee \langle\mathcal{A}\rangle\phi)$$
$$\leftrightarrow \langle\mathcal{F}\rangle\phi \vee \langle\mathcal{A}\rangle\phi \vee \langle\mathcal{A}\rangle\langle\mathcal{F}\rangle\phi \vee \langle\mathcal{A}\rangle\langle\mathcal{A}\rangle\phi$$
$$\leftrightarrow \langle\mathcal{F}\rangle\phi \vee \langle\mathcal{A}\rangle\phi \vee \langle\mathcal{A}\rangle\langle\mathcal{F}\rangle\phi$$

And since $\langle\mathcal{F}\rangle\phi \rightarrow \langle\mathcal{A}\rangle\langle\mathcal{F}\rangle\phi$ and $\langle\mathcal{A}\rangle\phi \rightarrow \langle\mathcal{A}\rangle\langle\mathcal{F}\rangle\phi$ the formula can be simplified to $\langle\mathcal{A}\rangle\langle\mathcal{F}\rangle\phi$.

Case (A.4): Using the result of case (A.3), it follows that $\langle\mathcal{F}\rangle\langle\mathcal{A}\rangle\langle\mathcal{F}\rangle\phi$ and then $\langle\mathcal{F}\rangle\langle\mathcal{F}\rangle\phi \vee \langle\mathcal{A}\rangle\langle\mathcal{F}\rangle\phi$, and again, since $\langle\mathcal{F}\rangle\phi \rightarrow \langle\mathcal{A}\rangle\langle\mathcal{F}\rangle\phi$ this is equivalent to $\langle\mathcal{A}\rangle\langle\mathcal{F}\rangle\phi$.

The second part, for box operators can be proved straightforwardly by applying the result of the first part:

$$[*]...[*]\phi \leftrightarrow \neg\neg[*]...[*]\phi \leftrightarrow \neg\langle*\rangle...\langle*\rangle\neg\phi$$
$$\leftrightarrow \neg\langle\mathcal{A}\rangle\langle\mathcal{F}\rangle\neg\phi \leftrightarrow [\mathcal{A}][\mathcal{F}]\phi$$

$\square$

Practical Policy Patterns

Dan Thomsen
Independent Consultant
Minneapolis, MN
612 789-0559
d.j.thomsen@ieee.org

ABSTRACT

The paper attempts to encourage deeper thinking about the nature of security enforcement policies with the intent of fostering a practical engineering design approach for building security enforcement policy. The paper suggests several approaches to lower the cost of developing security enforcement policies by developing technology to share enforcement policies like open source software, including patterns, isolation of site specific policy and tools to increase the ability of humans to understand the implemented policy. The paper also suggests research avenues for increasing human understanding of enforcement policy.

Categories and Subject Descriptors

D.4.6 [**Operating Systems**]: Security and Protection – *Access controls*
D.2.4 [**Software Engineering**]: Software/Program Verification.

General Terms

Security.

Keywords

Security pattern engineering, computer security, access control.

1. INTRODUCTION

A security enforcement policy represents the configuration of an enterprise's security mechanisms. Creating a secure enforcement policy requires a deep understanding of the software involved and a deep understanding of the protection goals. A good least privilege policy requires a large amount of detailed knowledge on how users and applications interoperate and consume enterprise resources. The complexity of developing a good security enforcement policy approaches that of software engineering. While the implementation of an enforcement policy requires less effort than developing software, the software engineering mindset produces more effective and secure enforcement policies.

Most enforcement policies evolve from the reaction to day-to-day events, as opposed to a thoughtful design process. Functionality drives this day-to-day viewpoint more than security requirements. Effective security requires a mandatory policy that satisfies easy to understand properties. A discretionary policy leaves security in

the hands of the users, who simply will not enforce a consistent policy even without the threat of Trojan horses.

As Figure 1 shows, this paper proposes to shift the burden of creating the security policy away from day-to-day administration tasks to a structured, bottom up, design process accomplished by security policy engineers. The approach applies engineering design patterns to creating security enforcement policies.

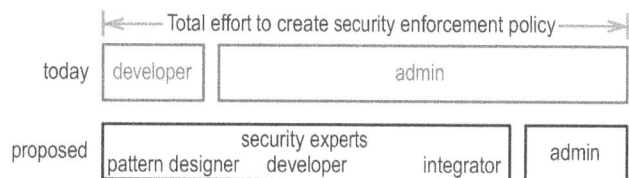

Figure 1. Shift effort from administrator to security experts.

Unlike software development, the simpler implementation of enforcement policies makes it possible to create an architecture that automates the translation from easily understood enforcement policy to site specific enforcement mechanism policies.

The paper discusses the challenges that have prevented a software engineering mentality in the past, and sketches a solution for each. Section 3 summarizes how all the elements fit together to create an architecture that reduces costs for creating enforcement policy.

2. CHALLENGES

There are four key challenges in making an engineering discipline for security enforcement policies;

1) Overcoming the incorrect mentality that creating security enforcement policy is easy.

2) Creating translation tools that spans the existing security models and enforcement mechanisms to allow designers to choose the best tool for the job.

3) Separating site specific details from generic patterns.

4) Understanding the impact of the resulting enforcement policy.

The paper discusses each challenge below.

2.1 Taking Enforcement Policy Seriously

Creating an accurate, secure enforcement mechanism that meets the security needs of an organization takes a great deal of effort. Often the enforcement policy evolves over time as the organization installs new capabilities, obscuring the full cost and resulting in a poorly understood, and insecure policy. Researchers often fare no better, often underestimating the effort to create a good enforcement policy for a 4new mechanism or security model.

Economics provides the most effective motivation for taking enforcement policy seriously. Organizations need a return on investment argument to motivate giving enforcement policy more attention. A good enforcement policy has reduced security incidents and limits the potential damage a malicious insider could do. However, it is often simply cheaper for organizations to cover the losses than invest in building an effective policy.

Reducing the cost of developing enforcement policy to nearly free becomes the only way to solve the problem. The open source software development model presents an effective "nearly" free approach that researchers could apply to creating enforcement policy. Currently much of the same policy engineering happens at every organization. Eliminating this duplicated effort spreads the development cost across many organizations, reducing the cost for a specific organization to provide a clear return on investment.

Just as a small business does not develop its own web server, it should also not develop its own security enforcement policy, if that is not its expertise. Many software vendors do provide policy elements for their product. However the diversity of security mechanisms and models means the local administrator must still understand each one. This tower of babble also obscures the total enterprise policy by distributing it through a variety of mechanisms. Strong security requires tools that manage this diversity to improve understanding.

2.2 Security Mechanism and Model Diversity

Security models and enforcement mechanisms range from permission bits on a file system to stored procedures in a database management system. Consider the Protection Proxy [5] pattern that runs arbitrary code to check some security condition. Once a security mechanism incorporates a proxy capability, all sound access control models and mechanisms become isomorphic. In other words you cannot express some policy in one mechanism that cannot be expressed by all other sound mechanisms. Clearly some security models make expressing some policy types easier, and some models require extensive proxies to express the policy. Diverse security models allow developers to select the model with the ideal cognitive fit for capturing key protection goals. Unfortunately, in practice often the security model fits the protection goals poorly, leading to human error. Creating an understanding that spans security models, allows policy developers to choose the best tool for the job.

All sound security models being isomorphic requires a formal proof. However, incorporating the word "sound" eliminates many fringe models that cannot implement effective security policy. Consider a primitive Unix file system with only nine permission bits. Such a model can implement an assured pipeline, which is a series of proxies connected together [1] but it cannot satisfy the requirement for the later stages to only read data from the prior stage because of globally readable files [13]. Models that cannot control the flow of information cannot implement serious security.

The isomorphic claim comes from practical experience creating a series of enterprise spanning policy specification tools that translate into existing enforcement mechanisms [14][15][8][12]. These tools allowed for specification of the policy in a single model and translated to a variety of mechanisms like; file permissions, firewall rules, authentication tools, and databases. The approaches represent a bottom up approach that group resources into a hierarchy of capabilities.

This yields an interesting question, "What is the simplest access control model that spans all sound security models?" What is the Turing machine of access control? The Lampson access matrix that maps all subject to all objects, certainly could express all policies [6], but does not aid humans in understanding the resulting enforcement policy. Engineers do not write flight controllers on Turing machines. Conceptual tools for proofs do not necessarily yield engineering tools.

A universal security policy represents an interesting academic question. However, from a practical engineering viewpoint the value comes from the ability to translate between security models to increase human understanding of the policy. Economics often dictate the enforcement mechanism, but with translation, designers can select the best model for the security requirements and simply translate it to the economically dictated mechanism.

This paper presents a simple variant of the NIST RBAC model [9] to aid understanding the benefits of translation. The model consists of actors and resources. Resources represent the finest granularity object the policy can reference. Assigning a resource to an actor implies the actor can access the resource. Resources allow designers to abstract out permissions and mechanism differences and work with simple sets of resources. The model organizes resources needed to perform a specific task into a set for easy assignment to actors who perform those tasks. Designers can choose to group sets together to conveniently capture common patterns. The set structure forms a hierarchy of membership, equivalent to an object-oriented design hierarchy for assigning resources to actors.

2.3 Separating Site Specific Details

When an application developer creates an application, they understand the tasks users can perform with it. The developer can also list the resources the application needs to accomplish these tasks. The developer can statically define some resources, like the password file, while other resources depend on local configurations, such as the path to user directories.

If applications defined the resources they need along with the necessary security properties, these classes could be expanded and mapped to the local environment. This requires more effort on the application developer's part, but it results in embedding security understanding directly in the development process. It also makes it possible to systematically separate out the common engineering patterns in access control.

Figure 2 shows the NIST core RBAC model for quick comparison [9]. Figure 3 show a slightly adjusted model that enables better site independence. Figure 3 changes *user* to *actor*, divides *role* into *role* and *task*, refines permission assignments into *resource interface*, *container*, and adds an *object class*. The role and task concepts are 100% equivalent, except application developers define tasks independent of any local configuration information. In essence, Tasks become the site independent roles in the role hierarchy.

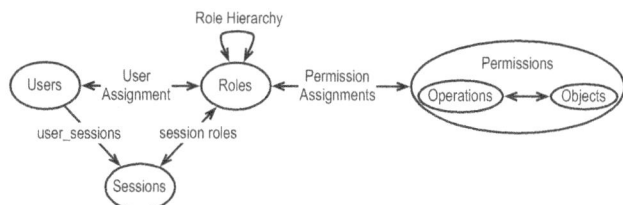

Figure 2. Standard NIST Core RBAC model.

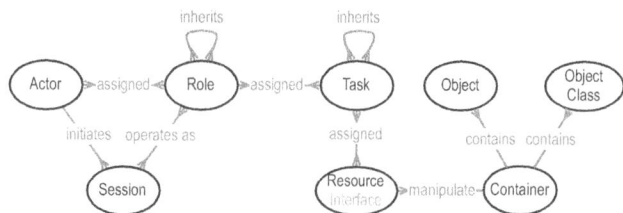

Figure 3. Modified NIST RBAC model.

Figure 3 replaces the user in the NIST model with actor to allow for more extensive definition of policy. Actors include users, programs, or hosts. Actors also include implied actors that define a set of actors based on some predicate, such as all users that have access to this network segment, or all actors in the enterprise. The actor definition allows the policy developers to define constraints independent of the actual users and configuration information.

Figure 3 also refines the NIST permission assignments. The approach defines objects and object classes. Object classes define a set of objects with the same security context pattern. Object classes allow the model to express a class of access control patterns. Different actors often access objects the same way. For example, suppose each user has a unique home directory, with specific permissions as the directory owner. Rather than tediously specifying the permissions for each home directory, the developer can define an object class that captures the pattern. The object class expands into a set of objects when translated to the enforcement system.

The model also introduces the *resource interface* concept. The resource interface defines the access to the object, such as read/write or a database view that selects some subset of rows and columns from a database table. The resource interface represents the proxy pattern that determines access for all objects in the container and could represent permissions or custom proxy code.

The *container* concept improves human understanding of the security policy when complex security constraints interact, which the next section explains further.

2.4 Adding "Why" to Security Enforcement

Enforcement policies have a life cycle that spans years just like software. Good software development includes documentation on the intent of the software model, but the intent of the original policy creator rarely gets documented.

Software exists to provide functionality. Functionality is the "why" of software and good regression testing can catch when a software modification destroys needed functionality. The "why" of enforcement policy exists outside the implementation and remains untestable. Standard regression testing can ensure that enforcement policy changes do not impact functionality, but it cannot ensure the change meets the original intent of the policy.

For example, why do Alice and Bob have to communicate via an encrypted channel? Regression testing could show that the policy changes still allow access to the cryptographic keys and network, but cannot show Alice's sensitive data doesn't fall into the malicious Chuck's hands via some new channel.

Clark and Wilson formalized the need for adding the "how" to the "who" and "what" of access control to create the Clark-Wilson triple [2]. Understanding the policy requires adding a fourth element to the access control tuple, the "why". Without the "why" it becomes impossible to understand the intent of the policy.

A day-to-day evolutionary approach to enforcement policy rarely results in documenting the intent of the policy, simply due to the required extra investment of time. However, amortizing the cost across organizations through reusable patterns reduces the cost.

The container concept was added to the NIST model to create better human understanding of the resulting policy. Most systems have hundreds of thousands of objects, which policy designers cannot address individually. A container groups objects into sets. All the objects in the container are accessed the same way, through the resource interface. Each object belongs to one and only one container. Actors can access an object only through the defined resource interfaces. Containers cannot contain other containers, because it would violate the rule that an object belongs to only one container.

The container concept aids human understanding by clarifying to the user that the only way to access an object in the container is to go through the resource interface. For example, suppose a container contains a medial record object. A variety of user roles need access to the record depending on the current situation; for example, an emergency room doctor might only be allowed to access the record for patients currently in the emergency room. To support this constraint a resource interface must define an emergency physician interface and what constraints must be satisfied before allowing access. This allows for implementing a Team Based access control [11].

The interfaces to the container provide a list of all access to objects in the container, allowing a human to review and understand who can access objects at any time in the life cycle. For example, if the object contains a database table, interfaces may slice and dice what information actors can see. Without access to a container interface an actor cannot see anything in the container. Many different interfaces may in fact grant access to an element in a table under different conditions, but the interfaces represent a complete list of the conditions. Humans must still understand the interactions of these conditions to ensure the conditions meet the intended policy. Proper container design can limit the need for understanding complex conditional interactions.

Encoding the intent of a policy element requires further study. Other concepts may improve human understanding of the policy more effectively than containers. Once possible approach may capture what threat the interface was designed to protect against. While a text description clearly captures the intent, it may be possible to build a model of the threat the resource interface addresses. Then automated reasoning tools could ensure validity of the protection goals over the policies life cycle. Clearly a variety of constraints and security invariant clauses could be created, but often such constraints do not include the active nature of an adversary trying to bypass the security policy. For software, humans still out perform software tools for reasoning about intent. However, the simpler domain of enforcement policy makes automated reasoning more tractable.

3. PATTERN ARCHITECTURE

Figure 4 shows an abstract architecture that capitalizes on the ability to create security enforcement patterns that separate local constraints from universal enforcement patterns. The architecture also enables automated policy translation and increased human understanding.

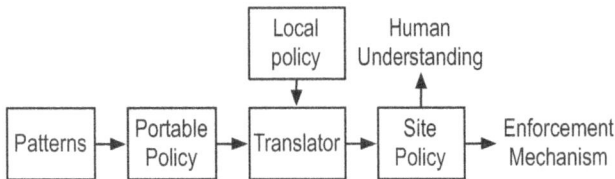

Figure 4. A system for applying patterns.

The patterns in the architecture represent the security engineering patterns that span organizations. Researchers have started applying pattern engineering to security [4][10]. Much of the research focuses on applied security software patterns, but many high level abstract patterns exist such as private data, or shared data. Engineering patterns arise from real world examples. However, the simplicity of the implementation space for enforcement policy allows for general descriptions of the pattern space.

Consider a model where every object has an owner. The system can share the object data in several ways. Figure 5 organizes these sharing patterns into an object-oriented hierarchy on a continuum of control.

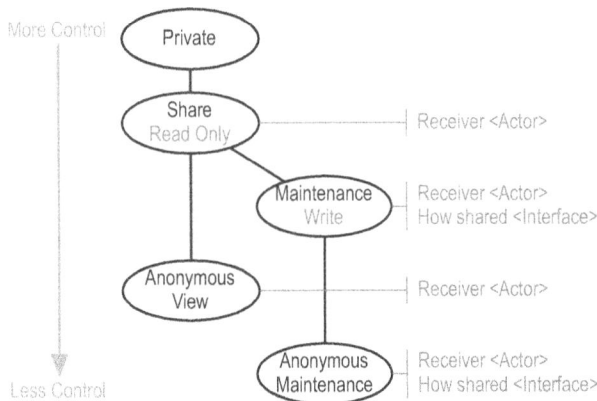

Figure 5. A simple object-oriented view of pattern space.

How strongly the policy designer can define the actor becomes an important factor in determining the control the owner or system retains over the data. Strong authentication yields the most control, anonymous the least control. However, a variety of interesting policies arise in the middle of the continuum. Consider a web server on an internal network. The web server allows anyone who has access to the network segment to read its web pages. The web server does not explicitly identify the users, but implicitly identifies them as all users that can access the network segment. Other examples of sets of implicit actors

include all users who can access a host, or all users in an enterprise. Often these implicit actor sets open the door for human error by obscuring the impact of policy changes. For example, suppose only employees should access the internal web server. Suppose an outside auditor needs access to some internal resource. Without a clear understanding of all the implicit actor sets once the auditor gets the needed access to the network segment, they could erroneously receive access to the web server.

Similarly, experience has shown a second continuum for data sharing starting with: no sharing, read only, controlled write, and uncontrolled write. A controlled write represents a Clark-Wilson triple that controls "how" the actor modifies the object.

Figure 6 sketches a two dimensional view of the pattern space on the dimensions of control and accountability. Entries in the table show popular examples of the pattern in that portion.

	Read Only	Controlled Write	Uncontrolled Write
Explicit Identity		Transformation Procecure	Wiki
Implicit Identity	Web page on internal network		
Anonymous	Web Page		anonymous ftp with upload

Owner has Less control →

← Less Accoutability

Figure 6. Sketch of enforcement pattern space.

One could imagine creating additional continuums to make an n-dimensional space. Many parts of this pattern space represent undesirable security policies, but recognizing undesirable patterns represents the first step towards fixing them.

Patterns occur at different levels in an enforcement policy;

- Object class definitions – patterns of resource definitions.
- Actors – explicit, implicit as well as degree of trust organize actors into patterns
- Resources interfaces – patterns of how to access objects
- Constraints – a subset of resource interfaces that control who and when an actor can access the interface
- Trusted Procedures – patterns that control how the data can change.

Policy designers can combine these patterns into larger patterns that span all these elements. For example, an auditor role pattern implies a strong identified actor, read only access to the data, and append access to an audit log.

The architecture in Figure 4 incorporates these high-level pattern descriptions in the first stage. Application developers and vendors would then implement those patterns to create the specific policy specification for the target application. The vendor must list each of the resources the application consumes, and define them in a site independent manner to create the portable policy.

When the local administrators install the application they provide the necessary details for the local site. Using the portable policy and these local details the translator can produce the local site policy. Since the portable policy embeds the policy intent, a policy tool can show the local administrator the impact of proposed changes. Since the supported access control models are isomorphic, the translator can also produce specific enforcement mechanism policy for all the applications in the enterprise.

A prototype exemplar implementation using a similar architecture translated policy patterns written in java into a variety of enforcement mechanisms for the enterprise. Choosing java allowed policy developers to use a wide variety of existing object-oriented design tools. While many enforcement mechanisms have attractive graphical user interfaces, the exemplar showed the benefit of a language approach for sharing policy as with open source software. Given the assertion that creating enforcement policy exemplifies a complex design problem, approach that have worked for complex designs in the past should apply to security enforcement policies.

The exemplar showed that good patterns save engineering effort by clarifying thinking and provide easier mapping to requirements. This savings in effort and the resulting structure opens the door to do research into adding new capabilities to the enforcement policy to increase human understanding of the impact of changes. In particular, tools that show the impact of implicitly defined actors sets could clearly show the impact a malicious insider could have on an organization.

4. SUMMARY
Economics represents the biggest hurdle to developing high assurance systems. Technology that reduces the cost of developing secure systems will greatly improve the likelihood of getting solid security systems deployed. Every security system has an enforcement policy that developers must engineer. This paper provides several practical points that can reduce the cost for creating enforcement policies.

- Creating security enforcement policy has many of the complexities of software engineering and can benefit from many of same cost saving techniques, such as patterns and open source development.
- Effective security requires clarity and understanding.
- The expressiveness of different security models and translating between them requires further study to allow policy designers to pick the proper tool for the job and integrate policies from different models together.
- Creating enforcement policy must become part of secure system engineering. Evolutionary approaches to writing enforcement security result in higher cost and poorer polices.
- The intent of a security enforcement policy requires further research to ensure continued human understanding of the policy over its life cycle. It should include a model of what the system attempts to protect against.
- An open source enforcement policy approach can reduce the security costs for individual enterprises and better ensure the enforcement policy meets its intended purpose.

Overall, people need to recognize that creating enforcement policy represents a complex engineering discipline that needs further refinement. That shift in mindset can have a great impact on the quality and effectiveness of secure systems.

5. ACKNOWLEDGMENTS
My thanks to the Sandia National Lab cyber forum for creating a venue for discussion of critical computer security topics like policy management.

6. REFERENCES
[1] Boebert, W.E. and Kain, R.Y. 1985. A practical alternative to hierarchical integrity policies. *Proc. 8th National Computer Security Conference* (1985).

[2] Clark, D.D. and Wilson, D.R. 1987. A Comparison of Commercial and Military Computer Security Policies. *Proc. of the 1987 IEEE Symposium on Research in Security and Privacy.* (Mar. 1987), 184–194.

[3] Epstein, P. and Sandhu, R.S. 2001. Engineering of role/permission assignments. *Proc. 17th Annual Computer Security Applications Conference.* (2001), 127–136.

[4] Fernandez, E. et al. 2008. Patterns and Pattern Diagrams for Access Control. *Proc. of the 5th international conference on Trust, Privacy and Security in Digital Business.* (2008), 38–47.

[5] Gamma, E. et al. 1995. *Design patterns: elements of reusable object-oriented software.* Addison-Wesley Reading, MA.

[6] Lampson, B.W. 1973. A note on the confinement problem. *Commun. ACM.* 16, 10 (1973), 613-615.

[7] Neumann, G. and Strembeck, M. 2002. A scenario-driven role engineering process for functional RBAC roles. *Proc. 7th ACM symposium on Access control models and technologies* (2002), 33–42.

[8] Payne, C. et al. 1999. Napoleon: a recipe for workflow. *Proc. of the 15th Annual Computer Security Applications Conference* (1999), 134–142.

[9] Sandhu, R.S. et al. 2000. The NIST model for role-based access control: towards a unified standard. *Proc. 5th ACM Workshop on Role-based Access Control.* (Jan. 2000).

[10] Schumacher, M. 2006. *Security Patterns Integrating Security & Systems Engineering.* Wiley-India.

[11] Thomas, R.K. 1997. Team-based access control (TMAC): a primitive for applying role-based access controls in collaborative environments. *Proc. 2nd ACM workshop on Role-based Access Control* (1997), 13–19.

[12] Thomsen, D.J. 2007. Patterns in Security Enforcement Policy Development. *International Conference on Database and Expert Systems Applications (DEXA).* (2007), 744–748.

[13] Thomsen, D.J. and Haigh, T. 1990. A comparison of type enforcement and Unix setuid implementation of well-formed transactions. *Proc. 6th Annual Computer Security Applications Conference.* (Jan. 1990).

[14] Thomsen, D.J. et al. 1998. Role based access control framework for network enterprises. *Proc. 14th Annual Computer Security Applications Conference.* (1998), 50–58.

[15] Thomsen, D.J. et al. 1999. Napoleon: network application policy environment. *Proc. 4th ACM workshop on Role-based access control.* (1999), 145–152.

The Optimization of Situational Awareness for Insider Threat Detection

Kenneth Brancik
Northrop Grumman Corporation
7575 Colshire Drive
McLean, VA 22102
703-883-8333
Kenneth.Brancik@ngc.com

Gabriel Ghinita
Purdue University
305 N. University St.
W. Lafayette, IN 47907
765-496-9390
gghinita@purdue.edu

ABSTRACT

In recent years, organizations ranging from defense and other government institutions to commercial enterprises, research labs, etc., have witnessed an increasing amount of sophisticated insider attacks that manage to bypass existing security controls. Insider threats are staged by either disgruntled employees, or employees engaged in malicious activities such as industrial espionage. The objectives of such threats range from sabotage, e.g., in order to disrupt the completion of a project, to exfiltration of sensitive data such as trade secrets, patents, etc. Insiders are often skilled and motivated individuals with good knowledge of internal security measures in the organization. They devise effective and carefully planned attacks, prepared over long periods of time and customized to inflict maximum damage. Such attacks are difficult to detect and protect against, because insiders have the proper credentials to access services and systems within the organization, and possess knowledge that may allow them to deceive network defense controls. As a result, a large number of hosts may be taken over, allowing malicious insiders to maintain control over the network even after leaving the organization.

The objective of this study is to identify a high-level architecture and mechanisms for early detection and protection against insider threats. One of the main aspects we focus on is preventing data exfiltration, which is known to cost billions of dollars in losses annually. The goal is to either *(i)* detect attacks as they occur and prevent insiders from gaining control over the network, or *(ii)* detect early hosts and services that are compromised such that malware is prevented from spreading/morphing, hence insiders are no longer able to control the network or to exfiltrate sensitive data. We envision a data-intensive approach that leverages large amounts of events collected from a diverse set of sources such as network sensors, intrusion detection systems, service logs, as well as known attack databases (e.g., virus signature collections, digital artifacts), security and service logs, etc. The proposed approach aims to study and understand the relationships and correlations between events, with the purpose of detecting anomalous and/or malicious behavior.

Categories and Subject Descriptors

K.6.5 [**Management of Computing and Information Systems**]: Security and Protection – *Access controls, Authentication, Cryptographic controls, Information flow controls, Invasive software (e.g., viruses, worms, Trojan horses)*

General Terms

Management, Design, Security.

Keywords

Insider Threat, Data Exfiltration.

1. INTRODUCTION

Ever since the creation of the Internet more than two decades ago, cyber-attacks have increased in sophistication and frequency. Malware capabilities have gained more disruptive power, as well as faster velocity of spreading from one system to another. However, the conventional paradigm for cyber-attacks was to target a relatively small number of system vulnerabilities, write exploits, and then mass-distribute them indiscriminately to an as-large-as-possible number of Internet hosts. In many cases, the attacked hosts were not even running software that was subject to vulnerability, but the number of hosts that did and got compromised was still large enough to warrant the cyber-criminals' efforts. Defending against malware was thus a matter of making sure that all systems are timely patched with the most up-to-date version of operating systems, application libraries, etc. Therefore, most security tools to-date rely on signature-based detection that identifies malware based on the code structure of binaries and prevents execution of malicious programs.

However, conventional defenses are often insufficient to defend against a more powerful type of attacks staged by insiders. An insider is a current or former employee, a contractor or consultant, a software vendor, who possesses similar access rights and provisioning to data and systems as an employee. Insider threats have been identified as a very dangerous source of cyber-attacks. The motivation of insiders ranges from revengeful acts, in the case of disgruntled employees, to more serious scenarios of espionage. In the former case, employees or ex-employees that are not happy with the way that the organization treated them are infecting the network with malware, corrupting or deleting data, sabotaging projects, etc. On the other hand, the latter case typically involves the theft of trade secrets, patents or other confidential data. Exfiltration of such data can have disastrous effects, either in the form of financial losses, or the compromise of national security, e.g., in the case of military secrets.

The effectiveness of insider attacks is often higher than conventional attacks for a number of reasons:

- Insiders already possess credentials that allow them legitimate access to machines and service inside the organization network.

- Actions of insiders originate at a trusted domain within the network, and are not subjected to thorough security controls in the same way as external accesses. For instance within the organization network there is often no internal firewall, which allows insiders to stage a broader range of attacks.

- Insiders, especially trained computer technicians, have good knowledge about the internal configuration of the network and the security and auditing control deployed. Therefore, they may be able to by-pass security mechanisms.

- Insiders have physical access to organization machines. They could, for instance, insert removable media with malware in an organization machine and easily infect a large number of hosts.

The insider threat component is one of the more elusive and insidious components of the threat landscape and represents a national security concern given its implications on all sectors of the critical infrastructure. There is little data available in the public domain that provides an accurate image of this threat. Consequently, the insider threat modeling is a process that has been long overlooked, leaving many organizations exposed to it.

A 2005 study by McAfee [1] presents several statistics about insider threats, covering both malicious insiders, as well as situations where insiders pose a security threat due to negligence. In the former category, the study found that five percent of employees have knowingly accessed areas of the corporate IT infrastructure that they were not supposed to access. In the latter category, the statistics show that one in five employees allow family and friends to use company laptops and PCs to access the Internet and install software. In addition, more than half of employees connect their own devices or gadgets to the company PC, creating the opportunity for malware to spread within the corporate network.

In this paper, we discuss the main elements of a solution to the problem of insider threat with focus on protecting against data exfiltration. Such elements are as follows:

- Techniques to identify data sources (e.g., security and service logs, network flow captures, etc.) that provide valuable information which helps in identifying malicious insider behavior
- A data-intensive architecture for a system that collects, indexes and processes event data. Data analysis and correlation is performed in order to identify malware based on signatures of known attacks and digital artifacts

Note that, with respect to the sophistication and complexity of the attack strategies used, there are many common characteristics between insider threats and advanced persistent threats (APT). Furthermore, the objectives of both categories of cyber attackers are often the same (e.g., data exfiltration). In our view, it is becoming increasingly more challenging to segregate insider threat attacks against other threat vectors which comprise the entire threatscape (e.g., external and APT attacks). Throughout the paper, we will emphasize the symbiotic relationship which exists between the three threat vectors (External, Insider and APT).

The rest of the paper is organized as follows: In Section 2, we present two representative insider attack scenarios. Section 3 outlines the proposed data-intensive architecture for detection and protection against insider threats. We survey related work in Section 4 and conclude with directions for future research in Section 5.

2. INSIDER THREAT ATTACK SCENARIOS

To illustrate the severe consequences and the difficult challenges posed by insider threats, we present two real-life attack scenarios that have as object a financial services institution. In the first case, an insider named Mallory is able to take control over a restricted organization machine in order to commit fraud and obtain financial gains by placing illegal trades. In the second case, Mallory exfiltrates a database with customers and trading positions which he can sell to a competitor financial services organization.

Case 1: Insider accesses unauthorized machine for own benefit. Mallory is a long-time employee who has been working with the *"sweat.equity.com"* investment company for more than ten years. He has been recently passed over for a long-waited promotion, and he is now planning to get his revenge and at the same time get rich quickly through misrepresentation and fraud. Mallory is a FX trader for private retail customers and all his accounts have a daily limit on the amount of money that can be invested. In addition, his accounts are audited daily. On the other hand, Alice is a recently hired and impressionable employee who is in charge of trades for large institutional investors. Institutional trades are placed from a restricted machine *MAE (Machine Attack and Exploit)* and trades are not subject to confirmation by the accounting department. Furthermore, auditing is only done on a monthly basis.

As a seasoned veteran with the company, Mallory is aware of the absence of daily checks for MAE trades, and he plans to use this to his own benefit. Specifically, Mallory sends an e-mail to Alice with a document that she must urgently review. The e-mail contains malware that installs a split VPN channel between the MAE and Mallory's machine. Even if the e-mail is marked as potentially malicious by the e-mail filter, Mallory sends follow-up messages to Alice claiming that false alarms often happen in the organization. He pressures Alice to open the document containing malware under the pretext of urgency.

Once the VPN channel is active, Mallory places his own orders into the MAE, and it appears as the trades are placed by Alice. Mallory transfers the trade proceeds to his own bank account, and then leaves the country long before the next monthly audit is scheduled. This way, he enjoys the financial benefits of the committed fraud, and he also feels vindicated for not getting the promotion, as the organization has to suffer both financially, as well as due to the loss of credibility in front of its customers.

Case 2: Insider exfiltrates sensitive data with the intent to sell critical information. Trade orders from both private and institutional investors are stored in a database as they are received, and then trade-specialized computers read the information from the database and execute the trades. Knowing the trades in advance, even by just a few minutes, provides a competitor with valuable information. For instance, a competitor that learns that a large buy order exists for shares of company *XYZ* can buy the shares himself in advance, knowing that the price is very likely to increase.

This time, Mallory sends an email message to the database administrator (DBA). The e-mail contains a malicious attachment that connects to the database, queries the trades that are scheduled to be executed in that day, and immediately transmits the information to an adversary. To avoid detection, the malware first encrypts data contents, and may also use another machine to perform the transfer. This way, network sensor monitors are not able to detect unusual activity between the database server and a machine from outside the organization.

3. DATA-INTENSIVE ARCHITECTURE FOR DETECTION OF INSIDER THREATS

There is a broad area of insider threats in terms of the complexity of the attacks, the attack vectors employed, as well as the specific objective pursued by the attackers. Typical areas of concern in the case of insider threats are:

- *Compromise of information privacy*: e.g., identity theft, extortion against top executives in the organization, etc.

- *Unauthorized Transfer of Funds*

- *Unauthorized Manipulation of Data Input:* e.g., data suppression (denial of service), destruction and/or corruption

Note that, each insider attack typically consists of a combination of the above factors. In order to fully understand the intricacies and interrelationships between each of these components, the leadership and operational personnel need a full understanding the following areas [2]:

- The Insider Threat Planning Process
- Enterprise Architecture
- Protection of Web Sites from Insider Abuse and the IT Infrastructure
- Web Services and Control Considerations for Reducing Transaction Risks
- Application Security and Methods for Reducing Insider Computer Fraud (ICF)
- ICF Taxonomy and the Art of a Key Fraud Indicator (KFI) Selection Process
- Key Fraud Signatures (KFS)
- Application and System Journaling and the Software Engineering Process

3.1 Technical Aspects

Fighting against insider threats involves two distinct aspects: profiling the behavioral aspects of the insider and profiling the behavior of the data. Although the two approaches can be performed individually, studying them collectively helps developing a better understanding of threats. We envision detection and protection against the insider threat as a set of coordinated processes that collect network and service data,

analyze patterns of network accesses and interactions, and correlate events in order to expose the tracks of malicious behavior. Typically, organizations collect large amounts of data, in the form of security and audit logs, traces of network flows, service logs such as email, web access, etc. All these represent valuable sources of information that we include in our insider threat detection framework.

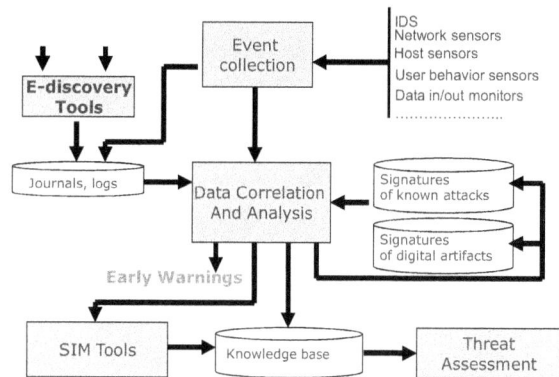

Figure 1: Data-intensive Architecture for Detection and Protection against Insider Threats

The proposed data-intensive architecture is presented in Figure 1, and consists of the following components:

- **Event and anomaly collection.** An essential component of the architecture is concerned with collection of data from a variety of sources, such as intrusion detection systems (IDS), network sensors, security and service logs, etc. As large amounts of data are available in an organization, this component will address issues such as effective and efficient data indexing, storage, querying and classification.

- **Data analysis and correlation.** Sophisticated attackers may customize their attack strategy in a manner that evades conventional signature-based detection systems (e.g., IDS). Still, some common traits do exist that allow the identification of common attack patterns. Such common characteristics can be found in the type of malware that is being used, the pattern of network communication and access to storage, etc. An essential component for insider threat anomaly detection will be represented by *Neural Networks and Associative Memories (NAM)*, which are able to recognize and predict patterns of activity and identify normalcy benchmarks for data/metadata values and associations between all the key people, processes, entities and data attributes. Any event identified as not fitting the benchmark needs to be surfaced and reported as a "red-flag": an early-warning indicator of malicious activity.

- **E-discovery tools.** Detected malicious activity must be properly documented to facilitate subsequent forensic analysis and prosecution of attackers. E-discovery tools allow the collection of necessary evidence, including e-mail, data and service access audit logs, etc.

- **Security Information Systems (SIM) tools.** The proposed threat detection architecture will interface with SIM tools that can process alarms and take appropriate action to confine and fight the attack.

An important aspect of data collection is to generate and maintain provenance and lineage information, in addition to the data contents. Data exfiltration is another major concern in the case of insider threats. To prevent exfiltration, malicious insiders will attempt to disguise the data such that security controls (e.g., deep packet inspection tools) will not detect the leakage of sensitive information. Maintaining secure and accurate provenance and lineage of data helps identifying and preventing attempts of data exfiltration.

3.2 Governance Aspects

At the organizational level, understanding insider threats is a very complex task that involves various methods and means to evaluate many existing interacting factors in order to achieve a complete situational awareness. In brief, there are three fundamental components which need to be evaluated and addressed in any insider threat solution and to strengthen Cyber Situational Awareness (CSA) between all related components:

1) Enterprise Risk Management (ERM): Performing a continuous assessment and evaluation of the integrated business/operational/technology risks is critical to evaluating asset vulnerabilities and requisite layers of protection

2) Threat Modeling: The ability to accurately assess the likelihood and probability of a specific threat vector impacting an enterprise will facilitate the ability to assign a more accurate threat rating which factors in probability and damage potential, as well as operational resiliency into a quantitative and/or qualitative scoring

3) Enterprise Security Architecture (ESA): The effectiveness of establishing the appropriate governance processes over the insider threat issue as well as its many interconnections between other threat vectors (namely, external and APT scenarios), will allow for a greater insight and fusion of seemingly disparate pieces and parts of the insider threat challenge

Using ERM and threat modeling as a backdrop and general context prior to evaluating feasible insider threat solutions, the thrust of the following proposed solution should not be a point in time solution, but rather a solution which originates from continuous monitoring of the enterprise risk assessments, which should include an evaluation of the overall cyber-hygiene of each individual IT infrastructure component, in addition to factoring the situational awareness implications of pervasive cyber risks which factors the confluence of external and insider threats.

An important component in the layered defense associated with insider threat detection is represented by journaling. Keeping logs of events and activities is required from an investigatory, legal and compliance perspective. There needs to be a logical and repeatable process for identifying when journaling for various IT infrastructure components are necessary for digital forensics, trace-back and attribution purposes. To meet the digital forensics purpose, there needs to be some means of capturing data at key points in the creation, transference and storage of these key data attributes at various control points or gates, where personally-identifiable information (PII), classified data or other key information is either inputted into a system, processing is occurring, data is being output and/or transferred within an enterprise or beyond and eventually into storage. The ultimate goal for journaling to detect an insider threat early in the process is to avoid the many complications associated within Massive Information Management (MIM) and data archiving challenges involved with this process, based on the myriad of legal, regulatory and other organizational requirements to ensure the integrity of that data. The second benefit of performing the journaling in the context of insider computer fraud is the importance of having this information to establish a profile of the nominal data values, i.e., values that occur in the absence of attacks. For example, if the normal data value for a given financial transaction ranges between $5 – 10 million and the transaction occurs consistently from only one static IP address, then being able to establish a journaling "clipping level" will be important in the identification of anomalous activity which either exceed or falls below a particular level of normalcy based on the pattern of that data profile.

Finally, the confluence between various cyber attack vectors often make outsiders look like insiders and insiders appear as outsiders. Through enhanced situational awareness, the ability to effectively connect the dots between cyber attack tactics, techniques and procedures and general modus operandi of seemingly disparate conventional network attacks will allow the security architecture designers and others to proactively identify changes in the security architecture of an enterprise from a preventive and not a reactive perspective.

3.3 An Overview of Data Exfiltration Threats

One important aspect in detecting malicious insiders is to track closely their activities. So far we have discussed the importance of monitoring and logging network events. However, tracking individual, disparate events may not always give a clear indication of malicious activity. In addition, in order to correlate multiple events, it is often required to track data items, and to know what were the activities that led to the generation of those data items.

Consider that an insider plants malware in one of the organization machines. In turn, the malware will affect certain files, either local or remote. Since insiders may try to cover their tracks before staging an attack, the malware may travel across several hosts before starting to execute the attack proper. Provenance and lineage techniques can help in the early identification of malware propagation.

Tracking data and event lineage may be achieved using additional tags that can be attached at various layers of abstraction (e.g., inside each network packet). On the other hand, such explicit tags may be visible to the attacker, and alert the insider that his or her actions are being monitored. Therefore, it is desirable to devise tracking mechanisms that are implicit and transparent, in the form of watermarks.

A watermark embedded in the network packets can serve the purpose of tracking malicious activities in a stealthy fashion. Furthermore, unauthorized access to data by malicious insiders may also be achieved with watermarks. Consider that an insider gathers sensitive data from within the organization and stores them on a compromised staging machine or server with the purpose of exfiltrating them at a later time. If data are watermarked, then a simple scanning software function can detect

Method	Frequency
Native Remote Access Applications	27%
Microsoft Windows Network Shares	28%
Malware Capability: FTP	17%
Malware Capability: IRC	2%
Malware Capability: SMTP	4%
HTTP File Upload Site	1.5%
Native FTP Client	10%
SQL Injection	6%
Encrypted Backdoor	<1%

Figure 2: Breakdown of Data Exfiltration Attacks
per Transport Mechanism Used

the presence of such data (e.g., a plug-in for an anti-virus tool may achieve this functionality).

In practice, full protection against attacks may be an unfeasible goal, due to the complexity of organization-level networks that often include a large variety of applications, protocols, services, etc. This heterogeneity provides adversaries with a broad spectrum of attack vectors, which complicates the task of defending such networks. Heterogeneity is one of the reasons why conventional firewalls/IDS are not able to defend against data exfiltration, because insiders and APT may choose among many available venues to transfer data beyond organizational boundaries. Often, exfiltrated data are piggybacked on top of conventional traffic, such as web, email or instant messaging. Figure 2 shows the result of a study [3] that measures the breakdown of attacks involving data exfiltration with respect to the network protocols and services used for transport. Note that, due to the flexibility available to attackers, traditional filtering/blocking approaches are not feasible. If attackers use the same channel of communication that is used by legitimate applications, then filtering will block non-malicious traffic as well. Deep-packet inspection is also not suitable, as attackers often use encryption before shipping data off-site. Thus, packet inspection tools that check for tokens that may indicate sensitive packet contents are easily circumvented. Therefore, a data-intensive architecture that relies on correlation of large amount of captured events is required to detect exfiltration.

4. RELATED WORK

Insider threat has been widely acknowledged [1,2] as a very serious and difficult to address cyber-security concern. There are several factors [2] that make insider threats very effective, such as knowledge of the organization network, possession of valid credentials, and the benefit of trust.

Data Exfiltration has been recently acknowledged as an important research problem, and studied in several contexts. In [5], it is shown how data can be exfiltrated by embedding sensitive information in conventional browser HTTP requests. In [6], the authors study exfiltration through covert channels. For instance, the rate of sending packets to a destination can be tuned such that the frequency or inter-arrival time of packets corresponds to an encoding of the data.

Protection of data in the presence of untrusted users or software has been addressed in [4], where a virtual machine monitor is deployed to separate sensitive data and applications from other malicious or untrusted software, e.g., malware, compromised operating system, etc.

5. CONCLUSION

Insider attacks are very effective and often highly damaging, due to the fact that insiders reside within the trust domain of an organization, they are not subject to many security controls that keep external attackers at bay, and they have valid credentials to access systems and services within the organization. In addition, they have knowledge about security configurations that safeguard the network, and they are able to exploit more easily technical, as well as human factor weaknesses within the organization.

The creation of an effective insider threat cyber ecosystem is a significant challenge and requires a robust and mature cybersecurity governance process, which effectively incorporates: enterprise risk management, threat modeling and the enterprise security architecture, which should be a manifestation of understanding the integrated risks and selected mitigated controls, through the addition of new or reinforced security access layers from the network perimeter through to the data layer. The new frontier for anomalistic insider threat detection, monitoring and mitigation will include means of capturing data normalcy and patterns of suspicious activity and predictive modeling that can incorporate "what-if" scenarios that can make the correct associations between various activities and events for optimizing situational awareness for insider threat detection.

6. REFERENCES

[1] J. Leyden, "Geeks, squatters and saboteurs threaten corporate security", http://www.theregister.co.uk/2005/12/15/mcafee_internal_se curity_survey/

[2] K. Brancik, "Insider Computer Fraud – An In-Depth Framework for Detecting and Defending Against Insider IT Attacks.", Taylor and Francis Group LLC, 2008.

[3] N. J. Percoco, "Data exfiltration: how data gets out", Spiderlabs report. Available online at http://www.csoonline.com/article/570813/data-exfiltration-how-data-gets-out

[4] X. Chen et al, "Overshadow: A Virtualization-Based Approach to Retrofitting Protection in Commodity Operating Systems", In Proc. Of the 13th Intl. Conf. on Architectural Support for Programming Languages and OS, 2008

[5] K. Born, "Browser-Based Covert Data Exfiltration", In Proceedings of the 9th Annual Security Conference, Las Vegas, NV, April 7-8, 2010

[6] A. Giani, V. H. Berk, G. V. Cybenko, "Data exfiltration and covert channels", In Proceedings of Sensors, and Command, Control, Communications, and Intelligence (C3I) Technologies for Homeland Security and Homeland Defense, 2006

Fair and Dynamic Proofs of Retrievability

Qingji Zheng
Department of Computer Science
University of Texas at San Antonio
qzheng@cs.utsa.edu

Shouhuai Xu
Department of Computer Science
University of Texas at San Antonio
shxu@cs.utsa.edu

ABSTRACT

Cloud computing is getting increasingly popular, but has yet to be widely adopted arguably because there are many security and privacy problems that have not been adequately addressed. A specific problem encountered in the context of cloud storage, where clients outsource their data (files) to untrusted cloud storage servers, is to convince the clients that their data are kept intact at the storage servers. An important approach to achieve this goal is called Proof of Retrievability (POR), by which a storage server can convince a client — via a concise proof — that its data can be recovered. However, existing POR solutions can only deal with static data (i.e., data items must be fixed), and actually are not secure when used to deal with dynamic data (i.e., data items need be inserted, deleted, and modified). Motivated by the need to securely deal with dynamic data, we propose the *first* dynamic POR scheme for this purpose. Moreover, we introduce a new property, called *fairness*, which is necessary and also inherent to the setting of dynamic data because, without ensuring it, a dishonest client could legitimately accuse an honest cloud storage server of manipulating its data. Our solution is based on two new tools, one is an authenticated data structure we call *range-based 2-3 trees* (rb23Tree for short), and the other is an incremental signature scheme we call *hash-compress-and-sign* (HCS for short). These tools might be of independent value as well.

Categories and Subject Descriptors

C.2.4 [**Communication Networks**]: Distributed Systems; D.4.6 [**Security and Protection**]: Authentication; H.3.4 [**Information Storage and Retrieval**]: Systems and Software

General Terms

Security

Keywords

Cloud computing, cloud storage, cloud security, proof of retrievability, 2-3 tree, ranged-based 2-3 tree, verifiable data integrity, integrity checking, outsourced storage, authenticated data structures

1. INTRODUCTION

Most people believe that cloud computing will be the next paradigm of computing. However, cloud computing has not been widely deployed arguably because there are security and privacy problems that remain to be tackled. The specific problem we focus on in this paper is: How can a cloud storage client (i.e., data owner, user) be assured that its data outsourced to a cloud storage service provider (i.e., server) is kept intact? The trivial solution is to let the client download its whole data periodically, which is unfortunately not acceptable in practice. For this purpose, efficient cryptographic techniques have been proposed. Among existing solutions (see Section 1.2 below for details on related prior work), the arguably most powerful one is the so-called Proof of Retrievability (POR), which was first introduced by Juels and Kaliski (ACM CCS'07) [15] and later significantly improved by Shacham and Waters (Asiacrypt'08) [20]. POR allows a cloud storage provider to cryptographically convince the data owner — via some succinct interactions — that its outsourced data are kept intact.

Existing POR schemes can only deal with static data and are actually not secure when used to deal with dynamic data, as we will show in Section 6.1 through a concrete attack. However, dynamic data are more realistic because they allow to insert, delete, and modify data items. The importance of maintaining dynamic data can also be justified by the fact that researchers have proposed dynamic Proof of Data Possession (PDP) (ACM CCS'09) [13], which follows the static PDP proposed by Ateniese et al. (ACM CCS'07) [2]. Note that PDP is a weaker security property. Indeed, it is already observed in [13] that accommodating dynamic data in the setting of POR is more challenging than accommodating dynamic data in the setting of PDP. Intuitively, the difficulty can be attributed to the fact that the *retrievability* property is more demanding than the *possession* property. More specifically, this is because the former additionally needs to allow the data owner to derive its data from the transcripts of successful sessions of the proof-of-retrievability protocol, which is reminiscent of the cryptographic notion of Proof of Knowledge [4].

Another problem inherent to dynamic POR is what we call *fairness*, which roughly speaking assures that a dishonest data owner cannot legitimately accuse an honest cloud storage service provider of manipulating its data. If the service provider has no means to prove (say, to a judge in court) that it is innocent, then the provider could be imposed with a big financial burden because a dispute of this nature may often be biased against the service provider. Note that fairness in the setting of static POR is easily solved by, for example, requiring the client to digitally sign its data before the data are outsourced to the server. In the setting of dynamic POR, however, the problem is challenging because the updated data are not at the owner's end anymore. One trivial solution is to download and sign the whole data after each update operation, which is also clearly not acceptable in practice because of the linear communication cost.

1.1 Contributions

In this paper, we introduce the concept of fair and dynamic proof of retrievability (FDPOR), a useful extension of static POR in practice. Then, we present a formal definition of FDPOR and its security properties called *soundness* and *fairness*. We explain why the extension of static POR to FDPOR is non-trivial. We discuss in detail: (i) The state-of-the-art static POR scheme is insecure when directly used in the setting of dynamic POR; (ii) We need a new authenticated data structure to ensure soundness in the setting of dynamic POR; (iii) We need a special kind of technique to ensure fairness in the setting of dynamic POR; (iv) We need to use error-correcting code in a fashion different from its counterpart in the setting of static POR. These observations guided us in designing an efficient FDPOR scheme, which simultaneously offers both retrievability and fairness in the setting of dynamic data. Specifically, our scheme is built on top of two new building-blocks, which might be of independent value.

- The first building-block is a new authenticated data structure we call *range-based 2-3 tree*, or rb23Tree for short. A rb23Tree not only inherits the properties of 2-3 trees that dynamic maintenance only incurs logarithmic complexity while allowing to prove membership, but also offers an additional important assurance that a specific value is stored at a specific leaf node.

- The second building-block is a new incremental signature scheme called *hash-compress-and-sign* or HCS for short. Our tailored incremental signature scheme is more efficient than the literature ones that operate in a more general setting because our incremental signing incurs constant hash operations (due to the use of flat trees, which are related to but separate from the range-based 2-3 trees) rather than logarithmic many hash operations. Despite the fact that hash functions can be very efficient, the improvement of our scheme would still be significant because of the harddisk input/output operations incurred by the read/write accesses associated with the hash operations.

1.2 Related Work

As mentioned above, the concept of POR was introduced by Juels and Kaliski [15], whose scheme adopted the idea of "spot-checking" [16]. This approach assumes that files are encrypted before outsourcing so that data blocks and "sentinel" blocks are indistinguishable (in a cryptographic sense). Because each query will expose a number of sentinels, this approach is limited by its bounded usage (i.e., when all sentinels have been queried). The scheme was later significantly improved by Shacham and Waters [20] by adapting a tool (implicitly introduced by Ateniese et al. [2]) now known as "homomorphic linear authenticator." Putting informally, this tool allows a data owner to affiliate data blocks with some tags, which will allow the storage provider to produce (via the homomorphism property) a succinct authenticator with respect to any random challenge vector provided by the data owner. Other extensions and improvements include [11], which however still only deals with static data. POR has been experimentally tested [8, 9].

The related concept of PDP was introduced by Ateniese et al. [2], who were motivated by various drawbacks of previous relevant approaches (we refer to [2] for a nice thorough review on earlier relevant studies). Note that the scheme of [2] is insecure in dynamic data setting because of replay attacks. In order to defeat replay attacks, one needs to utilize an authenticated tree structure that incurs logarithmic complexity. This was realized by Erway et al. [13], whose $O(\log n)$ cost is justified by the bound given in [12]. On the other hand, if it is appropriate to assume that the number of challenges issued by data owner is bounded from above and the dynamic data operations are only append-like, then a very efficient PDP scheme can be found in [3].

Organization. We define FDPOR and its security properties in Section 2. We briefly review some preliminary materials in Section 3. We present the two building-blocks in Section 4-5, respectively. We describe the main FDPOR construction in Section 6, and analyze its security in Section 7. We conclude the paper in Section 8.

2. DEFINITIONS

A data file F is divided into blocks $F = (F_1, \ldots, F_n)$ and is updated block-by-block via an update operation (op, i, α), where i is the block index, and α is the new block value, op corresponds to deletion (denoted by $\mathcal{D}$), modification (denoted by $\mathcal{M}$), or insertion (denoted by $\mathcal{I}$). Specifically,

- $(\mathcal{D}, i, \texttt{null})$ means that the ith block F_i will be deleted;

- $(\mathcal{I}, i, \alpha)$ means that a new block will be inserted after the current i^{th} block F_i, namely that the new $F_{i+1} = \alpha$;

- $(\mathcal{M}, i, \alpha)$ means that the ith block F_i will be replaced with new value α.

Note that the initial uploading of a file F can be achieved via a series of $\mathcal{I}$ operation; in specific schemes, it can be simplified as a simpler batch process. We stress that, unlike in the setting of static POR [15, 20], the indices of blocks in dynamic POR or FDPOR are dynamic, namely that block F_{i+1} may become block F_i after deleting block F_i, and block F_{i+1} may become block F_{t+2} after adding a new block F_{i+1}. It is also worthwhile to note that, unlike static POR, we need to divide a file into blocks in the setting of dynamic POR or FDPOR because, otherwise, it is not clear how to define file operations. Nevertheless, this does not jeopardize the resulting scheme because, for performance reason, files are always divided into blocks in the case of static POR [15, 20].

Each file F is identified through an identity fid, which remains unchanged until after F is deleted. Each F is also accompanied with some auxiliary information, denoted by au, which can be various cryptographic tags that will be used (for example) as part of input in the process of verifying the retrievability of F. Moreover, au may have two variants: au_c is the auxiliary information stored at the client end, and au_s is the auxiliary information stored at the storage server end.

For better clarity, we assume that the communication between a client and a storage server is authenticated. This can be readily realized using a digital signature scheme or a message authentication scheme. Note that in practice the data file F is often encrypted by the client before outsourcing to the server, which justifies why the underlying channel does not have to be private.

The following definition of FDPOR is built on top of previous studies of static POR [15, 20].

Definition 1. (FDPOR; extended from [15, 20]) A FDPOR scheme consists of the following:

- FDPOR.KeyGen. This randomized algorithm takes as input a security parameter κ, and generates a collection of public keys, denoted by pk, and private/secret keys, denoted by sk. pk is publicly known but sk is kept as the client's secret.

- FDPOR.Update. This is a protocol executed between a client C on input $(pk, sk, \mathsf{fid}, \mathsf{au}_c, (op, i, \alpha))$ and a server S on input $(pk, \mathsf{fid}, F, \mathsf{au}_s)$. The protocol allows the client to update its file F according to (op, i, α). At the end of the protocol execution, if the server S accepts (outputs 1), it updates according to (op, i, α) the client's file F (identified by fid) to F' and the auxiliary information au_s to au'_s; otherwise, S aborts and outputs $(0, \bot, \bot)$. In addition, the server S sends to the client C possibly updated auxiliary information au'_c as well as some additional information evi that will allow C to verify that S faithfully updated C's file F according to (op, i, α). The client C verifies whether to accept that the server has faithfully updated the file based on $pk, sk, \mathsf{fid}, \mathsf{au}_c, (op, i, \alpha), \mathsf{au}'_c, \mathsf{evi}$. If C accepts (outputs 1), C also updates its local auxiliary information au_c to au'_c; otherwise, C aborts and outputs $(0, \bot)$. Formally, we denote this by:

$$((b_C, \mathsf{au}'_c); (b_S, F', \mathsf{au}'_s)) \leftarrow \\ (\mathrm{C}(pk, sk, \mathsf{fid}, \mathsf{au}_c, (op, i, \alpha)) \leftrightarrow \mathrm{S}(pk, \mathsf{fid}, F, \mathsf{au}_s)),$$

where $b_C \in \{0, 1\}$, $b_S \in \{0, 1\}$, $(b_C = 1, \mathsf{au}'_c)$ is the client C's output and $(b_S = 1, F', \mathsf{au}'_s)$ is the server S's output upon a successful execution of the FDPOR.Update protocol.

- FDPOR.Por. This is a protocol between a prover algorithm P and a verifier algorithm V, by which P (which often is the server S) convinces V (which can be, but not necessarily, the client C) about the retrievability of a data file F. For the execution, P takes as input pk, the file F (corresponding to file identity fid provided by V) and auxiliary information au_s. V takes as input pk, possibly also sk, and the auxiliary information au_c. When the execution of the protocol halts, V outputs 1 (meaning that the file is kept intact at the storage server) and 0 otherwise. Formally, we denote the protocol as $b \leftarrow (\mathrm{P}(pk, \mathsf{fid}, F, \mathsf{au}_s) \leftrightarrow \mathrm{V}(pk, sk, \mathsf{fid}, \mathsf{au}_c))$, where $b \in \{0, 1\}$.

We require a FDPOR protocol to be correct, sound (against dishonest storage provider) and fair (against dishonest client). Intuitively, we say a FDPOR scheme is correct if both the client and the storage provider are honest (i.e., execute according to the protocols), then FDPOR.Update and FDPOR.Por always execute successfully as long as the previous system state and the operation (op, i, α) are legitimate. Formally, we say a FDPOR scheme is correct if:

$$\Pr \left[\begin{array}{l} (pk, sk) \leftarrow \mathsf{FDPOR.KeyGen}(1^\kappa); \\ \forall\ \mathsf{fid}, F, v, \mathsf{au}_c, \mathsf{au}_s\ \text{s.t.} \\ 1 \leftarrow (\mathrm{P}(pk, \mathsf{fid}, F, \mathsf{au}_s) \leftrightarrow \mathrm{V}(pk, sk, \mathsf{fid}, \mathsf{au}_c)) : \\ \forall\ (op, i, \alpha), \\ (((1, \mathsf{au}'_c); (1, F', \mathsf{au}'_s)) \leftarrow \\ (\mathrm{C}(pk, sk, \mathsf{fid}, \mathsf{au}_c, (op, i, \alpha)) \leftrightarrow \mathrm{S}(pk, \mathsf{fid}, F, \mathsf{au}_s))) \wedge \\ (1 \leftarrow (\mathrm{P}(pk, \mathsf{fid}, F', \mathsf{au}'_s) \leftrightarrow \mathrm{V}(pk, sk, \mathsf{fid}, \mathsf{au}'_c))) \end{array} \right] = 1$$

The following definition of soundness is built on [20]. Intuitively, a FDPOR scheme is sound if any cheating storage provider, who successfully executed the FDPOR.Por protocol with an honest verifier, is actually keeping the data file F intact. This is captured, as in the case of Proof of Knowledge [4], by that an extractor algorithm that can efficiently derive the data file F. Formally, we consider an adversary $\mathcal{A}$ that operates in an environment, which is bootstrapped via an honest execution of FDPOR.KeyGen and gives the resulting pk to $\mathcal{A}$. Furthermore, $\mathcal{A}$ can query oracles corresponding to the protocol FDPOR.Update, which causes the storage/update of a file, and to the protocol FDPOR.Por, which causes the execution of the proof-of-retrievability protocol with respect to a file. Finally, $\mathcal{A}$ outputs a cheating prover P′ with respect to a file F. The cheating prover P′ is ϵ-*admissible* if it succeeds in executing FDPOR.Por with an honest verifier V with a non-negligible (in κ) probability ϵ, where the probability is taken over the coins of both the cheating prover P′ and the honest verifier V.

Definition 2. (soundness) Let ϵ be a non-negligible function of κ. We say a FDPOR scheme is ϵ-sound if there exists an extraction algorithm EXTRACTOR that, for every adversary $\mathcal{A}$ that outputs an ϵ-*admissible* cheating prover P′ for a file F, can recover F from P′ except a negligible probability. Formally, we define

$$\mathsf{Retrievability}_{\mathcal{A}}^{\mathsf{FDPOR}}(\kappa)$$

$$= \Pr \left[\begin{array}{l} (pk, sk) \leftarrow \mathsf{FDPOR.KeyGen}(1^\kappa); \\ \mathrm{P'} \leftarrow \mathcal{A}^{\mathsf{FDPOR.Update, FDPOR.Por}}(pk); \\ \Pr[1 \leftarrow (\mathrm{P'} \leftrightarrow \mathrm{V}(pk, sk, \mathsf{fid}, \mathsf{au}_c))] \geq \epsilon; \\ F' \leftarrow \mathrm{EXTRACTOR}(pk, sk, \mathsf{au}_c, \mathrm{P'}) : \\ F = F' \end{array} \right],$$

where $\mathcal{A}$ may play the role of the server S in the oracle access to FDPOR.Update and the role of the prover P in the oracle access to FDPOR.Por. We say a FDPOR scheme is ϵ-sound if $\mathsf{Retrievability}_{\mathcal{A}}^{\mathsf{FDPOR}}$ is a non-negligible.

The following definition of fairness is newly introduced. Intuitively, a FDPOR scheme is fair if no honest storage server will be legitimately accused of manipulating any client's data. This is captured by ensuring that the dishonest client, who essentially knows everything including the private keys, is still unable to generate $F' \neq F''$, but F' and F'' corresponds to successful executions of the FDPOR.Update protocol starting from the same sever state $(pk, \mathsf{fid}, F, \mathsf{au}_s)$. The idea is that, if a dishonest client can find such F' and F'', then the client can demonstrate that the server has manipulated its data from F' to F'', or from F'' to F'.

Definition 3. (fairness) Let adversary $\mathcal{A}$ have access to oracle FDPOR.KeyGen for generating keys, to oracle FDPOR.Update while $\mathcal{A}$ may play the role of the client C and choose file operations adaptively, to oracle FDPOR.Por while $\mathcal{A}$ may play the role of the verifier V. Define

$$
\mathsf{UnFairness}_{\mathcal{A}}^{\mathsf{FDPOR}}(\kappa) =
$$

$$
\Pr\left[
\begin{array}{l}
(pk, \mathsf{fid}, F, F', F'', \mathbf{au}_s) \leftarrow \\
\quad \mathcal{A}^{\mathsf{FDPOR.KeyGen,FDPOR.Update,FDPOR.Por}}(1^\kappa): \\
F' \neq F'' \quad \wedge \\
(((1, *); (1, F', *)) \leftarrow \\
\quad (\mathrm{C}(pk, sk, \mathsf{fid}, \mathbf{au}_c, (op, i, \alpha)) \leftrightarrow \mathrm{S}(pk, \mathsf{fid}, F, \mathbf{au}_s))) \wedge \\
(((1, *); (1, F'', *)) \leftarrow \\
\quad (\mathrm{C}(pk, sk, \mathsf{fid}, \mathbf{au}_c, (op, i, \alpha)) \leftrightarrow \mathrm{S}(pk, \mathsf{fid}, F, \mathbf{au}_s))) \wedge
\end{array}
\right],
$$

where $*$ indicates that no restriction on the respective value is imposed. We say a FDPOR protocol is fair, if for every polynomial-time algorithm $\mathcal{A}$, the probability $\mathsf{UnFairness}_{\mathcal{A}}^{\mathsf{FDPOR}}$ is negligible in κ.

3. PRELIMINARIES

A standard 2-3 tree is a tree where all leaves are at the same height and each node (except leaves) has two or three children. It has the nice property that leaf removal and insertion incur only logarithmic complexity because these operations only involve the nodes related to the path from the relevant leaf to the root. We refer to, for example, [1] for a comprehensive treatment of 2-3 trees. For the sake of a modular construction and representation, let us briefly review the maintenance algorithms for a standard 2-3 tree T; the details of these algorithms can be found in, for example, [1].

- 23Tree.M($\mathcal{T}, i, e$): This algorithm modifies the value of the ith leaf e.

- 23Tree.I($\mathcal{T}, i, e$): This algorithm inserts a leaf storing e immediately after the ith leaf.

- 23Tree.D($\mathcal{T}, i$): This algorithm deletes the ith leaf.

Let $h : \{0,1\}^* \to \{0,1\}^\ell$ be a collision-resistant hash function. Let $\{f_k\}_k$ be a family of secure pseudorandom function (PRF) $f : \{0,1\}^\ell \times \{0,1\}^* \to \{0,1\}^\ell$. Let SIG = (KeyGen, Sign, Ver) be a secure digital signature scheme, where SIG.KeyGen is the key generation algorithm, SIG.Sign is the signing algorithm, and SIG.Ver is the signature verification algorithm. These primitives and their security properties are standard and can be found for example in [14].

The motivation of incremental cryptography [5] was to speed up the cryptographic computation, especially when dealing with a large amount of data. Notable incremental cryptosystems including [5, 6, 7, 18].

Let $ECC(m, z, d)$ be any error-correcting code that encodes m symbols (e.g., elements in $\mathbb{Z}_p$ for an $\ell+1$ bits prime p) into z symbols such that the distance between any pair of codewords is at least d.

4. BUILDING-BLOCK I: RANGE-BASED 2-3 TREES

There have been some authenticated data structures that are constructed based on 2-3 trees [19, 6, 18]. Specifically,

[19] used a variant 2-3 tree for membership query; [6, 18] used another variant 2-3 tree for authenticating leaves while allowing fast searching. However, these data structures are not sufficient for our purpose because we not only need to authenticate the value at a leaf, but also want to authenticate the index of the leaf (i.e., we want to authenticate that a specific value is exactly stored at a specific leaf). This motivates us to propose *range-based 2-3 trees*, or rb23Tree, that have the desired properties.

4.1 Constructing Range-Based 2-3 Trees

For a set of n elements $S = \{e_1, e_2, \ldots, e_n\}$, we can create a 2-3 tree of n leaves such that each node stores $(l(v), r(v), x(v))$, where

- $l(v)$ is the height of node v, with each leaf having height 1.

- $r(v)$ is the *range value* of v, namely the number of leaves corresponding to the subtree rooted at v. If $v = \mathtt{null}$, define $r(v) = 0$. If v is a leaf, define $r(v) = 1$.

- $x(v)$ is the *authentication value* of v. It is defined as

$$
x(v) = \begin{cases}
h(l(v)\|r(v)\|x(c_1)\|x(c_2)\|x(c_3)) & \text{if } l(v) > 1 \\
e_i & v \text{ is the } i^{th} \text{ leaf} \\
0 & v = \mathtt{null}
\end{cases}
$$

where $\|$ is the concatenation operation, c_1, c_2, c_3 are the three left-to-right children of an inner node v (when v has two children c_1 and c_2, we treat $c_3 = \mathtt{null}$), and h is a collision-resistant hash function.

Let $\min(v)$ and $\max(v)$ denote the minimum and maximum leaf indices that can be reached via node v, respectively. Given $\min(v)$, $\max(v)$, and the ranges of v's children $r(c_1), r(c_2), r(c_3)$, we have:

$$
\begin{aligned}
\min(c_1) &= \min(v), \\
\max(c_1) &= \min(c_1) + r(c_1) - 1, \\
\min(c_2) &= \max(c_1) + 1, \\
\max(c_2) &= \min(c_2) + r(c_2) - 1, \\
\min(c_3) &= \max(c_3) - r(c_3) + 1, \\
\max(c_3) &= \max(v).
\end{aligned}
$$

Observe that a node v is on the path π_i from the ith leaf to the root if and only if $i \in \{\min(v), \max(v)\}$. We call π_i a *proof path* for locating the ith leaf by traversing the path starting at the root.

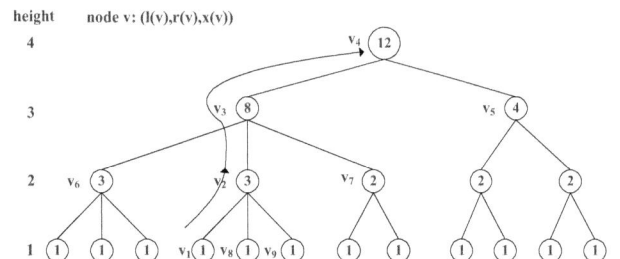

Figure 1: An example of range-based 2-3 tree. Each inner node v stores $(l(v), r(v), x(v))$.

Example. Let us look at the example tree shown in Figure 1. In this example, we have $\min(v_4) = 1$ and $\max(v_4) = 12$. Suppose we want to find the 4th leaf in Figure 1. We observe:

$$\begin{aligned}
\min(v_4) = 1 &\wedge \max(v_4) = 12 &\implies v_4 \in \pi_4 \\
\min(v_3) = 1 &\wedge \max(v_3) = 8 &\implies v_3 \in \pi_4 \\
\min(v_6) = 1 &\wedge \max(v_6) = 3 &\implies v_6 \notin \pi_4 \\
\min(v_2) = 4 &\wedge \max(v_2) = 6 &\implies v_2 \in \pi_4 \\
\min(v_1) = 4 &\wedge \max(v_1) = 4 &\implies v_1 \in \pi_4.
\end{aligned}$$

As a result, we find the path (represented as an ordered set) $\pi_4 = \{v_1, v_2, v_3, v_4\}$.

4.2 Utilizing Range-Based 2-3 Trees

Now let us put the above tree-construction method into the context of the present paper. Suppose a range-based 2-3 tree with n leaves $e_1, \ldots, e_n$. The tree was constructed by a client using the above method, and was outsourced to the storage server. The client always keeps $x(root)$, which is the authentication value of the root. Suppose further that the client wants to verify not only that e_i is stored at a leaf but also that e_i is stored exactly at the ith leaf, where $1 \le i \le n$. For this purpose, the server provides a proof path (or ordered set) $\pi_i = \{v_1, \ldots, v_k\}$, where v_1 is the ith leaf, v_k is the root, and each node $v_j \in \pi_i$ ($1 \le j \le k$) is associated with an 8-element tuple

$$Token(v_j) = (l(v_j), r(v_j), r(c_1), x(c_1), r(c_2), x(c_2), r(c_3), x(c_3)),$$

where c_1, c_2, c_3 are v_j's three left-to-right children, and $r(c_\ell) = -1$ and $x(c_\ell) = -1$ if $c_\ell \in \pi_i$ and $l(c_\ell) > 1$, where $1 \le \ell \le 3$. In other words, the proof is a sequence of

$$(Token(v_1), \ldots, Token(v_k)).$$

Example (continued). Take v_1 in Figure 1 as an example. Suppose we want to verify that the value in v_1 is e_4 and the index of v_1 is 4. Then the tuples along the proof path

	$l(v)$	$r(v)$	$r(c_1)$	$x(c_1)$	$r(c_2)$	$x(c_2)$	$r(c_3)$	$x(c_3)$
v_4	4	12	-1	-1	4	$x(v_5)$	0	0
v_3	3	8	3	$x(v_6)$	-1	-1	2	$x(v_7)$
v_2	2	3	-1	-1	1	$x(v_8)$	1	$x(v_9)$
v_1	1	e_4	0	0	0	0	0	0

Table 1: Proof path for that v_1 is the 4th leaf and $x(v_1) = e_4$

are shown in Table 1. Given a proof path, the clients can verify that element e_i of (ordered set) $S = \{e_1, \ldots, e_n\}$ is stored exactly at the ith leaf using Algorithm 1, denoted by rb23Tree.Examine($x(root), \pi_i$).

4.3 Verifiably Maintaining Range-Based 2-3 Trees

The maintenance of range-based 2-3 trees is essentially the same as the maintenance of standard 2-3 trees (which was briefly reviewed in Section 3), except that we need to take care of issues relevant to our extension, namely the updating of both range values and authenticated values of the relevant nodes. Specifically, the maintenance algorithms of range-based 2-3 trees are described as follows.

- rb23Tree.P($\mathcal{T}, i$): This algorithm allows the client to verify that a specific element is exactly stored at the ith leaf of $\mathcal{T}$. The algorithm traverses a range-based

---

Algorithm 1 rb23Tree.Examine($x(root), \pi_i$): This algorithm allows a client, who knows $x(root)$, to verify the ith element e_i of (ordered set) $S = \{e_1, \ldots, e_n\}$ is stored exactly at the ith leaf by examining proof path (ordered set) $\pi_i = \{v_1, \ldots, v_k\}$ provided by the server

1: initialize array $position[1..k] = 0$
2:   {$position$ tracks the index of the leaf with $x(\cdot) = e_i$}
3: initialize array $f[1..k] = 0$
4:   {$f[j]$ tracks $x(v_j)$ where $v_j \in \pi_i$}
5: $position[1] := 1$
6: $f[1] := e_i$
7: **for** $j = 2, \ldots, k$ **do**
8:   {v_i has three children c_1, c_2, c_3}
9:   **if** $r(c_1) = -1$ and $x(c_1) = -1$ **then**
10:    $position[j] := position[j-1]$
11:    $f[j] := h(l(v_i), r(v_i), f_{i-1}, x(c_2), x(c_3))$
12:   **end if**
13:   **if** $r(c_2) = -1$ and $x(c_2) = -1$ **then**
14:    $position[j] := position[j-1] + r(c_1)$
15:    $f[j] := h(l(v_j), r(v_j), x(c_1), f_{i-1}, x(c_3))$
16:   **end if**
17:   **if** $r(c_3) = -1$ and $x(c_3) = -1$ **then**
18:    $position[j] := position[j-1] + r(c_1) + r(c_2)$
19:    $f[j] := h(l(v_j), r(v_j), x(c_1), x(c_2), f_{j-1})$
20:   **end if**
21: **end for**
22: **if** $f[k] = x(root)$ and $i = position[k]$ **then**
23:   **return** true
24: **else**
25:   **return** false
26: **end if**

2-3 tree $\mathcal{T}$ from the root to the ith leaf, and returns a proof path (ordered set) $\pi_i = \{v_1, \ldots, v_k\}$, where each v_j is associated with an 8-element tuple as mentioned above.

- rb23Tree.M($\mathcal{T}, i, e$): This algorithm allows the client to update the value of ith leaf of $\mathcal{T}$ to the new value e and refresh $\mathcal{T}$ correctly. It executes as follows.

  1. Call rb23Tree.P($\mathcal{T}, i$), which returns (ordered set) $\pi_i = \{v_1, \ldots, v_k\}$, where each v_j is associated with an 8-element tuple as mentioned above.

  2. Call 23Tree.M($\mathcal{T}, i, e$) to replace the value of ith leaf of $\mathcal{T}$ with a new value e, then update the range value $r(v_j)$ and authentication value $x(v_j)$ for $j = 1, \ldots, k$. Denote the updated range-based 2-3 tree as $\mathcal{T}'$.

  3. Call 23Tree.P($\mathcal{T}', i$), which returns updated proof path $\pi_i' = \{v_1, \ldots, v_k\}$, where each v_j is associated with an updated 8-element tuple.

  4. Return π_i and π_i'.

- rb23Tree.I($\mathcal{T}, i, e$): This algorithm allows the client to insert a new leaf with the value e after i^{th} leaf of $\mathcal{T}$ correctly. It executes as follows.

  1. Call rb23Tree.P($\mathcal{T}, i$), which returns proof path (ordered set) $\pi_i = \{v_1, \ldots, v_k\}$, where each v_j is associated with an 8-element tuple as mentioned above.

2. Call 23Tree.I$(\mathcal{T}, i, e)$ to insert a new leaf with the value e after i^{th} leaf of $\mathcal{T}$, then update range value $r(v_j)$ and authentication value $x(v_j)$ for $j = 1, \ldots, k$. Denote the updated range-based 2-3 tree as $\mathcal{T}'$.

3. Call 23Tree.P$(\mathcal{T}', i+1)$, which returns updated proof path $\pi_i' = \{v_1', \ldots, v_{k'}'\}$, where each v_j is associated with an updated 8-element tuple.

4. Return π_i and π_i'.

- rb23Tree.D$(\mathcal{T}, i)$: This algorithm allows the client to delete the ith leaf of $\mathcal{T}$ correctly. It executes as follows.

  1. Call rb23Tree.P$(\mathcal{T}, i)$, which returns proof path (ordered set) $\pi_i = \{v_1, \ldots, v_k\}$, where each v_j is associated with an 8-element tuple as mentioned above.

  2. Call rb23Tree.P$(\mathcal{T}, i+1)$, which returns proof path (ordered set) $\pi_{i+1} = \{v_1, \ldots, v_k\}$, where each v_j is associated with an 8-element tuple as mentioned above.

  3. Call 23Tree.D$(\mathcal{T}, i)$ to delete the ith leaf of $\mathcal{T}$, then update the range value $r(v_j)$ and authentication value $x(v_j)$ for $j = 1, \ldots, k$. Denote the updated range-based 2-3 tree as $\mathcal{T}'$.

  4. Call 23Tree.P$(\mathcal{T}', i)$, which returns updated proof path $\pi_i' = \{v_1', \ldots, v_{k'}'\}$, where each v_j is associated with an updated 8-element tuple.

  5. Return π_i, π_{i+1}, π_i'.

- rb23Tree.Ver$((op, i, e), \pi_i, \pi_{i+1}, \pi_i')$: This algorithm allows a client, who knows $x(root)$, to verify π_i, π_{i+1}, π_i' that are received from the server at the end of executing one of the above update algorithms, where possibly $\pi_{i+1} = \texttt{null}$. The client executes as follows.

  1. If rb23Tree.Examine$(x(root), \pi_i)$ returns true, meaning that π_i is a legitimate proof path, then it executes the following; otherwise, it aborts.

  2. If $op \in \{\mathcal{M}, \mathcal{I}\}$, replace $x(v_1')$ with e where $\pi_i' = (v_1', \ldots, v_{k'}')$, and execute rb23Tree.Examine $(x(v_k'), \pi_i')$.

  3. If $op = \mathcal{D}$, execute rb23Tree.Examine$(x(root), \pi_{i+1})$. If rb23Tree.Examine$(x(root), \pi_{i+1})$ returns true, replace $x(v_1')$ with $x(v_1)$, where $\pi_{i+1} = (v_1, \ldots, v_k)$ and $\pi_i' = (v_1', \ldots, v_{k'}')$, and execute rb23Tree.Examine $(x(v_k'), \pi_i')$.

5. BUILDING-BLOCK II: A TAILORED IN-CREMENTAL SIGNATURE SCHEME

Recall that $h : \{0,1\}^* \to \{0,1\}^\ell$ is a collision-resistant hash function, and SIG = (SIG.KeyGen, SIG.Sign, SIG.Ver) is a secure digital signature scheme. Suppose W is a data file that we want to protect via an incremental signature scheme. We divide W into n blocks, namely $W = (W_1, \ldots, W_n)$. Let $(G, \odot)$ be a group, which can be, for example, $\mathbb{Z}_p$ such that $W_i \in \mathbb{Z}_p$ for $1 \leq i \leq n$.

In what follows we specify our incremental signature scheme HCS = (HCS.KeyGen, HCS.InitSign, HCS.IncSign, HCS.Ver).

- HCS.KeyGen(1^κ): This algorithm executes SIG.KeyGen by taking as input security parameter κ to generate a pair of public and secret keys (PK, SK).

- HCS.InitSign(SK, W): This algorithm executes as follows in the case of a new file:

  1. For $1 \leq i \leq n$, we define
  $$H_i = h(W_i).$$

  2. Construct a range-based 2-3 tree $\mathcal{T}$ by storing the n values $H_1, \ldots, H_n$ at the corresponding leaves.

  3. Apply h to each pair of $(H_i || H_{i+1})$ for $1 \leq i \leq n - 1$ to obtain
  $$\lambda_i \leftarrow h(H_i || H_{i+1}).$$
  where $||$ is the concatenation operation.

  4. Take group operation $\odot$ on $\lambda_1, \ldots, \lambda_{n-1}$ to obtain
  $$\lambda = \bigodot_{i=0}^{i=n-1} \lambda_i.$$

  5. Let $\delta \leftarrow$ SIG.Sign(SK, λ) and return $\mathcal{T}, \lambda$ and δ.

- HCS.IncSign(SK, $\mathcal{T}, \lambda, (op, i, \alpha), H_{i-1}, H_i, H_{i+1}$): This algorithm executes as follows in the case of an update operation (without loss of generality, assume $2 \leq i \leq n - 1$):

  1. $op = \mathcal{D}$: Update the signature as follows:
  $$\lambda' = \lambda \odot h^{-1}(H_{i-1}||H_i) \odot h^{-1}(H_i||H_{i+1}) \\ \odot h(H_{i-1}||H_{i+1}),$$
  $$\delta' = \text{SIG.Sign}(\text{SK}, \lambda').$$
  and call rb23Tree.D$(\mathcal{T}, i)$. Denote the updated range-based 2-3 tree as $\mathcal{T}'$

  2. $op = \mathcal{I}$: Update the signature as follows:
  $$\lambda' = \lambda \odot h^{-1}(H_i||H_{i+1}) \odot h(H_i||H(\alpha)) \\ \odot h(h(\alpha)||H_{i+1}),$$
  $$\delta' = \text{SIG.Sign}(\text{SK}, \lambda').$$
  and call rb23Tree.I$(\mathcal{T}, i, \alpha)$. Denote the updated range-based 2-3 tree as $\mathcal{T}'$

  3. $op = \mathcal{M}$: Update the signature as follows:
  $$\lambda' = \lambda \odot h^{-1}(H_{i-1}||H_i) \odot H^{-1}(H_i||H_{i+1}) \\ \odot h(H_{i-1}||h(\alpha)) \odot h(H(\alpha)||H_{i+1}),$$
  $$\delta' = \text{SIG.Sign}(\text{SK}, \lambda').$$
  and call rb23Tree.M$(\mathcal{T}, i, \alpha)$. Denote the updated range-based 2-3 tree as $\mathcal{T}'$

Then return $\mathcal{T}', \lambda'$ and δ'.

- HCS.Ver(PK, $W, \mathcal{T}, \lambda, \delta, (op, i, \alpha)$): This algorithm executes as follows (without loss of generality, assume $2 \leq i \leq n - 1$):

  1. If verifying the file W at the first time:
  $$H_i = h(W_i) \ 1 \leq i \leq n, \\ \lambda_i = h(H_i || H_{i+1}) \ 1 \leq i \leq n-1, \\ \lambda' = \bigodot_{i=1}^{n-1} \lambda_i.$$

  2. Else the verifier possesses $\mathcal{T}, \lambda, (op, i, \alpha)$
  - $op = \mathcal{D}$: execute the followings:
  $$\lambda' = \lambda \odot h^{-1}(H_{i-1}||H_i) \odot h^{-1}(H_i||H_{i+1}) \\ \odot h(H_{i-1}||H_{i+1}).$$

$-\ op = \mathcal{I}$: execute the following

$$\lambda' = \lambda \odot h^{-1}(H_i\|H_{i+1}) \odot h(H_i\|H(\alpha)) \\ \odot h(h(\alpha)\|H_{i+1}).$$

$-\ op = \mathcal{M}$: execute the following

$$\lambda' = \lambda \odot h^{-1}(H_{i-1}\|H_i) \odot H^{-1}(H_i\|H_{i+1}) \\ \odot h(H_{i-1}\|h(\alpha)) \odot h(H(\alpha)\|H_{i+1}).$$

In either case, execute $\mathsf{SIG.Ver}(\mathrm{PK}, \lambda', \delta)$ and return its outcome.

6. MAIN CONSTRUCTION

Recall that a file F is divided into n blocks, denoted by $F = (F_1, \ldots, F_n)$, where each block F_i contains m symbols of elements in $\mathbb{Z}_p$ for some large prime P, namely $F_i = (F_{i1} \cdots F_{im})$ with $F_{ij} \in \mathbb{Z}_p$ for $1 \le j \le m$. To be specific, we can instantiate the $(G, \odot)$ mentioned in building-block-II (Section 5) as $(\mathbb{Z}_p, \cdot)$, while noting that $(G, \odot)$ can be instantiated as other groups as well.

6.1 Design Rationale

A brief review of static POR. We now briefly review the static POR proposed in [20], which used a kind of homomorphic linear authenticator (HLA) and serves as a starting point for the present paper. Partition each data file into blocks $F = (F_1, \ldots, F_n)$. Assume each block is a single symbol $F_i \in \mathbb{Z}_p$ for some large prime p (this is for the purpose of highlighting the basic idea, while in the actual scheme each F_i will consist of multiple symbols). The client chooses a random $\theta \in \mathbb{Z}_p$ and a key k for pseudorandom function f, which are the client's secrets. The client computes an authentication tag for each block F_i as:

$$\sigma_i = f_k(i) + \theta F_i \quad (\text{in } \mathbb{Z}_p). \tag{1}$$

Then, the file $F = (F_1, \ldots, F_n)$ and the authentication tags $(\sigma_1, \ldots, \sigma_n)$ are stored on the server, which allow the following proof-of-retrievability protocol. The verifier (or client) chooses and sends to the prover (or server) a subset I of indices, namely $I \subseteq \{1, \ldots, n\}$, along with $|I|$ random challenges in $\mathbb{Z}_p$, denoted by $(random_i)_{i \in I}$. The server responds with

$$\sigma = \sum_{i \in I} random_i \cdot \sigma_i \quad \text{and} \quad \mu = \sum_{i \in I} random_i \cdot F_i \quad (\text{in } \mathbb{Z}_p),$$

which are very short messages. This works because the verifier, who knows the key k, can verify if:

$$\sigma \overset{?}{=} \sum_{i \in I} random_i \cdot f_k(i) + \theta \cdot \mu \quad (\text{in } \mathbb{Z}_p). \tag{2}$$

Why is the static POR **not applicable to the dynamic setting?** Note that the above elegant verification Eq. (2) works because the client can compute by itself $\sum_{i \in I} random_i \cdot f_k(i)$, where the i's are block indices that are *fixed* in the case of static POR. Unfortunately, this method is not applicable to the setting of dynamic POR anymore, as we now elaborate.

1. It is not secure when used to deal with dynamic data. To see this, suppose the ith block F_i is updated to new value F_i', where the block index i is kept unchanged. Then, Eq. (1) implies that the server sees:

$$\sigma_i = f_k(i) + \theta F_i \quad (\text{in } \mathbb{Z}_p) \\ \sigma_i' = f_k(i) + \theta F_i' \quad (\text{in } \mathbb{Z}_p),$$

where $F_i \neq F_i'$ but both are known to the server, and both σ_i and σ_i' are known to the server as well. As a consequence, the server can derive both θ and $f_k(i)$, which are the secrets of the data owner and will allow the server to cheat the data owner via Eq. (2) by (for example) choosing σ and then deriving the corresponding μ.

2. Even under some extreme cases (e.g., only insertion or deletion operations are required), the above idea still does not work because the client has to keep record of the indices of deleted blocks or the indices of yet-to-be inserted indices (otherwise, the verification is not well-defined). This requires significant (which can be proportional to n in the worst case) extra storage at the client end (this is something we want to avoid at the first place in cloud storage). One may suggest, as a rescue, to waste some storage space at the server (e.g., by setting each deleted or yet-to-be inserted block as some special value). But this would require to know the exact upper bound n, which may not be possible in many settings.

The basic ideas underlying our scheme. The core idea, by which we circumvent the above attack, is to use the following verification equation to replace Eq. (1):

$$\sigma_i = f_k(h(F_i)) + \theta F_i \quad (\text{in } \mathbb{Z}_p), \tag{3}$$

where $h : \{0,1\}^* \to \mathbb{Z}_p$ is a collision-resistant hash function. While this does break the tight binding between the authentication tag σ_i and the block index i, it does introduce new attacks as we now explain. Specifically, let us consider an example of before and after the insertion of block F_i. Because the client should be stateless (i.e., does not keep record of the block indices that have been inserted and deleted), a dishonest server can certainly pass the proof-of-retrievability by rolling back to the system state before the insertion of F_i. Therefore, in order to take full advantage of Eq. (3), we need to make the client keep an (ideally) constant state of the data stored at the server. This calls for a data structure which has the following features:

1. It allows fast update of data, meaning that an update operation only incurs very small amount of computation at the server end, while minimizing the involvement of the client in the process.

2. It allows short "summaries" of dynamic data files. Moreover, the update of a summary incurs only small amount of computation at both the server end and, if necessary, at the client end.

3. It allows fast query of the ith block F_i of a file F. This is important because for updating or querying file, we need to quickly identify F_i.

The above requirements led us to design a new data structure we call *range-based 2-3 trees*, which will be detailed in Section 4. (Note that Merkle trees [17] do not have all the required properties.)

On the other hand, in order to achieve fairness in the setting of dynamic remote data, it is intuitive to use some kind of incremental digital signature scheme. Actually, existing incremental signature schemes [5, 6, 7, 18] used 2-3 trees, which however are not sufficient for the purpose of

FDPOR as we discussed above. Nevertheless, it is possible to further extend our rb23Tree to serve the need of fairness assurance. However, this approach has the following drawback: incremental signing requires $O \log(n)$ hash operations corresponding to the path from the leaf to the root. Instead, we will build another flat tree (i.e., with height 1) directly based on the leaves of the rb23Tree, which will only incur constant hash operations when there is an update to a data file. Although hash functions can be made very efficient, this improved complexity still might be significant in practice because the hash operations will incur correspondingly the same number of read/write accesses. In other words, we use a tailored variant of incremental digital signature scheme for better performance.

Yet another important difference between dynamic POR and static POR is manifested by the way of error correcting codes is used. Specifically, in order to maintain dynamic data, we need to apply an error correct code at the block level, which is in contrast to the setting of static POR where an error correcting code is applied to the whole data file [15, 20]. Applying error-correcting code at the block lever is important because, otherwise, the accommodation of an update operation would always involve the entire data file, which is clearly not acceptable in practice.

Putting the pieces together. The high-level idea is described in Figure 2. Roughly speaking, there are four steps. The first step is to encode the original data file $F = (F_1, \ldots, F_n)$ into $F' = (F_0', \ldots, F_{n+1}')$. The second step is to compute $H_i = h(F_i')$ for $0 \leq i \leq n+1$. The third step is to construct a rb23Tree with leaves $(H_0, \ldots, H_{n+1})$, which leads to obtain the authentication value at root $x(root)$. The fourth step is to construct a flat tree for achieving fairness, where

$$\lambda = \bigodot_{j=0}^{n} \lambda_j = \bigodot_{j=0}^{n} h(H_j || H_{j+1}) = \bigodot_{j=0}^{n} h(h(F_j') || h(F_{j+1}')).$$

This allows us to construct incremental signatures efficiently because any update operation only incurs constant complexity in deriving the new root λ'.

6.2 Construction

The scheme is described as follows.

FDPOR.KeyGen: Taking as input a primary security parameter κ and a secondary security parameter ℓ, it chooses two secret keys $k_1, k_2 \in_R \{0,1\}^\ell$, executes HCS.KeyGen by taking as input security parameter κ to generate a pair of public and secret keys (PK, SK). The keys (k_1, k_2, SK) will be kept secret by a client, and the key PK will be made public.

FDPOR.Update: This protocol allows a client C to store a file $F = (F_1, \ldots, F_n)$ at the first time at the server S (Case 1 below), or to update a file F that was already stored at the server S (Case 2 below).

Case 1: Uploading a new file F.

1. The client C executes as follows:

    (a) Generate two random blocks F_0 and F_{n+1}, with each consisting of m symbols of random elements in $\mathbb{Z}_p$.

    (b) Insert F_0 in front of F_1 and append F_{n+1} to the tail of F_n. Then, we have $F = (F_0, F_1, \ldots, F_n, F_{n+1})$.

    (c) Apply ECC to $F = (F_0, F_1, \ldots, F_n, F_{n+1})$ in a block-by-block fashion. Denote the output file by

$F' = (F_0', F_1', \ldots, F_n', F_{n+1}')$, where each block F_j' for $0 \leq j \leq n+1$ contains z symbols of elements in $\mathbb{Z}_p$. For $0 \leq i \leq n+1$, we define

$$H_i = h(F_i').$$

    (d) $(\lambda, \delta, \mathcal{T}) \leftarrow \text{HCS.InitSign}(\text{SK}, F')$.

    (e) Compute *integrity tag* for the ith block as follows $(0 \leq i \leq n+1)$:

$$\sigma_i = f_{k_1}(H_i) + \sum_{j=1}^{z} f_{k_2}(j) F_{ij}' \qquad (\text{in } \mathbb{Z}_p)$$

    (f) Output the file $F' = (F_0', \ldots, F_{n+1}')$ with $\text{au}_c = (x(root), \lambda, \text{fid})$, which is kept by the client, and $\text{au}_s = (\text{fid}, (\sigma_0, \ldots, \sigma_{n+1}), \mathcal{T}, \lambda, \delta)$, where fid is a unique string chosen by the client.

    (g) Send (F', au_s) to the server over the authenticated channel.

2. The server S executes $\text{HCS.Ver}(\text{PK}, F', \text{null}, \text{null}, \delta, \text{null})$. If it returns true, meaning that δ is a valid signature with respect to the client's public key PK and F', the server stores F' and $\text{au}_s = (\text{fid}, (\sigma_0, \ldots, \sigma_{n+1}), \mathcal{T}, \delta, \lambda)$; otherwise, the server outputs 0 and aborts.

Case 2: Updating an existing file F with $(op, i - 1, \alpha)$, where $2 \leq i \leq n+1$.

Note that operation $(op, i - 1, \alpha)$ with respect to the raw file F means (op, i, α) with respect to the ECC-encoded file F', where α is an ECC-encoded block of z symbols in $\mathbb{Z}_p$, namely $\alpha = (\alpha_1 \cdots \alpha_z), \alpha_i \in \mathbb{Z}_p$. There are three legitimate subcases.

- Subcase 2.1: $op = \mathcal{D}$.

    1. The client C sends three leaf indices $i - 1, i, i + 1$ to the server S.

    2. The server S executes $\text{rb23Tree.P}(\mathcal{T}, j)$ for $j = i-1, i, i+1$ to obtain three respective proof paths $\pi_{i-1}, \pi_i, \pi_{i+1}$, which are returned to the client. Note that $\mathcal{T}$ is the range-based 2-3 tree with leaves $H_0 = h(F_0'), \ldots, H_{n+1} = h(F_{n+1}')$.

    3. The client C executes $\text{rb23Tree.Examine}(x(root), \pi_j)$ for $j = i-1, i, i+1$ in order to verify $\pi_{i-1}, \pi_i, \pi_{i+1}$ are valid with respect to the range-based 2-3 tree $\mathcal{T}$. If C accepts, it derives three block hash values H_{i-1}, H_i, H_{i+1} stored at the three leaves.

    4. The client C applies $\text{HCS.IncSign}(\text{SK}, \mathcal{T}, \lambda, (op, i, \alpha), H_{i-1}, H_i, H_{i+1})$ and obtain δ' and λ'.

    5. The client C sends $(\delta', (op, i, \alpha), \text{fid})$ to the server S and keeps λ'.

    6. The server S verifies δ' by executing $\text{HCS.Ver}(\text{PK}, \text{null}, \mathcal{T}, \lambda, \delta', (op, i, \alpha))$. If accepts, then S deletes the $(i-1)^{th}$ block, and applies $\text{rb23Tree.D}(\mathcal{T}, i)$ to obtain proof paths $(\pi_i, \pi_{i+1}, \pi_i')$, which are then returned to C.

    7. The client C verifies $(\pi_i, \pi_{i+1}, \pi_i')$ by executing $\text{rb23Tree.ver}((op, i, \alpha), \pi_i, \pi_{i+1}, \pi_i')$. If accepts, C updates $x(root)$ which is included in π_i'.

- Subcase 2.2: $op = \mathcal{I}$.

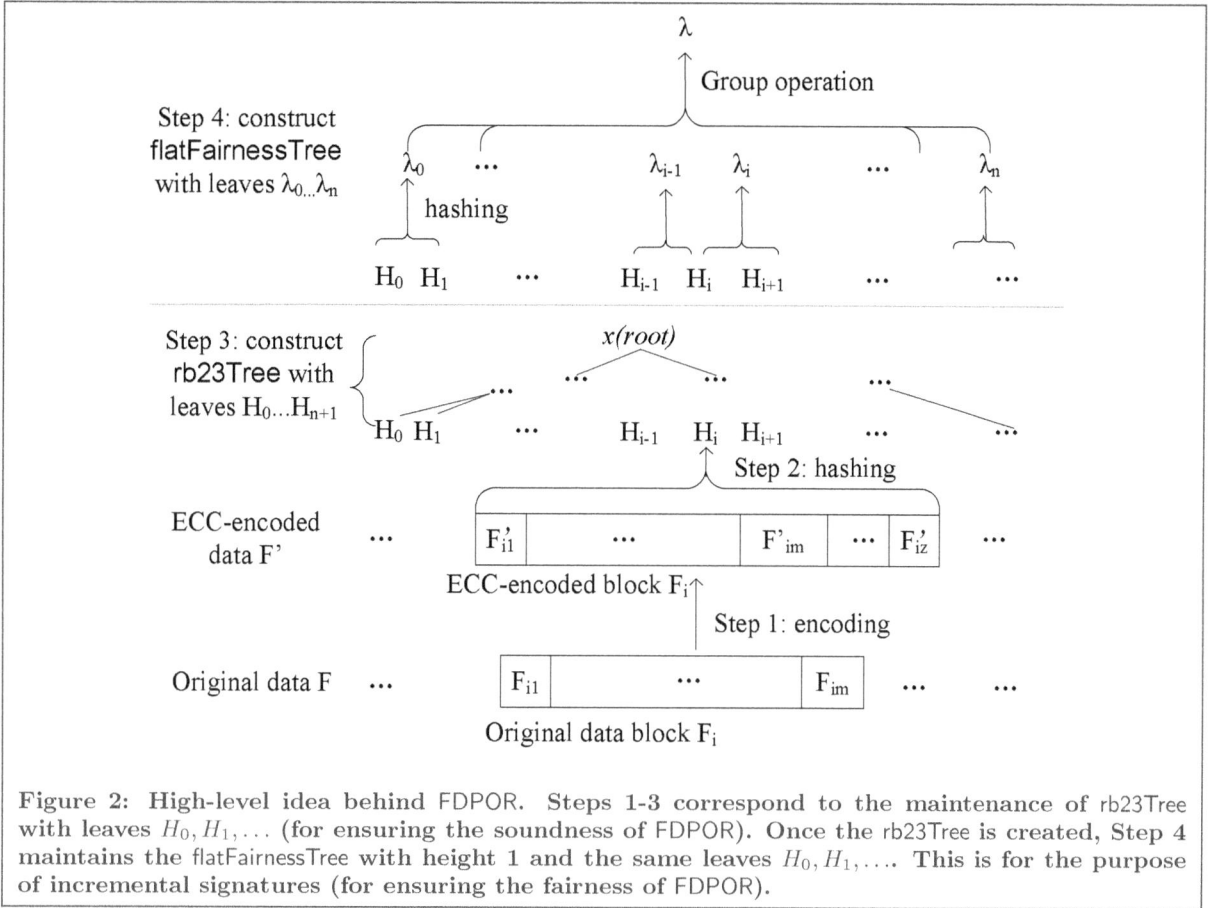

Figure 2: High-level idea behind FDPOR. Steps 1-3 correspond to the maintenance of rb23Tree with leaves $H_0, H_1, \ldots$ (for ensuring the soundness of FDPOR). Once the rb23Tree is created, Step 4 maintains the flatFairnessTree with height 1 and the same leaves $H_0, H_1, \ldots$. This is for the purpose of incremental signatures (for ensuring the fairness of FDPOR).

1. The client C sends two leaf indices $i, i+1$ to the server.

2. The server S returns π_i, π_{i+1}, which are obtained by executing rb23Tree.P$(\mathcal{T}, j)$ for $j = i, i+1$.

3. The client C executes rb23Tree.Examine$(\mathrm{x(root)}, \pi_j)$ for $j = i, i+1$, in order to verify π_i, π_{i+1} are valid with respect to $\mathcal{T}$. If accept, it derives two block hash values H_i, H_{i+1} stored at the three leaves.

4. The client C applies HCS.IncSign$(\mathrm{SK}, \mathcal{T}, \lambda, (op, i, \alpha),$ null$, H_i, H_{i+1})$ and obtain δ' and λ'. It also computes the integrity tag for the new block α as follows:

$$\sigma_\alpha = f_{k_1}(h(\alpha)) + \sum_{j=1}^{z} f_{k_2}(j)\alpha_j.$$

It then sends $(\delta', \sigma_\alpha, (op, i, \alpha), \mathsf{fid})$ to the server.

5. The server S verifies δ' by executing HCS.Ver$(\mathrm{PK},$ null$, \mathcal{T}, \lambda, \delta', (op, i, \alpha))$. If accepts, then it inserts the new block α after $(i-1)^{th}$ block, applies rb23Tree.I$(\mathcal{T}, i, h(\alpha))$ to obtain a pair of proof paths (π_i, π_i'), and updates δ to δ'.

6. the client C verifies π_i, π_i' by executing rb23Tree.ver $((op, i, \alpha), \pi_i, $ null$, \pi_i')$. If accept, C updates $\mathrm{x(root)}$.

- Subcase 2.3: $op = \mathcal{M}$.

    1. The client C sends three leaf indices $i-1, i, i+1$ to the server.

2. The server S returns $\pi_{i-1}, \pi_i, \pi_{i+1}$, which are obtained by executing rb23Tree.P$(\mathcal{T}, j)$ for $j = i-1, i, i+1$.

3. The client C execute rb23Tree.Examine$(\mathrm{x(root)}, \pi_j)$ for $j = i-1, i, i+1$, in order to verify $\pi_{i-1}, \pi_i, \pi_{i+1}$ are valid with respect to $\mathcal{T}$. If C accepts, it derives two block hash values H_{i-1}, H_i, H_{i+1} stored at the three leaves.

4. The client C applies HCS.IncSign$(\mathrm{SK}, \mathcal{T}, \lambda, (op, i, \alpha),$ $H_{i-1}, H_i, H_{i+1})$ and obtains δ' and λ'. It also computes the integrity tag for the new block α as follows:

$$\sigma_i = f_{k_1}(h(\alpha)) + \sum_{j=1}^{z} f_{k_2}(j)\alpha_j.$$

It sends $(\delta', \sigma_i, (op, i, \alpha), \mathsf{fid})$ to the server.

5. The server S verifies δ' by executing HCS.Ver$(\mathrm{PK},$ null$,$ $\mathcal{T}, \lambda, \delta', (op, i, \alpha))$. If accept, then it updates the $(i-1)^{th}$ data block with value α, and applies rb23Tree.M$(\mathcal{T}, h(\alpha))$ to obtain a pair of proof paths (π_i, π_i').

6. The client C executes rb23Tree.ver$((op, i, \alpha), \pi_i, $ null$, \pi_i')$ to verify π_i, π_i'. If accept, C updates $\mathrm{x(root)}$.

FDPOR.Por: This protocol is executed between the client C and the server S as follows.

1. The client C chooses a set of c elements: $I = \{\alpha_1, \cdots, \alpha_c\}$, $\alpha_i \xleftarrow{r} [1, n]$, randomly selects β_i from $\mathbb{Z}_p$ for $1 \leq i \leq c$, and sends the challenge $\mathcal{C} = \{(\alpha_i, \beta_i)\}$ to the server.

2. The server S computes:

$$u_j = \sum_{i \in I} \beta_i F'_{ij} \qquad 1 \leq j \leq z$$

$$\sigma' = \sum_{i \in I} \beta_i \sigma_i$$

$$H_i = h(F'_i) \qquad i \in I$$

and $\pi_i = \mathsf{rb23Tree.P}(\mathcal{T}, i+1)$ for $i \in I$. It then sends the response $\mathcal{R} = \{u_j, \sigma', H_i, \pi_i\}$ back to the client.

3. The client C verifies the response $\mathcal{R}$ and outputs true if the two following conditions hold, and outputs false otherwise:

   - $\mathsf{rb23Tree.Examine}(x(root), \pi_i)$ returns true for $i \in I$.

   - It holds that

   $$\sigma' = \sum_{i \in I} \beta_i f_{k_1}(H_i) + \sum_{j=1}^{z} f_{k_2} u_j$$

7. SECURITY ANALYSIS

The correctness of our scheme can be easily checked. Now we prove the soundness and fairness of our construction in the random model. Specifically, we show the soundness in two steps: First, we prove that no dishonest server can pass the verification with a non-negligible probability. Second, we show that our construction allows to extract the original data file from an ϵ-admissable prover with a certain non-negligible probability. We show the fairness of our scheme is ensured by the incremental signature scheme.

THEOREM 1. *Assume $\{f_k\}_k$ is a family of secure PRF, h is collision-resistant hash function, and $ECC(m, z, d)$ is an error-correcting code. Then one can recover the file F from the ϵ-admissable prover with at least the probability $(1 - e^{d/2-\mu}(d/2\mu)^{-d/2})^n$, where $\mu = (1-\epsilon)z/\epsilon$ with the condition $d > 2\mu$.*

PROOF. The theorem is proved by showing:

- A dishonest server cannot execute FDPOR.Por with an honest client successfully with a non-negligible probability (Lemma 1).

- Given a ϵ-admissable cheating prover, one can recover the original file F with probability $(1 - e^{d/2-\mu}(d/2\mu)^{-d/2})^n$, where $\mu = (1-\epsilon)z/\epsilon$ with the condition $d > 2\mu$ (Lemma 2).

$\square$

LEMMA 1. *If $\{f_k\}_k$ is a family of secure PRF and h is collision-resistant hash function, then no dishonest server can execute FDPOR.Por i times to convince an honest client successfully with a non-negligible probability.*

PROOF. According to Definition 2, a dishonest server successfully executes FDPOR.Por to convince the client when the client outputs 1. Let us now consider the probability that event happens. Recall that block F_i is associated with tag σ_i, where $1 \leq i \leq n$, that $I = \{\alpha_1, \ldots, \alpha_c\}$ is the set of block indices randomly selected by the client and $\mathcal{C} = \{(\alpha_i, \beta_i)\}_{1 \leq i \leq c}$ is the corresponding challenge, which caused the server to return the response $\{u'_1, \ldots, u'_z, \sigma'\} \bigcup \{H_i | (i \in I)\}$. Let $\{u_1, \ldots, u_z, \sigma\} \bigcup \{H'_i | (i \in I)\}$ be the expected response returned by an honest prover. Here we have $H_i = H'_i$ for all $i \in I$ because of the guarantee in the proof pathes verification. Hence, we have the two equations:

$$\sigma = \sum_{i \in I} \beta_i f_{k_1}(H'_i) + \sum_{j=1}^{z} f_{k_2}(j) u_j \quad (\text{in } \mathbb{Z}_p)$$

$$\sigma' = \sum_{i \in I} \beta_i f_{k_1}(H'_i) + \sum_{j=1}^{z} f_{k_2}(j) u'_j \quad (\text{in } \mathbb{Z}_p)$$

Let $\Delta\sigma = \sigma' - \sigma$ and $\Delta u_j = u'_j - u_j$, $1 \leq j \leq z$. Then we have

$$\Delta\sigma = \sum_{j=1}^{z} f_{k_2}(j)\Delta u_j \quad (\text{in } \mathbb{Z}_p) \qquad (4)$$

In order to successfully execute FDPOR.Por the dishonest server has to provide an instance of the $z+1$ values of the $z+1$ variables $\Delta u_1, \ldots, \Delta u_z$ that satisfy Eq. (4). Because f_{k_2} is a secure PRF, the z random coefficients $f_{k_2}(1), \ldots, f_{k_2}(z)$ are randomly distributed over $\mathbb{Z}_p$ and are not known to the server. This means that any given $\Delta u_1, \ldots, \Delta u_z$ and $\Delta\sigma$ satisfying Eq. (4) with probability $1/p$. Therefore, the probability of convincing the client after i attempts is:

$$1 - (1 - 1/p)(1 - 1/(p-1)) \ldots (1 - 1/(p-i))$$

Let $1 \leq i \leq p/2$, then we have

$$1 - (1 - 1/p)(1 - 1/(p-1)) \ldots (1 - 1/(p-i))$$
$$\leq 1 - (1 - 2/p)^i$$
$$\leq 1 - (1 - 2/p) = 2/p$$

For the large ℓ-bits prime p and within polynomial attempts, the probability of convincing the client will be negligible. $\square$

LEMMA 2. *Given an ϵ-admissible prover, one can recover the original file F with the probability $(1 - e^{d/2-\mu}(d/2\mu)^{-d/2})^n$, where $\mu = (1-\epsilon)z/\epsilon$ with the condition $d > 2\mu$..*

PROOF. Since the prover is ϵ-admissible, there are at most $(1-\epsilon)nz$ symbols corrupted in the file. Let us consider the probability that a corrupted symbol exists in a given block. It has the maximum probability while other $(1-\epsilon)nz - 1$ corrupted symbols appear in other blocks. Therefore, the probability of a corrupted symbol in a given block will be less than $z/(nz - (1-\epsilon)nz) = 1/\epsilon n$.

Let us define the event X_i whether i^{th} corrupted symbol will be in a given block $(0 \leq i \leq (1-\epsilon)nz)$, and $X_i = 1$ means i^{th} corrupted symbol is in the given block. Then $\Pr[X_i = 1] \leq 1/\epsilon n$ So $X_1, \ldots, X_{(1-\epsilon)nz}$ are the independent Bernoulli variables. Let us consider the number of corrupted symbols being in the given block, denoted by X. We have $X = \sum_{i=1}^{(1-\epsilon)nz} X_i$ and $\mathbf{E}[X] = \mu \leq (1-\epsilon)z/\epsilon$.

According to the Chernoff Bound [10], if $X_1, \ldots, X_N$ are independent bernoulli variables, then for $X = \sum_{i=1}^{N} X_i$ and any $\delta > 0$, $\Pr[X > (1 + \delta)\mu] < (e^\delta/(1 + \delta)^{(1+\delta)})^\mu$ with $\mu = \mathbf{E}[X]$.

For a given block, if it is not recoverable, it should contains at least $d/2$ corrupted symbols. Let $(1 + \delta)\mu = d/2$ and have $\delta = d/2\mu - 1$. So $\Pr[X > d/2] = \Pr[X > (1 + \delta)\mu] \leq (e^\delta/(1+\delta)^{(1+\delta)})^\mu$, by letting $\delta = d/2\mu - 1$ and $\mu = (1-\epsilon)z/\epsilon$. By simplification, we have $\Pr[X > d/2] \leq e^{d/2-\mu}(d/2\mu)^{-d/2}$ where $\mu = (1-\epsilon)z/\epsilon$ and under condition $d > 2\mu$. Hence, the probability of recovering(or retrieving) a given block will be at least $1 - e^{d/2-\mu}(d/2\mu)^{-d/2}$. Because the file is composed of n blocks, the probability of retrieving the original file will be at least $(1 - e^{d/2-\mu}(d/2\mu)^{-d/2})^n$ where $\mu = (1-\epsilon)z/\epsilon$ with the condition $d > 2\mu$. $\square$

Fairness of our FDPOR scheme is based on the hardness of the so-called *balance problem*, which is reviewed below.

LEMMA 3. ([7]; the balance problem and its hardness) *Given a group G, and elements $a_1, \ldots, a_n$ randomly selected from G, find disjoint subsets $\mathcal{U}, \mathcal{W} \subseteq \{1, \ldots, n\}$, s.t. $\bigodot_{i \in \mathcal{U}} a_i = \bigodot_{j \in \mathcal{W}} a_j$, $\mathcal{U}, \mathcal{W}$ not both empty, where $\bigodot$ is the group operation. When choosing G as $\mathbb{Z}_p$ for a suitable prime P, the hardness of the balance problem instantiated over $(\mathbb{Z}_p,)$ would be equal to, or even greater than, the discrete logarithm problem in $\mathbb{Z}_p$.*

THEOREM 2. *Assume h is a collision-resistant hash function and SIG is a secure signature scheme, our FDPOR scheme is fair.*

PROOF. According to Definition 3, a dishonest client may break the fairness of the scheme only when it can generate two files F and F', such that (i) $F \neq F'$, and (ii) the honest server verifies that $1 \leftarrow \mathsf{HCS.Ver}(\mathrm{PK}, F, \mathcal{T}, \lambda, \delta, \mathtt{null})$ and $1 \leftarrow \mathsf{HCS.Ver}(\mathrm{PK}, F', \mathcal{T}', \lambda', \delta, \mathtt{null})$.

Let us first review the signing process: computing hash value for each file block, $H_i = h(F_i)$, hashing $(H_i H_{i+1})$, i.e.. $\lambda_i = h(H_i||H_{i+1})$, then taking group operation on λ_i, namely $\lambda = \bigodot \lambda_i$. At last Let $\mathsf{SIG.Sign}(\mathrm{SK}, \lambda) \to \delta$. We denote this process by $F \to \mathcal{T} \to \lambda \to \delta$. Here $\mathcal{T}$ is a range-based 2-3 tree which stores H_i at the leaves. Two range-based 2-3 trees are said to be identical, denoted by $\mathcal{T} = \mathcal{T}'$, if both have the same number of leaves, and the corresponding leaves store the same hash value.

Now Let us consider the probability of the dishonest client breaking the fairness.

Let us consider the probability of the dishonest client successfully generating (F, F', δ). It can achieve this goal with three possible means:

- It can find two different λ and λ' such that
  $$1 \leftarrow \mathsf{SIG.Ver}(\mathrm{PK}, \lambda, \delta) \wedge 1 \leftarrow \mathsf{SIG.Ver}(\mathrm{PK}, \lambda', \delta).$$
  This is investigate in Case 1 below.

- It can obtain two distinct $\mathcal{T}$ and $\mathcal{T}'$ but get identical $\lambda = \lambda'$. This is investigated in Case 2 below.

- It can obtain two distinct file F and F', but have identical $\mathcal{T}$ and T'. This is investigated in Case 3 below.

Case 1: $\lambda \neq \lambda'$. Let us define event E_1 as
$$\{\lambda \neq \lambda'|1 \leftarrow \mathsf{SIG.Ver}(\mathrm{PK}, \lambda', \delta) \wedge 1 \leftarrow \mathsf{SIG.Ver}(\mathrm{PK}, \lambda', \delta)\}.$$
Because SIG is a secure signature scheme, $\Pr[E_1]$ is negligible.

Case 2: $\mathcal{T}' \neq \mathcal{T}$ but $\lambda = \lambda'$. Let us define event E_2 as
$$\{\lambda = \lambda'|\mathcal{T} \neq \mathcal{T}' \wedge \mathcal{T} \to \lambda \wedge \mathcal{T}' \to \lambda'\}.$$
Let us consider the probability $\Pr[E_2]$.

Assume that there exists a polynomial-time algorithm $\mathcal{A}$ that can obtain two different strings $x = x_1 x_2 \cdots x_n$ and $y = y_1 y_2 \cdots y_m$, which are stored at the leaves of $\mathcal{T}$ and $\mathcal{T}'$ such that $\lambda = \bigodot_{i=1}^{n-1} h(x_i||x_{i+1})$, $\lambda' = \bigodot_{j=1}^{m-1} h(y_j||y_{j+1})$ and $\lambda = \lambda'$. Then we have
$$h(x_1||x_2) \bigodot h(x_2||x_3) \cdots \bigodot h(x_{n-1}||x_n)$$
$$= h(y_1||y_2) \bigodot h(y_2||y_3) \cdots \bigodot h(y_{m-1}||y_m).$$
Let
$$\mathcal{U} = \{\alpha_i = h(x_i||x_{i+1}), 1 \leq i \leq n - 1\}$$
and
$$\mathcal{W} = \{\beta_j = h(y_j||y_{j+1}), 1 \leq j \leq m - 1\},$$
where α_i, β_j are randomly distributed over the $\mathbb{Z}_p$. Then we have
$$\bigodot_{i=1}^{n-1} \alpha_i = \bigodot_{j=1}^{m-1} \beta_j.$$
Since $x \neq y$, we have $\mathcal{U} \neq \mathcal{W}$. Hence we have
$$\bigodot_{i=1}^{l} \alpha_i = \bigodot_{j=1}^{k} \beta_j, \quad 0 \leq l \leq n-1, 0 \leq k \leq m-1$$
by eliminating identical values at both sides. Note that k and l cannot be zero simultaneously.

If the polynomial time algorithm $\mathcal{A}$ can obtain two different range-based 2-3 trees $\mathcal{T}, \mathcal{T}'$ (meaning two different strings x and y) such that $\lambda = \lambda'$, then we can adopt $\mathcal{A}$ to find a solution to the balance problem by satisfying $\bigodot_{i=1}^{n-1} \alpha_i = \bigodot_{j=1}^{m-1} \beta_j$, where α_i, β_j are randomly selected from the group $\mathbb{Z}_p$, $\bigodot$ is the group operation and l, k cannot be zero simultaneously. In other words, the probability that we find a solution to the balance problem is the same as the probability that $\mathcal{A}$ find two different range-based 2-3 trees such that $\lambda = \lambda'$.

According to Theorem 3, $\Pr[E_2]$ is negligible.

Case 3: $F \neq F'$ but $\mathcal{T}' = \mathcal{T}, \lambda = \lambda'$. Let us consider the event E_3 as
$$\{\mathcal{T} = \mathcal{T}'|F \neq F' \wedge F \to \mathcal{T} \wedge F' \to \mathcal{T}'\}.$$
The identical range-based 2-3 tree means that the two files have the same length, and the hash values of each block are identical. However, since h is a collision-resistant hash function, $\Pr[E_3]$ is negligible.

In summary, $\Pr[E_1] + \Pr[E_2] + \Pr[E_3]$ is negligible, meaning that a dishonest client can break the fairness of the scheme with only negligible probability. This completes the proof. $\square$

8. CONCLUSION

We presented FDPOR, a useful extension of the static POR. We also presented the first FDPOR scheme, which is proven secure in random oracle. Our scheme is based on two new building-blocks that might be of independent value.

Our future work includes: (i) realizing public verifiability so that a third party can verify the retrievability of data. (ii) utilizing erasure code rather than ECC so as to achieve possibly better performance.

Acknowledgements.

This work was supported in part by an AFOSR MURI grant and a State of Texas Emerging Technology Fund grant.

9. REFERENCES

[1] J. D. U. Alfred V.Aho, John E. Hopcroft. *The Design and Analysis of Computer Algorithms.* Addison Wesley, 1974.

[2] G. Ateniese, R. Burns, R. Curtmola, J. Herring, L. Kissner, Z. Peterson, and D. Song. Provable data possession at untrusted stores. In *CCS '07: Proceedings of the 14th ACM conference on Computer and communications security*, pages 598–609, 2007.

[3] G. Ateniese, R. Di Pietro, L. V. Mancini, and G. Tsudik. Scalable and efficient provable data possession. In *SecureComm '08: Proceedings of the 4th international conference on Security and privacy in communication netowrks*, pages 1–10, 2008.

[4] M. Bellare and O. Goldreich. On defining proofs of knowledge. In *CRYPTO*, pages 390–420, 1992.

[5] M. Bellare, O. Goldreich, and S. Goldwasser. Incremental cryptography: The case of hashing and signing. In *CRYPTO '94: Proceedings of the 14th Annual International Cryptology Conference on Advances in Cryptology*, pages 216–233, 1994.

[6] M. Bellare, O. Goldreich, and S. Goldwasser. Incremental cryptography and application to virus protection. In *STOC '95: Proceedings of the twenty-seventh annual ACM symposium on Theory of computing*, pages 45–56, 1995.

[7] M. Bellare and D. Micciancio. A new paradigm for collision-free hashing: incrementality at reduced cost. In *EUROCRYPT'97: Proceedings of the 16th annual international conference on Theory and application of cryptographic techniques*, pages 163–192, 1997.

[8] K. D. Bowers, A. Juels, and A. Oprea. Hail: a high-availability and integrity layer for cloud storage. In *ACM Conference on Computer and Communications Security*, pages 187–198, 2009.

[9] K. D. Bowers, A. Juels, and A. Oprea. Proofs of retrievability: theory and implementation. In *CCSW '09: Proceedings of the 2009 ACM workshop on Cloud computing security*, pages 43–54, 2009.

[10] H. Chernoff. A measure of asymptotic efficiency for tests of a hypothesis based on the sum of observations. *The Annals of Mathematical Statistics*, 23(4):493–507, 1952.

[11] Y. Dodis, S. Vadhan, and D. Wichs. Proofs of retrievability via hardness amplification. In *TCC '09: Proceedings of the 6th Theory of Cryptography Conference on Theory of Cryptography*, pages 109–127, 2009.

[12] C. Dwork, M. Naor, G. N. Rothblum, and V. Vaikuntanathan. How efficient can memory checking be? In *Theory of Cryptography (TCC'09)*, pages 503–520, 2009.

[13] C. Erway, A. Küpçü, C. Papamanthou, and R. Tamassia. Dynamic provable data possession. In *CCS '09: Proceedings of the 16th ACM conference on Computer and communications security*, pages 213–222, 2009.

[14] O. Goldreich. *The Foundations of Cryptography*, volume 1. Cambridge University Press, 2001.

[15] A. Juels and B. S. Kaliski, Jr. Pors: proofs of retrievability for large files. In *CCS '07: Proceedings of the 14th ACM conference on Computer and communications security*, pages 584–597, 2007.

[16] M. Lillibridge, S. Elnikety, A. Birrell, M. Burrows, and M. Isard. A cooperative internet backup scheme. In *ATEC '03: Proceedings of the annual conference on USENIX Annual Technical Conference*, pages 3–3, 2003.

[17] R. C. Merkle. Protocols for public key cryptosystems. *IEEE Symposium on Security and Privacy*, pages 122–134, 1980.

[18] D. Micciancio. Oblivious data structures: Applications to cryptography. In *In Proceedings of the 29th Annual ACM Symposium on the Theory of Computing*, pages 456–464, 1997.

[19] M. Naor and K. Nissim. Certificate revocation and certificate update. In *SSYM'98: Proceedings of the 7th conference on USENIX Security Symposium*, pages 17–17, 1998.

[20] H. Shacham and B. Waters. Compact proofs of retrievability. In *ASIACRYPT '08: Proceedings of the 14th International Conference on the Theory and Application of Cryptology and Information Security*, pages 90–107, 2008.

RASP: Efficient Multidimensional Range Query on Attack-Resilient Encrypted Databases

Keke Chen, Ramakanth Kavuluru, Shumin Guo
Department of Computer Science and Engineering
Wright State University
Dayton, Ohio 45435, USA
{keke.chen,ramakanth.kavuluru, guo.18}@wright.edu

ABSTRACT

Range query is one of the most frequently used queries for online data analytics. Providing such a query service could be expensive for the data owner. With the development of services computing and cloud computing, it has become possible to outsource large databases to database service providers and let the providers maintain the range-query service. With outsourced services, the data owner can greatly reduce the cost in maintaining computing infrastructure and data-rich applications. However, the service provider, although honestly processing queries, may be curious about the hosted data and received queries. Most existing encryption based approaches require linear scan over the entire database, which is inappropriate for online data analytics on large databases. While a few encryption solutions are more focused on efficiency side, they are vulnerable to attackers equipped with certain prior knowledge. We propose the Random Space Encryption (RASP) approach that allows efficient range search with stronger attack resilience than existing efficiency-focused approaches. We use RASP to generate indexable auxiliary data that is resilient to prior knowledge enhanced attacks. Range queries are securely transformed to the encrypted data space and then efficiently processed with a two-stage processing algorithm. We thoroughly studied the potential attacks on the encrypted data and queries at three different levels of prior knowledge available to an attacker. Experimental results on synthetic and real datasets show that this encryption approach allows efficient processing of range queries with high resilience to attacks.

Categories and Subject Descriptors

H.2.0 [**Database Management**]: General—*Security, integrity, and protection*; E.3 [**Data Encryption**]

General Terms

Security, Algorithms

Keywords

Multidimensional Range Query, Random Space Encryption, Attack Analysis, Outsourced Databases

1. INTRODUCTION

With the increasing popularity of web-based applications and the support from widely available cloud infrastructures, service-based computing has become a major computing paradigm. Service providers take advantage of low cost cloud infrastructures, while service users enjoy convenient services without worrying about the cost of maintaining hardware and software. On the other hand, large datasets have been collected, stored, and analyzed in business intelligence and scientific computing for several years. It was reported that maintaining data and supporting query-based services incur much higher cost than initial data acquisition [12]. An appealing solution is to delegate data services to a service provider, which, however, raises the question: how to protect the private information in the outsourced data, considering the service provider might be curious about the data.

Range query is the most frequently used query in online data analytics (OLAP) that requires the service provider to quickly respond to concurrent user queries. To efficiently process range queries, indexing is a necessary step. However, most existing encryption approaches [30, 4, 5, 29] require linear scan over the entire database, thus, impractical for OLAP. Fully homomorphic encryption [13] in theory allows any operation on encrypted data that can be traced back to an equivalent operation on the corresponding plaintexts. However, as the author of [13] mentioned, this is still too expensive to be practical even for a simple application like encrypted keyword search.

Several methods that consider different tradeoffs between data security and efficiency of query processing were proposed in the recent years. Both Crypto-index [20, 21] and order-preserving encryption (OPE) [1, 3] assume the attacker does not have sufficient prior knowledge about the data; thus powerful attacks cannot be conducted. Specifically, they assume the attacker knows only the ciphertext. However, we have found that if the attacker has some prior knowledge, such as the attribute domains (maximum and minimum values), the attribute distributions, and even a few pairs of plaintext and ciphertext, these encryption methods will be vulnerable to attacks. Therefore, although they can allow the service provider to build indices on encrypted data and perform efficient query processing, they can only be applied to very restricted applications. Wang and Lakshmanan [31] use OPE in querying encrypted XML database and address the prior-knowledge enhanced attacks on OPE with duplicated fake index entries that point to the same data item in the encrypted data block. However, their approach requires the data owner to build indices for the server, which is expensive and not convenient when the database is large and frequently updated.

Challenge: Therefore, the challenge is to provide an encryption scheme that allows efficient, index based query processing, and is also resilient to prior knowledge enhanced attacks on both data and queries. Our goal is to develop such an encryption scheme.

1.1 Our Contributions and Scope of Research

We propose the RAndom SPace encryption (RASP) approach for efficient range query processing on encrypted data. We assume the outsourced data are multidimensional data and thus the data records can be treated as vectors (or points) in the multidimensional space. The RASP method randomly transforms the multidimensional space, while preserving the convexity of datasets, which allows indexing and query processing with the encrypted multidimensional data. The framework assumes a secure proxy server at the client side that handles data encryption/decryption and query encryption. The data owner and authorized users submit the original data and queries to the proxy server; the proxy server then sends the encrypted data/queries to the service provider. The service provider is able to index the encrypted data and use it to efficiently process encrypted queries.

Our approach has several important features: (1) The RASP approach uses a random space transformation method that allows the service provider to build indices and process queries with multidimensional indices. With the support of indices, the proposed two-stage query processing algorithm can achieve much better performance than linear scan. (2) The existing indexable encryption schemes hold strong assumptions on attacker's lack of prior knowledge on the data; thus they are vulnerable to many attacks enhanced with prior knowledge. Our work categorizes attacker's prior knowledge into three levels and the proposed schemes are resilient to these knowledge-enhanced attacks. To increase resilience against known plain text attacks we use a straightforward composition of Agarwal et al.'s OPE [1] with RASP. (3) Attacks based on queries were rarely discussed in existing schemes. We show that with prior knowledge, attacks on queries can seriously undermine the encryption. We design certain methods to enhance the resilience to the query-based attacks. (4) Some approaches, such as crypto-index, may return a lot of encrypted records irrelevant to the query and burden the client side to filter out these irrelevant records. Our approach always returns the exact result to the client, eliminating the unnecessary additional costs.

We also conduct a number of experiments on synthetic and real datasets to evaluate the performance and the attack resilience. The experimental results show that the proposed method is efficient and resilient to the knowledge enhanced attacks.

The rest of this paper is organized as follows. Section 2 briefly describes range queries and the privacy problems with outsourced databases. Section 3 gives the definition of random space perturbation. In section 4 we present the algorithms for query transformation on the client side and efficient query processing on the server side. In Section 5, we formally analyze the security of the scheme, describe various attacks and discuss the resilience of our scheme to these attacks. The algorithms outlined in Section 4 and Section 5 are summarized at the end of Section 5. The cost of encryption, the resilience to attacks, and the efficiency of query processing are further evaluated through extensive experiments in Section 6.

2. PRELIMINARIES

First, we establish the notation used in this paper. A database table consists of n records and k searchable attributes. We also frequently refer to an attribute as a dimension or column. These three names are exchangeable in our context. Each record can be represented as a vector, and notated with bold lower cases, while lower

cases are used to represent scalars. Each column is defined on a domain. For categorical domain, we use integers to represent the categorical values. A table is also represented as a $k \times n$ matrix, notated with capital characters. In the following, we briefly describe the definition of range queries and the importance of indexability to the performance of query processing.

Range Queries: Range query is an important type of query for many data analytic tasks from simple aggregation to more sophisticated machine learning tasks. Let T be a table and X_i, X_j, and X_k be the real valued attributes in T, and a and b be some constants. Take the counting query for example. A typical SQL-style range query looks like

select count(*) from T
where $X_i \in [a_i, b_i]$ and $X_j \in (a_j, b_j)$ and $X_k = a_k$,

which calculates the number of records in the range defined by conditions on X_i, X_j, and X_k. Range queries may be applied to arbitrary number of attributes and conditions on these attributes combined with conditional operators "and"/"or". We call each part of the query condition that involves only one attribute as a *simple condition*. A simple condition like $X_i \in [a_i, b_i]$ can be described with two half space conditions $X_i \leq b_i$ and $-X_i \leq -a_i$. Without loss of generality, we will discuss how to process half space conditions like $X_i \leq b_i$ in this paper. A slight modification will extend the discussed algorithms to handle other conditions like $X_i < b_i$ and $X_i = b_i$.

3. RANDOM SPACE ENCRYPTION

In this section, we propose the basic Random Space Encryption (RASP) approach for secure range query processing on the encrypted outsourced data. First, we give the system framework and assumptions held for the attack models. Second, we present the definition of the basic random space encryption method and distinguish it from order preserving encryption methods. Finally, we describe how to generate outsourced data and answer queries with the encrypted data.

3.1 System Framework and Attack Models

System Framework. We assume the outsourced data are multidimensional data and thus the data records can be treated as vectors (or points) in the multidimensional space. Figure 1 shows the framework for processing range query services on outsourced data. In the client side, the data owner has all rights to upload/query data, and may also grant the query right to the trusted users. The proxy server receives original data and queries, encrypts and submits them, and decrypts the query results. It keeps the security key, the encryption functions $E_T()$, $E_Q()$, the decryption function $D()$, and controls the access rights. The traffic between the proxy server and the service provider contains only the encrypted data and queries. Although the proxy server does not handle the large dataset and process queries, it might still become a bottleneck for a large number of users and frequent query submissions. However, the cost to scale the proxy server should be much lower than that to host the entire query processing service.

This framework includes several key components. (1) *Encrypted auxiliary data generation.* This approach will generate the auxiliary data encrypted with the proposed scheme for indexing purpose through the encryption function $E_T()$ in Figure 1. It applies a type of multiplicative perturbation [9, 27] on the searchable attributes in the original database to generate the auxiliary data. The goal is to keep the topology of original data vectors in the auxiliary data but

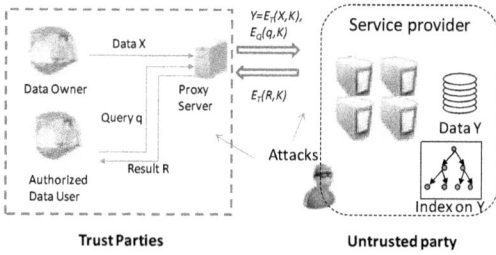

Figure 1: A framework for hosting range query services.

obscure the original data values so that they cannot be possibly inferred from the auxiliary data. (2) *Query Encryption.* A submitted query should also be appropriately transformed so that the server can use the index on the encrypted auxiliary data to process the query. This query transformation should be secure, not reveal any information that helps curious service providers breach privacy. We denote it as the $E_Q()$ function. (3) *Server side indexing and query processing.* The service provider is able to build multidimensional index on the auxiliary data. However, processing the transformed queries requires algorithms different from the existing ones. Our framework also includes the algorithms for query processing.

Attack Models. In our framework, we study the attack models based on the popular honest-but-curious service provider assumption. We assume the service provider will honestly provide the services and perform the computations following the protocol (e.g., public cloud providers). However, the provider might be curious about the data and the users' queries. Also, we assume that the attacker knows the algorithms used to encrypt data and queries (i.e., the algorithms for $E_T()$, $E_Q()$). Active attackers will also try to obtain as much prior knowledge as possible to help break the encryption, or estimate the encrypted data and queries. To better evaluate the strength of an encryption scheme, we categorize attacks into different levels based on the prior knowledge the attacker may have.

- Level 1: the attacker observes only the encrypted data and queries, without any additional knowledge. This corresponds to the ciphertext-only attack (COA) in cryptography [15].

- Level 2: Apart from the encrypted data, the attacker also knows some dimensional distribution information about the original data, including the attribute domain (the maximum and minimum values) and distribution (e.g., the Probability Density Function (PDF) or histogram). In practice, for some applications such as hosting query services for census data, the dimensional distribution might be known by the public.

- Level 3: In addition to Level 2 knowledge, the attacker observes a small set of plaintext tuples X and the corresponding encrypted tuples Y in the outsourced data. This corresponds to the known-plaintext attack (KPA) in cryptography. In our special context, the attacker may also observe a small number of plain queries and the corresponding encrypted queries.

The three levels also correspond to the difficulty level of obtaining the required prior knowledge. Both Level 2 and Level 3 knowledge are difficult to obtain and it is possible only when the attacker, e.g., the curious service provider, resorts to social engineering or gains temporary unauthorized access to some user accounts at the data owner location. For example, the related database applications may reveal some knowledge about the domain; the compromised

user may use queries to probe the encrypted database. The prior knowledge based attacks have also been used in attack analysis for privacy preserving data mining [2, 22, 9] and kNN queries [33] on outsourced data. We will study attacks under these three different levels after we present the basic encryption methods.

3.2 Definition of Random Space Encryption

Random Space Encryption (RASP) is one type of multiplicative perturbation [8], with relaxed constraints on the encryption parameters. Let's consider the multidimensional data are numeric and in multidimensional vector space − For categorical attributes, we use a simple mapping of integers to categorical values to convert them to integers[1]. Assume the database has k searchable dimensions and n records, i.e., a $k \times n$ matrix X. Let $\mathbf{x}$ represent a k-dimensional record. Note that in the k-dimensional vector space, the range query conditions are represented as half space conditions and a range query is correspondingly translated to finding the point set in a hyper-cube [6]. The RASP encryption involves two steps. For each k-dimensional input vector $\mathbf{x}$,

1. the vector is first extended to $k+2$ dimensions as $(\mathbf{x}^T, 1, v)^T$, where the $(k+1)$-th dimension is always a 1 and v is drawn from $(0, \alpha]$ using a random number generator R_α, with some private α and distribution [2].

2. After this extension the $(k+2)$-dimensional vector is then subjected to the transformation

$$E_T(\mathbf{x}, K = \{A, R_v\}) = A \begin{pmatrix} \mathbf{x} \\ 1 \\ v \end{pmatrix}, \qquad (1)$$

where A is a $(k+2) \times (k+2)$ randomly generated invertible matrix (see Appendix for matrix generation) with $a_{ij} \in \mathbb{R}$ such that there are at least two non-zero values in each row of A and the last column of A is also non-zero.

Note that A is shared by all vectors in the database, but v is randomly generated with the random number generator R_α for each individual vector. Note that only A is needed in the trusted proxy server for decryption (and hence forms the key) - we don't need to keep v in the proxy server. The design of extended data vector $(\mathbf{x}^T, 1, v)^T$ is to address the query-based attacks: the $k+1$ dimension is a homogeneous dimension for hiding the query content; the $k+2$ dimension is used to counter the inherent linearity in transforming the queries. The rationale behind different aspects of this encryption will be discussed clearly in later sections. Also, the structure of A will be slightly changed to withstand known plain text attacks in Section 5.

RASP has two important features. First, we want to show that RASP does not preserve the ordering of dimensional values, which distinguishes itself from order preserving encryption schemes, and thus does not suffer from the bucket-based attack (details in Section 7). Second, we show that RASP is *convexity preserving*, which allows range queries on the encrypted data.

RASP is Not Order Preserving. In the following, we show that RASP is not order preserving; thus the attacks on OPE schemes cannot be applied to RASP. An OPE scheme maps a set of dimensional values to another, while keeping the value order unchanged.

---

[1] For a categorical attribute X_i, the values $\{c_1, \ldots, c_m\}$ in the domain are mapped to $\{1, \ldots, m\}$. A query condition $X_i = c_j$, is converted to $j - \delta \leq X_i \leq j + \delta$, where $\delta \in (0, 1)$
[2] We used $\alpha = 1$ and uniform random distribution for the experiments

Let $\mathbf{x}$ be any record in the dataset, and $\mathbf{f}^i$ be the selection vector $(0, \ldots, 1, \ldots, 0)$ i.e., only the i-th dimension is 1 and other dimensions are 0. For simplicity we use unextended vectors – the extended dimensions are not related to this discussion and can be safely removed. Then, $(\mathbf{f}^i)^T\mathbf{x}$ will return the value at dimension i of $\mathbf{x}$.

PROPOSITION 1. *Let A be an invertible matrix with at least two non-zero entries in each row. For any vector $\mathbf{s}$, let $\mathbf{s}' = A\mathbf{s}$. Then for any $i \in \{1, \ldots, k\}$ there exist vectors $\mathbf{x}$, $\mathbf{y}$ for which A preserves the order of dimension i (that is, $(x_i - y_i)(x_i' - y_i') > 0$) and there exist vectors $\mathbf{u}$, $\mathbf{v}$ for which A reverses the order of dimension i. That is, RASP does not preserve order for arbitrary input vector pairs.*

PROOF. Using the same dimensional selection vector, we have $s_i' = (\mathbf{f}^i)^T A\mathbf{s}$ and $t_i' = (\mathbf{f}^i)^T A\mathbf{t}$. Thus, we get

$$
\begin{aligned}
(s_i - t_i)(s_i' - t_i') &= (s_i - t_i)(\mathbf{f}^i)^T A(\mathbf{s} - \mathbf{t}) \\
&= (s_i - t_i)\sum_{j=1}^{k} a_{i,j}(s_j - t_j), \quad (2)
\end{aligned}
$$

where $a_{i,j}$ is the i-th row j-th column element of A. Without loss of generality, let's assume $s_i > t_i$ (for $s_i < t_i$ the same proof applies). It is straightforward to see that given the fixed values of A, the values of s_j and t_j for all $j \neq i$ can be chosen so that $(s_i - t_i)\sum_{j=1}^{k} a_{i,j}(s_j - t_j)$ is either negative or positive. Note that since each row of A has at least two non-zero entries, even if $a_{i,i}(s_i - t_i)^2 > 0$ $(or < 0)$, using the other non-zero value in the i-th row of A, say $a_{i,k}$, the sign of $(s_i - t_i)\sum_{j=1}^{k} a_{i,j}(s_j - t_j)$ can be adjusted to either positive or negative by appropriately choosing the values s_k and t_k. □

RASP is Convexity Preserving. Let's treat data records as points in a real multidimensional space. In the following, we will show that although RASP does not preserve ordering, it preserves convexity, which forms the basis of our query processing strategy. The following definitions of convex set and convexity preserving function can be found in most textbooks on convex optimization, e.g., [6].

DEFINITION 1. *A set S is a convex set, if and only if for $\forall \mathbf{x}_1$, $\mathbf{x}_2 \in S$, and $\forall \theta \in [0, 1]$,*

$$\theta\mathbf{x}_1 + (1 - \theta)\mathbf{x}_2 \in S$$

DEFINITION 2. *A convexity preserving function $E()$ preserves the convexity of sets. Concretely, if S is a convex set in the original data space, the function $E()$ always transforms S to another convex set $E(S)$.*

The following proposition cited from [6] is critical to the proof of convexity preserving property of RASP encryption and our query processing algorithm.

PROPOSITION 2. *(1) Every convex set is a (possibly infinite) intersection of halfspaces, i.e., $\bigcap H_i$, where H_i defines a halfspace; and (2) the intersection of (possibly infinite) convex sets is also convex.*

With this proposition we can prove that

PROPOSITION 3. *RASP encryption is convexity preserving.*

PROOF. We assume an original convex set in $\mathbb{R}^k$ (that is closed) is the intersection of a set of halfspaces $\bigcap H_i$, where a halfspace

H_i can be represented as $\mathbf{w}_i^T\mathbf{x} \leq a_i$ ("=" for the closed set), and $\mathbf{w}_i \in \mathbb{R}^k$ and $a_i \in \mathbb{R}$ are parameters for the halfspace. By replacing $\mathbf{x}$ with a column vector $\mathbf{z} = (\mathbf{x}^T, 1, v)^T$ and $\mathbf{w}_i$ with $\mathbf{u}_i = (\mathbf{w}_i^T, -a_i, 0)^T$, the set enclosed by H_i is transformed to the set enclosed by the halfspace H_i^{ext}: $\mathbf{u}_i^T\mathbf{z} \leq 0$. With the RASP function, we have $\mathbf{y} = A\mathbf{z}$, and thus this halfspace H_i^{ext} can be further transformed to H_i' as follows

$$\mathbf{u}_i^T A^{-1}\mathbf{y} \leq 0. \quad (3)$$

Each of the halfspace conditions, H_i', in the transformed space represents a convex set. Thus, the intersection of them is convex as well. Therefore, the RASP encryption is convexity preserving. □

Since a range query defines a convex set, the transformation method (Eq. 3) gives a basic method for transforming the range query for the RASP encrypted data - we name it RASP query transformation method. The following proposition shows that by searching with the transformed conditions in the encrypted data space, we can get the exact set of points that is the image of the query result in the original data space.

PROPOSITION 4. *Let H_i and H_i' be halfspaces defined as in the proof of Proposition 3. The RASP query transformation uniquely maps the convex set S enclosed by halfspaces $\bigcap H_i$ to the convex set S' enclosed by $\bigcap H_i'$.*

It is straightforward to show that by using the RASP query transformation, any point in S cannot be mapped to a point outside S' and any point not in S cannot be mapped to a point in S'. So we skip the details of the proof.

Note that duplicate records in the original set might be mapped to different records in the encrypted space due to the randomly generated additional dimension $k + 2$. However, this query transformation method guarantees all of such records are still exactly found in the encrypted space. This proposition forms the basis for the proposed query processing strategy, which will be discussed in details.

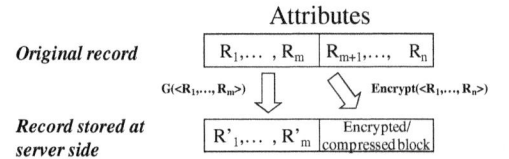

Figure 2: The records stored on the server.

Generating Auxiliary Vectors for Outsourcing. With the RASP encryption function, we generate the outsourced data as follows. First, we normalize each attribute to avoid the attacks based on the value ranges. The normalization process is briefly described as follows. Let the mean of the attribute distribution be μ_i and the variance be σ_i^2. For any value x of the i-th attribute, the transformation $(x - \mu_i)/\sigma_i$ is applied. For the sake of simplifying presentation, we assume the data columns are already normalized - when we say the vector $\mathbf{x}$ we mean it is the normalized version. Second, we assign an unintelligible name to each attribute, e.g. "X_1" for the first attribute. Finally, Eq. 1 is applied to the searchable dimensions $\mathbf{x}$ to generate the encrypted auxiliary record $\mathbf{y}$. $\mathbf{y}$ and the original record that is compressed and encrypted with any existing methods are used for outsourcing (as shown in Figure 2). The service provider may build indices or perform linear scan on the auxiliary data vectors to answer queries. The cost for generating an outsourced record consists of one RASP encryption perturbation

252

$(\mathcal{O}(k^2)$ multiplications; k is the number of searchable dimensions) and the compression/encryption operations applied to the whole record. Here note that the RASP transformation is applied only to those attributes that are actually queried. Thus like mentioned earlier, conventional encryption can be used on compressed values of attributes that will not be queried.

4. EFFICIENT RANGE QUERY PROCESSING WITH RASP

We have shown that the RASP encryption is convexity preserving. This result is closely related to how a query can be transformed and processed. A range query can be represented as a convex set query. Thus, in the encrypted space there is a unique convex set that is the answer to the query. However, there are challenges in (1) efficiently processing it, and (2) making sure query processing does not reveal significant information about the encryption key and the original data. One may already notice that the simple query transformation method described in this section is vulnerable to attacks. However, in this section, we will focus on the first challenge. It will be revisited and significantly improved in security analysis in Section 5.

In the encrypted space, a simple dimensional condition in the original space is transformed to a general halfspace condition (as Figure 4 shows). It would be straightforward to scan each auxiliary vector with the transformed conditions and return the result. We want to explore more efficient index-based processing methods in this section. The normal processing strategies are based on multidimensional index trees, such as R-Tree [28], that handles axis-aligned minimum bounding boxes (MBR). If we still depend on multidimensional tree indexing to process the transformed queries, the processing algorithm should be slightly modified to handle arbitrary convex areas, the boundaries of which are not necessarily axis-aligned. We will start with the method of query transformation, briefly discuss the normal range query processing algorithms using multidimensional indices, and then present the proposed solution for processing the transformed queries.

4.1 Query Transformation

Since the auxiliary vectors are in the encrypted space, to query on this space, range queries should also be appropriately transformed. We have mentioned that the transformation method used in proving Proposition 3 can be used for query transformation. In this section, we discuss how to transform an original range query into the encrypted space in details.

First, let's look at the general form of a range query condition. Let X_i be an attribute in the database. A simple condition in a range query involves only one attribute and is of the form "X_i $<op>$ a_i", where a_i is a constant in the normalized domain of X_i and $op \in \{<, >, =, \leq, \geq, \neq\}$ is a comparison operator. For convenience we will only discuss how to process $X_i \leq a_i$, while the proposed method can be slightly changed for other conditions. Any complicated range query can be transformed into the disjunction of a set of conjunctions, i.e., $\bigcup_{j=1}^{n}(\bigcap_{i=1}^{m} C_{i,j})$, where m, n are some integers depending on the original query conditions and $C_{i,j}$ is a simple condition about X_i. Again, to simplify the presentation we restrict our discussion to single conjunction condition $\cap_{i=1}^{m} C_i$. A simple condition $X_i \leq a_i$ is a halfspace condition. Following the previous discussion, $X_i \leq a_i$ is converted to the extended vector representation first: $\mathbf{u}^T \mathbf{z} \leq 0$, where $\mathbf{u}$ is a $k+2$ dimensional vector with $u_i = 1, u_{k+1} = -a_i$, and $u_j = 0$ for $j \neq i, k+1$, (for $X_i \geq a_i$, $u_i = -1, u_{k+1} = a_i$), and $\mathbf{z} = (\mathbf{x}^T, 1, v)^T$. Then, let

$\mathbf{y}$ be the auxiliary vector, i.e., $\mathbf{y} = A\mathbf{z}$. The original condition is transformed to the form of Eq. 3 in the encrypted space.

As Proposition 4 shows, searching with the transformed queries on the auxiliary vectors is equivalent to searching with the original queries and data. Note that this simple query transformation is vulnerable to attacks as shown in Section 5.2; we will eventually use slightly different query transformation method. (In the Appendix, we also give the details of the transformed query.) Next, we show how to efficiently process these transformed queries.

4.2 A Two-Stage Query Processing Strategy with Multidimensional Index Tree

With the transformed queries, the first important task is to process queries efficiently. A commonly used method is to use tree indices to improve the search performance. However, multidimensional tree indices are normally used to process axis-aligned "bounding boxes"; whereas, the transformed queries are in arbitrary convex shape, not necessarily aligned to axes. In this section, we propose a two stage query processing strategy to handle such irregular shape queries in the encrypted space. First, we briefly introduce the query processing algorithm based on multidimensional index trees. Then, we describe the two stage processing algorithm.

Multidimensional Index Tree. Most multidimensional indexing algorithms are derived from R-tree like algorithms [19], where the minimum bounding region (MBR) is the construction block for the multidimensional data. For 2D data, an MBR is a rectangle. For higher dimensions, the concept of a MBR is extended to a hypercube. Figure 3 shows the MBRs in the R-tree for a 2D dataset, where each node is bounded by a node MBR.

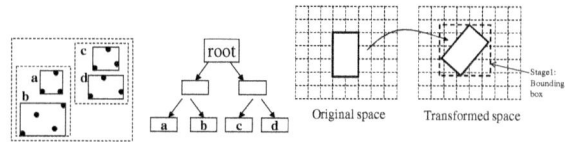

Figure 3: R-tree index.

Figure 4: Illustration of the two-stage processing algorithm.

Range query processing with a multidimensional indexing tree can be described as follows. The conjunction of a set of simple range conditions can be represented as a query MBR. The goal is to find the MBRs in the tree that are contained by or intersected with the search MBR. If the query MBR contains a node MBR, all points in the subtree should be included in the query result. If the query MBR intersects a node MBR, further checking should be performed for the children nodes. If the query MBR intersects a leaf MBR, each point included by the leaf node should be checked and only those inside the query MBR are selected.

The Two-Stage Processing Algorithm. The transformed query describes an irregular convex shape that cannot be directly processed by multidimensional tree algorithms. New tree search algorithms can be designed to use arbitrary polyhedron conditions, i.e., the transformed query, directly for search. However, we use a simpler two-stage solution that keeps the existing tree search algorithms unchanged.

At the first stage, the proxy in the client side finds the MBR of polyhedron (as a part of the submitted transformed query) and the server uses the MBR to find the initial result set. We use the simple *vertex-based algorithm* for finding the MBR of the polyhedron. The original query condition constructs a hyper-cube shape. With the query transformation, the vertices of the hyper cube are also transformed to vertices of the polyhedron. Therefore, we can calculate the MBR with only the transformed vertices. Figure 4 illustrates the relationship between the vertices and the MBR. There are a maximum number of 2^k vertices for one conjunctive range query condition on k dimensions, i.e., each dimension has its lower and upper bounds. It is straightforward to construct these vertices based on the dimensional bounds. In practice, the MBR of the polyhedron needs to be calculated by the proxy server for security reason, and then sent to the server together with the transformed queries.

At the second stage, the server uses the transformed halfspace conditions [3] to filter the initial result and find the final result. In most cases, the initial result set will be reasonably small so that it can be filtered in memory with linear scan. In the worst case, the MBR of the polyhedron will possibly enclose the entire dataset and the second stage is reduced to linear scan of the entire dataset.

Cost Analysis. Assume the query ranges are selected uniformly at random. For small ranges the first stage average cost is $\mathcal{O}(\log_B N)$ index block accesses plus a few of data block accesses [28], where N is the number of records and B is the number of children an index node has. Due to the randomness associated with the RASP transformation, the data distribution, and the unpredictable query ranges, the cost to get the initial result could vary, which will be investigated in experiments. If the initial result has n records, a linear scan at the 2nd stage with $2k$ simple conditions will cost $\leq 2kn$ checks of the form in Eq. 3. In Section 6, we study the cost distribution between the two stages and experimentally demonstrate that this two-stage processing is efficient and orders of magnitudes faster than the linear scan approach.

5. ATTACK ANALYSIS

We categorize the possible attacks into two types: (1) Attacks on auxiliary vectors; (2) Attacks based on range queries. There has been some related work on attack analysis methods for similar encryption methods, e.g., geometric data perturbation for data mining [9], which can be migrated to analyze the first type of attacks. However, attacks on range queries are entirely new for our approach.

5.1 Attacks on Auxiliary Vectors

According to the three levels of knowledge the attacker may have, we categorize the attacks into three classes: (1) Naive estimation; (2) Distributional Attacks; and (3) Known Input/Output Attacks. Due to the random component in the RASP encryption, some attacks are actually estimation attacks, i.e., the goal of the attack is to estimate the original values. If the estimation result is sufficiently accurate, we say the encryption is broken.

5.1.1 Attack Description and Analysis

Naive Estimation. With the level 1 knowledge, the attacker observes only the encrypted data. The only attack is to blindly guess the matrix A. It has been discussed to find a matrix A to maximize the difference between the encrypted data and the original data [9]. However, since there is no way to verify how accurate a random guess is, this type of attack is ineffective, in general.

Distributional Attack. With the level 2 knowledge, the attacker also knows column domains and distributions. This knowledge can be possibly used to perform more effective attacks. In particular,

---

[3]The final form of the security-enhanced transformed query is represented with the matrices Θ_is that are described in Section 5.2.

when the original data have independent columns and no more than one column having Gaussian distribution, an attack called Independent Component Analysis (ICA) [23] can be applied to effectively recover the original data from the perturbed data. Originally developed for signal processing, ICA is used to discover components A (the mixing matrix) and X (the original signals) from the mixed data $Y = AX$. Since ICA recovers columns in an arbitrary order, it has to rely on the known distributional information to distinguish the columns and order them correctly. Furthermore, the effectiveness of ICA heavily depends on the independence of the columns and the number of columns having non-Gaussian distributions . In practice, since the independence condition and the Gaussian distribution condition are often not satisfied, the ICA attack can only result in approximate estimation to the original data. However, the previous study [9] shows that if the matrix A is not carefully selected, the ICA attack can still result in serious damage.

Another distributional attack is to enumerate the matrix A and then check the column distributions of $A^{-1}Y$ to find the best match between the known column distributions and the distributions of the estimated columns. However, since there is no constraint on the elements of A, with uniformly discretized domains, the number of candidate matrices will be extremely large. Concretely, if the discretized domain has d values, the total candidate matrices will be $d^{(k+2)^2}$, where k is the number of dimensions. Even for extremely low dimensionality, e.g., k=2, this attack could be computationally intractable.

Known Input/Output Attack. With the level 3 knowledge, the attacker knows a number of input/output (plaintext/ciphertext) record pairs. Concretely, let $P_{k \times m}$ be the known m k-dimensional original records $(\mathbf{x}_1, \ldots, \mathbf{x}_m)$, $m > k + 2$, that include $k + 2$ linearly independent records, and $Q_{k+2 \times m}$ be the corresponding perturbed $k + 2$-dimensional records $(\mathbf{y}_1, \ldots, \mathbf{y}_m)$. The typical method is to use the linear regression method to get an estimate of the key and then recover the entire original data. In the following, we show how to use the regression method to attack the encryption. Let A decomposed into blocks $A = (A_1, A_2, A_3)$, where A_1, A_2 and A_3 have block sizes $(k + 2) \times k$, $(k + 2) \times 1$ and $(k + 2) \times 1$, respectively, and the extended data be $\begin{pmatrix} P \\ \mathbf{1} \\ \mathbf{v} \end{pmatrix}$ where $\mathbf{1}$ is the row vector with '1' and $\mathbf{v}$ is a row vector with random positive values, corresponding to the two additional dimensions in RASP. Thus, the encryption can be represented as

$$Q = (A_1, A_2, A_3) \begin{pmatrix} P \\ \mathbf{1} \\ \mathbf{v} \end{pmatrix} = A_1 P + A_2 \mathbf{1} + A_3 \mathbf{v}, \quad (4)$$

where $A_2 \mathbf{1}$ is a translation matrix that adds the vector A_2 to each of the column vectors in $A_1 X$; $A_3 \mathbf{v}$ is a random noise matrix. With sufficient number of known record pairs ($m > k + 2$), first, the translation component can be canceled out; then, the regression method can be applied to estimate A_1. With the estimate $\hat{A}_1$ of A_1, A_2 can be estimated as well. Therefore, for an encrypted dataset Y, the estimate of the original data X is $\hat{X} = (\hat{A}_1^T \hat{A}_1)^{-1} \hat{A}_1^T (Y - \hat{A}_2 \mathbf{1})$.

5.1.2 Countering Attacks on Auxiliary Data

Countering ICA-based Distributional Attack. Since the enumeration based attack is computationally intractable, we focus on the ICA-based attack. We propose two approaches to increase the resilience to the attack. The first approach is to simulate the ICA attack in sufficient rounds to find a statistically resilient A matrix as the previous work does [9]. However, a more attack-resilient approach is using the composition encryption scheme (CES) that consists of two steps: transforming the original data with an order preserving encryption scheme E_o first; then followed by the basic RASP encryption, which can be represented as follows.

$$E(X, K, K_o) = A \begin{pmatrix} E_o(X, K_o) \\ 1 \\ \mathbf{v} \end{pmatrix} \quad (5)$$

We use the OPE scheme by Agarwal et al. [1] that allows us to change all column distributions to normal distributions. Thus, the requirement of non-Gaussian distribution is not satisfied, which renders ICA ineffective. Since the composition scheme is not order preserving, the attacks on OPE schemes will not be applicable either. However, can the two-stage query processing strategy still be applied? The following proposition indicates that it can still be applied.

PROPOSITION 5. *Order preserving encryption functions transform a hyper-cubic query range to another hyper-cubic query range.*

PROOF. Assume the original range query condition consists of simple conditions like $b_i \le X_i \le a_i$ for each dimension. Since the order is preserved, each simple condition is transformed as follows: $E_o(b_i) \le E_o(X_i) \le E_o(a_i)$, which means the transformed range is still a hyper-cubic query range. $\quad\square$

When processing a query, the proxy server needs to transform the ranges to OPE encrypted ranges first, and then apply the query transformation method. We will show in the experiments how the resilience to the ICA attack is improved with the composition scheme.

Countering Known Input/Output Attacks. As we have mentioned earlier, the random noise matrix $A_3\mathbf{v}$ in Eq. 4 determines how effective the linear regression estimation can be done. The more intense (in terms of variance) the noise component is, the less accurate the estimation can be. A randomly generated matrix A does not allow us to control the noise intensity, however. We propose to use the following method to generate A_3 that satisfying a specified noise intensity. (1) generate a $k + 2$ by β random matrix Ψ according to the required noise distribution and intensity, with sample size β that is sufficiently large, or larger than the maximum number of known Input/Output records that an attacker may have access to; (2) generate β positive random values $\mathbf{v}$; (3) apply $A_3 = \Psi\mathbf{v}^T/(\mathbf{v}\mathbf{v}^T)$ to get A_3. The last column of the randomly generated A is then replaced with A_3. Note here that having a value of zero for say the i-th entry in A_3 would mean that the noise values are never added to i-th attribute. So the random generation process is repeated until all elements of A_3 are not zero. Previous study shows that Principle Component Analysis (PCA) can be used to possibly filter out the noise component or reduce the effect of noise in some circumstances [22]. We will investigate the relationship between the noise component and the accuracy of estimation, and study whether PCA can help improve the estimation in experiments.

A more attack-resilient solution is using the previous discussed composition encryption scheme. If the OPE scheme uses a nonlinear transformation, the composition of OPE and RASP will create a nonlinear mapping from the original data to the encrypted data. Therefore, the linear regression attack will not be effective by simply using the known pairs of input and output records, if the OPE key is unknown.

5.2 Attacks on Transformed Queries

As we have discussed, in query processing, the proxy server will submit the MBR and the transformed query to the server. We refer to the original query as the *input* query, and the transformed query that is submitted to the server as the *output* query. With the knowledge of a number of pairs of input/output queries, the following attacks can be performed on the current query conditions, e.g., $\mathbf{u}^T A^{-1}\mathbf{y} \le 0$, to break the encryption.

5.2.1 Attack Description and Analysis

First, we will show that the row vectors of A^{-1} can be probed if the attacker has the level 3 knowledge on query conditions. Second, we show a more serious attack that can reveal columns of data if the attacker has the level 2 knowledge about dimension distributions.

A^{-1} **Probing Attack.** With the level 3 knowledge, the attacker knows a pair of input query conditions on the same dimension, say $X_i \le a_i$ and $X_i \le b_i$, and their output forms, $\mathbf{u}_{a_i}^T A^{-1}\mathbf{y} \le 0$ and $\mathbf{u}_{b_i}^T A^{-1}\mathbf{y} \le 0$, respectively. Then, $\mathbf{u}_{a_i}^T A^{-1}\mathbf{y} - \mathbf{u}_{a_i}^T A^{-1}\mathbf{y} = \mathbf{u}_{a_i-b_i}^T A^{-1}\mathbf{y}$, where $\mathbf{u}_{a_i-b_i}^T = (0, \ldots, a_i - b_i, 0)$, only the non-zero $(k+1)$-th element remains. Let $\mathbf{r}_j$ be the j-th row of A^{-1}. The constant part of the condition represents $(a_i - b_i)\mathbf{r}_{k+1}$, thus revealing $\mathbf{r}_{k+1}$. While the single condition like $\mathbf{u}_{a_i}^T A^{-1}\mathbf{y} \le 0$ has the constant part $\mathbf{r}_i + a_i\mathbf{r}_{k+1}$, with known a_i and $\mathbf{r}_{k+1}$, $\mathbf{r}_i$ can be revealed. Repeating this process for all dimensions with known input/output conditions, the attacker can recover $k + 1$ rows of the matrix A^{-1}, which leaves very weak security.

Dimensional Selection Attack. With the level 2 knowledge, i.e., the column domains and the column distributions, the attacker can perform a *dimensional selection attack*. Assume the condition is applied to some unknown dimension i. Applying the query parameters $\mathbf{u}_i^T A^{-1}$ to each record $\mathbf{y}$ in the server, the attacker can get $\mathbf{u}_i^T A^{-1}\mathbf{y} = x_i - a_i$, where x_i is the i-th dimension of the corresponding original record $\mathbf{x}$. After getting all the values, the attacker can build up a histogram to compare with the known column distributions. It is thus easy to identify what dimension is queried. With the knowledge of the column domain, the constant a_i can be easily removed, which leads to complete breach of the entire column i.

In summary, the original query transformation method can be exploited to construct very effective attacks. It needs to be carefully redesigned to address these attacks.

5.2.2 Countering Query-based Attacks

The additional dimension X_{k+2} is used to construct secure query conditions. Instead of processing a half space condition $X_i \le a_i$, we use $(X_i - a_i)X_{k+2} \le 0$ instead. These two conditions are equivalent because the additional dimension X_{k+2} satisfies $X_{k+2} > 0$. Using the extended vector form $\mathbf{z}^T = (\mathbf{x}^T, 1, v)$, we have $X_i - a_i = \mathbf{z}^T\mathbf{u}$ and $X_{k+2} = \mathbf{w}^T\mathbf{z}$, where $u_i = 1$, $u_{k+1} = -a_i$, $u_j = 0$, for $j \ne i, k+1$; $w_{k+2} = 1$ and $w_j = 0$, for $j \ne k + 2$. With the transformation $\mathbf{y} = A\mathbf{z}$, we get the transformed quadratic query condition

$$\mathbf{y}^T (A^{-1})^T \mathbf{u}\mathbf{w}^T A^{-1}\mathbf{y} \le 0. \quad (6)$$

Let $\Theta = (A^{-1})^T \mathbf{u}\mathbf{w}^T A^{-1}$. In the two-stage processing strategy, the bounding box of the transformed query area is calculated in the proxy server as we discussed earlier. Then, this bounding box and the parameters Θ_i for each condition i, are submitted to the server. Thus, assume each dimension is represented with two half space conditions, the encrypted query E_Q is represented as {MBR, $\{\Theta_1, \ldots, \Theta_{2k}\}$}. The server will use the bounding box to get the first-stage results and then use the conditions, e.g., $\mathbf{y}^T\Theta_i\mathbf{y} \leq 0$, to filter out the results. We now show that this query transformation is resilient to both query-based attacks.

Assume the attacker knows two pairs of input/output query conditions, e.g., for $X_i \leq a_i$ and $X_i \leq b_i$. We use the same method used in the A^{-1} probing attack to find the difference of the two conditions. Let Θ_a and Θ_b notate the parameters for these two conditions, respectively. The simplified form for a single condition, e.g., Θ_a, is $(\mathbf{r}_i^T - a_i\mathbf{r}_{k+1}^T)\mathbf{r}_{k+2}$, where $\mathbf{r}_i, \mathbf{r}_{k+1}$, and $\mathbf{r}_{k+2}$ are the row vectors of matrix A^{-1}. Thus, the result of $\Theta_a - \Theta_b$ is $(b_i - a_i)\mathbf{r}_{k+1}^T\mathbf{r}_{k+2}$. But knowing $\Theta_a, \Theta_b, a_i, b_i$ does not help find the unknown vectors — in fact there are an infinite number of solutions because $\mathbf{r}_{k+1} = \frac{(\Theta_a - \Theta_b)\mathbf{r}_{k+2}}{(b_i - a_i)\|\mathbf{r}_{k+2}\|}$. Therefore, knowing pairs of input/ouput queries does not help probing A^{-1}.

This quadratic query transformation method counters the dimensional selection attack as well. For any perturbed record $\mathbf{y}$, $\mathbf{y}^T\Theta_a\mathbf{y}$ recovers $(x_i - a_i)x_{k+2}$, where x_i and x_{k+2} are the dimensional values of the corresponding original vector $\mathbf{x}$. Since x_{k+2} is a randomly generated positive value, knowing X_i's domain and distribution does not help recover x_i. Therefore, dimensional selection attack does not work either.

In the appendix, we put together all the algorithms after considering the attacks discussed in this section.

6. EXPERIMENTS

In this section, we present three sets of experimental results to investigate the following questions: (1) How costly are the RASP encryption scheme and the composition scheme involving OPE scheme? (2) How effective are the ICA attack and the known input/output attack, if the composition scheme is not applied? (3) How efficient is the two-phase query processing?

6.1 Setup

Two datasets are used in experiments: (1) a synthetic dataset that draws samples from uniform distribution in the range [0, 1]; and (2) the Adult dataset from UCI machine learning database[4]. For the adult dataset, we assign numeric values to the categorical values using a simple one-to-one mapping scheme. For each dataset, we generate multiple versions with different numbers of records by using sampling with replacement. We also change the dimensionality of the datasets by randomly selecting a number of dimensions of the data. All experiments were done in a quad-core AMD Opteron server (2.5GHz CPU and 120GB memory).

6.2 Cost of Encryption

In this experiment, we study the cost of the components in the composition scheme. We implement the OPE scheme [1] by mapping original column distributions to normal distributions. The OPE algorithm partitions the target distribution into buckets, first. Then, the sorted original values are proportionally partitioned according to the target bucket distribution to create the buckets for the original distribution. With the aligned original and target buckets, an original value can be mapped to the target bucket and appropriately scaled. Therefore, the encryption cost mainly comes from the bucket search procedure (proportional to $\log D$, where D is the number of buckets). Both encryption schemes are implemented with Matlab. Figure 5 shows the cost distribution for 20K records at different number of dimensions of data for the two components in the composite scheme. The dimensionality has less effect on the cost of RASP than on that of OPE.

---

[4]http://archive.ics.uci.edu/ml/

6.3 Resilience to Estimation Attacks

We have discussed the methods for countering the estimation attacks, primarily the ICA attack and the known input/output attack. In this set of experiments, we explore the resilience of both the RASP-Only scheme and the composition scheme to the estimation attacks. Although the composition scheme is more resilient to attacks, it incurs the additional cost that might not be favored by some applications. Therefore, it is worth looking at how resilient the RASP-Only scheme is to the attacks.

Metric for Evaluating Estimation Attacks. The accuracy of estimation attacks can be evaluated with the well-known mean square error (MSE). Let the number of records be n and the value of the i-th attribute in the j-th record be $x_{i,j}$ and the corresponding estimated value be $\hat{x}_{i,j}$. Model the i-th attribute with a random variable X_i and its estimate as $\hat{X}_i$. The estimation error can be estimated with the root of mean square error (RMSE): $m_i = \sqrt{1/n \sum_{j=1}^{n} (x_{i,j} - \hat{x}_{i,j})^2}$, i.e., $X_i = \hat{X}_i \pm m_i$. $2m_i$ can be used to roughly represent the effective estimation range. Apparently, m_i has different meaning for different value range. For example, ± 10 means ineffective estimation for an attribute "age" (in the range [0,100]), while very effective for "salary" (often > 10000). One of the common methods is to normalize all attributes to approximately the same range. For large data, the assumption that each attribute has approximately normal distribution would be reasonable [25]. Therefore, standardization can be used to normalize all attributes to normal distribution with mean zero and standard deviation one. For a standardized domain, four times of the standard deviation (i.e., $4\sigma = 4$) covers the majority of records (> 95%). Then, we can use the rate $p_i = 2m_i/(4\sigma) = m_i/2$ to represent the relative effectiveness of the estimation attack. The larger the m_i, the less effective the estimation is. To evaluate the resilience across all attributes, we also define dataset-wise metrics, such as the minimum security guarantee $p^{min} = \min\{p_i, 1 \leq i \leq k\}$, which is used in our experiment.

Results. We simulate the ICA attack for randomly chosen matrices A. The data used in the experiment is the 10-dimension Adult data with 10K records. The x-axis in Figure 6 represents the sequence number of randomly chosen matrix A and the y-axis represents the minimum security guarantee among all dimensions. The label "Best" means the most resilient A to the ICA attack; "Worst" means the A shows the weakest resilience; "Average" is the progressive average resilience for the generated A matrices. Figure 6 shows that the effectiveness of the ICA attack can vary with different matrices A and we can find some ones that are more resilient to the attack. In addition, if applied is the composition method that uses the OPE scheme to change column distributions to Gaussian distributions, the resilience of a randomly chosen A is significantly increased.

We also simulate the known input/output attack with a number of randomly selected input/output records pairs (10% of the entire dataset). The original data is generated with the method mentioned in Section 5.2.2 by generating the noise matrix with standard normal distribution $N(0, 1)$. Due to the randomness, we repeat the experiment 10 times and record the variance of the estimation. The PCA based noise filtering technique [22] is also applied as a part of the attack. Let Y be the encrypted data. The PCA method finds the eigenvalue decomposition of YY^T. Let Q be the eigenvectors corresponding to the largest p preserved eigenvalues (i.e., the principal components). The noise filtering algorithm uses YQQ^T to represent Y. Figure 7 shows the result for the known I/O attack

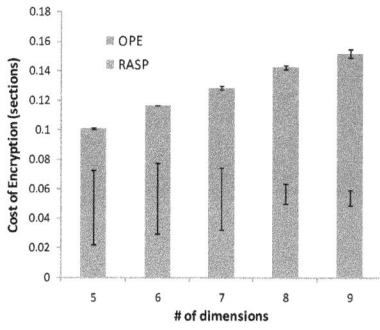

Figure 5: The cost distribution of the composition encryption scheme. Data: Adult (20K records,5-9 dimensions)

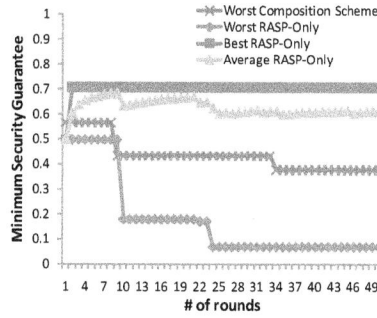

Figure 6: Randomly generated matrix A and the resilience to ICA attack. Data: Adult (10dimensions, 10K records)

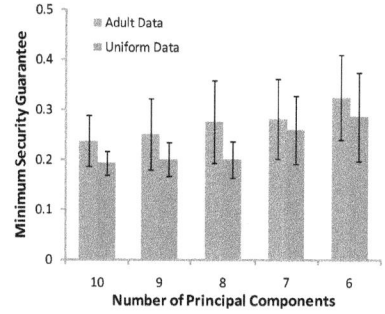

Figure 7: Known input/output attacks on both Adult and Uniform data.

with the PCA noise filtering step. The x-axis represents the number of principal components preserved. Since the data dimensionality is 10, 10 principal components means no noise reduction is applied. For both datasets, the average estimation errors are higher than 0.2. Also, the PCA noise filtering does not help much — when the number of principle components is reduced (trying to remove the noises), the estimation error does not reduce. This result shows that with appropriately set noise component, the known I/O attack is not effective either.

6.4 Performance of Two-stage Range Query Processing

In this set of experiments, we study the performance aspects of polyhedron range query processing. We use the two-stage processing strategy described in Section 4, and explore the additional cost incurred by this processing strategy. We implement the two-stage query processing based on an R*-tree implementation provided by Dr. Hadjieleftheriou at AT&T Lab http://www2.research.att.com/ marioh/spatialindex/. The block size is 4KB and we allow each block to contain only 20 entries to mimic a large database with many disk blocks. Samples from the three databases in different size (10,000 − 50,000 records, i.e., 500-2500 data blocks) are encrypted as the auxiliary data and then indexed for query processing. Another set of indices are also built on the original data for setting up the performance baseline of query processing on non-encrypted data. We will use the number of disk block accesses, including index blocks and data blocks, to assess the performance to avoid the possible variation caused by other parts of the computer system. In addition, we also show the wall-clock time for some results for comparison.

Recall the two-stage processing strategy: (1) calculate the MBR of the transformed query and use the MBR to search the indexing tree; (2) filter the returned result with the transformed query. We will study the performance of the first stage by comparing it to two additional methods: (1) the original queries with the index built on the original data, which is used to identify how much additional cost is paid for querying the MBR of the transformed query; (2) the linear scan approach, which is the worst case cost. Range queries are generated randomly within the domain of the datasets, and then transformed with the method described in the Section 4.1. We also control the range of the queries to be [10%,20%,30%,40%,50%] of the total range of the domain, to observe the effect of the scale of the range to the performance of query processing.

Results. The first pair of figures (the left subfigures of Figure 8 and 9) shows the number of block accesses for 10,000 queries on differ-

ent sizes of data with different query processing methods. For clear presentation, we use $\log_{10}$(# of block accesses) as the y-axis. The cost of linear scan is simply the number of blocks for storing the whole dataset. The data dimensionality is fixed to 5 and the query range is set to 30% of the whole domain. Obviously, the first stage with MBR for polyhedron has a cost much cheaper than the linear scan method and only moderately higher than R*tree processing on the original data. Interestingly, different distributions of data result in slightly different patterns. The costs of R*tree on transformed queries are very close to those of original queries for Adult data, while the gap is larger on uniform data. The costs over different dimensions and different query ranges show similar patterns.

	Linear Scan	R*Tree-Orig	Stage-1	Stage-2	rpq	purity
Uniform	6.32	0.132	0.805	0.041	60	1.3%
Adult	5.42	0.091	0.20	0.017	24	2.2%

Table 1: Wall clock cost distribution and comparison.

We also studied the cost of the second stage. We use "purity" to represent the rate (final result count)/(1st stage result count), and records per query (RPQ) to represent the average number of records per query for the first stage results. The quadratic filtering conditions are used in experiments. Table 1 compares the average wall-clock time (milliseconds) per query for the two stages, the RPQ values for stage 1, and the purity of the stage-1 result. The tests are run with the setting of 10K queries, 20K records, 30% dimensional query range and 5 dimensions. Since the 2nd stage is done in memory, its cost is much lower than the 1st-stage cost. Overall, the two stage processing is much faster than linear scan and comparable to the original R*Tree processing.

7. RELATED WORK

We review the two most related methods: OPE and crypto-index first, and then give other related work.

OPE. As the name indicates, order preserving encryption (OPE) [1] preserves the dimensional value order after encryption. It can be described as a function $y = F(x), \forall x_i, x_j, x_i < (>, =)x_j \Leftrightarrow y_i < (>, =)y_j$. A well-known attack is based on attacker's prior knowledge of original distributions of attribute values. If the attacker knows the original distributions and manages to identify the mapping between the original attribute and its encrypted counterpart, the following bucket-based attack can be performed to break the encryption for the attribute. (1) Model the original distribution for the attribute with a histogram of a number of buckets; (2)

257

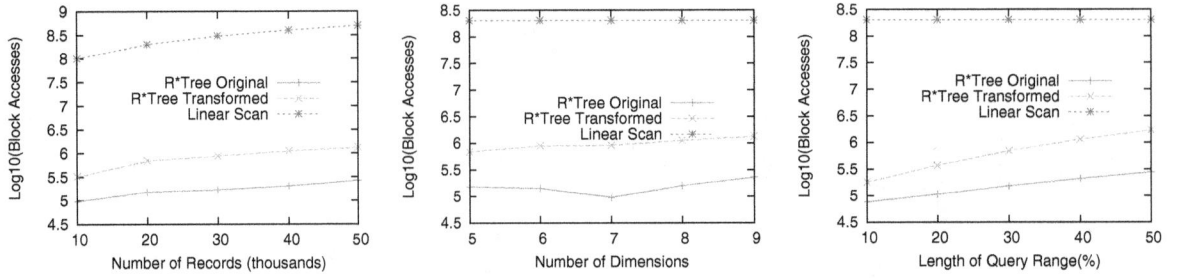

Figure 8: Performance comparison on Uniform data. Left: data size vs. cost of query; Middle: data dimensionality vs. cost of query; Right: query range (percentage of the domain) vs. cost of query

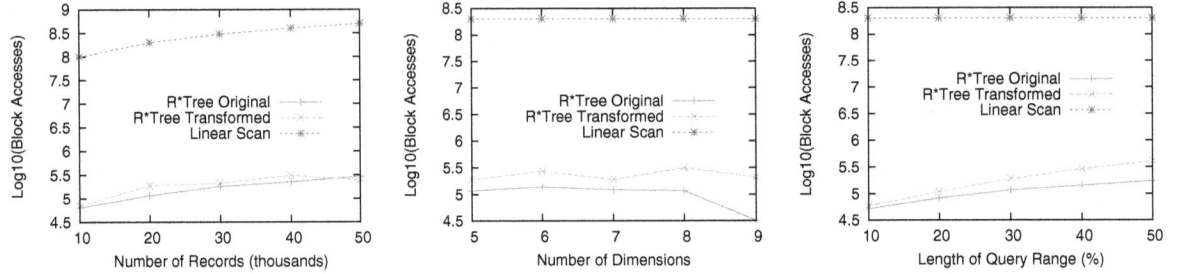

Figure 9: Performance comparison on Adult data. Left: data size vs. cost of query; Middle: data dimensionality vs. cost of query; Right: query range (percentage of the domain) vs. cost of query

Calculate the percentage of each bucket to the entire distribution; (3) Sort the encrypted values; (4) According the bucket's percentages, sequentially partition the sorted encrypted values to generate buckets; (4) Sequentially map the encrypted buckets to the original buckets and get the estimate of the encrypted value. The precision of estimation is determined by the width of the buckets - the narrower the buckets are the higher the precision will be. Since the number of buckets can be arbitrarily chosen, the bucket width can be very small. It is also not difficult to get the mapping between the original attribute and the encrypted attribute, if the attacker knows a number of plain queries and their encrypted queries. In developing our schemes, we have carefully studied whether the known query patterns will also damage the proposed encryption scheme in our framework.

Crypto-Index. Crypto-Index is also based on column-wise bucketization. It assigns a random ID to each bucket; the values in the bucket are replaced with the bucket ID to generate the auxiliary data for indexing. To utilize the index for query processing, a normal range query condition has to be transformed to a set-based query on the bucket IDs. For example, $X_i < a_i$ might be replaced with $X'_i \in [ID_1, ID_2, ID3]$. If the attacker manages to know the mapping between the input original query and the output bucket-based query, the range that a bucket ID represents could be estimated. The width of the bucket determines how precise the estimation could be done. A bucket-diffusion scheme [21] was proposed to address this problem, which, however, has to sacrifice the precision of query results. Another drawback of this method is that the client, not the server, has to filter out the query result. Low precision results raise large burden on the network and the client system. Furthermore, due to the randomized bucket IDs, the index built on bucket IDs is not so efficient for processing range queries as the index on OPE encrypted data is.

Other Related Work. Private information retrieval (PIR) [10, 24] tries to fully preserve the privacy of access pattern, while the data may not be encrypted. PIR schemes are normally very costly. Focusing on the efficiency side of PIR, Williams et al. [32] use a pyramid hash index to implement efficient privacy preserving datablock operations based on the idea of Oblivious RAM [16]. It is different from our setting of high throughput range query processing. Another line of research [5, 29] facilitates authorized users to access only the portion of data in the authorized range with a public key scheme. The underlying identity based encryption used in these schemes does not produce indexable encrypted data. Also the setting for which Shi et al. [29] propose the multidimensional range query is different from ours. The untrusted service provider in our setting is responsible for both indexing and query processing. Secure keyword search on encrypted documents [30, 17, 14, 4, 11] scans each encrypted document in the database and finds the documents containing the keyword, which is more like point search in database. The research on privacy preserving data mining has discussed multiplicative perturbation methods [7, 9, 27, 26, 18], which are similar to the RASP encryption, but with more emphasis on preserving the utility for data mining.

8. CONCLUSION AND FUTURE WORK

In this paper we propose the random space encryption approach to efficient range queries over encrypted data and analyze the unique attacks to this approach. Our approach uses a random space transformation to generate indexable auxiliary data. The auxiliary data is exported to the service provider, indexed and used for processing range queries. We present an efficient server-side two-stage query processing strategy. Experimental results show that this processing strategy is highly efficient. In addition, we analyzed the attacks on encrypted data and queries. Experiments are performed to show the resilience of the encryption to estimation attacks. Note that this

258

attack analysis is just the first step to rigorous analysis of security. We will continue to explore more attacks and formally study the security. As an important extension to our approach, we would like to further investigate how database update operations, such as record deletions, insertions, and updates, affect data utility and security. The goal is to allow the data owner and authorized users update the encrypted data without undermining the security.

9. REFERENCES

[1] R. Agrawal, J. Kiernan, R. Srikant, and Y. Xu, "Order preserving encryption for numeric data," in *Proceedings of ACM SIGMOD Conference*, 2004.

[2] R. Agrawal and R. Srikant, "Privacy-preserving data mining," in *Proceedings of ACM SIGMOD Conference*. Dallas, Texas: ACM, 2000.

[3] A. Boldyreva, N. Chenette, Y. Lee, and A. O'Neill, "Order preserving symmetric encryption," in *Proceedings of EUROCRYPT conference*, 2009.

[4] D. Boneh, G. D. Crescenzo, R. Ostrovsky, and G. Persiano, "Public-key encryption with keyword search," in *Proceedings of Advances in Cryptology, (EUROCRYPT)*. Springer, 2004.

[5] D. Boneh and B. Waters, "Conjunctive, subset, and range queries on encrypted data," in *the Theory of Cryptography Conference (TCC*. Springer, 2007, pp. 535–554.

[6] S. Boyd and L. Vandenberghe, *Convex Optimization*. Cambridge University Press, 2004.

[7] K. Chen and L. Liu, "A random rotation perturbation approach to privacy preserving data classification," in *Proceedings of International Conference on Data Mining (ICDM)*. Houston, TX: IEEE, 2005.

[8] K. Chen and L. Liu, "A survey of multiplicative data perturbation for privacy preserving data mining," *Privacy-Preserving Data Mining: Models and Algorithms, Edited by Charu C. Aggarwal and Philip S. Yu*, 2008.

[9] K. Chen, L. Liu, and G. Sun, "Towards attack-resilient geometric data perturbation," in *SIAM Data Mining Conference*, 2007.

[10] B. Chor, E. Kushilevitz, O. Goldreich, and M. Sudan, "Private information retrieval," *ACM Computer Survey*, vol. 45, no. 6, pp. 965–981, 1998.

[11] R. Curtmola, J. Garay, S. Kamara, and R. Ostrovsky, "Searchable symmetric encryption: improved definitions and efficient constructions," in *Proceedings of the 13th ACM conference on Computer and communications security*. New York, NY, USA: ACM, 2006, pp. 79–88.

[12] I. Gartner, "Server storage and raid worldwide," *Technical Report*, 1999.

[13] C. Gentry, "Fully homomorphic encryption using ideal lattices," in *STOC '09: Proceedings of the 41st annual ACM symposium on Theory of computing*. New York, NY, USA: ACM, 2009, pp. 169–178.

[14] E.-J. Goh, "Secure indexes," Cryptology ePrint Archive, Report 2003/216, 2003, http://eprint.iacr.org/2003/216/.

[15] O. Goldreich, *Foundations of Cryptography*. Cambridge University Press, 2001.

[16] O. Goldreich and R. Ostrovsky, "Software protection and simulation on oblivious ram," *Journal of the ACM*, vol. 43, pp. 431–473, 1996.

[17] P. Golle, J. Staddon, and B. Waters, "Secure conjunctive keyword search over encrypted data," in *ACNS 04: 2nd International Conference on Applied Cryptography and Network Security*. Springer-Verlag, 2004, pp. 31–45.

[18] S. Guo and X. Wu, "Deriving private information from arbitrarily projected data," in *Proceedings of the 11th European Conference on Principles and Practice of Knowledge Discovery in Databases (PKDD07)*, Warsaw, Poland, Sept 2007.

[19] A. Guttman, "R-trees: A dynamic index structure for spatial searching," in *SIGMOD'84, Proceedings of Annual Meeting, Boston, Massachusetts, June 18-21, 1984*, B. Yormark, Ed. ACM Press, 1984, pp. 47–57.

[20] H. Hacigumus, B. Iyer, C. Li, and S. Mehrotra, "Executing sql over encrypted data in the database-service-provider model," in *Proceedings of ACM SIGMOD Conference*, 2002.

[21] B. Hore, S. Mehrotra, and G. Tsudik, "A privacy-preserving index for range queries," in *Proceedings of Very Large Databases Conference (VLDB)*, 2004.

[22] Z. Huang, W. Du, and B. Chen, "Deriving private information from randomized data," in *Proceedings of ACM SIGMOD Conference*, 2005.

[23] A. Hyvarinen, J. Karhunen, and E. Oja, *Independent Component Analysis*. Wiley, 2001.

[24] E. Kushilevitz and R. Ostrovsky, "Replication is not needed: Single database, computationally-private information retrieval," in *In Proc. of the 38th Annu. IEEE Symp. on Foundations of Computer Science*, 1997, pp. 364–373.

[25] E. L. Lehmann and G. Casella, *Theory of Point Estimation*. Springer-Verlag, 1998.

[26] K. Liu, C. Giannella, and H. Kargupta, "An attacker's view of distance preserving maps for privacy preserving data mining," in *European Conference on Principles and Practice of Knowledge Discovery in Databases (PKDD)*, Berlin, Germany, September 2006.

[27] K. Liu, H. Kargupta, and J. Ryan, "Random projection-based multiplicative data perturbation for privacy preserving distributed data mining," *IEEE Transactions on Knowledge and Data Engineering (TKDE)*, vol. 18, no. 1, pp. 92–106, 2006.

[28] Y. Manolopoulos, A. Nanopoulos, A. Papadopoulos, and Y. Theodoridis, *R-trees: Theory and Applications*. Springer-Verlag, 2005.

[29] E. Shi, J. Bethencourt, T.-H. H. Chan, D. Song, and A. Perrig, "Multi-dimensional range query over encrypted data," in *IEEE Symposium on Security and Privacy*, 2007.

[30] D. X. Song, D. Wagner, and A. Perrig, "Practical techniques for searches on encrypted data," in *IEEE Symposium on Security and Privacy*. Washington, DC, USA: IEEE Computer Society, 2000, p. 44.

[31] H. Wang and L. V. S. Lakshmanan, "Efficient secure query evaluation over encrypted xml databases," in *VLDB '06: Proceedings of the 32nd international conference on Very large data bases*. VLDB Endowment, 2006, pp. 127–138.

[32] P. Williams, R. Sion, and B. Carbunar, "Building castles out of mud: Practical access pattern privacy and correctness on untrusted storage," in *ACM Conference on Computer and Communications Security*, 2008.

[33] W. Wong, D. W. Cheung, B. Kao, and N. Mamoulis, "Secure knn computation on encrypted databases," in *Proceedings of ACM SIGMOD Conference*, 2009.

Appendix: the Attack-Resilient Algorithms

There are four key algorithms in the proposed research — two deployed at the proxy server: (1) Data Encryption and Decryption; (2) Query Transformation and Encryption; and two at the service provider: (3) Data Indexing; (4) Query Processing. We will use the existing multidimensional tree algorithms for data indexing, thus we skip the procedure (3). For simplicity, we process the conditions like $X_i \leq a_i$ or $X_i \geq b_i$. The algorithms can be slightly changed to handle other types of conditions.

In Algorithm 1, the key matrix A is generated with the resilience to known input/output attack in mind. First, A is randomly generated with elements drawn from a random real number generator R_A (We used the normal distribution N(0,1) for R_A in experiments). Second, according to the desired noise distribution (i.e., $N(0, \sigma^2)$) for enhancing the resilience to known input/output attack, the algorithm described in Section 5.1 is used to find the last column of A (i.e., A_3) and A_3 replaces the last column of the generated A. The invertibility of A is checked to make sure decryption can be done. The data encryption function extends each original data vector $\mathbf{x}$ to the $(k + 2)$ dimensional vector with the homogeneous $(k + 1)$-th dimension and the random positive $(k + 2)$-th dimension with the random real number generator R_α. Then, it uses an OPE scheme E_o to transform the original k dimensions, followed by the RASP encryption with the key matrix A. Note that the proxy server needs only A and the key for OPE in decryption.

In Algorithm 2, the query transformation and encryption function takes the $2k$ simple conditions (assume two for each dimension: the upper and lower bounds for each conjunction clause) and the key matrix A as the input, and transforms each condition with the method described in Section 5.2. The MBR is calculated by the following steps: (1) calculate the vertices of the original query range with the dimensional bounds (the (k+1)-th dimension is 1 and the (k+2)-th dimension is bounded by $(0, \alpha]$); (2) transform the vertices with the composite encryption; (3) Find the bounding box of the transformed vertices as the MBR.

Algorithm 2 Query transformation and encryption.

1: **QueryEnc**$(Cond, A)$
2: Input: Cond: $2k$ simple conditions, 2 for each dimensions. A:the key;

3: **for** each condition C_i in Cond **do**
4:     $\mathbf{u}_i \leftarrow zeros(k + 2, 1)$;
5:     **if** C_i is like $X_j \leq a_j$ **then**
6:         $u_{ij} \leftarrow 1, u_{i,k+1} \leftarrow -a_j$;
7:     **end if**
8:     **if** C_i is like $X_j \geq a_j$ **then**
9:         $u_{ij} \leftarrow -1, u_{i,k+1} \leftarrow a_j$;
10:     **end if**
11:     $\mathbf{w}_i \leftarrow zeros(k + 2, 1)$;
12:     $w_{i,k+2} \leftarrow 1$;
13:     $\Theta_i \leftarrow (A^{-1})^T \mathbf{u}\mathbf{w}^T A^{-1}$;
14: **end for**
15: Use the vertex transformation method to find the MBR of the transformed queries;
16: submit MBR and the filtering conditions $\{\Theta_i\}$ to the server;

In Algorithm 3, the two-stage query processing uses the MBR to find the initial query result and then filters the result with the transformed query conditions $\mathbf{y}^T \Theta_i \mathbf{y} \leq 0$, where the matrices $\{\Theta_i\}$ are passed by the client and $\mathbf{y}$ is a record in the first-stage query result.

Algorithm 3 Two-Stage Query Processing.

1: **ProcessQuery**$(MBR, \{\Theta_i\})$
2: Input: MBR: MBR for the transformed query; $\{\Theta_i\}$:filtering conditions;

3: $Y \leftarrow$ use the indexing tree to find answers for MBR;
4: $Y' \leftarrow \emptyset$;
5: **for** each record $\mathbf{y}_i$ in Y **do**
6:     success $\leftarrow 1$
7:     **for** each condition Θ_i **do**
8:         **if** $\mathbf{y}^T \Theta_i \mathbf{y} > 0$ **then**
9:             success $\leftarrow 0$;
10:             break;
11:         **end if**
12:     **end for**
13:     **if** success = 1 **then**
14:         add $\mathbf{y}_i$ into Y';
15:     **end if**
16: **end for**
17: return Y' to the client;

Algorithm 1 Data encryption and decryption algorithms

1: **Encrypt**$(X, R_\alpha, R_A, K_o, \alpha, \beta, \sigma)$
2: Input: X: $k \times n$ data records, R_α and R_A : random real value generators for generating the $(k + 2)$-nd dimension (i.e., $\mathbf{v}$) and the invertible $(k + 2) \times (k + 2)$ matrix A with at least two non-zero values in each row, K_o: key for OPE E_o, α: the upper bound for $\mathbf{v}$, β:sample size, σ: noise intensity; Output: the matrix A

3: $A \leftarrow 0$;
4: **while** A is not invertible **do**
5:     generate the elements in A with R_A;
6:     $\mathbf{v} = (v_1, \ldots, v_\beta) \leftarrow$ generate β random positive values in range $(0, \alpha)$ with R_α;
7:     $A_3 \leftarrow 0$;
8:     **while** A_3 contains zero elements **do**
9:         generate the $(k + 2) \times \beta$ noise matrix Ψ use $N(0, \sigma^2)$;
10:         $A_3 \leftarrow \Psi \mathbf{v}^T / (\mathbf{v}\mathbf{v}^T)$;
11:     **end while**
12:     Replace the last column of A with A_3;
13:     Check the invertibility of the matrix A;
14: **end while**
15: **for** each record $\mathbf{x}$ in X **do**
16:     $v \leftarrow$ random positive value in range $(0, \alpha)$ with R_α
17:     $\mathbf{y} \leftarrow A(E_o(\mathbf{x}^T, K_o), 1, v)^T$;
18:     submit $\mathbf{y}$ to the server;
19: **end for**
20: return A;

1: **Decrypt**(Y, A, K_o)
2: Input: Y: $k \times n$ matrix, the encrypted records, A:the RASP key, K_o: the OPE key; Output: the decrypted records X

3: $X \leftarrow A^{-1}Y$;
4: $X' \leftarrow$ the first k dimensions of X;
5: return OPE decryption $D_o(X')$

Privacy-Preserving Activity Scheduling on Mobile Devices

Igor Bilogrevic   Murtuza Jadliwala   Jean-Pierre Hubaux
Laboratory for Computer communications and Applications (LCA 1)
EPFL, CH-1015 Lausanne, Switzerland
firstname.lastname@epfl.ch

Imad Aad   Valtteri Niemi
Nokia Research Center
CH-1015 Lausanne, Switzerland
firstname.lastname@nokia.com

ABSTRACT

Progress in mobile wireless technology has resulted in the increased use of mobile devices to store and manage users' personal schedules. Users also access popular context-based services, typically provided by third-party providers, by using these devices for social networking, dating and activity-partner searching applications. Very often, these applications need to determine common availabilities among a set of user schedules. The privacy of the scheduling operation is paramount to the success of such applications, as often users do not want to share their personal schedules with other users or third-parties. Previous research has resulted in solutions that provide privacy guarantees, but they are either too complex or do not fit well in the popular user-provider operational model. In this paper, we propose practical and privacy-preserving solutions to the server-based scheduling problem. Our novel algorithms take advantage of the homomorphic properties of well-known cryptosystems in order to privately compute common user availabilities. We also formally outline the privacy requirements in such scheduling applications and we implement our solutions on real mobile devices. The experimental measurements and analytical results show that the proposed solutions not only satisfy the privacy properties but also fare better, in regard to computation and communication efficiency, compared to other well-known solutions.

Categories and Subject Descriptors

C.2.4 [**Distributed Systems**]: Client/server; K.4.1 [**Public Policy Issues**]: Privacy

General Terms

Algorithms, Design, Performance, Security

Keywords

Activity scheduling, Client-server architecture, Homomorphic encryption

1. INTRODUCTION

Users rely increasingly on mobile devices such as smartphones and netbooks to access information while on the move [7], and very often they use the same equipment to store personal information about their daily schedules and activities [2]. Although many context and data sharing applications such as Google Maps, Facebook and Twitter are popular, activity management and synchronization applications are also gaining more and more attention [4]. Applications such as Microsoft Outlook [5], Apple iCal [1] and Nokia Ovi [6] are available on mobile devices and they all offer time and activity management services. One desirable feature in such applications is activity *scheduling*: colleagues can schedule meetings at common available time slots, groups of friends can organize parties on weekends and people unbeknownst to each other can engage in dating based on their common free/busy hours.

One concern in such scheduling applications is that users would prefer not to share all personal information with everyone. For example, they may only want to share common availabilities, but not details about other records. They may also have reservations about sharing personal information with third-party service providers. Therefore, privacy of personal information, *vis-à-vis* service providers and peers, is paramount for the success of such scheduling applications. For instance, a well-known service that allows users to find all common availabilities is Doodle [3]. However, Doodle does not provide privacy: Each user and the doodle server see the free/busy state of every user, and the private information that is leaked to all users and the central server is well beyond just the common available slots. Cultural, religious and many other private information can be easily inferred from availability patterns. Even if pseudonyms are used instead of real names, the server and all peers still know what time slots are available for everyone and how many users are free or busy.

Privacy-preserving scheduling problems have been extensively studied in the past by researchers from the theoretical perspective, for instance, by modeling them as set intersection problems [20, 11], distributed constraint satisfaction problems [27, 28, 24, 25], secure multi-party computation problems [18, 12] and by framing them in the e-voting context [19]. Traditionally, there are two possible approaches to the scheduling problems: distributed and centralized. Distributed solutions do not rely on a third-party provider (and thus they prevent revealing information to the provider), but have several limitations. For instance, due to the frequent and intensive message exchanges among peers, scalability and computational complexity is an issue when dealing with a large number of (resource-limited) mobile devices; moreover, the need of sequencing among peers and the unpredictability of scheduling results (if a user interrupts the protocol) are two additional drawbacks. The centralized approaches, such as cloud-based computing, are better in terms of scalability, communication cost, complexity, synchronization and resilience but usually do not provide privacy, because users are required to transmit their personal information to the provider.

Our goal is to provide simple, practical and feasible solutions to the scheduling problem which, in addition to ensuring reasonable privacy guarantees, are easily integrated with existing operational models and mobile service providers. In this paper, we follow a centralized approach for addressing the problem of efficient and privacy-preserving scheduling. In the proposed schemes, users are able to determine common time slots without revealing any other information to either the other participants or to the central scheduling server. Our specific contributions are as follows. First, by building on the work of authors in related domains, we formally define the basic privacy requirements for users in a scheduling scenario. Second, we propose three novel privacy-preserving scheduling algorithms that take advantage of the homomorphic properties of asymmetric cryptosystems. Third, we implement the proposed algorithms on real mobile devices and perform extensive experiments using these devices in order to verify their computation and communication overheads. Finally, we explain how the system can be further made resilient to collusion and other well-known active attacks. To the best of our knowledge, we believe this is the first implementation and extensive testing of privacy-preserving scheduling schemes on commercial mobile devices.

The paper is organized as follows. We introduce the state-of-the-art in Section 2 and the system model and problem definition in Section 3. We formalize the privacy requirements for the scheduling problem in Section 4 and outline our algorithms in sections 5, 6 and 7. We present a comparative analysis and implementation results in Section 8, and we discuss the extensions of our schemes in Section 9. We conclude the paper in Section 10.

2. STATE OF THE ART

In the literature, the four most relevant bodies of work that address privacy in scheduling or similar scenarios are based on techniques from private set-intersection [20, 11], distributed constraint satisfaction [27, 28, 24, 25], secure multi-party computation [18, 12] and e-voting [19]. Hereafter, we review the most relevant aspects of such approaches.

In the private set-intersection domain, Kissner and Song [20] use mathematic properties of polynomials to design privacy-preserving union, intersection and element reduction operations on private multisets by leveraging on the Goldwasser-Micali homomorphic encryption scheme [17]. De Cristofaro and Tsudik [11] provide efficient variations of private-set intersection protocols and present a comparison in terms of

computational and communication complexity, adversarial model and privacy. The authors also give informal definitions of client and server privacy. However, PSI approaches are generally distributed, and an efficient extension to an n-party protocol is challenging. In the meeting scheduling scenario, for instance, a trivial extension of the 2-party PSI to n parties (by running a 2-party protocol between each pair of users) would undermine the privacy of users' schedules as well; knowing the personal availability and the aggregate availability is sufficient to infer the other party's schedule.

Distributed constraint satisfaction approaches were investigated by Wallace and Freuder [27]: they study the tradeoff between privacy and efficiency and show that the information that entities learn during the negotiation of a common schedule has, in some cases, a tremendous impact on privacy. Details of an accept/reject response are exploited by intelligent agents in order to successfully infer the availabilities of other peers involved in the scheduling process. Similarly, Zunino and Campo [29] design a scheduling system in which entities learn and refine their knowledge about user preferences by using a Bayesian network. Yokoo et al. [28] use secret sharing among third-party servers in order to determine a suitable agreement among entities in a collusion-resistant way.

Solutions based on secure multi-party computation were investigated in [12] and a practical scheme was proposed in [18]. Herlea et al. [18], for instance, design and evaluate a distributed secure scheduling protocol by relying on properties of the XOR operation over binary values, in which all users contribute to the secrecy of individual schedules while ensuring the correctness of the results. Although not a pure e-voting scheme, Kellerman and Böhme [19] proposed an event scheduling protocol that inherits several security and privacy requirements from the e-voting context. However, a formal study of such properties and experimental performance results are missing in their work.

In contrast to most of the above solutions, we take a more centralized approach (with a single third-party server) for the privacy-preserving scheduling problem. Our solutions overcome communication and computational complexities intrinsic to most distributed approaches discussed above, as well as ensure that no private information (other than the resulting common availabilities) is exposed. Moreover, our protocols can easily fit into today's popular provider-consumer service architectures without incurring a huge communication cost on the service-provider.

3. SYSTEM MODEL

In this section, we outline the network and adversary model and formally define the scheduling problem.

3.1 Network Model

We assume that there is a total of N users u_i, $i \in \{1 \ldots N\}$, that want to schedule an activity (meeting, party) at a common available time slot. Each user has a private schedule x_i represented by a string of bits $x_i = [b_{i,1}, b_{i,2}, \ldots, b_{i,m}]$, where each bit $b_{i,j} \in \{0, 1\}$ expresses the availability of user u_i in a particular time slot j; $b_{i,j} = 1$ means that user u_i is available at time slot j, whereas $b_{i,j} = 0$ means that the user is not available.[1] We assume that the length m of x_i,

---

[1] In general, however, users may assign not only a binary value (available or busy) for each time slot, but they could

i.e. the time horizon of the individual schedules, is constant for all users. The value of m can either be predecided by the participants or fixed by the application.

Moreover, we assume that each user's device is able to perform public key cryptographic operations and that there is a semi-honest [16] (as detailed in Section 3.2) third-party performing the scheduling computations. The latter must be able to communicate with the users and run public key cryptographic functions as well. For instance, a common public-key infrastructure using the RSA [23] cryptosystem could be employed. All communications between a user and the third-party server will be encrypted with the latter's public key for the purposes of confidentiality of the schedules with respect to other users, for authentication and integrity protection. Thus, all users know the public key of the server but nobody, except the server, knows the corresponding private key. For simplicity of exposition, in our algorithms we do not explicitly show the cryptographic operations involving the server's public/private key.

We assume that the N users share a common secret, which is used to derive (i) a fresh common key pair (K_P, K_s), where K_p is the public key and K_s is the private key, and (ii) a fresh bit permutation function $\sigma = [\sigma_1, \ldots, \sigma_m]$ before initiating the scheduling operation. This could be achieved, for example, through a secure credential establishment protocol [9, 10, 21]. Thus, these keys and permutations are derived and known to each member of the group but not to the server. We refer to the encryption of a message M with the group public key as $E_{K_P, r}(M) = C$, where r is a random integer that is eventually needed, and to the decryption of the encrypted message C as $D_{K_s}(C) = M$. The permutation σ, although not strictly required, is used in order to randomize the order of bits sent to the server. This prevents the server from gaining any knowledge about which time slot is being evaluated in each computation.

3.2 Adversarial Model

Server

The third-party server is assumed to execute the scheduling protocols correctly, but it tries to learn any information it can from the input it gets by the users and the computations it performs. The server can accumulate the knowledge about users in each computation it performs. We refer to this adversarial behavior as *semi-honest*. More details about the semi-honest model can be found in [16].

Users

Users also want to learn private information about other users' schedules and, in addition to the passive eavesdropping attacks, users could act maliciously by generating fake users, manipulating their own schedules or by colluding with other users or the scheduling server. Initially, we assume that users are honest but curious (or semi-honest), and afterwards we present more active (or malicious) types of user adversaries in Section 9.2.

Although the semi-honest adversarial model is sufficient

in most practical settings, considering the commercial interest of service providers and the mutual trust among participants, it does not include possible malicious behavior by the server or users. For instance, the server could collude with the participants or generate fake participants in order to obtain private information of the participants. Similarly, users might collude with other users or try to maliciously modify their schedules in order to disrupt the execution of the protocol or to gain information about other users' schedules. We address such active attacks by both users and server in Section 9.2, and we describe how such attacks can be thwarted by using existing cryptographic mechanisms.

3.3 Centralized Scheduling Algorithm

Given a group of N users $u_i, i \in \{1 \ldots N\}$, each with private schedules $x_i = [b_{i,1}, \ldots, b_{i,m}]$, the scheduling problem is to find time slots j such that $\forall i = 1 \ldots N$, $b_{i,j} = 1$, i.e. all users are available in the same time slot j. We refer to an algorithm that solves the scheduling problem as a *scheduling algorithm*. Formally, a scheduling algorithm A accepts the following inputs and produces the respective outputs:

- Input: a transformation of individual schedules
$$f(b_{i,1}, \ldots, b_{i,m}), \quad \forall i = 1 \ldots N.$$
where f is a transformation function such that it is hard (success with only a negligible probability) to determine the input of the function by just observing the output.

- Output: a function $g(Y), Y = y^1, \ldots, y^j, \ldots, y^m$ where:
$$y^j = \begin{cases} YES & \text{if } b_{i,j} = 1, \quad \forall i = 1 \ldots N \\ NO & \text{otherwise} \end{cases}$$

such that each user is able to compute $Y = g^{-1}(g(Y))$ using its local data. As we will see later on, we use the well-known cryptosytems ElGamal [13], Paillier [22] and Goldwasser-Micali [17] as our transformation and output functions f and g.

A centralized scheduling process works as follows. Each user $u_i, i \in \{1 \ldots N\}$ computes $f_i = f(b_{i,1}, \ldots, b_{i,m})$ and sends it to the third-party server, which then executes the scheduling algorithm A on the received inputs f_i, $\forall i$, and produces $g(Y) = A(f_1, \ldots, f_N)$. Finally, the server sends $g(Y)$ to each user who then obtains $Y = g^{-1}(g(Y))$. Figure 1 shows one execution of a generic centralized scheduling process.

4. PRIVACY DEFINITIONS

As mentioned earlier, in this paper we follow a centralized approach to solve the privacy-preserving scheduling problem. In other words, we assume that a third-party, given users' individual private schedules, computes their common availabilities (time slots). /The privacy provided by a centralized scheduling algorithm can be defined in terms of the following two components: a) User-privacy and b) Server-privacy. Hereafter, we formally define each of these components. The symbols used throughout the paper are summarized in Table 1.

User-privacy

The *user-privacy* of any centralized scheduling algorithm A measures the probabilistic advantage that any user $u_i, i \in$

---

express preferences [14, 15]. For example, $b_{i,j} \in 0, \ldots, 10$ where $b_{i,j} = 0$ means that user u_i is busy in the time slot j, whereas its preference would increase if $b_{i,j} \geq 1$. For simplicity of exposition, we assume a binary value here. We later discuss a more general case with non-binary costs in Section 9.

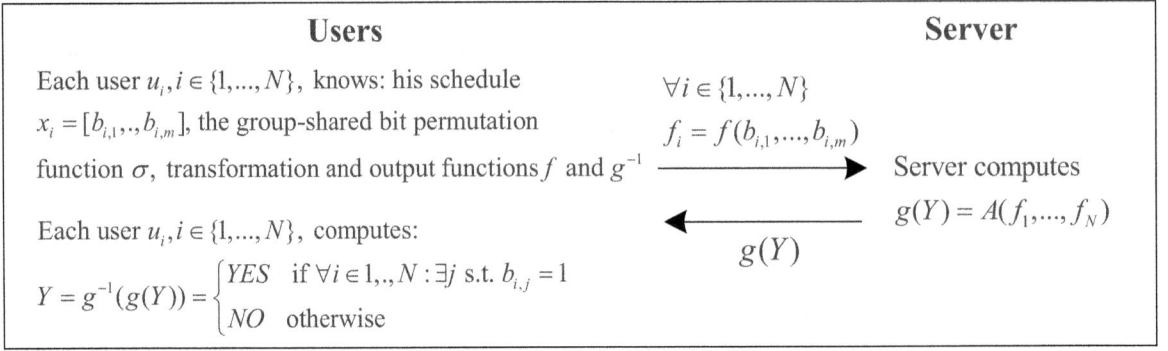

Figure 1: A generic scheduling protocol. Users first send their transformed schedules f_i to the server, which then performs the scheduling algorithm A on the received data and sends the encrypted output $g(Y)$ back to each user.

Table 1: Table of symbols.

SYMBOL	DEFINITION
$Adv^{LNK}(A)$	Linkability advantage
$Adv^{IDT}(A)$	Identifiability advantage
$D(C)$	Decryption of a ciphertext C
$E_{K,r}(m)$	Encryption of a message m using the key K and a random number r
K_P	Shared public key of the N users
K_S	Shared private key of the N users
m	Number of slots of each individual schedule
N	Number of users
$x_i=[b_{i,1},..,b_{i,m}]$	Schedule of user u_i, where $b_{i,j}$ is the availability at time slot j
$\sigma=[\sigma_1,..,\sigma_m]$	Schedule permutation function

$\{1\ldots N\}$ gains towards learning the private schedules of at least one other user $u_j, j \neq i$, except their common availabilities, after all users have participated in the execution of the algorithm A. In order to accurately measure users' privacy, we need to compute the following two advantages. First, we measure the *Identifiability Advantage*, which is the probabilistic advantage of an adversary in correctly guessing a schedule bit (which is not a common availability) of any other user. We denote it as $Adv_{u_i}^{IDT}(A)$. Second, we measure the *Linkability Advantage*, which is the probabilistic advantage of an adversary in correctly guessing that any two or more other users have exactly the same corresponding schedule bit (not a common availability bit) without necessarily knowing the values of those bits. We denote this advantage as $Adv_{u_i}^{LNK}(A)$. We make the following straightforward observation.

Observation 1. If an adversary has identifiability advantage over two corresponding schedule bits of two different users, this implies that it has linkability advantage over those two bits as well. However, the inverse is not necessarily true.

We semantically define the identifiability and linkability advantages using a challenge-response methodology. Challenge-response games have been widely used in cryptography to prove the security of cryptographic protocols. We now de-

scribe such a challenge-response game for the identifiability advantage $Adv_{u_i}^{IDT}(A)$ of any user u_i participating in the algorithm A as follows.

1. Initialization: Challenger privately collects $x_i = [b_{i,1}, \ldots, b_{i,m}]$ and $f_i = f(b_{i,1}, \ldots, b_{i,m})$ from all users $u_i, i \in \{1 \ldots N\}$.

2. Scheduling: Challenger computes $g(Y) = A(f_1, f_2, \ldots, f_N)$ with the users and sends $g(Y)$ to all users $u_1, u_2, \ldots, u_N$.

3. Challenger randomly picks a user u_i, $i \in \{1 \ldots N\}$, as the adversary.

4. u_i picks $j \in \{1 \ldots N\}$, *s.t.* $j \neq i$ and sends it to the challenger.

5. Challenge: the challenger picks a random time slot $p \in \{1 \ldots m\}$, *s.t.*, $\exists b_{k,p} = 0$ for at least one $k \in 1, \ldots, N$. Challenger then sends (j, p) to the user u_i. This is the challenge.

6. Guess: User u_i sends $b'_{j,p} \in \{0, 1\}$ to the challenger as a response to his challenge. If $b'_{j,p} = b_{j,p}$, the user u_i (adversary) wins; otherwise, he loses.

The identifiability advantage $Adv_{u_i}^{IDT}(A)$ can be defined as

$$Adv_{u_i}^{IDT}(A) = \left| Pr_{u_i}[b'_{j,p} = b_{j,p}] - \frac{1}{2} \right| \quad (1)$$

where $Pr_{u_i}[b'_{j,p} = b_{j,p}]$ is the probability of user u_i winning the game (correctly answering the challenge in the challenge-response game), computed over the coin flips of the challenger, $b'_{j,p}$ is u_i's guess about the schedule of user u_j in the time slot p and $b_{j,p}$ is u_j's true availability. An external attacker, having no access to the output of the algorithm, has obviously no advantage at all. Thus, we focus on the non-trivial case with participating users only.

Similarly, we describe the challenge-response game for the linkability advantage $Adv_{u_i}^{LNK}(A)$ of any user u_i as follows.

1. Initialization: Challenger privately collects $x_i = [b_{i,1}, \ldots, b_{i,m}]$ and $f_i = f(b_{i,1}, \ldots, b_{i,m})$ from all users $u_i, i \in \{1 \ldots N\}$.

2. Scheduling: Challenger computes $g(Y) = A(f_1, f_2, \ldots, f_N)$ with the users and sends $g(Y)$ to all users $u_1, u_2, \ldots, u_N$.

3. Challenger randomly picks a user u_i, $i \in \{1 \dots N\}$, as the adversary.

4. u_i picks $h, j \in \{1 \dots N\}$, s.t. $j \neq h, j \neq i, h \neq i$ and sends (h, j) to the challenger.

5. Challenge: Challenger randomly picks a time slot $p \in \{1 \dots m\}$, s.t., $\exists b_{k,p} = 0$ for at least one $k \in 1, \dots, N$. Challenger then sends (j, p) and (h, p) to the user u_i. This is the challenge.

6. Guess: User u_i decides if $b_{j,p} = b_{h,p}$ or not. User u_i sets $b' = 1$ if he decides $b_{j,p} = b_{h,p}$ and $b' = 0$ if he decides $b_{j,p} \neq b_{h,p}$. User u_i sends b' to the challenger as a response to his challenge. If $b_{j,p} = b_{h,p}$ and $b' = 1$ or if $b_{j,p} \neq b_{h,p}$ and $b' = 0$, the user u_i (adversary) wins; otherwise, he loses.

The linkability advantage $Adv_{u_i}^{LNK}(A)$ can be defined as

$$Adv_{u_i}^{LNK}(A) = |Pr_{u_i}[((b_{j,p} = b_{h,p}) \wedge b' = 1)$$
$$\vee ((b_{j,p} \neq b_{h,p}) \wedge b' = 0)] - \frac{1}{2}| \quad (2)$$

where $Pr_{u_i}[.]$ is the probability of user u_i winning the game, computed over the coin flips of the challenger. As for the identifiability advantage, an external attacker has no linkability advantage at all.

We now define the user-privacy of the scheduling algorithm A on a per-execution basis as follows:

Definition 1. An execution of the centralized scheduling algorithm A is *user-private* if both the identifiability advantage $Adv_{u_i}^{IDT}(A)$ and the linkability advantage $Adv_{u_i}^{LNK}(A)$ of each participating user $u_i, i \in \{1, \dots, N\}$ is negligible.

A function $f(x)$ is called *negligible* if, for any positive polynomial $p(x)$, there is an integer B such that for any integer $x > B$, $f(x) < 1/p(x)$ [16].

Definition 1 says that a particular execution of the scheduling algorithm is user-private if and only if users do not gain any (actually, negligible) additional knowledge about the schedule bits of any other user, except the schedule bits that have a value 1 for all users (common availabilities).

Server-privacy

The *server-privacy* of any (centralized) scheduling algorithm A measures the probabilistic advantage that the server (which executes the scheduling algorithm A and observes the inputs from the users) gains towards learning the private schedules of at least one user $u_i, i \in \{1 \dots N\}$. As in the case of user-privacy, we need to compute the following two advantages. First, the advantage of the server in guessing correctly any schedule bit of any user participating in the scheduling algorithm, called as *Identifiability Advantage* and denoted as $Adv_S^{IDT}(A)$. Second, the advantage of the server in guessing correctly that any two (or more) participating users have exactly the same corresponding schedule bits without necessarily knowing the values of those bits, called the *Linkability Advantage* and denoted as $Adv_S^{LNK}(A)$.

The server identifiability and linkability advantages are defined in a similar fashion as the user advantages. The challenge-response game for the server identifiability advantage $Adv_S^{IDT}(A)$ is defined as follows.

1. Initialization: Challenger privately collects $x_i = [b_{i,1}, \dots, b_{i,m}]$ and the server privately collects $f_i = f(b_{i,1}, \dots, b_{i,m})$ from all users $u_i, i \in \{1 \dots N\}$.

2. Scheduling: Server computes $g(Y) = A(f_1, f_2, \dots, f_N)$ with the users and sends $g(Y)$ to all users $u_1, u_2, \dots, u_N$.

3. Server picks $i \in \{1 \dots N\}$ and sends it to the challenger.

4. Challenge: Challenger randomly picks a time slot $p \in \{1 \dots m\}$. Challenger then sends (i, p) to the server. This is the challenge.

5. Guess: server sends $b'_{i,p} \in \{0, 1\}$ to the challenger as a response to his challenge. If $b'_{i,p} = b_{i,p}$, the server (adversary) wins; otherwise, he loses.

The identifiability advantage $Adv_S^{IDT}(A)$ is defined as

$$Adv_S^{IDT}(A) = \left| Pr_S[b'_{j,p} = b_{j,p}] - \frac{1}{2} \right| \quad (3)$$

where $Pr_S[b'_{j,p} = b_{j,p}]$ is the probability of the server winning the game, computed over the coin flips of the challenger.

The challenge-response game for the server linkability advantage $Adv_S^{LNK}(A)$ is defined as follows.

1. Initialization: Challenger privately collects $x_i = [b_{i,1}, \dots, b_{i,m}]$ and the server privately collects $f_i = f(b_{i,1}, \dots, b_{i,m})$ from all users $u_i, i \in \{1 \dots N\}$.

2. Scheduling: Server computes $g(Y) = A(f_1, f_2, \dots, f_N)$ with the users and sends $g(Y)$ to all users $u_1, u_2, \dots, u_N$.

3. Server picks $h, j \in \{1 \dots N\}$, s.t. $j \neq h$ and sends (h, j) to the challenger.

4. Challenge: Challenger randomly picks $p \in \{1 \dots m\}$ and then sends (j, p) and (h, p) to the server. This is the challenge.

5. Guess: Server decides if $b_{j,p} = b_{h,p}$ or not. Server sets $b' = 1$ if he decides $b_{j,p} = b_{h,p}$ and $b' = 0$ if he decides $b_{j,p} \neq b_{h,p}$. Server sends b' to the challenger as a response to his challenge. If $b_{j,p} = b_{h,p}$ and $b' = 1$ or if $b_{j,p} \neq b_{h,p}$ and $b' = 0$, the server (adversary) wins; otherwise, he loses.

The linkability advantage $Adv_S^{LNK}(A)$ is defined as

$$Adv_S^{LNK}(A) = |Pr_S[(b_{j,p} = b_{h,p}) \wedge b' = 1)$$
$$\vee (b_{j,p} \neq b_{h,p}) \wedge b' = 0)] - \frac{1}{2}| \quad (4)$$

where $Pr_S[.]$ is the probability of the server winning the game, computed over the coin flips of the challenger.

The server-privacy of the scheduling algorithm A on a per-execution basis can then be defined as follows:

Definition 2. An execution of the centralized scheduling algorithm A is *server-private* if both the identifiability advantage $Adv_S^{IDT}(A)$ and the linkability advantage $Adv_S^{LNK}(A)$ of the server is negligible.

Now, it is reasonable to assume that in practice users will be able to perform multiple executions of the scheduling algorithm with possibly different participating sets of users.

This is especially true if such an algorithm is offered, for example, as a service by mobile service providers to their subscribers. Thus, privacy of the scheduling algorithm should be defined over multiple executions. First, we define a *private execution* as follows:

Definition 3. A *private* execution is an execution which does not reveal more information than what can be derived from its result and the prior knowledge.

Based on how memory is retained over sequential executions, we define two types of algorithm executions, namely, independent and dependent:

Definition 4. An *independent* (respectively, *dependent*) *execution* is a single private execution of the scheduling algorithm defined in Section 3.3 in which *no* (respectively, *some*) information of an earlier and current execution is retained and passed to future execution.

The information retained can include past inputs to the algorithm, intermediate results (on the server) and the outputs of the algorithm. Based on the type of executions, we define a privacy-preserving scheduling algorithm as follows:

Definition 5. A scheduling algorithm A is *execution* (respectively *fully*) *privacy-preserving* if and only if for every *independent* (respectively *all*) execution(s):

1. A is correct; All users are correctly able to compute $y^j = 1, \forall j = 1 \ldots m$ if and only if $b_{i,j} = 1, \forall i = 1 \ldots N$.

2. A is user-private in every execution.

3. A is server-private in every execution.

A fully privacy-preserving algorithm is a much stronger (and difficult to achieve) privacy requirement. In this work, similar to earlier efforts, we focus on achieving execution privacy. The following observation gives the relationship between fully privacy-preserving and execution privacy-preserving scheduling algorithms.

Observation 2. Any scheduling algorithm A, as defined in Section 3.3, is execution privacy-preserving if it is fully privacy-preserving, but the inverse is not true.

Next, we outline our centralized scheduling algorithms.

5. SCHEDELG ALGORITHM

In this section, we describe our first privacy-preserving centralized scheduling scheme, which is based on the El-Gamal [13] cryptosystem. The security of the ElGamal encryption relies on the intractability of the discrete logarithm problem (DLP), which assumes that it is computationally infeasible to obtain the private key K_s given the public key (g, h), where g is a generator of a multiplicative cyclic group G of prime order q and $h = g^{K_s} \mod q$.

Our protocol *SchedElG* uses the *homomorphic* property of the ElGamal cryptosystem in order to allow the scheduling server to compute the aggregated availabilities by working only on the encrypted individual schedules. For instance, it can be verified that the ElGamal scheme satisfies:

$$D(E_{K_P, r_1}(m_1) \cdot E_{K_P, r_2}(m_2)) =$$
$$D((g^{r_1}, m_1 h^{r_1}) \cdot (g^{r_2}, m_2 h^{r_2})) =$$
$$D(g^r, (m_1 \cdot m_2)h^r) = m_1 \cdot m_2$$

where $r = r_1 + r_2 \in \mathbb{Z}_q$ is a random integer. Moreover, being a probabilistic encryption scheme, it follows that if $r_1 \neq r_2$, $E_{K_P, r_1}(m) \neq E_{K_P, r_2}(m)$.

For the *SchedElG* algorithm, we assume that the meeting participants represent their availabilities in the following way: $b_{i,j}^* = 1$ if $b_{i,j} = 1$, but $b_{i,j}^* = R$ (where $R \in \mathbb{Z}_q, R > 1$ is a random integer) if $b_{i,j} = 0$.

Scheme

The privacy-preserving scheduling protocol *SchedElG* is shown in Figure 2. All users first select the sequence of time slots according to the permutation σ, i.e., $\sigma_j, \forall j = 1..m$, and then encrypt individually the corresponding schedule availabilities, i.e., $E_i = [E_{i,\sigma_1}, \ldots, E_{i,\sigma_m}]$ where $E_{i,\sigma_j} = E_{K_P, r_{i,j}}(b_{i,\sigma_j}^*)$. Then, each user sends its E_i privately to the scheduling server that performs the multiplication $\prod_{i=1}^N E_{i,\sigma_j}$ of all users' encrypted schedules E_{i,σ_j}, for $j = 1, \ldots, m$. The results of such operation are the (encrypted) aggregated availabilities of all users for each time slot j. Next, the server replies with the aggregated encrypted result E_{sched} back to each user. Each slot in E_{sched} contains a product of the individual time-slot bits encrypted with the users' shared key. Finally, each user decrypts the result and obtains the aggregated availabilities $[y^1 = B_{\sigma_1}^*, \ldots, y^m = B_{\sigma_m}^*]$ of all users u_i for each time slot σ_j. If $B_{\sigma_j}^* = 1$, it means that all users are available at time slot σ_j; if $B_{\sigma_j}^* > 1$, then at least one user is not available and therefore σ_j is not a suitable time slot. The following result shows the correctness and privacy properties of *SchedElG*.

LEMMA 1. *The protocol SchedElG is correct and execution privacy-preserving.*

Due to space constraints, we omit the proof of Lemma 1 here. Interested readers can find the proof in the full paper [8]. In Figure 3, we plotted the identifiability and linkability advantages of an adversary for *SchedElg*, compared with polynomially (in terms of the number of participants N) decreasing functions $p(N)$, for increasing values of N. As confirmed by our analysis, the plot shows that there is always an integer N such that for any integer $x > N$, the identifiability and linkability advantages are smaller than $1/p(x)$.

6. SCHEDPA ALGORITHM

In this section, we define our second privacy-preserving scheduling scheme, which is based on the Paillier cryptosystem [22]. The security of the Paillier encryption scheme is based on the intractability of determining whether an integer r is an n-residue mod n^2, where n is a composite number. In our protocol, we use the homomorphic properties of the Paillier cryptosystem to compute in a privacy-preserving fashion the availability of all users involved in the scheduling process. In particular, one can verify that the Paillier scheme satisfies the following:

$$D[E_{K_P, r_1}(m_1) \cdot E_{K_P, r_1}(m_2) \mod n^2] = m_1 + m_2 \mod n$$
$$D[E_{K_P, r}(m_1)^{m_2} \mod n^2] = m_1 \cdot m_2 \mod n$$

where $r_i, r \in \mathbb{Z}_n^*$ are random numbers chosen by the encrypters, $m \in \mathbb{Z}_n$ is the message to encrypt and $n = pq$ where p, q are two large primes. The randomness in the encryption ensures that if $r_1 \neq r_2$, $E_{K_P, r_1}(m) \neq E_{K_P, r_2}(m)$.

Users		Server

Users

1. Each user $u_i, i \in \{1,...,N\}$, encrypts $b^*_{i,\sigma_j}, j = 1..m$,

   obtaining $E_i = [E_{i,\sigma_1},..,E_{i,\sigma_m}]$, where $E_{i,\sigma_j} = E_{K_P,r_{i,j}}(b^*_{i,\sigma_j})$

   $\xrightarrow{\forall i, E_i}$

3. Each user $u_i, i \in \{1,...,N\}$, obtains $[B^*_{\sigma_1},..B^*_{\sigma_m}]$, the

   aggregated availabilities of all users for all time slots

   $\xleftarrow{E_{sched}}$

Server

2. $\forall j = 1..m$, compute

$$E_{K_P,r}(B^*_{\sigma_j}) = E_{K_P}(\prod_{i=1}^{N} b^*_{i,\sigma_j}) = \prod_{i=1}^{N} E_{i,\sigma_j}$$

$$E_{sched} = [E_{K_P,r}(B^*_{\sigma_1}),..,E_{K_P,r}(B^*_{\sigma_m})]$$

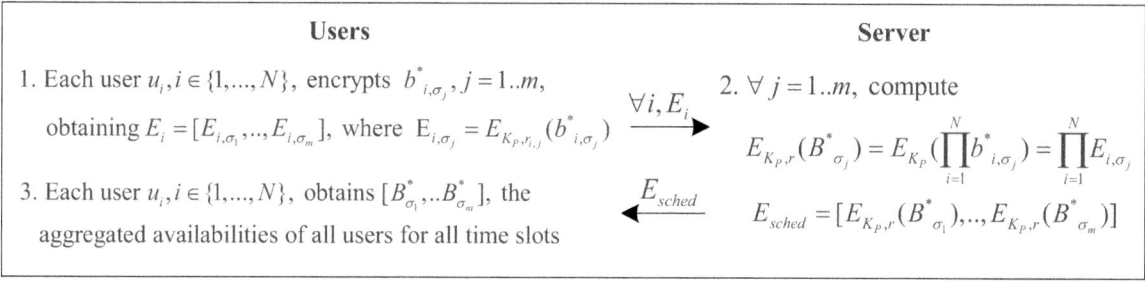

Figure 2: *SchedElg* protocol.

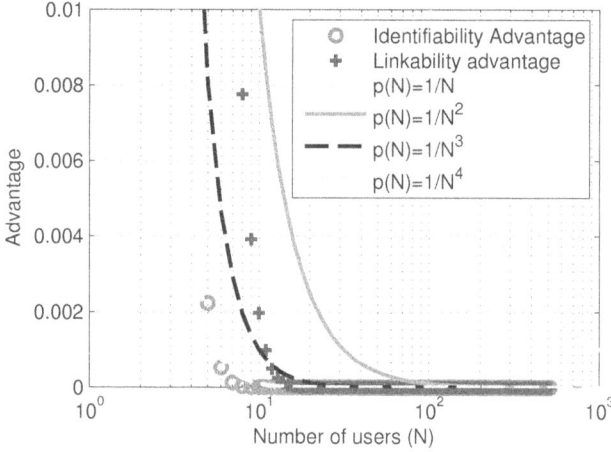

Figure 3: **Identifiability and linkability advantages of an adversary.**

To adapt our scheme to the addition property of Paillier's homomorphism, we take the bit value $\bar{b}_{i,j}$ in the computation instead of the original bit value $b_{i,j}$ as follows: $\bar{b}_{i,j} = 0$ if $b_{i,j} = 1$, and $\bar{b}_{i,j} = r$ (where $r \in \mathbb{Z}_n^*, r > 1$ is a random integer) if $b_{i,j} = 0$.

Scheme

The corresponding privacy-preserving scheduling protocol is shown in Figure 4. First, all users select the sequence of time slots according to the permutation σ, i.e., $\sigma_j, \forall j = 1,\ldots,m$, and then encrypt individually the corresponding availabilities, i.e. $E_i = [E_{i,\sigma_1},\ldots,E_{i,\sigma_m}]$ where $E_{i,\sigma_j} = E_{K_P,r_{i,j}}(\bar{b}_{i,\sigma_j})$. Then, each user sends its E_i privately to the scheduling server that performs the multiplication and exponentiation $(\prod_{i=1}^{N} E_{i,\sigma_j})^R$ of all users' encrypted schedules E_{i,σ_j}, for $j = 1,\ldots,m$, in order to obtain the encryption of the value V_{σ_j} that is needed by the users. Afterwards, the server sends the aggregated encrypted result E_{sched} back to each user. Each slot in E_{sched} contains a randomly scaled sum of the individual time-slot bits $\bar{b}_{i,\sigma_j}$ encrypted with the users' shared key. Finally, each user decrypts the result and knows that if $V_{\sigma_j} = 0$, the time slot σ_j is available for everybody. If $V_{\sigma_j} > 1$, then at least one user is not available. Note that even if the server chooses $R = 1$, the privacy of the users is preserved with $\bar{b}_{i,j}$. The following result shows the correctness and privacy properties of *SchedPa*.

LEMMA 2. *The protocol* SchedPa *is correct and execution privacy-preserving.*

Due to space constraints, we omit the proof of Lemma 2 here. Interested readers can find the proof in the full paper [8].

7. SCHEDGM ALGORITHM

In this section, we present our last privacy-preserving scheduling algorithm, which is based on the Goldwasser-Micali (GM) cryptographic scheme [17]. The security of the GM encryption relies on the intractability of the quadratic residuosity problem, i.e. on the infeasibility of determining whether or not an integer r is a quadratic residue mod n when the Jacobi symbol for r is 1, given $n = pq$ where p, q are large primes. *SchedGM* makes use of the following homomorphic property of the GM cryptosystem:

$$D[E_{K_P,r_1}(m_1) \cdot E_{K_P,r_2}(m_2)] = m_1 \oplus m_2$$

The intuition behind the protocol is based on the work by Herlea *et al.* [18], in which users privately establish a global bit mask (unknown to any user) and then compare all the masked availabilities without knowing the true bit value b_{i,σ_j} of the other users. If all users have the same masked bit value for a given time slot σ_j, then each user knows that everybody else has the same availability, which can be inferred by looking at the private unmasked bit value b_{i,σ_j}. Although initially used in a distributed scenario, we extend the general idea to the centralized scheme as well.

Assumption

Each user u_i generates a private random bit mask $s_i = [c_{i,1}, c_{i,2}, \ldots, c_{i,m}], c_{i,j} \in \{0,1\}$, of the same length of the schedule x_i.

Scheme

The privacy-preserving scheduling algorithm is shown in Figure 5. Each user first selects the sequence of time slots according to the permutation σ, i.e., $\sigma_j, \forall j = 1,\ldots,m$, and then masks the corresponding schedule bits, i.e. $b^{\oplus}_{i,\sigma_j} = b_{i,\sigma_j} \oplus c_{i,j}$. Then, each user encrypts individually both its bit mask, i.e. $E^c_i = [E_{K_P,r_{i,1}}(c_{i,1}),\ldots,E_{K_P,r_{i,m}}(c_{i,m})]$, and the masked availabilities, i.e. $E_i = [E_{i,\sigma_1},\ldots,E_{i,\sigma_m}]$, where $E_{i,\sigma_j} = E_{K_P,r_{i,j}}(b^{\oplus}_{i,\sigma_j})$. Afterwards, each user u_i sends its E_i and E^c_i to the server, which computes the multiplication of the received E_{i,σ_j} with the encrypted masks of all other users $u_k, \forall k \neq i$, obtaining $E^{\oplus}_{i,\sigma_j} = E_{i,\sigma_j} \cdot \prod_{k \neq i} E_{K_P}(c_{k,j})$, $\forall i \in 1,\ldots,N$ and $\forall j = 1,\ldots,m$. Afterwards, the server

267

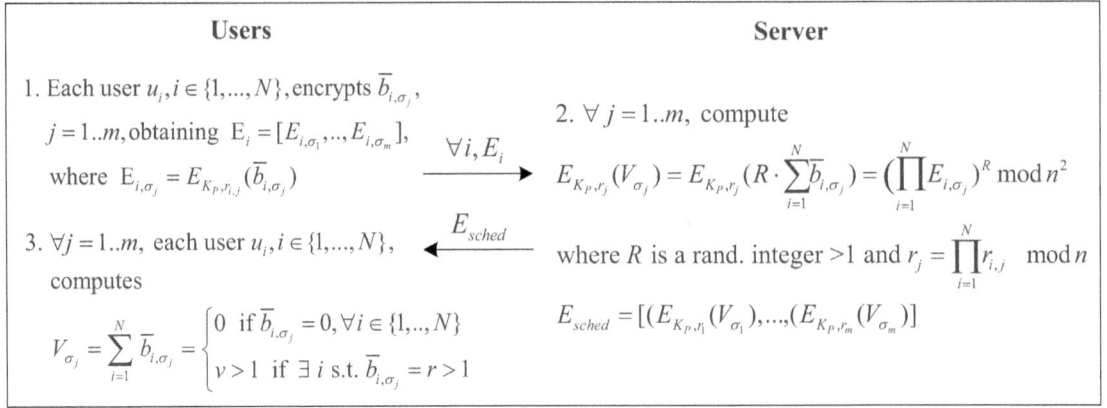

Users

1. Each user $u_i, i \in \{1,...,N\}$, encrypts $\overline{b}_{i,\sigma_j}$,
$j = 1..m$, obtaining $E_i = [E_{i,\sigma_1},..,E_{i,\sigma_m}]$,
where $E_{i,\sigma_j} = E_{K_p, r_{i,j}}(\overline{b}_{i,\sigma_j})$

$\xrightarrow{\forall i, E_i}$

3. $\forall j = 1..m$, each user $u_i, i \in \{1,...,N\}$,
computes

$\xleftarrow{E_{sched}}$

$V_{\sigma_j} = \sum_{i=1}^{N} \overline{b}_{i,\sigma_j} = \begin{cases} 0 \ \ \text{if } \overline{b}_{i,\sigma_j} = 0, \forall i \in \{1,..,N\} \\ v > 1 \ \ \text{if } \exists \, i \text{ s.t. } \overline{b}_{i,\sigma_j} = r > 1 \end{cases}$

Server

2. $\forall \, j = 1..m$, compute

$E_{K_p, r_j}(V_{\sigma_j}) = E_{K_p, r_j}(R \cdot \sum_{i=1}^{N} \overline{b}_{i,\sigma_j}) = (\prod_{i=1}^{N} E_{i,\sigma_j})^R \bmod n^2$

where R is a rand. integer >1 and $r_j = \prod_{i=1}^{N} r_{i,j} \mod n$

$E_{sched} = [(E_{K_p, r_1}(V_{\sigma_1})),...,(E_{K_p, r_m}(V_{\sigma_m})]$

Figure 4: *SchedPa* protocol.

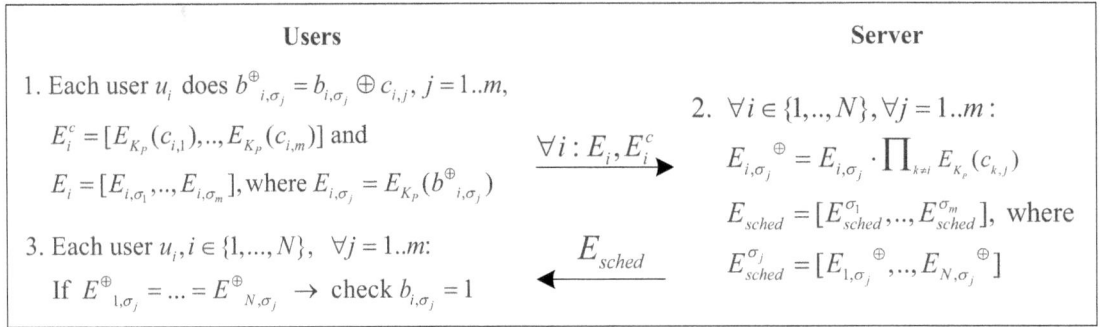

Users

1. Each user u_i does $b^{\oplus}_{i,\sigma_j} = b_{i,\sigma_j} \oplus c_{i,j}$, $j = 1..m$,
$E_i^c = [E_{K_p}(c_{i,1}),..,E_{K_p}(c_{i,m})]$ and
$E_i = [E_{i,\sigma_1},..,E_{i,\sigma_m}]$, where $E_{i,\sigma_j} = E_{K_p}(b^{\oplus}_{i,\sigma_j})$

$\xrightarrow{\forall i: E_i, E_i^c}$

3. Each user $u_i, i \in \{1,...,N\}$, $\forall j = 1..m$:
If $E^{\oplus}_{1,\sigma_j} = ... = E^{\oplus}_{N,\sigma_j} \rightarrow$ check $b_{i,\sigma_j} = 1$

$\xleftarrow{E_{sched}}$

Server

2. $\forall i \in \{1,..,N\}, \forall j = 1..m$:
$E_{i,\sigma_j}^{\oplus} = E_{i,\sigma_j} \cdot \prod_{k \neq i} E_{K_p}(c_{k,j})$
$E_{sched} = [E_{sched}^{\sigma_1},..,E_{sched}^{\sigma_m}]$, where
$E_{sched}^{\sigma_j} = [E_{1,\sigma_j}^{\oplus},..,E_{N,\sigma_j}^{\oplus}]$

Figure 5: *SchedGM* protocol.

sends all individual schedules, masked by a global mask $c_{1,j} \oplus ... \oplus c_{N,j}$, to each user in a random order. As a result, a user will not know his own schedule (masked with the global mask), otherwise he would be able to determine the global mask. Finally, each user decrypts the received messages and compares all masked individual schedules. If for a given time slot σ_j they all have the same value, then each user u_i can infer whether the time slot σ_j is available by looking at its own schedule b_{i,σ_j}. The following result shows the correctness and privacy properties of *SchedGM*.

LEMMA 3. *The protocol* SchedGM *is correct and server-private.*

Due to space constraints, we omit the proof of Lemma 3 here. Interested readers can find the proof in the full paper [8].

8. IMPLEMENTATION AND DISCUSSION

Before presenting the implementation details, let us first perform a comparative analysis of the asymptotic complexities of the proposed protocols, as shown in Table 2. In order to compare our three algorithms with an equivalent security, we set the bit-lengths of the ElGamal modulus q and the Paillier and GM modulus n to 1024 bits. A time-slot availability would then be encrypted to a 2-tuple of 1024-bit ciphertexts for ElGamal, to a 1024-bit ciphertext for GM and to a 2048-bit ciphertext for the Paillier encryption scheme.

From Table 2 we can see that the *SchedElG* and *SchedPa* protocols are very efficient, both in terms of communication

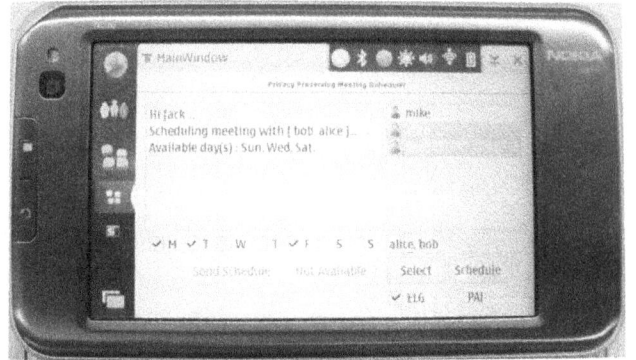

Figure 6: Frontend of the scheduling application on a Nokia N810.

$O(m)$, where m is the number of time slots, and computation complexity $O(m)$. Moreover, these two algorithms provide strong privacy guarantees. *SchedGM*, on the other hand, is comparatively less efficient due to the greater number of exchanged messages ($O(N \cdot m)$), where N is the number of participants). From the privacy perspective, *SchedGM* reveals more information: users can infer the ratio of free/busy participants for each time slot without identifying the ones that are busy and the ones that are free. Because in all schemes, the server operates only on encrypted data, it cannot gain any knowledge about the users' private schedules.

Distributed [24, 18] and hybrid [28] solutions proposed

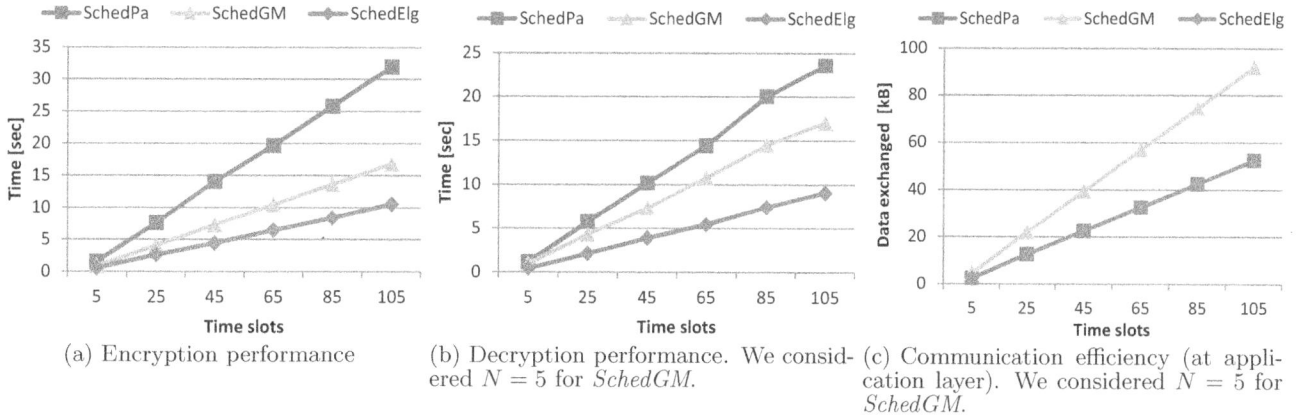

(a) Encryption performance

(b) Decryption performance. We considered $N = 5$ for *SchedGM*.

(c) Communication efficiency (at application layer). We considered $N = 5$ for *SchedGM*.

Figure 7: Client implementation performance.

in the literature are less efficient from the communication standpoint as compared to the proposed protocols. Moreover, the computational complexity of these schemes is higher than *SchedElG* and *SchedPa*, and this undermines their applicability on resource-constrained mobile platforms. Even though the hybrid approach [28] has comparable computation complexity, it is not completely reliable from the privacy point of view because it assumes that the server(s) can get clear-text access to the individual availabilities.

Table 2: Efficiency and privacy of scheduling protocols (DisCSP [28], MPC-DisCSP2 [24] and SDC [18])

		Per-user encr.	Per-user decr.	Per-user comm.	Order of an encr. availab.	Privacy properties
Centralized	SchedElG	O(m)	O(m)	O(m)	1024 bits	User-private Server-private
	SchedPa	O(m)	O(m)	O(m)	2048 bits	User-private Server-private
	SchedGM	O(m)	O(N · m)	O(N · m)	1024 bits	User-private # Server-private
	Naïve	0	0	O(m)	1 bit *	None
Hybrid	DisCSP protocol	O(m)	O(m)	O(N · m)	1024 bits	Private
Distributed	MPC-DisCSP2 protocol	O(N · m)	O(m)	O(N · m)	2048 bits	Private
	SDC protocol	O(N² · m)	O(N · m)	O(N · m · ⌈log₂(N)⌉)	1024 bits	Private

(*) The naïve algorithm does not encrypt the schedule bits
(#) Adv^{IDT} is a negligible function, whereas, for some output Y of the algorithm, Adv^{LNK} is non-negligible

We further evaluate the performance of *SchedElg*, *SchedPa* and *SchedGM* by implementing the client component of the protocols and primitives on Nokia N810 mobile devices with 400 MHz CPU and 128 MB RAM (Figure 6), and the server component on a desktop computer with 2 GHz CPU and 3 GB RAM. The results of the experimentation are shown in Figure 7 and 8.

Client encryption

As we can see from Figure 7, the time required to perform the scheduling operations increases with the number of time slots for all the proposed algorithms, which is intu-

itive. With respect to encryption performance, Figure 7(a) shows that *SchedElg* is the most efficient scheduling algorithm, requiring 4 seconds to encrypt 45 time slots (a typical weekly schedule on a per hour basis). The same task is accomplished by *SchedGM* and *SchedPa* in 7 and 14 seconds respectively. These results might be explained by the following. First, the cryptographic primitives for the ElGamal scheme are implemented in a standard well-optimized library, *libgcrypt*, present in most Unix-based operating systems. *SchedGM*, on the contrary, does not use a standard library. We implemented the Goldwasser-Micali cryptosystem libraries, and as such it is likely that further optimization could significantly improve the performance. Second, the encrypted elements in *SchedPa* have twice the bit-length of the ones used in the other two algorithms, and therefore the same operations (multiplications and exponentiations) require more time.

Client decryption

Figure 7(b) shows the time required for decrypting the final result (common availabilities) of the scheduling algorithms at the client. Similarly to the encryption time, the fastest algorithm for the decryption is *SchedElg*, which takes 4 seconds in order to obtain the aggregated availabilities for a 45 time-slot period. For the same number of time slots, *SchedPa* takes approx. 7 seconds, which is almost twice the best performance. The decryption times for both *SchedElg* and *SchedPa* are independent of the number of participants. The performance of *SchedGM*, due to the fact that the final output of the algorithm is a sequence of vectors instead of just a single aggregated vector, is decreasing with the number of users as well as with the number of time slots. Thus, for a reasonable number of participants (e.g. $N = 5$), *SchedGM* is still practical enough to be implemented on resource-constrained mobile devices, although it is not the preferred solution.

Client communication

Figure 7(c) shows the (application layer) data that each client exchanges during one execution of the scheduling algorithm. In general, all the proposed privacy-preserving scheduling algorithms have reasonable communication costs. *SchedElg* and *SchedPa* are the most efficient algorithms and they require 22 kB of data in order to compute the aggre-

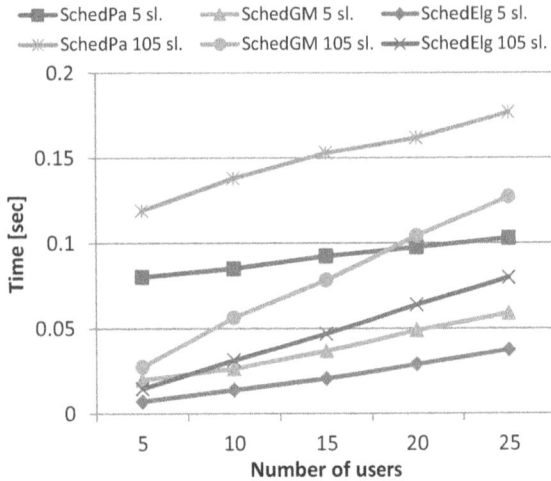

Figure 8: Server processing performance.

gated availabilities of a 45 time-slot period, whereas *SchedGM* requires 39 kB for the same result. As previously mentioned, *SchedGM* uses a sequence of masked vectors in order to compute the final availabilities of the users, and therefore the amount of data is proportional both to the number of users and time-slots.

Server performance

The scheduling server's performance is shown in Figure 8. As it can be seen, the time required to perform the scheduling operations on encrypted values increases with both the number of users and time slots, which is intuitive. Even with a large number of users and time slots, the amount of time required for the operations is still below 0.2 second, which suggests that the load on the server is limited, which allows it to efficiently handle multiple scheduling events, without incurring in huge computational overhead.

9. EXTENSIONS

In this section, we show how *SchedPa* can be easily extended to the case where user schedules are non-binary, i.e., each time slot is a non-negative cost $C_{i,j}$ that indicates u_i's preference for time-slot j. We also describe several active attacks on the proposed scheduling schemes, such as collusion between users-server and data modification by the users, and how these attacks can be mitigated by using existing cryptographic mechanisms. Finally, we discuss some further enhancements for the privacy of users' schedules and how to implement them.

9.1 Non-binary Schedules

The goal here is to find, in a privacy-preserving fashion, the time-slot with the minimum aggregated cost. The scheme works as follows:

1. Each user u_i reorders its cost sequence $C_{i,1} \ldots C_{i,m}$ using the shared permutation σ and encrypts each cost C_{i,σ_j} in the sequence using the Paillier cryptosystem with the shared group key K_P. It then passes the result $(E_{K_P,r_{i,1}}(C_{i,\sigma_1}) \ldots E_{K_P,r_{i,m}}(C_{i,\sigma_m}))$ to the server.

2. The server computes the encrypted sum of costs $E_{K_P,r_j}(R \cdot$

$\sum_{i=1}^{N} C_{i,\sigma_j}), \forall j$, where R is a random integer greater than one chosen by the server.

3. The server selects a pre-determined user u_k and passes a *randomly ordered* (different from σ) sequence of the encrypted aggregated costs to it. This is to prevent u_k from learning the aggregated cost function.

4. User u_k decrypts all the elements passed from the server, and identifies the minimum aggregated cost.

5. User u_k then queries the server for the index of the (encrypted) minimum aggregated cost. The server then distributes the queried index to all users.

It can be easily shown that the above scheme is execution privacy-preserving. For conciseness, we do not discuss the details of the privacy analysis here.

9.2 Active Attacks

There are five kinds of possible active attacks on the scheduling schemes: (i) collusion between the scheduling server and users, (ii) collusion among users, (iii) fake user generation by the server, (iv) individual user schedule modification and (v) integrity and replay attacks.

In order to thwart the first issue, the invited participants could agree on establishing a shared secret using techniques from threshold cryptography, such as [26]. The server should then collude with at least a predefined number of participants in order to obtain the shared secret and learn the individual availabilities. The second concern may arise if k colluding users set their schedules to *all-available*, and try to learn the schedules of other users. Assuming that N is the total number of participants and k the number of colluding ones, our schemes would provide some level of schedule privacy to honest users as long as $N - k \geq 2$. Only if all but one users collude, then they are able to determine the schedule of the remaining user. In order for the third attack to succeed, the server would need to generate fake users and convince the true participants about the legitimacy of the fake users. In practice, this is a non-trivial task to achieve, and thus the attack has a very slim chance of succeeding. Moreover, the effectiveness of such attack could be further reduced by adopting the threshold cryptographic scheme mentioned previously, because the server would then need to generate k fake users and validate them as true participants.

The fourth attack is also not able to succeed in revealing the availability of other meeting participants, as the best a malicious user can do is to set its own schedule to all-available, and then guess the availabilities of the other $N-1$ participants. Even if a malicious user attempts to modify its own schedule with invalid values, such as negative values, the message domain restrictions of cryptosystems (such as ElGamal and Paillier) would prevent such modifications. Thus, malicious attacks consisting of manipulating the final result by using invalid negative values as schedule values are not possible in the proposed protocols.

The last attack concerns the integrity and freshness of the encrypted schedules. The participants are the only entities in the system that know the secret that has been used to generate the public/private key pair, and therefore they are the only ones that can generate and verify the integrity of the encrypted data. Moreover, using the shared common secret, each participant could generate a fresh *nonce* at each

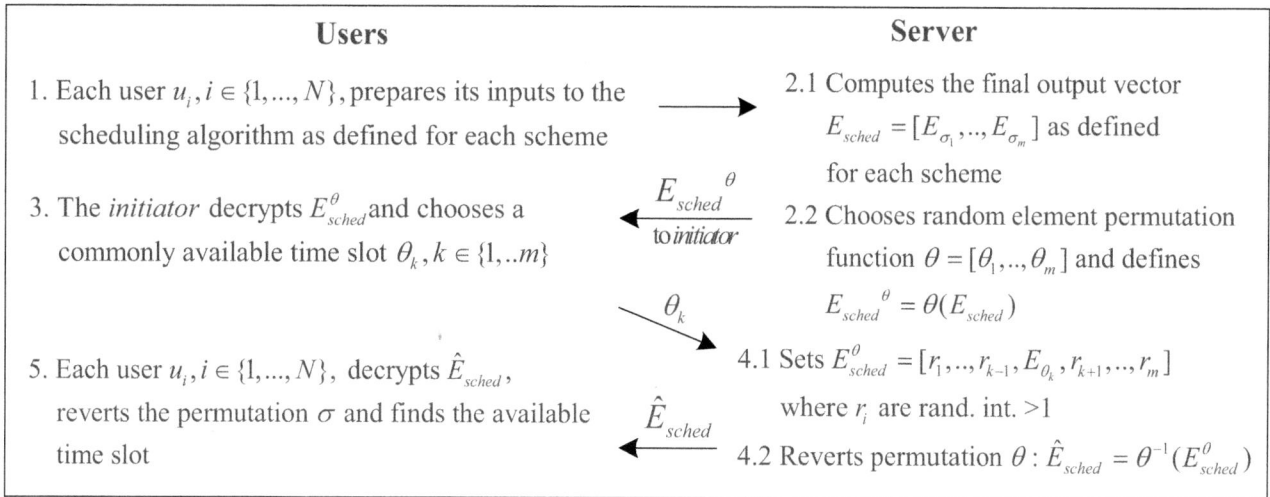

Figure 9: Extended algorithm scheme for revealing a single available time slot.

algorithm execution and send it (in encrypt form) to the server during the scheduling process. The server would then forward these encrypted nonces to each participant, who could verify that all received nonces are equal. If not all nonces are equal, then the participants know that there has been at least one replay attack, and thus the schedule results are not to be trusted.

9.3 Single Available Time Slot

The output of conventional, not privacy-preserving scheduling services (such as Doodle [3] or Outlook [5]) consists of time slots in which all participating users are available. The proposed schemes follow this paradigm and they provide, in an efficient and privacy-preserving way, all time-slots for which all users are available.

In some cases, however, it might be desirable to limit the disclosure of common availabilities to only one time-slot, instead of the set of all available time-slots. This would provide an additional layer of privacy for the individual schedules, as the participants would be given a single feasible solution. Hereafter we describe one simple way to adapt the proposed schemes to support this feature (Figure 9).

First, all users participating in the scheduling process perform step 1 of the respective algorithm (*SchedElg*, *SchedPa* or *SchedGM*). Second, the server performs step 2 but it does not send the final output to each user. Instead, it randomly chooses a private time-slot permutation function $\theta = [\theta_1, \ldots, \theta_m]$ and applies it to the elements of the final output vector(s) E_{sched}. We call this new vector(s) E_{sched}^{θ}. At this point, the schedules have been permuted twice, once by the users prior to the encryptions (with σ) and once by the server (with θ).

Next, the server sends E_{sched}^{θ} to the user who started the activity scheduling (the *initiator*), which then gets the common availabilities but in a doubly permuted order. The initiator is able to determine the *available* slots in this doubly permuted time slot list, but he is not able to determine the time slots they correspond to in the original schedule. The initiator selects one commonly available time slot θ_k and securely sends the index θ_k to the server. Fourth, the server (i) replaces all availabilities other than θ_k in E_{sched}^{θ}

with random numbers, (ii) reverts the permutation θ, and (iii) sends this new vector(s) $\hat{E}_{sched}$ to each user. Finally, each user decrypts and reverts the initial permutation σ of the received vector(s) and determines which time slot j is the only commonly available time slot.

This simple solution that reveals only a single available time slot to all the participants involves one extra message exchange between the initiator and the scheduling server, as shown in step 3 of Figure 9. Although the permutation θ performed by the server preempts the initiator from knowing the true common availabilities, he might still want to maliciously modify the permuted availabilities. However, the only action the initiator can do is to choose one of the permuted time slots and communicate its index θ_k to the server, as it is the server who will then revert the permutation θ and send the final vector(s) $\hat{E}_{sched}$ to all users.

10. CONCLUSION AND FUTURE WORK

Activity scheduling applications are increasingly used by people on-the-move to efficiently and securely manage their time. In addition to privacy, which is paramount, such services should also be practical and feasible to implement, given the client-server paradigm that most providers are using. In this paper, we have provided a framework for the formal study of privacy properties in such applications, and we have proposed three novel privacy-preserving protocols that, in addition to guaranteeing privacy, are more efficient than similar solutions in terms of computation and communication complexities. Moreover, the implementation and extensive performance evaluation on real mobile devices showed that our privacy-preserving schemes are well suited to practical network architectures and services.

As part of our future work, we intend to further optimize the implementation of the proposed scheduling algorithms for performance on mobile devices, and to include user preferences and security related features described in the previous section. We also plan to release the source code of the proposed scheduling schemes to the general public under the GPL licence.

Acknowledgment

We would like to thank Sudeep Singh Walia and Praveen Kumar for the implementations, Mathias Humbert, Anthony Durussel and Gianpaolo Perrucci for their constructive input that helped improving the quality of this work, as well as the Nokia Research Center (Lausanne) for supporting this project.

11. REFERENCES

[1] Apple iCal. http://apple.com/ical.

[2] Chilabs PDA (Personal Digital Assistants) use study. http://personal.bgsu.edu/~nberg/chilabs/pda.htm.

[3] Doodle: easy scheduling. http://www.doodle.com/.

[4] Google smart rescheduler. http://gmailblog.blogspot.com/2010/03/smart-rescheduler-in-google-calendar.html.

[5] Microsoft Outlook. http://office.microsoft.com/outlook.

[6] Nokia Ovi. http://ovi.nokia.com.

[7] dailywireless.org. http://www.dailywireless.org/2009/03/24/smartphone-users-100m-by-2013, 2009.

[8] I. Bilogrevic, M. Jadliwala, J.-P. Hubaux, I. Aad, and V. Niemi. Privacy-preserving activity scheduling on mobile devices. EPFL Technical Report 161569, https://infoscience.epfl.ch/record/161569, 2010.

[9] C. Cachin and R. Strobl. Asynchronous group key exchange with failures. In *PODC '04: Proceedings of the twenty-third annual ACM symposium on Principles of distributed computing*, pages 357–366, New York, NY, USA, 2004. ACM.

[10] C.-H. O. Chen, C.-W. Chen, C. Kuo, Y.-H. Lai, J. M. McCune, A. Studer, A. Perrig, B.-Y. Yang, and T.-C. Wu. Gangs: Gather, authenticate 'n group securely. In *MobiCom '08: Proceedings of the 14th ACM international conference on Mobile computing and networking*, pages 92–103, New York, NY, USA, 2008. ACM.

[11] E. De Cristofaro and G. Tsudik. Practical private set intersection protocols with linear complexity. *Financial Cryptography and Data Security FC'10*, 2010.

[12] W. Du and M. Atallah. Secure multi-party computation problems and their applications: a review and open problems. In *Proceedings of the 2001 workshop on New security paradigms*, pages 13–22. ACM New York, NY, USA, 2001.

[13] T. ElGamal. A public key cryptosystem and a signature scheme based on discrete logarithms. *IEEE transactions on information theory*, 31(4):469–472, 1985.

[14] E. Ephrati, G. Zlotkin, and J. S. Rosenschein. Meet your destiny: A non-manipulable meeting scheduler. In *CSCW '94: Proceedings of the 1994 ACM conference on Computer supported cooperative work*, pages 359–371, New York, NY, USA, 1994. ACM.

[15] M. Franzin, E. Freuder, F. Rossi, and R. Wallace. Multi-agent meeting scheduling with preferences: Efficiency, privacy loss, and solution quality. *Computational Intelligence*, 20(2), 2004.

[16] O. Goldreich. *Foundations of Cryptography*, volume 1. Cambridge University Press, 2001.

[17] S. Goldwasser and S. Micali. Probabilistic encryption. *JCSS*, 28(2):270–299, 1984.

[18] T. Herlea, J. Claessens, B. Preneel, G. Neven, F. Piessens, and B. De Decker. On securely scheduling a meeting. In *Trusted information: the new decade challenge: IFIP TC11 16th International Conference on Information Security (IFIP/Sec'01), June 11-13, 2001, Paris, France*, pages 183–198. Kluwer Academic Pub, 2001.

[19] B. Kellermann and R. Böhme. Privacy-Enhanced Event Scheduling. In *IEEE International Conference on Computational Science and Engineering*, volume 3, pages 52–59, 2009.

[20] L. Kissner and D. Song. Privacy-preserving set operations. *Advances in Cryptology - CRYPTO 2005*, 3621:241–257, 2005.

[21] Y.-H. Lin, A. Studer, H.-C. Hsiao, J. M. McCune, K.-H. Wang, M. Krohn, P.-L. Lin, A. Perrig, H.-M. Sun, and B.-Y. Yang. Spate: Small-group PKI-less authenticated trust establishment. In *MobiSys '09: Proceedings of the 7th international conference on Mobile systems, applications, and services*, pages 1–14, New York, NY, USA, 2009. ACM.

[22] P. Paillier. Public-key cryptosystems based on composite degree residuosity classes. *Advances in Cryptology - EUROCRYPT '99*, 1592:223–238, 1999.

[23] R. Rivest, A. Shamir, and L. Adleman. A method for obtaining digital signatures and public-key cryptosystems. *Communications of the ACM*, 21(2):126, 1978.

[24] M. Silaghi and D. Mitra. Distributed constraint satisfaction and optimization with privacy enforcement. *3rd IC on Intelligent Agent Technology*, pages 531–535, 2004.

[25] M. C. Silaghi. Meeting scheduling guaranteeing n/2-privacy and resistant to statistical analysis (applicable to any discsp). In *WI '04: Proceedings of the 2004 IEEE/WIC/ACM International Conference on Web Intelligence*, pages 711–715, Washington, DC, USA, 2004. IEEE Computer Society.

[26] M. Stadler. Publicly verifiable secret sharing. In *Advances in Cryptology - EUROCRYPT '96*, pages 190–199, 1996.

[27] R. Wallace and E. Freuder. Constraint-based reasoning and privacy/efficiency tradeoffs in multi-agent problem solving. *Artificial Intelligence*, 161(1-2):209–227, 2005.

[28] M. Yokoo, K. Suzuki, and K. Hirayama. Secure distributed constraint satisfaction: Reaching agreement without revealing private information. *Artificial Intelligence*, 161(1-2):229 – 245, 2005. Distributed Constraint Satisfaction.

[29] A. Zunino and M. Campo. Chronos: A multi-agent system for distributed automatic meeting scheduling. *Expert Systems with Applications*, 36(3, Part 2):7011 – 7018, 2009.

Privacy-Enhanced Reputation-Feedback Methods to Reduce Feedback Extortion in Online Auctions

Michael T. Goodrich

Dept. of Computer Science
University of California, Irvine
Irvine, California 92697-3435 USA
goodrich(at)acm.org

Florian Kerschbaum

SAP Research
Vincenz-Priessnitz-Str. 1
76131 Karlsruhe, Germany
florian.kerschbaum(at)sap.com

ABSTRACT

In this paper, we study methods for improving the utility and privacy of reputation scores for online auctions, such as used in eBay, so as to reduce the effectiveness of feedback extortion. The main idea behind our techniques is to escrow reputations scores until appropriate external events occur. Depending on the degree of utility and privacy needed, these external techniques could depend on the number and type of reputation scores collected. Moreover, if additional privacy protection is needed, then random sampling can be used with respect reputation scores in such a way that reputation aggregates remain useful, but individual reputation scores are probabilistically hidden from users. Finally, we show that if privacy is also desired with respect to the the reputation aggregator, then we can use zero-knowledge proofs for reputation comparisons.

Categories and Subject Descriptors

F.2.0 [**Analysis of Algorithms and Problem Complexity**]: General; H.3.5 [**Information Storage and Retrieval**]: Online Information Services—*Commercial services*; J.4 [**Social and Behavioral Sciences**]: Economics; K.4.4 [**Computers and Society**]: Electronic Commerce; K.6.0 [**Management of Computing and Information Systems**]: General—*Economics*; K.6.5 [**Management of Computing and Information Systems**]: Security and Protection

General Terms

Algorithms, Economics, Security

Keywords

online auctions, game theory, prisoner's dilemma game, stag hunt game, Internet security, privacy, reputation, escrow, zero-knowledge proofs

1. INTRODUCTION

Now that online auctions are a mature Internet enterprise, online auctions are a common source of complaints of Internet fraud. The most common first line defense for dealing with auction fraud is to provide a feedback system, so that buyers and sellers can rate each other. That is, to provide a means for deterring cheating and fraud, the managers of online auction systems allow sellers to rate buyers on how quickly and honestly they pay for the items for which they are the highest bidder and buyers to rate sellers on how honestly they described their goods and how well they shipped them. Not surprisingly, the feedback rating score of a buyer or seller can have dramatic impacts on their ability to buy and sell goods [19].

Rating systems vary from those that rate on a numerical scale to those, such as eBay, that rate on a simple "negative," "neutral," and "positive" continuum. In practice, however, these different feedback mechanisms are similar, in that anything but the highest, most positive rating is seen as a bad score. Thus, we take the simplified view in this paper that feedback evaluations are essential binary, being either "positive" or "negative."

Because of the importance of reputation in online auctions, there is a strong incentive for buyers and sellers to work hard to get highly positive ratings. Naturally, the intent of this incentive is that buyers and sellers should be on their best behavior, with buyers being fast and reliable with their payments and sellers being fast and reliable with their item descriptions and shipping methods.

Unfortunately, dishonest or incompetent buyers and sellers still want positive feedback, and some are even willing to manipulate the system to get it. In particular, some buyers and sellers who deserve negative feedback will nevertheless pressure their trading partner for positive feedback even if their behavior is more accurately classified as "negative." For example, a seller might threaten to provide negative feedback to an unhappy buyer if she provides negative feedback on the seller.

Such *feedback extortion* became such a problem within eBay, for example, that in January 2008 eBay changed its feedback policy so that sellers can only provide positive feedback for buyers. In addition, the eBay web site contains the following feedback extortion policy[1]:

---

[1] http://pages.ebay.com/help/policies/
feedback-extortion.html

Buyers aren't allowed to demand goods or services outside of the transaction while threatening negative Feedback, neutral Feedback, or low detailed seller ratings.

Sellers can't require buyers to leave specific Feedback or detailed seller ratings. Sellers also can't demand that buyers withdraw existing Feedback or detailed seller ratings. This applies to all Feedback activity, whether it happened before, during, or after delivery of items or services described in the original listing.

This solution removes the possibility of feedback extortion from sellers, of course, but it also completely negates the usefulness of feedback on buyers. Now the only influence that a seller can provide on the reputation of a poor buyer is to say nothing at all and hope that other, external methods can be used to resolve any disputes with buyers. Even then, this seller feedback restriction approach still does not stop feedback extortion from buyers, who can still threaten negative feedback on sellers unless they give the buyers positive feedback by a certain deadline. Thus, we are interested in this paper on schemes that can promote good-quality, accurate feedback, while discouraging or even preventing feedback extortion.

1.1 Prior Related Results

The positive impact of feedback on interacting parties has been studied by economists for a long time and even been experimentally verified [4]. Nevertheless only the bilateral feedback system enabled the emerging problem of feedback retaliation.

1.1.1 Feedback Correction and Evaluation

Feedback retaliation is well-known folklore in online auction sites. Resnick and Zeckhauser systematically evaluated eBay feedback data [19]. They noticed that only 0.3 percent of all transactions were rated negative, but in case one partner rated negative the probability of the other partner rating negative was over 37%. Furthermore, only roughly half of the transactions were rated at all. This data at least suggests that there is a problem of feedback extortion and reluctance to rate negatively.

Miller et al. suggest a payment mechanism to elicit honest feedback [14]. Such a payment mechanism can be implemented cost-neutral to the reputation platform and have a Nash equilibrium for truth-telling. Of course, its realization involves another accounting mechanism not necessary in our implementation.

Traupman and Wilensky suggest a statistical method in order to correct the error from negative ratings [20]. Nevertheless they evaluate their system only under synthetic data from current reputation systems. Clearly this does not take into account the game changing effect a change in the reputation scoring algorithm has. For example, if it becomes less threatening for someone to be rated negative, he might be inclined to even lower his ratings or perform worse.

1.1.2 Feedback Computation Privacy

Privacy as a mechanism to protect against feedback extortion has been proposed previously by Kerschbaum [12], in that he presents a protocol for a private and reliable reputation system using two mutually distrustful service providers,

i.e., where there is no single trusted reputation provider anymore. Nevertheless, the proposed mechanism still suffers from a long delay before publishing results, which this paper removes via sampling and escrow.

Note that, in the context of this paper, privacy deals with the secrecy of a rating score, i.e., *how* an agent was rated. Other private reputation systems, e.g., [1, 15, 18], only protect the identity of the rater, i.e., *who* has rated, which does not protect against feedback extortion.

Privately computing a reputation score is an instance of secure computation (SC) [2, 11, 21]. SC allows a number of parties to compute a function (such as a reputation score) on joint inputs (such as the ratings) without disclosing anything except what can be inferred from one party's input and output. We stress that a straight-forward application of SC does not protect the rating by itself. The continuous release of the reputation score, i.e., the result of the aggregation mechanism, reveals the input and breaks privacy. Protocols that implement secure computation therefore either use a more complicated reputation mechanism, e.g. collaborative filtering [5], or simply do not reveal the result [17].

1.1.3 Differential Privacy

The work of this paper is also related to approaches used in the context of *differential privacy* (e.g., see [9]) for hiding the contribution of a single value to the whole through the introduction of random noise or assumed randomness. Unfortunately, such approaches are not a good fit for protecting the privacy of reputation scores in online auctions. There are two primary reasons for this difficulty.

First, most existing schemes, such as that by Dinur and Nissim [7], for protecting the privacy of individual values that contribute to a sum require that one at least knows the number of items included in the sum. But reputation scores have an arbitrary, unbounded number of items that can be included—they are the total number of items bought or sold by a member of an auction—and making such previous differential-privacy methods work for such unbounded summations appears difficult.

Second, a reputation score evolves over time. So we cannot assume that such scores are drawn uniformly at random from some distribution, say, as is needed in the differential-privacy scheme of Duan [8]. Likewise, a participant that queries his or her own reputation after every transaction can be modeled as issuing correlated summation queries, but existing techniques, such as that of Li *et al.* [13], for obfuscating such queries, appear to introduce too much noise to be of practical use for reputation aggregation.

1.2 Our Results

In this paper, we first present a game-theoretic analysis of simple reputation escrow. In simple reputation escrow we consider a single transaction and its feedback. We show that when players are forced to leave feedback concurrently they are inclined to leave correct feedback. This applies even in case both players experienced a negative transaction.

We then extend this result to a reputation system that keeps feedback escrowed forever, i.e., it remains entirely private. This may seem impossible at first sight, since changes in the reputation score reveal the type of left feedback. Nevertheless we introduce a randomized sampling technique that can compute reliable averages while still providing privacy of the feedback. We show the error bounds of this sampling

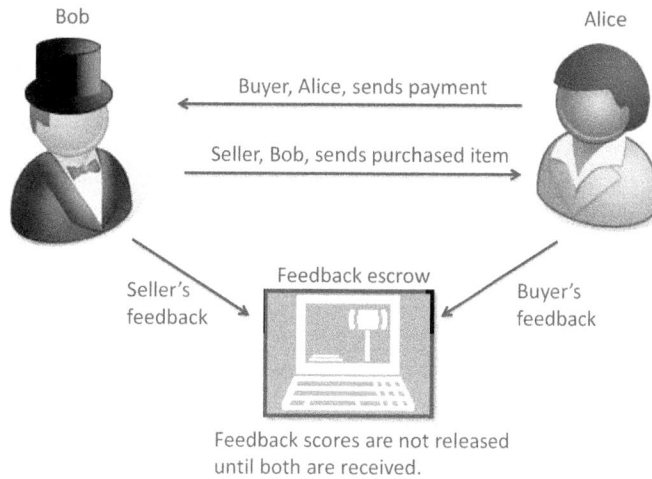

Figure 1: Feedback escrow.

technique and conclude that it is a reliable estimator of performance.

As a last result, we remove the need for a trusted reputation service provider. We adapt the previous result of Kerschbaum [12] to include the randomized sampling technique. This adaption requires an additional zero-knowledge proof for correct sampling. The challenge in its construction is that the input for the proof is distributed.

In summary, this paper contributes

- a *game-theoretic analysis of reputation escrow*

- a *randomized feedback sampling mechanisms* that provides privacy of ratings despite immediate publishing

- a *secure computation of a zero-knowledge proof* for correct sampling that removes the need for a trusted reputation service provider

The remainder of the paper is structured as follows: Section 2 introduces reputation escrow and presents its game-theoretic analysis. Section 3 describes the sampling algorithm and analyses its error bounds. Section 4 explains how to remove the need for a trusted reputation provider and the secure computation protocol for the necessary zero-knowledge proof including a security proof. We conclude in Section 5.

2. SIMPLE REPUTATION ESCROW

The first solution we consider is a simple one—escrow the feedback from a buyer or seller, which ever comes first, until the second party in the transaction posts feedback on the first. (See Figure 1.)

This simple approach removes the sequential nature of feedback scoring for determining a person's reputation in the online auction; hence, it prevents quid pro quo retaliation or reward, for non-repeated transactions. When an online auction uses a reputation escrow, a buyer or seller cannot know the feedback score they are receiving from the other until they post their own feedback score for the other. Rather than argue the benefits of a reputation escrow in an ad hoc manner, however, let us analyze its benefits using game theory.

2.1 Studying Reputation Escrow Through a Game Theoretic Lens

When a buyer, Alice, and seller, Bob, are contemplating the feedback to give one another after a transaction, there are several factors that impact their respective decisions. Let us model what we feel are the most important of these factors using the following non-negative parameters (where we let x represent A for "Alice" or B for "Bob" and we let y denote the other party, i.e., "Bob" or "Alice")

- Δ_x: the utility that x receives by having his or her reputation factor increase from the receipt of a positive feedback score. So $-\Delta_x$ is the amount by which x's reputation utility would decrease from his/her receiving a negative feedback score.

- f_x: the normalized utility that x receives from giving a correct feedback (e.g., from the satisfaction of doing the right thing and/or helping other auction users learn the true reputation of y better).

- r_x: the normalized utility that x receives from performing a revenge punishment on y for a negative feedback from y. It is a recognition of human nature to allow for this parameter, but we nevertheless assume that revenge satisfaction cannot fully overcome negative feedback, even when one is also giving out the correct feedback (so $r_x + f_x < \Delta_x$).

There are four different games that Alice and Bob can play, depending on whether each wants to give the other a positive (P) feedback or a negative feedback (N). We can model these games using a two-by-two payoff matrix, where we let Alice be the row player and let Bob be the column player. These are shown in Figure 2 in generic form.

If Alice and Bob both want to give positive feedback (the P-P game), then this is either a game strictly dominated by the (P,P) response (if $r_x < f_x$), which is the unique Nash equilibrium in this case, or (if $r_x > f_x$) it is an instance

	P	N
P	$(\Delta_A + f_A, \Delta_B + f_B)$	$(-\Delta_A + f_A, \Delta_B)$
N	$(\Delta_A, -\Delta_B + f_B)$	$(-\Delta_A + r_A, -\Delta_B + r_B)$

(a)

	P	N
P	$(\Delta_A + f_A, \Delta_B)$	$(-\Delta_A + f_A, \Delta_B + f_B)$
N	$(\Delta_A, -\Delta_B)$	$(-\Delta_A + r_A, -\Delta_B + r_B + f_B)$

(b)

	P	N
P	$(\Delta_A, \Delta_B + f_B)$	$(-\Delta_A, \Delta_B)$
N	$(\Delta_A + f_A, -\Delta_B + f_B)$	$(-\Delta_A + f_A + r_A, -\Delta_B + r_B)$

(c)

	P	N
P	(Δ_A, Δ_B)	$(-\Delta_A, \Delta_B + f_B)$
N	$(\Delta_A + f_A, -\Delta_B)$	$(-\Delta_A + f_A + r_A, -\Delta_B + f_B + r_B)$

(d)

Figure 2: The four games that come from Alice and Bob respectively wanting to give (a) P-P feedback, (b) P-N feedback, (c) N-P feedback, and (d) N-N feedback.

of a generic stag hunt game[2]. In the case of a stag hunt game (i.e., if $r_x > f_x$), there two Nash equilibria for this game, the (P,P) response and the (N,N) response. Clearly, however, the (P,P) response is preferred by both parties, even in this case, so it is the most likely response, as one would expect, even if $r_x > f_x$.

The N-P and P-N games are less interesting, from a game theoretic point of view, in that one player has a dominating N strategy and, given that choice, the other player's best choice is either P or N depending on the relative utility they receive from altruism (their f_x value) or revenge (their r_x value). So, if $r_x > f_x$, then (N,N) is the unique Nash equilibrium for both of these games. Alternatively, if $r_x < f_x$, then (N,P) or (P,N) is the unique Nash equilibrium, depending on whether it is Alice or Bob that feels the other deserves a negative feedback (i.e., whether they are playing the N-P game or the P-N game).

The N-N game, on the other hand, is an instance of a generic prisoner's dilemma game[3]. In spite of the dilemma posed by the fact that (P,P) is a highest payoff choice for both players, the Nash equilibrium for this game is (N,N).

So as to provide more concrete examples of these games, we show examples of these games and in Figure 3 using the concrete values, $\Delta_x = 5$, $f_x = 3$, and $r_x = 1$. Note that

[2]In a *stag hunt* game, two players are hunting a stag. If they cooperate, they both share the prize. If one of them does not cooperate, while the other still does, then the non-cooperator gets a hare (which is worth less than half a stag), while the stag hunter gets nothing. If they both defect, they both get hares.

[3]In a *prisoner's dilemma* game, two prisoner's are accused of a crime. If they both deny the other is guilty, then they both go free. If only one testifies against the other, on the other hand, then he gets a reward and goes free, while the other gets a heavy sentence. But if both of them testifies against the other, they both get modest prison terms.

in this case, where revenge is less powerful than altruism, i.e., when $r_x < f_x$, then we get that the Nash equilibrium for each game is the desired feedback that we would like to see for this reputation system. That is, the system works in this case, in that the optimal choice for each player in this system is to provide the feedback that they feel is most appropriate for the other player.

	P	N
P	$(8, 8)$	$(-2, 5)$
N	$(5, -2)$	$(-4, -4)$

(a)

	P	N
P	$(8, 5)$	$(-2, 8)$
N	$(5, -5)$	$(-4, -1)$

(b)

	P	N
P	$(5, 8)$	$(-5, 5)$
N	$(8, -2)$	$(-1, -4)$

(c)

	P	N
P	$(5, 5)$	$(-5, 8)$
N	$(8, -5)$	$(-1, -1)$

(d)

Figure 3: The four games that come from Alice and Bob respectively wanting to give (a) P-P feedback, (b) P-N feedback, (c) N-P feedback, and (d) N-N feedback, for the concrete values, $\Delta_x = 5$, $f_x = 3$, and $r_x = 1$.

Of course, even in the case when revenge is stronger than altruism, the two parties don't know with certainty which game they are actually playing, between the games P-P, P-N, N-P, and N-N. At best, they can eliminate two of these games, based on what they think is the appropriate feedback to give the other person. But they don't know the feedback the other person feels is most appropriate to give them. Based on the above analysis, if a person feels the other player deserves a negative feedback (N), then they should give them a negative feedback. But, even if revenge is stronger than altruism (i.e., $r_x > f_x$), a player who feels the other person deserves a positive rating (P), has to make an educated guess as to whether they are playing the P-P game or the N-P or P-N game (depending on whether they are the buyer or seller). By assigning probabilities, based on how satisfied they think the other person is, a player can calculate an expected return based on their probabilities that they are playing, say, the P-P game or the P-N game. In most cases, the optimal choice in this instance will be to provide positive feedback for the other person when they deserve it. Thus, even if revenge is stronger than altruism, the reputation system should work and it should score people with their appropriate feedback scores most of the time.

2.2 Why Non-Escrowed Systems Breakdown

In a nutshell, a crucial property that allows the reputation escrow system to work is that the buyer and seller have a degree of uncertainty about what the other person is going to do. In fact, they don't know for certain even what game they are playing, between the choices of P-P, N-P, P-N, and N-N. And that uncertainty pushes each person to provide the appropriate level of feedback as their optimal response. In this subsection, we outline why removing this uncertainty, as in a non-escrowed system, allows for feedback extortion.

Suppose now that the feedback game is played sequentially, so that player x first makes their choice, which is revealed to player y, and then y makes their choice. For simplicity, let us assume that it is the buyer, Alice, who goes first and the seller, Bob, who goes second (the reverse scenario is similar). Notice immediately that as soon as Alice provides her feedback, Bob knows her response and can react to that choice with certainty. Moreover, Alice now knows that Bob is going to realize her response as soon as she reveals it, and this can in fact influence the choice Alice is going to make.

This influence doesn't make much of a difference, however, in three of the feedback games. In the P-P game, for instance, Alice reveals a positive response and Bob replies with a positive response, as these are the optimal choices for them. Likewise, in the P-N game, Alice reveals her positive or negative response depending on whether she favors altruism over revenge, just as in the synchronized version, and then is hit with a negative feedback from Bob either way. And in the N-N game, Alice reveals a negative response and is immediately hit with negative feedback from Bob, as this is the equilibrium choice for both of them.

Something interesting happens in the N-P game, however, where Alice feels that the correct assessment of her satisfaction with the transaction is negative while Bob feels that the correct assessment of his satisfaction with the transaction is positive. Let's looks at the possible scenarios:

- *Alice reveals a positive response.* In this case, Bob's optimal response is also positive, and the payoff is $(\Delta_A, \Delta_B + f_B)$.

- *Alice reveals a negative response.* In this case, depending on Bob's relative utility between altruism and revenge, his optimal response is either positive, with payoff $(\Delta_A + f_A, -\Delta_B + f_B)$, or negative, with payoff $(-\Delta_A + f_A, -\Delta_B + r_B)$.

Thus, Alice knows that if she reveals a positive response, she is giving up on a higher payoff, of $\Delta_A + f_A$, which she might get from Bob should he be an altruistic person. But this is exactly the decision that Bob can now influence. Should he reveal to Alice ahead of her choice (e.g., using an email threat or even just a snide comment) that he prefers revenge over altruism, then her optimal choice is now to give him positive feedback. That is, she is making a suboptimal choice for herself, based on pressure from Bob, which is extortion. Of course, Bob would not know at the point of his threats whether Alice and he are playing the P-P, N-P, P-N, or N-N game, but he loses nothing in the P-P, P-N, or N-N game from revealing his preference for revenge

over altruism. Since he gains something in the N-P game from this revelation, Bob is therefore motivated to threaten Alice with retaliation should she give him negative feedback. The reputation escrow system reduces the possibility of this abuse, however, by making it impossible for Bob to know with certainty the feedback he is getting from Alice (and vice versa) until after he reveals his feedback score.

Of course, if Bob strongly suspects that Alice has given him negative feedback, then he may refuse to give Alice any feedback, so as to avoid getting her feedback. So this simple reputation escrow approach has the drawback that it allows for Bob to effectively block feedback that he anticipates will be negative. The simple reputation escrow system returns the feedback process to have the players giving their honest feedback when they are both motivated to complete the feedback process. But it doesn't stop this feedback blockage that either Alice or Bob could initiate against the other. The next solution we describe addresses this drawback.

3. SAMPLING FROM ARCHIVED REPUTATION SCORES

Let us now consider a more restrictive reputation escrow system, where we escrow all feedback and never release it in its raw form, ever. That is, let us consider an *archived* reputation escrow. At first, this might seem to be a wasted effort, which could never yield useful reputation data, but there is a work around.

Since one of the main reasons for having a reputation feedback score is so that we can compute reputation averages for each participant in an online auction, let us consider how we could use an archived reputation escrow to compute a reputation score.

Suppose that Alice has just left feedback for Bob, and, like all of his feedback scores, this score is not released. We nevertheless would like to compute a reputation score, which is the average of his reputation scores (e.g., on a scale of 1 to 5, for degree of satisfaction, 0 to 1, for positive-negative, or -1 to 1, for negative-neutral-positive). Let n denote the number of feedback scores that Bob now has and let S denote the sum of these scores. Thus, we are interested in computing S/n, Bob's average feedback score. But if we directly release S/n and Bob has been keeping track of how this average score changes each time he receives a new feedback score (and, in particular, Bob knows this average before Alice gives her feedback), then Bob can figure out how Alice rated him.

So instead of directly computing S/n, we independently sample from Bob's feedback scores $r < n$ times, with each score being equally likely (and allowing for repetitions, since each selection is independent). We then compute the sum, T, of the chosen scores and we release Bob's computed average feedback score, F_B, as

$$F_B = \frac{Tn}{r},$$

where the parameter r is determined below in our analysis. So let us study the degree of accuracy and privacy that comes from this sampling approach.

3.1 Accuracy

Let us simplify our analysis by assuming that the scores are either 1, for "positive," or 0, for "negative." This is actually not much of a restriction in practice, since praise inflation in online auctions occurs to such a regular degree that anything but the highest feedback score is considered negative. That is, buyers tend to rate sellers by the percentage of feedbacks that are the highest possible.

Let X_i be a random variable that is 1 if the ith feedback score chosen from Bob's feedbacks is positive, so $X_i = 0$ if this score is negative. So we can write

$$T = \sum_{i=1}^{r} X_i.$$

To analyze the accuracy of this random sampling method, let us consider the expected error that occurs from this approach,

$$E\left(\left|\frac{T}{r} - \frac{p}{n}\right|\right),$$

where p is the number of positive feedbacks that Bob has.

For relatively small values of n and r, we can compute this expected value directly as

$$\sum_{i=0}^{r} \left|\frac{T}{r} - \frac{p}{n}\right| \Pr(T = i),$$

which is the same as

$$\sum_{i=0}^{r} \left|\frac{i}{r} - \frac{p}{n}\right| \binom{r}{i} \left(\frac{p}{n}\right)^i \left(1 - \frac{p}{n}\right)^{r-i}.$$

The expected error is maximized for $p = \frac{n}{2}$. This implies that the necessary sample size r for achieving an expected error of 5% or 10%, respectively, is constant and independent of the number of feedback scores n. Figure 4 depicts the expected error for sample sizes of 1 to 75. We conclude that 16 samples are sufficient to lower the expected error below 10% and 64 samples for 5%. Consequently it is sufficient and efficient to sample a (small) fixed number of feedback scores.

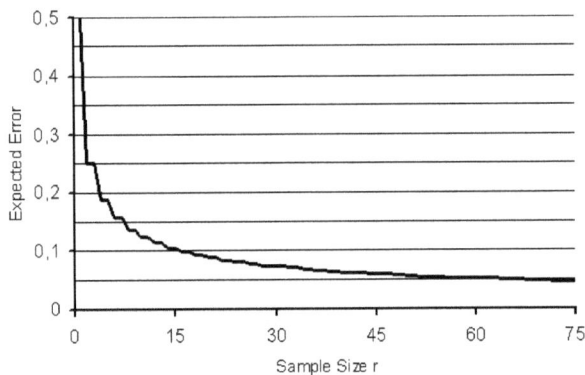

Figure 4: Expected Error over Sample Size

3.2 Privacy

An objective commonly opposing accuracy is privacy, and this remains the case with respect to sampled reputation scores. The question is how well does sampling protect a single feedback score. Assume an attacker is observing

its average feedback score F_B, e.g., after each transaction. We need to determine the probability that if he observes a lower score, a negative feedback was left. This probability determines the reliability of the observation.

We conduct the following experiment. Given n and p we take r random samples and compute F_B. Now we introduce two cases:

(a) a positive feedback is left

(b) a negative feedback is left.

We choose r random samples again and compute F'_B. We define a *privacy breach* as the event, if

- in case a: $F'_B > F_B$
- in case b: $F'_B < F_B$.

We conducted this experiment for a range of values and in most cases the probability of a privacy breach was so low that we did not observe one even for very large sample sizes. Nevertheless, interesting situations arise in the borderline cases, where privacy breaches are likely.

In the remainder of this section, we assume a sampling rate $\frac{r}{n} = \frac{1}{2}$. As we have seen in Section 3.1, this rate quickly leads to accurate estimations.

The first borderline case is when there is a very low number of feedback scores (as would occur, say, with a buyer or seller just starting out). Clearly new feedback can result in a significant change of the score. For example, if a seller has one positive score and one negative score, then the next feedback will change the score $\frac{p}{n}$ by an absolute value of $\frac{1}{6}$.

Figure 5: Probability of privacy breach for a small number of feedback scores.

In Figure 5, we depict the results of our experiments for a small number of feedback scores. The probability of a privacy breach for such small numbers of feedback scores is shown. We assume a score $\frac{p}{n} = \frac{1}{2}$ that minimizes accuracy. The probability is depicted on a logarithmic scale and from the graph we conclude an exponential decrease. Even for two feedbacks we measured only a privacy breach probability of less than 17%. For four feedbacks this probability is already less than 4%. Thus, one way to mitigate the risk of a privacy breach in this case is to simply delay the release of an agent's average feedback score until he or she has reached some reasonable threshold, of, say, 5 or 10 scores.

The second borderline case is when an agent has a high number of positive feedback scores. Clearly, negative feedback is easier to spot in a sea of positive feedback. Assuming one has a set of nearly uniformly positive feedback scores, then another positive feedback will maintain the high average or slightly increase it and a negative feedback will lower the average score if it is sampled. Therefore the probability of a privacy breach is exactly the sampling rate $\frac{r}{n}$ in case of previous scores being uniformly positive.

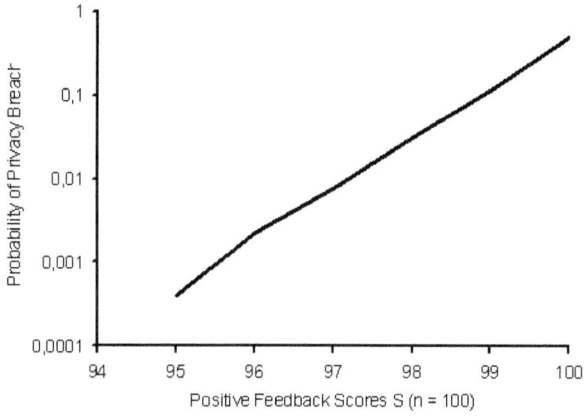

Figure 6: Probability of Privacy Breach for High Feedback Score

In Figure 6, we show the results of our experiments for the probability of a privacy breach for high feedback scores. We assume $n = 100$ feedback ratings have been left. The probability is depicted on a logarithmic scale for $p = 95$ to $p = 100$ positive ratings among this set of scores. From the graph, we conclude an exponential decrease of the probability of privacy breach with decreasing positive ratings. Nevertheless, for 99% positive ratings, the privacy breach probability is already lower than 12%. Again, as with the borderline case of too few scores, a possible countermeasure in the case of many positive scores is to wait until a minimum number of additional ratings has been received before publishing a score. This waiting period does not have to be large, since we have seen that already a second negative feedback rating is hard to detect. We therefore only have to wait until it is likely that one negative feedback has been left.

We stress that these experiments rely on a single sample for each feedback score. If the feedback score is computed multiple times with different sampling sets, but identical feedback ratings, the probability of a privacy breach increases. This risk can be reduced, however, by using a sampling rate that is not too close to 1, so that it would be difficult for an adversary to know when the scores from various agents are included.

4. UNTRUSTED REPUTATION PROVIDER

So far we have considered methods for protecting the rater and ratee in an online auction, but the service provider aggregating the reputation scores was assumed to be fully trustworthy. Ideally, the rater and ratee should not have to fully trust the reputation provider. For instance, in [12], a scheme has been presented for distributing trust over two reputation providers SP_1 and SP_2.

The advantage of this scheme is that the first reputation provider, SP_1, only learns the ratings and the ratee whereas the second reputation provider only learns the rater (in addition to the reputation score). This distribution ensures privacy of the rating against a single service provider. Furthermore, using verification algorithms, rater and ratee can ensure that all, but only valid, ratings have been aggregated into the reputation score, i.e., it is not possible for the service provider to invent or suppress ratings.

In the scheme from Kerschbaum [12], each transaction has a unique identifier g^r and rating z. The first service provider publishes a public key and we denote with $E()$ the encryption using this public key.[4] The scheme consists of the following protocols and algorithms:

- Alice (ratee) and Bob (rater): $A \longleftrightarrow B$ TokenIssue() $\rightarrow$ Alice: r, Bob: $g^r, \ldots$[5].

- Bob and SP_2: $B \longleftrightarrow SP_2$ RatingSubmission() $\rightarrow SP_2$: $g^r, E(z) \ldots$

- SP_2: PublishRatings() $\rightarrow g^r, E(z), \ldots$

- Alice or Bob: VerifyRatings() $\rightarrow \top \vee \bot$

- SP_1: PublishReputation() $\rightarrow s = f(z, \ldots), \ldots$

- Alice (ratee): VerifyReputation() $\rightarrow \top \vee \bot$

The scheme consists of two basic mechanisms for security. For integrity, it relies on the bilinear decisional Diffie-Hellman assumption and the idea that intermediate results are hard to compute, but can be used to solve an instance of the problem. We refer the reader to [12] for details. For confidentiality, it relies on encryption. A rating z is encrypted using the public key of the first reputation provider SP_1, such that only he will learn the rating, but he will not learn who it is from.

Homomorphic encryption is used in order to compute the reputation score on encrypted ratings. For instance, Paillier encryption [16] is an instance of homomorphic encryption that is public-key and semantically secure. Semantic security in this case means that a ciphertext is indistinguishable from any other ciphertext due to randomization. We can make this randomization explicit in our notation. A plaintext x with randomization r is denoted by $E(x, r)$.[6]

The randomization carries through the homomorphic property, i.e.,

$$E(x_1, r_1)E(x_2, r_2) = E(x_1 + x_2, r_1 r_2)$$

$$E(x_1, r_1)^{x_2} = E(x_1 x_2, r_1^{x_2})$$

---

[4]We omit the identity as a subscript, since there is only one public key in the system.
[5]We omit the details for achieving security against false ratings or false aggregation.
[6]We omit the randomization, if it is irrelevant for the exposition.

4.1 Escrow

The scheme in [12] was designed for the unilateral scheme and therefore obviously does not apply to a scheme with feedback escrow.

Before extending this scheme to handle escrow, we need to make it bilateral. Therefore, for each transaction let there now be two TokenIssue() protocols. One where Alice is the ratee and obtains r_A and Bob is the rater and obtains g^{r_A} and another one with the roles reversed and the identifiers r_B and g^{r_B}.

The basic idea for implementing escrow is that SP_2 now only publishes ratings for transactions where both parties have submitted ratings. Note that SP_1 cannot implement escrow, since it implies learning both parties—ratee and rater—of the transaction. Instead, SP_2 implements escrow learning both parties of the transactions, but not the rating z.

The rater submits next to g^{r_A} also $g^{r_A r_B}$ to SP_2 in the protocol RatingSubmission(), which is a common value to both instances belonging to the same transactions. The reputation provider SP_2 only publishes ratings for which both ratings with $g^{r_A r_B}$ have been received. Alice and Bob can prevent SP_2 from suppressing ratings by signaling their submissions to each other.

4.2 Sampling

In order to extend this scheme further to handle sampling, we let the second reputation provider SP_2 select the subset of ratings. Two questions immediately arise: First, how can we ensure that he chooses the selection fairly (i.e., non-adaptive to the rating) and, second, how can we still verify the aggregation.

The idea for solving the first issue is that the reputation provider chooses the samples first and binds himself to them using a commitment. The idea for the second is to extend the zero-knowledge proof for aggregation by sampling.

Let us start with the simplest zero knowledge proof that $E(x, r)$ is an encryption x. The verifier (encryptor) reveals r and the prover encrypts x with r and verifies that the ciphertexts match.

This basic idea has been used to verify that the reputation score s has been correctly aggregated. The ciphertext of the reputation score $E(s, r)$ can be computed as the product of the ciphertexts of the ratings. Then the reputation provider SP_2 publishes s and the corresponding r, and the ratee verifies that this corresponds to the product of the ciphertexts.

Of course, when introducing sampling, this sampling needs to be considered in the aggregation. A sampling is nothing else than a product with a bit $b \in \{0, 1\}$, however. If the bit b is one, the rating is selected; if the bit is zero, it is not. So we now let the second reputation provider SP_1 select this bit and instead of publish the rating $E(z)$, he publishes $E(bz)$.

The zero-knowledge proof of the first reputation provider SP_1 then remains unchanged. Furthermore, SP_2 can even prove that it adhered to the sampling rate by revealing the sum and randomness of the ciphertext of the sum of the sampling bits in the same way.

The remaining problems are for SP_2 to commit to b and prove in zero-knowledge that $E_{SP_1}(bz)$ has a plaintext of the product of the committed bit and the rating.

As a commitment we let SP_2 publish $c = E_{SP_1}(b, r)$. In [6], there is a zero-knowledge proof (ZKP) that c is a ciphertext for one-out-of-two plaintexts (which are 0 and 1 in our case). SP_2 publishes such a ZKP along with c and keeps b and r for his private records. In order to make each ZKP non-interactive the first reputation provider SP_1, which is not involved in any such ZKP, publishes a common random string. We can then use the techniques from [3] in order to make all proofs non-interactive.

In [6], another ZKP is given for proving, for $E(\alpha, r_\alpha)$, $E(\beta, r_\beta)$, $E(\gamma, r_\gamma)$ that $\gamma = \alpha\beta$. We can use this proof for our scheme, since if SP_2 also publishes $E_{SP_1}(z)$ and proves that $E_{SP_1}(bz)$ is indeed a ciphertext of the product, then the privacy of the rating against SP_2 is still maintained, but Alice and Bob can still verify the ratings using VerifyRating().

We briefly review the ZKP from [6].
Public Input: $e_\alpha = E(\alpha, r_\alpha)$, $e_\beta = E(\beta, r_\beta)$, $e_\gamma = E(\gamma, r_\gamma)$
Private Input of the Prover: α, r_α, β, r_β, γ, r_γ

The prover chooses random values d, r_d, $r_{d\beta}$ and publishes $e_d = E(d, r_d)$ and $e_{d\beta} = E(d\beta, r_{d\beta})$. The prover retrieves u from the common random string and publishes $v = u\alpha + d$ and $r_1 = r_\alpha^u r_d$. Finally, the prover publishes $r_2 = r_\beta^v (r_{d\beta} r_\gamma^u)^{-1}$.

The verifier also retrieves u from the common random string and verifies that $e_\alpha^u e_d = E(v, r_1)$ and $e_\beta^v (e_{d\beta} e_\gamma^u)^{-1} = E(0, r_2)$.

In summary, the ZKP consists of:

- $E(d, r_d)$

- $E(d\beta, r_{d\beta})$

- $v = u\alpha + d, r_1 = r_\alpha^u r_d$

- $r_2 = r_\beta^v (r_{d\beta} r_\gamma^u)^{-1}$

Lemma 1: *The ZKP is complete and honest-verifier zero-knowledge.*

There are two differences in our scheme to the setup of [6]. First, the two ciphertexts for the factors a and b are distributed over two parties: Bob and SP_2. The reputation service provider SP_2 holds the sampling bit b and the rater Bob the rating z. Second, neither of those two parties has the secret key for the encryption scheme, but that is with the first service provider SP_1. Fortunately, the ZKP can be computed without knowledge of the secret key, as long as the randomness for the ciphertexts is known, but that is, of course, distributed over the two parties, again.

The basic idea is to perform a secure computation for the zero-knowledge proof, i.e., SP_2 and Bob jointly engage in a computation of the result of the ZKP without either learning the other party's input. We can make use of the following observation: Plaintext and randomization computations in Paillier's encryption system are in similar groups. Plaintext computations are in $\mathbb{Z}_n$ and randomization computations are in $\mathbb{Z}_{n^2}^*$. Both share the modulus n of secret factorization.

Fortunately, there exists a corresponding encryption scheme by Damgard and Jurik [6] operating with plaintexts in $\mathbb{Z}_{n^2}$ for each Paillier encryption scheme [16] operating with plaintexts in $\mathbb{Z}_n$. The other homomorphic properties are preserved and even the private and public keys are identical. We denote $E'(x, r)$ the encryption of plaintext $x \in \mathbb{Z}_{n^2}$ with randomization $r \in \mathbb{Z}_{n^3}^*$ in Damgard and Jurik's encryption scheme.

In the SubmitRating() protocol, Bob then not only sends $E(z, r_z)$ (his encrypted rating), but also chooses d, r_d, and r'. Bob publishes $E(d, r_d)$ and $v = uz + d$ and chooses $r_1 = r_z^u r_d$, i.e., we set $z = \alpha$ and $b = \beta$ in the previous proof. The random numbers $r_{d\beta}$ and r_γ in the previous proof are (secretly) shared between Bob and SP_2. Bob also submits the ciphertext $E'(r_z^u r_d, r')$.

Once the the second reputation provider SP_2 received Bob's submission, he chooses r_{zb} and publishes the multiplication of the sampling bit b and the rating z: $E(zb, r'_{zb}) = E(z, r_z)^b E(0, r_{zb})$ $(r'_{zb} = r_z^b r_{zb})$. Then he chooses r_{db} and publishes $E(db, r'_{db}) = E(d, r_d)^b E(0, r_{db})$ $(r'_{db} = r_d^b r_{db})$. If the sampling bit $b = 1$ is one, then SP_2 computes

$$E'(r_2^{-1}, r'') = E'(r_z^u r_d, r')^{(r_b^v)^{-1} r_{db} r_{zb}^u}$$

If the sampling bit $b = 0$ is zero, then SP_2 computes

$$E'(r_2^{-1}, r'') = E'((r_b^v)^{-1} r_{db} r_{zb}^u, r'')$$

Note that this only works, because of the small domain of the sampling, since we can avoid exponentiation of encrypted values.

The first reputation provider SP_1 decrypts and publishes (the inverse) r_2. During VerifyRating() Alice and Bob can now verify that $E(zb, r'_{zb})$ is indeed an encryption of the product of $E(b, r_b)$ and $E(z, r_z)$. They only need to verify that

$$E(z, r_z)^u E(d, r_d) = E(v, r_1)$$

and that

$$E(b, r_b)^v \left(E(db, r_{db}) E(z, r_z)^u \right)^{-1} = E(0, r_2)$$

Note that the first reputation provider SP_1 still does not learn the rater and the second reputation provider SP_2 still does not learn the rating. The sampling bit is known to both reputation providers, but remains entirely secret from the rater and ratee. The first service provider learns the sampling bit from the ciphertext, but he would learn it with some error from the rating anyway.

Lemma 2: *The protocol above is secure in the semi-honest model, i.e., neither Bob nor the second reputation SP_2 learn anything that cannot be derived from their input and output.*

PROOF. We give standard simulators for the views of the parties following the seminal work of [10]. First the reputation providers view can be simulated by ciphertexts and two random numbers for v and r_1. Both v and r_1 are perfect secret shares where one share is only known Bob (d and r_d). Note that ciphertexts are under the private key of SP_1 and therefore cannot be decrypted by either party. Bob's view can be simulated by ciphertexts and one random number for r_2. Also r_2 is a perfect secret share due to r_{zb}. □

Our scheme does not require security against malicious attackers. Instead, following the proposal from [12], we can implement a detection procedure based on signed messages. In the case of a dispute, all parties could then open their messages and the culprit would be identified.

5. CONCLUSION

In this paper, we have studied the problem of reputation feedback extortion and how it can be mitigated. We advocated the use of feedback escrow to increase the likelihood of the various parties giving honest feedback, random sampling to decrease the ability of either party tying a specific feedback score to a specific individual, and zero-knowledge proofs as a means to reduce the need for a trusted reputation provider.

6. REFERENCES

[1] E. Androulaki, S. Choi, S. Bellovin, and T. Malkin. Reputation systems for anonymous networks. In *Proceedings of the 8th International Symposium on Privacy Enhancing Technologies*, pages 202–218, 2008.

[2] M. Ben-Or, S. Goldwasser, and A. Wigderson. Completeness theorems for non-cryptographic fault tolerant distributed computation. In *Proceedings of 20th ACM Symposium on Theory of Computing*, pages 1–10, 1988.

[3] M. Blum, P. Feldman, and S. Micali. Non-interactive zero-knowledge and its applications. In *Proceedings of the 20th ACM Symposium on Theory of Computing*, pages 103–112, 1988.

[4] C. Camerer and K. Weigelt. Experimental tests of a sequential equilibrium reputation model. *Econometrica*, 56(1):1–36, 1988.

[5] J. Canny. Collaborative filtering with privacy. In *Proceedings of the IEEE Symposium on Security and Privacy*, pages 45–57, 2002.

[6] I. Damgård and M. Jurik. A generalisation, a simplification and some applications of pailliers probabilistic public-key system. In *Proceedings of International Conference on Theory and Practice of Public-Key Cryptography*, pages 119–136, 2001.

[7] I. Dinur and K. Nissim. Revealing information while preserving privacy. In *PODS '03: Proceedings of the twenty-second ACM SIGMOD-SIGACT-SIGART symposium on Principles of database systems*, pages 202–210, New York, NY, USA, 2003. ACM.

[8] Y. Duan. Privacy without noise. In *Proc. of 18th ACM Conf. on Information and Knowledge Management*, pages 1517–1520, 2009.

[9] C. Dwork. Differential privacy: a survey of results. In *Proc. of the 5th Int. Conf. on Theory and Applications of Models of Computation (TAMC)*, pages 1–19. Springer, 2008.

[10] O. Goldreich. Secure multi-party computation. Available at www.wisdom.weizmann.ac.il/~oded/pp.html, 2002.

[11] O. Goldreich, S. Micali, and A. Wigderson. How to play any mental game. In *Proceedings of the 19th Symposium on the Theory of Computing*, pages 218–229, 1987.

[12] F. Kerschbaum. A verifiable, centralized, coercion-free reputation system. In *Proceedings of the ACM Workshop on Privacy in the Electronic Society*, pages 61–70, 2009.

[13] C. Li, M. Hay, V. Rastogi, G. Miklau, and A. McGregor. Optimizing linear counting queries under differential privacy. In *Proc. of 29th ACM*

Symp. on Principles of Database Systems of Data (PODS), pages 123–134, 2010.

[14] N. Miller, P. Resnick, and R. Zeckhauser. Eliciting informative feedback: The peer prediction method. *Management Science*, 51(9):1359–1373, 2005.

[15] V. Naessens, L. Demuynck, and B. De Decker. A fair anonymous submission and review system. In *Proceedings of the 10th IFIP International Conference on Communications and Multimedia Security*, pages 43–53, 2006.

[16] P. Paillier. Public-key cryptosystems based on composite degree residuosity classes. In *Advances in Cryptology – EUROCRYPT*, pages 223–238, 1999.

[17] E. Pavlov, J. Rosenschein, and Z. Topol. Supporting privacy in decentralized additive reputation systems. In *Proceedings of the 2nd International Conference on Trust Management*, pages 108–119, 2004.

[18] F. Pingel and S. Steinbrecher. Multilateral secure cross-community reputation systems for internet communities. In *Proceedings of the 5th International Conference on Trust, Privacy and Security in Digital Business*, pages 69–78, 2008.

[19] P. Resnick and R. Zeckhauser. Trust among strangers in internet transactions: Empirical analysis of ebay' s reputation system. *Advances in Applied Microeconomics*, 11:127–157, 2002.

[20] J. Traupman and R. Wilensky. Robust reputations for peer-to-peer marketplaces. In *Proceedings of the 4th International Conference on Trust Management*, pages 382–396, 2006.

[21] A. Yao. How to generate and exchange secrets. In *Proceedings of the 27th IEEE Symposium on Foundations of Computer Science*, pages 162–167, 1986.

Panel

Research Agenda for Data and Application Security

Organizer and Chair
X. Sean Wang
National Science Foundation & University of Vermont
Arlington, Virginia
+1-703-292-5311
xwang@nsf.gov

PANEL SUMMARY

Data and application security is traditionally viewed as a subfield of cybersecurity. The goal is still the same, namely to provide trustworthy computing infrastructure. However, in data and application security, we are dealing with the infrastructural aspects that are closer to humans, their interactions with the system, their perceptions, and their values. Data should not be treated as just bits, but as semantically rich content. Hence, securing data may be different from securing bits. Application software is much more diverse than system software, often directly responding to particular end-user needs. Hence, usability of security may be of more importance.

The above may be just a small sample of the uniqueness of data and application security. What else? What particular research agenda does this uniqueness call for? What about research methodologies?

With the above questions in mind, this panel will bring 4-5 panelists to discuss their experiences and their views of future research directions in data and application security.

Categories & Subject Descriptors: J.0 [Computer Applications] General, E.0 [Data] General, I.m [Computing Methodologies] Miscellaneous

General Terms: Algorithms, Design, Documentation, Economics, Experimentation, Human Factors, Languages, Legal Aspects, Management, Measurement, Performance, Reliability, Security, Standardization, Theory, Verification.

Keywords: Application security, Data security, Research directions, Research methodologies.

Background Information

Critical infrastructures of modern societies rely heavily on computing; data become critical assets of governments, businesses and even individuals; applications have become more complex and closer to "common" users (a cursory look at the huge availability of "apps" on smartphones may make people concerned about the security of the users and their data). Security research has come a long way to defend users and systems, but attackers seem to have an upper hand in the race of attack and defense. A general

question is: can we have a "science of security" so that a set of fundamental principles may be used to guide the design and implementation of data and application security [1]?

Recently, National Coordination Office (NCO)'s Networking and Information Technology Research and Development (NITRD) program presented new Federal cybersecurity game-change R&D themes [2]. The idea is to reverse the trend of defense lagging behind attacks, calling for methods to increase attacker cost, enable tailored security environments, and incentivize security deployment, socially responsible behavior, and deter cyber crimes. These are all very relevant to data and application security. A general question is: is there a specific research agenda suitable to advance the NITRD R&D themes?

Questions for the Panel

To start off the panel discussion, the panelists will be asked to respond to the following questions:

1. What are some general research directions in data and application security? What are the hardest problems in this area?

2. How does data and application security interface with system and network security? What are the critical issues in dealing with this interface?

3. Is there a "science of data and application security"? If yes, how is it defined?

4. How are the NITRD themes relevant to the data and application security? What specific research directions can be spurned by these themes?

5. What are the most important research questions regarding human factors and usability in data and application security?

6. How to evaluate research results in this area?

The panel is promised to be an interactive one, involving the panelists and audience.

References

[1] JASON, MITRE, "Science of Cyber-Security", Report number JSR-10-102, November 19, 2010

[2] http://cybersecurity.nitrd.gov/

CODASPY'11, February 21–23, 2011, San Antonio, Texas, USA.
ACM 978-1-4503-0465-8/11/02.

Author Index

Aad, Imad 261
Asokan, N. 13
Barker, Ken 213
Bilogrevic, Igor 261
Brancik, Kenneth 231
Cadenhead, Tyrone 133
Carminati, Barbara 51
Chen, Keke 249
Chen, You 63
Conti, Mauro 39
Crispo, Bruno 39
Dickson, John B. 25
Ekberg, Jan-Erik 13
Ferrari, Elena 51
Fong, Philip W. L. 191, 213
Ghinita, Gabriel 231
Goodrich, Michael T. 273
Gunter, Carl A. 97
Guo, Shumin 249
Hasani, Arbnor 39
Hoque, Imranul 97
Hubaux, Jean-Pierre 261
Inan, Ali 179
Jadliwala, Murtuza 261
Jafari, Mohammad 213
Jahid, Sonia 97
Jiang, Wei 169
Jin, Lei 27
Joshi, James B. D. 27
Kantarcioglu, Murat 133, 179
Kavuluru, Ramakanth 249
Kerr, Sam 203
Kerschbaum, Florian 273
Khadilkar, Vaibhav 133
Kirkpatrick, Michael S. 203
Komlenovic, Marko 121
Kostiainen, Kari 13
Kuhn, Jens-Michael 85

Kumari, Prachi 85
Li, Zhitang 75
Liu, Peng 75
Lorenzi, David 157
Malin, Bradley 63
Malkin, Tal 3
Mayer, Daniel A. 109
Meyer, Ulrike 109
Morasca, Sandro 51
Murugesan, Mummoorthy 169
Nergiz, Ahmet Erhan 169
Niemi, Valtteri 261
Okhravi, Hamed 97
Peschla, Jonas 85
Pretschner, Alexander 85
Qian, Haifeng 145
Reshetova, Elena 13
Safavi-Naini, Reihaneh 213
Sandhu, Ravi 1
Sheppard, Nicholas Paul 213
Taibi, Davide 51
Takabi, Hassan 27
Teranishi, Isamu 3
Teubert, Dominik 109
Thomsen, Dan 225
Thuraisingham, Bhavani 133
Tripunitara, Mahesh 121
Uzunbaz, Serkan 169
Vaidya, Jaideep 157
Wang, X. Sean 283
Wetzel, Susanne 109
Xi, Bowei 179
Xu, Shouhuai 145, 237
Yu, Junfeng 75
Yung, Moti 3
Zhang, Shengzhi 75
Zheng, Qingji 237
Zitouni, Toufik 121